PELOUBET'S
NOTES
1976-1977

PELOUBET'S NOTES
1976-1977

Based on the International Bible Lessons

for Christian Teaching

Uniform Series

by

Ralph Earle

103rd Annual Volume

Founded by Francis N. Peloubet

BAKER BOOK HOUSE ● GRAND RAPIDS, MICHIGAN

Scripture passages from the New International Version (NIV) copyrighted 1973 by the
New York International Bible Society are used with permission.

ISBN: 0-8010-3323-3

Lessons based on International Sunday School Lessons; the International Bible
Lessons for Christian Teaching, copyright by the Committee on the Uniform
Series.

Printed in the United States of America

PREFACE

1905361

In *Peloubet's Notes, 1976-77*, Ralph Earle continues to present detailed Bible studies based on the *International Bible Lessons for Christian Teaching*. In his commentary he blends Scripture exposition with application. His own commentary is enriched by quotations from a wide spectrum of commentators, making this a particularly rich source of information for the teacher who may not have wide resources at his fingertips.

In the first quarter Dr. Earle applies first-century truths to life in the seventies—"The Message of Reconciliation." The second and third quarters present the life and ministry of Jesus as recorded in the Gospels of Mark and Luke, and the lessons of practical Christianity from James. In the fourth quarter he transports his students to the times of Israel's beginnings: their slavery in Egypt, their wilderness wanderings en route to the Promised Land, and their subsequent conquest of the people living there. Finally he takes the student through the times of the Judges and the people's request for a king. But this is not just history. Each lesson is applied to the life of the student in the here and now—a confrontation with the human situation that changes only in style, not in essence.

Each week the teacher will find the same helpful features as those featured in past issues of this helpful book:

Devotional Reading for heart preparation

Background Scripture to provide the larger context of the lesson

Scripture Lesson that focuses the attention of the class on the lesson for the week

Memory Verse that pinpoints the main thrust of the lesson

Lesson Topics directed to the particular age group

Daily Bible Readings to supply a sustained interest in the lesson topic and provide daily inspiration

Lesson Aim, Setting, and **Outline** to present the total scope of the lesson at a glance

Suggested Introduction for Adults, Suggested Introduction for Youth, and **Concepts for Children** to allow the teacher to select the appropriate approach to his class

Lesson Commentary that explains and applies the truths presented in the lesson

Discussion Questions to clinch the meat of the lesson for the life of the students

Contemporary Application that builds a bridge between the Scriptural context and living today

A Bibliography of Commentaries further assists the teacher in the preparation of the lesson.

Baker Book House is happy to present to the wide church family using the *International Bible Lessons for Christian Teaching* this comprehensive study guide and prays that its use will stimulate Christians to better understand God's Word and become brighter lights in our spiritually darkened world.

CONTENTS

FIRST QUARTER

The Message of Reconciliation

Unit I: The Freedom of the Christian

Unit II: The Meaning of Reconciliation

Unit III: The Life of the Reconciled

SECOND QUARTER

The Life and Ministry of Jesus: Mark and Luke

Unit I: God Comes to Man in Jesus

Unit II: Jesus Begins His Ministry

Unit III: Jesus Demonstrates His Power

THIRD QUARTER

The Life and Ministry of Jesus: Mark and Luke (continued)

Unit IV: Jesus Teaches His Way

Unit V: Jesus Climaxes His Mission

Unit VI: Faith in Action: James

FOURTH QUARTER

From Slavery to Nationhood

Unit I: A People in Need of Deliverance

Unit II: God Creates a Covenant People

Unit III: The Struggle to Survive

THE MESSAGE OF RECONCILIATION

JUSTIFICATION BY FAITH

DEVOTIONAL READING	Hebrews 11:1-12

ADULTS

Topic: *Justification by Faith*

Background Scripture: Galatians 1:1—3:18

Scripture Lesson: Galatians 2:15-16; 3:1-14

Memory Verse: *. . . a man is not justified by works of the law but through faith in Jesus Christ.* Galatians 2:16

YOUTH

Topic: *Faith: The Beginning Point*

Background Scripture: Galatians 1:1—3:18

Scripture Lesson: Galatians 2:15-16; 3:1-14

Memory Verse: *. . . a man is not justified by works of the law but through faith in Jesus Christ.* Galatians 2:16

CHILDREN

Topic: *An Enemy Becomes a Friend*

Background Scripture: Acts 9:1-22; Galatians 1:1-24

Scripture Lesson: Galatians 1:11-24

Memory Verse: *I live by faith in the Son of God, who loved me and gave himself for me.* Galatians 2:20

DAILY BIBLE READINGS

Mon., Aug. 30: No Other Gospel, Galatians 1:1-10.
Tues., Aug. 31: Not Man's Gospel, Galatians 1:11-24.
Wed., Sept. 1: Free in Christ Jesus, Galatians 2:1-10.
Thurs., Sept. 2: Justified by Faith Not by Works, Galatians 2:11-21.
Fri., Sept. 3: The Example of Abraham's Faith, Galatians 3:1-9.
Sat., Sept. 4: "The Law Does Not Rest on Faith," Galatians 3:10-18.
Sun., Sept. 5: Living by Faith, Hebrews 11:1-12.

LESSON AIM

To show that we are justified by faith in Christ and what He has done for us, not by our own deeds.

LESSON SETTING

Time: The Epistle to the Galatians was written sometime between A.D. 48 and 55.

Place: Unknown

11

Justification by Faith

SUGGESTED INTRODUCTION FOR ADULTS

Today we begin a new quarter of lessons under the general heading, "The Message of Reconciliation"—the central theme of the Bible. This is divided into three units: (1) "The Freedom of the Christian," lessons 1—4; (2) "The Meaning of Reconciliation," lessons 5—10; (3) "The Life of the Reconciled," lessons 11—13. The Scripture passages for the first unit are taken from the Epistle to the Galatians. The other two units are based on the Epistle to the Romans. These are the two books of the New Testament that particularly emphasize justification by faith. In fact, it is sometimes called the general theme of both of these letters of Paul.

Justification by faith was the central focus of the Protestant Reformation of the sixteenth century. Martin Luther made it the rallying cry for a Christ-centered and Bible-centered Christianity, in contrast to the church-centered faith of his day. As heirs of the Reformation, we should treasure and propagate this truth.

SUGGESTED INTRODUCTION FOR YOUTH

Sinful man is alienated from a holy God. We are very conscious of this. So the most important topic that should "grab" us is "The Message of Reconciliation."

What is "the beginning point"? The only correct answer is: "Justification by faith." We cannot justify ourselves by our own efforts. This is utterly futile. We can only trust in what Christ did for us on the cross. By faith in His finished work of redemption there, we become reconciled to God.

<table>
<tr><td>CONCEPTS FOR
CHILDREN</td><td>1. By nature we are enemies of God.
2. By grace we become friends of God.
3. Paul is an excellent example of this.
4. Children need to come to Christ and trust in Him as their Savior.</td></tr>
</table>

THE LESSON COMMENTARY

I. THE MEANS OF JUSTIFICATION:
Galatians 2:15-16

A. By Faith in Jesus Christ: vv. 15-16a

Paul was a Jew. So he begins with "we": "We who are Jews by nature [that is, by birth] and not sinners of the Gentiles." The Jews considered all Gentiles (non-Jews) to be "sinners," separated from God. Only the Jews were united to Him by the covenant made to Abraham and confirmed through Moses at Mount Sinai.

He goes on to say that we know "that a man is not justified by the works of the law [that is, by observing the Mosaic Law] but by the faith of Jesus Christ." The wording of this last part could be misunderstood, as if it were Christ's faith. The correct translation is: "by faith in Jesus Christ" (NIV). It is trusting in what He has done for us, not what we are trying to do for ourselves.

B. Not by the Law: v. 16b

Paul ends this verse with the emphatic statement quoted from Psalm 143:2: "For by the works of the law no flesh shall be justified"; or better, "because by observing the law no one will be justified" (NIV). This is the central thrust, on the negative side, of this Epistle. There is absolutely no way that we can justify ourselves before God.

Perhaps we should look further at the meaning of the word *justified* which occurs three times in verse 16. The popular use of the term today is often, "He justified himself"; that is, "He defended himself," or "He tried

to prove his innocence." But in the Bible *justify* has the theological connotation: "To free (man) of the guilt and penalty attached to grievous sin" (*American Heritage Dictionary*, p. 712).

II. THE IMPLICATIONS OF JUSTIFICATION:
Galatians 2:17-21

A. Does Not Promote Sin: vv. 17-18

"If, while we seek to be justified in Christ, it becomes evident that we ourselves are sinners, does that mean that Christ promotes sin? Absolutely not!" (v. 17, NIV). The key to understanding this somewhat difficult passage seems to lie in the previous paragraphs. Peter had acted like a Gentile by eating with Gentiles (v. 12). According to the Pharisees, this made him a Gentile "sinner." So when some representatives of the Jewish Christian church in Jerusalem, whose pastor was James the brother of Jesus, came to Antioch, he separated himself from the Gentile believers. Paul reproved him publicly for doing this (v. 14). He had no right to compel Gentile Christians to Judaize!

So it appears that Paul is still using "sinners" in verse 17 in the same sense as "Gentile sinners" (v. 15), that is, men outside the Mosaic Law, or violators of that Law, disregarding the Mosaic statutes concerning clean and unclean meats for instance. E. D. Burton says about Peter and Paul: "That they had become sinners by seeking to be justified in Christ, Paul would admit in the sense that they had become violators of law, but deny what the Judaizers would affirm, that this was equivalent to saying that they had become actual sinners, wrong-doers, violators of God's will" (*A Critical and Exegetical Commentary on the Epistle to the Galatians*, International Critical Commentary, p. 125).

In answer to his rhetorical question Paul exclaims, "God forbid" (KJV)—"Absolutely not!" (NIV). The Greek expression literally means "Let it not be." It is used only by Paul (14 times) in his Epistles, except for Luke 20:16. It has the force of "By no means!"

In verse 18 Paul declares that if he rebuilt what he had destroyed—slavery to the Jewish Law—he would prove that he was a transgressor. That is exactly what he accused Peter of having done.

B. Brings a New Life in Christ: vv. 19-21

What was Paul's relationship to the Law of Moses? He expresses it well in verse 19: "For through the law I died to the law so that I might live for God" (NIV).

What is suggested here by the figure of death? Burton comments: "In the usage of Paul, 'to die to' a thing is to cease to have any relation to it, so that it has no further claim upon or control over one" (Burton, *Galatians*, p. 132).

But how did this come "through the law"? Perhaps the best explanation is to be found in the seventh chapter of Romans. Paul had discovered that a legalistic adherence to the Mosaic Law brought only frustration and defeat, and so he had turned to Christ for salvation.

Galatians 2:20 is one of the outstanding verses in this Epistle. In the King James Version the first part reads: "I am crucified with Christ: nevertheless I live; yet not I, but Christ liveth in me." But the Greek does not say "nevertheless I live"; it says "no longer do I [*ego*] live." The correct rendering is: "I have been crucified with Christ and I no longer live, but Christ lives in me" (NIV). By identify-

ing himself with Christ on the cross, the apostle was able to say that his self-centered ego had died there and no longer dominated his life; instead Christ had become the dominant force. This is the real secret of victorious Christian living: to make what was provisional at Calvary experiential in the here and now. That was the purpose of Christ's death (v. 21).

III. THE AGENT OF JUSTIFICATION:
Galatians 3:1-5

A. Reception of the Spirit by Faith: vv. 1-2

Paul chides his readers: "O foolish Galatians." The Greek word translated "foolish" means "mindless, senseless," or at the least "thoughtless." Then he asks, "Who hath bewitched you?"—literally, "fixed his evil eye on you?" ("That ye should not obey the truth" is not in the earliest Greek manuscripts.) "Hath been evidently set forth" is all one word in Greek, *proegraphe*, which means "has been placarded"—"clearly portrayed" (NIV).

The Galatian converts were without excuse. In Paul's life and preaching they had clearly seen the crucified Christ. Charles J. Ellicott gives a beautiful paraphrase: "Who could have bewitched you by his gaze, when you had only to fix your eyes on Christ to escape the fascination?" (*St. Paul's Epistle to the Galatians*, p. 65). The Judaizers had hypnotized the Galatians!

Then Paul asked a very pertinent question. He said, "I would like to learn just one thing from you: Did you receive the Spirit by observing the law, or by believing what you heard?" (v. 2, NIV). He is reminding them of the beginnings of their Christian life. He had preached to them the simple gospel of salvation through faith in Jesus Christ and His atoning death at Calvary. They had believed this message and had received the witness of the Spirit that their sins were forgiven.

The Holy Spirit had regenerated their hearts. They had been justified by faith alone.

Was it by observing the Mosaic Law that all this had come to them? No, it was through believing what they heard, the true gospel of Jesus Christ, from the lips of the apostle.

B. Perfection by the Spirit: vv. 3-5

Now Paul makes the logical application: "Are you so foolish having begun in the Spirit, are ye now made perfect by the flesh?"—that is, "by human effort?" (NIV). What the apostle is saying is that every step taken in the Christian life is a step of faith. The very first steps—confession, repentance, forsaking the old life—are taken by faith, not by human effort. They are responses to God's Word speaking to us. And they are taken only by the enablement that the Spirit gives. We can neither repent nor believe without the help of the Holy Spirit.

Justification is a work of the Holy Spirit through faith in Jesus Christ, and so is sanctification. We cannot attain to perfection by our own efforts, but only through letting the Holy Spirit do it in us.

It is almost plaintively that Paul asks, "Have you suffered so much for nothing—if it really was for nothing?" (v. 4, NIV). Like all new converts, especially in that day, the Galatian Christians had suffered for their faith. If they now turned back from Christ to the Mosaic Law, all their suffering would be in vain.

The apostle continues to ask his readers: "He therefore that ministereth to you the Spirit [Greek, "the one supplying to you the Spirit"] and worketh miracles among you, doeth he it by the works of the law, or by the hearing of faith?" (v. 5). To put it a little more plainly: "Does God give you his Spirit and work miracles among you because you observe the law, or because you believe what you heard?" (NIV). The answer is obvious. All that they had received from God had come to them through faith. It was all of God, not of themselves.

IV. THE EXAMPLE OF JUSTIFICATION:
Galatians 3:6-9

A. Abraham Justified by Faith: v. 6

In the Old Testament the statement is made that Abraham "believed in the Lord, and he counted it to him for righteousness" (Genesis 15:6). This important assertion is also quoted in Romans 4:3. It was a basic foundation of Paul's doctrine of justification by faith.

The apostle enlarges and enforces this point later on in the chapter (vv. 15-17). He says that even a human covenant, once established, cannot be set aside. So it is with the divine covenant made with Abraham; it was not annulled by the Law. Paul writes: "What I mean is this: The law, introduced 430 years later, does not set aside the covenant previously established by God and thus do away with the promise" (v. 17, NIV). Justification by faith takes precedence over the Mosaic regulations.

B. Children of Abraham: vv. 7-9

The true children of Abraham are not his physical descendants but those who are "of faith"—that is, saved by faith, as was Abraham. Put most simply, the truth is this: "Those who believe are children of Abraham" (NIV). So today all of us who are saved by faith are the spiritual descendants of the venerable founder of the Hebrew race. We, just as truly as the Jews, can call him "Father Abraham."

In the Scriptures it was foreseen that God would justify the Gentiles by faith, not works (v. 8). So the gospel was announced in advance to Abraham in the promise, "In thee shall all nations be blessed" (Genesis 12:3). This sweeping assertion has found its fulfillment in Christ, the true "seed" of Abraham (v. 16).

Paul concludes this paragraph by saying, "So those who have faith are blessed along with Abraham, the man of faith" (v. 9, NIV). Faith is the sure route of blessing. The fellowship of faith takes in a vast multitude of God's believing people across the many centuries. What a heritage and what a privilege!

V. THE PROVISION OF JUSTIFICATION:
Galatians 3:10-14

A. The Curse of the Law: vv. 10-12

"All who rely on observing the law are under a curse, for it is written: 'Cursed is everyone who does not continue to do everything written in the book of the Law' " (v. 10, NIV). The quotation is from Deuteronomy 27:26.

This verse sounds a significant note. No human being but Jesus Christ has ever kept the Law perfectly. For all others it has been a practical impossibility. But since everyone who fails to do so is under a curse, it follows that those who depend on observance of the Law of Moses for their salvation are going to find themselves under God's curse, not His blessing. With this one quotation Paul dealt a death blow to the whole idea of salvation through keeping the Law.

DISCUSSION QUESTIONS

1. What are some modern forms of "works-religion"?
2. Why was Paul so stirred up when he wrote his Epistle to the Galatians?
3. How did his own experience affect his message?
4. How would you analyze Peter's action?
5. What do you think was the secret of Abraham's great faith?
6. How may we develop a strong faith in God?

It was a master stroke in his fight for the freedom of his converts, whose faith was being threatened by the attacks of the Judaizers.

Having assailed the legal concept of salvation from the negative side, supported by Scripture, Paul now quotes another passage from the Old Testament on the positive side: "The just shall live by faith" (v. 11). This is one of the most important statements made in the older Scriptures. It is found in Habakkuk 2:4. This was the cornerstone of Paul's great doctrine of justification by faith. He found the truth stated already by an Old Testament prophet. One of the functions of the prophets was to interpret the Law. They called people back to its true spiritual meaning.

Once more the apostle reiterates for emphasis the basic truth he is trying to get these Galatians to see. The Law is not based on faith, but on works (v. 12). This is supported by another quotation: "The man who does these things will live by them" (NIV). The citation is from Leviticus 18:5. Since no one can do all these things—meet all the demands of the Law—he will find death, not life.

B. The Curse Put on Christ: vv. 13-14

"Christ redeemed us from the curse of the law by becoming a curse for us, for it is written: 'Cursed is everyone who is hanged on a tree' " (v. 13, NIV). The quotation is from Deuteronomy 21:23. This is the price that our Lord had to pay for our salvation. But He is willing to do it for us. What amazing love! And how grateful we ought to be! The whole curse of the Law we had broken came on Him. And so we can go free through faith in Him and His finished work for us. How this should make our hearts rejoice!

The result is that all the blessing promised to Abraham might come to us Gentiles "through Jesus Christ" (v. 14). The greatest blessing is "the promise of the Spirit," which we receive by faith. But all the blessings that we get from God come to us through Jesus Christ. This is a central truth in Paul's Epistles, and it is supported by the rest of the New Testament. It is a fact that we should never forget. And it should evoke our deepest love and gratitude.

CONTEMPORARY APPLICATION

The idea that we cannot save ourselves, that we can only let Christ save us, cuts across human pride. That is one reason that so many people reject justification by faith. They want to work their own way through. But we can no more build a stairway to heaven by our efforts than the men working on the tower of Babel could reach the sky by putting one stone on top of another. Faith in Christ's work for us is the only way.

HEIRS OF GOD'S GRACE

DEVOTIONAL READING | Romans 3:21-31

ADULTS
Topic: *Heirs of God's Grace*

Background Scripture: Romans 4:1-25; Galatians 3:19—4:7

Scripture Lesson: Galatians 3:23—4:7

Memory Verse: *In Christ Jesus you are all sons of God, through faith.* Galatians 3:26

YOUTH
Topic: *God's Gift of Grace*

Background Scripture: Romans 4:1-25; Galatians 3:19—4:7

Scripture Lesson: Galatians 3:23—4:7

Memory Verse: *In Christ Jesus you are all sons of God, through faith.* Galatians 3:26

CHILDREN
Topic: *God's Love Is for All*

Background Scripture: Acts 15:1-21; Galatians 2:1-2; 3:26-28

Scripture Lesson: Galatians 3:23—4:7

Memory Verse: *You are all one in Jesus Christ.* Galatians 3:28

DAILY BIBLE READINGS

Mon., Sept. 6: "Heirs According to Promise," Galatians 3:19-29.

Tues., Sept. 7: "God Sent Forth His Son," Galatians 4:1-7.

Wed., Sept. 8: "Until Christ Be Formed in You," Galatians 4:8-20.

Thurs., Sept. 9: Faith Accounted as Righteousness, Romans 4:1-8.

Fri., Sept. 10: Father of All Who Believe, Romans 4:9-15.

Sat., Sept. 11: Faith in God's Grace, Romans 4:16-25.

Sun., Sept. 12: Justified by God's Grace, Romans 3:21-31.

LESSON AIM | To help us see some of the glorious privileges we have as children of God.

LESSON SETTING
Time: A.D. 48-55

Place: Unknown

18

Heirs of God's Grace

I. Purpose of the Law: Galatians 3:19-20

II. Prisoners of Sin: Galatians 3:21-22

III. Prisoners of the Law: Galatians 3:23-25
   A. The Confinement by the Law: v. 23
   B. The Function of the Law: v. 24
   C. The New Era of Faith: v. 25

IV. Sons of God: Galatians 3:26-29
   A. Sons Through Faith in Christ: vv. 26-27
   B. All One in Christ: v. 28
   C. Heirs to the Promise: v. 29

V. Heirs of God: Galatians 4:1-7
   A. The Status of the Heir as a Child: vv. 1-2
   B. The Application to the Readers: v. 3
   C. The Full Rights of Sons: vv. 4-7

LESSON OUTLINE

SUGGESTED INTRODUCTION FOR ADULTS

The Epistle to the Galatians and the Epistle to the Romans have much in common. This shows up especially in a comparison of Romans 4—5 with Galatians 3—4. And the most striking parallelism is found in the treatment of Abraham, who was justified by faith, not by works.

The whole of the fourth chapter of Romans, which should be read carefully, deals with the example of Abraham. In the third verse we have the quotation from the Old Testament that we noted last week cited in Galatians 3:6: "[Abraham] believed in God, and it was credited to him as righteousness" (NIV). (There is also an added testimony from David [v. 6] in a quotation from Psalm 32:1-2.)

The point is emphasized that this happened before Abraham was circumcised (v. 10). So circumcision is not a prerequisite for justification. Abraham is "the father of all who believe but have not been circumcised," as well as of "the circumcised who not only are circumcised but also walk in the footsteps of the faith that our father Abraham had before he was circumcised" (vv. 11-12, NIV). The point made in both Epistles is that justification is by faith, not by the Law.

SUGGESTED INTRODUCTION FOR YOUTH

Young people have a great heritage. It began with Abraham, the father of those who are saved by faith. It reaches down through Moses, David, and the prophets to the apostles of the New Testament and the saints of all the centuries since, especially the Reformers, who recaptured the great truth of justification by faith. We should thank God for this glorious inheritance.

CONCEPTS FOR CHILDREN	1. God's love is for all people. 2. He makes no distinction for race or status. 3. We, as His children, should love all people. 4. The church should try to reach all people for Christ.

THE LESSON COMMENTARY

I. THE PURPOSE OF THE LAW: Galatians 3:19-20

In the previous paragraph (vv. 15-18) Paul emphasized the fact that the Law of Moses, given at Sinai, could not set aside the covenant made with Abraham four hundred years earlier. The covenant was graciously given by God's promise, not through the Law.

The question would naturally come to the minds of his readers: "What, then, was the purpose of the law?" The apostle's answer is: "It was added because of transgressions until the Seed to whom the promise referred had come" (v. 19, NIV). The "Seed" promised to Abraham is Jesus Christ, the Messiah and Savior.

The word *added* indicates that the Law was supplementary to the promise, and so was subordinate to it. The promise was permanent, beginning before the Law and continuing after it. The Law was temporary, and fixed within its chronological boundaries. It began with Moses and ended with the coming of Christ.

The word *transgressions* is significant. There was sin, lots of it, before the giving of the Law, at Sinai. But a transgression is a violation of a specific law. It was only when the Mosaic Law had been given that people could be found guilty of transgressions.

Paul adds an interesting detail about the Law: "And it was ordained by angels in the hand of a mediator" (cf. Acts 7:53; Hebrews 2:2). This idea is found in the Septuagint, but not the Hebrew text, of Deuteronomy 33:2. It is perhaps an interpretation of the phrase, "written with the finger of God" (Exodus 31:18). The whole passage here reflects Paul's understanding of the Law as secondary. The promise was primary, given directly by God (v. 20).

II. PRISONERS OF SIN: Galatians 3:21-22

"Is the law, therefore, opposed to the promises of God? Absolutely not!" (v. 21, NIV). Paul here employs his favorite device of asking a rhetorical question—one that might naturally be deduced from his previous discussion—and then answering it with an emphatic *me genoito*, "By no means!"

The rest of verse 21 supports his answer. Law is not opposed to promise, because the two have distinct functions; they operate in different spheres. The Law has to do with transgression and penalty, the promise with forgiveness of sins and relationship to God. The Law brings death; the promise brings life.

"But the Scripture declares that the whole world is a prisoner of sin" (v. 22, NIV). Perhaps the reference is to Deuteronomy 27:26, quoted in verse 10. All men are in the prison of sin, held there until they accept by faith the gracious promise of God.

III. PRISONERS OF THE LAW: Galatians 3:23-25

A. The Confinement by the Law: v. 23

"Before this faith came, we were held prisoners by the law, locked up until faith should be revealed" (NIV). The emphasis is on the temporary nature of the Law; it held people in confinement until Christ came, bringing freedom through faith.

Legalism is a prison. Legalists are not free persons. This was true of the

Pharisees in Jesus' day, and it is true of legalists in the church today. There is no joy in legalism, just a dull sense of drab duty. Legalists are to be pitied, not imitated. The life of faith is a life of freedom.

B. The Function of the Law: v. 24

This verse is a familiar one, often quoted. But the word "schoolmaster" in the King James Version is somewhat misleading and not quite accurate.

It is true that the Greek word is *paidagogos*, from which comes the English term "pedagogue." But this was not the connotation of the word at that time. William F. Arndt and F. Wilbur Gingrich define it this way: *"attendant (slave), custodian, guide,* lit. 'boy-leader,' the man, usually a slave, whose duty it was to conduct the boy or youth to and from school and to superintend his conduct generally; he was not a 'teacher' (despite the present meaning of the derivative 'pedagogue')" (*Greek-English Lexicon of the New Testament*, p. 608).

In a similar vein J. B. Lightfoot writes: "The pedagogue or tutor, frequently a superior slave, was entrusted with the moral supervision of the child. Thus his office was quite distinct from that of the *didaskolos* (Greek word for 'teacher'), so that the English rendering 'schoolmaster' conveys a wrong idea" (*Epistle of St. Paul to the Galatians*, p. 148).

E. D. Burton adds a specific detail. He says: "A *paidagogos* was a slave employed in Greek and Roman families to have general charge of a boy in the years from about six to sixteen, watching over his outward behaviour and attending him whenever he went from home, as *e.g.* to school" (*A Critical and Exegetical Commentary on the Epistle to the Galatians*, International Critical Commentary, p. 200).

The Law could not justify, Paul says again. It is only through Christ that we are "justified by faith." The main thrust of this whole section of Galatians (chapters 3 and 4), as well as

Romans 3—5, is that justification cannot come through the Mosaic Law but only through faith in Jesus Christ.

C. The New Era of Faith: v. 25

With the coming of Christ the age of Law came to an end. Its rule over God's people was abolished. Now we are free individuals in Christ, under His direct care and guidance.

IV. SONS OF GOD: Galatians 3:26-29

A. Sons Through Faith in Christ: vv. 26-27

The *we* of verses 23-25 refers primarily to Jewish Christians, of whom Paul was one. But the *ye* of vv. 26-29 means "all you Gentiles," or at least "all you Galatians." From the account in Acts we would assume that the Galatian Christians were mostly Gentiles, and many passages in this Epistle imply that this was the case.

Paul declares that his readers in the churches of Galatia were "all sons of God through faith in Christ Jesus" (v. 26, NIV). "Sons" is a more accurate translation than "children" (KJV). John in his First Epistle is fond of the expression "little children," a term of endearment. But Paul uses "sons" here, for he is emphasizing the idea of liberty, of maturity. Lightfoot says that the stress of this verse lies on two words, *all* and *sons*. He puts it this way: " 'all,' Jews and Gentiles alike, those under the law and those without the law; 'sons,' claiming therefore the privileges, the liberty of sons, so that the rigorous supervision of the tutor (*paidagogos*) ceases when you cease to be children" (*Galatians*, p. 149). Of the phrase "in Christ Jesus" he continues: "You are sons by your union with, your existence in Christ Jesus."

Those who have been baptized into Christ "have put on Christ" (v. 27). The verb here literally means "have been clothed with." Luther comments: "To put on Christ according to the Gospel means to clothe oneself with the righteousness, wisdom, power, life, and Spirit of Christ. By nature we are clad in the garb of Adam. This garb Paul likes to call 'the old man.' Before we can become the children of God this old man must be put off, as Paul says, Ephesians 4:22. Then we are clothed with the righteousness of Christ. With this change of garments a new birth, a new life stirs in us. New affections toward God spring up in the heart. New determinations affect our will. All this is to put on Christ according to the Gospel" (*A Commentary on St. Paul's Epistle to the Galatians*, abridged translation, p. 147).

Burton observes: " 'To put on Christ' is to become as Christ, to have his standing; in this context to become objects of the divine favour, sons of God, as he is the Son of God" (*Galatians*, p. 203).

B. All One in Christ: v. 28

Paul declares that in Christ there is "neither Jew nor Greek, slave nor free, male nor female, for you are all one in Christ Jesus" (NIV). Luther suggests, "The list might be extended indefinitely: There is neither preacher nor hearer, neither teacher nor scholar, neither master nor servant, etc. In the matter of salvation, rank, learning, righteousness, influence count for nothing" (*Commentary on Galatians*, p. 148). In Christ we are all equal. And we are all "one"; there must be no division in the body of Christ.

It is only in Christ that this true unity takes place. All attempts to legislate equality must necessarily fail, because of the sinful nature of man. But in Christ there is loving unity and a willingness to treat all our fellow Christians as our equals.

C. Heirs to the Promise: v. 29

If we belong to Christ, we are Abraham's true "seed" and so are "heirs according to the promise." The Judaizers claimed that circumcision would make them children of Abraham and heirs to the promise. But Paul

asserted that this inheritance comes only to those who belong to Christ.

Lightfoot paraphrases verses 28-29 this way: "In Christ ye are all sons, all free. Every barrier is swept away. No special claims, no special disabilities exist in Him, none *can* exist. The conventional distinctions of religious caste or of social rank, even the natural distinction of sex, are banished hence. One heart beats in all: one mind guides all: one life is lived by all. Ye are all *one man*, for ye are members of Christ. And as members of Christ ye are Abraham's seed, ye claim the inheritance by virtue of a promise, which no law can set aside" (*Galatians*, p. 150). In Christ there is no room, no place, for these distinctions.

V. HEIRS OF GOD:
Galatians 4:1-7

Burton sums up the force of this paragraph in this way: "Still pursuing his purpose of persuading the Galatians that they would lose, not gain, by putting themselves under the law, Paul compares the condition under the law to that of an heir who is placed under a guardian for a period fixed by the father and in that time has no freedom of action, and describes it as a bondage under the elements of the world. Over against this he sets forth the condition into which they are brought by Christ as that of sons of God, living in filial and joyous fellowship with God" (*Galatians*, p. 210).

A. The Status of the Heir as a Child: vv. 1-2

Paul begins with the words, "What I am saying is [this]" (NIV). He is thereby "introducing an expansion or explanation of what has gone before" (Lightfoot, *Galatians*, p. 166).

He goes on to say that "as long as the heir is a child, he is no different from a slave, although he owns the whole estate" (NIV). As Lightfoot continues, "The minor was legally in much the same position as the slave. He could not perform any act, except through his legal representative" (*Galatians*, p. 166).

Describing the case of the child-heir more specifically, Paul says that he is subject to "guardians and trustees" until the time set by his father (v. 2). There has been considerable discussion as to the exact nature of these two terms, and the distinction beween them. Lightfoot suggests the translation: "controllers of his person and property," which fits well with "guardians and trustees."

The problem is that we do not know whether Paul had in mind Roman law, Greek law, Jewish custom, or just a general principle applying to young heirs. Under Roman law (at a slightly later period at least) "the minor was under a *tutor* till his fourteenth year, and thereafter under a *curator* until his twenty-fifth year" (Burton, *Galatians*, p. 212). But Paul says "until the time set by his father" (NIV). So many scholars prefer the context of a general principle.

B. The Application to the Readers: v. 3

"So also, when we were children, we were enslaved by the basic principles of the world" (NIV). What is meant by these "basic principles," or "elements" (KJV)? Lightfoot translates the word as "elementary teaching" and comments: "This is probably the correct interpretation, both as simpler in itself and as suiting the context better. St. Paul seems to be dwelling still on the rudimentary character of the law, as fitted for an earlier stage in the world's history" (*Galatians*, p. 167).

But there were Gentile as well as Jewish Christians in Galatia. Probably, then, Paul is thinking of all knowledge of religion up to that time as elementary.

C. The Full Rights of Sons: vv. 4-7

"But when the time had fully come, God sent his Son, born of a woman, born under law, to redeem those under law, that we might receive the full rights of sons" (vv. 4-5, NIV). "The fulness of the time" (KJV) was God's appointed time for sending His Son into the world as the Savior of mankind. This had been prepared for by many centuries of teaching and preaching. Long the Israelites had waited for their Messiah. But finally, in God's time, He came.

Christ was "born of a woman." This has a twofold thrust. It underscores the fact of His true humanity. And it perhaps hints at His virgin birth, which underlies His deity.

He was also "born under law," a true Jew. Only thus could He be the nation's Messiah, "son of David, the son of Abraham" (Matthew 1:1). But it may hint too at the fact that He, and He alone, perfectly fulfilled the righteous demands of the Law, and so was able to be the perfect sacrifice for our sins.

"Because you are sons, God sent the Spirit of his Son into our hearts, the Spirit who calls out, '*Abba*, Father.' So you are no longer a slave, but a son; and since you are a son, God has made you also an heir" (vv. 6-7, NIV). In Christ we are sons of the Father, and this is certified to us by the Holy Spirit. Thus all three members of the Trinity are beautifully involved in our salvation.

Abba is the Aramaic word for

DISCUSSION QUESTIONS

1. Why did God keep the Jews under Law until Christ came?
2. In what sense were we prisoners of sin?
3. What was the main function of the Law?
4. How do we become children of God?
5. In what sense are we heirs of God?
6. What will we inherit with Christ?

father. Aramaic was evidently the common language of Palestine in the time of Christ, the Jews having brought it back from their Babylonian exile. So when Jesus was praying in agony in the Garden of Gethsemane, He naturally cried out in His mother tongue, "Abba" (Mark 14:36). Paul also uses it in a parallel passage (Romans 8:15). These are the only three places in the New Testament where the term occurs.

CONTEMPORARY APPLICATION

The doctrine of assurance of salvation, or the witness of the Spirit, was set forth by Augustine but rejected by the Roman Catholic Church in the Middle Ages. It was recovered in large measure by Luther, Calvin, and the other Reformers in the sixteenth century and emphasized still more by Wesley in the great Evangelical Revival of the eighteenth century. It is one of the most precious truths of the gospel that we can *know* we are children of God.

SET FREE!

DEVOTIONAL READING	I Corinthians 6:12-20

ADULTS

Topic: *Set Free!*

Background Scripture: Galatians 4:8—5:12

Scripture Lesson: Galatians 4:8-11; 5:1-10

Memory Verse: *For freedom Christ has set us free; stand fast therefore, and do not submit again to a yoke of slavery.* Galatians 5:1

YOUTH

Topic: *Set Free!*

Background Scripture: Galatians 4:8—5:12

Scripture Lesson: Galatians 4:8-11; 5:1-10

Memory Verse: *For freedom Christ has set us free; stand fast therefore, and do not submit again to a yoke of slavery.* Galatians 5:1

CHILDREN

Topic: *Believing in God's Son*

Background Scripture: Matthew 16:13-17; Galatians 4:4-7

Scripture Lesson: Galatians 4:4-7

Memory Verse: *But when the time had fully come, God sent forth his Son.* Galatians 4:4

DAILY BIBLE READINGS

Mon., Sept. 13: Not Slave, but Free, Galatians 4:21-31.
Tues., Sept. 14: "Christ Has Set Us Free," Galatians 5:1-12.
Wed., Sept. 15: "The Truth Will Make You Free," John 8:31-36.
Thurs., Sept. 16: Free from Fear of Rulers, Acts 4:5-12.
Fri., Sept. 17: Speaking the Word with Boldness, Acts 4:13, 18-31.
Sat., Sept. 18: Freedom of Spirit, Even in Prison, Philippians 1:21-21.
Sun., Sept. 19: "United to the Lord," I Corinthians 6:12-20.

LESSON AIM

To help us see how we may be set entirely free in Christ.

LESSON SETTING

Time: A.D. 48-55

Place: The Roman province of Galatia was in the central part of Asia Minor (modern Turkey).

Set Free

I. The Peril of Being Enslaved: Galatians 4:8-11
   A. Former Slavery to Idolatry: v. 8
   B. Turning Back to Slavery: v. 9
   C. Enslaved to Jewish Law: v. 10
   D. Paul's Concern for the Galatians: v. 11

II. The Early Zeal of the Galatians for Paul: Galatians 4:12-16

III. The Zeal of the Judaizers: Galatians 4:17-20

IV. The Allegory of Hagar and Sarah: Galatians 4:21-31

V. Freedom in Christ: Galatians 5:1

VI. Slavery Through Circumcision: Galatians 5:2-6
   A. Renunciation of Christ: v. 2
   B. Obligation to Keep the Whole Law: v. 3
   C. Falling from Grace: v. 4
   D. Freedom Through Faith: vv. 5-6

VII. The Evil Work of the Judaizers: Galatians 5:7-10

SUGGESTED INTRODUCTION FOR ADULTS

Legalism is slavery; true freedom comes only in Christ. This is the theme of today's lesson. And it is still pertinent in the twentieth century.

In the first century the issue was between the slavery of Judaism and the freedom of Christianity. In Judaism salvation was through keeping the Law; in Christianity salvation is through faith in Christ.

Today the problem is legalism within the church. People assert that you have to conform to certain meticulous rules and regulations in order to be saved. The one who does not conform is not a Christian!

This is exactly what Paul is attacking in the Epistle to the Galatians. He warns his Galatian converts against being enslaved to the Law. They have been made free in Christ and must maintain this freedom.

SUGGESTED INTRODUCTION FOR YOUTH

Young people crave freedom; many of them demand it. But the kind of freedom they want—the privilege of doing their own "thing"—can turn out to be a terrible slavery. That is what thousands of youth are finding out today. They are determined to do as they please, but soon find they can't. There is no slavery worse than being a slave to one's own sinful desires and habits. Those, for instance, who have sought freedom from hard reality through drugs have soon discovered a far more horrible reality of inescapable slavery. We are only truly free when we are in Christ.

CONCEPTS FOR CHILDREN	1. We become children of God through faith in Christ.
	2. That is why God sent His Son into the world.
	3. Jesus is the proof that God loves us.
	4. We need to accept God's love in Christ.

THE LESSON COMMENTARY

I. THE PERIL OF BEING EN-SLAVED:
Galatians 4:8-11

A. Former Slavery to Idolatry: v. 8

Most of Paul's converts in the province of Galatia were Gentiles. This is clearly indicated by his statement here: "Formerly, when you did not know God, you were slaves to those who by nature are not gods" (NIV).

Idolatry is slavery. Anyone who has studied pagan religions knows that. The false gods of the heathen are not gods of love but gods of hate and cruel vengeance. Fear is the main controlling factor in these religions. In no other religion but Christianity do we hear the glorious Good News: "For God so loved the world that he gave his only begotten Son, that whosoever believeth in him should not perish, but have everlasting life" (John 3:16).

B. Turning Back to Slavery: v. 9

Paul chides his readers for turning back from their knowledge of the true God to enslavement by "the weak and beggerly elements" ("those weak and miserable principles" [NIV]) to which he has already referred in verse 3. E.D. Burton writes: "The present expression emphasizes the ineffectualness and poverty of the old religious systems in contrast with the power and richness of the gospel" (*A Critical and Exegetical Commentary on the Epistle to the Galatians*, International Critical Commentary, p. 231).

The Greek word for *beggarly* comes from a verb meaning to "crouch" or "cower," as a beggar does. The adjective finally came to be used in the sense of "poor," in con-trast to "rich." All other religions, Paul declares, are poverty-stricken and bankrupt.

What is meant by Paul's added clause, "or rather are known by God" (NIV)? Burton indicates that the true meaning is "having become objects of his favourable attention" (*Galatians*, p. 229).

C. Enslaved to Jewish Law: v. 10

Here Paul points out some of the "weak and beggarly elements" of legalism. He writes: "You are observing special days and months and seasons and years!" (NIV).

It is generally recognized that the main distinguishing feature of Judaism in that day was sabbath-observance. The Jews were very rigid in avoiding all travel and work on the sabbath, which ran from sunset Friday to sunset Saturday. Even today in Israel tourists are warned against taking a taxi on Friday afternoon unless they are sure they can reach their destination before sundown.

"Months" would refer especially to the religious celebration at the time of the new moon, with which each month began in their lunar calendar. In Colossians 2:16-17 Paul writes (also to Asia Minor): "Therefore do not let anyone judge you by what you eat or drink, or with regard to a religious festival, a new moon celebration, or a sabbath day. These are a shadow of the things that were to come; the reality, however, is found in Christ" (NIV).

"Seasons" would refer to any appointed times of religious observance. "Years" might refer to the sabbatical years specified in the Mosaic

Law. The Christian is not bound by these.

D. Paul's Concern for the Galatians: v. 11

"I fear for you, that somehow I have wasted my efforts on you" (NIV). If these converts were going to return to the slavery of legalism, Paul might as well not have preached to them. It is a sad note that the apostle sounds here. Was all his sacrifice and labor in vain?

II. THE EARLY ZEAL OF THE GALATIANS FOR PAUL: Galatians 4:12-16

Turning from argument to entreaty, Paul says: "I plead with you, brothers, become like me, for I became like you. You have done me no wrong" (v. 12, NIV). Appropriately Burton calls this verse "enigmatical and paradoxical." He offers this explanation: "The apostle desires the Galatians to emancipate themselves from bondage to law as he had done, and appeals to them to do this on the ground that he, who possessed the advantages of the law, had foregone them and put himself on the same level, in relation to law, with them" (*Galatians*, p. 236).

The King James Version says in verse 13: "Ye know how through infirmity of the flesh I preached the gospel unto you at the first." The Greek, however, does not say "through" but "on account of." The correct translation is: "It was because of an illness that I first preached the gospel to you" (NIV). It would seem that an attack of chronic malaria in the swampy land surrounding Perga had forced Paul to go up into the highlands around Pisidian Antioch (Acts 13:14), in the province of Galatia.

He goes on: "Even though my illness was a trial to you, you did not treat me with contempt or scorn" (v. 14, NIV). Malarial victims often appear weak and emaciated, not pleasant to look at. Yet the Galatians had received the apostle "as an angel of God, even as Christ Jesus."

Now Paul asks, "What has happened to all your joy?" (v. 15, NIV). If possible, the Galatians would have torn out their own eyes and given them to the one who brought them the Good News. (Paul may also have had poor eyesight.) Pathetically the apostle asks, "Have I now become your enemy by telling you the truth?" (v. 16, NIV).

III. THE ZEAL OF THE JUDAIZERS: Galatians 4:17-20

Verse 17 is very obscure in meaning in the King James Version. The New International Version offers a helpful translation: "Those people are zealous to win you over, but for no good. What they want is to alienate you from us, so that you may be zealous for them." "Alienate you" is literally "shut you out." "From us" is not in the Greek, as indicated by half-brackets in the New International Version. Burton thinks that "shut you out" goes more naturally with the idea of exclusion from the privileges of the gospel. J. B. Lightfoot agrees basically with this. He paraphrases verses 15-18 thus: "I once held the first place in your hearts. Now you look upon me as an enemy. Others have supplanted me. Only enquire into their aims. True, they pay court to you: but how hollow, how insincere is their interest in you! Their desire is to shut you out from Christ. Thus you will be driven to pay court to them" (*Epistle of St. Paul to the Galatians*, p. 176).

If the Galatian converts submitted themselves to the Law they would lose the benefits of their new birth. Paul writes: "My dear children, for whom I am again in the pains of childbirth until Christ is formed in you" (v. 19, NIV). Again he cries out, "I am perplexed about you" (v. 20).

IV. THE ALLEGORY OF HAGAR AND SARAH:
Galatians 4:21-31

The apostle contrasts Ishmael, who was born of the slave woman Hagar, with Isaac, the son of promise, born to the free woman Sarah. He says that these historical facts have allegorical meaning (Greek, *allegoroumena*, v. 23). The two women represent two covenants. Hagar stands for the covenant given at Mount Sinai "and corresponds to the present city of Jerusalem, because she is in slavery with her children" (v. 25, NIV). But Sarah represents the New Jerusalem and the freedom of the children of God in Christ (v. 26). Paul concludes: "Therefore, brothers, we are not children of the slave woman, but of the free woman" (v. 31, NIV).

V. FREEDOM IN CHRIST:
Galatians 5:1

The Greek reads this way: "It is for freedom that Christ has set us free. Stand firm, then, and do not let yourselves be burdened [or, "held in"] again by a yoke of slavery" (NIV). Here Paul uses a familiar figure of that day. A yoke was fastened around the neck of two oxen, so that they had to walk side by side and work together. They could not escape each other. The apostle likens this to the bondage of the Law. The Galatians had been made free in Christ. They must not insert their necks in the yoke of the Law of Moses.

In contrast to the yoke of legalism, with its dreadful burden of duty, is the yoke of Christ. There are no more beautiful words in the New Testament than this invitation of Jesus: "Come unto me, all you that labour and are heavy laden, and I will give you rest. Take my yoke upon you, and learn of me; for I am meek and lowly in heart: and ye shall find rest unto your souls. For my yoke is easy, and my burden is light" (Matthew 11:28-30).

VI. SLAVERY THROUGH CIRCUMCISION:
Galatians 5:2-6

A. Renunciation of Christ: v. 2

The apostle now sounds a solemn warning: "Behold, I Paul say unto you, that if ye be circumcised, Christ shall profit you nothing." He lays it right on the line: To be circumcised is to renounce Christ and His free grace.

Burton points out the force of this: "The acceptance of circumcision is, under the circumstances then existing in the Galatian churches, the acceptance of the principle of legalism, the committal of the Galatians to a relation to God wholly determined by conformity to statutes and leaving no place for Christ or the development of spiritual life through faith in him and spiritual fellowship with him" (*Galatians*, p. 272).

B. Obligation to Keep the Whole Law: v. 3

In this verse Paul gives another reason why the Galatians should not submit to circumcision: "For I testify again to every man that is circumcised, that he is a debtor to do the whole law." Again Burton makes the issues clear. He writes: "The acceptance of circumcision is in principle the acceptance of the whole legalistic scheme. The reasons that can be urged in favour of circumcision apply equally to every statute of the law."

He goes on to say: "That Paul points out this logical consequence of circumcision implies that the Judaisers had not done so. They were now urging the Galatians to accept circumcision as the rite by which they could become sons of Abraham and participators in the blessings of the Abrahamic covenant ...; they had already persuaded them to adopt the cycle of Jewish festivals (4:10)" (*Galatians*, p. 274). The noose was closing more tightly on the necks of these Galatian converts.

C. Falling from Grace: v. 4

"You who are trying to be justified by law have been alienated from Christ; you have fallen away from grace" (NIV). The expression "fallen from grace" (KJV) has been greatly misused by Christians. If a person slips up in his spiritual life or seems to become a little bit "worldly," people are quick to say that he has "fallen from grace." But that is not at all the meaning of the phrase as used here by Paul. He is talking about people in his day "falling away" from faith in Christ to a system of salvation by legalism; they have fallen away from grace to law. This has nothing to do with what we now commonly refer to as "backsliding."

It is not a matter of our faith in Christ becoming weak. Rather, Paul is talking about giving up reliance on Christ for salvation and depending on conformity to the Law to save us.

D. Freedom Through Faith: vv. 5-6

"But by faith we eagerly await through the Spirit the righteousness for which we hope" (v. 5, NIV). The apostle is pleading with his recent converts to stay in the path of faith. On that way we have the constant assistance of the Holy Spirit. Legalism stifles the Spirit; faith opens the door for Him to work in our lives. The final righteousness before God, which we all eagerly hope for, is possible to us only through the Spirit. It cannot be won by conformity to the Law, or by any legalistic endeavors.

The way of legalism is the way of the flesh, for it is dependence on our own efforts. In Christ, and only in Him, we are set free from the treadmill of trying to save ourselves, and we rest in Him and in His finished work for us on the cross.

"For in Christ Jesus neither circumcision nor uncircumcision has any value. The only thing that counts is faith expressing itself through love" (v. 6, NIV). Not legalism, but faith and love. This was Paul's message to the Galatians in the first century, and it is God's message to us today.

What does the apostle mean by "faith"? Burton writes: "Faith is for Paul, in its distinctively Christian expression, a committal of one's self to Christ, issuing in a vital fellowship with him, by which Christ becomes the controlling force in the moral life of the believer." He adds: "But the principle of Christ's life is love. . . . Faith in Christ, therefore, generates love, and through it becomes effective in conduct" (*Galatians*, p. 280).

This is Paul's answer to any objection that might be raised that freedom from Law leaves a person without moral control. It is faith working through love that is the moral dynamic of life.

VII. THE EVIL WORK OF THE JUDAIZERS: Galatians 5:7-10

Again the apostle's deep concern for the Galatians comes to the fore. He says to them: "You were running a good race. Who cut in on you and kept you from obeying the truth?" (v. 7, NIV). The figure is a familiar one. As the runners go around the track, one runner cuts in on a competitor and blocks him. This is what the Judaizers were doing to the Galatians. Paul affirms that the persuasion put forth by the Judaizers did not come from God ("him that calleth you"). Its origin was Satanic rather than divine. The

---

DISCUSSION QUESTIONS

1. How does Christ set us free?
2. How can we maintain this freedom?
3. Why do people prefer slavery?
4. Why does legalism have so much appeal?
5. What is the relation of faith and love?
6. What are some modern forms of religious slavery?

Judaizers posed as exponents of "the old-time religion," as against this new gospel of free grace preached by Paul. But it was not a call back to foundations of faith. Rather it was a summons to dead legalism, which in the final analysis is a denial of life.

Verse 9 is a proverb that is also quoted in exactly the same form in I Corinthians 5:6. So it should be put in quotation marks, as in the New International Version: "A little yeast works through the whole batch of dough." It refers to "the tendency of an influence seemingly small to spread until it dominates the whole situation. [Here it is used to indicate the fact that] the doctrine of the necessity of circumcision, insidiously presented by a few, is permeating and threatening to pervert the whole religious life of the Galatian churches" (Burton, *Galatians*, p. 283).

Optimistically Paul writes to them: "I have confidence in you through the Lord, that ye will be none otherwise minded" (v. 10). But the one who is causing them confusion will pay the penalty for it. The apostle realized the seriousness of the destructive work being carried on by the Judaizers.

CONTEMPORARY APPLICATION

Paul had been set free from the slavish legalism of the Pharisees of his day. And we can be set free from the Pharisaic legalisms of our time. It was in Christ that he found this glorious freedom, and that is the only place where we can find it.

That we can be completely free in Christ is good news, the best news ever heard by man. Legalism is bad news. To be given an endless list of dos and don'ts is to face frustration and ultimate failure. Christ is our victory.

SET FREE TO SERVE

DEVOTIONAL READING	I Peter 2:9-17

ADULTS

Topic: *Set Free to Serve*

Background Scripture: Galatians 5:13—6:18

Scripture Lesson: Galatians 5:13-15, 25—6:10

Memory Verse: *If we live by the Spirit, let us also walk by the Spirit.* Galatians 5:25

YOUTH

Topic: *Set Free to Serve*

Background Scripture: Galatians 5:13—6:18

Scripture Lesson: Galatians 5:13-15, 25—6:10

Memory Verse: *If we live by the Spirit, let us also walk by the Spirit.* Galatians 5:25

CHILDREN

Topic: *Serving One Another*

Background Scripture: John 13:1-20; Galatians 5:13-15

Scripture Lesson: John 13:16-17; Galatians 5:13-14

Memory Verse: *Through love be servants of one another.* Galatians 5:13

DAILY BIBLE READINGS

Mon., Sept. 20: Serve One Another with Love, Galatians 5:13-15.
Tues., Sept. 21: "Walk by the Spirit," Galatians 5:16-26.
Wed., Sept. 22: "Bear One Another's Burdens," Galatians 6:1-10.
Thurs., Sept. 23: "Glory . . . in the Cross," Galatians 6:11-18.
Fri., Sept. 24: "As One Who Serves," Luke 22:24-27.
Sat., Sept. 25: An Example of Service, John 13:1-5, 12-17.
Sun., Sept. 26: "Live as Servants of God," I Peter 2:9-17.

LESSON AIM

To help us see what true freedom is: freedom to love and serve others.

LESSON SETTING

Time: Between A.D. 48 and 55

Place: The place where Galatians was written is uncertain.

32

Set Free to Serve

LESSON OUTLINE

SUGGESTED INTRODUCTION FOR ADULTS

Christ does not set us free to do as we please. True freedom is freedom to love and serve others.

Those who want to be free to please themselves soon find themselves in abject slavery to the worst tyrant on earth—the sinful self. The self-centered self is arbitrary, brutal, capricious, demanding, envious, fitful, grabbing, hateful, insatiable, jealous, kicking, lustful, mean, narrow, obstinate, proud, querulous, resentful, selfish, temperamental, unreasonable, vicious, warlike, xenophobic, yapping, zigzagging—the whole thing!

The only way we can be freed from slavery to self is to let the Holy Spirit fill our hearts with divine love. Then we will be unselfish and will seek the best good of others.

SUGGESTED INTRODUCTION FOR YOUTH

What is the main sign of maturity? The best answer is "thinking of others." The immature person is always thinking of himself or herself.

This can be observed in restaurants. Most people would rather have older waitresses serving them, rather than teenagers waiting on them. The reason is obvious to any who "eat out" frequently.

Of course, there are many exceptions. There are "adult" ladies who fail to come back and offer a second cup of coffee. And there are teenage girls—many of them—who are extremely thoughtful of the ones they are waiting on. God bless them! It's a beautiful sight to see kind, thoughtful young people, and we see them often.

CONCEPTS FOR CHILDREN

1. Jesus washed His disciples' feet.
2. We should be willing to wait on others.
3. The Christian should be known for acts of humble, loving service.
4. We should seek to find opportunities for these.

THE LESSON COMMENTARY

I. LIMITATIONS OF FREEDOM: Galatians 5:13-15

A. Serving Others: v. 13

In our last lesson we noted that Paul describes with zest and enthusiasm the wonderful freedom we have in Christ. In Him we are set free from slavery to sin and the multifarious requirements of the Mosaic Law.

But lest we should glory selfishly in this freedom and think we can now do as we please, he reminds us that we are set free to serve. Our liberty must always be limited by love. And only unselfish love brings complete freedom. We have been called to liberty. But Paul warns: "Only use not liberty for an occasion to the flesh, but by love serve one another."

And herein lies a paradox: The more we serve others, the more free we find we actually are. For in loving service to others we are freed from the self-centeredness that is actually the worst slavery.

B. Loving One's Neighbor: v. 14

The Jewish rabbis counted 613 precepts in the Law: 248 commands and 365 prohibitions. Paul had studied all these under Gamaliel in Jerusalem. But now by the Holy Spirit he had come to realize that all of these were summed up in one commandment: "Love your neighbor as yourself." Love is the real fulfillment of the Law.

So we do not need to spend our time trying to check out hundreds of minute details in the Law. Rather, we are to let God's love fill our hearts and flow out through our lives to others. When we do this we are keeping the divine Law in the way that God wants us to.

This command implies that we must love ourselves before we can love our neighbor. Self-love has often been categorically condemned as entirely sinful. But it has now been increasingly recognized that the one who hates himself cannot love others. It is a true psychological insight: We cannot accept others until we accept ourselves.

Do we love our neighbors as we love ourselves? This is the constant test we must apply to our daily living. It is not natural; it is supernatural. Only God's grace can enable us to do it.

C. Avoiding Unkindness to Others: v. 15

"If you keep on biting and devouring each other, watch out or you will be destroyed by each other" (NIV). Evidently Paul sensed that there were some people even in the churches of Galatia that were picking on each other. The danger was that they would pick each other to pieces!

If we truly love each other we will not be indulging in cutting criticism. John says in his First Epistle that we are to have perfect love. We are to love others as Christ loves us.

II. LIFE IN THE SPIRIT: Galatians 5:16-26

A. The Spirit-led Life: vv. 16-18

How are we to avoid "biting and devouring each other"? Paul gives us the answer: "Walk in the Spirit, and ye shall not fulfill the lust of the flesh"

(v. 16). Walking in the Spirit means living in close fellowship with the Holy Spirit. It means that we let His holy presence pervade and permeate our intellect, emotions, and will. It is letting His love be the pattern of our thinking, feeling, and deciding. The only way that we can escape being dominated by fleshly desires is to submit ourselves completely to the Holy Spirit, to let Him dominate our lives. Ultimately, the controlling force in our lives will be either the "sinful nature" (NIV) or the Holy Spirit Himself. But we have to keep on walking in the Spirit day by day to avoid "the lust of the flesh."

"For the sinful nature desires what is contrary to the Spirit, and the Spirit what is contrary to the sinful nature. They are in conflict with each other so that you do not do what you want" (v. 17, NIV). (The King James Version has the Holy Spirit "lusting." By today's meaning of the word *lust* this almost sounds blasphemous.) Only the cleansing of the Holy Spirit can free us from this conflict.

Again Paul warns his Galatian converts against slavery to the Mosaic Law. He says that if they are led by the Spirit they are "not under the law" (v. 18).

B. The Works of the Flesh: vv. 19-21

In these three verses Paul lists fifteen works of the flesh. (The first item in the King James Version, "adultery," is not in the earliest Greek manuscripts.) This list divides itself naturally into four groupings, as indicated by semicolons in the New International Version. The first group consists of three sins connected with sensuality; the second, of two associated with pagan religions; the third, of eight describing a bad spirit or attitude toward people; the fourth, of two that are related to drunkenness. Lack of space forbids any extended treatment of these. But we should like to note a few.

"Fornication" is a general term for sexual immorality and includes what we call "adultery." "Lasciviousness" is better translated "sensuality" (NASB). "Witchcraft" is *pharmaceia* in the Greek; probably the earliest "pharmacists" were like witch-doctors! "Hatred" is literally "enmities." The term "variance" in the King James Version hardly communicates; the correct translation is "quarreling" or "discord." The word "emulations" is even more archaic; the Greek word simply means "jealousy." "Wrath" is *thymoi* (plural). Joseph H. Thayer says that the noun means "anger forthwith boiling up and soon subsiding again" (*Greek-English Lexicon of the New Testament*, p. 293). It is best translated "outbursts of anger" (NASB) or "fits of rage" (NIV). "Strifes" means "disputes" (NASB).

"Seditions" and "heresies" both suggest now something quite different from what the Greek says. The correct translation is "dissensions" and "factions." Today "sedition" has to do with rebellion against governmental authority, and "heresy" is wrong doctrine. Paul was talking about a spirit of division, probably in the church.

"Revellings" is a rather innocent word today. The Greek term means "carousings" (NASB) or "orgies" (NIV). These are the consequence of "drunkenness." The apostle declares that those who indulge in such things will "not inherit the kingdom of God" (v. 21).

C. The Fruit of the Spirit: vv. 22-24

We should not fail to note the tremendous contrast suggested by the word "but." The "works of the flesh" are the extreme opposite of "the fruit of the Spirit."

There is also a contrast implicit between "works" (plural) and "fruit" (singular). The "works of the flesh" are all *divisive*—divisive of countries, of communities, of churches, of homes, and of hearts. For instance, hatred and jealousy tear the individual's heart to pieces. To indulge in the works of the flesh is to destroy one's self.

But all the virtues listed under the fruit of the Spirit are *uniting*—uniting people and the individual heart. Love and humility unite us with others.

The first thing mentioned is "love." John Wesley says that this is "the root of all the rest." That is, love is the root from which all this fruit grows. Perhaps that is the reason Paul writes: "The fruit of the Spirit is love." The other eight things mentioned are then epexegetical of love; they describe how love manifests itself in daily living.

Again we can comment only briefly. "Joy" is always a fruit of love. Loving people are happy people. "Peace" comes when love and joy reign in the heart. Someone has defined peace as "the consciousness of adequate resources to meet every emergency of life." Only the Holy Spirit can give that peaceful sense of adequacy.

"Longsuffering," or "patience," is what all of us must have as long as we live or associate with other people. We differ so much in tastes and temperament that we will always have to be patient with each other.

"Gentleness" is perhaps better translated "kindness" (NASB, NIV). There is no manifestation of love that is more significant than "kindness." Spirit-filled Christians should always be kind!

"Faith" should be "faithfulness." The Greek word *pistis* is used for both, but here obviously means the latter. "Meekness" is "gentleness"—a characteristic of the dovelike Spirit that He wants to impart to us. "Temperance" means "self-control."

D. Keeping in Step with the Spirit: vv. 25-26

The word for "walk" in verse 25 is not the common verb for that in the New Testament—*peripateo*. Rather it is *stoicheo*, which suggests keeping in

line, or walking step by step. So a good translation of this verse would be: "If we live in the Spirit, let us also keep in step with the Spirit." That is the greatest secret of successful Christian living. If we do this we will never fail or go astray.

"Let us not be desirous of vain glory" (v. 26) is literally, "Let us not become conceited" (NIV), or "vain-minded." E. D. Burton suggests that the adjective means "glorying in vain things" or "setting value on things not really valuable" (*A Critical and Exegetical Commentary on the Epistle to the Galatians*, International Critical Commentary, p. 324).

We are not to provoke one another. The verb may be translated "challenging." Nor are we to envy each other. These two verbs, found only here in the New Testament, suggest actions and attitudes that are contrary to the Spirit of God.

III. BEARING EACH OTHER'S BURDENS: Galatians 6:1-5

A. Restoring the Fallen: v. 1

The apostle now proceeds to deal with relationships between the members of the church. He says that if a man is "overtaken" (surprised, caught, trapped) in a "fault" (Greek, "trespass"), those who are spiritual should restore him in the spirit of "meekness," or "gentleness." In other words, they should manifest the fruit of the Spirit in dealing with all people, even offenders. Then he adds: "But watch yourself; you also may be tempted" (NIV). All of us are subject to temptation. So we should be gentle and patient with those who stumble, treating them as we would want to be treated under the same circumstances.

B. Fulfilling the Law of Christ: v. 2

Paul declares that we fulfill the law of Christ when we bear each other's burdens. The law of Christ is the law of love. James (2:8) quotes "Thou shalt love thy neighbour as thyself" (Leviticus 19:18) and calls it "the royal law"—that is, the kingly law, given by the King of kings. As His children we should keep this royal law, acting in a kingly manner. Burden-bearing is one of the important responsibilities of Christians.

C. Appraising Ourselves Honestly: vv. 3-4

The logic of verse 3 is so utterly obvious that it hits us squarely in the face. Are we rating ourselves higher than we should? If so, we are foolish.

In the last analysis, everyone of us is "nothing" apart from Christ. It is only in Him that we are "something." So there is no ground for our boasting.

Paul goes on to say: "Each man should test his own actions. Then he can take pride in himself, without comparing himself to somebody else" (v. 4, NIV). This business of comparing ourselves with others is always wrong and unchristian. It is what each of us is before God that counts.

D. Carrying One's Own Load: v. 5

On the face of it, this verse seems to be in contradiction to verse 2. There we read, "Bear ye one another's burdens." Here it says, "For every man shall bear his own burden."

The seeming conflict does not exist in the original Greek, for there are two quite different words that are translated "burden." The one in verse 2 is *baros*, which comes from the verb *bareo*, "depress, weigh down." So it means a crushing weight, something that burdens and depresses a person.

But in verse 5 the word is *phortion*, which comes from *phero*, "carry." It was used in that day for the pack that a soldier had to carry on his back. So here it refers metaphorically to one's proper responsibilities in life. The correct translation is:

"For every man should carry his own load." When crushing burdens come on our fellow Christians, we should lend a helping hand. But we should not shift our own responsibilities on to others.

IV. SHARING WITH OTHERS: Galatians 6:6-10

A. Pupil with Teacher: v. 6

"Let him that is taught in the word communicate unto him that teacheth in all good things." What does this mean? Today it is the teacher who (hopefully) communicates knowledge to the pupil, not vice versa.

It is obvious that "communicate" is not the right word here. The Greek word means "share." The correct meaning of the verse is: "And let the one who is taught the word share all good things with him who teaches" (NASB).

The Greek words for "who is taught" and "who teaches" are interesting. Literally it is "the catechumen" and the one "who is catechising." This refers to the method of instruction in the early church. It was the question-and-answer method of the catechism.

What Paul is saying here is that teachers should be paid by their pupils. This agrees with what he says elsewhere (I Corinthians 9:14).

DISCUSSION QUESTIONS

1. Is there any such thing as absolute freedom?
2. How does love limit freedom?
3. How does it enhance our freedom?
4. What does it mean to "walk in the Spirit"?
5. How can we bear one another's burdens?
6. What are some advantages of a life of sharing?

B. Sowing and Reaping: vv. 7-9

The word translated "mocked" is a strong term in the Greek. Literally the verb means "to turn up one's nose at," and so "to sneer at, to mock." But no one can mock God successfully. Those who have tried it have found it didn't pay to attempt it.

The last part of the verse expresses one of the most significant principles of life: "A man reaps what he sows" (NIV). It is an inescapable law of life, demonstrated daily in thousands of ways.

The solemn truth is this: We can choose what to sow, but we cannot decide the consequences of that sowing. If we sow wheat, we will reap wheat. If we sow oats, we will reap oats. If we sow "wild oats," we will reap wild oats! And eating wild oats can be a very tragic experience for the one who has sown them.

There is another principle involved: "A man reaps more than he sows." This is true of wheat and oats. It is also true of wild oats.

Then Paul draws the contrast: "For the one who sows to his own flesh shall from the flesh reap corruption, but the one who sows to the Spirit shall from the Spirit reap eternal life" (v. 8, NASB). This twofold truth is being abundantly demonstrated in the lives of people all around us. In view of this fact it is hard to understand why young people, especially, will go ahead and sow to the flesh. We have all seen the results in the sad end of drunkards and profligates. On the other hand, we have seen the happy, fulfilled lives of those who have sowed to the Spirit. They have shown that they had eternal life—a new life in Christ—while here on earth. And they have died in the faith, leaving a testimony of assurance of eternal salvation in the Lord's presence. The choice is clear. How can anyone miss it?

We are urged not to be "weary in well doing," or "in doing good" (NIV). Why not? "For in due season we shall reap if we faint not"—"for at the proper time we will reap a harvest if we do not give up" (NIV). So let us not give up doing good! Let us keep on sowing good deeds, even if the harvest seems slow in coming. God has promised that it will come "in due time."

C. Doing Good to All: v. 10

We are admonished to do good to all people, but "especially to those who belong to the family of believers" (NIV). Both of these obligations are important. We should try to give help to all who need it—regardless of who they may be—as opportunity affords. But as Christians we have a special responsibility to our fellow Christians, just as we all have special obligations to our own families.

CONTEMPORARY APPLICATION

The last verse of the lesson (v. 10) ties in with verse 2. We are to help our fellow Christians in whatever way they need us.

One of the beautiful developments in some churches today has been the formation of "circles of concern." These are small groups within the church. Someone in the group is to contact by phone every other member of the group each week. If anyone in the group has an emergency arise, he is to contact the leader immediately, so that prayers, cards, calls, or whatever fits the need will be forthcoming. This is the kind of a thing Paul is advocating.

OUR NEED TO BE RECONCILED

DEVOTIONAL READING	Psalm 53
ADULTS	Topic: *Our Need to Be Reconciled* Background Scripture: Romans 1:16—2:11 Scripture Lesson: Romans 1:28—2:11 Memory Verse: *All have sinned and fall short of the glory of God.* Romans 3:23
YOUTH	Topic: Sinners: *One and All* Background Scripture: Romans 1:16—2:11 Scripture Lesson: Romans 1:28—2:11 Memory Verse: *All have sinned and fall short of the glory of God.* Romans 3:23
CHILDREN	Topic: *A Man with a Mission* Background Scripture: Acts 28:11-22; Romans 1:1-18 Scripture Lesson: Romans 1:15-17 Memory Verse: *For I am not ashamed of the gospel.* Romans 1:16
DAILY BIBLE READINGS	Mon., Sept. 27: Good News of Salvation, Romans 1:16-25. Tues., Sept. 28: God's Verdict, Romans 1:26-32. Wed., Sept. 29: "To Lead You to Repentance," Romans 2:1-11 Thurs., Sept. 30: "Return . . . to the Lord," Hosea 14. Fri., Oct. 1: Love and Law, Romans 13:8-14. Sat., Oct. 2: Forgiveness of Injuries, Matthew 18:15-22. Sun., Oct. 3: "Call upon God," Psalm 53.
LESSON AIM	To highlight the fact that all men have to be reconciled to God.
LESSON SETTING	Time: The Epistle to the Romans was written probably in A.D. 56. Place: It was written in Corinth.

LESSON OUTLINE	**Our Need to Be Reconciled**
	
	I. **Revelation of Righteousness:** Romans 1:16-17
	   A. The Power of the Gospel: v. 16
	   B. A Righteousness by Faith: v. 17

39

II. Revelation of Wrath: Romans 1:18-27
    A. The Revelation of God in Nature: vv. 18-20
    B. The Rejection of This Revelation: vv. 21-23
    C. The Rejection by God in Judgment: vv. 24-25
    D. The Results of This Rejection: vv. 26-27

III. Revelation of Human Sin: Romans 1:28-32
    A. Divine Judgment: v. 28
    B. Depraved Living: vv. 29-31
    C. Death as the Consequence: v. 32

IV. Revelation of Judgment: Romans 2:1-11
    A. The Fallacy of Human Judgment: vv. 1-3
    B. The Refusal to Repent: v. 4
    C. Repentance or Wrath: vv. 5-6
    D. The Rewards of Good and Evil: vv. 7-11

SUGGESTED INTRODUCTION FOR ADULTS

We have had four lessons from the Epistle to the Galatians. The remaining lessons of this quarter are taken from the Epistle to the Romans.

The relationship between these two letters is striking. Both emphasize strongly the truth of justification by faith, not by observing the Mosaic Law. Both go on to discuss sanctification, the inner life of the Spirit.

But the approach is different. In Galatians Paul is dealing with a crucial problem that had risen in the churches of Galatia, which he had founded on his first journey. His treatment is remedial. On the other hand, in Romans his purpose is preventative against what might happen there.

In Galatians the apostle sharply attacks the Judaizers who were undoing his work in that region. In Romans he is writing to a church he had never seen. So his approach is more positive. Instead of strong medicine to counteract a disease, it is solid food to build good health.

Redemption is the keynote of Romans. And the meaning of reconciliation is the main topic for these next six lessons.

SUGGESTED INTRODUCTION FOR YOUTH

"Sinners: One and All." That is the title of today's lesson. The golden text says: "All have sinned and fall short of the glory of God" (Romans 3:23).

This statement needs no documentation. We all know that we have sinned, and we all are conscious that we fall short of God's glory. We were made in the image of God, but we don't act like it. But the Good News is that there is redemption and reconciliation.

CONCEPTS FOR CHILDREN

1. Paul was a man with a mission—to save men.
2. He wanted to carry this mission to Rome.
3. We should all have a missionary concern.
4. We can show this by giving, and by showing Christ to those around us.

THE LESSON COMMENTARY

I. REVELATION OF RIGHTEOUS-NESS:
Romans 1:16-17

A. The Power of the Gospel: v. 16

This verse sounds the keynote of the Epistle. Paul says: "I am not ashamed of the gospel ["of Christ" (KJV) is not in the best Greek text] because it is the power of God for the salvation of everyone who believes: first for the Jew, then for the Gentile" (NIV).

Sidney Martin, for many years pastor of the Parkhead Church of the Nazarene in Glasgow, Scotland, once said in an address: "The gospel does not become articulate to any generation until it has first become incarnate in Christians." When the gospel transforms our lives it will become the power to save others.

What is meant by "power"? The Greek word here is *dynamis*—from which we get "dynamite, dynamic, dynamo." It means "strength, ability, power." Someone has said, "Power is the production of intended effects." The gospel is the power of God to effect man's salvation. William Sanday and Arthur C. Headlam make this inspiring observation: "The Gospel has all God's omnipotence behind it" (*A Critical and Exegetical Commentary on the Epistle to the Romans*, International Critical Commentary, p. 23).

B. A Righteousness by Faith: v. 17

The King James Version says "the righteousness of God." The Greek, however, does not have the definite article. It is "a righteousness from God" (NIV). But why not both? It is God's righteousness imparted to us through faith. "From faith to faith" is literally "out of faith into faith," or "faith from first to last" (NIV).

Again Paul quotes from Habakkuk 2:4, "The just shall live by faith" (cf. Galatians 3:11). This can also be translated "He who is righteous by faith shall live."

"Therein" means "in the gospel" (NIV). The gospel reveals to us the fact that through the death of Christ, the Righteous One, God has provided a righteousness for those who believe. When we by faith identify ourselves with Christ, His righteousness becomes ours.

II. REVELATION OF WRATH:
Romans 1:18-27

A. The Revelation of God in Nature: vv. 18-20

"The wrath of God is being revealed from heaven against all the godlessness and wickedness of men who suppress the truth by their wickedness" (v. 18, NIV). The King James Version says "hold the truth." The Greek, however, is not *echo*, "hold," but *katecho*, "hold down." It is true that the prefix *kata* sometimes has the perfective force, "hold fast." But practically all modern versions have "suppress" (RSV, NASB) or "hold back" (Beck). The New English Bible says, "stifling the truth."

Truth is not only mental, but also moral. True doctrine is hindered by wrong conduct.

Paul goes on to say that "what may be known about God is plain to them, because God has made it plain to them" (v. 19, NIV). There is no excuse for men being ignorant about God.

This important truth is spelled out carefully in verse 20. "God's invisible qualities—his eternal power and divine nature—have been clearly seen." How? "Understood by the things that are made." That is, the things in visible nature around us reveal the invisible qualities of God, for what a person does is a projection of his personality.

Admittedly the revelation of God in nature is limited and incomplete.

We see in nature something of the power of God, His love of beauty and variety, the orderliness of His mind. But we need to supplement this with the written revelation, the Bible, if we are going to understand His redemptive love.

B. The Rejection of This Revelation: vv. 21-23

Darwin's epochal work, *The Descent of Man*, pictured the human race as evolving from lower forms of life. But the true story of the descent of man is given in Romans 1:21-32. It shows man descending from the heights of knowing God down to the depths of depravity in religion and morals. This is one of the blackest sections of divine revelation in the Bible.

It starts with men on the high plane of "when they knew God" (v. 21). The first step downward was unthankfulness and a refusal to glorify God. The second step was intellectual darkness: They "became vain [empty] in their imaginations [thinking], and their foolish heart was darkened." The third step was folly. "Professing themselves to be wise, they became fools" (v. 22). The fourth step was idolatry (v. 23). And this idolatry had four stages of devolution: making images of man, birds, beasts, and reptiles. The cellar of idolatry is snake worship, which is still carried on in some parts of the world. And we must remember that a human being rises no higher than the gods he worships. If people worship animal images—as we once saw in a "Monkey Temple" in India—they will live like animals.

C. The Rejection by God in Judgment: vv. 24-25

Because men deliberately rejected God's revelation of Himself in nature, God rejected them and released them to suffer the consequences. There are no sadder words than "God gave them up."

This expression occurs three times in this section of Scripture (vv. 24, 26, 28). In verse 28 the King James Version has "God gave them over." But "gave them up" or "gave them over" is one word in Greek, *paredoken*, and it is the same in all three places and should be translated the same. Since the basic meaning of the verb is "hand over," some versions use "God gave them over" (NASB, NIV).

In either case it is the statement of a judicial act of God. If people will not follow Him but insist on rejection and disobedience, God hands them over to live as they wish. But the tragedy is that they become the miserable slaves of those things that they have chosen in place of God.

Idolatry leads to immorality. This sequence is clearly indicated here. Because the people rejected God and chose idols (v. 23), "God gave them over in the sinful desires of their hearts to sexual impurity for the degrading of their bodies with one another" (v. 24, NIV).

They "exchanged the truth of God for a lie" (v. 25, NIV), worshiping and serving creation rather than the Creator. The New English Bible says "they have bartered away the true God for a false one." This suggests the topic, "A Bad Bargain," which is also supported by the translation "exchanged . . . for" (vv. 23, 25, 26). It was a bad trade.

D. The Results of This Rejection: vv. 26-27

"Because of this, God gave them over to shameful lusts. Even their women exchanged natural relations for unnatural ones" (v. 26, NIV). This is what is called "lesbianism," which has become extremely common today.

What was true of the women also became true of the men: "In the same way the men also abandoned natural relations with women and were inflamed with lust for one another. Men committed indecent acts with other men, and received in themselves the due penalty for their perversion" (v. 27, NIV). The growth of homosexuality in the United States and Europe in the last few years is almost unbelievable. Probably it is more rampant than at anytime since the first century, when Paul wrote.

There is a great deal of effort today to put the cloak of respectability over this sin. There is now a denomination made up of homosexual churches. Some denominations are ordaining practicing homosexuals. But God's Word still condemns it as sin.

III. REVELATION OF HUMAN SIN: Romans 1:28-32

A. Divine Judgment: v. 28

There is a play on words here in the Greek that does not come out in English. "Like" is *edokimasan*; "reprobate" is *adokimon*. The first is the verb *dokimazo*, "approve after testing"; the second is the adjective *adokimon*, "rejected after testing." Men tested God, and refused to approve Him; they set Him aside. So God gave them over to rejection after He had tested them. The truth emphasized throughout this section is that divine judgment is fair. Coupled with it is the idea of the punishment fitting the crime. This basic principle is emphasized in both the Old Testament and the New and is vividly portrayed in Dante's *Inferno*.

One of the worst forms of penal justice is for God to give us over to do what we want to do. This means hell on earth and hell hereafter. A. T. Robertson says of the expression, "God gave them over," "The words sound to us like clods on the coffin as God leaves men to work their own wicked will" (*Word Pictures in the New Testament*, IV, 330). This clause spells moral abandonment.

B. Depraved Living: vv. 29-31

This is one of the longest catalogs of sin—twenty-three in all—in the Bible. The Greek word for "filled" means "filled to the full." So we might label this section, "Brimful with Badness."

It would be impossible to comment on each item. The first term in

verse 29, "unrighteousness" (KJV) or "wickedness" (NIV), may well be "a comprehensive term, including all that follows" (Sanday and Headlam, *Romans*, p. 47). "Fornication" (KJV) is not in the oldest Greek manuscripts. "Covetousness" we would call "greed" today. "Debate" should be "strife." "Malignity" should not be confused with "malignancy"! A better translation today would be "malice." The word "whisperers" means "gossips" (RSV, NASB, NIV).

"Backbiters" (v. 30) should be "slanderers." "Despiteful" ("spiteful"?) means "insolent." "Proud" is a compound word meaning "haughty" (RSV) or "arrogant" (NASB, NIV). "Disobedient to parents" is a very common sin today, but one that is condemned in both the Old and New Testaments.

In verse 31 each of the four items—"implacable" is not in the best Greek text—is one word in Greek; and they all begin with alpha-negative—*asynetous, asynthetous, astorgous, aneleemonas*. This can be represented appropriately in English by four adjectives ending in "less"—"senseless, faithless, heartless, ruthless" (NIV).

C. Death as the Consequence: v. 32

These sinners know that God's sentence on sin is death (cf. 6:23). In spite of that, they not only keep on in these sins, "but also approve of those who practice them" (NIV). They thus become partners in sin. Here is moral confusion and depth of guilt.

IV. REVELATION OF JUDGMENT: Romans 2:1-11

A. The Fallacy of Human Judgment: vv. 1-3

In these three verses we find (in the Greek) the verb *judge* four times and the noun *judgment* twice. In fact, divine judgment is the main topic of verses 1-16.

But in the first verse the main

emphasis is against judging others. Paul declares that the one who judges other people is "inexcusable." The Greek is *anapologetos*, "without apology." But the original meaning of "apology" was "defense." So the adjective literally means "defenseless." This is really stronger than "inexcusable." A person's mistakes may be inexcusable. "But 'defenseless' suggests a court scene, where the defendant stands before the judge condemned because he has not been able to defend his action. It is exactly this legal or forensic use which is found in early Greek writers, such as Polybius (second century B.C.). So the implication here is that the self-righteous Jew was defenseless before God and would be so at the final judgment" (Ralph Earle, *Word Meanings in the New Testament*, III, 42). That Paul is here addressing Jews is explicitly indicated in verse 17 and implied throughout the chapter. For the Jews were constantly sitting in judgment on the Gentiles.

The key phrase of this chapter is "the judgment of God" (vv. 2, 3). Three things are said about God's judgment: (1) It is "according to truth," v. 2; (2) It is "according to his deeds," v. 6; (3) It is "according to my gospel," v. 16.

All three of these are significant. Divine judgment will be according to the truth of God's Word, and it will be according to the truth of the situation, not hearsay. In the second place, it will be according to one's deeds. It is not enough to be sincere; we must be doing right. And in the third place, it will be according to the gospel. Sincerity and morality are not enough; we must be saved by Christ.

The fallacy of human judgment is underscored in verse 3. The one who is judging others for what they do is usually guilty of doing much the same things himself—not necessarily outwardly, but inwardly.

The second "thou" in this verse is emphatic in the Greek. It means "*you*, of all people"—will *you* escape the judgment of God? No! The fact that the man was a descendant of Abraham did not guarantee him exemption from divine judgment. Nor will church membership do it today.

B. The Refusal to Repent: v. 4

"Or do you show contempt for the riches of his kindness, tolerance and patience, not realizing that God's kindness should lead you to repentance?" (NIV). Too many people take kindness and patience—both human and divine—as signs of weakness. But God's kindness is intended to lead us to a place of repentance. To refuse to repent is to place ourselves at the judgment with no plea.

C. Repentance or Wrath: vv. 5-6

Paul spells this truth out more precisely and emphatically in verse 5: "But because of your stubbornness and your unrepentant heart, you are storing up wrath against yourself for the day of God's wrath, when his righteous judgment will be revealed" (NIV). A holy God, who is all-knowing and all-loving, will give righteous judgment. But refusal to repent, and rejection of infinite love, will finally eventuate in inescapable judgment. This is the note that needs to be sounded in our modern permissive society. Ultimately it is repentance or wrath.

The statement that God "will give

DISCUSSION QUESTIONS

1. Are we ever "ashamed of the gospel"?
2. In what way is it the power of God for salvation?
3. To what extent is God revealed in nature?
4. How can we suppress the truth by wickedness?
5. What sins named in 1:28-32 are especially prominent today?
6. Why is it dangerous to judge others?

to each person according to what he has done" (v. 6, NIV) is quoted from Psalm 62:12 and Proverbs 24:12. It is a clear Old Testament truth, reiterated in the New Testament. There is no way that a sinner can escape the righteous judgment of God.

D. The Rewards of Good and Evil: vv. 7-11

Verse 7 states that those who persist in doing good—and thus seek glory, honor, and immortality—will be rewarded with eternal life. Then Paul delineates the results of disobedience (vv. 8-9) and the rewards of obedience (v. 10).

The unrighteous are given a threefold description: "those who are self-seeking and who reject the truth and follow evil" (v. 8, NIV). Upon them will come "wrath and anger" (v. 8), plus "trouble and distress" (v. 9). These four things will be the reward "for every human being who does evil: first for the Jew, then for the Gentile." But to everyone who does good will come "glory, honor and peace"—"first for the Jew, then for the Gentile" (v. 10). Here we have repeated twice the expression we found in 1:16. The Jews were first in privilege. But that means that they were first in responsibility. And the same is true of church members today. Our added light makes us doubly responsible for what we do.

Paul closes this discussion by saying, "For there is no respect of persons [literally, "receiving of face"] with God" (v. 11). God's judgment will be impartial. "For God does not show favoritism" (NIV). No one can "get by" with Him.

CONTEMPORARY APPLICATION

Faced with these facts, we realize that man desperately needs to be reconciled. Rebellion calls for repentance. Dishonesty requires restitution. Disobedience must change to obedience.

Every Christian should be an agent of reconciliation—between man and God first of all, but also between man and man. Divine love can enable us to fulfill this crucial role.

RECONCILED THROUGH JESUS CHRIST

DEVOTIONAL READING | Isaiah 53

ADULTS

Topic: *Reconciled Through Jesus Christ*

Background Scripture: Romans 5:1-21

Scripture Lesson: Romans 5:1-11

Memory Verse: *God shows his love for us in that while we were yet sinners Christ died for us.* Romans 5:8

YOUTH

Topic: *At One Through Christ*

Background Scripture: Romans 5:1-21

Scripture Lesson: Romans 5:1-11

Memory Verse: *God shows his love for us in that while we were yet sinners Christ died for us.* Romans 5:8

CHILDREN

Topic: *God's Love for Us*

Background Scripture: Luke 15:3-7; Romans 5

Scripture Lesson: Luke 15:3-7

Memory Verse: *We have peace with God through our Lord Jesus Christ.* Romans 5:1

DAILY BIBLE READINGS

Mon., Oct. 4: Christ Died for Sinful Men, Romans 5:1-11.
Tues., Oct. 5: The Verdict of Grace, Romans 5:12-21.
Wed., Oct. 6: A Life Turned Around, Acts 22:3-16.
Thurs., Oct. 7: The Lord Listens, Psalm 69:13-18, 31-36.
Fri., Oct. 8: The Lord Cares, Psalm 138.
Sat., Oct. 9: "I Have Redeemed You," Isaiah 43:1-7.
Sun., Oct. 10: The Lord Saves, Isaiah 53.

LESSON AIM | To help us see the privileges that are ours in being reconciled to God through Christ.

LESSON SETTING

Time: A.D. 56

Place: Corinth

LESSON OUTLINE

Reconciled Through Jesus Christ

I. Results of Justification: Romans 5:1-5
   A. Peace: v. 1
   B. Joy: vv. 2-4
   C. Love: v. 5

46

II. **Redeeming Death of Christ:** Romans 5:6-8
   A. For Helpless Humanity: v. 6
   B. For Sinners: vv. 7-8

III. **Reconciling Death of Christ:** Romans 5:9-11
   A. Saved from God's Wrath: v. 9
   B. Reconciled Through Christ's Death: v. 10
   C. Rejoicing in God: v. 11

IV. **Results from Adam and Christ:** Romans 5:12-21
   A. Death Through Adam: vv. 12-14
   B. Life Through Christ: vv. 15-17
   C. Justification Through Christ: vv. 18-19
   D. Eternal Life Through Christ: vv. 20-21

SUGGESTED INTRODUCTION FOR ADULTS

The Epistle to the Romans divides itself naturally into three main sections. The first (chaps. 1—8) is doctrinal. The second (chaps. 9—11) is eschatological, discussing prophetically God's dealings with Israel. The third (chaps. 12—16) is practical.

In the doctrinal section we again have three divisions, treating three doctrines: I. Sin (1:18—3:20); II. Justification (3:21—5:21); III. Sanctification (chaps. 6—8). We also find three sections on Sin: I. The Sins of the Gentiles (1:18-32); II. The Sins of the Jews (2:1—3:8); III. The Sins of the Whole World (3:9-20). The main sins of the Gentiles were idolatry and immorality. The sins of the Jews were insincerity and inconsistency. The sins of all mankind are delineated in a quotation from the Old Testament (3:10-18). This long quotation includes material from six different psalms, plus Isaiah and Ecclesiastes.

Under the doctrine of Justification we again have three divisions: I. Justification by Faith (3:21-31); II. Example of Justification (chap. 4); III. Results of Justification (chap. 5). The example of justification is Abraham. In today's lesson we look at the results of justification. It is an exciting picture.

SUGGESTED INTRODUCTION FOR YOUTH

"At One Through Christ." That means at one with God through Christ and at one with fellow believers in Christ. This is the meaning of reconciliation.

The most important thing is that we, as sinners, should be reconciled to God. That is what happens in justification. But we also must be reconciled to others. This is the desperate need in the world today.

CONCEPTS FOR CHILDREN

1. God's love for us was shown in sending His Son to save us.
2. We were all lost sheep, who had gone astray.
3. Christ is the Good Shepherd who seeks the lost sheep.
4. God's love reaches out to everyone of us.

THE LESSON COMMENTARY

I. RESULTS OF JUSTIFICATION: Romans 5:1-5

A. Peace: v. 1

Paul declares that since we have been justified, "we have peace with God through our Lord Jesus Christ." But the earliest Greek manuscripts have the hortatory subjunctive, "let us have." This is found in both of our manuscripts of the fourth century (Vaticanus and Sinaiticus), as well as the three great manuscripts from the fifth century. All scholars agree that the manuscript evidence is overwhelmingly in favor of "let us have." But most commentators feel that the context demands the indicative, "we have." Which is it?

Most committee versions of the Bible (ASV, RSV, NASB, NIV) follow the majority of the commentators in reading, "we have." However, the English Revised Version (1881) had "let us have." This hortatory subjunctive was adopted in several translations done by individuals in this century. The New English Bible (1970) has, "Let us continue at peace with God. . . ." This implies that we have it.

It seems to us that the best solution is to combine these two ideas in one translation. Weymouth (1903) was reaching in this direction: "Let us enjoy peace with God." This is also found in Verkuyl's Berkeley Version (1945). Moffatt (1926) moved a long step nearer when he rendered it, "Let us enjoy the peace we have. . . ." But it was Phillips (1947) who went all the way in his meaningful translation of this verse: "Since then it is by faith that we are justified, let us grasp the fact that we *have* peace with God through our Lord Jesus Christ." That says it all. In his two-volume *Commentary on the Epistle of Paul to the Romans*, in the New International Commentary series, John Murray makes this helpful suggestion: "May not the exhortation here, as in other cases, presuppose the indicative (cf. 6:12 with 6:14)? And the thought would be: 'since we have peace with God, let us take full advantage of this status.' Paradoxically stated, it would mean: 'since we have it, let us have it.' 'Peace with God' is a gift of grace flowing from justification and inseparable from it, but exhortation is relevant and necessary to the cultivation of the privilege" (I, 159). That is exactly the way we see it.

B. Joy: vv. 2-4

An old Scots preacher is credited with saying, "Peace is joy resting; joy is peace dancing." Joy has zip and zest; it has a lilt and a lift. Joyless living is drab, unendurable living.

Paul declares that through Christ we have "access by faith into this grace wherein we stand." God's grace is a firm foundation for our feet.

He goes on to say that "we rejoice in hope of the glory of God." It is hope that lends wings to our faith.

What is our hope? That one day we will share God's glory. Even in this life we experience divine glory in our souls. But in the coming Kingdom, we are told, we shall reign with Christ in glory. All the limitations of this life will be gone. In our glorified body we will live the full life of glory in God's presence.

We are to rejoice not only in this glorious hope, but also "in tribulations" (v. 3). The translation of the verb here as "glory" (KJV) is unfortunate, for the English reader will naturally connect this with "glory" in verse 2. But there is no such connection in the Greek. Actually the two verbs—"rejoice" (v. 2) and "glory" (v. 3) are exactly the same in the original (*kauchometha*). Obviously they should be translated the same in English, as they are in modern versions. We rejoice in hope of sharing God's glory. We also rejoice in tribulations or "sufferings" (NIV).

The Greek noun translated "tribulation" comes from the verb meaning "to press," used metaphorically in the sense of "oppress." So it suggests the pressures of life. It can be translated "affliction" or "distress."

How can we rejoice in such circumstances? Paul gives us the answer: "knowing that tribulation worketh patience." A better translation is, "because we know that suffering produces perseverance" (NIV).

With three exceptions the King James Version always translates the Greek word *hypomone* by "patience" (29 times). But all lexicons and commentaries are agreed that this is not the correct meaning. The word means "endurance, steadfastness, perseverance." The term "patience" is too passive; the Greek word is positive and active. Joseph H. Thayer in *Greek-English Lexicon of the New Testament*, explains it this way: "In the NT the characteristic of a man who is unswerved from his deliberate purpose and his loyalty to faith and piety by even the greatest trials and sufferings" (p. 644).

It is through suffering that we develop perseverance, the steadfast determination to obey God, no matter what happens. Realizing this, we rejoice in our sufferings. They are an inevitable factor in our growth as strong Christians.

This perseverance that comes through suffering produces "character" (v. 4). The King James Version says "experience." But this is inadequate, if not indeed inaccurate.

The Greek word is *dokime*, which comes from the adjective *dokimos*, "tested, accepted, approved." William Sanday and Arthur C. Headlam give a good definition, which fits this passage perfectly: "The character which results from the process of trial, the temper of the veteran as opposed to that of the raw recruit" (*A Critical and Exegetical Commentary on the Epistle to the Romans*, International Critical Commentary, p. 125). James Denney defines it as "a spiritual state which has shown itself proof under trial" (*Expositor's Greek Testament*, II, 624). He also says, "Perhaps the best English equivalent of *dokime* would be *character*." True character is always costly.

Paul goes on to say that character produces "hope." Without hope life is worthless. It is the hope of a glorious future that enables us to forget the past and keep going in a trying present. We sing, "It will be worth it all when we see Jesus," and then we press on toward the goal. Paul lists hope as one of the three most important ingredients of life—"faith, hope, love" (I Corinthians 13:13). As far as this world is concerned, when hope is gone life is gone.

C. Love: v. 5

"And hope does not disappoint us, because God has poured out his love into our hearts by the Holy Spirit, whom he has given us" (NIV). What a beautiful picture: God's love poured out into our hearts by the Holy Spirit. The only way that our hearts can be filled with divine love is for them to be filled with the Holy Spirit. For the Holy Spirit is God, and God is love. This is what John is talking about when he says that God's "love is perfected in us" (I John 4:12).

These first five verses of Romans 5 portray some of the glories of the Christian life. The fruits of justification are peace, joy, hope, and love. The peace comes when we are made right with God. The joy results from our contemplation of the glorious future that awaits us as the children of God. The hope is made firm as the end result of suffering, perseverance, and character. And the Holy Spirit, who fills our hearts with divine love, gives us the constant assurance that this hope will not disappoint us.

II. REDEEMING DEATH OF CHRIST: Romans 5:6-8

A. For Helpless Humanity: v. 6

"You see, at just the right time, when we were still powerless, Christ died for the ungodly" (NIV). The Greek word for "powerless" is *asthenos*. It comes from *a*—negative— and *stenos*, "strength." So it literally means "without strength" (KJV). In

Acts 4:9 it is used for the "impotent" man who was powerless to walk.

"Hence it aptly describes the unregenerated man, who is 'weak' and 'helpless,' unable to help himself but completely dependent on a Higher Power. Until the unsaved person is willing to recognize and confess his utter helplessness and hopelessness he cannot be a recipient of God's redeeming grace in Christ Jesus" (Ralph Earle, *Word Meanings in the New Testament*, III, 100-101).

B. For Sinners: vv. 7-8

"Very rarely will anyone die for a righteous man, though for a good man someone might possibly dare to die" (v. 7, NIV). Paul is registering this obvious truth as a backdrop for the startling contrast that he presents in the next verse. He wants to point up the infinite distance between the human and the divine. And so he declares: "But God demonstrates his own love for us in this: While we were sinners, Christ died for us" (v. 8, NIV).

The word for "sinner" literally means "one who misses the mark." Heinrich Cremer says that it is used in the Septuagint (Greek Old Testament) for "missing the divinely appointed goal, deviation from what is pleasing to God" (*Biblico-Theological Lexicon of New Testament Greek*, p. 99).

"A 'sinner,' then, is not necessarily one who has gone far astray in wicked living. Rather, every man without Christ is a sinner because he has missed the goal of God's purpose for us as human beings; namely, that we should live holy lives in fellowship with God" (Earle, *Word Meanings*, III, 101). This is why all people outside Christ are correctly called "sinners."

III. RECONCILING   DEATH   OF CHRIST:
Romans 5:9-11

A. Saved from God's Wrath: v. 9

The term translated "wrath" (KJV) is in Greek "the wrath." It obviously means "God's wrath" (NIV). Even the New American Standard Bible, which is a highly literal, word-for-word translation, says "the wrath *of God*."

We are justified by Christ's "blood," that is, by His death for us on the cross. Hebrews 9:22 echoes the Old Testament statement that without the shedding of blood there is no remission of sins. Only the blood of the sinless Son of God could atone for our sins. Through faith in that blood we are made just, or righteous, in the sight of God.

B. Reconciled   Through   Christ's Death: v. 10

In this verse Paul gives the third stage in his description of those for whom Christ died. In verse 6 he says, "when we were still powerless" (NIV)—weak, helpless. In verse 8 he says, "when we were God's enemies" (NIV).

These are climactic in progression. Not only are people outside of Christ "powerless"; they are "sinners." But worst of all they are "enemies" of God. The Greek word originally meant "hated" or "hateful." In the New Testament it means "hostile."

"This term shows the seriousness of sin. Reduced to the final analysis, sin is rebellion against God. It is not only a failure, but a refusal, to do God's will. Only when understood thus can the serious consequences of sin be properly appreciated" (Earle, *Word Meanings*, III, 102).

Having been reconciled to God by the death of His Son, we shall be "saved by his life." The Greek has *en*, which most literally means "in." Some prefer the translation "in his life." It is in His life that we find full life. It is only as we are "in Christ" that we are fully saved.

C. Rejoicing in God: v. 11

In verse 2 Paul says that we "rejoice in hope." In verse 3 he says that we "rejoice in our sufferings." In the third place, he now says that we "rejoice in God."

This is another threefold climax. We are to rejoice in hope. But when the clouds of sorrow and suffering close in on us, we are still to rejoice in these circumstances. And when it seems impossible to rejoice in anything future or present, we can still "rejoice in God." (It is odd that the same Greek verb is translated in the King James Version as "rejoice" in verse 2, "glory" in verse 3, and "joy" in verse 11.)

When the Revised Standard Version came out in 1952 it was severely criticized for robbing us of the great word "atonement," because it had "reconciliation" in this verse in place of "atonement" (KJV). But in the Old Testament the Revised Standard Version has "atonement" eighty-seven times as against seventy-four times in the King James Version. In the second place, the word *atonement* occurs only once in the King James Version New Testament (here). And in the third place, the Greek word used here is translated "reconciling" in 11:5 and "reconciliation" in II Corinthians 5:18-19—the only other places in the New Testament where it occurs! We might also add that the Greek verb derived from this noun occurs six times in the New Testament and is always translated "reconcile" in the King James Version (cf. verse 10 here). In I Corinthians 7:11 it is used of a wife being reconciled to her husband. It is obvious that "reconciliation" is the correct translation here (RSV, NASB, NIV).

Thayer says that the Greek noun is used for the "adjustment of a difference, reconciliation, restoration to favor," and "in the New Testament, of the restoration of the favor to sinners that repent and put their trust in the expiatory death of Christ" (*Lexicon*, p. 333).

We should not fail to note that we "receive" this reconciliation. We cannot earn it or buy it. We have to accept it as a free gift from a loving God. The infinite price of it was paid by Christ in His death for us on the cross.

IV. RESULTS FROM ADAM AND CHRIST: Romans 5:12-21

A. Death Through Adam: vv. 12-14

"Sin" and "death" both carry the definite article here and seem to be personified. Like a sneaking, stalking animal of prey, Sin came into the world, with the frightful monster Death hard on its heels. Because all men were trapped by Sin, all men were the victims of Death. Even without the Law given at Sinai, "Death reigned from Adam to Moses" (v. 14).

B. Life Through Christ: vv. 15-17

Death came as the penalty for the sin of "one man" (v. 12), Adam. In contrast to that is the free gift of God's grace that comes by "one man, Jesus Christ" (v. 15). Condemnation came as the result of one sin, Adam's (v. 16). But in spite of many trespasses since, the gift of justification has been offered to all. This is "God's abundant provision of grace and of the gift of righteousness" (v. 17, NIV). And it all comes "through the one man, Jesus Christ."

C. Justification Through Christ: vv. 18-19

Adam's sin was cosmic in significance. But so was Christ's sacrificial

---

DISCUSSION QUESTIONS

1. How can we retain the peace that comes through justification?
2. What is the Christian's hope?
3. How can we keep our hearts filled with love?
4. How is "character" produced?
5. What is the value of suffering?
6. What is meant by reconciliation?

death on the cross. Verse 18 puts them together: "Consequently, just as the result of one trespass was condemnation for all men, so also the result of one act of righteousness was justification that brings life for all men" (NIV). Potentially and provisionally the death of Christ offers justification for all men. But they only receive it by faith. The disobedience of Adam brought sin and death on all men; the obedience of Christ results in "the many" being "made righteous" (v. 19).

D. Eternal Life Through Christ: vv. 20-21

The Law at Sinai "was added" so that disobedience of specific commands would make people more conscious of their sinning—"so that the trespass might increase" (v. 20, NIV). Then comes the beautiful statement: "But where sin abounded, grace did much more abound." God's grace is greater than man's sin. That's the Good News.

Sin has reigned in death. But God's purpose is that "grace might reign through righteousness to bring eternal life through Jesus Christ our Lord" (v. 21, NIV). Through the reign of grace we will be brought to the ultimate goal of salvation—eternal life. And this comes to us, like everything else good in this chapter, through Jesus Christ.

CONTEMPORARY APPLICATION

Commenting on "let us have peace" (v. 1), A. B. Simpson tells of an evangelist who led a lady into the assurance of her salvation by a verse of Scripture. He then wrote this verse on a slip of paper and gave it to her.

The next morning she said to her son, who had been with her: "I don't feel as if I'm saved this morning." Quickly he ran to the bedroom, took out of her purse the slip of paper and said joyfully, "Why, mother, it says the same thing as last night." That brought peace again. By faith in God's unchanging Word, we are to enjoy the peace He has given us.

THE NEW LIFE IN CHRIST

DEVOTIONAL READING	Colossians 3:5-17

ADULTS	Topic: *Alive in Christ* Background Scripture: Romans 6 Scripture Lesson: Romans 6:12-23 Memory Verse: *If anyone is in Christ, he is a new creation.* II Corinthians 5:17

YOUTH	Topic: *Alive in Christ* Background Scripture: Romans 6 Scripture Lesson: Romans 6:12-23 Memory Verse: *If anyone is in Christ, he is a new creation.* II Corinthians 5:17

CHILDREN	Topic: *Growing as Christians* Background Scripture: Luke 2:41-52; Romans 6 Scripture Lesson: Luke 2:41-52 Memory Verse: *And Jesus increased in wisdom and stature and in favor with God and man.* Luke 2:52

DAILY BIBLE READINGS	Mon., Oct. 11: Dead to Sin, Alive to God, Romans 6:1-11. Tues., Oct. 12: Offer Yourselves to God, Romans 6:12-23. Wed., Oct. 13: Our Life in Christ, Philippians 2:1-11. Thurs., Oct. 14: A Different Heart, a New Spirit, Ezekiel 11:14-25. Fri., Oct. 15: God's Law in Our Hearts, Jeremiah 31:27-34. Sat., Oct. 16: The Reality in Christ, Colossians 3:5-17. Sun., Oct. 17: Rules of Christian Behavior, Colossians 3:5-17.

LESSON AIM	To discover the secret of finding a new life in Christ.

LESSON SETTING	Time: Romans was written about A.D. 56. Place: It was written in Corinth.

LESSON OUTLINE	The New Life in Christ I. Life Through Death: Romans 6:1-4

II. Life Through Union with Christ: Romans 6:5-7

III. Life Through Faith in Christ: Romans 6:8-10

IV. Dead to Sin, Alive to God: Romans 6:11

V. Living the New Life: Romans 6:12-14
  A. Rejecting Sin's Reign: v. 12
  B. Offering Our Bodies to God's Rule: v. 13
  C. Denying Slavery to Sin: v. 14

VI. Slaves to Righteousness: Romans 6:15-18
  A. No More Sinning: v. 15
  B. Slaves to Someone: v. 16
  C. Freed from Sin, Slaves to Righteousness: vv. 17-18

VII. Freed from Sin, Slaves to God: Romans 6:19-23
  A. A New Slavery: v. 19
  B. Results of Slavery to Sin: vv. 20-21
  C. Results of Slavery to God: vv. 22-23

SUGGESTED INTRODUCTION FOR ADULTS

We have already noted that Paul expounds three main doctrines in the Epistle to the Romans. The first is the doctrine of sin (1:18—3:20). The second is the doctrine of justification (3:21—5:21). Now we take up the third doctrine, sanctification (chaps. 6—8).

There are two sides to sanctification. Negatively it is through death to self. This is highlighted in chapter 6. Positively it is through the fullness of the Spirit. This is described in chapter 8. Chapter 7, which intervenes, we are to study in our next lesson.

Some people differentiate between justification and sanctification by saying that justification is objective, a change in our record, whereas sanctification is the subjective side of salvation—what happens to us inside. But regeneration, or the new birth, is also an inner experience, a change of heart. Perhaps it is better to think of sanctification in terms of the Holy Spirit living the Christ-life in us, as He fills our hearts with His presence and power.

SUGGESTED INTRODUCTION FOR YOUTH

"Alive in Christ!" That is the only way we can live a new life.

Most young people are at least a bit unhappy about the life they are living. They would like a new life. But where or how can they find it?

Christ is the answer! Without Him we are dead in our sins. By faith we can become alive in Christ. That brings supreme satisfaction.

CONCEPTS FOR CHILDREN

1. We must belong to Christ before we can grow as Christians.

2. Jesus had a normal growth—physically, mentally, socially, spiritually (Luke 2:52).
3. We should seek to develop in these four ways.
4. The Holy Spirit will help us to grow as Christians, if we ask Him to guide us.

THE LESSON COMMENTARY

I. LIFE THROUGH DEATH:
Romans 6:1-4

In Paul's Epistles we frequently find him countering the arguments of his opponents. The first verse here is a typical example: "What shall we say then? Shall we continue in sin, that grace may abound?" This could be taken as a false inference from his statement in 5:20—"But where sin abounded, grace did much more abound." Some were evidently assuming that the more they sinned the more God's grace was demonstrated in their lives.

What was Paul's answer to this? "God forbid. How shall we, that are dead to sin, live any longer therein?" (v. 2). We have noted before that "God forbid" is literally "May it not be." It is a strong ejaculatory expression, meaning "By no means!" (NIV). Paul uses this fourteen times in his Epistles and it occurs in one other place in the New Testament (Luke 20:16).

The apostle's answer is that as Christ's people we are to be dead to sin. How then can we live longer in it?

He goes on to say that when we were baptized into Christ we were baptized into His death (v. 3). Through baptism we were buried with Him into death, so that as He was raised from the dead, we also should "walk in newness of life" (v. 4).

In St. Paul's Epistle to the Romans W. H. Griffith Thomas points out the transition that takes place at the beginning of chapter 6. He writes: "But at once comes the important question of the life to be lived by the justified man. The past may have been met (ch. v.); but what about the present? This

is the problem now to be considered. From ch. iii. 21 to ch. v. 21 the theme has been Justification by Faith in the Crucified Savior; now, from ch. vi. 1 to ch. viii. 39, it is Sanctification by Faith in the Risen Lord. . . . Justification is the strait gate through which we enter the narrow way of holiness, and from this point we are to deal with the way, not with the gate. Hitherto the contrast has been between wrath and justification; now it is to be between sin and holiness" (p. 163).

Joseph Agar Beet likewise underscores the marked change that comes at the beginning of chapter 6. Using the same three divisions for chapters 1—8 that we noted in our introduction, he says: "DIV. I revealed to us the anger of God against all sin; DIV. II has now revealed deliverance from this anger, and restoration to His favour. DIV. III will reveal deliverance from the power of sin, and a new life free from sin" (A Commentary on St. Paul's Epistle to the Romans, pp. 171-72).

II. LIFE THROUGH UNION WITH CHRIST:
Romans 6:5-7

Verse 5 further explicates and enforces the truth of verse 4. "Planted together" translates the Greek adjective symphytos, found only here in the New Testament. It comes from the verb symphyo, which means "make to grow together." So it signifies "grown along with, united with." William Sanday and Arthur C. Headlam say of this adjective: "The word exactly expresses the process by which a graft becomes united with the life of a tree.

So the Christian becomes 'grafted into' Christ" (*A Critical and Exegetical Commentary on the Epistle to the Romans*, International Critical Commentary, p. 157).

John Murray writes: "The word used to express our union with Christ in his death and resurrection means, strictly, 'grown together'. . . . No term could more adequately convey the intimacy of the union involved. It is not that this relationship is conceived of as a process of growth progressively realized. The terms of the clause in question and the context do not allow for this notion. The death of Christ was not a process and neither is our conformity to his death a process. We are in the condition of having become conformed to his death" (*Commentary on the Epistle of Paul to the Romans*, New International Commentary on the New Testament, I, 218).

Romans 6:6 is one of the crucial verses of this Epistle: "Knowing this, that our old man is crucified with him that the body of sin might be destroyed, that henceforth we should not serve sin." What is "our old man"? Most recent versions agree that it is "our old self" (RSV, NASB, NIV). It is the carnal, selfish, self-willed, self-centered self that must be crucified.

The Greek says that our old man "was crucified." In the plan and purpose of God this took place at Calvary. But we must know that what was potential and provisional at the cross has become actual and experiential in us.

Verse 7 sums up the main thrust here: "For he that is dead is freed from sin." We are not saved *in* sin but saved *from* sin.

III. LIFE THROUGH FAITH IN CHRIST:
Romans 6:8-10

Verse 8 should be translated: "Now if we died with Christ, we believe that we will also live with him" (NIV). Christ's crucifixion was a definite event in history. And our crucifixion must likewise be a definite event in our history. But we must also believe that we shall live together with Him—both here and hereafter.

This thought is reinforced by verses 9 and 10. When Christ died, sin had no more dominion over Him. When we die with Him, we too are dead to sin's dominion. And, like Christ, we are to live to God.

It should be obvious from this Scripture that sinning everyday is not God's will for His children. We are to die with Christ to sin, so that we shall no longer be slaves to sin (the literal meaning of verse 6b). Rather, we are to live the resurrection life of victory over sin in Christ!

IV. DEAD TO SIN, ALIVE TO GOD:
Romans 6:11

In view of all this Paul says: "Likewise reckon ye also yourselves to be dead indeed unto sin, but alive unto God through Jesus Christ our Lord." In the best Greek text the last clause reads: "but alive to God in Christ Jesus."

The word "reckon" requires a word of comment. Someone asks, "Do you think it will rain tomorrow?" and we answer, "Well, I reckon it will." Obviously in popular colloquial use "reckon" simply means "guess" or "think."

But the Greek word here was a technical commercial term in the first century. It meant "count" or "account." By faith we are to account ourselves dead to sin.

But the last part of the verse is also important. The only way we can stay dead to sin is to keep ourselves continuously and increasingly alive to God. This is the most significant secret of spiritual victory.

V. LIVING THE NEW LIFE:
Romans 6:12-14

A. Rejecting Sin's Reign: v. 12

"Therefore, do not let sin reign in your mortal body so that you obey its evil desires" (NIV). *Mortal* means "subject to death," and that is what our physical bodies are, as we well know.

Instead of letting sin reign in our bodies, we are to let Christ reign. When He is "Lord of all," we will not be in slavery to evil desires, to passions and lust, but by His power we are to live a holy life.

B. Offering Our Bodies to God's Rule: v. 13

The message of verse 12 is spelled out in more detail and extended here. We are to stop offering the parts of our body as instruments of sin. Rather, we are to offer ourselves to God, as those He has made alive from the dead. And we are to offer the parts of our body to Him as instruments of righteousness.

An important truth for every Christian to realize is that we are to give ourselves in a decisive commitment (aorist tense in the Greek) to God—body, soul, and spirit. God does not want just a part of us; He wants us to be completely His. This is the only way we can live a true Christian life. We are not fully Christian unless we belong wholly to God.

Beet writes: "Instead of obeying the desires of our body, and thus permitting sin to erect its throne there and use our bodily powers for its own ends, Paul bids us place our whole personality at the disposal of God, resolving that henceforth our hands shall do His work, our feet run on His errands, and our lips speak His message, in His conflict against sin" (*Romans*, p. 181).

C. Denying Slavery to Sin: v. 14

"For sin shall not be your master, because you are not under law, but under grace" (NIV). This continues what Paul has just said in verse 13.

VI. SLAVES TO RIGHTEOUSNESS: Romans 6:15-18

A. No More Sinning: v. 15

Again Paul has to challenge the false deductions that might be made from what he has just said. Some people might draw wrong conclusions from the last part of verse 14. So in similar language to verse 1, the apostle writes: "What then? shall we sin, because we are not under the law, but under grace? God forbid."

Griffith Thomas points out the difference between the questions in verse 1 and here. He writes: "The first question is 'Shall we continue *in* sin?' The second is 'Shall we continue *to* sin?' The former deals with the permanent state; the latter with the isolated act. The Apostle has already shown that the justified believer will not be able to continue the life of sin which he formerly led. He has now to show that he will not even commit a single act of sin, if he realizes what it means to be 'under grace'" (*Romans*, p. 175).

B. Slaves to Someone: v. 16

The word *servants* occurs twice in this verse and several times in the remaining verses of this chapter. The Greek word is *doulos*, which is found 125 times in the New Testament. In the King James Version it is rendered "servant" 118 of these times.

But the word *doulos* literally means "one who is bound"—that is, legally to his master who owns him. And so the real meaning is "slave." It is claimed that one-half of the population of the Roman Empire in the first century consisted of slaves. On *doulos* William F. Arndt and F. Wilbur Gingrich make this observation: "'Servant' for 'slave' is largely confined to Biblical translations and early American times.... In normal usage at the present time the two words are carefully distinguished" (*Greek-English Lexicon of the New Testament*, p. 204). So the correct translation here is "slaves," as in most modern versions. Paul is not talking about hired servants, who can come and go as they wish, but about slaves, who are subject to the will of their masters. Adolph Deissmann bemoans the fact that "the word *slave* with its satellites has been translated servant, to the total effacement of its ancient significance, in our Bibles" (*Light from the Ancient East*, p. 319).

The apostle declares that "when you offer yourselves to someone to obey him as slaves, you are slaves to the one whom you obey" (NIV). We take our choice as to whether we will be slaves to sin, which leads to death, or slaves to obedience (to God), which leads to righteousness.

C. Freed from Sin, Slaves to Righteousness: vv. 17-18

"But thanks be to God that, though you used to be slaves to sin, you wholeheartedly obeyed the form of teaching to which you were committed" (v. 17, NIV). He then goes on to say: "You have been set free from sin and have become slaves to righteousness" (v. 18, NIV). We are either slaves to sin or slaves to righteousness.

The expression "set free from sin" occurs again in verse 22. Deissmann points out the fact that the same verb and preposition were used in the time of Christ as a technical expression in legal documents for freeing slaves. So Paul's readers were familiar with the language he uses here. Perhaps some of them had been freed from slavery.

But the striking truth of verses 18 and 22 is that we are freed from one slavery to enter another! The fact is that we are all slaves of something. But

we are freed from the lower slavery to sin in order that we might enjoy the glorious liberty of a higher slavery to God (cf. v. 22). We become His love slaves, which is true freedom.

VII. FREED FROM SIN, SLAVES TO GOD: Romans 6:19-23

A. A New Slavery: v. 19

"I put this in human terms because you are weak in your natural selves. Just as you used to offer the parts of your body in slavery to impurity and to ever-increasing wickedness, so now offer them in slavery to righteousness and holiness" (NIV). Sanday and Headlam say that "because of the infirmity of your flesh" (KJV) means "because of the difficulties of apprehension, from defective spiritual experience, which prevents the understanding of its deeper truths" (*Romans*, p. 168).

This verse implies that we either go deeper into sin or higher in holiness. This truth is implied in the last chapter of the Bible: "He that is unjust, let him be unjust still: and he which is filthy, let him be filthy still: and he that is righteous, let him be righteous still: and he that is holy, let him be holy still" (Revelation 22:11).

B. Results of Slavery to Sin: vv. 20-21

"When you were slaves to sin, you were free from the control of righteousness. What benefit did you reap at that time from the things you are now ashamed of? Those things result in death!" (NIV). The truth of this passage is being vividly and tragically illustrated today in the case of those who are addicted to drugs or alcohol. But the principle holds good for all who are slaves to sin—even the inner sin of selfishness. All sin brings death. That truth is emphasized over and over in this chapter. The results of slavery to sin are spiritual death now and eternal death hereafter.

DISCUSSION QUESTIONS

1. What does it mean to be dead to sin?
2. How can we be united with Christ in His death and resurrection?
3. How do we reckon ourselves dead to sin?
4. What is the Christian view of the body?
5. What does it mean to be freed from sin?
6. What is the final result of sin?

C. Results of Slavery to God: vv. 22-23

"But now that you have been set free from sin and have become slaves to God, the benefit you reap leads to holiness, and the result is eternal life" (v. 22, NIV). It seems clear that "slaves to God" here is parallel to "slaves to righteousness" in verse 18 and helps to explain the meaning of that earlier phrase. We actually are slaves to a person. As we noted before, "Sin" is personified in this chapter. It is a horrible slave-master, beating to death its helpless victims.

Slavery to God, however, leads to holiness and results in eternal life. Why is it that people cannot see this simple truth and decide accordingly? Paul gives the answer: "The god of this world hath blinded the minds of them which believe not, lest the light of the glorious gospel of Christ . . . should shine unto them" (II Corinthians 4:4).

Verse 23 is often quoted. Here we have a most striking contrast. "Gift" is literally "free gift" or "gracious gift"— *charisma*, from *charis*, "grace." If we serve sin all our lives, the only wages we get will be eternal death. But if we serve God, He gives us eternal life as a free gift of His love.

CONTEMPORARY APPLICATION

In his commentary on Romans, Griffith Thomas quotes this: "The missionary Casilis told us that he was one day questioning a converted Bechuana as to the meaning of a passage analogous to that before us. . . . The latter said to him: Soon I shall be dead, and they will bury me in my field. My flocks will come to pasture above me. But I shall no longer hear them, and I shall not come forth from my tomb to take them and carry them with me to the sepulchre. They will be strange to me, as I to them. Such is the image of my life in the midst of the world since I believed in Christ" (*Romans*, p. 172). That must be our relationship to the old life of sin.

THE NEW LIFE AS FREEDOM

DEVOTIONAL READING | Romans 7:1-6

ADULTS

Topic: *The New Life as Freedom*

Background Scripture: Romans 7:1—8:17

Scripture Lesson: Romans 7:14—8:2

Memory Verse: *All who are led by the Spirit of God are sons of God.* Romans 8:14

YOUTH

Topic: *Free to Live!*

Background Scripture: Romans 7:1—8:17

Scripture Lesson: Romans 7:14—8:2

Memory Verse: *All who are led by the Spirit of God are sons of God.* Romans 8:14

CHILDREN

Topic: *Free to Choose the Good*

Background Scripture: Romans 7:15-25

Scripture Lesson: Romans 7:15-20

Memory Verse: *For I do not do what I want, but I do the very thing I hate.* Romans 7:15

DAILY BIBLE READINGS

Mon., Oct. 18: Function of the Law, Romans 7:7-13.
Tues., Oct. 19: The Inward Struggle, Romans 7:14-25.
Wed., Oct. 20: Life in the Spirit, Romans 8:1-11.
Thurs., Oct. 21: The Witness of the Spirit, Romans 8:12-17.
Fri., Oct. 22: Strength Through the Spirit, Ephesians 3:7-19.
Sat., Oct. 23: Free to See the Highest, Colossians 2:16—3:4.
Sun., Oct. 24: Free to Serve, Romans 7:1-6.

LESSON AIM | To help us understand and experience what it means to be free to live.

LESSON SETTING

Time: A.D. 56

Place: Corinth

LESSON OUTLINE

The New Life as Freedom

    I. Freedom from the Law: Romans 7:1-3

II. **Union with Christ:** Romans 7:4-6

III. **Function of the Law:** Romans 7:7-13

IV. **A Slave to Sin:** Romans 7:14-20
   A. Spiritual Law, Unspiritual Man: v. 14
   B. The Inner Struggle: v. 15
   C. Indwelling Sin: vv. 16-20

V. **Two Laws at Work:** Romans 7:21-25
   A. God's Law: vv. 21-22
   B. Law of Sin: vv. 23-24
   C. Victory in Christ: v. 25

VI. **Life Through the Spirit:** Romans 8:1-4
   A. No Condemnation: v. 1
   B. Freedom from the Law of Sin: v. 2
   C. Freedom in the Spirit: vv. 3-4

SUGGESTED INTRODUCTION FOR ADULTS

In the Introduction to our previous lesson, we noted that the sixth chapter of Romans describes sanctification through death to self, while the eighth chapter shows that it is through the infilling of the Spirit. We would like to suggest that the seventh chapter has to do with sanctification as union with Christ (v. 4).

A large part of this chapter is autobiographical. In the first six verses it is mostly "you" and "we." But in verses 7-25 Paul constantly uses "I." It seems evident that he is describing his own experience. But when?

In verses 7-13 he writes in the past tense, describing his struggle under the Law as a conscientious Pharisee. But at verse 14 he changes to the present tense and retains this to the end of the chapter. We shall discuss the implications of this in our Lesson Commentary. For the moment we leave the question unanswered.

SUGGESTED INTRODUCTION FOR YOUTH

"Free to Live!" Is that what you are? Or are you a slave of habits that keep you from being fully alive?

The new life in Christ is freedom to live as Christ would have us live. It is freedom from sin and the sinful self. It is a free life of victory and peace and joy.

Deep down inside, every young person wants joy and peace. But how to find it—that's the question. The answer is, "In Christ." He can free us from sin to follow Him. In Him we are free to live the way we know we ought to live.

CONCEPTS FOR CHILDREN

1. We all have to make choices every day.
2. Our future depends on the choices we make now.
3. Bad choices have costly consequences.
4. We need to ask Jesus every day to help us choose what is best.

THE LESSON COMMENTARY

I. FREEDOM FROM THE LAW:
Romans 7:1-3

Commenting on verses 1-6, William Sanday and Arthur C. Headlam say: "The text of this section—and indeed of the whole chapter—is still, 'Ye are not under Law but under Grace' " (*A Critical and Exegetical Commentary on the Epistle to the Romans*, International Critical Commentary, p. 171). Dr. William Greathouse heads this chapter: "Sanctification through death to the law" (*Beacon Bible Commentary*, VII, 145).

"Brethren" (v. 1) means "fellow Christians." Paul says that he is speaking to those that "know the law." But in the Greek there is no definite article here. Sanday and Headlam make this comment: "At once the absence of the article and the nature of the case go to show that what is meant here is not Roman Law (Weiss) ... nor yet the Law of Moses more particularly considered (Lips.), but a general principle of all Law; an obvious axiom of political justice—that death clears all scores, and that a dead man can no longer be prosecuted or punished" (*Romans*, p. 172). And so Paul says that "the law has authority over a man only as long as he lives" (NIV).

In verses 2 and 3 he gives an illustration from marriage. A married woman is bound to her husband as long as he lives. But if he dies, she is released from "the law of her husband." If she marries another man while her husband is still living, she will be called an adulteress. But if her husband dies, she is free to marry another man.

II. UNION WITH CHRIST:
Romans 7:4-6

Now Paul makes the application of this to Christians. He writes: "Wherefore, my brethren, ye also are become dead to the law [the law of Moses (definite article in the Greek)] by the body of Christ; that ye should be married to another, even to him who is raised from the dead, that we should bring forth fruit unto God" (v. 4).

Then he contrasts this with the old life: "For when we were controlled by our sinful nature, the sinful passions aroused by the law were at work in our bodies, so that we bore fruit for death" (v. 5, NIV). James Denney comments: "It is through the law that these passions became actualized: we would never know them for what they are, if it were not for the law." Regarding the last clause of the verse he says: "Death is personified here as in v. 17: this tyrant of the human race is the only one who profits by the fruits of the sinful life" (*Expositor's Greek Testament*, II, 638).

But now, having died to the Law, we are released from its authority, so that we may "serve in newness of spirit, and not in the oldness of the letter" (v. 6). H. Emil Brunner comments: "Being bound to the Law is captivity, being bound to the living Christ is freedom. There it is enslavement in the letter, here freedom in the Holy Spirit" (*Letter to the Romans*, p. 58).

Griffith Thomas gives a good summary of these first six verses. He writes:

"1. The 'wife' is that inmost self or personality which is the same under all conditions of existence: 'I myself.'

"2. The first husband is 'our old man' (ch. vi. 6), our unregenerate self; and as long as he was alive we were under his law.

"3. The death of the first husband is the crucifixion of the 'old man' with Christ (ch. vi. 6).

"4. The wife, set free through her first husband's death and thereby become dead to the law of that husband, is the soul set free by the crucifixion of the old man and thereby made dead to its law."

III. FUNCTION OF THE LAW:
Romans 7:7-13

Griffith Thomas also gives an excellent summary of this section, as follows:

I. Law Reveals the Fact of Sin (ver. 7).
II. Law Reveals the Occasion of Sin (ver. 8).
III. Law Reveals the Power of Sin (ver. 9).
IV. Law Reveals the Deceitfulness of Sin (ver. 11).
V. Law Reveals the Effect of Sin (vers. 10, 11).
VI. Law Reveals the Sinfulness of Sin (vers. 12, 13).

We have already noted that beginning with verse 7 the rest of the chapter is autobiographical. This is indicated not only by the writer's frequent use of *I*, *me*, and *my*, but by the depth and intensity of the feeling expressed. But what stage of his life is Paul describing?

Denney handles this well. He says: "The much discussed question, whether the subject of this passage (vers. 7-24) is the unregenerate or the regenerate self, or whether in particular vers. 7-13 refer to the unregenerate, and vers. 14-24 to the regenerate, is hardly real. The distinction in its absolute form belongs to doctrine, not to experience. No one could have written the passage but a Christian: it is the experience of the unregenerate, we may say, but seen through regenerate eyes, interpreted in a regenerate mind" (*Expositor's Greek Testament*, II, 639).

Again Paul asks, "What shall we say then?" (cf. 6:1, 15). This is introductory to another question that might be raised as a false deduction: "Is the law sin?" (v. 7). He had spoken so disparagingly of the Law as something to which we must die (v. 4) that someone might offer this conclusion.

Once more the apostle comes back with an emphatic, "God forbid." He goes on to say that he would not have known what sin was except through the Law: "For I had not known lust, except the law had said, Thou shalt not covet" (KJV). This translation ignores the fact that the noun "lust" and the verb "covet" are the same root in Greek. The correct rendering is: "For I would not have known what it was to covet if the law had not said, 'Do not covet' " (NIV). This is the tenth commandment. The Greek verb means to have evil desire, and wrong desire is the root of all sin. So, as Denney suggests, this was the most appropriate commandment to quote.

Confronted by the commandment, Paul had felt rebellion rising within him, producing "every kind of covetous desire" (v. 8, NIV). ("Concupiscence," KJV, is a Latinism that is certainly not current English.) Without the Law sin was dead (v. 8) and Paul was alive (v. 9). When the Law came, sin sprang to life and Paul died.

Is the Law sin? No, it is holy, just and good (v. 12). But was it made death to Paul? (v. 13). Again he replies, "God forbid." No, it was not the Law, but sin, that brought death.

IV. A SLAVE TO SIN:
Romans 7:14-20

A. Spiritual Law, Unspiritual Man: v. 14

"We know that the law is spiritual; but I am unspiritual, sold as a slave to sin" (NIV). The word translated "unspiritual" is *sarkinos*, which means "fleshly," or "carnal" (KJV, a Latinism).

This is often taken, because of the present tense, as Paul's testimony about his condition at the time he wrote. But this is denied by I Corinthians 3:1-4, where the apostle severely criticizes the Corinthian believers for being "carnal." It is obvious that he is using the present tense for vividness but is still describing an earlier stage in his life. To say that Paul was at this time a slave to sin is to ignore all the evidence.

B. The Inner Struggle: v. 15

"I do not know what I am doing. For what I want to do I do not do, but what I hate I do" (NIV). This is a haunting cry from an honest soul that is trying to do right, but failing.

Again we raise the question as to the time when Paul had this inner struggle, marked by defeat. Griffith Thomas says that "it seems in every way best to regard the description from verses 7-25 as that of a Jew under the Mosaic law, who valued its spirituality but failed to fulfil its requirements. . . . It is therefore a picture of a Jew under law, not a Christian under grace" (*Romans*, p. 192).

Griffith Thomas goes on to say: "The key to the meaning of the entire section is found in the repetition of 'I' thirty times in the chapter, without a single mention of the Holy Spirit. It indicates what 'I' am struggling to do, and utterly fail to do in my own strength" (pp. 192-93).

C. Indwelling Sin: vv. 16-20

The statement of verse 16 seems at first sight a bit obscure. What he means is that if he hates the wrong he does, he is agreeing that the Law is right and good.

In verse 17 we come to the heart of the problem: "Now then it is no more I that do it, but sin that dwelleth in me." At last we have discovered the culprit, the tyrant Sin that had caused Paul to do what he didn't want to do.

Why do men sir? Because of indwelling sin that exerts such power over them that they falter and fail. Everyone is born with this old Adamic nature that motivates people to sin. We remember Dr. George Croft Cell saying in class one day at Boston University School of Theology: "When I began teaching here I didn't believe in the doctrine of original sin. But thirty years of reading church history has compelled me to believe in it. There is no other way to explain the evil that men have perpetrated." Every man has observed this in others and felt it in himself.

And so Paul says: "I know that nothing good lives in me, that is, in my sinful nature. For I have the desire to do what is good, but I cannot carry it out" (v. 18, NIV). This is a tragic testimony of defeat. It describes the natural man with an awakened conscience, but powerless to obey it. His wish was right, but his will was weak.

Verse 19 is almost a repetition of verse 15. It shows in what a desperate situation Paul had found himself in his preconversion days.

Again the apostle identifies the culprit: "sin that dwelleth in me" (v. 20). In his unregenerate state Paul found that it was "no more I . . . but sin." After his conversion it was: "not I, but Christ" (Galatians 2:20). This is the vast difference between the two. In himself the natural man is a pathetic failure. In Christ he is "more than conqueror."

V. TWO LAWS AT WORK: Romans 7:21-25

A. God's Law: vv. 21-22

There has been considerable debate as to the meaning of "law" in verse 21 (it carries the definite article). At the end of a considerable discussion, Denney writes: "Hence I agree with those who make *ton nomon* the Mosaic law" (*Expositor's Greek Testament*, II, 642)—that is, God's law. Sanday and Headlam, however, connect it with "another law" (v. 23), which seems more reasonable.

In verse 22 Paul clearly mentions "the law of God." He says that he delights in it "after the inward man." Some have taken this as an indication that in these last verses of the chapter the apostle is referring to his regenerate state.

B. Law of Sin: vv. 23-24

Now the description becomes more clear and precise. Paul writes: "But I see another law at work in the members of my body, waging war against the law of my mind and making me a prisoner of the law of sin at work within my members" (v. 23, NIV). The law of his mind was perhaps his moral conscience. Warring against this was a fleshly nature that he calls "the law of sin," or a sin-principle. This seems to be the same as "the flesh" used for "the sinful nature" (NIV).

So there was a battle going on, and Paul had found that the law of sin was stronger than the law of conscience. The result was defeat.

And so he cries out for deliverance. He wants to be delivered from his wretched state (v. 24).

Of this wail of anguish and cry for help Denney says: "The words are not those of the Apostle's heart as he writes; they are the words which he knows are wrung from the heart of the man who realises that he is himself in the state just described. Paul has reproduced this vividly from his own experience, but 'O wretched man that I am' is not the cry of the Christian Paul, but of the man whom sin and law have brought to despair" (*Expositor's Greek Testament*, II, 643).

C. Victory in Christ: v. 25

Who can deliver him? "I thank God through Jesus Christ our Lord." That is victory! Why then does he end with the melancholy picture of the rest of the verse? Godet puts it well: "He simply sums up in order to conclude" (*Romans*, p. 291). It is a summary of what he has been saying in chapter 7.

VI. LIFE THROUGH THE SPIRIT: Romans 8:1-4

A. No Condemnation: v. 1

"There is therefore now no condemnation to them which are in Christ Jesus." The rest of the verse in the King James Version is not in the oldest Greek manuscripts. It was evidently imported from verse 4, where it is genuine.

The word for "no" (first in the

Greek) is very emphatic; there is no condemnation at all! As long as we are actually in Christ, by faith and obedience, we are free from condemnation.

The second word in the Greek is *ara*, a strong inferential particle. It looks back to the exclamation of victory in verse 25: "I thank God through Jesus Christ our Lord." Denney says of this ejaculatory outburst: "The exclamation of thanksgiving shows that the longed-for deliverance has actually been achieved" (*Expositor's Greek Testament*, p. 643). From his vantage point of freedom the apostle praises God.

B. Freedom from the Law of Sin: v. 2

Paul mentions two laws in this verse. And their relationship is clearly expressed. He writes: "For the law of the Spirit of life in Christ Jesus hath made me free from the law of sin and death." It is the latter law that he has been discussing mostly in chapter 7 (cf. 7:23). Now he introduces the new law of the Spirit of life, which has set him free from the other. It would be folly to deny that Paul's present state when he wrote this Epistle is portrayed in the eighth chapter, not the seventh.

In this second verse we are introduced to the dominant feature of this

DISCUSSION QUESTIONS

1. Are some Christians today living in the seventh chapter of Romans?
2. What is the secret of moving over into the eighth chapter?
3. What is meant by "the law of sin"?
4. How is union with Christ allegorized?
5. What was the function of the Law?
6. What is the secret of victorious living?

chapter—the Holy Spirit. The Spirit is mentioned only once in the previous pages of the Epistle, but in chapter 8 we find Him referred to nearly twenty times. The eighth chapter describes life in the Spirit. Griffith Thomas remarks: "In contrast with the thirty occurrences of 'I' in ch. vii. are the twenty references to the Holy Spirit in ch. viii." (*Romans*, p. 201).

C. Freedom in the Spirit: vv. 3-4

In chapter 5 Paul shows that the Law was powerless to justify; in chapter 8 he shows that it was powerless to sanctify. Why? Because of the weakness of the flesh.

But God had a remedy. He sent His own Son "in the likeness of sinful flesh, and for sin" (v. 3)—or, "for a sin-offering." The expression can be translated either way, and both ways have significance. But the exact phrase used here occurs in the Septuagint (Greek Old Testament) constantly for "sin-offering," over fifty times in Leviticus alone. So that is probably what it means here.

In so doing God "condemned sin in the flesh, that the righteousness of the law might be fulfilled in us, who walk not after the flesh, but after the Spirit" (v. 4). The true Christian life is life in the Spirit, not life in the flesh.

CONTEMPORARY APPLICATION

Paul asked the question that his opponents might raise: "Is the Law sin?" His answer is: "No, the Law is not sin; it is that which makes me conscious of sin."

A. T. Robertson makes this apt observation: "Some people today oppose all inhibitions and prohibitions because they stimulate violations. That is half-baked thinking" (*Word Pictures in the New Testament*, IV, 367). We agree.

SECURE IN GOD'S LOVE

DEVOTIONAL READING	Psalm 90:13-17

ADULTS

Topic: *Secure in God's Love*

Background Scripture: Romans 8:18-39

Scripture Lesson: Romans 8:28-39

Memory Verse: *We know that in everything God works for good with those who love him, who are called according to his purpose.* Romans 8:28

YOUTH

Topic: *God's Love: A Sure Thing*

Background Scripture: Romans 8:18-39

Scripture Lesson: Romans 8:28-39

Memory Verse: *We know that in everything God works for good with those who love him, who are called according to his purpose.* Romans 8:28

CHILDREN

Topic: *Trusting in God's Love*

Background Scripture: Acts 9:10-19; Romans 8:28-39

Scripture Lesson: Romans 8:28, 37-39

Memory Verse: *We know that in everything God works for good with those who love him.* Romans 8:28

DAILY BIBLE READINGS

Mon., Oct. 25: "In This Hope We Were Saved," Romans 8:18-25.
Tues., Oct. 26: "In Everything God Works for Good," Romans 8:26-30.
Wed., Oct. 27: "The Love of Christ," Romans 8:31-39.
Thurs., Oct. 28: "God Is Love," I John 4:13-21.
Fri., Oct. 29: "God So Loved the World," John 3:16-21.
Sat., Oct. 30: "My Refuge and My Fortress," Psalm 91.
Sun., Oct. 31: God's Steadfast Love, Psalm 90:13-17.

LESSON AIM

To show that in Christ we are secure in God's love.

LESSON SETTING

Time: A.D. 56

Place: Corinth

LESSON OUTLINE

Secure in God's Love

I. A Suffering Creation: Romans 8:18-22

II. A Firm Hope: Romans 8:23-27

III. The Blessings of God's People: Romans 8:28-30
   A. All Things for Good: v. 28
   B. Conformity to Christ: v. 29
   C. Called, Justified, Glorified: v. 30

IV. Secure in Christ: Romans 8:31-39
   A. The Guarantee of God's Love: vv. 31-32
   B. No Condemnation: vv. 33-34
   C. No Separation: vv. 35-36
   D. More Than Conquerors: v. 37
   E. Nothing Can Separate: vv. 38-39

SUGGESTED INTRODUCTION FOR ADULTS

Most people want security. Men choose jobs that will give them financial security. Our government offers Social Security—something that is more financial than social.

But these things are outward and material. Far more important is an inward sense of security. And this is something that money cannot buy, nor can any government guarantee it. What people need to realize is that true security of heart and mind can be found only in Christ.

Husbands and wives need to feel secure in each other's love. Children need a real sense of security in their parents' love. In the last analysis, love is the only adequate source of a satisfying security. This lesson points out the fact that we are "secure in God's love"—and only there!

SUGGESTED INTRODUCTION FOR YOUTH

Do you feel secure? Too many young people do not. They find themselves caught in a very insecure society socially and morally. So they drift and don't care.

Is there any "sure thing" in life? The answer is an emphatic "Yes!" Salvation is a sure thing, for those who will accept it. Faith, hope, and love—these are sure things for those who are fully yielded to Christ. And while we are in Christ we are eternally secure. What more could a young person ask?

CONCEPTS FOR CHILDREN

1. When we are on God's side, He takes care of us.
2. Nothing in this world can separate us from God's love.
3. God's love comes to us through others.
4. We must accept this love as from Him.

THE LESSON COMMENTARY

I. A SUFFERING CREATION:
   Romans 8:18-22

Paul writes: "I consider that our present sufferings are not worth comparing with the glory that will be revealed in us" (v. 18, NIV). That belief will hold us steady when the sufferings of this life seem unbearable. And it is the only explanation that makes sense in life.

Almost any person would be willing to endure hardship and privation for a few months if he knew that he was going to have an abundance of health and wealth for the following fifty years. How much more should we be willing to suffer for even a few years in this life when we have the assurance of limitless blessings in Christ's presence throughout a never-ending eternity. It makes very good sense!

In Romans 3:21—5:21 we find redemption applied to the *sins* of man. In chapters 6—8 we see redemption applied to the *sin* of man. But in this paragraph (8:19-22) we have redemption applied to all creation. We are told that "the creation waits in eager expectation for the sons of God to be revealed" (v. 19, NIV). This revelation will take place in connection with the second coming of Christ.

"For the creation was subjected to frustration, not by its own choice, but by the will of the one who subjected it, in hope that the creation itself will be liberated from its bondage to decay and brought into the glorious freedom of the children of God" (vv. 20-21, NIV). The curse on Adam for his disobedience was extended to material creation. Adam was told that the soil would bring forth thorns and thistles (Genesis 3:18). When the redemption of humanity is completed, then the curse on creation will be lifted. Human liberation from sin will be followed by creation's freedom from the curse.

What is the condition of creation now? Paul, under the inspiration of the Spirit, spells it out this way: "We know that the whole creation has been groaning as in the pains of childbirth right up to the present time" (v. 22, NIV). There is a sense in which creation awaits a new birth. (In the King James Version the same Greek word, *ktsis*, is translated "creature" in verses 19, 20, and 21 but "creation" in verse 22. It should be "creation" throughout.)

On verses 19-22 Griffith Thomas writes: "This is one of the most striking passages in St. Paul's writings. It suggests to us some of the most wonderful lessons connected with the universe. Science, philosophy, and Christianity all unite in testifying to the essential unity of the universe, with man as the crown and culmination, and there seems no reason to doubt that the fact of sin has in some way affected the entire constitution of things created. . . . Very much that we see around us goes to show that nature is not now in normal condition, or in that state in which it was originally created by God" (*St. Paul's Epistle to the Romans*, p. 220).

Isaiah 11:6-9 gives a beautiful picture of redeemed creation: The most ferocious animals, as we know them now, will associate freely with domestic animals (vv. 6-7); children will play freely with snakes that are now deadly (v. 8); "they shall not hurt or destroy in all my holy mountain" (v. 9). Some would apply all this to the Christian life now. But why not *both* now *and* in the Millennium?

II. A FIRM HOPE: Romans 8:23-27

It is not alone creation that groans; we do too. Paul writes: "Not only so, but we ourselves, who have the first-fruits of the Spirit, groan inwardly as we wait eagerly for our adoption as sons, the redemption of our bodies" (v. 23, NIV). Our conversion experience includes justification, regeneration, and adoption. But there is a very real sense in which our adoption as God's sons will reach its culmination in our glorification, when we are at last at home forever with our Father. In spiritual experience here we have "the firstfruits of the Spirit." The final fruits await our resurrection.

It was in the hope of this that we were saved (v. 24). Hope relates to what we have not yet seen, what we still anticipate. And this hope enables us to wait patiently for the time of fulfillment (v. 25).

Meanwhile, "the Spirit helps us in our weakness" (v. 26). The Greek word translated "helps" is a long double compound, *synantilambanetai.*

A. T. Robertson beautifully describes its full meaning: "The Holy Spirit lays hold of our weakness along with (*syn*) us and carries his part of the burden facing us (*anti*) as if two men were carrying a log, one at each end" (*Grammar of the Greek New Testament in the Light of Historical Research*, p. 573). With the Holy Spirit taking the heavy end of the load, we can make it!

Here the apostle especially emphasizes the help that the Holy Spirit gives us in our prayer life. We do not know how we ought to pray. But the Spirit intercedes for us with groans that cannot be uttered in words. Every consecrated Christian has experienced this aspect of intercessory prayer. And the Spirit helps us to pray in accordance with God's will (v. 27).

III. THE BLESSINGS OF GOD'S PEOPLE: Romans 8:28-30

A. All Things for Good: v. 28

When life seemed to be turning against Jacob, that venerable patriarch wailed, "All these things are against me" (Genesis 42:36). Paul had suffered far more than Jacob, but he declared: "We know that all things work together for good to them that love God, to them who are the called according to his purpose." That is the Christian's perspective. The striking fact is that just when Jacob thought everything was going wrong, things were miraculously coming out right. He would soon see his supposedly dead son Joseph, who was now prime minister of Egypt.

Three of our most ancient Greek manuscripts—Papyrus 46 (third century), Vaticanus (fourth century), and Alexandrinus (fifth century) read: "God works all things together for good." We know that it is actually He who does it.

Griffith Thomas gives two good, homely illustrations of the truth of Romans 8:28. He says: "A staircase may wind, but each step is higher than the preceding one, and it is 'still upward.' The diamond setter cuts and polishes the jewel very long and thoroughly before its facets of brilliancy are visible" (*Romans*, p. 225). By faith we can see God's hand at work shaping and beautifying our lives. And when we cannot trace, we can trust.

There is an important restriction here that we must not fail to notice. God works all things together for good to those who love Him, those who are called according to His purpose. It is only when we submit ourselves completely to the will of God and truly love Him that we can claim this wonderful promise.

B. Conformity to Christ: v. 29

Divine predestination is based on divine foreknowledge. That fact is clearly stated in this verse. It is those whom God foreknew that He predestined to be conformed to the likeness of His Son. This conformity begins at conversion, continues throughout our life here on earth, and will find its culmination when we meet Christ face to face. John writes: "We know that, when he shall appear, we shall be like him; for we shall see him as he is" (I John 3:2). This is the blessed hope of the Christian.

The Greek word translated "conformed" does not indicate conformity in outward appearance, but likeness of inner nature and character. The very essence of our being is to be made constantly more Christlike by the operation of the Holy Spirit in our hearts.

C. Called, Justified, Glorified: v. 30

This is the order of Christian experience. We are first "called." Many passages in both the Old Testament (e.g., Isaiah 55:1-3) and the New Testament indicate that we must respond to the divine call if we are to be saved. John 3:16 clearly declares that. And in the closing chapter of the Bible it is "whosoever will" (Revelation 22:17) that may accept the invitation and receive eternal life.

The next stage is "justified." When we accept God's call we are justified by faith, as Paul repeatedly asserts in his Epistles to the Galatians and Romans.

The final act of human redemption is that we are "glorified" at the resurrection morning. But our glorification is dependent on our prior justification. Glorification is what Paul has already described as "the redemption of our body" (v. 23).

IV. SECURE IN CHRIST:
Romans 8:31-39

A. The Guarantee of God's Love: vv. 31-32

Paul throws out the challenge: "If God be for us, who can be against us?"—that is, in any effective way. With God on our side, we have no excuse for worry. If we really believe in Romans 8:28 we should never wring our hands in despair when everything seems to go wrong. Even if people hurt us in this life, as they did Jesus, they can never harm our eternal life. We are secure in Christ.

Then Paul reinforced this truth with one of the most inspiring questions in the New Testament: "He that spared not his own Son, but delivered him up for us all, how shall he not with him also freely give us all things?" (v. 32). If God gave us His most precious gift, His Son, surely He will not withhold anything good from us!

B. No Condemnation: vv. 33-34

The second part of both these verses may well be put in the form of a question, as Weymouth did long ago, and as Kenneth Taylor has done more recently in *The Living Bible*. This— with its clearly implied answer, "No!"—seems to us to make the passage not only more dramatic but far more forceful. And the Greek can just as well be translated as a question.

The logic of these verses is well described by an older writer, Marcus Rainford. He says: "There is no ground for condemnation since Christ has suffered the penalty; there is no law to condemn us since we are not under law but under grace; there is no tribunal for judgment since ours is now a Throne of Grace, not a judgment; and, above all, there is no Judge to sentence us since God Himself, the only Judge, is our Justifier" (quoted by Griffith Thomas, *Romans*, p. 230).

C. No Separation: vv. 35-36

Paul asks the crucial question: "Who shall separate us from the love of Christ?" He names a number of things that might seem threatening: "Shall tribulation or distress or persecution or famine or nakedness or peril or sword?" He bolsters this with a quotation from Psalm 44:22.

D. More Than Conquerors: v. 37

To all of this the apostle replies with the mighty affirmation: "Nay, in all these things we are more than conquerors through him that loved us." The five words "we are more than conquerors" are all one word in Greek, *hypernikomen*. This is compounded of the Greek word for "victory," *nike* (cf. "nike rockets") and the preposition *hyper*, which is the Greek equivalent of the Latin *super*. So it literally

DISCUSSION QUESTIONS

1. What are some evidences of the curse on creation?
2. What will happen when the curse is lifted?
3. How does the Holy Spirit help us in our praying?
4. How much do we believe Romans 8:28?
5. What is the greatest evidence of God's love?
6. How can we be more than conquerors daily?

means, "We are supervictors" through Christ. Paul did not believe in barely getting by, in being pushed back against the wall. He believed in abundant victory. In ourselves we are failures, defeated. But in Christ we are to be more than conquerors.

E. Nothing Can Separate: vv. 38-39

The apostle declares: "For I am convinced that neither death nor life, neither angels nor demons, neither the present nor the future, nor any powers, neither height nor depth, nor anything else in all creation, will be able to separate us from the love of God that is in Christ Jesus our Lord" (NIV).

This is a very sweeping statement and takes in a lot of territory. In fact, it includes about everything in the material world and the spirit world.

We can only take time to comment on one point. Some people say, "I think I can face today, but I'm afraid of what tomorrow may bring." Paul says, "neither the present nor the future." In Christ we can face the future with faith, not with fear.

It is said that a Christian leader once saw a weathervane with the words on it, "God is love." His reaction was, "You mean that God's love is as changeable as the wind?" The answer came back, "No, God is love whichever way the wind blows."

That's the concept we need to have. No matter what the changing circumstances of life, "God is love." His love never changes.

Paul declares that nothing in all creation can separate us from the love of God in Christ. There is only one thing that can do it—our will. Just as we can accept Christ by faith, so we can by an act of our will reject Him.

Some people have the cat-hold theory of salvation. They believe that just as the mother cat picks up her kitten by the nape of the neck and carries it wherever she wishes, so God takes His elect to heaven, no matter what they do or don't do. Others have the monkey-hold theory. They believe that they must grab hold of Christ by faith and then hold on for dear life.

Both these extremes are unscriptural. The true concept is the kangaroo-hold. As long as the baby kangaroo stays inside its mother's pouch it is perfectly safe. If it jumps out, it may be devoured. We are eternally secure in Christ, and only in Him.

CONTEMPORARY APPLICATION

Griffith Thomas gives this interesting illustration of Romans 8:28: "Many years ago an eminent French engineer was detained in the Mediterranean by a tedious quarantine. It was hard for one of his active temperament to endure such confinement; but as he waited on the deck of the vessel he read, and the book, to which he gave extra attention, prompted him to the conception of the Suez Canal, the execution of which has made him so famous and has been of such great service to the world. Did M. de Lesseps afterwards regret those dragging days of quarantine?" (Romans, p. 228).

GOD'S MERCY FOR ALL

DEVOTIONAL READING	Isaiah 42:5-9

ADULTS

Topic: *Together Under God*

Background Scripture: Romans 10:1-13; 11

Scripture Lesson: Romans 10:5-13; 11:33-36

Memory Verse: *There is no distinction between Jew and Greek; the same Lord is Lord of all and bestows his riches upon all who call upon him.* Romans 10:12

YOUTH

Topic: *Together Under God*

Background Scripture: Romans 10:1-13; 11

Scripture Lesson: Romans 10:5-13; 11:33-36

Memory Verse: *There is no distinction between Jew and Greek; the same Lord is Lord of all and bestows his riches upon all who call upon him.* Romans 10:12

CHILDREN

Topic: *Hearing the Good News*

Background Scripture: Romans 10:1-17

Scripture Lesson: Romans 10:14-17

Memory Verse: *So faith comes from what is heard, and what is heard comes by the preaching of Christ.* Romans 10:17

DAILY BIBLE READINGS

Mon., Nov. 1: "No Distinction Between Jew and Greek," Romans 10:1-13.
Tues., Nov. 2: "A Remnant, Chosen by Grace," Romans 11:1-6.
Wed., Nov. 3: "Salvation Has Come to the Gentiles," Romans 11:7-12.
Thurs., Nov. 4: God's Kindness and Severity, Romans 11:13-24.
Fri., Nov. 5: God's Inscrutable Ways, Romans 1:25-26.
Sat., Nov. 6: Saved Through Grace, Acts 15:6-11.
Sun., Nov. 7: "A Light to the Nations," Isaiah 42:5-9.

LESSON AIM

To help us learn to live "together under God" in a spirit of love and respect.

LESSON SETTING

Time: A.D. 56

Place: Corinth

73

God's Mercy for All

I. Paul's Prayer for Israel's Salvation: Romans 10:1-4
   A. The Prayer: v. 1
   B. The Problem: vv. 2-3
   C. The Solution: v. 4

II. Two Kinds of Righteousness: Romans 10:5-13
   A. Righteousness by the Law: v. 5
   B. Righteousness by Faith: vv. 6-10
   C. One Righteousness for All: vv. 11-13

LESSON OUTLINE

III. The Redeemed Remnant of Israel: Romans 11:1-6

IV. The Rebellious Rejects of Israel: Romans 11:7-10

V. The Relation of Jews and Gentiles in God's Plan: Romans 11:11-24
   A. Loss and Gain: vv. 11-12
   B. Rejection and Reconciliation: vv. 13-16
   C. Wild and Natural Branches: vv. 17-21
   D. Kindness and Sternness of God: vv. 22-24

VI. All Israel Will Be Saved: Romans 11:25-32

VII. Closing Doxology: Romans 11:33-36

As is Paul's usual procedure in his Epistles, we have in Romans first a doctrinal presentation (chaps. 1—8) and finally a practical application (chaps. 12—16). In between we find a prophetic interpretation (chaps. 9—11), dealing with God's plan and purpose for Israel.

The message of these three chapters might be summed up as follows:

I. Some of Israel Were Already Saved (chap. 9)

II. All Israel Might Be Saved But for Unbelief (chap. 10)

SUGGESTED INTRODUCTION FOR ADULTS

III. All Israel Will Ultimately Be Saved (chap. 11).

Another way of putting it is this:

I. God's Choice of Israel (chap. 9)

II. Israel's Rejection of God's Righteousness (chap. 10)

III. God's Final Purpose for Israel (chap. 11).

These chapters are what we call "eschatological"; that is, they deal with the doctrine of future things.

Throughout the three chapters the message of "God's mercy for all" rings loud and clear. And the proof of this truth was demonstrated dramatically at Calvary, when Christ died for all men.

SUGGESTED INTRODUCTION FOR YOUTH

"Together under God"—that is the way we were made to live. It is only when we submit to His lordship that we can fully live in peace with each other.

This goes for the home, first of all. When parents and children really love the Lord they can love each other. When both husband and wife are submitted to the will of God, they can live in unity. There is no true living without loving each other. We can only be "together" if we are "under God."

CONCEPTS FOR CHILDREN

1. The good news of salvation is for children as well as grown-ups.
2. We should listen as this good news is preached.
3. Faith comes through hearing the message.
4. We should seek opportunities for sharing the good news.

THE LESSON COMMENTARY

I. PAUL'S PRAYER FOR ISRAEL'S SALVATION: Romans 10:1-4

A. The Prayer: v. 1

There are those who would spiritualize all references to Israel in these three chapters. But we should notice how this section of Romans begins: "I speak the truth in Christ . . . I have great sorrow and unceasing anguish in my heart. For I could wish that I myself were cursed and cut off from Christ for the sake of my brothers, those of my own race, the people of Israel" (9:1-4a, NIV). Paul is unquestionably talking about the Jews.

And so he declares in the first verse of the tenth chapter that his "heart's desire and prayer to God" for the Israelites is that they might be saved. The great apostle still had a deep compassion and concern for his fellow Jews, even though his particular assignment was to the Gentiles (Galatians 2:9). In our lesson today he calls himself "the apostle of the Gentiles"

(11:13). But he still loved the Jews and wanted them to be saved.

B. The Problem: vv. 2-3

The Jews of that day were zealous for God, but their zeal was not based on knowledge. Disregarding the righteousness that God gives to men in response to faith (1:17; 3:22), they were trying to establish their own righteousness. But all this was futile. (We shall see a little later in the lesson what their righteousness was.)

C. The Solution: v. 4

"Christ is the end of the law so that there may be righteousness for everyone who believes" (NIV). This is Paul's answer to the problem, the "hang-up" that the Jews had. They did not have to strive to keep the Law in order to be saved. Christ brought an end to the Law as a means of attaining righteousness. He perfectly fulfilled the Law's demands for us.

II. TWO KINDS OF RIGHTEOUS-NESS:
Romans 10:5-13

A. Righteousness by the Law: v. 5

"Moses describes in this way the righteousness that is by the law: 'The man who does these things will live by them' " (NIV). The quotation is from Leviticus 18:5.

James Denney says of this: "Moses, of course, in writing this did not mock his people; the O.T. religion, though an imperfect one, was a real religion, under which men could be right with God" (*Expositor's Greek Testament*, II, 670). But now God was operating through a new covenant in Christ.

B. Righteousness by Faith: vv. 6-10

In verses 6-8 Paul quotes from Deuteronomy 30:12-14 to point out the nature of "the righteousness that is by faith." One does not have to ascend into heaven or descend into the abyss (Greek *abyssos*) in order to find Christ. The word of faith is right within one's heart, where the Holy Spirit is speaking the gospel message.

Verses 9-10 are often quoted in doing personal evangelism or counseling with seekers, and so they should be memorized by every Christian worker. They plainly state we are not only to believe in our heart that Christ has risen from the dead to be our Savior, but we are to confess with our mouth, "Jesus is Lord" (NIV). If we meet these two conditions, we are "saved." This obviously refers to justification as the initial act of salvation.

Paul goes on to say (v. 10) that it is with the heart that one believes and is justified, and it is with the mouth "that you confess and are saved" (NIV). This seems to indicate that a public confession of Christ is essential to salvation. Jesus Himself said, "Whosoever therefore shall be ashamed of me ... of him also shall the Son of man be ashamed" (Mark 8:38). But He also declared, "Whosoever therefore shall confess me before men him will I confess also before my Father" (Matthew 10:32).

However, we should not make a sharp distinction between the righteousness that comes by faith and the salvation that comes by confession Denney writes: "To separate the two clauses, and look for an independent meaning in each, is a mistake; a heart believing unto righteousness, and a mouth making confession unto salvation, are not really two things, but two sides of the same thing" (*Expositor's Greek Testament*, II, 671). That is, if faith is genuine, it will express itself in confessing Christ to others.

It may seem cruel to ask one who has just accepted Jesus as Savior to give public testimony to that fact. But it is really an important kindness. For the witnessing strengthens the faith of the new believer and brings added spiritual blessing. That is why Jesus required the woman healed of her hemorrhage to step out and confess it (Mark 5:25-34).

C. One Righteousness for All: vv. 11-13

The quotation in verse 11 is taken from Isaiah 28:16. The one who truly believes in Christ will never be "ashamed," never be "disappointed" (Weymouth, Moffatt, Goodspeed). The Septuagint uses this verb to express the idea of being ashamed because of unfulfilled hopes. The truth taught here is that the one who really believes in Jesus will not fail to have his hopes realized. Specifically this will be true of his hope of eternal salvation.

In verse 12 Paul asserts one of the important principles of his gospel: "For there is no difference between Jew and Gentile" (NIV). In Old Testament times the Jews were God's chosen people. But when they rejected His Son as their Messiah they forfeited this special privilege. On the cross Christ died for all men without any distinction. So salvation is offered to both Jews and Gentiles on exactly the same condition. And that condition is faith in Jesus as the only Savior from sin.

As a result of Calvary, "the same Lord is Lord of all and richly blesses all who call on him" (NIV). Leading commentators (Sanday and Headlam, Denney, etc.) agree that the reference is to Christ. One of the amazing features of the New Testament is that it takes the Old Testament word "Lord" (*Yahweh* in the Hebrew, *Kyrios* in the Greek Septuagint) and applies it to Christ. Paul does this not only here, but also in quotations from the Old Testament in II Thessalonians 1:9; I Corinthians 2:16; 10:21; II Corinthians 3:16—and perhaps other places. In the eyes of the Jews, who applied the term only to God, this was a daring and dramatic assertion of the full deity of Jesus, who was thus equated with God.

That salvation is available to all people is clearly declared in verse 13, in a beautiful quotation from Joel 2:32. Christ will receive *all* who come to Him.

III. THE REDEEMED REMNANT OF
    ISRAEL:
    Romans 11:1-6

In the last part of chapter 10 Paul documents from the Old Testament the sad story of Israel's rejection of her God. The chapter ends with the sad quotation from Isaiah 65:2—"All day long I have held out my hands to a disobedient and obstinate people" (NIV). This summarizes much of the history of Old Testament times.

In the light of this, Paul asks the logical question, "Did God reject his people?" (11:1, NIV). He answers with his favorite expression, *me genoito*, "By no means!" Then he gives the evidence: "I am an Israelite

myself, a descendant of Abraham. . . . God did not reject his people, whom he foreknew" (vv. 1-2, NIV). Paul himself was a living proof that God had not rejected His ancient people. His covenant with Abraham still stood firm. Divine mercy had saved the sinner Saul.

The Greek of verse 2 very clearly and simply says, "Don't you know?" That communicates better than the "Wot ye not?" of the King James Version! "Actually 'wot' here is a translation of the very common verb *oida*, which occurs 317 times in the New Testament and is almost always (281 times) rendered 'know' " (Ralph Earle, *Word Meanings in the New Testament*, III, 204).

Then the apostle calls attention to what the Scripture says "of Elias"— literally, "in Elijah," that is, "in the passage about Elijah" (NIV). This prophet informed the Lord that he was the only one left who was a true worshiper. But God informed *him* that He had seven thousand faithful followers who had not bowed the knee to Baal (v. 4).

Now Paul makes the application: "So too, at the present time there is a remnant chosen by grace. And if by grace, then it is no longer by works; if it were, grace would no longer be grace" (vv. 5-6, NIV). Salvation by works is rejected; even in the Old Testament times it was God's grace that saved men.

The doctrine of the faithful remnant is prominent in the Old Testament (see Genesis 45:7; Jeremiah 23:3; Haggai 2:2; Zechariah 8:11). But its clearest presentation is by Paul in this passage. In all periods of time God has had His remnant of followers, even if it was down to only eight, as in Noah's day.

Once more the apostle brings in his doctrine of grace. It is not as a result of good works that the remnant is chosen, but by the grace of God. We are not saved by grace *and* works, as some teach, but by grace alone. All we do is respond to that grace in accepting it.

IV. THE REBELLIOUS REJECTS OF ISRAEL:
Romans 11:7-10

"What then? What Israel sought so earnestly it did not obtain, but the elect did. The others became hardened" (v. 7, NIV). This is followed by two quotations from the Old Testament. The first (v. 8) is from Deuteronomy 29:4 and Isaiah 29:10. The second (vv. 9-10) is from Psalm 69:22-23. These verses show the tragic consequences of a spirit of rebellion and of rejection of God.

Some have used these verses to support a rigid doctrine of election: God hardens those He does not wish to save. But William Sanday and Arthur C. Headlam make this observation on the last part of verse 7: "They have not failed because they have been hardened, but they have been hardened because they have failed; cf. i. 24ff., where sin is presented as God's punishment inflicted on man for their rebellion" (*A Critical and Exegetical Commentary on the Epistle to the Romans*, International Critical Commentary, p. 313). Rejection of God's grace is the cause of eternal loss.

DISCUSSION QUESTIONS

1. How may we learn to live "together under God"—internationally, nationally, and locally?
2. What part is played by love? by knowledge?
3. What is the basic cause of prejudice?
4. How should a "godly" person act toward others?
5. What part can the church have in better relations?
6. What are the dimensions of true love?

V. THE RELATION OF JEWS AND GENTILES IN GOD'S PLAN:
Romans 11:11-24

A. Loss and Gain: vv. 11-12

"Again I ask, Did they stumble so as to fall beyond recovery? Not at all! Rather because of their transgression, salvation has come to the Gentiles to make Israel envious" (v. 11, NIV). The rebellion of Israel has been overruled by God as the occasion for Gentile salvation. This, in turn, should make the Jews envious so that they will seek God's favor again.

Then Paul declares that if the loss of the Jews brings gain to the Gentiles, how much more will their fullness bring riches to all the world. That is, the return of the Jews to God's full favor will result in blessing for all mankind.

B. Rejection and Reconciliation: vv. 13-16

The same topic is pursued further in this paragraph. As "the apostle to the Gentiles," Paul is yet deeply concerned for the salvation of his fellow Jews. He wants his very success among the Gentiles to arouse his own people to envy, so that some of them might be saved. Again he argues that if their rejection of the gospel has resulted in "the reconciliation of the world," through Christ's death on the cross, their acceptance of the gospel will be "life from the dead."

C. Wild and Natural Branches: vv. 17-21

Some of the natural branches (Israelites) were broken off. A wild olive branch (the Gentiles) had been grafted in among the natural branches. This was what was taking place in the salvation of both Jews and Gentiles in the first century. But Paul warns that if the new branches fell into unbelief, they too would be broken off (vv. 20-21).

D. Kindness and Sternness of God: vv. 22-24

God's sternness was shown toward the rebellious Israelites, and His kindness toward the Gentiles who were saved. But Paul sounds a solemn warning: "provided you continue in his kindness. Otherwise you also will be cut off" (v. 22, NIV). Our salvation is contingent on our continued faith and obedience. Then Paul adds: God is able to graft the natural branches (Jews) in again.

VI. ALL ISRAEL WILL BE SAVED: Romans 11:25-32

"And so all Israel shall be saved" (v. 26). What does this mean? Certainly not that every Jew will be saved, any more than that every Gentile will be saved. The New Testament is very clear in teaching that individuals are saved through personal faith in Jesus Christ. And nineteen hundred years of Christian history demonstrates vividly the fact that not all people respond to the gospel.

It is our opinion that what this passage teaches is that Israel as a nation will turn to the Lord and accept Jesus as Messiah when He returns to earth. This seems to us to fit into the tenor of these three chapters.

There are many things today that point in this direction. Two are particularly significant. The first is the return of the Jews to Palestine, setting up their own nation there for the first time since A.D. 70. The second is the conversion of Jews in large numbers.

Many, if not most, of us have heard all our lives that before Jesus comes back the Jews would return to Palestine, though in unbelief, and would accept Jesus as their Messiah when He appeared. They *have* returned—nearly three million of them—and are established as a nation in the land promised to Abraham, Isaac, and Jacob. But apparently most of them have no vital belief in God, to say nothing of accepting Jesus as Messiah and Savior.

That picture, however, is changing. For the first time since the first century, Jews are turning to Christ in large numbers. In the June 12, 1972, issue of *Time* magazine the rabbi who was a chaplain at the U.C.L.A. campus was reported as saying, "Young Jews are converting to Christianity at the rate of six or seven thousand a year." Can anyone doubt that prophecy is being fulfilled and the way prepared for Christ's return?

VII. CLOSING DOXOLOGY: Romans 11:33-36

"O the depth of the riches, the wisdom and the knowledge of God!" (v. 33, NIV). Griffith Thomas comments: "There are three elements of adoring wonder at the Divine attributes contemplated here, and they are in view throughout the whole section (ch. ix.-xi.)" (*St. Paul's Epistle to the Romans*, p. 307). He thinks that the word *depth* refers to "inexhaustible fulness rather than unfathomable mystery"—though it may mean both.

The rest of the verse should read (as in the NIV):

How unsearchable his judgments, and his paths beyond tracing out!

The finite human mind can never trace out the richness and fullness of God's grace. We can never fully know the mind of the Lord; no one can advise Him (v. 34, from Isaiah 40:13). The beautiful doxology ends by noting that all things are "from him and through him and to him."

CONTEMPORARY APPLICATION

This morning's paper carried an article on the editorial page that is very relevant to the lesson today. It told how in the summer of 1964 at least thirty-seven black churches were destroyed by fire. Feelings on both sides ran high, inflamed by extreme oratory.

The picture is very different today, the article pointed out. At an anniversary celebration of the rebuilding of one of these churches, whites were present. An interracial Committee of Concern had helped to produce a new atmosphere of mutual respect and toleration in that community. This is the true role of Christianity.

THE RECONCILED LIFE

DEVOTIONAL READING	Romans 12:1-2, 19-21
ADULTS	Topic: *The Reconciled Life* Background Scripture: Romans 12 Scripture Lesson: Romans 12:3-18 Memory Verse: *Do not be overcome by evil but overcome evil with good.* Romans 12:21
YOUTH	Topic: *Living as a Christian* Background Scripture: Romans 12 Scripture Lesson: Romans 12:3-8 Memory Verse: *Do not be overcome by evil but overcome evil with good.* Romans 12:21
CHILDREN	Topic: *Living as Christians* Background Scripture: Romans 12 Scripture Lesson: Romans 12:6-18, 20-21 Memory Verse: *Do not be overcome by evil but overcome evil with good.* Romans 12:21
DAILY BIBLE READINGS	Mon., Nov. 8: "One Body in Christ," Romans 12:1-8. Tues., Nov. 9: "Live Peaceably with All," Romans 12:9-21. Wed., Nov. 10: "The New Nature," Ephesians 4:17-32. Thurs., Nov. 11: "Imitators of God," Ephesians 5:1-14. Fri., Nov. 12: "Be Filled with the Spirit," Ephesians 5:15-20. Sat., Nov. 13: "The Whole Armor of God," Ephesians 6:10-20. Sun., Nov. 14: "Partakers of the Divine Nature," II Peter 1:3-11.
LESSON AIM	To see what it really means to live as a Christian.
LESSON SETTING	Time: A.D. 56 Place: Corinth

LESSON OUTLINE	Living as a Christian
	
	I. A Living Sacrifice: Romans 12:1-2
	  A. Crucial Commitment: v. 1
	  B. Continuing Renewal: v. 2

II. **One Body in Christ:** Romans 12:3-5
   A. The Need for Humility: v. 3
   B. The Human Body: v. 4
   C. The Body of Christ: v. 5

III. **Different Gifts:** Romans 12:6-8

IV. **Living in Love:** Romans 12:9-13
   A. Sincere Love: v. 9
   B. Brotherly Love: v. 10
   C. Abounding Love: vv. 11-12
   D. Practical Love: v. 13

V. **Living in Harmony:** Romans 12:14-18
   A. Responding in Love: v. 14
   B. Community of Spirit: v. 15
   C. Harmony Based on Humility: v. 16
   D. Living in Peace: vv. 17-18

SUGGESTED INTRODUCTION FOR ADULTS

The lessons this quarter have been devoted to a study of "The Message of Reconciliation." The first unit was on "The Freedom of the Christian," going through Galatians. The second unit was "The Meaning of Reconciliation," using passages from the first eleven chapters of Romans. Today we begin our study of "The Life of the Reconciled," as described in chapters 12, 14, and 15.

What is the richest devotional chapter in the New Testament? Various answers might be given: I Corinthians 13, Ephesians 1, I John 4, etc. But we would suggest that the twelfth chapter of Romans has as much devotional help for the Christian life as perhaps any chapter in the Bible.

The suggested Adult Topic for today is "The Reconciled Life." But we have chosen to use the Youth Topic, "Living as a Christian." This seems to us to fit the contents of this wonderful chapter better than the other. In looking closely at Romans 12, we want to learn better how to live the Christian life.

SUGGESTED INTRODUCTION FOR YOUTH

How can we live as Christians? The twelfth chapter of Romans will give us a lot of help in answering that question. It shows us that we must begin with a crucial commitment to Christ. This must be followed by a change of life-style—"Do not conform any longer to the pattern of this world." Then there must be an increasing transformation of our characters by a change in our thinking. Added to this, we must learn to live daily lives of love and humility, of sharing and concern for others.

CONCEPTS FOR CHILDREN

1. A Christian is one who belongs to Christ.
2. The Christian life involves both believing and doing.
3. Our actions show whether we are Christians.
4. The way to avoid doing wrong is to be busy doing right.

THE LESSON COMMENTARY

I. A LIVING SACRIFICE:
Romans 12:1-2

A. Crucial Commitment: v. 1

The word "therefore" is important. It ties the twelfth chapter to the preceding eleven chapters. In view of "the mercies of God"—shown in our justification and sanctification, as well as in His dealings with Israel—Paul urges his hearers to a full commitment to God.

He does not say, "I command," but, "I beseech." Instead of asserting his apostolic authority, Paul pleads with his readers. Johann A. Bengel well remarks: "Moses commands; the apostle exhorts" (*Gnomon of the New Testament*, III, 159).

What does he beseech his readers to do? "That ye present [literally, "to present"] your bodies a living sacrifice." There is considerable agreement among commentators that "your bodies" means "yourselves." W. H. Griffith Thomas describes it this way: "A comprehensive phrase, meaning *themselves*—spirit, soul, and body. The body is the instrument of the inner life, and if this is really consecrated it carries the soul and spirit with it" (*St. Paul's Epistle to the Romans*, p. 324). James Denney writes: "The body is in view here as the instrument by which *all* human service is rendered to God" (*Expositor's Greek Testament*, II, 687). A contemporary British scholar, C. K. Barrett, says, "By 'body' Paul means the whole human person" (*A Commentary on the Epistle to the Romans*, p. 231). And John Wesley comments: "Your bodies—that is, yourselves; a part is put for the whole" (*Explanatory Notes upon the New Testament*, p. 568).

We are to offer ourselves as "a living sacrifice"—not as the dead animal sacrifices of ancient Judaism. The claim could well be made that it is easier to die for Christ than to live for Him. The latter takes greater, more consistent consecration.

These sacrifices are to be "holy and pleasing to God" (NIV). Only a holy life is pleasing to Him.

The expression "reasonable service" has occasioned much discussion. The adjective *logicen* (from which we get "logical") first meant "pertaining to the *logos*, or reason." The noun *latreia*, is used for both "service" and "worship." A check of recent versions will reveal a wide variety of translations of the Greek. C. K. Barrett comments: "Paul means, a worship consisting not in outward rites but in the movement of man's inward being. This is better described as 'spiritual worship' than as 'rational,' for Paul is not thinking of what is meant in modern English by 'rational'" (*Romans*, p. 231).

B. Continuing Renewal: v. 2

"Be not conformed" could be taken as meaning, "Do not become conformed." But the Greek clearly says, "Do not conform any longer to the pattern of this world" (NIV).

Instead, we are to be "transformed by the renewing of your mind." In the previous verse "to present" is the aorist infinitive, indicating a crisis of complete consecration. But "transformed" is in the present tense of continuous action. We are to go on, day by day, being more and more "transformed." In the Greek this is the same verb that is rendered "transfigured" in connection with the transfiguration of Jesus (Matthew 17:2; Mark 9:2). The word is *metamorpho-o*, which gives us *metamorphosis*. We are to experience a spiritual metamorphosis as Christians.

But how? Paul says, "by the renewing of your mind." Our thoughts change our character. Charles Reznikoff is quoted as saying, "The fingers of your thoughts are molding your face ceaselessly."

As a result of this renewal of our thinking we will be able "to test and approve what God's will is—his good, pleasing and perfect will" (NIV). That is the goal of Christian living.

II. ONE BODY IN CHRIST: Romans 12:3-5

A. The Need for Humility: v. 3

True consecration produces humility, because we belong wholly to God and realize that all our goodness comes from Him. We have nothing in ourselves to boast about.

There is a play on words in the Greek of this verse that is difficult to bring out in English: "*hyperphronein ... phronein ... phronein ... sophronein* literally "not to think more highly than one ought to think, but to think so as to think soberly." We are to be sober-minded, not high-minded, Sober thinking will always bring humility, which is honest self-appraisal.

B. The Human Body: v. 4

Paul is fond of using the human body as a type of the body of Christ. The physical body is composed of many "members," or "parts." These do not all have the same "office"—better, "function" (NIV). This is true of both the visible and invisible parts of the body. Yet each part is important to the whole.

C. The Body of Christ: v. 5

The same is true of the church which is the body of Christ. It is composed of millions of members, yet they are all one body in Christ. And each member has his particular function assigned to him by God.

An important corollary truth is that we are "every one members one of another"—"each member belongs to all the others" (NIV). As Christians we not only belong to Christ but we also belong to each other.

What a challenging truth! We may differ somewhat in doctrinal formulations and practical customs. But we all belong to each other. For fellow Christians to be criticizing and fighting each other is just as ridiculous as for a person's hand to injure his own foot or eye. Worse still, it is morally wrong, for it is a denial of Christ's love in us.

Griffith Thomas writes strongly of the implications of this section (vv. 3-5). He says: "As the vine has many branches, and the body many members, so the Christian Church is made up of a large number of individual members, each with his own gift, intended to be exercised in its proper place and way. Our duty, therefore, is to note our province and to stay there, to recognize our limitations and work accordingly" (*Romans*, p. 332). He goes on to note: "Three great words are thus emphasized ... : Unity, Diversity, and Harmony. And it is only when all three are realized and blended that the Church of Christ can live its true life and do its proper work" (p. 333).

Charles Gore puts the matter graphically: "What good work is there which is not in more or less continual danger of suffering ... because fellow Christians ... will plainly ... yield to the ambition to be first: will not be content to be second or third: will not do unobtrusive work: will think 'How can I shine?' rather than 'How can I serve?'" (*St. Paul's Epistle to the Romans*, I, 112).

III. DIFFERENT GIFTS: Romans 12:6-8

Seven ministerial gifts are mentioned in this paragraph. The first four may be thought of as more or less official: prophecy, ministry, teaching, exhortation. The other three are general: giving, ruling, shewing mercy.

It is generally agreed that in the New Testament "prophesying" (NIV) means preaching, not predicting. We are to prophesy according to the measure of the faith God has enabled us to have.

"Ministry" (*diaconia*) may be translated "serving" (NIV). But the context would suggest that here it refers to what we now call the ministry. For it comes between the gifts of "prophecy" and "teaching." The same should probably be said of "exhortation," which may mean "encouraging" (NIV), but is in the context here more likely related to preaching—or to one with an "exhorter's license"!

Our giving should be with "simplicity." William Sanday and Arthur C. Headlam comment: "The word is used by St. Paul alone in the N.T., and was specially suited to describe the generous unselfish character of Christian almsgiving: and hence occurs in one or two places almost with the signification of liberality, 2 Cor. ix. 11, 13" (*A Critical and Exegetical Commentary on the Epistle to the Romans*, International Critical Commentary, p. 357). Perhaps the best meaning here is: "If it is contributing to the needs of others [compound verb in the Greek] let him give generously" (NIV).

"He that ruleth" is literally "one who is set before or over, one who presides." Hence Barrett translates here: "Let the president act with zeal." But there is no clear indication that the Christian church had a president, as does the Jewish synagogue. Probably it is better to take it in a more general sense: "If it is leadership, let him govern diligently" (NIV).

The one who shows mercy is to do it "with cheerfulness." The Greek says: *en hilaroteti*, with "hilarity." Gore says that the term "denotes the joyful eagerness, the amiable grace, the affability going the length of gaiety, which makes the visitor, whether man or woman, a sunbeam penetrating into the sick chamber and to the heart of the afflicted" (*Romans*, p. 293).

IV. LIVING IN LOVE:
Romans 12:9-13

A. Sincere Love: v. 9

"Without dissimulation" is one word in the Greek, literally meaning "unhypocritical." So what Paul is saying here is simply, "Love must be sincere" (NIV). There is nothing sadder in life than insincere love. To claim that we love when we actually do not is a travesty and a tragedy.

The next command is significant and needs emphasis: "Abhor that which is evil; cleave to that which is good." We cannot cling to the good unless we hate the evil. The compound Greek verb meaning to "abhor" is found only here in the New Testament. It means to hate a thing so that one turns utterly away from it.

That is what one has to do with evil if he is going to love what is good. Griffith Thomas writes: "The power of love to hate that which is not good is one of the prime marks of a true life" (*Romans*, p. 338).

"Cleave" is literally "be glued." Divine moral love will act like glue, to stick us fast to what is good and pure.

B. Brotherly Love: v. 10

We are exhorted to be "kindly affectioned"—the Greek adjective (a single word) is found only here in the New Testament—toward each other with "brotherly love." This also is one word, *philadelphia*. Griffith Thomas comments: "It is a little unfortunate that our English versions render this 'brotherly love,' which means 'brother-like love,' or love similar to that of brethren. But the true idea is very much more, and means 'brother-love,' that is, love because we are brethren" (*Romans*, p. 337). He goes on to say, "This brother-love is one of the proofs of real discipleship" (p. 339).

Then Paul adds: "In honour preferring one another." Someone has described the church as "the noblest school of courtesy." The tragedy is that the church too often has not lived up to this description. What a difference it would have made in church history if this admonition had been consistently obeyed!

C. Abounding Love: vv. 11-12

These two verses contain no less than six guidelines for Christian living. The first is "Not slothful in business." But the Greek is more accurately translated, "Never be lacking in zeal" (NIV). There is no place for laziness in the Christian's life. Even in the Old Testament we read, "Whatsoever thy hand findeth to do, do it with thy might" (Ecclesiastes 9:10).

The next admonition is to be "fervent in spirit"—"that is, the human spirit instinct with and inspired by the Divine Spirit" (Sanday and Headlam, *Romans*, p. 361). The word for "fervent" means "boiling hot." It is only the Holy Spirit who can fire our human spirits with holy love. Paul admonishes us: "Keep your spiritual fervor" (NIV). A cold heart is a backslidden heart.

In all this we are to be "serving the Lord," not ourselves. The story of the sheep and the goats (Matthew 25: 31-46) clearly shows that we are serving the Lord when we are serving others in His name.

The fourth admonition is "rejoicing in hope" (v. 12). No matter how bad things may look right now, we can always rejoice in hope of the glorious future that awaits every believer. This is not whistling in the dark; it is simply taking God at His word.

"Patient in tribulation" fits right in with this. The word translated "patient" here conveys the idea of holding steady, of patient endurance. The Greek word for "tribulation" comes from the verb meaning to

"press." So it refers to the pressures of life that sometimes seem unbearable. The English word "tribulation" is derived from the Latin *tribulum*, which was a flail used for beating out the grain. Putting these two ideas together, we have the picture of enduring the pressures and poundings of life in this world.

"Continuing instant in prayer" means "continuing steadfastly" (one word in Greek) in prayer. No matter what happens, we must keep up our prayer life. In this lies our only safety as Christians.

D. Practical Love: v. 13

"Share with God's people who are in need" (NIV). If we have true brother-love we will gladly do this. We will also "practice hospitality" as the need arises.

V. LIVING IN HARMONY: Romans 12:14-18

A. Responding in Love: v. 14

To bless those who curse us takes real love—divine love. This is one of the greatest tests of our Christian experience, and so becomes one of the most effective ways we can prove that Christ has regenerated our hearts and changed our lives.

B. Community of Spirit: v. 15

Griffith Thomas has written cogently on this verse. He says: "It is comparatively easy to 'weep with them that weep,' but much more difficult to 'rejoice with them that rejoice.' We find it a simple matter to condole, but not so simple to congratulate. The reason is that the latter calls for much more unselfishness and the entire absence of any envy or jealousy at another's success. But self-forgetfulness will enable us to do both, and thereby to manifest the true spirit of Christ in deep interest for others" (*Romans*, p. 344).

DISCUSSION QUESTIONS

1. How do we present ourselves wholly to God?
2. What is conformity to the world?
3. How can we renew our thinking?
4. What is the antidote to pride?
5. How may we maintain the spiritual glow?
6. How can we live harmoniously with others?

C. Harmony Based on Humility: v. 16

"Be of the same mind one toward another" means "Live in harmony with one another" (NIV). Paul goes on to say, "Mind not high things, but condescend to men of low estate." The Greek of this last part can be taken either as neuter ("lowly things") or masculine ("lowly men"). Sanday and Headlam say, "probably neuter; 'allow yourself to be carried along with, give yourself over to, humble tasks'" (*Romans*, p. 364). But the majority of the versions take it as masculine: "be willing to associate with people of low position" (NIV).

Barrett handles the problem well. He writes: "It is impossible to feel confident that either translation is correct to the exclusion of the other. . . . Paul may have been aware, and may have approved, of both ways of taking his words" (*Romans*, pp. 241-42). That makes sense.

D. Living in Peace: vv. 17-18

"Do not repay anyone evil for evil. Be careful to do what is right in the sight of everybody" (v. 17, NIV). The first part of this verse is expanded in verse 19: "Do not take revenge, my friends, but leave room for God's wrath, for it is written: 'It is mine to revenge, I will repay,' says the Lord" (NIV).

"If it be possible, as much as lieth in you, live peaceably with all men" (v. 18) has often been misused, due to a misunderstanding of its true meaning. People excuse their lack of peaceful relations by saying, "It doesn't lie within me to live at peace with So-and-So!"

The correct rendering of the verse is this: "If it is possible, as far as depends on you, live at peace with everyone" (NIV). It simply means that unpeaceful attitudes or words are not to originate on our side. As far as depends on us, there will be peace.

CONTEMPORARY APPLICATION

The Memory Selection says: "Do not be overcome by evil, but overcome evil with good" (v. 21). This is one of the greatest secrets of victorious Christian living. When temptations bombard us with seemingly relentless pressure, the way to meet them successfully is not to struggle and wrestle with them. A far more effective strategy is to begin immediately to think of some very pleasant experience in life, exciting enough to "grab" our attention. Or get busily occupied in doing some good thing that will absorb our mind and body. The good will soon drive out the evil, since we can only think of one thing at a time.

November 21, 1976

WALKING IN LOVE

| DEVOTIONAL READING | I Corinthians 8 |

ADULTS

Topic: *Walking in Love*

Background Scripture: Romans 14:1—15:7; I Corinthians 8

Scripture Lesson: Romans 14:10-23

Memory Verse: *Then let us no more pass judgment on one another, but rather decide never to put a stumbling block or hindrance in the way of a brother.* Romans 14:13

YOUTH

Topic: *Love in Action*

Background Scripture: Romans 14:1—15:7; I Corinthians 8

Scripture Lesson: Romans 14:10-23

Memory Verse: *Then let us no more pass judgment on one another, but rather decide never to put a stumbling block or hindrance in the way of a brother.* Romans 14:13

CHILDREN

Topic: *Love in Action*

Background Scripture: Romans 14:10-13; 15:1-7

Scripture Lesson: Romans 15:1-7

Memory Verse: *Love does no wrong to a neighbor; therefore love is the fulfilling of the law.* Romans 13:10

DAILY BIBLE READINGS

Mon., Nov. 15: "Live to the Lord," Romans 14:1-9.
Tues., Nov. 16: "Pursue What Makes for Peace," Romans 14:13-23.
Wed., Nov. 17: Live in Harmony, Romans 15:1-6.
Thurs., Nov. 18: "Love Builds Up," I Corinthians 8:1-6.
Fri., Nov. 19: Protect the Weak, I Corinthians 8:7-13.
Sat., Nov. 20: The Way of Love, I Corinthians 13.
Sun., Nov. 21: Love As Jesus Loved, John 15:12-17.

LESSON AIM

To show us how to walk in love, especially toward our fellow Christians.

LESSON SETTING

Time: A.D. 56
Place: Corinth

LESSON OUTLINE

Walking in Love
  I. Love Toward Weak Christians: Romans 14:1-9
    A. Vegetarians: vv. 1-4
    B. Legalists: vv. 5-9

88

II. **Love Not Judgment: Romans 14:10-12**
   A. God Is Judge: vv. 10-11
   B. Individual Responsibility: v. 12

III. **Love, Not Stumbling Blocks: Romans 14:13-21**
   A. The Danger of Stumbling Blocks: v. 13
   B. No Distinction Between Foods: v. 14
   C. Avoiding Hurting a Brother: vv. 15-16
   D. The Spiritual Nature of Christianity: vv. 17-18
   E. Peace and Mutual Edification: v. 19
   F. Consideration for Others: vv. 20-21

IV. **Love and Faith: Romans 14:22-23**
   A. Not Hindering Others: v. 22
   B. Acting in Faith: v. 23

V. **Love and Unity: Romans 15:1-7**

SUGGESTED INTRODUCTION FOR ADULTS

Romans 14 is one of the most important chapters in the Bible on the relationship of Christians within the church fellowship. Combined with chapter 12, we have enough guidelines to keep us busy the rest of our lives.

Last week's lesson (chap. 12) dealt more with the recognition of unity in diversity within the congregation. We are to recognize other Christians' gifts and functions, and work together in a spirit of love and unity.

Today's lesson carries much the same emphasis. But the diversity here is between the "weak" and the "strong," who must practice mutual forbearance and understanding. Walking in love requires this.

There always will be differing types of personality in the church—and there should be! We need to learn to get along with those who entertain ideas different from ours about Christian practices. Above all, we must let love control all our attitudes and actions.

SUGGESTED INTRODUCTION FOR YOUTH

Charles R. Erdman says, " 'Goodness' is love in action" ("Galatians," *Commentaries on the New Testament Books*, p. 112). That is far and away the best definition of goodness that I have ever encountered.

We are not good because of anything we *don't* do. Goodness is positive, not negative. We are only good when we are acting in love.

This is a penetrating, probing, disturbing truth. Do we always act in love? Probably none of us would dare to say we do. But that should be our goal. Every act, every word, every attitude showing love—that is the ideal of the Christian life.

CONCEPTS FOR CHILDREN

1. Christian love must be expressed in our words and actions.
2. We should be charitable toward those who differ from us.
3. Christian love should help us to live in harmony.
4. We should look for ways to show our love.

THE LESSON COMMENTARY

I. LOVE TOWARD WEAK CHRISTIANS:
Romans 14:1-9

A. Vegetarians: vv. 1-4

"Him that is weak in the faith receive ye, but not to doubtful disputations" (v. 1, KJV). What does the last clause mean?

Admittedly this is a difficult passage to translate and interpret. The Greek literally says, "not for judgment of thoughts." But what does that mean?

The versions go in two different directions. One is that "weak" Christians should be accepted in the church but not allowed to decide for others: "yet not for decision of scruples" (ASV); "but not for disputes over opinions" (RSV). They must not be permitted to create dissension.

The other view is that the weak ones should not be suppressed: "Do not criticize their views" (Goodspeed); "but not for the purpose of passing judgment on his scruples" (Moffatt); "but not with the idea of arguing over his scruples" (Phillips). Since the Greek is ambiguous, we would allow both. This is well expressed in the translation suggested by William F. Arndt and F. Wilbur Gingrich: "but not for the purpose of getting into quarrels about opinions" (*Greek-English Lexicon of the New Testament*, p. 184). If a person is quarrelsome, he should be excluded from the fellowship on that basis.

What is meant by "him that is weak in the faith"? Fortunately we are on firmer ground here. The second verse clearly states that it refers to a vegetarian, not to one who is careless or worldly. The "weak" person is the one who is "overscrupulous" about unimportant things. He makes a major issue out of minor matters. Paul repeatedly declares that Christ has freed us from slavery to the Law, with its meticulous rules and regulations. William Sanday and Arthur C. Headlam put it well: " 'Weakness in faith' means an inadequate grasp of the great principle of salvation by faith in Christ" (*A Critical and Exegetical Commentary on the Epistle to the Romans*, International Critical Commentary, p. 384).

Verse 2 puts the matter squarely: "One man's faith allows him to eat everything, but another man, whose faith is weak, eats only vegetables" (NIV). People who are overscrupulous about such things usually think they have a stronger faith than others, a superior Christianity. But Paul categorically rejects this. Legalism is a sign of weak faith.

The point that the apostle is particularly emphasizing here, however, is that all our relationships to our fellow Christians must be governed by love. The one who eats meat must not despise the vegetarian, and the vegetarian must not condemn the man who is free in Christ to eat all foods.

"Who are you to judge someone else's servant?" (v. 4, NIV). God is his master, and you have no right to judge him. Let the Lord take care of His own servants. The last clause of this verse shows that "another man's servant" (KJV) is an incorrect translation. The Greek simply says "another's servant." The "another" is "the Lord" (best Greek text; not "God").

B. Legalists: vv. 5-9

Now Paul introduces a new element: the observance of special days as sacred. This is a clear reference to Judaism, with its many sacred days—the Sabbath each week, the new moon each month, and the seven annual feasts (Leviticus 23). For Paul these were no longer legally binding. But each Christian should be "fully persuaded in his own mind" about such matters (v. 5).

Inevitably the question comes to mind: "But what about sabbath observance?" Probably the first thing that should be said is that the first day of the week is not, properly speaking, "the sabbath." Rather, it is "the Lord's Day." We are to do on Sunday whatever we feel is pleasing to our Lord.

Frederic L. Godet makes these helpful suggestions: "It has been concluded from these sayings of Paul, that the obligation to observe *Sunday* as a day divinely instituted, was not compatible with Christian spirituality, as this was understood by St. Paul. The context does not allow us to draw such a conclusion. The believer who observes Sunday does not in the least do so under the thought of ascribing to this day a *superior holiness* to that of other days. To him all days are, as the apostle thinks, equal in holy consecration." He goes on to say: "The Christian does not cease to be a man by becoming a spiritual man. And as one day of rest in seven was divinely instituted at the creation in behalf of natural humanity, one does not see why the believer should not require this periodical rest as well as the unregenerate man" (*Commentary on the Epistle to the Romans*, p. 456). Personally, we feel that everyone needs to spend one day a week in rest and/or spiritual exercises for the good of his body and soul.

The seventh verse states a great principle: "For none of us liveth to himself, and no man dieth to himself." Rather, "we live unto the Lord" and "we die unto the Lord" (v. 8). That is the reason for Christ's death and resurrection (v. 9). We are to do everything "to the Lord." Godet writes: "May I allow myself this or that pleasure? Yes, if I can enjoy it to the Lord, and while giving Him thanks for it; no, if I cannot receive it as a gift from His hand, and bless Him for it" (*Romans*, p. 457).

II. LOVE, NOT JUDGMENT: Romans 14:10-12

A. God Is Judge: vv. 10-11

The "you" is emphatic in the Greek—"You, then, why do you judge your brother? Or why do you look down on your brother?" (v. 10, NIV). Instead of judging others, we should realize that we ourselves are going to be judged: "For we shall all stand before the judgment seat of Christ" (the oldest Greek manuscripts have "of God"). This statement is supported by a quotation (v. 11) from Isaiah 45:23.

B. Individual Responsibility: v. 12

Again the truth is underscored: Instead of judging others, we should remember that "every one of us shall give account of himself to God." We won't have to give an account for others; so we should leave them in God's hands. But we will have to give an account of ourselves. This is one of the most solemn truths we can contemplate. It should make us walk carefully before God each day.

III. LOVE, NOT STUMBLING BLOCKS: Romans 14:13-21

A. The Danger of Stumbling Blocks: v. 13

Paul begins this section by saying, "Therefore, let us stop passing judgment on one another" (NIV). In verse 10 he rather obviously was addressing the "strong" brother, who was tempted to judge and despise the "weak" brother. But the "one another" here seems to indicate that he now includes also the weak who might condemn the strong. However, what follows is mainly a warning against hurting the weak.

Godet (*Romans*, p. 459) divides the rest of the chapter into two main parts: "1st. Vv. 13-19a, the duty of not wounding the heart of the weak or producing inward irritation; 2nd. Vv. 19b-23, the fear of destroying God's work within him by leading him to do something against his conscience." It is obvious that this whole chapter is addressed primarily to those in the church who were strong in faith (cf. v. 1). This carries over into chapter 15, as the first verse clearly shows.

Rather than judging others, Paul says, one should reach a decision (aorist tense) not to "put a stumbling block or an occasion to fall in his brother's way." Here we find two interesting terms in the Greek. The word for "stumbling-block" is *proskomma*. It comes from *proskopto*, "strike against" or "stumble" (strike one's foot against). "An occasion to fall" is *scandalon* (cf. "scandal"). This originally meant the bait stick of a trap or snare and then the trap or snare itself, in which one is caught.

Godet makes this comment on these two words: "The wise decision to take is, according to Paul, to avoid anything that might cause a *shock* (*proskomma*), or even a *fall* (*scandalon*) to your neighbor.... One *strikes against* (*proskoptein*), the result is a *wound*; but one stumbles against an obstacle (*scandalizesthai*), the result is a *fall*. The second case is evidently graver than the first. It is easy even to recognize in these two terms the theme of the two following developments: the first relates to the *wounded feeling* of the weak, with all its vexing consequences; the second is the *sin* which one is in danger of making him commit by leading him into an act contrary to his conscience" (*Romans*, p. 460).

B. No Distinction Between Foods: v. 14

The Mosaic Law gave considerable attention to "clean" and "unclean" animals. The flesh of the former could be eaten; that of the latter was forbidden (Leviticus 11:1-47).

The apostle's clear teaching is that in Christ all these distinctions are obliterated. "The principle which Paul is enunciating here is that in and of themselves *things* are nonmoral. It is the use we make of them which constitutes them pure or impure. That is true, for instance, of the human body. Morality does not attach to matter, but to spirit.... Paul recognized the fact that there can be no such thing as 'unclean' animals.... Our choice of foods should not be based on religious scruples but on scientific knowledge" (Ralph Earle, *Word Meanings in the New Testament*, III, 247).

C. Avoiding Hurting a Brother: vv. 15-16

"If your brother is distressed because of what you eat, you are no longer acting in love. Do not by your eating destroy your brother for whom Christ died" (v. 15, NIV). Walking in love—our topic today—involves seeking to avoid doing anything that would hurt our Christian brother (or sister). "Destroy" here means "cause to perish." If what we do thoughtlessly and selfishly can cause some soul to be lost forever, it is obvious that we need to heed carefully the admonitions of verse 13.

A further responsibility is enjoined in verse 16: "Do not allow what you consider good to be spoken of as evil" (NIV). "It is not enough to do what we feel is right. We must guard against doing anything that could cause criticism from others. Of course, this is not always possible. But the principle holds good, nevertheless. We should be concerned about the impression we make on others, as well as the relation of our own consciences to God" (Earle, *Word Meanings*, p. 249).

D. The Spiritual Nature of Christianity: vv. 17-18

"For the kingdom of God is not a matter of eating and drinking, but of righteousness, peace and joy in the Holy Spirit" (v. 17, NIV). The Jews have traditionally placed a great deal of emphasis on the matter of "clean" and "unclean" foods, as well as the cooking and serving of food. We once heard an Orthodox rabbi introduced as an authority in this field: He had devoted a total of twelve years to a study of Jewish dietary laws!

Paul declares that the kingdom of God is not a matter of what we eat or drink. Christianity is not a religion of externals—though some Christians unfortunately put the emphasis there. Rather, it is a religion of the spirit. It is concerned with an inward, spiritual transformation, a new life in Christ. What we eat or drink is not a vital part of our religion, unless it has moral implications.

Instead, it is three things. The first is "righteousness"—being right with God and living a righteous life. Then it is "peace," which comes only as a result of being right with the Lord (Romans 5:1) and is maintained by our having right relationships to our fellowmen. Peace is always based on righteousness. That is why we have so little peace in the world today; it is because we have so little righteousness. But some day Christ will set up His kingdom of righteousness and peace, and it will last forever.

The third thing is "joy." This follows from righteousness and peace, and is based upon them. But we should not forget that "joy in the Holy Spirit" is a basic element of the Christian life. Some "pious" people seem only to have righteousness, but not peace or joy. Others seem to have peace also. But our life in Christ is not complete unless His Spirit is generating joy in our hearts. The joy of the Lord is our strength, and without it we are weak. Legalism majors on externals, but true Christianity emphasizes what is spiritual.

E. Peace and Mutual Edification: v. 19

"Let us therefore make every effort to do what leads to peace and to mutual edification" (NIV). The Revised Standard Version gives it even more literally: "Let us then pursue what makes for peace and for mutual upbuilding." The consecrated believer will seek to build his fellow Christians up, not tear them down.

F. Consideration for Others: vv. 20-21

Paul warns against overthrowing the work of God just over the matter of food. But this is the kind of thing that has happened too often in the history of the church. Arguments over nonessentials have caused strife that tore a church to pieces.

All food is pure (religiously), the apostle declares, but it is wrong to eat anything that causes someone to fall. Better abstain from eating meat than cause a brother to stumble. This is the policy that Paul himself followed: "Wherefore, if meat make my brother to offend, I will eat no flesh while the world standeth, lest I make my brother to offend" (I Corinthians 8:13). That is the true spirit of Christian charity.

IV. LOVE AND FAITH: Romans 14:22-23

A. Not Hindering Others: v. 22

"So whatever you believe about these things keep between yourself and God. Blessed is the man who does not condemn himself by what he approves" (NIV). In this verse Paul is addressing the "strong" brother. To him he says: "If you have faith that these things are pure matters of indifference, keep that faith to yourself; do not parade it in public and shock your weak brother. At the same time be quite sure that in this attitude of liberty you are not condemning yourself and going beyond your con-

DISCUSSION QUESTIONS

1. What is the religious basis of vegetarianism?
2. What is the difference between being scrupulous and being overscrupulous?
3. What does Paul mean by a "strong" Christian?
4. How may we maintain mutual brotherhood?
5. How are love and humility related to unity?
6. To what extent should we try to please others?

science. Happy is he who has no misgivings in that of which he approves; happy is the man whose practice does not go beyond his convictions" (W. H. Griffith Thomas, *St. Paul's Epistle to the Romans*, p. 376).

B. Acting in Faith: v. 23

In this last verse of the chapter the apostle makes an appeal to the "weak" brother. To him he says: "Here is your danger; if you have any doubt or hesitation about a matter of food, you are thereby self-condemned. If you cannot exercise faith about it, you must by all means leave it alone. When you are in doubt, give Christ the benefit of the doubt, and if you cannot do a thing as Christ's follower, do not do it at all" (Griffith Thomas, *Romans*, pp. 376-77). He adds: "The weak and the strong are still with us, and if we would maintain that Christian fellowship which is of the very essence of true life we must constantly learn how the weak is to regard the strong, and, even more, how the strong is to regard the weak" (p. 377).

The King James rendering of the first part of this verse is obviously an unfortunate one: "And he that doubteth is damned if he eat." The correct translation is: "But the man who has doubts is condemned if he eats." Paul is not talking here about eternal damnation.

V. LOVE AND UNITY:
Romans 15:1-7

It is immediately evident that the first verse of this chapter is closely related to the entire discussion of the previous chapter. Here the apostle says: "We then that are strong ought to bear the infirmities of the weak, and not to please ourselves." Today we would probably say, "bear with." We must be willing to put up patiently with the failings of the overscrupulous ones in the church and try to help, not hurt, them. The general principle is expressed in verse 2: "Each of us should please his neighbor for his good, to build him up" (NIV).

Verse 5 has one of Paul's beautiful wishes for his readers: "May the God who gives endurance and encouragement give you a spirit of unity among yourselves as you follow Christ Jesus" (NIV). And he pleads: "Accept one another, then, just as Christ accepted you" (v. 7, NIV). This is essential to having a real fellowship: We must accept each other.

CONTEMPORARY APPLICATION

A friend of ours was selling religious mottoes to help pay his way through college. To a prospective customer he showed one that read: "For even Christ pleased not himself" (Romans 15:3). Her immediate response was: "O no, I wouldn't want that hanging on my wall, for I like to please myself."

Most people would probably not be as frank as this woman. But her attitude is altogether too common. We want to please ourselves, to have our own way. But in doing so, we deny Christ. As Christians we are to please Christ and seek to please others also, when it is for their good.

OUR MINISTRY OF RECONCILIATION

DEVOTIONAL READING	Colossians 1:21-29
ADULTS	Topic: *Our Ministry of Reconciliation* Background Scripture: Romans 1:16; 15:7-33 Scripture Lesson: Romans 1:16; 15:8-21 Memory Verse: *All this is from God, who through Christ reconciled us to himself and gave us the ministry of reconciliation.* II Corinthians 5:18
YOUTH	Topic: *Living Harmoniously* Background Scripture: Romans 1:16; 15:7-33 Scripture Lesson: Romans 1:16; 15:8-21 Memory Verse: *All this is from God, who through Christ reconciled us to himself and gave us the ministry of reconciliation.* II Corinthians 5:18
CHILDREN	Topic: *Sharing the Good News* Background Scripture: Matthew 28:16-20; Romans 1:16; 15:14-33 Scripture Lesson: Romans 15:22-29 Memory Verse: *I am not ashamed of the gospel.* Romans 1:16
DAILY BIBLE READINGS	Mon., Nov. 22: Hope for the Gentiles, Romans 1:16; 15:7-13. Tues., Nov. 23: A Minister to the Gentiles, Romans 15:14-21. Wed., Nov. 24: The Ministry of Reconciliation Continues, Romans 15:22-33. Thurs., Nov. 25: "Ambassadors for Christ," II Corinthians 5:16-21. Fri., Nov. 26: Marks of the Ministry, II Corinthians 6:1-10. Sat., Nov. 27: "He . . . Has Made Us Both One," Ephesians 2:11-22. Sun., Nov. 28: "The Hope of Glory," Colossians 1:21-29.
LESSON AIM	To understand the nature and importance of our ministry of reconciliation.
LESSON SETTING	Time: A.D. 56 Place: Corinth

Our Ministry of Reconciliation

LESSON OUTLINE

I. The Good News for Jews and Gentiles: Romans 1:16

II. Christ's Ministry to Jews and Gentiles: Romans 15:8-12
   A. The Servant of the Jews: v. 8
   B. The Effect on the Gentiles: vv. 9-11
   C. The Ruler of All Nations: v. 12

III. The Joyous Hope of the Christians: Romans 15:13

IV. Paul's Ministry to the Gentiles: Romans 15:14-16
   A. The Roman Christians: v. 14
   B. His Boldness in Writing Them: v. 15
   C. Paul's Priestly Duty to the Gentiles: v. 16

V. The Nature and Extent of His Ministry: Romans 15:17-21
   A. The Power of His Ministry: vv. 17-19a
   B. The Extent of His Ministry: v. 19b
   C. The Nature of His Ministry: vv. 20-21

VI. Paul's Plan to Visit Rome: Romans 15:22-29
   A. His Plan to Go to Spain: vv. 22-24
   B. His Mission to Jerusalem: vv. 25-27
   C. His Subsequent Visit to Rome: vv. 28-29

VII. Paul's Closing Plea: Romans 15:30-33

SUGGESTED INTRODUCTION FOR ADULTS

The seventh verse of Romans 15 reads: "Accept one another, then, just as Christ accepted you, in order to bring praise to God" (NIV).

The most important thing in life is the assurance that God has accepted us as His children. Then we must accept ourselves for what we are, and learn to live with ourselves. Only when we have taken these first two steps can we take the third: "Accept one another."

This truth is being increasingly emphasized by psychologists today. The reason that people do not accept others is that they have never accepted themselves. Openness and honesty, with ourselves and with others, is essential to happy, successful living.

But we must never forget that the beginning of all this must be our reconciliation to God. Only reconciled people can have a ministry of reconciliation to others.

The great need of our day is for reconciliation. But it must begin with a recognition of sin and our need for forgiveness. Christ, for us and through us, is the great Reconciler.

SUGGESTED INTRODUCTION FOR YOUTH

How can we live harmoniously? We must first accept the fact that we are sinners, and become reconciled to God. Then we must, as forgiven people, forgive others and be reconciled to them. In that way we become ministers of reconciliation to those around us.

This must begin in the home. It must then extend to school or work, taking in all those we are associated with from day to day. The nations of the world will never live together harmoniously until individuals do it.

CONCEPTS FOR CHILDREN

1. Paul was deeply concerned to reconcile the Jews and Gentiles of his day.
2. He showed this by preaching the gospel to all.
3. He was eager to reach new places of ministry.
4. We are to carry the gospel to the whole world.

THE LESSON COMMENTARY

I. THE GOOD NEWS FOR JEWS AND GENTILES:
Romans 1:16

"I am not ashamed of the gospel ["of Christ" (KJV) is found in only very late Greek manuscripts], because it is the power of God for the salvation of everyone who believes: first for the Jew, then for the Gentile" (NIV). This is the keynote of the Epistle to the Romans.

The Greek word for "gospel" is *euangelion*, which means "good news." The good news is that Christ died for our sins and that by accepting His salvation we are saved.

Paul declares that the gospel is God's "power." The Greek word is *dynamis*, from which we get "dynamite, dynamo, dynamic." The gospel is like dynamite, blasting sin out of our lives. It becomes in us a dynamo, generating power for holy living. And it should make us dynamic Christians, different from the person of the world.

This gospel is received by faith. And it is for all who will believe, both Jews and Gentiles. First preached to Jews, it reached out to the Gentile world.

II. CHRIST'S MINISTRY TO JEWS AND GENTILES:
Romans 15:8-12

A. The Servant of the Jews: v. 8

"Minister" (KJV) or "servant" (NIV), which should it be? The answer is that either fits very well. The Greek word is *diaconos*, from which we get "deacon." It is used in this technical sense three times in the New Testament (Philippians 1:1; I Timothy 3:8, 12). On the other hand, in the Gospels (e.g., Matthew 22:13; 23:11; John 2:5, 9) it clearly means "servant." Occurring thirty times in the New Testament, *diaconos* is used most frequently in connection with a spiritual ministry. It emphasizes the fact that the minister of Jesus Christ is a servant. He is obligated to render service.

Christ became a servant of the Jews "for the truth of God, to confirm the promises made unto the fathers." James Denney comments: "The truth of God, as the giver of the promises to the fathers, was vindicated by Christ's ministry; for in Him they were all fulfilled, 2 Cor. i. 20" (*Expositor's Greek Testament*, II, 710).

B. The Effect on the Gentiles: vv. 9-11

The ultimate purpose of Christ's ministry to the Jews was "that the Gentiles might glorify God for his mercy" (v. 9). God's mercy to the Gentiles was a fulfillment of His promise to the fathers. For God promised Abraham: "In thee shall all families of the earth be blessed" (Genesis 12:3). Through Christ and His salvation this promise is being fulfilled today.

Fitting this into the background of the previous chapter (our last lesson),

Denney writes: "Hence the Gentiles must not be contemptuous of scruples or infirmities, especially such as rise out of any associations of the old covenant; nor should the Jews be censorious of a Gentile liberty which has its vindication in the free grace of God" (*Expositor's Greek Testament*).

The quotation in the last part of verse 9 is from Psalm 18:49. The psalmist was aware that God's name should be praised among the Gentiles.

In verse 10 we find a quotation from Deuteronomy 32:43, and in verse 11 one from Psalm 117:1. Paul is concerned to show his Jewish readers that God's redemptive purposes took in both Jews and Gentiles, and that the Old Testament declared this truth.

C. The Ruler of All Nations: v. 12

In this verse the apostle quotes from Isaiah 11:10. "The root of Jesse" refers to Christ, "the Son of David" (Matthew 1:1), whose father was Jesse. The Messiah would "rule over the nations; the Gentiles will hope in him" (NIV)—not "trust" (KJV).

William Sanday and Arthur C. Headlam sum up well the purpose of this passage: "St. Paul has a double object. He writes to remind the Gentiles that it is through the Jews that they are called, the Jews that the aim and purpose of their existence is the calling of the Gentiles. The Gentiles must remember that Christ became a Jew to save them; the Jews that Christ came among them in order that all the families of the earth might be blessed" (*A Critical and Exegetical Commentary on the Epistle to the Romans*, International Critical Commentary, p. 397).

III. THE JOYOUS HOPE OF THE CHRISTIAN: Romans 15:13

The apostle picks up the idea of "hope" (Greek text) in verse 12 and enlarges on it. He uses a new designation: "the God of hope." This One will fill us with "all joy and peace in believing," so that we may "abound in hope." How? Through the power of the Holy Spirit.

W. H. Griffith Thomas writes beautifully on this verse. He says: "Now comes a prayer, summing up and concluding the entire subject, and, indeed, the whole of the doctrinal part of the Epistle. After showing in the frankest and yet tenderest way the necessity for both parties, Jew and Gentile, weak and strong, to unite in their one Lord and Master, he lifts up his heart for them in this exquisite prayer, feeling sure that if these spiritual realities are experienced there will be no further difficulty or difference, still less division, in the Church" (*St. Paul's Epistle to the Romans*, p. 337). Prayer is the most important way to solve our problems.

H. C. G. Moule writes at greater length about Paul's intent: "He closes here his long, wise, tender appeal and counsel about the 'unhappy divisions' of the Roman Mission. He has led his readers as it were all round the subject. With the utmost tact, and also candour, he has given them his own mind, 'in the Lord,' on the matter in dispute. He has pointed out to the party of scruple and restriction the fallacy of claiming the function of Christ, and asserting a divine rule where He has not imposed one. He has addressed the 'strong,' (with whom he agrees in a certain sense) at much greater length, reminding them of the moral error of making more of any given application of their principle than of the law of love in which the principle was rooted. He has brought both parties to the feet of Jesus Christ as absolute Master" (*The Epistle to the Romans*, The Expositor's Bible, p. 402).

IV. PAUL'S MINISTRY TO THE GENTILES: Romans 15:14-16

A. The Roman Christians: v. 14

Paul speaks very highly of his readers. They are "full of goodness" and "filled with all knowledge." Yet the message of chapters 14 and 15 would seem to indicate that there was some strife and division in the Roman church, involving misunderstandings between the Jewish and Gentile Christians: a reconciliation was needed.

These people excelled in knowledge, but they were lacking in love. Too often this situation is found today. People substitute learning for love. But, as the thirteenth chapter of I Corinthians says so eloquently, there is *no* substitute for love. One may get into heaven with a lack of knowledge and ability, but not without love. For "God is love," and so a loveless person is a godless person. The primacy of love is one of the main emphases of the New Testament.

B. His Boldness in Writing Them: v. 15

The apostle was writing boldly to the Christians at Rome on some of these points, to remind them of their need of love and unity. He was doing this because of God's grace given to him.

C. Paul's Priestly Duty to the Gentiles: v. 16

The apostle declares that he was "minister" and ministering" in the King James Version have no similarity God." The first observation we would make is that the terms translated "minister" and "ministering" in the King James Version have no similarity in the Greek. The noun is *leitourgos*, which is used technically in the Septuagint (Greek Old Testament) for a priest officiating in the tabernacle or temple. The verb is *hierourgeo* (only here in the New Testament). It comes from *hierourgos*, "a sacrificing priest." So the verb means to "minister in priestly service." Paul says that he is acting as a priest at the altar, offering the Gentiles as a sacrifice to God (cf. Romans 12:1), acceptable because "sanctified by the Holy Spirit."

V. THE NATURE AND EXTENT OF HIS MINISTRY: Romans 15:17-21

A. The Power of His Ministry: vv. 17-19a

Sanday and Headlam offer this paraphrase of verse 17: "I have therefore my proper pride, and a feeling of confidence in my position, which arises from the fact that I am a servant of Christ, and a priest of the Gospel of God" (*Romans*, p. 405).

Though he has much to "glory" about, he says that he will speak only of what Christ had accomplished through him to make the Gentiles obedient "by word and deed" (v. 18)—literally "by word and work"; that is, by Paul's preaching and his other activity.

What his "work" consisted of is suggested in the first part of verse 19: "through mighty signs and wonders, by the power of the Spirit of God" (KJV). But the Greek says quite simply: "in the power of signs and wonders, in the power of the Spirit." (The definite article is not here expressed, but necessary for smooth English.)

Unlike some modern "miracle-workers," Paul was very humble and reticent about the miracles that the Holy Spirit had enabled him to perform. But he does mention them here as evidences of his apostolic authority. It will be remembered that Jesus conferred this power on His chosen apostles (Matthew 10:1).

B. The Extent of His Ministry: v. 19b

The scope of Paul's missionary work is astounding. He says, "From Jerusalem, and round about unto Illyricum, I have fully preached the gospel of Christ."

"Jerusalem" is familiar to us today as the capital of modern Israel, as it was of ancient Israel. But where was "Illyricum"? It was a Roman province in the western part of the Balkan peninsula, north of Greece and across the Adriatic Sea from Italy. The area is now occupied by Yugoslavia and Albania.

On his three missionary journeys Paul had preached in the Roman provinces of Cilicia and Syria, Galatia, Asia, Macedonia, and Achaia. This covered the eastern Mediterranean world. And most of his travel, with the exception of some voyages, was done on foot. The apostle could honestly say, in comparison with his critics, "I have worked much harder" (II Corinthians 11:23, NIV).

C. The Nature of His Ministry: vv. 20-21

Paul was a pioneer missionary. He writes: "It has always been my ambition to preach the gospel where Christ was not only the greatest missionary building on someone else's foundation" (v. 20, NIV). As usual, he supports his action with Scripture (Isaiah 52:15). The vital outreach of the church around the world has depended on men with this kind of a vision.

Paul was a remarkable person. He was not only the greatest missionary of the first century, but also its greatest theologian. This is a rare combination. The part that Paul played in establishing Christianity throughout the Roman Empire is without parallel. A tireless worker, a keen thinker, an

---

DISCUSSION QUESTIONS

1. How can we show that we accept each other?
2. What are some parallels in our day to the situation in Paul's day?
3. How much of the world has been evangelized?
4. How may we help to build unity in the church?
5. What are some areas where reconciliation is needed?
6. What characteristics of Paul impress you?

---

immortal writer—he was all of these and more. His life is a constant challenge to all of us.

VI. PAUL'S PLAN TO VISIT ROME: Romans 15:22-29

A. His Plan to Go to Spain: vv. 22-24

"This is why I have often been hindered from coming to you" (v. 22, NIV). What was the reason? The immediately preceding context suggests that it was his desire to evangelize the eastern part of the Roman Empire. He had done this from Jerusalem all the way around the eastern shore of the Mediterranean to Illyricum, the boundary of the West. He had been so busy doing this that he had not had any opportunity to move on to Rome.

But now there was no more place for Paul to work in these eastern areas (v. 23). This statement could be taken in two ways: (1) The apostle felt that he had sufficiently evangelized that part of the empire; (2) He was running into increasing opposition, so that he had no more opportunity to work there. It may have been a combination of these two. He also had had a "great desire," or longing, for many years to visit Rome. Now the time had come.

Paul was planning to go to Spain, to do pioneer work in the far west. But he wanted to stop at Rome on the way and visit the Christians there (v. 24). After enjoying their company for awhile, he hoped that they would assist him on his further journey to Spain.

B. His Mission to Jerusalem: vv. 25-27

Before going to Spain, however, Paul had a very important errand to take care of. He must go to Jerusalem first. Why? "For it hath pleased them of Macedonia and Achaia to make a certain contribution for the poor saints which are at Jerusalem" (v. 26).

The apostle goes on to say that this was altogether proper: "For if the

Gentiles have been made partakers of their [the Jews'] spiritual blessings, their duty is also to minister unto them in carnal things" (v. 27). It is obvious that "carnal," which carries a bad connotation today, is not the proper word here. The correct translation is "material." Those who receive spiritual blessings should share their material assets.

From this passage and Paul's two Epistles to the Corinthians we learn that this Jerusalem mission weighed heavily on his heart at this time. In I Corinthians (A.D. 54) he devoted four verses of the last chapter to this subject (16:1-4). But in II Corinthians (A.D. 55) his discussion of the special offering for the saints at Jerusalem covers two whole chapters (8 and 9). He is concerned about the fact that the Corinthians had pledged the year before, but hadn't paid (9:2-5). Meanwhile the churches of Macedonia (Philippi, Thessalonica, and Berea) had already given generously out of their deep poverty (8:1-5).

C. His Subsequent Visit to Rome: vv. 28-29

Paul said that after he had completed raising the offering and had made sure that the poor saints in Jerusalem had received it, he would head for Spain and stop off at Rome on the way (v. 28). He assured his readers that when he came to them it would be "in the fulness of the blessing of the gospel of Christ" (v. 29).

VII. PAUL'S CLOSING PLEA: Romans 15:30-33

"I urge you, brothers, by our Lord Jesus Christ and by the love of the Spirit, to join me in my struggle [Greek, "agonize together with me"]

by praying to God for me" (v. 30, NIV).

What did he want them to pray for? There were three petitions. First, "that I may be delivered from them that do not believe in Judaea" (v. 31). Paul knew that he had many enemies in Judea. The Jews there who had not believed in Jesus considered him a traitor. He had been their most zealous leader in the persecution of the Christians. But something had happened on the Damascus road. Now he was the most zealous preacher and propagator of the faith he had once persecuted. His life wasn't safe in Jerusalem, and he knew it.

The second petition was "that my service which I have for Jerusalem may be accepted of the saints." Denney describes the situation: "There was a real danger that the contributions he brought from the Gentile Churches might not be graciously accepted, even accepted at all; it might be regarded as a bribe, in return for which Paul's opposition to the law was to be condoned, and the equal standing of his upstart churches in the Kingdom of God acknowledged" (*Expositor's Greek Testament*, II, 717).

One of the main concerns that Paul had for the offering was that it might bring together in a loving fellowship the Jewish and Gentile Christians. Any possibility that this would fail would be agonizing to his heart.

The third petition was "that I may come unto you by the will of God." He was very eager to visit the church at Rome. He did finally arrive there, but as a prisoner of the emperor.

The main part of the Epistle closes with chapter 15. (Chapter 16 is composed almost entirely of greetings.) So the last verse is a benediction: "Now the God of peace be with you all."

CONTEMPORARY APPLICATION

One of the encouraging signs of our day is the increasing recognition given to the so-called "younger

churches." At the second Berlin Conference on Evangelism (1974) the delegates from the Third World made up a large segment of the three thousand or so attending—in decided contrast to the 1966 Conference. More and more the nationals are being given places of strategic leadership.

This is as it should be. The more closely the parts of the body of Christ work together in loving harmony, the more effective will be the witness for its Lord.

SECOND QUARTER

THE LIFE AND MINISTRY OF JESUS: MARK AND LUKE

Unit I: God Comes to Man in Jesus

Unit II: Jesus Begins His Ministry

Unit III: Jesus Demonstrates His Power

THE COMING ANNOUNCED

DEVOTIONAL READING

Luke 1:11-17

ADULTS

Topic: *The Coming Announced*

Background Scripture: Mark 1:1-3; Luke 1:1-38

Scripture Lesson: Luke 1:26-38

Memory Verse: *"You shall call his name Jesus. He will be great, and will be called the Son of the Most High."* Luke 1:31-32

YOUTH

Topic: *The Coming Announced*

Background Scripture: Mark 1:1-3; Luke 1:1-38

Scripture Lesson: Luke 1:26-38

Memory Verse: *"You shall call his name Jesus. He will be great, and will be called the Son of the Most High."* Luke 1:31-32

CHILDREN

Topic: *Joyous News of Jesus and John*

Background Scripture: Isaiah 9:6; 40:3; Mark 1:1-3; Luke 1:1-38

Scripture Lesson: Luke 1:26-38

Memory Verse: *Declare his glory among the nations, His marvellous works among all the peoples!* Psalm 96:3

DAILY BIBLE READINGS

Mon., Nov. 29: The Messianic King, Isaiah 11:1-5.
Tues., Nov. 30: The Deliverer from Bethlehem, Micah 4:1-4; 5:2.
Wed., Dec. 1: Preparing the Way of the Lord, Isaiah 40:1-11.
Thurs., Dec. 2: Luke's Orderly Account, Luke 1:1-4.
Fri., Dec. 3: The Forerunner Promised, Luke 1:15-17.
Sat., Dec. 4: A Priest Struck Dumb, Luke 1:18-25.
Sun., Dec. 5: The Announcement to Mary, Luke 1:26-38.

LESSON AIM

To see how the coming of Christ was announced.

LESSON SETTING

Time: Probably 7 and 6 B.C.

Place: Zechariah received his vision in the temple at Jerusalem. Mary received hers in Nazareth, north of Jerusalem, in Galilee.

The Coming Announced

I. The Introduction to the Gospel of Mark: Mark 1:1-3

II. The Prologue to the Gospel of Luke: Luke 1:1-4

III. The Announcement to Zechariah: Luke 1:5-25
   A. Zechariah and Elizabeth: vv. 5-7
   B. Zechariah's Big Moment: vv. 8-10

LESSON OUTLINE
   C. Announcement of John's Birth: vv. 11-17
   D. Zechariah's Doubt and Penalty: vv. 18-22
   E. Fulfillment of Promise: vv. 23-25

IV. The Announcement to Mary: Luke 1:26-38
   A. Gabriel's Greeting to Mary: vv. 26-28
   B. Announcement of Jesus' Birth: vv. 29-33
   C. Mary's Surprise: v. 34
   D. The Angel's Explanation: vv. 35-37
   E. Mary's Response of Submission: v. 38

SUGGESTED INTRODUCTION FOR ADULTS

Today we begin a series of twenty-one sessions devoted to the study of the life and ministry of Jesus as recorded in the Gospels of Mark and Luke. Special attention is given to passages that are found in these Gospels but not in Matthew or John. The purpose is to catch something of the personal nature of devotion exhibited in Luke and the power and immediacy of Mark's Gospel. Jesus is presented as Lord of all, sovereign over creation and over His people.

The first unit of study is entitled "God Comes to Man in Jesus." It takes in the four Sundays in December, presenting the beautiful Christmas story as Luke alone records it in the first two chapters of his Gospel. We owe a great debt to Luke, for without his Gospel most of the immediate happenings of that first Christmas day would be unknown to us.

Let us prepare our hearts and minds for an especially joyous Christmas this year—a Christ-centered Christmas. Luke will help us to do it.

SUGGESTED INTRODUCTION FOR YOUTH

Christmas is the story of the Incarnation—that is, Christ coming to earth and becoming a man like us. He did this for two reasons: (1) that He might share our human nature; (2) that we might share His divine nature, as the result of His death for us on the cross.

We ought to be eternally grateful to Him for coming. Let's show our gratitude to Him in love and service.

CONCEPTS FOR CHILDREN

1. Jesus came as the promised Savior.
2. The Old Testament foretold that He would come.
3. The announcement of His birth was made to Mary.
4. She accepted her role as mother of the Messiah.

THE LESSON COMMENTARY

I. THE INTRODUCTION TO THE GOSPEL OF MARK:
Mark 1:1-3

"The beginning of the gospel of Jesus Christ, the Son of God" (v. 1). This is the heading of the Gospel of Mark. *Gospel* means "good news." This Gospel gives us the good news about Jesus, His coming to earth to be our Savior.

The immediate preparation for the appearance of Jesus was the ministry of John the Baptist. The coming of this Forerunner of the Messiah was predicted in the Old Testament. So Mark quotes from Malachi 3:1 (in v. 2) and Isaiah 40:3 (in v. 3). Instead of "in the prophets" (v. 2), the oldest Greek manuscripts have "in Isaiah the prophet," since the main quotation is from that book (cf. Matthew 3:3). Because Malachi is here quoted first, some later scribe substituted "in the prophets" (KJV).

John the Baptist came as God's "messenger." The Greek word is *angelos*, which came to be used mainly for *angel*. John was a "voice," crying out that Christ was coming.

II. THE PROLOGUE TO THE GOSPEL OF LUKE:
Luke 1:1-4

Luke's name is mentioned only three times in the Bible (Colossians 4:14; II Timothy 4:11; Philemon 24), and then only very briefly. Yet this man wrote the two longest books in the New Testament—the third Gospel and Acts. He is the leading historian of the apostolic church.

With a style similar to that of the great Greek historians, Herodotus and Xenophon, Luke says that other men had "undertaken to draw up an account of the things that have been fulfilled among us" (v. 1, NIV). He had read these written narratives and had also checked with "eyewitnesses" (v. 2), as any good historian would do.

"Having had perfect understanding of all things from the very first" (v. 3). is more accurately translated "since I myself have carefully investigated everything from the beginning" (NIV). Luke, a Greek, had not known Jesus personally. But he had made a thorough investigation of what happened. Now he writes an "orderly account" to "most excellent Theophilus," who was probably a Roman nobleman.

III. THE ANNOUNCEMENT TO ZECHARIAH:
Luke 1:5-25

A. Zechariah and Elizabeth: vv. 5-7

Typical of an historian, Luke locates the event he now describes as being in the time when Herod was king of Judea (v. 5). This was Herod the Great, who reigned between 40 B.C. and 4 B.C., but who actually *ruled* all of Palestine 37-4 B.C. We know from secular records that Herod died in the latter year. Since "Jesus was born in Bethlehem of Judaea in the days of Herod the king" (Matthew 2:1), we know that Christ's birth was at least as early as 4 B.C. and very probably in 5 B.C.—the wisemen arrived months later while Herod was still living.

Zechariah—the Hebrew Old Testament form of his name should be used—was a priest belonging to "the priestly division of Abijah." The thousands of priests in that day were divided into twenty-four classes, or "courses." Each division served for a week at a time in the temple.

In accordance with the best custom, Zechariah had married a descendant of Aaron. In fact, she had the same name as Aaron's wife (Exodus 6:23). *Elizabeth* means "God is an oath"—that is, the faithful, covenant-keeping God. *Zechariah* means "The Lord is strength." These two people were both "righteous before God," living blameless lives in keeping with the Law of Moses (v. 6).

This godly couple had one great sorrow. Elizabeth was barren, and now both of them were "well along in years" (NIV). Among the Jews it was considered a disgrace, and a sign of God's disfavor, if a married woman had no children (I Samuel 1:2-11).

B. Zechariah's Big Moment: vv. 8-10

On one of the weeks when the division of Abijah was on duty, Zechariah "was chosen by lot, according to the custom of the priesthood, to go into the temple of the Lord and burn incense" (v. 9, NIV). The Mosaic Law specified that fresh incense must be burned on the altar each morning and evening (Exodus 30:7-8). Each day one priest was chosen by lot to perform this special duty, and he could only do it once during his lifetime. (There were twenty thousand priests.) So this was the high moment of Zechariah's entire life. While he was in the Holy Place, where the altar of incense was, the people were praying outside (v. 10).

C. Announcement of John's Birth: vv. 11-17

We may be sure that Zechariah was in a very spiritual frame of mind as he entered the sanctuary. He probably felt more fully than ever before that he was in God's presence.

Suddenly an angel of the Lord appeared to him, standing at the right side of the altar of incense (v. 11). "When Zechariah saw him, he was startled and was gripped with fear" (v. 12, NIV). Immediately the angel quieted his fears. Literally he said, "Stop being afraid, Zechariah" (v. 13). "Fear not" is God's favorite approach to His people. Johann A. Bengel comments here: "This is the first address from heaven in the opening dawn of the New Testament which is most charmingly described by Luke" (*Gnomon of the New Testament*, II, 12).

Then Zechariah was told that his wife would bear a son, whom they were to name John (which means "God is gracious"). "He will be a joy and delight to you, and many will rejoice because of his birth" (v. 14, NIV). Further instructions were given that this son was never to take wine or any other fermented drink. Instead, "he will be filled with the Holy Spirit even from birth" (v. 15, NIV). The same contrast between being drunk and being filled with the Spirit is found in Ephesians 5:18.

Why would John's birth cause such great rejoicing? The answer includes verse 16: "And many of the children of Israel shall he turn to the Lord their God." This is enlarged upon in verse 17. John would go on before the Lord "in the spirit and power of Elijah" (cf. Malachi 4:5), "to make ready a people prepared for the Lord."

The angel said to Zechariah, "Your prayer has been heard" (v. 13, NIV). Was he praying again for a son? Perhaps so. But he may also have been praying for the restoration of Israel, as was now promised.

D. Zechariah's Doubt and Penalty: vv. 18-22

Zechariah's immediate reaction to the angel's words was one of doubt: "Whereby shall I know this? for I am an old man, and my wife well stricken in years" (v. 18). Donald Miller, in *The Laymen's Bible Commentary* (XVIII, 26), takes this verse as evidence that Zechariah was not praying in the temple for a son; he and his wife had already given up all hopes of this. Rather, Miller says, "As Israel's representative before God, he was praying for the redemption of Israel." The angel's answer in verse 13 was twofold: "First, your prayer for the redemption of Israel is heard. Second, as an instrument of preparing the way for this redemption, you will have a son."

In any case, Zechariah's doubt brought its penalty—as doubt always does. The angel identified himself as Gabriel, one of the archangels who stands in the presence of God. (He is mentioned again in verse 26 and also in Daniel 8:16; 9:21.) He announced that Zechariah would lose his power of speech until the promise had been fulfilled in the birth of his son (v. 20). The priest had asked for a sign ("Whereby," v. 18). Now he got one, but not what he wanted!

Meanwhile the people praying outside were wondering why Zechariah stayed so long in the sanctuary. When he finally emerged, he was speechless. "They realized he had seen a vision in the temple, for he kept making signs to them but remained unable to speak" (v. 22, NIV).

E. Fulfillment of Promise: vv. 23-25

When his duties in the temple were completed, Zechariah returned home. "After this his wife Elizabeth became pregnant and for five months remained in seclusion" (v. 24, NIV). She was very grateful for the miracle God had performed. He had shown His favor toward her and removed her disgrace among the people (v. 25). There was now joyous anticipation at her house.

IV. THE ANNOUNCEMENT TO MARY:
Luke 1:26-38

A. Gabriel's Greeting to Mary: vv. 26-28

"In the sixth month" after Zechariah's vision God sent the same angel, Gabriel, to announce the birth of Jesus. He was sent to "a city of Galilee, named Nazareth." Galilee was, and is, the northern part of Palestine. Nazareth, now a flourishing town, was then a little, obscure village in the hills above the Plain of Esdraelon.

The angel was sent "to a virgin pledged to be married to a man named Joseph" (v. 27, NIV). This was more binding than a modern engagement. In those days the betrothal was a legal contract, that could be broken only by a divorce (see Matthew 1:18-19, NIV). Alfred Plummer writes: "The interval

between betrothal and marriage was commonly a year, during which the bride lived with her friends. But her property was vested in her future husband, and unfaithfulness on her part was punished, like adultery, with death" (*A Critical and Exegetical Commentary on the Gospel According to St. Luke*, International Critical Commentary, p. 21).

The man to whom the virgin, Mary, was betrothed was Joseph, a descendant of David. This fact gave Jesus legal right to the throne of David. He was "the son of David"—a title for the Messiah.

The angel said to Mary: "Greetings, you who are highly favored! The Lord is with you" (v. 28, NIV). The Roman Catholic hymn *Ave Maria* ("Hail, Mary"), dating in its present form from the sixteenth century, is based on this verse.

"You who are highly favored" is all one word in Greek. Literally it means "having been graced" (by God). In the Latin Vulgate it was translated *gratia plena*, "full of grace." This led to the idea that Mary had surplus grace that she could bestow on those who prayed to her. But Bengel (eighteenth century) had a good answer for this: "She is so called, not as the mother of grace, but as the daughter of grace" (*Gnomon*, II, 15-16). She was the recipient of, not the bestower of, grace.

The last clause of this verse in the King James Version is not in the two oldest Greek manuscripts. It was probably imported here from verse 42.

B. Announcement of Jesus' Birth: vv. 29-33

"Mary was greatly troubled at his words and wondered what kind of greeting this might be" (v. 29, NIV). The King James Version has "troubled" both here and in verse 12. But in verse 29 a strong compound is used. Zechariah was "startled" when he suddenly saw the angel. But Mary was "greatly troubled" at the import of the angel's words. What did he mean by them?

Gabriel comforted Mary with the same words that he had said to Zechariah (v. 13): "Do not be afraid" (v. 30). Why? Because "you have found favor with God." When we are under divine favor we do not need to fear, no matter what happens to us.

Then came the definite, startling announcement: "You will be with child and give birth to a son, and you are to give him the name Jesus" (v. 31, NIV). *Jesus* is the Greek form of the Hebrew name *Joshua*, which means "salvation of Yahweh." In general it means "Savior."

The angel went on to say that this child would be great and would be called "the Son of the Most High" (v. 32). The language is reminiscent of Isaiah 9:6-7.

It is further declared that God will give to Him "the throne of his father David." This One, who was both Son of God and Son of David, will "reign over the house of Jacob for ever; and of his kingdom there shall be no end" (v. 33). One is reminded of Daniel 2:44; 7:13-14, 27; Micah 4:7.

C. Mary's Surprise: v. 34

" 'How can this be,' Mary asked the angel, 'since I am a virgin?' " (NIV). The announcement made to Mary was far more incredible than the one made to Zechariah. Yet while the priest expressed doubt, and was penalized for it, Mary simply asked for information: "How shall this be?" This is amazing.

One can imagine how shattering the angel's announcement must have been to a pure virgin, who knew she was innocent. She showed a beautiful spirit.

D. The Angel's Explanation: vv. 35-37

Mary's question was answered precisely: The Holy Spirit would come upon her and the power of the Most High would overshadow her. As a result, the holy one born to her would be called the Son of God (v. 35). The Holy Spirit would take the place of a human father.

The Virgin Birth is undeniably a mystery. But Bishop John C. Ryle has well said: "In a religion which really comes down from heaven there must needs be mysteries. Of such mysteries in Christianity, the incarnation is one" ("Luke," *Expository Thoughts on the Gospels*, p. 27). And F. F. Bruce writes: "The more we appreciate the uniqueness of this incarnation, the more may we recognize how fitting—indeed, how inevitable—it is that the means by which it was brought about should also be unique" ("The Person of Christ: Incarnation and Virgin Birth," *Basic Christian Doctrines*, p. 128).

What is the theological meaning of the Virgin Birth? It is put well by Donald Miller: "One must believe that in the Virgin Birth God entered human life redemptively, and that *he did so for me*" (*Laymen's Commentary*, p. 32).

The child that would be born to Mary would be "holy." In his excellent *Commentary on the Gospel of Luke* in The New International Commentary on the New Testament series, J. Norval Geldenhuys writes: "The angel in these words does not merely announce that the incarnation of Jesus will take place through the direct influence of the Holy Ghost, but also expressly declares that He who will

---

DISCUSSION QUESTIONS

1. How do the first two chapters of Mark and Luke differ?
2. How does this fit their distinctive purposes?
3. How did Zechariah and Mary differ in their reactions to the angelic announcement?
4. Why was the Virgin Birth necessary?
5. What sacrifices may God ask us to make?
6. How are faith and obedience related?

through Him be begotten as Man will be free from all taint of sin—He will be the Holy One. It was necessary for the Redeemer to be 'born of a woman' (Gal. iv. 4) so that He should be of the same nature as those He came to save. But it was just as imperative that He should be perfectly holy, since no sinful being can accomplish reconciliation for the sins of others" (p. 77). Jesus was the only one who could be an acceptable sacrifice for our sins.

The angel went on to say: "Even Elizabeth your relative is going to have a child in her old age, and she who was said to be barren is in her sixth month" (v. 36, NIV). The Greek word for "cousin" in the King James Version really means "kinswoman," or, as we would say now, "relative."

The reason Gabriel told Mary about Elizabeth's expected child was to strengthen her faith. As William Arndt observes, "If God worked such an astounding miracle in the case of Elisabeth, then Mary could with confidence await the fulfillment of God's promise made to her" (*Gospel Accord-*

ing to St. Luke, p. 51). The advent of the Messiah was a time of miracles.

Verse 37 reads literally: "For no word from God shall be void of power" (ASV). When God speaks, He speaks with authority and with power to carry out what He says.

E. Mary's Response of Submission: v. 38

We cannot appreciate the amazing consecration of Mary unless we face the implications involved. Miller points out some of these: "To be God's servant, Mary had to expose herself to the misunderstanding of Joseph (Matt. 1:18-25), to the possible loss of her reputation and the curse of being considered a sinful woman, and to possible death by stoning (Deut. 22:23-24)" (*Laymen's Commentary*, p. 29).

In spite of all these very real hazards, Mary said, "I am the Lord's servant; let it happen to me as you have said" (NIV). It was a costly consecration—to do God's will, regardless of the consequences.

CONTEMPORARY APPLICATION

"In the fullness of time" Christ came. And He will come again at God's appointed hour. The first time He came to a humble home in a little town in a foreign-dominated country. The next time He will come in power, to rule the whole world.

We should be forever grateful that He came long ago for our salvation. And we must be ready for His return, to rule with Him.

THE COMING ANTICIPATED

DEVOTIONAL READING	Luke 1:68-79

ADULTS

Topic: *The Coming Anticipated*

Background Scripture: I Samuel 2:1-10; Luke 1:39-79

Scripture Lesson: Luke 1:39-55

Memory Verse: *"My soul magnifies the Lord, and my spirit rejoices in God my Savior."* Luke 1:46-47

YOUTH

Topic: *The Coming Anticipated*

Background Scripture: I Samuel 2:1-10; Luke 1:39-79

Scripture Lesson: Luke 1:39-55

Memory Verse: *"My soul magnifies the Lord, and my spirit rejoices in God my Savior."* Luke 1:46-47

CHILDREN

Topic: *A Great Day A Comin'*

Background Scripture: Luke 1:39-80

Scripture Lesson: Luke 1:39-58

Memory Verse: *"And you, child . . . will go before the Lord to prepare his ways . . . to give light to those who sit in darkness . . . to guide our feet into the way of peace."* Luke 1:76-79

DAILY BIBLE READINGS

Mon., Dec. 6: Hannah's Song of Praise, I Samuel 2:1-10.
Tues., Dec. 7: A New Song of Praise, Psalm 96.
Wed., Dec. 8: The Lord's Messenger, Malachi 3:1-5.
Thurs., Dec. 9: Mary Visits Elizabeth, Luke 1:39-45.
Fri., Dec. 10: Mary's Song of Praise, Luke 1:46-56.
Sat., Dec. 11: John the Baptist Born, Luke 1:57-66.
Sun., Dec. 12: Zechariah's Song of Praise, Luke 1:67-79.

LESSON AIM

To note the joyful anticipation expressed by Mary and Zechariah, and to challenge us to show our gratitude to God.

LESSON SETTING

Time: About 6 B.C.

Place: Some town in Judea

112

The Coming Anticipated

I. **Mary's Visit to Elizabeth**: Luke 1:39-45
   A. The Hill Country of Judea: v. 39
   B. Elizabeth Filled with the Spirit: vv. 40-41
   C. Elizabeth's Prophetic Pronouncement: vv. 42-45

II. **Mary's Song of Praise**: Luke 1:46-55
    A. Her Personal Rejoicing: vv. 46-50
    B. God's Mercy to the Needy: vv. 51-53
    C. God's Special Mercy to Israel: vv. 54-55

III. **The Birth of John the Baptist**: Luke 1:57-66
     A. Rejoicing at His Birth: vv. 57-58
     B. The Question of His Name: vv. 59-61
     C. The Miracle of Speech: vv. 62-66

IV. **Zechariah's Song of Praise**: Luke 1:67-79
    A. Spirit-inspired Prophecy: v. 67
    B. Divine Redemption: vv. 68-75
    C. The Role of John: vv. 76-79

LESSON OUTLINE

SUGGESTED INTRODUCTION FOR ADULTS

Last week our lesson was on "The Coming Announced." Today it is "The Coming Anticipated." We are getting nearer to the actual birth of Jesus.

One of the striking features of the first two chapters of Luke is the inclusion of several hymn-poems not found elsewhere. This shows that Luke was not only a great historian, physician, and artist (as the early Church Fathers tell us), but he was also a poet. This does not mean that he composed these hymns, but only a poet would record them.

The two longest, found in today's lesson, are the *Magnificat* (1:46-55) and the *Benedictus* (1:68-79). Both are named after the first word in the Latin translation.

In the second chapter we find the *Gloria in Excelsis* (v. 14) and the *Nunc Dimittis* (vv. 29-32). All four of these have been used in Christian churches.

Luke's Gospel is the Gospel of Joy. D. A. Hayes comments: "This Gospel begins with songs and ends with songs, and there is singing and rejoicing all the way along" (*Synoptic Gospels and the Book of Acts*, p. 262).

SUGGESTED INTRODUCTION FOR YOUTH

One of the most exciting events in the life of a young couple is the birth of their first baby. But the birth of Jesus was to be something more than this. He would be the Messiah of Israel, the Savior of the world. No wonder there was great excitement in anticipation of His birth!

The Old Testament, from Genesis to Malachi, has many prophetic predictions of the coming of the Messiah. In the period just before the birth of Jesus this anticipation had been heightened. Many were looking for Him to come (Luke 2:38).

CONCEPTS FOR
CHILDREN

Today there is a fresh anticipation of His coming again—among both Jews and non-Jews. We ought to sense something of the excitement of this and be ready and waiting for the Second Coming.

1. The Jews had suffered for a long time under foreign domination.
2. They were looking for the promised Messiah to come and free them from foreign rule.
3. Only Christ can bring peace to Israel today.
4. And only He can bring peace to the whole world.

THE LESSON COMMENTARY

I. MARY'S VISIT TO ELIZABETH: Luke 1:39-45

A. The Hill Country of Judea: v. 39

The angel had told Mary that her relative Elizabeth was expecting a child. Probably Mary was well aware of the sorrow of the aged couple through years of disappointed hopes. So now she hurried to Elizabeth's side to rejoice with her in her new anticipation. The two expectant mothers would celebrate together. Though one was a young virgin and the other an elderly woman, they had much in common.

Mary's southward journey of at least eighty miles would take most of the week between sabbath days—on which Jews could travel only half a mile. The average rate of travel at that time was fifteen or twenty miles a day—all on foot, of course. With our modern motorized transportation it is hard for us to envision the situation then.

We are told that Mary "hurried to a town in the hill country of Judah" (v. 39, NIV). It is not identified. Since many priests lived in Hebron (Joshua 21:10-11), some think that this was the town. Hebron is twenty miles south of Jerusalem, and the total distance from Nazareth is a hundred miles. Tradition places the birth of John the Baptist in Ain Karem, a village about four miles west of Jerusa-

lem. This would be about eighty miles from Nazareth.

The vicinity of Jerusalem is about twenty-five hundred feet above sea level; Hebron has an elevation of about three thousand feet. The main part of "the hill country of Judah" was between these two.

In either case, such an extended journey (for those times) would require considerable preparation. (A young girl would not be allowed to travel alone.) "Mary arose" (KJV) is better translated "Mary got ready" (NIV).

B. Elizabeth Filled with the Spirit: vv. 40-41

As Mary entered Zechariah's home, she greeted Elizabeth. The typical Jewish greeting was, and is, "Shalom"—that is, "Peace!"

Immediately Elizabeth felt the unborn baby leap within her. She was "filled with the Holy Spirit" (v. 41, NIV). J. Norval Geldenhuys comments: "This prophetic action of the Spirit differs completely from the outpouring of and the filling with the Holy Ghost on and from Pentecost (Acts ii), seeing that it is only temporary and again recedes" (Commentary on Luke, New International Commentary on the New Testament, p. 83, n. 3).

Frederic L. Godet makes this comment concerning Elizabeth: "The emotion which possesses her is communicated to the child whose life is as yet one with her own; and at the sudden leaping of this being, who she knows is compassed about by special blessing, the veil is rent. The Holy Spirit, the prophetic Spirit of the old covenant, seizes her, and she salutes Mary as the mother of the Messiah" (*Commentary on the Gospel of St. Luke*, p. 98).

C. Elizabeth's Prophetic Pronouncement: vv. 42-45

"Blessed are you among women" (NIV) is the same as saying, "Blessed are you above all other women." Elizabeth adds: "and blessed is the child you will bear!" (v. 42, NIV). Then she asks why she should be so favored, "that the mother of my Lord should come to me" (v. 43). Only the Holy Spirit could have shown her this.

"Mother of my Lord" doesn't mean that Mary is the "mother of God," as heretics asserted in the early church and as the Roman Catholic Church still teaches. Mary was the mother of Jesus' human nature but not of His divine nature.

Then Elizabeth told Mary about the unborn baby leaping within her at the sound of Mary's greeting. This seems to have been a prophetic premonition to Elizabeth that Mary was to be the mother of the Messiah.

The exact translation of verse 45 cannot be determined with certainty. J. M. Creed explains the problem: "It is not easy to decide whether *hoti* should be taken to mean 'that,' in which case the following clause explains the content of what Mary believed, or whether it means 'because,' in which case the following clause gives the ground for Mary's blessedness. The latter is to be preferred" (*Gospel According to St. Luke*, p. 22). But that is debatable. Although the King James Version has "for" (meaning "because"), both the New American Standard Bible and the New International Version have "that": "Blessed is she who has believed that what the Lord has said to

her will be accomplished" (NIV). Godet affirms: "*Hoti* cannot be taken here in the sense of *because*" (*Luke*, p. 99).

Geldenhuys has a beautiful comment on Elizabeth's words. He says: "Elizabeth nobly and voluntarily placed herself in the background and acknowledged unreservedly and joyfully that her younger relative had received infinitely more honour than she. The gift of God to herself she accepted in grateful worship. But when she meets Mary, to whom a still greater gift has been given, she does not become jealous or unsympathetic. She humbles herself and sings to the honour of the all-excelling privileged one among women who is to become the Mother of her Lord. Because she was filled with the Holy Ghost, she was capable of such special magnanimity. Whilst jealousy would have darkened her life, her humble attitude opened for her the gates to true, deep and jubilant joy." Geldenhuys adds this helpful application: "He who elevates himself is constantly engaged in wrecking his own life. But he who is sincerely humble finds richness of life and happiness" (*Luke*, p. 83).

II. MARY'S SONG OF PRAISE: Luke 1:46-55

A. Her Personal Rejoicing: vv. 46-50

As noted in the Introduction, this song is called the *Magnificat*, the first word in the Latin version. It has striking parallels to the Song of Hannah (I Samuel 2:1-10). It is also similar to the Psalms in content and spirit. Maclaren observes: "Birds sing at dawn and sunrise. It was fitting that the last strains of Old Testament psalmody should prelude the birth of Jesus" ("Luke," *Expositions of Holy Scripture*, I, 17).

In similar manner van Oosterzee writes: "The Magnificat . . . and the Benedictus of Zechariah, vv. 68-79, . . . are the Psalms of the New Testament, and worthily introduce the history of Christian hymnology. They prove the harmony of poetry and religion. They are the noblest flowers of Hebrew lyric poetry, sending their fragrance to the approaching Messiah. They are full of reminiscences of the Old Testament, entirely Hebrew in tone and language, and can be rendered almost word for word" ("Luke," *Commentary on the Holy Scriptures*, J. P. Lange, ed., p. 25).

With regard to the timing of these two hymns of praise, van Oosterzee continues: "The angel's visit was vouchsafed to Mary later than to Zacharias, yet her song of thanksgiving is uttered long before his: faith is already singing for joy, while unbelief is compelled to be silent."

Concerning the general structure and content of the song, William Arndt makes this suggestion: "There are three great thoughts which Mary's song stresses. (1) She thanks God for having favored her, a humble maid of Israel, in such extraordinary fashion (46-50). (2) She praises God for resisting the haughty, the proud, and the self-righteous, and for aiding the poor, the lowly, that is, the humble sinners (51-53). (3) She exalts the name of God because the Lord fulfills the promises which he made to the fathers in the Messianic prophecies (54-55)" (*Gospel According to St. Luke*, p. 60).

The verb "magnify" (v. 46) literally meant "enlarge," as in Matthew 23:5. But more often in the New Testament it is used, as here, in the derived sense of "extol" or "magnify." It may here be translated "exalts" (NASB) or "praises" (NIV).

What is the difference between "soul" (v. 46) and "spirit" (v. 47)? Godet explains it this way: "When the human spirit is referred to in Scripture, the word indicates the deepest part of our humanity, the point of contact between man and God. The *soul* is the actual centre of human life, the principle of individuality, and the seat of those impressions which are of an essentially personal character" (*Luke*, p. 102). Concerning the use of the two terms here he says: "Thus,

while the expression, '*My soul* doth magnify,' refers to the personal emotions of Mary, to her feelings as a woman and a mother, all of which find an outlet in adoration, these words, '*My spirit* hath rejoiced,' appear to indicate the moment when, in the profoundest depths of her being, by the touch of the Divine Spirit, the promise of the angel was accomplished in her" (*Luke*). Other scholars feel that we have here simply the parallelism of Hebrew poetry, with no intended distinction.

Mary gives the reason why she rejoices in spirit: "for he has been mindful of the humble state of his servant" (v. 48, NIV). Then she adds: "From now on all generations will call me blessed." That has certainly been true.

She rejoices that "the Mighty One" has done great things for her (v. 49), and she reveres His name as "holy." God alone is absolutely holy, eternally without sin or any imperfection.

God's mercy is extended to those who "fear" Him in every generation (v. 50). Geldenhuys comments: "To 'fear' God means to cherish reverence and respect for Him—not to be afraid, but to honour Him lovingly by avoiding what is contrary to His will and by striving after what pleases Him" (*Luke*, p. 85).

B. God's Mercy to the Needy: vv. 51-53

"He hath showed strength with his arm" (v. 51). The arm is the symbol of power or force. With His almighty arm God has "scattered the proud in the imagination of their hearts." Geldenhuys writes: " 'Heart' is used in the Bible to indicate the pivot of human life in its fullest extent with regard to man's thoughts, desires and emotions" (*Luke*, p. 88, n. 8).

The Greek word for "mighty" (v. 52) is *dynastas*, from which we get "dynasties." The word for "seats" is *thronon*, "thrones." And "them of low degree" is all one word, *tapeinous*, "humble." So the correct translation of this verse is: "He has brought down rulers from their thrones but has lifted up the humble" (NIV).

God also ministers in mercy to the hungry, filling them with good things (v. 53). On the other hand, He sends the rich away empty.

Godet gives the application of these verses to the situation then: "The *proud*, the *mighty*, and the *rich*, denote Herod and his court, the Pharisees and the Sadducees, as well as the foreign oppressors, Caesar and his armies, and all the power of heathendom" (*Luke*, p. 104). All these would be "put down."

C. God's Special Mercy to Israel: vv. 54-55

It is obvious that "holpen" (KJV) should be "helped." Mary now exults in the way God has "helped his servant Israel," being merciful to Abraham and his descendants. This is not only a glance at God's mercy shown in the past, but also a prophetic preview of the future. Through the coming of the Messiah divine mercy would be demonstrated in its highest measure.

After staying about three months with Elizabeth, Mary returned home to Nazareth (v. 56). It is not stated whether this was before or after the birth of John the Baptist. Creed says: "Mary returns to her home before the birth of Elizabeth's child" (*Luke*, p. 24). Richard C. H. Lenski agrees and suggests a reason: "We judge that Mary hastens home because she wanted to avoid people who would soon throng the house of Elizabeth" (*The Interpretation of Luke's Gospel*, p. 94). This seems to us reasonable.

III. THE BIRTH OF JOHN THE BAPTIST: Luke 1:57-66

A. Rejoicing at His Birth: vv. 57-58

"When it was time for Elizabeth to have her baby, she gave birth to a son" (v. 57, NIV). When her neighbors and

relatives heard of this evidence of God's mercy to her, "they rejoiced with her." This would seem to indicate that her seclusion (v. 24) covered the last five months, rather than the first five months. It appears that people were not aware that she was expecting a baby.

Luke loves to describe homey scenes, and this is one. Godet describes it this way: "These verses are like a pleasing picture of Jewish home-life. We see the neighbours and relations arriving one after the other—the former first, because they live nearest. Elizabeth, the happy mother, is the central figure of the scene; every one comes up to her in turn" (*Luke*, p. 108). It was an unexpected, joyous occasion.

B. The Question of His Name: vv. 59-61

"On the eighth day they came to circumcise the child, and they were going to name him [the Greek has the imperfect tense of attempted action] after his father Zechariah, but his mother spoke up and said, 'No! He is to be called John' " (vv. 59-60, NIV). They immediately protested: " 'There is no one among your relatives who has that name' " (v. 61, NIV).

On this custom Godet writes: "As an Israelitish child by its birth became a member of the human family, so by

DISCUSSION QUESTIONS

1. What are some advantages of a Christian home?
2. What do you suppose Mary and Elizabeth talked about for three months?
3. How were they alike and how were they different?
4. In what ways was Mary "blessed"?
5. How can we apply her song to our day?
6. What are some spiritual values in Zechariah's song?

circumcision, on the corresponding day of the following week, he was incorporated into the covenant (Gen. xvii); and it was the custom on this occasion to give him his name" (*Luke*, p. 108). Henry Alford makes this suggestion: "The names of children were given at circumcision, because at the institution of that rite, the names of Abram and Sarai were changed to Abraham and Sarah" (*Greek Testament*, I, 451).

C. The Miracle of Speech: vv. 62-66

Perplexed, the neighbors and relatives made signs to the father, "to find out what he would like to name the child" (v. 62, NIV). Zechariah "asked for a writing tablet [not "table" (KJV)] and to everyone's astonishment he wrote, 'His name is John' " (v. 63, NIV). That settled it!

This was an expression of faith and obedience. Consequently the penalty on Zechariah for his unbelief was lifted: "And his mouth was opened immediately, and his tongue loosed, and he spake, and praised God" (v. 64). What a thrilling moment this must have been for Zechariah, who had been unable to speak for nine months.

It is no wonder that we read: "The neighbors were all filled with awe, and throughout the hill country of Judea people were talking about all these things" (v. 65, NIV). People were asking, " 'What manner of child shall this be!' "—"For the Lord's hand was with him" (v. 66, NIV).

IV. ZECHARIAH'S SONG OF PRAISE: Luke 1:67-79

A. Spirit-inspired Prophecy: v. 67

This song is called the *Benedictus*, after the first word in the Latin version. It was given after Zechariah was "filled with the Holy Spirit," as Elizabeth had been three months before. Under the inspiration of the Holy Spirit he "prophesied"; that is, he spoke for God with prophetic utterance. It does not mean "predicted," as the word is popularly taken today.

B. Divine Redemption: vv. 68-75

The first thing Zechariah said was: " 'Blessed be the Lord God of Israel; for he hath visited and redeemed his people' " (v. 68). In the birth of John the Baptist God was already beginning to visit His people and inaugurate their redemption.

In the Old Testament the "horn" (v. 69) is a symbol of strength (I Samuel 2:10; Psalm 132:17; Ezekiel 29:21). The "horn of salvation" was Christ, who was of the house of David, whereas John the Baptist was of the tribe of Levi.

This salvation was first to be a matter of being "saved from our enemies" (v. 71), in accordance with the "holy covenant" (v. 72). But man's greatest enemy is sin, and it is only as we are saved from sin that we can "serve him without fear." "This implies that holiness of heart and righteousness of life are part of what *salvation* means" (Ralph Earle, *Wesleyan Bible Commentary*, IV, 218).

C. The Role of John: vv. 76-79

In this second half of the song Zechariah addresses his son prophetically. John would be called "a prophet of the Most High" (v. 76, NIV). He would "go on before the Lord," as the Forerunner of the Messiah, to prepare the way for Christ. His message would center on forgiveness of sins (v. 77). The "day-spring" (v. 78), or "rising sun" (NIV) was Christ, who would give light to those sitting in darkness and guide their feet into the path of peace (v. 79).

CONTEMPORARY APPLICATION

While John the Baptist filled a special, assigned role as the Forerunner of Christ, turning people's hearts toward God, every Christian worker has this mission in a measure. For this reason the birth of every child into a Christian home is a significant event and should be accompanied by much prayer. Perhaps the newborn infant will become a great soul-winner, helping to precipitate gracious revivals. Christian parents should never take lightly the birth of a child into their home.

THE COMING CELEBRATED

DEVOTIONAL READING	Isaiah 52:7-10

ADULTS

Topic: *The Coming Celebrated*

Background Scripture: Luke 2:1-20

Scripture Lesson: Luke 2:7-20

Memory Verse: *The Word became flesh and dwelt among us, full of grace and truth; we have beheld his glory, glory as of the only Son from the Father.* John 1:14

YOUTH

Topic: *The Joyful Day*

Background Scripture: Luke 2:1-20

Scripture Lesson: Luke 2:7-20

Memory Verse: *The Word became flesh and dwelt among us, full of grace and truth; we have beheld his glory, glory as of the only Son from the Father.* John 1:14

CHILDREN

Topic: *Good News for All the People*

Background Scripture: Luke 2:1-20

Scripture Lesson: Luke 2:7-20

Memory Verse: *"Be not afraid . . . I bring you good news of a great joy which will come to all the people."* Luke 2:10

DAILY BIBLE READINGS

Mon., Dec. 13: Tidings of Good, Isaiah 52:7-10.
Tues., Dec. 14: Luke's Account of Jesus' Birth, Luke 2:1-7.
Wed., Dec. 15: The Angel and the Shepherds, Luke 2:8-14.
Thurs., Dec. 16: The Visit of the Shepherds, Luke 2:15-20.
Fri., Dec. 17: Matthew's Account of Jesus' Birth, Matthew 1:18-25.
Sat., Dec. 18: "When the Time Had Fully Come," Galatians 4:1-7.
Sun., Dec. 19: The Exalted Servant, Isaiah 52:13-15.

LESSON AIM

To help us join in celebrating the coming of Christ to earth.

LESSON SETTING

Time: Probably 5 B.C.

Place: Bethlehem, six miles south of Jerusalem

The Coming Celebrated

LESSON OUTLINE

SUGGESTED INTRODUCTION FOR ADULTS

The first two chapters of Matthew and Luke contain the so-called Infancy Narratives, not found elsewhere in the New Testament. Many people assume that the two Gospels give much the same incidents. But the truth is that the two accounts are entirely different. They are not contradictory, however; rather, they are complementary.

Matthew gives the announcement to Joseph that Christ was to be born (1:18-25), the visit of the Wisemen (2:1-12), the escape to Egypt (2:13-18) and the return to Nazareth (2:19-23). On the other hand, Luke gives the announcement to Zechariah that John the Baptist was to be born (1:5-25), the announcement to Mary that Christ was to be born (1:26-38), the visit of Mary to Elizabeth (1:39-56), the birth of John the Baptist (1:57-80), the birth of Jesus (2:1-7), the visit of the shepherds (2:8-20), the circumcision of Jesus (2:21), the presentation of the baby Jesus in the temple (2:22-40), the boy Jesus in the temple (2:41-50), and the growth of Jesus as a young man (2:51-52). It will readily be seen that Luke has an entirely different set of Infancy Narratives.

SUGGESTED INTRODUCTION FOR YOUTH

What was the most joyful day in all history? It was the day Jesus was born. Only a few humble shepherds rejoiced with Mary and Joseph. But in the light of nineteen hundred years we can say that that day has brought more joy to the world than any other day. That is why all events are dated B.C. (before Christ) or A.D. (Anno Domini, in the year of our Lord).

1. The birth of Jesus is good news for all people.
2. We should respond as the shepherds did, by coming to Jesus.
3. We should tell others, as they did.
4. Our lives should then be filled with praise, as theirs was.

THE LESSON COMMENTARY

I. THE ROMAN CENSUS:
Luke 2:1-3

In order to get this short paragraph of Scripture before us accurately it will be helpful to quote it from the New International Version: "In those days Caesar Augustus issued a decree that a census should be taken of the entire Roman world. (This was the first census that took place while Quirinius was governor of Syria.) And everyone went to his own town to register."

"All the world" (KJV) does not mean the whole globe, as that phrase now would suggest, but only "the entire Roman world." That was the extent of the jurisdiction of Caesar Augustus (30 B.C.–A.D. 14). Both parts of this ruler's name are titles. *Caesar* is similar to *Czar* or *Kaiser*. *Augustus* means "reverend," a title assumed by the Roman emperors. The forty-four-year reign of Caesar Augustus, bringing peace and order to the whole Mediterranean world, prepared the way for the coming of Christ and the rapid spread of Christianity. Never before or after the Roman era has this great area, including large segments of three continents (Europe, Asia, and Africa) been under one government and with one language used throughout the whole. God had set the stage for the coming of His Son to earth.

The King James Version says "taxed" (vv. 1, 3, 5) and "taxation." The Greek words, however, both verb and noun, refer to an enrollment or census. The actual taxation came later.

Secular history describes a census that Quirinius took in A.D. 6 (not 6 B.C.), which provoked much opposition in Palestine. Negative critics have challenged the historicity of Luke's account, claiming that he has confused the facts. But more recent archaeological evidence supports Luke (see Ralph Earle, *Wesleyan Bible Commentary*, IV, 219).

Critics have also found fault with Luke's statement: "And everyone went to his own town to register" (v. 3, NIV). They say that there is no evidence for such a requirement. But Adolph Deissmann gives the actual text of such an edict (*Light from the Ancient East*, p. 271).

James Moulton and George Milligan write: "The deduction so long made from Luke's shocking blunders about the census apparently survives the demonstration that the blunder lay only in our lack of information: the microbe is not yet completely expelled. Possibly the salutary process may be completed by our latest inscriptional evidence that Quirinius was a legate in Syria for census purposes in B.C. 8-6" (*The Vocabulary of the Greek New Testament*, p. 60).

Across the last two centuries the Bible has successfully withstood the vicious assaults of destructive critics. These men only break their puny hammers on the anvil of God's Word.

II. THE BIRTH IN BETHLEHEM:
Luke 2:4-7

A. The Reason for Going to Bethlehem: v. 4

We are told that Joseph "went up" from Nazareth in Galilee to Bethlehem in Judea. A glance at the map shows that he was going south, which for us is "down." But the Jews always spoke of going "up" to Jerusalem and its surroundings.

"Bethlehem" is compounded of two Hebrew words—*beth*, which means "house," and *lehem*, which means "bread." So Bethlehem signifies "House of Bread." Here was born Jesus, who would be "the bread of life" to all humanity (John 6:35).

Bethlehem was known as "the city of David," because David, Israel's greatest king, was born there. So "the Son of David," the Messiah, must be born there. But Mary and Joseph were living in Nazareth, far north in Galilee. Is it too much to say that God arranged a Roman census just at this time so that Christ could be born in Bethlehem?

Joseph was from the line of David. Many scholars feel—and we would agree with them—that Luke gives us the genealogy of *Mary* in 3:23-38 (see comments by Earle in *Wesleyan Commentary*, IV, 230). This would be in proper keeping with the obvious fact that Matthew's Infancy Narratives are all told from Joseph's point of view, while Luke's are all told from Mary's standpoint.

If this conclusion is accepted, then Mary was also a descendant of David, and so only related by marriage to Elizabeth, who was of the tribe of Levi (1:5). Jesus would then have double right to the throne of David—legally through His foster-father Joseph, and by blood descent through His mother Mary. God works everything out beautifully.

B. The Registration of Joseph and Mary: v. 5

This verse seems to support the above deduction. "He went there to register with Mary, who was pledged to be married to him and was expecting a child" (NIV). They were both descended from David.

C. The Babe in a Manger: vv. 6-7

"While they were there, the time came for the baby to be born, and she gave birth to her firstborn, a son. She wrapped him in strips of cloth and placed him in a manger, because there was no room for them in the inn" (NIV).

God's timing was perfect. Probably only a Roman decree would have caused Mary to make that long journey of five or six days in the condition in which she was at that time. She made it safely to Bethlehem, but then the baby arrived.

"Firstborn" does not prove, but it does imply, that Mary later had other children. The fact that *she* had to wrap the swathing bands around the baby suggests that no midwife was present at the birth of Jesus. Mary placed Him in a manger. Tradition says that this was in a cave stable in the hillside. Actually it may have been warmer there, because of animal heat, than in a cold room in the crowded inn.

III. THE ANNOUNCEMENT TO THE SHEPHERDS: Luke 2:8-12

A. Shepherds Watching Their Flocks: v. 8

The statement that shepherds were keeping watch over their flocks by night in the open field has led many to say that Christ could not have been born on December 25. It is true that there is no conclusive evidence for this date. But after carefully checking the data, Samuel Andrews wrote: "There seems, then, so far as climate is concerned, no good ground to affirm that shepherds could not have been pasturing their flocks in the field during the month of December" (*Life of Our Lord*, p. 16). Edersheim agrees (*Life and Times of Jesus the Messiah*, I, 186). At Christmastime one can usually walk around in Bethlehem and Jerusalem in the middle of the day without wearing a topcoat. The nights are cool at the twenty-five-hundred-feet elevation, but frost and snow are rare.

B. The Appearance of an Angel: v. 9

Suddenly an angel of the Lord appeared to these shepherds in the field, and the glory of the Lord was shining around them. No longer were they shrouded in darkness. The scene symbolized the fact that "the light of the world" (John 8:12) had come.

The shepherds were "sore afraid." The Greek literally says that they "feared with a great fear." They were "terrified" (NIV), as normal human beings would be.

C. The Message of the Angel: vv. 10-12

"Good news of great joy"—that's what Christmas is all about. How sad that in the modern commercializing of Christmas so few hear the news and feel the joy!

This good news is "for all the people" (NIV). Primarily "the people" (so the Greek) would mean the Jews, God's Chosen People. But it also reaches out to all the people of the Gentile world.

Concerning verse 11 we have written elsewhere: "No newspaper ever carried headlines more significant than this. No more important event was ever heralded. It was particularly fitting that this announcement should be made by an angel. He came as God's 'messenger' (literal meaning of 'angel'), to deliver the greatest divine message man had ever heard" (Earle, *Wesleyan Commentary*, IV, 221).

In this verse we find three titles given to the newborn baby. The first is "Savior." That is the meaning of *Jesus* (Matthew 1:21). He comes to us first as our Savior. The second is "Christ." The Greek *Christos* and Hebrew *Messiah* both mean "anointed one." Jesus came as the promised Messiah of Israel. The third title is "Lord." The Greek word is *kyrios*, which is used in the Septuagint to translate *Yahweh* (or, *Jehovah*), the regular name for the God of Israel. Jesus is God, and He is Lord over all creation.

The implications of verse 12 are most striking. "What a paradox! The *Eternal One* caught in a moment of time. *Omnipresence* corralled in a cave manger. *Omnipotence* cradled in a helpless infant who could not even raise His head from the straw. *Omniscience* confined in a baby who could not say a word. The *Christ* who created the heavens and the earth cradled in a cave stable. What condescending love! And what divine wisdom! For when God would draw near to cold, cruel, sinful, suffering humanity, He placed a baby in a manger at Bethlehem. The quickest way to the human heart is by way of an innocent little child. In infinite wisdom God planned it thus. And so today the story most loved the world around is the one found in Luke 2:1-20" (Earle, *Wesleyan Commentary*, IV, 221).

Because Christ was born in such circumstances and brought up in at least relative poverty, He can sympathize today with the humble and the poor. He identifies with suffering humanity.

IV. THE GLORIA IN EXCELSIS: Luke 2:13-14

"Glory to God in the highest" is in the Latin *Gloria in Excelsis Deo*, which we often hear sung at Christmastime. The first Christmas it was sung by "a multitude of the heavenly host," who "suddenly" appeared. They were "praising God" and proclaiming "peace." This was good news!

It is almost universally agreed that "good will toward men" is not the correct reading in the second line of verse 14. Instead of *eudokia* (nominative), "good will," all the oldest Greek manuscripts have *eudokias* (genitive), "of good will." But there is also general agreement that "among men of goodwill" is not the best translation. "Among men with whom he is pleased" (RSV, NASB) is better, as is "to men on whom his favor rests" (NIV). Humphry declared that the meaning is "God's peace among all to whom these tidings shall come, and who in accepting them become His dear children, the objects of His good pleasure" (quoted in *Luke*, Cambridge Greek Testament, p. 115).

V. THE RESPONSE OF THE SHEP-HERDS:
Luke 2:15

The value of a vision lies in its results. Too many so-called visions have no consequences of any worth; in fact, many of them have spawned heresies.

But this one brought men to find Christ. The shepherds lost no time in debating their decision. As soon as the angels left, the shepherds said to each other, "Let's go to Bethlehem"—right "now" (Greek, *de*).

"Go" is literally "go through" or "go across." This, with "even unto" (Greek, *heos*), suggests that they were some little distance from the village of Bethlehem. They must go across the fields to reach it. The present "Field of the Shepherds," owned by the YMCA, is about two miles out of town and may well be the authentic site, or nearly so. On Christmas Eve many Protestants gather at the Field of the Shepherds to celebrate with a meal in the open and with appropriate songs and passages of Scripture. Those who have been privileged to be at this spot on Christmas Eve have sensed something of the wonder of the angel's visit.

VI. THE SHEPHERDS AND CHRIST:
Luke 2:16-20

A. Finding the Baby in a Manger: v. 16

Hurrying off, the shepherds went into Bethlehem. There "they found both Mary and Joseph" (so the Greek), and the baby "lying" (singular participle in the Greek, indicating only the baby) in "the manger" (so the Greek)—*the* manger the angels had told them about.

"Found" is not the simple verb

heuron. Rather it is the compound *aneuron.* Alfred Plummer says, "The compound implies a *search* in order to find" (*A Critical and Exegetical Commentary on the Gospel According to Luke*, International Critical Commentary, p. 60). Similarly F. W. Farrar says that the verb means "discovered after search" (*Luke*, Cambridge Greek Testament, p. 115). The shepherds were not given any street and house number! It would necessarily take some inquiring around before they found the newborn baby.

The lesson here is obvious. Today we must be willing to search for Christ until we find Him. Difficulties and distractions must not deter us. The shepherds might well have reasoned that they could not afford to leave their sheep alone so long. But they persevered until they found Jesus.

B. Reporting to Others: vv. 17-18

When the shepherds finally found the infant Jesus in the manger, they at once began to tell others about Him. They reported the hymn of the angelic host, as well as the words of the announcement made by the angel who first appeared. The result was amazement on the part of all who heard.

With many it was more than amazement. Those who were caught up in Messianic expectation could not fail to see the implications of the

---

DISCUSSION QUESTIONS

1. How did the shepherds celebrate the first Christmas?
2. How should we celebrate it now?
3. What are some ways by which we can "put Christ back into Christmas"?
4. Why was the good news given to shepherds?
5. What are the prerequisites for our receiving the Good News?
6. How may we share the Good News?

angel's words. He had called the new-born babe "a Savior." That is what the devout Jews were waiting for. He had further identified him as "Christ," the Messiah, the One for whom they had waited long centuries. In the third place, he had called him "Lord": He would be a divine Messiah. No wonder the people were amazed! Those with spiritual discernment could see that now at last their hopes were to be fulfilled, their longings satisfied. Shepherds were the first preachers of the gospel.

C. Mary Pondering: v. 19

"But Mary kept all these things, and pondered them in her heart." How did Luke know? The probable answer seems very clear. On Paul's last fateful visit to Jerusalem, Luke had accompanied him. This we know from the use of "we" and "us" in Acts 20:6—21:17. The author of Acts was with Paul.

The apostle was mobbed and arrested in the temple (Acts 21:27-39). After he had recounted his conversion experience to the Jews, in a speech from the steps of the Tower of Antonia (chap. 22), Paul appeared before the Sanhedrin (23:1-10). Then he was taken down to Caesarea for safekeeping (23:12-35). There he spent two years in prison (24:27). When Paul was sent to Rome as an imperial prisoner, Luke was again with him (27:1-2).

What was Luke doing during those two years that Paul was in prison? The logical answer is that he was gathering the materials for his Gospel, talking with eyewitnesses who had known Jesus personally. There were plenty of them still living in Judea and Galilee. Jesus' brother James was head pastor of the church in Jerusalem.

But the most important person to talk to would have been Jesus' mother, Mary. By this time she would be about eighty years of age, reliving those memories of 6 and 5 B.C., sixty years before. Luke was a fine Christian gentleman, with a gracious appreciation for women, as his Gospel shows in many places. He was also a physician (Colossians 4:14). To whom would Mary more likely have opened her heart and told the intimate details connected with Jesus' birth and childhood? The whole picture falls into a logical pattern. Only Luke gives us the Infancy Narratives from Mary's point of view.

D. The Shepherd's Praising: v. 20

The hearts and mouths of the shepherds were filled with joy and praise—as well they might be! They were the first ones, aside from Mary and Joseph, who had the privilege of seeing the Messiah. It was a great honor.

They had found everything just as the angel had told them it would be. We have every right to believe that everything will happen that angels predicted about His second coming (Acts 1:9-11).

CONTEMPORARY APPLICATION

It was Christmas Eve in 1950. A small group of us gathered on a hilltop at the Field of the Shepherds. The YMCA crowd was gone; all was quiet. The lights of Bethlehem twinkled in the distance, but no sounds of the town reached our ears. The moon shone overhead, lighting up the hills of Judea that surrounded us. It was a perfect setting!

One of our number started singing softly:

Silent night, holy night.
All is calm, all is bright.

As the words and music of Christmas carols sounded out across the silent landscape from grateful, worshiping hearts, suddenly figures appeared, dressed in white robes. Not angels, but Bedouin children. Without a sound they squatted on the ground in front of us, looking up at us with wide-open eyes, ears, and mouths. We felt we had recaptured something of the wonder of that first Christmas night, so long ago.

THE PROMISE FULFILLED

DEVOTIONAL READING	Isaiah 9:2-7
ADULTS	Topic: *The Promise Fulfilled* Background Scripture: Luke 2:21-38 Scripture Lesson: Luke 2:25-38 Memory Verse: "... *mine eyes have seen thy salvation which thou hast prepared in the presence of all peoples.*" Luke 2:30-31
YOUTH	Topic: *God Keeps His Word* Background Scripture: Luke 2:21-38 Scripture Lesson: Luke 2:25-38 Memory Verse: ... *mine eyes have seen thy salvation which thou hast prepared in the presence of all peoples.*" Luke 2:30-31
CHILDREN	Topic: *They Brought Their Child* Background Scripture: Luke 2:21-40 Scripture Lesson: Luke 2:25-38 Memory Verse: *And the child grew and became strong, filled with wisdom; and the favor of God was upon him.* Luke 2:40
DAILY BIBLE READINGS	Mon., Dec. 20: "Unto Us a Child Is Born," Isaiah 9:2-7. Tues., Dec. 22: Jesus Presented in the Temple, Luke 2:21-24. Wed., Dec. 22: Simeon and Anna, Luke 2:25-38. Thurs., Dec. 23: Wise Men Come to Jesus, Matthew 2:1-12. Fri., Dec. 24: Sojourn to Egypt, Matthew 2:13-23. Sat., Dec. 25: The Eternal Word, John 1:1-5. Sun., Dec. 26: The Light of the World, John 1:6-18.
LESSON AIM	To see how Jesus was recognized by devout people as the expected Messiah.
LESSON SETTING	Time: 5 B.C. Place: Jerusalem
LESSON OUTLINE	**The Promise Fulfilled** I. The Circumcision of Jesus: Luke 2:21

II. The Presentation of Jesus: Luke 2:22-24
   A. The Time of Purification: v. 22
   B. The Requirement in the Law: v. 23
   C. The Sacrifice to Be Offered: v. 24

III. The Recognition by Simeon: Luke 2:25-32
   A. Waiting for the Messiah: v. 25
   B. Revelation from the Spirit: v. 26
   C. Guided by the Spirit: vv. 27-28
   D. The *Nunc Dimittis*: vv. 29-32

IV. The Prediction of Simeon: vv. 33-35
   A. The Wonder of the Parents: v. 33
   B. The Significance of Their Son: v. 34
   C. The Sword in Mary's Soul: v. 35

V. The Report of Anna: Luke 2:36-38
   A. An Old Prophetess: v. 36
   B. A Dedicated Saint: v. 37
   C. Sharing the Good News: v. 38

SUGGESTED INTRODUCTION FOR ADULTS

For too many people old age is a time of disappointed hopes, unfulfilled promises, and faded dreams. But for those who are in Christ it is a time of rich and rewarding fulfillment.

When one can look back on a full half century of Christian service (as this writer can) and realize that his highest hopes and fondest dreams have been far more than fulfilled—that is a foretaste of heaven!

It is not said that Simeon was an elderly person, but the fact that he blessed Mary and Joseph would imply that he was. It is stated that Anna was eighty-four years old. So here were two people who found their highest blessing and fulfillment in their old age.

That is God's will for those who walk with Him. We read in the Scriptures: "But the path of the just is as the shining light, that shineth more and more unto the perfect day" (Proverbs 4:18). We have found that promise abundantly fulfilled.

SUGGESTED INTRODUCTION FOR YOUTH

"God Keeps His Word." That statement, our topic for today, has proved true in the life of all who have believed it. And history documents its validity.

In today's lesson we find the fulfillment of the promise that the Messiah would come to His people. His real people, represented by two devout Jews in Jerusalem, greeted the fulfillment of that promise in the baby Jesus and witnessed to others about Him.

It is our privilege today to know Jesus and then to tell others that He has come and that He can come to them as their Savior. Older people can help us to understand and appreciate Him more. They play an important part in the church of Jesus Christ.

1. Joseph and Mary brought their child to God's house.
2. We should be very thankful for godly parents.
3. God has a mission in life for each of us.
4. We should grow physically, mentally, and spiritually (Luke 2:40).

THE LESSON COMMENTARY

I. THE CIRCUMCISION OF JESUS: Luke 2:21

Both John (1:59) and Jesus were circumcised when eight days old. This was in accordance with the command given to Abraham (Genesis 17:12) and incorporated in the Law of Moses (Leviticus 12:3). Circumcision was a symbol of "putting off the body of the sins of the flesh by the circumcision of Christ" (Colossians 2:11). Jesus did not need this, because He was sinless. But Christ was fulfilling all the righteous requirements of the Law for us. Sadler notes: "Thus His circumcision was the first stage in that outward life of submission to the will of His Father by which He redeemed us" (*St. Luke*, p. 53).

As in the case of John, Jesus received His name at the time of His circumcision. He was called "Jesus," which means "Jehovah [Yahweh] saves." Josephus mentions nineteen persons called Jesus in the first century. So it was a common Jewish name at that time. Christ is referred to as "Jesus" nearly a thousand times in the New Testament. He is *the* Savior of mankind.

II. THE PRESENTATION OF JESUS: Luke 2:22-24

A. The Time of Purification: v. 22

The King James Version has "her purification." But with the possible exception of one very late manuscript (76, from the twelfth century), no Greek manuscript has this reading. The Greek text says "their purification." Frederic L. Godet comments: "This pronoun refers primarily to Mary, then

to Joseph, who is, as it were, involved in her uncleanness, and obliged to go up with her" (*Commentary on the Gospel of St. Luke*, p. 136).

"According to the law of Moses" refers to Leviticus 12:1-4. There it is stipulated that after the birth of a male child the mother would be unclean for seven days. On the eighth day the boy was to be circumcised. Then the mother remained unclean for thirty-three more days, during which time she could not enter the sanctuary. So Jesus was forty days old when this purification ceremony for His mother took place. On the significance of all this H. D. Spence says: "These ancient rites—circumcision and purification—enjoined in the Mosaic Law were intended as perpetual witnesses to the deadly taint of imperfection and sin inherited by every child of man" ("Luke," *Pulpit Commentary*, p. 39).

B. The Requirement in the Law: v. 23

The purpose of the trip to Jerusalem was twofold: (1) to purify the mother; (2) to present the child to the Lord. The latter was in fulfillment of the command (Exodus 13:2) quoted rather freely in verse 23: "Every firstborn male is to be consecrated to the Lord" (NIV).

The background of this divine claim was the last of the ten plagues in Egypt—the death of the firstborn son in every home that did not have the Passover blood sprinkled on the door posts. So the Lord said that all the firstborn Israelite boys would belong to Him.

C. The Sacrifice to Be Offered: v. 24

The stipulation of the Law was that a mother must bring for her purification "a one year old lamb for a burnt offering, and a young pigeon or a turtledove for a sin offering" (Leviticus 12:6, NASB). However, a further provision was made: "But if she cannot afford a lamb, then she shall take two turtledoves or two young pigeons, the one for a burnt offering and the other for a sin offering; and the priest shall make atonement for her, and she shall be clean" (Leviticus 12:8, NASB).

The Law went even further. In connection with the trespass offering it is stated that a lamb was to be sacrificed. If the person could not afford this, two doves or two young pigeons would be accepted. And in cases of extreme poverty the provision was made: "But if he be not able to bring two turtledoves or two young pigeons, then he that sinned shall bring for his offering the tenth part of an ephah of fine flour for a sin offering" (cf. Leviticus 5:7-11).

In the light of all this, we deduce the fact that Jesus' parents were poor but that they were not entirely destitute. The eternal Son of God was willing to make Himself poor, that we through His poverty might be rich (II Corinthians 8:9).

III. THE RECOGNITION BY SIMEON:
Luke 2:25-32

A. Waiting for the Messiah: v. 25

In Jersualem at that time was a man named Simeon, who was "just and devout." The first adjective means "righteous." Simeon was careful to keep all the requirements of the Law—which is what "righteous" meant to the Jews of that day. But he was also "devout" in spirit. Both his outer and inner life were pleasing to the Lord.

Simeon was waiting for "the consolation of Israel," that is, for the fulfillment of the Messianic hope. F. W. Farrar writes: " 'May I see the consolation of Israel!' was a common Jewish formula and a prayer for the Advent of the Messiah was daily used; and Menachem 'the Consoler' was recognized as one of the names of the Messiah" (*St. Luke*, Cambridge Greek Testament, p. 177).

Godet makes this interesting observation at this point: "In times of spiritual degeneracy, when an official clergy no longer cultivates anything but the form of religion, its spirit retires amongst the obscurer members of the religious community, and creates for itself unofficial organs, often from the lowest classes. Simeon and Anna are representatives of this spontaneous priesthood" (*Luke*, p. 137).

B. Revelation from the Spirit: v. 26

Not only was Simeon righteous and devout, but the Holy Spirit was on him. And the Spirit revealed to him the fact that he would not die until he had seen "the Lord's Christ"—literally, "the Anointed of the Lord," that is, the One whom God had sent as His Messiah. So Simeon was on the alert, expecting the Messiah to appear at any time.

C. Guided by the Spirit: vv. 27-28

Simeon came "by the Spirit" into the temple. This does not mean that he was in a state of ecstasy but that he was under the influence of the Holy Spirit—"moved by the Spirit" (NIV). God always times things perfectly. Godet well remarks: "There are critical moments in life, when everything depends on immediate submission to the impulse of the Spirit" (*Luke*). Those who fail to hear or heed the voice of the Holy Spirit sometimes miss life's biggest blessings and opportunities. Anyone who is led by the Spirit knows what it is to find that God has arranged things precisely for us as we follow His guidance.

The Greek word for "temple" here is not *naos*, "sanctuary," meaning the building that contained the Holy Place and the Holy of Holies. Rather it is *hieron*, which means the temple area, covering twenty-five or thirty acres. It is correctly translated "temple courts" (NIV).

Right in front of the sanctuary was the Court of the Priests, containing the altar of sacrifice and the large laver. Surrounding this was the Court of Israel, where only Jewish adult males could go. Around this was the Court of the Women, where the treasury was situated. The largest of all was the outer Court of the Gentiles, covering many acres. Since Mary was offering a sacrifice, it was probably the Court of the Women where Simeon found her and her child.

The word *parents* has caused considerable comment by some critics who claim that it negates the Virgin Birth. But such an attitude reveals a lack of common sense. As Godet notes, "The word *parents* is simply used to indicate the character in which Joseph and Mary appeared at this time in the temple and presented the child" (*Luke*, p. 138).

Simeon took the baby Jesus "in his arms," acting as a priest as he "blessed God." The official priests were not in the Spirit and so were totally unaware of the Child's presence and the Messianic significance of the occasion. They failed utterly in their duty of welcoming the Messiah to His temple.

Obedience brings blessing. Plummer comments: "The parents bring Him in accordance with the Divine Law, and Symeon welcomes Him in accordance with the Divine impulse" (*A Critical and Exegetical Commentary on the Gospel According to Luke*, International Critical Commentary, p. 67).

D. The *Nunc Dimittis*: vv. 29-32

As we have noted before, this beautiful hymn is named after the two opening words in Latin, meaning "now lettest thou." Simeon is now ready to be dismissed in peace, willing to depart this life.

In his "Luke," *Expositions of Holy Scripture*, Alexander Maclaren gives this beautiful description of the scene: "Think of the old man, waiting there in the Sanctuary, told by God that he was thus about to have the fulfilment of his lifelong desire, and yet probably not knowing what kind of a shape the fulfilment would take. There is no reason to believe that he knew he was to see an infant; and he waits. And presently a peasant woman comes in with a child in her arms, and there arises in his soul the voice 'Anoint Him! for this is He!' And so, whether he expected such a vision or no, he takes the Child in his arms, and says, 'Lord! Now, now!—after all these years of waiting—lettest thou thy servant depart in peace'" (I, 56).

The Greek word for "Lord" in verse 29 is not the familiar *kyrios*, found about 750 times in the New Testament. Rather, it is *despotes* ("despot"), which occurs only 10 times and is translated "Lord" only 5 of those times. Joseph H. Thayer says that it "denoted absolute ownership and uncontrolled power" (*Greek-English Lexicon of the New Testament*, p. 130). It may well be translated "Sovereign Lord" (NIV). Plummer comments: "In using the word Symeon acknowledges God's absolute right to dispose of him, either in retaining or dispensing with his service" (*Luke*, p. 68).

Simeon is ready to depart "in peace." Plummer says, "It is the peace of completeness, of work finished and hopes fulfilled" (*Luke*). To die in peace is the final climax of blessing on earth for the true servant of God.

"For mine eyes have seen thy salvation" (v. 30). Simeon does not try to describe the child's appearance, as later legends do. For him the baby Jesus meant just one thing: God's "salvation," which He had sent to his people. This Child was what long generations of true Israelites had been waiting for.

In this verse the Greek word for "salvation" is not the usual *soteria* which occurs forty-five times in the New Testament, but *soterion*, which is found only four times. Godet says that it "denotes an apparatus fitted to save." He continues: "Simeon sees in this little child *the means of deliverance* which God is giving to the world" (*Luke*, p. 139).

This fits well with the next verse (31), which states that this *soterion* has been "prepared." God had prepared a means of salvation for the whole world by sending His Son. "All people" includes both Jews and Gentiles, as the following verse shows.

Moved by the Holy Spirit, Simeon had remarkable spiritual insight and prophetic power. He declared that Jesus would be "a light for revelation [Greek, *apocalypsis*] to the Gentiles, and for glory to your people Israel" (v. 32, NIV). Farrar comments: "A memorable prophecy, considering that even the Apostles found it hard to grasp the full admission of the Gentiles" (*Luke*, p. 118). Yet it had been clearly foretold in the Old Testament. Psalm 98:3 says: "All the ends of the earth have seen the salvation of our God" (also in Isaiah 52:10). In Isaiah 42:6 God declares: "I . . . will give thee . . . for a light of the Gentiles." In Isaiah 49:6 we read: "I will also give thee for a light to the Gentiles, that thou mayest be my salvation unto the end of the

earth." These words were spoken to Israel, but they only have their complete fulfillment in Christ.

IV. THE PREDICTION OF SIMEON: vv. 33-35

A. The Wonder of the Parents: v. 33

Instead of "Joseph and his mother" the oldest Greek manuscripts have "his father and mother." The substitution of "Joseph" by later scribes was evidently intended to protect the doctrine of the Virgin Birth. But Joseph was Jesus' foster-father and so is properly referred to as "his father."

It is no wonder that the parents "marvelled" at what Simeon said. That the baby Jesus would be the Light of the world (cf. John 8:12) was a startling truth.

B. The Significance of Their Son: v. 34

Acting again as a true, though unofficial, priest of God, Simeon "blessed them." Then he said to Mary: "This child is destined to cause the falling and rising again of many in Israel, and to be a sign that will be spoken against" (NIV). Plummer comments: "The coming of the Messiah necessarily involves a *crisis*, a separation, or judgment (*crisis*). Some welcome the Light; others 'love the darkness rather than the Light, because their deeds are evil' (Jn. iii.19), and are by their own conduct condemned. Judas despairs, Peter repents; one robber blasphemes, the other confesses" (*Luke*, p. 70).

Jesus would be a sign that would be "spoken against." The same Greek compound verb is used in Acts 28:22, where the Jews at Rome said to Paul: "for as concerning this sect, we know that every where it is spoken against." Jesus suffered much opposition and vicious slander during His earthly minisry. But men's destinies are settled by their attitude toward Jesus Christ.

DISCUSSION QUESTIONS

1. What Christian rite takes the place of circumcision?
2. In what ways did Jesus fulfill the Law for us?
3. Why are people today looking for the coming of Christ?
4. How may we be guided by the Spirit, as Simeon was?
5. How is suffering related to redemption (Mary's sword)?
6. How may we share the Good News?

C. The Sword in Mary's Soul: v. 35

This sobering prediction of Simeon found vivid fulfillment when Mary stood at the cross and witnessed the agony of her Son who was suffering there. Her mother heart was pierced with the sword of bitter pain on that awful day.

V. THE REPORT OF ANNA: Luke 2:36-38

A. An Old Prophetess: v. 36

"Anna" is in Hebrew "Hannah" (see I Samuel 1:20). The name means "grace" or "compassion." This Anna was a "prophetess," like Miriam, Deborah, and Huldah in the Old Testament. Her father's name was "Phanuel," which means "face of God"—the same as "Peniel" (Genesis 32:30). Perhaps there would be more Annas if there were more Phanuels! These people were from the tribe of "Aser"—rather, Asher.

This woman was "very old" (NIV). She had lived with her husband for seven years after their marriage. Then her husband had died.

B. A Dedicated Saint: v. 37

"And she was a widow of about fourscore and four years" (KJV) is rather ambiguous. Does it mean that she had been a widow for eighty-four years—which would make her ancient—or that she was now eighty-four years old? Instead of *hos*, "about," the best Greek text has *heos*, "until." So the correct translation is: "and then was a widow until she was eighty-four" (NIV).

This widow was a devout woman who dedicated herself completely to the service of the Lord. She never left the temple courts, "but worshiped night and day, fasting and praying" (NIV). Who knows how much blessing may have come to many people's lives through the sacrificial prayers of this good woman?

C. Sharing the Good News: v. 38

Coming up at that very moment, Anna gave thanks to God that she, too, was privileged to see the Messiah. Then she spoke about Him "to all who were looking forward to the redemption of Jerusalem" (NIV). God always has His faithful saints who believe His promises and are waiting patiently for the time of their fulfillment. Anna and Simeon were not the only ones who were eagerly expecting the coming of the Messiah. And they knew who the others were!

CONTEMPORARY APPLICATION

Anna told about the Christ child to all those who were looking for the redemption of Jerusalem. The Redeemer had come. But when He offered Himself publicly and prophetically (cf. Zechariah 9:9) in His so-called Triumphal Entry into Jerusalem on Palm Sunday (Matthew 21:1-11), the religious rulers of Israel rejected Him (Luke 19:39). The result was that Jesus wept over the city and predicted its destruction (Luke 19:41-44). He also said that its house (the temple) was left desolate and that the Jews would see Him no more until they echoed the cry of the crowd: "Blessed is he that cometh in the name of the Lord" (Matthew 23:37-39). This will happen at His second coming. We, like Anna, should be talking about this to those who await His return!

JESUS AFFIRMS HIS SONSHIP

DEVOTIONAL READING	I Timothy 4:12-16

ADULTS

Topic: *Jesus Affirms His Sonship*

Background Scripture: Luke 1:80; 2:39-52

Scripture Lesson: Luke 2:39-52

Memory Verse: *"How is it that you sought me? Did you not know that I must be in my Father's house?"* Luke 2:49

YOUTH

Topic: *My Relation with God*

Background Scripture: Luke 1:80; 2:39-52

Scripture Lesson: Luke 2:39-52

Memory Verse: *"How is it that you sought me? Did you not know that I must be in my Father's house?"* Luke 2:49

CHILDREN

Topic: *My Father's Work*

Background Scripture: Mark 1:4-8; Luke 1:80; 2:41-52

Scripture Lesson: Luke 2:41-52

Memory Verse: *They found him in the temple, sitting among the teachers, listening to them and asking them questions.* Luke 2:46

DAILY BIBLE READINGS

Mon., Dec. 27: The Son of Zion, Psalm 2:6-12.
Tues., Dec. 28: A Religious Heritage, Luke 2:41-45.
Wed., Dec. 29: My Father's Business, Luke 2:46-52.
Thurs., Dec. 30: The Beloved Son, John 3:13-18.
Fri., Dec. 31: The Power of the Son, John 5:19-23.
Sat., Jan. 1: Commissioned by the Father, John 6:31-38.
Sun., Jan. 2: Growing as God's Sons, I Timothy 4:12-16.

LESSON AIM

To note the development of Jesus' spiritual consciousness and its implications for our understanding of children today.

LESSON SETTING

Time: About A.D. 8

Place: Nazareth and Jerusalem

LESSON OUTLINE

Jesus Affirms His Sonship

    I. The Early Childhood of Jesus: Luke 2:39-40
       A. The Return to Nazareth: v. 39
       B. The Growth of Jesus: v. 40

II. **The Boy Jesus in the Temple:** Luke 2:41-50
   A. The Annual Passover Pilgrimage: v. 41
   B. The Twelve-Year-Old Boy: v. 42
   C. Neglectful Parents: vv. 43-44
   D. Anxious Parents: v. 45
   E. Jesus' Discussion with the Teachers: vv. 46-47
   F. Surprised Parents: v. 48
   G. Jesus' Affirmation of Sonship: v. 49
   H. Perplexed Parents: v. 50

III. **Jesus' Development as a Young Man:** Luke 2:51-52
   A. Subjection to His Parents: v. 51
   B. Normal Growth as a Young Man: v. 52

SUGGESTED INTRODUCTION FOR ADULTS

Today we begin a second unit of study in this quarter of lessons. It is entitled, "Jesus Beings His Ministry." Actually, the incident in the temple in which Jesus recognized and declared His unique sonship to the Father (treated in today's lesson), is a prelude to His ministry.

We have in these four lessons a series of significant firsts in Jesus' life and ministry—from His first expression of sonship to the calling of His first disciples. No longer is it the baby Jesus, but the boy and the young man.

One of the most important aspects of today's lesson is the gradual, normal development that Jesus had as a child and youth. This helps us to understand who and what He was. But it should also help us to know better how to deal with our own children as they grow up. Many parents and even Sunday school teachers hinder rather than help the growth of children under their care because they do not understand the changes of childhood.

SUGGESTED INTRODUCTION FOR YOUTH

Our topic today is "My Relation with God." This is the most important relationship in life. It governs all other relationships. We first have to be right with God if we are going to maintain right relationships to other people.

When we give our hearts to Christ we become the children of God. We need to work out the implications of that in our daily lives. Sonship is a great privilege, but also a great responsibility.

As we study how Jesus developed as a young man, it should help us to grow the same way. This is our task.

CONCEPTS FOR CHILDREN

1. Jesus grew up as a child just as we do.
2. He had to learn to read and write, and obey His parents.
3. At twelve years of age He realized that He was God's Son.
4. Children can accept Jesus into their hearts at a young age.

THE LESSON COMMENTARY

I. THE EARLY CHILDHOOD OF JESUS:
Luke 2:39-40

A. The Return to Nazareth: v. 39

Jesus was born in Bethlehem, in Judea, but He grew up in Nazareth, in Galilee. Just how long the family stayed around Bethlehem and Jerusalem we are not told. Frederic L. Godet comments: "It is easy to perceive that ver. 39 has a religious rather than a chronological reference. 'They returned to Nazareth *only* after having fulfilled every prescription of the law'" (*Commentary on the Gospel of Luke*, p. 144).

B. The Growth of Jesus: v. 40

The phrase "in spirit" (KJV) is not found in the Greek text. A later scribe inserted it here from 1:80, where we find a similar statement made about the boy John.

The description given here is significant indeed. Richard C. S. Lenski writes: "It is impossible for us to penetrate the mystery of this development in Jesus—body and soul untouched by sin, unchecked and unretarded by any result of sin, his mind and his soul absorbing the wisdom of God's Word as a bud drinks in the sunshine and expands. His mind and his soul, which were truly human indeed, grew in strength and in the range of wisdom but in perfection and in power beyond anything that is possible to sinful mortals. His development was absolutely normal, that of all others is to a great degree abnormal" (*Interpretation of St. Luke's Gospel*, p. 160).

In a similar vein Alfred Plummer says: "The intellectual, moral, and spiritual growth of the Child, like the physical, was *real*. His was a perfect humanity developing perfectly, unimpeded by hereditary or acquired defects. It was the first instance of such a growth in history. For the first time a human infant was realizing the ideal of humanity" (*A Critical and Exegetical Commentary on the Gospel According to St. Luke*, International Critical Commentary, p. 74).

This verse sums up the history of the first twelve years of Jesus' life. All four Gospels concentrate on His public ministry, culminating in His death and resurrection.

II. THE BOY JESUS IN THE TEMPLE:
Luke 2:41-50

A. The Annual Passover Pilgrimage: v. 41

As a devout couple, Joseph and Mary had the regular habit of going to Jerusalem every year for the Passover feast, which was in the latter part of March or in April. This festival, which commemorated the "passing over" of the firstborn Israelites on the night when the Egyptian firstborn boys were slain, was the most important of the annual feasts.

Why did Mary go? Godet writes: "According to Ex. xxiii. 17, Deut. xvi. 16, men were to present themselves at the sanctuary at the three feasts of Passover, Pentecost, and Tabernacles. There was no such obligation for women. But the school of Hillel required them to make at least the Passover pilgrimage" (*Luke*, p. 146). It is probable, however, that Mary went because she was such a devout person and not because Hillel had ordered it. She would want to take advantage of every possible contact with God, in order that she might give her miracle Son the best spiritual training.

B. The Twelve-Year-Old Boy: v. 42

Plummer declares definitely: "At the age of twelve a young Jew became 'a son of the Law,' and began to keep its enactments respecting feasts, fasts, and the like. The mention of the age implies that since the Presentation Jesus had not been up to Jerusalem" (*Luke*, p. 75). Godet agrees.

This religious significance of "twelve years old" is echoed by a number of more recent commentators. For instance, William Arndt says: "When a Jewish boy was twelve years old (the Talmud says, 'at the age of puberty'), he through a special ceremony similar to our confirmation was acknowledged a 'son of the Law.' At that age he was supposed to have learned enough to be sufficiently mature for following the mandates of the Law of God. From now on he would be expected to attend the festivals in Jerusalem whose attendance the Law prescribed" (*Gospel According to St. Luke*, p. 100). And Professor Ray Summers writes: "In many religious things a Jewish boy assumed the responsibility of a man when he became twelve. In reckoning population for building synagogues, a boy of twelve was counted as a man. At twelve he became a 'son of Torah' (son of the law) and was expected to learn it and live by it. This journey to share the Passover in the Temple area was an experience to be coveted" (*Commentary on Luke*).

J. Norval Geldenhuys, in his outstanding volume, *The Gospel of Luke* in the New International Commentary on the New Testament, takes a different view. In relation to Jesus going to the temple at twelve years of age he says: "That was probably in order to be prepared for the ceremony of the following year, when He would be permitted as a young Jewish boy to join the religious community as a responsible member—i.e. as 'son of the commandment' (*Bar Mitzvah*). This important event takes place when the Jewish boy is thirteen" (p. 126).

It is true that today a Jewish boy's Bar Mitzvah (Aramaic for the Hebrew Ben Torah, "son of the Law") is celebrated in connection with his thirteenth birthday. But we prefer to stay with the majority of commentators in

holding that Jesus was having His Bar Mitzvah at this visit to the temple. (Many Jewish boys from the United States now go to Israel for their Bar Mitzvah ceremony.) It seems to us psychologically and spiritually probable that it was when Jesus became "a son of the commandment"—the highest religious moment in His young life—that He realized that He was in a unique sense the Son of God. When would this more naturally happen?

This brings us to a much debated question: When did Jesus' "Messianic consciousness" begin? Some Roman Catholics have assumed that He had it from birth. Early "Gospels of the Nativity" picture Jesus performing miracles when He was in the cradle, and discoursing with people. But this point of view denies His true humanity and makes of Him a psychological monstrosity. Verses 40 and 52 both indicate clearly that Jesus had a normal development as a child and youth.

Some say that Jesus first received His Messianic consciousness at Caesarea Philippi. Peter's confession there (Matthew 16:13-18) confirmed to Jesus what He had begun vaguely to suspect! But this view rejects the clear testimony of the Gospel of John, as well as many passages in the Synoptic Gospels, that Jesus acted as God's Messiah during the preceding part of His ministry.

Others, with more reason, put the dawn of His Messianic consciousness at His baptism, when the voice from heaven said, "Thou art my beloved Son" (3:22). But we find it logical to hold that in this incident of Jesus in the temple at twelve years of age He had a clear intimation of His Sonship and Messiahship, and that this was completely confirmed at His baptism.

C. Neglectful Parents: vv. 43-44

"When they had fulfilled the days"—the seven days of the Feast of Unleavened Bread, then commonly called "the Passover"—they started to Nazareth. But Jesus, without Joseph and Mary knowing it, remained behind in Jerusalem. Assuming that He was in the "company," or "caravan," they traveled for a whole day without Him. It was only when they camped for the night that they discovered He was missing.

This seems to add considerable weight to the idea that Jesus had just had His Bar Mitzvah in Jerusalem. Up until that ceremony in his life, a Jewish boy worshiped with the women and the other children. But at his Bar Mitzvah he was inducted into "the congregation of Israel." After that he traveled and worshiped with the men.

Now the picture seems clear. Joseph was so accustomed to Jesus traveling with Mary and the children that he assumed the lad was still with her. On the other hand, Mary now expected her Son to be in the company of the men. At the close of the day, when they assembled again as families, the parents were distressed to find the boy missing. (Probably all the pilgrims from Nazareth traveled in one large caravan.)

One could find further argument for the Bar Mitzvah in the use of two different Greek words for "child" in verses 40 and 43. In the former it is *paidion*, which means "little child." In the latter it is *pais*, which simply means "child." The distinction is indicated well by using "child" in verse 40 and "boy" in verse 43 (NIV). Jesus was no longer thought of as a child, but rather as a boy among men. He did not feel quite so completely dependent on His parents as hitherto. So He "tarried" (KJV) or "stayed behind" (NIV) in Jerusalem (v. 43).

Godet has a good comment on why He remained: "Jesus spent these seven days of the feast in holy delight. Every rite spoke a divine language to His pure heart; and His quick understanding gradually discovered their typical meaning. This serves to explain the following incident. An indication of wilful and deliberate disobedience has been found in the term *hypemeinen, He abode* ["tarried"]. Nothing could be further from the

historian's intention (ver. 51). The notion of perseverance contained in this verb alludes simply to Jesus' love for the temple, and all that took place there. It was owing to this that, on the day for leaving, He found himself unintentionally separated from the band of children to which He belonged" (*Luke*, pp. 146-47).

D. Anxious Parents: v. 45

When the caravan stopped for the night, some fifteen or twenty miles north of Jerusalem, Jesus was not in evidence. So Joseph and Mary "began looking for him among their relatives and friends" (v. 44, NIV). When they could not find Him anywhere, they went back to Jerusalem to look for Him. Since it was difficult to travel at night, they doubtless waited until morning.

E. Jesus' Discussion with the Teachers: vv. 46-47

"After three days they found him in the temple." This does not mean that they searched for three days in Jerusalem before they found Him, but that three days had gone by since they left the city. The first day was spent going northward, the second day returning to Jerusalem, and the third day searching for Him there.

Jesus was in "the temple courts" (NIV). There He was sitting among the "doctors." The correct translation is "teachers" (NIV). The Oxford English Dictionary notes that for many centuries the only meaning of "doctor" was "teacher." That is why it is used here in the King James Version to translate the Greek word which has just one meaning—"teachers." (Later the physicians and surgeons "stole" this word from us teachers!)

It is not surprising that Jesus was listening to these teachers of the Law. But it may seem strange that He was "asking them questions." However, this was the custom of that day. In their German commentary on the Gospels, based on the Talmud and Midrash, Strack and Billerbeck say: "The asking of questions by the pupil formed an essential element in the ancient Jewish method of instruction."

But Jesus was an unusual case. We read that "all that heard him were astonished at his understanding and answers" (v. 47). This young lad showed exceptional spiritual insight.

F. Surprised Parents: v. 48

When Joseph and Mary finally found Jesus, "they were amazed." His mother said to Him: "Son, why have you treated us like this? Your father and I have been anxiously searching for you" (NIV). The Greek uses a strong term, indicating that they had sought with anguish of mind.

The reason for their surprise is described thus by Arndt: "When Joseph and Mary saw Jesus in such a dignified assembly and, at that, not merely as a spectator but as a participant, they were amazed. They themselves, humble Galileans that they were, would never have ventured to intrude into such circles; and their Son, merely twelve years old, was joining in the discussions of the learned Jerusalem theologians! His mother could not suppress a question of reproach, natural enough when one considers the worry she and Joseph had experienced, caused by Jesus' absence" (Luke, p. 101).

G. Jesus' Affirmation of Sonship: v. 49

After expressing surprise that they should have had to look for Him—where else would they expect to find Him but in the temple!—Jesus asked, "Wist ye not that I must be about my Father's business?" "Wist ye not"—the Greek simply says, "Didn't you know?" Most scholars agree that "about my Father's business" should be "in my Father's house" (NIV).

Arndt comments on this: "The answer of Jesus is the most significant part of the story. He replies, there

should have been no necessity to search for Him, they should have known that He was in the temple. Did He not have to be in His Father's house? Why did they not go directly to the temple? The words manifested that Jesus was conscious of being the Son of God in a special sense. Mary had spoken of Joseph as His father; Jesus, however, definitely states that it is God who is His Father. It is significant that He refers to God as *My* and not simply as *our* Father, which later expression any pious Israelite might have used" (*Luke*).

H. Perplexed Parents: v. 50

Why did Joseph and Mary not understand the meaning of Jesus' words? Godet comments: "That Mary and Joseph should not have been able to understand this speech appears inexplicable to certain critics. . . . But this word, *my Father*, was the first revelation of a relation which surpassed all that Judaism had realized" (*Luke*, p. 149). The Jews had a very strong monotheistic belief, as they have today. The idea of a unique Son of God was foreign to their thinking. It was a new Christian revelation.

DISCUSSION QUESTIONS

1. Why is it that so many conversions occur around the age of twelve?
2. What spiritual perceptions may a child have before then?
3. What things characterize a godly home?
4. How may children have a fourfold development today?
5. How was Jesus' sonship to the Father both like and unlike ours?
6. How can the church supplement the home?

III. JESUS' DEVELOPMENT AS A YOUNG MAN: Luke 2:51-52

A. Subjection to His Parents: v. 51

The years of Jesus' life between the ages of twelve and thirty—when He began His public ministry (3:23), NIV)—are often referred to as "the hidden years." All that we know about them is found in the two verses of this paragraph.

Jesus made no protest against now leaving the temple and returning to Nazareth. Back home, He "was subject" to them, living in submissive obedience. If Jesus, with His consciousness of being uniquely the Son of God, would live this way, certainly children today should do no less. In this regard, as in all His ways, Jesus set an example for all to follow.

Again (cf. v. 19) we read, "but his mother kept all these sayings hidden in her heart." Day after day she treasured His words and pondered over their meaning. These were high moments, utterly beyond human expectation. And it was probably mainly with Luke that she shared these early thoughts.

B. Normal Growth as a Young Man: v. 52

"And Jesus grew in wisdom and stature, and in favor with God and men" (NIV). Put very simply, He had a normal human development in four important ways—physically, mentally, socially, and spiritually. (This is the order we would probably use today in describing it.)

It may surprise us that Jesus had to have *spiritual* growth. But this truth is highlighted in Hebrews 5:8. In His incarnation Christ had to develop along all these lines. Plummer comments: "That He *advanced* in favour with God plainly indicates that there was moral and spiritual growth. At each stage He was perfect for that stage, but the perfection of a child is inferior to the perfection of a man; it is the difference between perfect innocence and perfect holiness" (*Luke*, p. 79).

Jesus is our perfect example. We ought to seek for every child this same fourfold development into true adulthood.

CONTEMPORARY APPLICATION

In his commentary on the Gospel according to Luke, Ernest Fremont Tittle points out the need for godly training in the home, such as Jesus had. He writes: "In today's world there is desperate need that children be brought under the influence of true religion. The movie, the radio, the comics, the billboard, the advertisement in newspaper or magazine—these, not in all but in all too many cases, present a view of life that is cruel, pagan and irresponsible. . . . The exclusion of religion from the public school curriculum inevitably leaves children under the impression that religion is a matter of no great importance. . . . The home must accept responsibility for the religious nurture of children if today's world is to be saved from godlessness, cynicism, and destruction" (p. 27).

JESUS FACES HIS FUTURE

DEVOTIONAL READING	Hebrews 4:12-16

ADULTS

Topic: *Jesus Accepts His Calling*

Background Scripture: Mark 1:4-13; Luke 3:1-22; 4:1-13

Scripture Lesson: Mark 1:4-13

Memory Verse: *The Spirit of the Lord shall rest upon him,*
the spirit of wisdom and understanding,
the spirit of counsel and might,
the spirit of knowledge and the fear
of the Lord. Isaiah 11:2

YOUTH

Topic: *Thinking of a Vocation?*

Background Scripture: Mark 1:4-13; Luke 3:1-22; 4:1-13

Scripture Lesson: Mark 1:4-13

Memory Verse: *The Spirit of the Lord shall rest upon him,*
the spirit of wisdom and understanding,
the spirit of counsel and might,
the spirit of knowledge and the fear
of the Lord. Isaiah 11:2

CHILDREN

Topic: *My Beloved Son*

Background Scripture: Mark 1:9-13; Luke 3:1-22

Scripture Lesson: Mark 1:9-13

Memory Verse: *"Thou art my beloved Son; with thee I am well pleased."* Luke 3:22

DAILY BIBLE READINGS

Mon., Jan. 3: John the Messenger, Mark 1:1-6.
Tues., Jan. 4: John's Message, Luke 3:4-9.
Wed., Jan. 5: Living Your Testimony, Luke 3:10-14.
Thurs., Jan. 6: The Price of Prophecy, Luke 3:15-20.
Fri., Jan. 7: Jesus' Baptism, Mark 1:7-11.
Sat., Jan. 8: Jesus' Temptation, Luke 4:1-13.
Sun., Jan. 9: Source of Mercy and Grace, Hebrews 4:12-16.

LESSON AIM

To see how Jesus accepted His calling, with all that was involved.

LESSON SETTING

Time: About A.D. 26

Place: The Jordan Valley and the Wilderness of Judea

Jesus Faces His Future

I. The Historical Setting: Luke 3:1-2

II. The Preaching of John the Baptist: Luke 3:3-18
   A. The Prophecy of Isaiah: vv. 3-6
   B. Warning to the People: vv. 7-9
   C. Questions and Answers: vv. 10-14
   D. The Prediction of the Messiah: vv. 15-18

LESSON OUTLINE

III. The Ministry of John the Baptist: Mark 1:4-8
   A. A Baptism of Repentance: v. 4
   B. The Popularity of John: v. 5
   C. The Appearance of John: v. 6
   D. The Message of John: vv. 7-8

IV. The Baptism of Jesus: Mark 1:9-11
   A. Baptism in the Jordan: v. 9
   B. The Descent of the Spirit: v. 10
   C. The Voice from Heaven: v. 11

V. The Temptation of Jesus: Mark 1:12-13

SUGGESTED INTRODUCTION FOR ADULTS

Today we study what is called "The Period of Preparation" for Jesus' public ministry. All three Synoptic Gospels agree that there were three parts to this preparation: (1) the ministry of John the Baptist; (2) the baptism of Jesus; (3) the temptation of Jesus.

Mark gives the briefest attention to this period of preparation, plunging into the public ministry of Jesus after only thirteen verses of introduction to his Gospel. He also has none of the Infancy Narratives found in the first two chapters of Matthew and Luke.

Mark's treatment of John's ministry is the briefest of the three, though closest to Matthew's account. But Luke adds several items of interest, which we look at under the second main heading of our outline.

The three accounts of the baptism of Jesus are much alike, with one addition in Matthew (3:14-15). But in the case of His temptation, Mark's account is exceedingly brief. Only Matthew and Luke describe the three specific temptations that Satan presented to Jesus. In the last part of our lesson we study Luke's description of these.

SUGGESTED INTRODUCTION FOR YOUTH

"Thinking of a Vocation?" That is our topic today. Aside from one's personal experience of salvation, this is probably the most significant decision a young person has to make.

In a sense it is a relief to have this settled by a definite divine call to some specific kind of ministry, at home or overseas. But this involves a grave responsibility to fulfill that call.

For all who do not sense such a call, there is the

necessity of choosing a career. God is able and eager to
guide in this decision. And we must not forget that all
Christians are called to serve Christ wholeheartedly.

**CONCEPTS FOR
CHILDREN**

1. Children must prepare for being adults.
2. As a man, Jesus was not only baptized and filled with
   the Spirit, but also tempted.
3. Both of these experiences helped to prepare Him for
   His ministry to others.
4. God has a plan and purpose for each of our lives.

THE LESSON COMMENTARY

I. THE HISTORICAL SETTING:
Luke 3:1-2

Like all good historians, Luke begins his account of John the Baptist's ministry by giving the historical setting. He says that it was "in the fifteenth year of the reign of Tiberius Caesar." This ruler was the second emperor of the Roman Empire, being the adopted stepson of the first emperor, Augustus (30 B.C.-A.D. 14). He became sole ruler in A.D. 14. Fifteen years from this would make John's ministry begin at A.D. 33, as held now by a number of scholars. If we hold to A.D. 30 for the crucifixion, we would say that the fifteenth year is to be reckoned from A.D. 11 or 12, when Tiberius was associated with his father in ruling. That would make A.D. 26 a likely date.

Pontius Pilate was the Roman governor of Judea (A.D. 26-36). Herod Antipas was "tetrarch of Galilee" (4 B.C.-A.D. 39), and also of Perea, east of the Jordan River. His brother Philip was "tetrarch of Ituraea and of the region of Trachonitis" (4 B.C.-A.D. 33)—northeast of Galilee. These two brothers were sons of Herod the Great, who was ruling Palestine at the time of Christ's birth. When Herod the Great died, his vast territory was divided among three of his sons.

Not much is known about Lysanias, "tetrarch of Abilene," a country far to the north, near Damascus. But after critics had accused Luke of being

inaccurate, an inscription was found that mentions Lysanias as a tetrarch in the time of Tiberius.

The expression "Annas and Caiaphas being the high priests" sounds very odd, since the Mosaic Law provided for only one high priest at a time, and he was to hold office for life. But the Roman rulers appointed and dismissed high priests as they wished. In the seventy-five years between the brith of Christ (5 B.C.) and the destruction of the temple in A.D. 70 (which ended the priesthood) there were no less than twenty-five different high priests—an average of one every three years.

Annas was high priest from A.D. 6 to 15. But he continued to dominate the high priesthood, which was held in succession by five of his sons, plus his son-in-law "Caiaphas" (A.D. 18-36). It will be remembered that it was Caiaphas who presided over the Sanhedrin that condemned Jesus to death.

Having identified the period of time in this sixfold manner, Luke now tells what happened: "The word of God came to John son of Zechariah in the desert" (NIV). The phrasing is similar to that found in several Old Testament passages (I Samuel 15:10; II Samuel 7:4; I Kings 17:2; Jeremiah 2:1). It was about four hundred years since the voice of the last Old Testament prophet, Malachi, had been heard. Donald Miller writes: "The belief was widespread, however, that when the Messianic Age came, prophecy would reappear (Joel 2:28; Malachi 3:1; 4:5). When, therefore, John the Baptist made his sudden and dramatic appearance in the Judean wilderness, it was like a bolt out of the blue" (*Laymen's Bible Commentary*, XVIII, 43).

II. THE PREACHING OF JOHN THE BAPTIST: Luke 3:3-18

A. The Prophecy of Isaiah: vv. 3-6

To identify John's ministry, Luke quotes Isaiah 40:3-5. (Matthew and Mark quote only verse 3.) This passage suggests God's fourfold formula for a revival: (1) Fill in the valleys; (2) cut down the hills; (3) straighten out the curves; (4) smooth out the bumps (Ralph Earle, *The Gospel of Luke*, pp. 21-22).

Verse 6 highlights a typical Lukan emphasis: salvation for all mankind. It is thought that Luke, a Greek, was the only non-Jewish writer of any book of the Bible. He gives strong emphasis to the universality of salvation.

B. Warning to the People: vv. 7-9

This paragraph is closely parallel to Matthew 3:7-10. There it says that the warning was addressed particularly to the Pharisees and Sadducees. Here it simply says "the multitude."

His greeting was: "You brood of vipers! Who warned you to flee from the coming wrath?" (v. 7, NIV). These seem like harsh words. But John saw through the casual curiosity that drew many of his hearers, and he wanted to jolt them awake to their danger. So he employed strong language.

He proceeded to warn them that what they needed to do was to show evidence of sincere repentance (v. 8). They must not trust in the fact that they were the children of Abraham; they had to obey God, as he did. If not, they would be cut down (v. 9). The coming of the Messiah would be a day of judgment on the nation.

C. Questions and Answers: vv. 10-14

This section is found only in Luke's Gospel. Here we find John giving specific instructions to three groups: (1) the crowd, vv. 10-11; (2) the tax collectors, vv. 12-13; (3) the soldiers, v. 14. All three of these groups asked the same question: "What shall we do?" But John gave varying answers, fitting the questioners.

When the crowd asked what to do, John replied: "The man with two tunics should share with him who has none, and the one who has food should do the same" (v. 11, NIV). The "tunics," worn underneath the outer robe, would hardly be "coats" as stated in the King James Version.

The love of God in our hearts requires us to share with those in deep need, as we may have opportunity. The essence of sin is selfishness, for which we must genuinely repent.

"Publicans" (KJV, v. 12) should be "tax collectors." These were not the wealthy *publicani*, who were responsible for large districts, but the ordinary tax collectors in the villages of Palestine.

Addressing John as "Teacher" (so the Greek), they asked what they should do. John told them, straight from the shoulder, "Don't collect any more than you are required to" (v. 13, NIV). The common practice was for everyone, from the *publicani* down to the local tax collector, to take a generous cut from whatever came to him. John condemned this.

Finally came some soldiers, asking the same question—perhaps wondering what John would say to them. He gave them just the instruction *they* needed: "Don't extort money and don't accuse people falsely—be content with your pay" (v. 14, NIV).

The Greek word for "extort" literally means to shake as with an earthquake. The soldiers were told not to force men, through threat of violence, to give them what they wanted. "Accuse falsely" is also a strong word, found only here and in 19:8 (of Zacchaeus). It gives us our noun "sycophant," which means a malignant informer. In those days soldiers often took unfair advantage of helpless civilians. John denounced this.

D. The Prediction of the Messiah: vv. 15-18

"The people were waiting expectantly and were all wondering in their hearts if John might possibly be the Christ" (v. 15, NIV)—that is, the Messiah. This verse is found only in Luke. It indicates the reason for John's words that follow. He told them that a greater One (the Messiah) was now coming.

His first words (v. 16) are found also in Matthew and Mark; so we bypass them now. But the significant words of verse 17 are not in Mark, though in Matthew (3:12). Luke adds: "And with many other words John exhorted the people and preached the good news to them" (v. 18, NIV).

III. THE MINISTRY OF JOHN THE BAPTIST: Mark 1:4-8

A. A Baptism of Repentance: v. 4

The first three verses of Mark were a part of our first lesson of this quarter. So we begin now with the fourth verse.

The very first word in the Greek is *egeneto*, which might be translated "appeared." Ezra P. Gould writes: "The verb is used to denote the appearance of a person on the stage of history" (*A Critical and Exegetical Commentary on the Gospel According to St. Mark*, International Critical Commentary, p. 6). The Greek says, "John appeared, baptizing." His sudden, abrupt appearance was like that of Elijah, whose prototype he was.

John was baptizing "in the wilderness." Matthew identifies it as "the wilderness of Judea" (3:1), between

the high plateau to the west and the Jordan Valley to the east. Luccock remarks that "wilderness" is an "up-to-the-minute description of much of our world" today (*Interpreter's Bible*, G. A. Buttrick, ed., VII, 649).

John was also preaching. The Greek verb signifies "proclaiming." Gould says: "The word means to exercise the office of a herald, to proclaim officially and with authority" (*Mark*, p. 6). "The verb comes from the noun *keryx*, which means 'herald.' It was used in a military sense of the herald who stepped out before the army to make an important announcement for the commanding officer. . . . John did not come on the scene to air his opinions or to discuss subtle theological questions. He came with an authoritative proclamation from God. The Messiah was coming and the people were to prepare the way for Him" (Earle, *The Gospel According to Mark*, p. 28).

But how? By a "baptism of repentance for the remission of sins," a repentance-baptism. That is the only kind of baptism that counts in God's sight.

The word translated *"repentance"* is *metanoia*, which literally means "a change of mind." Too often repentance is identified mainly with the emotions. Most people, if asked what repentance is, would say that it means being sorry for one's sins. A little girl came nearer the truth when she said it was "being sorry enough to quit." But actually it means a change of attitude. And there is no forgiveness without repentance.

B. The Popularity of John: v. 5

The Greek literally says: "And there was going out to him all the Judean country and all the Jerusalemites, and they were being baptized by him in the Jordan River as they were confessing out their sins." John baptized only those who confessed their sins. That should be the requirement. The language of this verse suggests a constant stream of people coming from all over Judea. It seemed that the whole population of Jerusalem turned out to hear him. Since this city was twenty miles from the Jordan and nearly four thousand feet higher in elevation, one can sense the earnestness of the crowds in coming. The people knew they would have a stiff climb back up the hill.

Why did John have such large crowds coming to him? Because he was saying something worth hearing! The people had been wanting to hear the voice of a prophet, one who spoke from God. Now such a prophet had appeared and everyone was excited. Could this be the Messiah?

C. The Appearance of John: v. 6

"John wore clothing made of camel's hair, with a leather belt around his waist, and he ate locusts and wild honey" (NIV). The camel's hair cloth would be coarse and rough. For that reason it was commonly used for sackcloth in connection with mourning or fasting. His clothes were held together by a leather belt around his waist.

Some people have thought that the "locusts" might refer to the blossoms of a locust tree. But it is altogether likely that John ate the grasshopper-like insects. These were "clean" according to the Mosaic Law and they are still eaten by the Bedouin. In fact, dried locusts can be bought for food in supermarkets in the United States.

Also some have suggested that the "wild honey" may have been the sweet sap of some tree. But the Wilderness of Judea has plenty of bees, and it seems best to take this as bees' honey.

John's diet and clothing were both of the rudest and simplest type. In contrast, Jesus wore the usual clothes and ate the usual food.

It might be noted that John's manner of living fitted his mission and message. J. C. Jones has put it well. He says that John was a "coarse man levelling mountains and filling up valleys, sternness in his looks, vehemence in his voice. The truth is—reformers must despise the conventionalities of society. They have rude work to do, and they must not be too dainty respecting the means they adopt to effect it. Adorn your frontispieces, embellish your corner-stones, but let the foundations be as rugged as you please. Decorations are for the superstructure, strength and solidity for the base" ("Mark," *Biblical Illustrator*, p. 8).

Josephus, the Jewish historian of the first century, says that John the Baptist "was a good man, and commanded the Jews to exercise virtue, both as to righteousness towards one another, and piety toward God" (*Antiquities*, xviii. 5.2.). John was a rugged pioneer, the very type that was needed at that time.

D. The Message of John: vv. 7-8

The people were wondering if John might be the expected Messiah. But John "proclaimed" ("And this was his message" [NIV]), "A mightier One is coming; I am only the forerunner" (literal Greek). In fact, said John, "I am not worthy to stoop down, like a humble servant, and untie the thongs of his sandals." There was no question about John's understanding of his role in relation to the Messiah.

Then he declared: "I indeed have baptized you with water: but he shall baptize you with the Holy Ghost" (v. 8). Both Matthew (3:11) and Luke (3:16) say "with the Holy Spirit and fire." That is, the baptism with the Holy Spirit is a fiery baptism that cleanses the heart from sin.

In view of the clear statement of John the Baptist here it is difficult to understand why the church has traditionally made much of water baptism but has been silent about the baptism with the Holy Spirit. Jews baptized converts, called "proselytes," in water. The distinctive Christian baptism is the baptism with the Holy Spirit.

IV. THE BAPTISM OF JESUS: Mark 1:9-11

A. Baptism in the Jordan: v. 9

Jesus came from Nazareth and was baptized by John in the Jordan River. But He had no sins to confess or of which to repent! That is true. But this act was a symbol of His whole earthly life, in which He identified Himself with humanity. Also it was necessary for Him to fulfill all the righteous demands of the Law (Matthew 3:14-15). In that way He could be the perfect Sacrifice for our sins.

B. The Descent of the Spirit: v. 10

"As Jesus was coming up out of the water, he saw heaven torn open and the Spirit descend on him like a dove" (NIV). Typically, Mark uses a stronger word for "open" than do Matthew and Luke. His Gospel reflects the rugged language of the fisherman Peter, whose preaching, according to the early church, Mark gives us in his Gospel.

The dove is a symbol of tenderness, purity, and gentleness. The Holy Spirit wants to bring those characteristics into our lives by His abiding presence.

C. The Voice from Heaven: v. 11

It is at the baptism of Jesus that the Trinity was first clearly and fully revealed. As Jesus, the Son, came up out of the water the Holy Spirit descended on Him. At the same time the Father's voice from heaven proclaimed: "Thou art my beloved Son, in whom I am well pleased." The expression "the Beloved" was one of the Jewish titles for the Messiah. So Jesus was declared to be God's Son in a unique sense, and also the expected Messiah.

The deity of Jesus is the touchstone of orthodoxy. Without a divine Savior there is no salvation and so no valid Christianity. The voice at the baptism was not only for Christ—what a comfort it must have been to Him—but it was also for us. Every Christian needs to have a firm, unshakable belief in the deity of our Lord. This is the absolutely essential foundation for our Christian faith.

V. THE TEMPTATION OF JESUS: Mark 1:12-13

Again Mark's account is the briefest. Yet he has some little, vivid additions.

All three Synoptic Gospels indicate that the temptation came right after the baptism. But Mark emphasizes this with his favorite word *euthys*, "immediately" (v. 12), which he uses some forty times.

Whereas Matthew and Luke say that Jesus was "led" by the Spirit into the wilderness to be tempted, Mark characteristically says that the Spirit "driveth him into the wilderness." This suggests some compelling power. In His humanity He would naturally shrink from temptation. But his public inauguration on the banks of the Jordan, where the large crowd was, must be followed by His private initiation alone in the desert.

Mark indicates, as does Luke, that

DISCUSSION QUESTIONS

1. What men in Christian history have been pioneers like John the Baptist?
2. How can we fulfill God's fourfold formula for a revival?
3. What is the importance of repentance?
4. How can we show our repentance?
5. What is the function of baptism today?
6. How did Jesus meet His temptations? (See Matthew and Luke.)

Satan tempted Jesus throughout the forty days. But Mark alone says that He was "with the wild beasts"—His only companions in the lonely wilderness. Both Matthew and Mark say that angels ministered to Him.

CONTEMPORARY APPLICATION

Men can never fathom the depths of the waters through which Christ passed in this period of temptation. It was a part of the tremendous price He paid for man's salvation. But because He "suffered being tempted, he is able to succour them that are tempted" (Hebrews 2:18).

Christ's temptation thus becomes to us a very comforting experience. Since He overcame, we can overcome in Him. He went through everything *for* us, while here on earth, and now He wants, through His Spirit, to go through everything *with* us.

JESUS DECLARES HIS MISSION

DEVOTIONAL READING | Isaiah 61:1-4

ADULTS

Topic: *Jesus Declares His Mission*

Background Scripture: Mark 1:14-15; Luke 4:14-30

Scripture Lesson: Luke 4:14-24

Memory Verse: *"The time is fulfilled, and the kingdom of God is at hand; repent, and believe in the gospel."* Mark 1:15

YOUTH

Topic: *Courage to Be*

Background Scripture: Mark 1:14-25; Luke 4:14-30

Scripture Lesson: Luke 4:14-24

Memory Verse: *"The time is fulfilled, and the kingdom of God is at hand; repent, and believe in the gospel."* Mark 1:15

CHILDREN

Topic: *A Christian's Mission*

Background Scripture: Mark 1:14-15; Luke 4:14-30

Scripture Lesson: Luke 4:16-24

Memory Verse: *"The Spirit of the Lord is upon me, because he has anointed me to preach good news to the poor*
He has sent me to proclaim release to the captives and recovering of sight to the blind, to set at liberty those who are oppressed, to proclaim the acceptable year of the Lord."
Luke 4:18-19

DAILY BIBLE READINGS

Mon., Jan. 10: A Mission of Helpfulness, Isaiah 58:6-9.
Tues., Jan. 11: A Mission of Salvation, Isaiah 55:1-6.
Wed., Jan. 12: A Mission of Fulfillment, Luke 4:14-19.
Thurs., Jan. 13: A Mission Spirit-filled, Isaiah 61:1-4.
Fri., Jan. 14: A Mission of Suffering, Psalm 22:1-2, 6-8, 14-15.
Sat., Jan. 15: Christ's Mission Interpreted, Luke 4:20-24.
Sun., Jan. 16: Christ's Mission Rejected, Luke 4:25-30.

LESSON AIM | To discover the true nature of Jesus' mission on earth.

LESSON SETTING

Time: Perhaps A.D. 26 or 27

Place: Galilee, in northern Palestine

149

Jesus Declares His Mission

LESSON OUTLINE

SUGGESTED INTRODUCTION FOR ADULTS

We sometimes hear it said that Jesus was born at Bethlehem in order that He might die at Calvary; the main purpose of His incarnation was His sacrificial death.

There is a great deal of truth to this, of course. But it is an oversimplification. We see in this lesson that Jesus' mission involved more than His death. It included His life of loving ministry to needy humanity.

We have already seen, in previous lessons, that Jesus fulfilled all righteousness for us. His circumcision, presentation in the temple, baptism, and temptation were all in preparation for His being the perfect Sacrifice for our sins.

But there was more to it than that. Jesus had a ministry of mercy and compassion to those in need around Him. In fulfilling this mission He left us an example of how we should live. So His life, as well as His death, is significant for us. Being justified by His death, we shall be saved by (literally, "in") His life (Romans 5:9).

SUGGESTED INTRODUCTION FOR YOUTH

"Courage to Be." That is what all of us need. Courage to be ourselves. But more importantly, courage to be what Christ wants us to be.

It does take courage to live the Christian life in today's world. Our life-style has to be different, and most people don't like anyone who is different from them. So we pay a price for following Christ.

But He is our Example. He ran into opposition right at the beginning of His ministry, and right in His own hometown. So it will not be surprising if we have a similar problem.

Life without a mission is wasted. We need to find a purpose, a mission in life, and then carry it out. That is what makes life worth the living.

CONCEPTS FOR CHILDREN

1. Jesus always went to the synagogue on the sabbath.
2. We should always go to church on Sunday.
3. His mission was to help others.
4. As Christians we should try to find ways in which we can help those around us.

THE LESSON COMMENTARY

I. THE BEGINNING OF HIS MINISTRY:
Mark 1:14-15

A. The Occasion for It: v. 14

Both Matthew and Mark indicate that it was the arrest and imprisonment of John the Baptist that became the occasion for Jesus beginning His public ministry. He did not want to stage competition with His illustrious predecessor. So he waited until John was out of the way.

The Greek verb translated "put in prison" may also mean "arrested." That is why we have used both terms above. It was Herod Antipas who arrested and imprisoned John. This was because John had reproved him for stealing his brother's wife and marrying her (Luke 3:19-20).

Jesus "came into Galilee," in the northern part of Palestine. This verse marks the beginning of His great Galilean ministry, which may have lasted about a year and a half. He was safer, and more accepted, in Galilee than in Judea.

He came "preaching the gospel of God." The added words "of the kingdom" (KJV) are not in the oldest Greek manuscripts. The "gospel" is

the "good news" (Greek, *euangelion*) of the salvation that God has provided.

B. The Heart of His Message: v. 15

"The time is fulfilled." These words are fraught with tremendous significance. The Greek word for "time" in this verse is not *chronos*, which indicates the passing of time (cf. "chronology"). Rather, it is *kairos*, which means "*the right, proper, favorable time . . . definite fixed time . . .* one of the chief eschatological terms *. . . the time of crisis, the last times*" (William F. Arndt and F. Wilbur Gingrich, *Greek-English Lexicon of the New Testament*, pp. 395-96). This was God's appointed time for His Son to appear on the scene.

It was also the "opportune moment" for the Jewish nation to accept "the kingdom of God" in the person of the Messiah. But the moment (His ministry) passed. The nation rejected Him and soon suffered severe punishment from Rome.

William Lane writes: "Jesus declares that the critical moment has come: God begins to act in a new and decisive way, bringing his promise of ultimate redemption to the point of fulfilment. By sovereign decision God makes this point in time the critical one in which all the moments of promise and fulfilment in the past find their significance in one awesome moment. In comparison with John's preaching, the distinctive note sounded by Jesus is the emphasis upon fulfilment" (*The Gospel According to Mark*, The New International Commentary on the New Testament, p. 64).

Herman Ridderbos sounds a similar note: " 'The time is fulfilled' indicates that the threshold of the great future has been reached, that the door has been opened, and the prerequisites for the realization of the divine work of consummation are present, so that now the concluding drama can start" (*The Coming of the Kingdom*, p. 48).

Today we think of a "kingdom" as a territory ruled by a king. But scholars are agreed that this is not the primary meaning of the word as used in the Bible. *Kingdom* means "reign" not "realm." "The kingdom of God," which Jesus proclaimed, is the *sovereign authority* of God. This is reflected in Psalm 103:19, which reads: "The Lord hath prepared his throne in the heavens; and his kingdom ruleth over all." It is His divine authority that rules over all creation.

Jesus echoed John's proclamation: "Repent ye" (Matthew 3:2). But he added a new, Christian note: "Believe the gospel." "John's main emphasis was on judgment. With stern voice and strict manner he called on men to repent and confess their sins. But Jesus' main emphasis was on the Gospel. Repentance is the prerequisite for believing. Too many people try vainly to believe without having really repented. But some fail to look up through their tears of repentance and believe the Gospel" (Ralph Earle, *The Gospel According to Mark*, p. 33). Matthew Henry writes: "Repentance will quicken faith, and faith will make repentance evangelical" (*Commentary*, V, 453).

II. HIS EARLY POPULARITY: Luke 4:14-15

A. Widespread Publicity: v. 14

After his temptation, "Jesus returned in the power of the Spirit into Galilee." This is a typically Lukan statement. Matthew and Mark simply say that He withdrew to Galilee (Matthew 4:12; Mark 1:14). Luke says far more about the Holy Spirit than either of the other two Synoptic writers. This is in keeping with the primary emphasis on the Holy Spirit in Acts, which Luke also wrote.

The statement here is significant. All three Synoptic Gospels say that the Holy Spirit came down on Jesus at His baptism and that the Spirit led Him into the wilderness to be tempted by Satan. Having overcome the temptations, He emerged "in the power of the Spirit" for His public ministry. This suggests that there is a fresh release of the Spirit in greater power in our lives when we are victorious in meeting temptation. Probably most Spirit-filled Christians have experienced this fact. Obedience brings God's greater blessing on us. And temptations test our obedience.

Empowered by the Spirit, Jesus had such an effective ministry that "news about him spread through the whole countryside" (NIV). This was the beginning of His great Galilean ministry, when His popularity was at its height.

B. A Synagogue Ministry: v. 15

In the early part of His ministry in Galilee, Jesus taught largely in the "synagogues." This word comes directly from the Greek *synagoge*, which literally means "a gathering together." As in the case of *church*, it first designated the congregation and later the building. By the time of Christ it was commonly used for the building, as here.

The synagogues sprang up during and after the Babylonian captivity, when the people no longer had the temple in which to worship. So they gathered in small groups to hear the Scriptures read and expounded. There were synagogues everywhere.

III. HIS PREACHING AT NAZA-RETH:
Luke 4:16-21

A. In the Synagogue on the Sabbath: v. 16

Jesus "came to Nazareth, where he had been brought up" (NIV). He had already chosen the larger city, Capernaum—some twenty miles away on the north shore of the Lake of Galilee—as the headquarters for His ministry (Matthew 4:13). But it was fitting that He should make a visit to His hometown.

"As his custom was, he went into the synagogue on the sabbath day." Observance of the sabbath was one of the main distinguishing features of the Jews, separating them from the pagans. Although He was God's Son—and also *because* He was—Jesus conformed to the custom of synagogue worship on the sabbath day. He thereby set us an example that we should go to church on the Lord's Day.

Ordained priests, all of whom were Levites, ministered in the temple at Jerusalem. But unordained rabbis taught the Scriptures in the synagogues. And any competent layman could read the Scripture lesson. They always "stood up" to do this.

Plummer describes the situation. "The lectern was close to the front seats, where those who were most likely to be called upon to read commonly sat. A lesson from the *Torah* or Law was read first, and then one from the Prophets. After the lesson had been read in Hebrew it was interpreted into Aramaic (Neh. viii. 8), or into Greek in places where Greek was commonly spoken. This was done verse by verse in the Law; but in the Prophets three verses might be taken at once, and in this case Jesus seems to have taken two verses. Then followed the exposition or sermon. The reader, interpreter, and preacher might be

one, two, or three persons. Here Christ was both reader and preacher; and possibly He interpreted as well. Although there were officers with fixed duties attached to each synagogue, yet there was no one specially appointed either to read, or interpret, or preach, or pray. Any member of the congregation might discharge them in turn at the invitation of the *archisynagogos* [that is, "ruler of the synagogue"]" (*A Critical and Exegetical Commentary on the Gospel According to St. Luke*, International Critical Commentary, p. 119). This is what we find in Acts 13:15.

B. Reading the Lesson from the Prophets: v. 17

When Jesus stood up "there was delivered to him the book of the prophet Esaias"—rather "Isaiah." The word for "book" (*biblion*) means "scroll." Fortunately we have a scroll of Isaiah from Dead Sea Cave I, near Qumran, dating from about 125 B.C. It is twenty-four feet long and about a foot wide. The Hebrew text is written in fifty-four columns on seventeen sheets of leather stitched end to end. Anyone who has seen this magnificent scroll on display in the Shrine of the Book outside Jerusalem cannot help being much impressed with the excellent condition of a leather scroll that is over two thousand years old. But this is because it was sealed airtight in a large clay jar—probably in A.D. 68, just before the Roman legions captured Qumran and largely destroyed it.

Probably the scroll that Jesus held in His hands was very similar to the Dead Sea Scroll of Isaiah. Unrolling it, He found the passage He wanted to read. Later there were assigned lessons for each sabbath, but there is no evidence that this was the case at this time.

C. The Passage from Isaiah: vv. 18-19

Jesus read from Isaiah 61:1-2. The bulk of the quotations in the New

Testament from the Old Testament are from the Septuagint (a Greek translation of the Old Testament made between 250 and 150 B.C.). This differs at times from the Massoretic text, the standard Hebrew text which comes to us from the Middle Ages. That will account for some of the differences that one finds if he compares Luke 4:18-19 with Isaiah 62:1-2.

On verse 18 Plummer writes: "In the original the Prophet puts into the mouth of Jehovah's ideal Servant a gracious message to those in captivity, promising them release and a return to the restored Jerusalem, the joy of which is compared to the joy of the year of jubilee. It is obvious that both figures, the return from exile and the release at the jubilee, admirably express Christ's work of redemption" (*Luke*, p. 121).

Any thoughtful Christian can see the logic of this. Christ, "the Servant of the Lord," sets people free from the captivity of sin. He opens sin-blinded eyes.

Jesus finished His Scripture reading with "to preach the acceptable year of the Lord" (v. 19), or "to proclaim the year of the Lord's favor" (NIV). Why did Jesus stop in the middle of a sentence? Because the next clause reads: "and the day of vengeance of our God" (Isaiah 61:2). If Jesus had read that, He could not have said, "This day is this scripture fulfilled in your ears" (v. 21). All that He read related to His first coming for our salvation. But the "vengeance," or judgment, will take place at His second coming.

D. Sitting Down to Speak: v. 20

"Then he rolled up the scroll, gave it back to the attendant and sat down" (NIV). It was the regular custom among the Jews to stand while reading the sacred Scriptures, out of reverence for God's Word, but to be seated while teaching or preaching. Today we follow the Greek and Roman custom of standing to speak. Obviously this is far more efficient with a group of any considerable size. It adds force to a man's speech. Also the people can see the preacher and hear him better.

The eyes of all those in the synagogue were fixed intently on Jesus, waiting to hear what He would have to say. The people of Nazareth had naturally been rather excited about the reports that had come in about the doings of their hometown boy (v. 14). They could hardly believe their ears. Was He as great as they had heard that He was? They were eager to find out. So they were all eyes and ears.

E. Jesus' Proclamation About Himself: v. 21

He started His message with the startling words, "This day is this scripture fulfilled in your ears." He was actually the One about whom Isaiah had written seven centuries earlier. The Spirit of the Lord had come on Him at His baptism and anointed Him to preach good news to the poor, and to do the rest of the things cited in verse 18. At last the Messiah, the true "Servant of the Lord" of Isaiah 40—60, had come to bring redemption to sinful mankind. He Himself was the Redeemer.

IV. THE REACTION OF THE AUDIENCE: Luke 4:22

"All spoke well of him and were amazed at the gracious words that came from his lips. 'Isn't this Joseph's son?' they asked" (NIV). "Gracious words" is literally "words of grace." When Jesus talked about God's gracious compassion for the poor and needy, the people were pleased and amazed. They were so used to hearing their rabbis urging them to keep all the meticulous details of the Law of Moses that they couldn't believe their ears now. This Teacher was telling them that God loved the poor, that He had sent His anointed Servant to heal their hurts!

There are some religious leaders today who preach more law than love.

But fortunately there has been a new emphasis on love in the last few years. For this we should be devoutly thankful.

Yet how could this man be preaching in this way? "Isn't this Joseph's son?" Matthew (13:55-56) and Mark (6:3) both say that the people mentioned knowing His mother, brothers, and sisters. How could the familiar village carpenter be such an outstanding preacher?

V. THE RESPONSE OF JESUS: Luke 4:23-27

A. A Popular Proverb: v. 23

Jesus declared: "Surely you will quote this proverb to me: 'Physician, heal yourself! Do here in your home town what we have heard that you did in Capernaum'" (NIV). The report of His miracles and mighty preaching had been sounding in their ears for some time. Curiosity led them to want to see some of the miraculous deeds.

B. Elijah and the Gentile Widow: vv. 24-26

Jesus countered by asserting, "No prophet is accepted in his own country." While perhaps not a popular proverb, this was certainly a truism. It is hard for people to believe that a hometown boy has become as great as they hear he is. They remember all his limitations and can't believe that he could have surmounted them completely. The proverb that does fit is, "Familiarity breeds contempt." That is too often the case.

Then the Master reminded them of an incident that had happened far back in the days of the kingdom period. Although there were many Israelite widows, Elijah (the familiar form of Old Testament characters should always be used) was not sent by the Lord to any of them. Rather, God told him go to Zarephath (KJV, "Sarepta"), between Tyre and Sidon. There he supplied the needs of a destitute widow.

C. Elisha and the Gentile Leper: v. 27

Likewise God did not send Elisha to any of the numerous lepers in Israel. Instead He had the prophet cure Naaman the Syrian of his leprosy.

What point was Jesus trying to make? Simply that God is interested in Gentiles as well as Jews, and that when His own people disobey and reject Him, He turns to others who will accept Him.

This, of course, is what happened in the case of Jesus. The Jewish nation rejected Him as its Messiah, and so the Gospel was given to the Gentiles, who gladly accepted Jesus as Savior.

VI. VIOLENT REJECTION OF JESUS: Luke 4:28-30

A. The Fury of the Crowd: v. 28

"All the people in the synagogue were furious when they heard this" (NIV). We find the same reaction when Paul told a crowd in Jerusalem that God had commissioned him to go to the Gentiles (Acts 22:21-23). The people there were so infuriated at the idea of God blessing the Gentiles that they shouted, threw off their outer cloaks, and threw dust in the air. God was not supposed to bless the Gentiles—just the Jews!

Plummer comments: "They see

DISCUSSION QUESTIONS

1. Why is it hard for a young man to preach in his hometown?
2. What does verse 22b reveal about Jesus' humanity?
3. How may verse 24 be applied?
4. Why do people speak of "The Gospel of Isaiah"?
5. How can you explain Nazareth's rejection of Jesus?
6. How can we help fulfill verse 18?

the point of His illustrations: He has been comparing them to those Jews who were judged less worthy of Divine benefits than the heathen. . . . His comparing Himself to such Prophets as Elijah and Elisha would add to the wrath of the Nazarenes. On the other hand, those early instances of God's special blessings being conferred upon heathen would have peculiar interest for Luke" (*Luke*, p. 129).

B. The Attempted Execution: v. 29

Nazareth is up in the Galilean hills just north of the plain of Esdraelon, which separates Samaria and Galilee. Overlooking the main part of the Arab town today is a hill on which is located a new Jewish settlement. It is not certain just where "the brow of the hill" is, over which the people tried to throw Jesus to His death.

C. Jesus' Escape: v. 30

Plummer writes: "The addition of *dia mesou* ["through the midst"] is for emphasis, and seems to imply that there was something miraculous in His passing through the very midst of those who were intending to slay Him, and seemed to have Him entirely in their power. They had asked for a miracle, and this was the miracle granted to them. Those who think that it was His determined look or personal majesty which saved Him, have to explain why this did not prevent them from casting Him out of the synagogue" (*Luke*, p. 130).

CONTEMPORARY APPLICATION

J. Norval Geldenhuys puts the matter beautifully: "No one will ever be able to do much for mankind unless he has a deep realization of the terrible need of the human race. An imperfect insight into the actual needs and misery of man results in giving inadequate prescriptions for finding relief. Now it is characteristic of the Savior's preaching that He referred in a remarkably plain manner to the unfathomable spiritual need of mankind. . . . He points to the condition of man as one of spiritual poverty, broken-heartedness, captivity, blindness and mutilation. This spiritual distress is caused by the sin of mankind. For sin makes man inwardly poor, sows destruction in his heart and life, makes him a captive in its stranglehold, makes him spiritually blind so that he loses all vision and all power of clear judgment, and crushes his personality" (*Commentary on the Gospel of Luke*, New International Commentary on the New Testament, pp. 169-170).

JESUS CALLS HIS DISCIPLES

DEVOTIONAL READING	John 17:6-19
ADULTS	Topic: *Jesus Calls His Disciples* Background Scripture: Mark 1:16-20; 3:13-19; Luke 5:1-11; 6:12-16; 9:1-6. Scripture Lesson: Luke 5:1-11 Memory Verse: *"Follow me and I will make you become fishers of men."* Mark 1:17
YOUTH	Topic: *Commitment to Serve* Background Scripture: Mark 1:16-20; 3:13-19; Luke 5:1-11; 6:12-16; 9:1-6 Scripture Lesson: Luke 5:1-11 Memory Verse: *"Follow me and I will make you become fishers of men."* Mark 1:17
CHILDREN	Topic: *Fishers of Men* Background Scripture: Mark 1:16-20; 3:13-19; Luke 5:1-11; 6:12-16; 9:1-6 Scripture Lesson: Luke 5:1-11 Memory Verse: *"Follow me, and I will make you fishers of men."* Matthew 4:19
DAILY BIBLE READINGS	Mon., Jan. 17: Four by the Sea, Mark 1:16-20. Tues., Jan. 18: A Call and a Supper, Matthew 9:9-13. Wed., Jan. 19: Job Description, Mark 3:13-19. Thurs., Jan. 20: A Disciple Lost, Matthew 19:16-22. Fri., Jan. 21: Living as a Disciple, Matthew 5:1-12. Sat., Jan. 22: Disciples Commissioned, Luke 9:1-6. Sun., Jan. 23: Jesus Prays for Disciples, John 17:6-19.
LESSON AIM	To see what is involved in being called by Jesus to follow and serve Him.
LESSON SETTING	Time: Probably A.D. 28 or 29 Place: Galilee

LESSON OUTLINE	Jesus Calls His Disciples
	
	  I. The Call of the First Four: Mark 1:16-20.
	      A. Simon and Andrew: vv. 16-18
	      B. James and John: vv. 19-20

II. **The Selection of Simon:** Luke 5:1-3
 A. The Big Crowd: v. 1
 C. Teaching from a Boat: vv. 2-3

III. **The Miraculous Catch of Fish:** Luke 5:4-9
 A. Jesus' Command: v. 4
 B. Simon's Response: v. 5
 C. The Big Catch: vv. 6-7
 D. The Amazed Fishermen: vv. 8-9

IV. **The Master's Commission:** Luke 5:10-11
 A. The Commission: v. 10
 B. The Response: v. 11

V. **The Selection of the Twelve Apostles:** Luke 6:12-16
 A. The All Night of Prayer: v. 12
 B. The Names of the Twelve: vv. 13-16

VI. **The Mission of the Twelve:** Luke 9:1-6

SUGGESTED INTRODUCTION FOR ADULTS

To be a Christian means to follow Christ. So everyone is called to follow Him.

But some are called to special service. Such were the twelve apostles, whom Jesus selected and commissioned to be His special representatives ("apostles"). They left their former vocations and devoted themselves fully to His service.

Jesus first called them to come after Him. Then He sent them out to preach His gospel. Being with Him precedes going for Him.

There is a real sense in which following Jesus involves complete commitment to Him, even for those who remain in secular employment. Every Christian must acknowledge Him as Master and Lord, and must be ready to do what He asks. In whatever task we may be engaged, we must be serving Him, doing what He wants us to do.

SUGGESTED INTRODUCTION FOR YOUTH

"Commitment to Serve." That is what it costs to be a Christian. We are all called to work with Christ in a redemptive ministry to people of all ages, classes, and needs.

There is no greater challenge than the call: "Follow me and I will make you fishers of men." When Christ speaks those words to us, we must rise out of our sin or lethargy of indifference and follow Him. Both by virtue of creation and because of Calvary He has a claim on our lives. We meet that claim by a complete commitment to Him.

Today, more than ever, Christ is looking for followers. We must be ready to leave all to follow Him.

CONCEPTS FOR CHILDREN

1. Because Peter obeyed Jesus, he was richly rewarded.
2. But he was also called to greater service.
3. Christ wants all of us to be "fishers of men."
4. This means that we lead others to Him.

THE LESSON COMMENTARY

I. THE CALL OF THE FIRST FOUR:
Mark 1:16-20

A. Simon and Andrew: vv. 16-18

Jesus was walking along the shore of "the sea of Galilee." Luke, who was used to sailing the Mediterranean, calls it a lake, for it was only about twelve miles long and seven miles wide. But to those who lived on its banks and fished in its waters it was "the sea." At that time there were several busy cities on its northern shore. Now there is only one city on the Lake of Galilee—Tiberias, on the west side.

Jesus saw "Simon"—a very common Jewish name in the first century—and his brother Andrew. They were "casting a net" in the lake. The Greek literally says "casting about," using a circular net with weights around the edge. This type of net would be used in the shallow water near the shore.

The two brothers were fishermen. This was the vocation of the first four men whom Jesus called as His disciples. They were accustomed to hard work and the dangers of the lake. Also, fishing begets patience. These were qualities they would need as Christ's servants.

It has often been observed that busy men make good prospects for Christian service. The seventeenth-century Puritan divine, John Trapp, wrote: "God calleth men when they are busy; Satan, when they are idle. For idleness is the hour of temptation, and an idle person the devil's tennis-ball, which he tosseth at pleasure, and sets to work as he liketh and listeth" (*Commentary on the New Testament*, p. 40).

Fishing was an honorable vocation. But Jesus had more important work for these men. And so He asked them to follow Him, and He would make them "fishers of men."

This is the first responsibility of those who are called to the full-time ministry. But it is also the duty of every follower of Christ. We rejoice in the fact that today thousands of Christian "laymen" are learning to do personal evangelism.

Without hesitation the two fishermen obeyed the call: "And straightway they forsook their nets, and followed him" (v. 18). Prompt obedience is necessary if we are going to fulfill God's purpose for our lives.

B. James and John: vv. 19-20

With His first two disciples following Him, Jesus went a little farther along the shore of the lake. Soon He spied James and John, two sons of Zebedee, "in the ship." Today we reserve the word "ship" for large vessels. A craft on a lake would properly be called a "boat."

These two brothers were busy "mending their nets." The Greek verb means to "make fit." The men were "preparing their nets" (NIV) for fishing the next night.

Immediately the Master called these two additional fishermen. They "left their father Zebedee in the ship with the hired servants, and went after him" (v. 20). The mention of hired men (only in Mark) shows that the father was not left in hardship by his sons.

II. THE SELECTION OF SIMON:
Luke 5:1-3

A. The Big Crowd: v. 1

One day Jesus was standing by "the lake of Gennesaret." This is the same as "the sea of Galilee" in Mark's account that we just studied. We noted that Luke, a wide traveler, calls it a "lake."

This is the only place in the New Testament where the name "lake of Gennesaret" occurs. It got this title from the Plain of Gennesaret on the northwest shore of the lake (Matthew 14:34; Mark 6:53).

A large crowd "pressed upon" Jesus to hear the word of God. At that time there was a heavy population on the northern shore of the Lake of Galilee, so that immense crowds could gather in only a short time.

This was the central year of Jesus' ministry, and it has often been called "the year of popularity." Wherever He went, large crowds followed Him. Often the main purpose was to be healed (Mark 3:10). But here it says, "to hear the word of God."

B. Teaching from a Boat: vv. 2-3

Two boats were at the water's edge. The fishermen were busy on the shore, washing their nets.

One of the boats belonged to Simon Peter. Jesus got into it and asked Simon to put out a little from shore. Then Jesus sat down—as was the custom of Jewish rabbis—and taught the people from the boat.

With the people pressing against Jesus, it was difficult for Him to speak effectively. But now that He was sitting in the boat, the situation was greatly improved. Anyone who has spent much time in a boat on the water has discovered that voices carry much farther across the water than they do on land. One can distinctly hear a conversation being carried on in ordinary tones a considerable distance away.

So it was here. The people were sitting on the sloping hillside in a sort of amphitheater. The surface of the lake was a perfect sounding board to carry Jesus' words to the large crowd on the shore.

III. THE MIRACULOUS CATCH OF FISH:
Luke 5:4-9

A. Jesus' Command: v. 4

When Jesus had finished speaking, He proceeded to pay His host for the loan of His boat. He said to Simon, "Put out into deep water, and let down the nets for a catch" (v. 4, NIV).

This was a simple order, and one that would have been familiar to any fisherman. But the timing of it did not seem auspicious.

B. Simon's Response: v. 5

Simon Peter was always quick to speak his mind, and this was no exception. His answer was clear-cut and emphatic, but also submissive: "Master, we've worked hard all night and haven't caught anything. But because you say so, I will let down the nets" (NIV).

In all four Gospels (in the King James Version) Jesus is addressed as "Master." Most frequently the Greek word is *didascalos*, which should be translated "Teacher." Often it is *kyrios*, which means "Lord." Less frequently it is *rabbi* (taken over from the Hebrew), which means "my teacher." But Luke alone (7 times) uses the word *epistata*, "commander." Plummer comments: "Here it is used of one who has a right to give orders" (*A Critical and Exegetical Commentary on the Gospel According to St. Luke*, International Critical Commentary, p. 143). Jesus was the real commander of the boat, and Peter acknowledged this. He was ready to take orders from his Commander.

As has often been the custom in modern times, the fishermen of that day did their fishing at night. Along the Atlantic or Pacific coast one can still see fishing boats coming back into the harbor in the morning. In the darkness the unsuspecting fish can be caught more easily.

Though Peter, seasoned fisherman that he was, could see no point in undertaking to fish in the daytime—especially after a fruitless night—yet "because you say so" he was willing to obey the order.

C. The Big Catch: vv. 6-7

Because Peter obeyed—"they" indicates that Andrew helped him—he got results. The net enclosed a large school of fish. The King James Version says: "and their net brake." Obviously this is incorrect, for if the net had broken they would have lost the fish. The Greek clearly says that "their nets began to break" (NIV).

So they had to get help immediately. They "signaled their partners in the other boat to come and help them" (v. 7, NIV). The result was that they filled both these small fishing boats so full of fish that they began to sink. This is a good example of God's generous abundance in giving.

It has been suggested that Jesus spotted a large school of fish and so gave the order. But why could not the eyes of experienced fishermen see this? It seems better to treat the whole incident as a divine miracle.

D. The Amazed Fishermen: vv. 8-9

Simon Peter's reaction was typical. Impulsively he fell down at Jesus' feet and said, "Depart from me; for I am a sinful man, O Lord."

It should be noted in this connection that a display of divine power almost always brings deep conviction of sin. When people are confronted by God they see themselves as they really are. In a purely humanistic atmosphere people can be complacent about their sins. But when God demonstrates His powerful presence, sinners tremble.

It was fitting that at the beginning of their following Jesus these disciples should have abundant evidence given to them of His divine power. They could never again doubt that Jesus was what He claimed to be. And they realized that they must follow Him as their authoritative Leader and Lord.

IV. THE MASTER'S COMMISSION: Luke 5:10-11

A. The Commission: v. 10

Here we learn that the partners of Peter and Andrew were James and John the sons of Zebedee. These four fishermen had worked closely together on the Lake of Galilee, and now they were called to work together in Jesus' vocation of saving men.

Jesus addressed Simon Peter directly: "Fear not: from henceforth thou shalt catch men." Up to this time his whole life had been wrapped up in the fishing business. It was not only his livelihood; it was his life. But now Jesus called him to a higher task—fishing for men's souls, to save them. It is the highest calling on earth.

B. The Response: v. 11

Jesus' commission was given specifically to Simon Peter. But all four men felt the impact of it. They "pulled their boats up on shore, left everything and followed him" (NIV). So here again we find the four fishermen disciples.

The Greek word for "catch" (v. 10) is literally "catch alive." J. Norval Geldenhuys comments: "By our Lord's words in verse 10, 'from henceforth thou shalt catch men,' it is clear that we should also understand this event symbolically in connection with evangelization. So the message comes to the church 'to launch out into the deep and there to cast the net of the Gospel.' In spite of all failures in the past, the church of Christ must again and again renew its energetic attempts under His guidance to gather in souls for His kingdom, and must do this not merely in the 'shallow waters' but in the 'deep water'—not only in the vicinity of settled ecclesiastical life, but also among the great masses of people where the need is so great" (*Commentary on the Gospel of Luke*, New International Commentary on the New Testament, p. 183).

V. THE SELECTION OF THE TWELVE APOSTLES: Luke 6:12-16

A. The All Night of Prayer: v. 12

Luke's Gospel is the Gospel of prayer. It alone has Jesus' three great parables on prayer: The Importunate

Friend at Midnight (11:5-8), The Unjust Judge (18:1-8), and The Pharisee and the Tax Collector (18:9-14). But Luke is also the only one of the Gospel writers who mentions Jesus praying at six crucial points in His life: at His baptism (3:21), after cleansing the leper, which caused opposition to Him (5:16), before choosing the twelve apostles (6:12), before Peter's great confession at Caesarea Philippi 9:18), at His transfiguration (9:28), and before giving the Lord's Prayer (11:1). It seems evident that Luke was a great man of prayer, or he would not have recorded these incidents of Jesus praying.

One of the most important decisions that Jesus ever made was the choice of His twelve apostles. They would be the nucleus of His church. On them would depend the ongoing of His ministry.

They must be selected with great care. And so Jesus spent all night in prayer, seeking the guidance of the Father in His selection of those who would have the responsibility of beginning the church and mediating Christ's ministry to mankind. A pertinent question is posed by this incident: If Jesus needed to pray all night before making this important decision, how much more do we need to pray about our decisions in life?

DISCUSSION QUESTIONS

1. Why does God call busy people into His service?
2. What is the advantage of having different types of personalities working in the church?
3. What were some types represented in the twelve apostles?
4. Why do we need to pray, as Jesus prayed?
5. How is Pentecost related to the miraculous catch of fish?
6. What part may healing play in the ministry of the church?

B. The Names of the Twelve: vv. 13-16

In the New Testament we find four lists of the twelve apostles. They are named in all three Synoptic Gospels (Matthew 10:1-4; Mark 3:16-19; Luke 6:14-16) and in Acts (1:13). All the lists begin with Peter and end with Judas Iscariot (except in Acts, when Judas was dead). The four fishermen are always named first. The second group of four names always begins with Philip, and the third group with James the son of Alphaeus. A comparison of these four lists will be found in the *Beacon Bible Commentary*, Volume 6, page 106.

After spending the entire night in prayer Jesus called His disciples to Him. From the whole group He chose twelve, "whom he also named apostles" (v. 13). Our word "apostle" is taken over from the Greek *apostolos*, which literally means "one sent on an errand, or with a message." It is closely equivalent to our word "missionary," which comes from the Latin with the same meaning. But it appears that in the early church the apostles acted with special authority as sort of general superintendents of the whole church.

To Simon Jesus gave the name *Peter* (Greek *petros*, "stone"). Peter became the main spokesman of the apostles. His brother Andrew was less prominent but played some important roles (e.g., John 6:8). James and John were the sons of Zebedee. There was a less well-known James "the son of Alphaeus." There was also another Simon, called "Zelotes"—better, "the Zealot." This could simply mean that he was a very zealous individual, but more probably it means that he had formerly belonged to the party of "the Zealots," whom Josephus describes as ardent nationalists (against Roman rule). Judas "the brother of James"—better, "son of James" (NIV)—is called "Thaddaeus" ("the warm-hearted one") in Matthew and Mark.

One of the sad notes of the four Gospels is that whenever Judas Iscariot is mentioned he is further designated as "the traitor" or "who also betrayed him"—except at the end of the Gospels in connection with the actual betrayal. The name "Judas" has gone down in history with this stigma attached. What a price to pay for a few pieces of silver!

The word *Iscariot* is thought to come from *ish* (Hebrew for *man*) and *Kerioth*, a village in Judea. Judas was probably the only one of the twelve apostles who was not from Galilee.

VI. THE MISSION OF THE TWELVE:
Luke 9:1-6

Mark's Gospel (3:14) tells us that Jesus "ordained twelve, that they should be with him, and that he might send them forth to preach." The first stage, being with Him, is suggested in the previous section of the lesson. Now we move to the second stage—sending them out to preach.

Jesus called together "the Twelve" (so the best Greek text). These were the twelve disciples that He had selected as His apostles. He "gave them power and authority over all devils" (v. 1). The Greek never speaks of "devils." There is only one devil (*diabolos*). But the Greek word here is *daimonia*, "demons"—which is the correct translation. He also gave them power "to cure diseases."

Then "he sent them to preach the kingdom of God, and to heal the sick" (v. 2). The word for "preach" is literally "proclaim." They were to proclaim that the Kingdom had come in the person of Jesus Christ. God was visiting His people.

The Twelve were to go on a brief mission in a hospitable country with a warm climate. So they were to travel light. Jesus instructed them: "Take nothing for the journey—no staff, no bag, no bread, no money, no extra tunic" (v. 3, NIV). The word for "bag" was sometimes used in connection with begging. These disciples were not to take along any food, any bag for begging food, or any money for buying food. They were to depend on the hospitality of the people. In that culture strangers were to be given food and shelter whenever needed.

Whenever they were preaching in any town, they were to stay in one house, not move about and create problems (v. 4). If people rejected them, they were to shake the dust off their feet as a testimony of God's rejection of those people (v. 5).

"So they set out and went from village to village, preaching the gospel and healing people everywhere" (v. 6, NIV). The question may well be raised as to whether the church today should give more attention to a healing ministry.

CONTEMPORARY APPLICATION

We are called to be "fishers of men." So we ought to learn how to fish.

There are two main methods of fishing—by hook and line, and by pulling in a net. These suggest two methods of soul-winning—personal evangelism and mass evangelism.

Traditionally there has been much dispute as to which is better, which one should be used. As is often true, the answer is, "Both!" The two supplement each other. Groups that have majored on mass evangelization are realizing increasingly that this must be supported by personal evangelism in order to be effective. And the reverse is also true.

POWER OVER THE DEMONIC

(Temperance)

DEVOTIONAL READING	Psalm 103:1-5

ADULTS	Topic: *Power over the Demonic* Background Scripture: Mark 1:21-39; Luke 4:31-44 Scripture Lesson: Mark 1:21-34 Memory Verse: *"What is this? A new teaching! With authority he commands even the unclean spirits, and they obey him."* Mark 1:27

YOUTH	Topic: *Becoming a Whole Person* Background Scripture: Mark 1:21-39; Luke 4:31-44 Scripture Lesson: Mark 1:21-34 Memory Verse: *"What is this? A new teaching! With authority he commands even the unclean spirits, and they obey him."* Mark 1:27

CHILDREN	Topic: *The Joy of Being Healed* Background Scripture: Mark 1:21-34; Luke 4:31-44 Scripture Lesson: Mark 1:21-28 Memory Verse: *O Lord my God, I cried to thee for help, and thou hast healed me.* Psalm 30:2

DAILY BIBLE READINGS	Mon., Jan. 24: The Demons and the Swine, Matthew 8:28-34. Tues., Jan. 25: Muted by a Demon, Matthew 9:32-38. Wed., Jan. 26: Demon-Possessed Daughter, Matthew 15:21-28. Thurs., Jan. 27: A Son Restored, Matthew 17:14-20. Fri., Jan. 28: A Demon in the Synagogue, Luke 4:31-37. Sat., Jan. 29: Demons Testify, Luke 4:38-44. Sun., Jan. 30: Healer of All, Psalm 103:1-5.

LESSON AIM	To help us realize that Christ can deliver us from all demonic forces in our lives.

LESSON SETTING	Time: About A.D. 27 Place: Capernaum, on the north shore of the Lake of Galilee

164

Power over the Demonic

LESSON OUTLINE

I. The Cure of a Demoniac: Mark 1:21-28
   A. Authority of Jesus' Teaching: vv. 21-22
   B. The Man with an Unclean Spirit: vv. 23-24
   C. The Power of Christ over Demons: vv. 25-26
   D. The Amazement of the People: vv. 27-28

II. The Healing of Peter's Mother-in-Law: Mark 1:29-31
   A. The Place: v. 29
   B. The Condition: v. 30
   C. The Cure: v. 31

III. A Sunset Healing Service: Mark 1:32-34
   A. The Many Needs: v. 32
   B. The Big Crowd: v. 33
   C. The Many Cures: v. 34

IV. An Early Prayer Time: Mark 1:35-39
   A. The Master Praying: v. 35
   B. The Disciples Seeking: vv. 36-37
   C. The Need to Go Farther: vv. 38-39

SUGGESTED INTRODUCTION FOR ADULTS

Power is costly. The Holy Spirit came on Jesus at His baptism (Luke 3:21-22). But this was followed by forty agonizing days of temptation by Satan in the wilderness (4:1-13). It was after this that "Jesus returned in the power of the Spirit into Galilee" (4:14). Soon His fame spread throughout that region (4:15).

But then came another form of opposition, this time from His own townspeople. When He preached in His boyhood synagogue at Nazareth, the people were infuriated and tried to kill Him (Luke 4:16-30). But then we read that He went to Capernaum and taught on the sabbath days in the synagogue, where the people were astonished at His teaching, "for his word was with power" (4:32).

The rest of the fourth chapter of Luke is comprised of the incidents that we study today in Mark's Gospel. We shall note some of the parallels in the two accounts. The striking differences reflect the personalities of the two authors, Mark and Luke.

SUGGESTED INTRODUCTION FOR YOUTH

One of the most important goals of youth is "Becoming a Whole Person." Actually, most "adults" (chronologically) never achieve this in satisfactory measure. But this is what we mean by maturity.

It is only in Christ that one can become a whole person. We have to submit ourselves wholly to Him, so that in Him we find a unified personality. Only divine love can unite the human heart and give it real unity. This is the secret of achieving true personhood. Perhaps it is better to say that we do not achieve it. Rather, we accept it by being identified with Him.

Christ is the only adequate answer to drugs and alcohol. When we are wholly committed to Him we are safe—and only then. The young person who is turned on by Christ has no desire to turn to drugs.

CONCEPTS FOR CHILDREN

1. Jesus has power to meet every human need.
2. He can cure the most difficult cases in modern, drug-ridden society.
3. The safest way is to give our hearts and lives fully to Him while we are young.
4. We can then know the joy of being healed inside.

THE LESSON COMMENTARY

I. THE CURE OF A DEMONIAC: Mark 1:21-28

A. Authority of Jesus' Teaching: vv. 21-22

Jesus made His headquarters at Capernaum, near the northwest corner of the Lake of Galilee, during His great Galilean ministry. The Greek name is *Capharnahum*, meaning "Village of Nahum." It was a sizable city in Jesus' day.

"Straightway"—a key word in Mark, occurring forty times—on the sabbath day Jesus went into the synagogue and taught. Today one can stand in the impressive ruins of an ancient synagogue at Capernaum. In common with most Palestinian synagogues of that day, it faces south, toward Jerusalem. While it is thought that this synagogue was built in the second century—since all the Jewish synagogues are said to have been destroyed by Titus and Hadrian—it may well be a reconstruction of the very one in which Jesus worshiped.

Synagogues served three purposes. First they were places of worship on the sabbath (Saturday). Second, they served as schools on weekdays. (Jesus very likely went to school in such a synagogue.) Third, they were places where the local court met to try cases.

The people were astonished at His "doctrine" (v. 22)—better, "teaching."

Why? Because "he taught them as one that had authority, and not as the scribes"—the official teachers of the law. The scribes had the habit of quoting the opinions of earlier rabbis. But Jesus spoke with direct divine authority.

In the *Expositor's Bible* G. A. Chadwick has a paragraph worth quoting. He says: "And the lapse of ages renders this 'authority' of Christ more wonderful than at first. The world bows down before something other than His clearness of logic or subtlety of inference. He still announces where others argue, He reveals, imposes on us His supremacy, bids us take His yoke and learn. And we still discover in His teaching a freshness and profundity, a universal reach of application and yet an unearthliness of aspect, which suit so unparalleled a claim. Others have constructed cisterns in which to store truth, or aqueducts to convey it from higher levels. Christ is Himself a fountain; and not only so, but the water which He gives, when received aright, becomes in the faithful heart a well of water springing up in new inexhaustible developments" (*Gospel According to St. Mark*, p. 23).

B. The Man with an Unclean Spirit: vv. 23-24

Even in the synagogue service on the sabbath day there was "a man with an unclean spirit." The Greek says literally "in an unclean spirit"—that is, under its power.

Mark prefers the expression "unclean spirit," using it ten times, as compared with twice in Matthew and six times in Luke. Here Luke says that the man "had a spirit of an unclean devil [demon]" (4:33).

The unclean spirit cried out through the man's vocal organs, "What do we have to do with thee?" This is literally "What to us and to thee?"—that is, "What is there between us, or common to us?" Moffatt renders it, "What business have you with us?" Goodspeed translates it, "What do you want of us?" Perhaps still better is "What do you want with us?" (NIV).

The unclean spirit continued with the challenge: "Have you come to destroy us?" Then it declared: "I know who you are—the Holy One of God" (NIV). It is obvious that the demon was afraid of Jesus. It recognized Him as "the Holy One of God," in contrast to its own uncleanness.

C. The Power of Christ over Demons: vv. 25-26

Jesus rebuked the demon. "Hold thy peace" is literally, "Be muzzled!"—that is, "Shut your mouth and keep it shut!" Why did Jesus silence the demon, when it was confessing His deity? The testimony was true, but the character of the witness was not the best! Christ didn't want to have support from such a source. Perhaps, too, He was not yet ready to have His Messiahship proclaimed publicly. That would have hindered His teaching ministry by risking a political revolution against Rome. This is exactly what Jesus was seeking to avoid. So He commanded the demon to come out of the man.

God's word is always spoken with power to carry it out. When Christ commanded, the unclean spirit obeyed Him and came out. But he showed his hateful cruelty, his malicious meanness, by taking out his spite on the man and screaming as he left. "Had

torn him" is better translated "throwing him into convulsions" (NASB) or "shook the man violently" (NIV), for Luke says that the man was left unharmed (Luke 4:35).

D. The Amazement of the People: vv. 27-28

The people were so amazed that they began to ask each other: "What is this? A new teaching—and with authority! He even gives orders to evil spirits and they obey him" (v. 27, NIV). They were used to the pious platitudes and sometimes innocuous sayings of their rabbis. But here was a man who spoke directly to the needs of their hearts and brought conviction of sin. Furthermore, His word was with power. He could even control the demon world. This was unbelievable!

The Greek word for "amazed" may also be translated "terrified." Mark is the only New Testament writer who uses this strong verb (*thambeo*). The early church says that Mark's Gospel gives us the preaching of Peter. The Big Fisherman was a man of the out-of-doors, not of books. As such, he was very observant. He may well have noted the terror that gripped the people as they saw this demonstration of power over demons.

The thing that astonished the crowd was the fact that Jesus cast out the demon by a simple word of command. The Jews of that day practiced exorcism by repeating magical formulae—a sort of mumbo-jumbo. But Jesus spoke briefly and directly, with divine authority. And the result was immediate and complete.

This casting out of the demon in the synagogue at Capernaum is the first miracle of Jesus recorded by Mark and Luke. Matthew omits it.

"News about him spread quickly over the whole region of Galilee" (v. 28, NIV). "Fame" (KJV) is an over-translation; the Greek word *akoe* simply means "a report" or "news." The most literal translation of this verse would be: "And the report of Him went out immediately in all directions into the whole surrounding region of Galilee." Everywhere people went they told excitedly about the wonderful miracle they had witnessed.

William Lane comments: "The people were utterly astonished and alarmed at Jesus' word. There had been no technique, no spells or incantations, no symbolic act. There had been only the word. There was no category familiar to them which explained the sovereign authority with which Jesus spoke and acted" (*The Gospel According to Mark*, The New International Commentary on the New Testament, p. 76).

II. THE HEALING OF PETER'S MOTHER-IN-LAW: Mark 1:29-31

A. The Place: v. 29

"Forthwith" is the same word in the Greek (*eutheos* or *euthys*) that is translated in the King James Version as "straightway" (vv. 10, 18, 20, 21), "immediately" (vv. 31, 42), "forthwith" (vv. 29, 43), and "anon" (v. 30). It is also rendered "as soon as" (5:36; 11:2) and "shortly" (III John 14). It is incorrectly translated "by and by" in Luke 17:7; 21:9. (Today the expression "by and by" means just the opposite of "immediately." It is this use of words in exactly the opposite sense of what they mean today [cf. "let" in II Thessalonians 2:7] that makes the King James Version inadequate for our time.)

When Jesus and His disciples came out of the synagogue, they entered the house of Simon and Andrew, "with James and John." This interesting addition (only in Mark) doubtless reflects Peter's preaching. He would tell it in the first person something like this: "And immediately having gone out of the synagogue we came into our house with James and John. Now my mother-in-law was lying prostrate with a fever, and immediately we tell Him about her. And having come near and taken her by the hand He raised her up. And the fever left her, and she began to wait on us." This reflects the

somewhat awkward changes of tense in the Greek. Mark is trying to reproduce Peter's style.

B. The Condition: v. 30

They found Peter's mother-in-law lying "sick of fever." This is one word in the Greek, *pyressousa*, which comes from *pyr*, "fire." She seemed to be burning up with a sudden, raging fever. Luke, as a physician, uses more technical medical language; he says that she was "taken with a great fever" (Luke 4:38), or as we would say today, "suffering from a high fever" (NIV). Her condition was reported at once to Jesus.

C. The Cure: v. 31

The Master went in "and took her by the hand, and lifted her up." His touch healed her body. The fever immediately disappeared. She got up and "ministered" to them. The Greek verb was commonly used for waiting on table, serving a meal.

This enables us to reconstruct the incident. Peter was taking the Master home for dinner after the service at the synagogue. Usually the Jews did not eat before such a service. The dinner that followed was the big meal of the day. Probably the mother-in-law had been well when they left and had planned to have the meal ready when they returned. But she was seized by one of the sudden fevers common to that region and was lying prostrate in bed.

"It was an embarrassing moment for the host. But the guest of honor quickly set everything right. As soon as Jesus heard about the situation He entered the room where the sick woman was, took her by the hand and lifted her up. Healed of the fever, she quickly went to work and soon the meal was ready. With what joy must she have waited on the One who had just healed her! It was another instance showing Jesus' love for the home and the family" (Ralph Earle, *The Gospel According to Mark*, pp. 37-38).

We can get at least the hint of a lesson here. We are not healed just to enjoy health for ourselves, but so that we can serve. We are "saved to serve," not just to enjoy life. A healed (or well) person has an added responsibility.

III. A SUNSET HEALING SERVICE: Mark 1:32-34

A. The Many Needs: v. 32

"That evening after sunset the people brought to Jesus all the sick and demon-possessed" (NIV). Why after sunset? The Jewish sabbath lasted from sunset Friday to sunset Saturday. The Mosaic Law forbade carrying any burden on the sabbath.

It was an exciting day in Capernaum. Doubtless what had happened in the synagogue that morning was being talked of all over town. Also many heard about the miraculous healing that had taken place in Peter's house.

People could hardly wait until the sun went down. Then they came hurrying to Peter's home, bringing their loved ones who were sick or demon-possessed. For that day Jesus had miraculously cured both of these severe ailments.

B. The Big Crowd: v. 33

"And all the city was gathered together at the door." Of course it would not be possible for the entire population to congregate in the narrow street in front of Peter's house. But as he looked out the front, it seemed to him that all the city was there. And we can easily imagine impetuous Peter describing it in those terms. This is one of the countless vivid touches in Mark's Gospel that give us an eye-witness view of scenes in Jesus' life.

C. The Many Cures: v. 34

Jesus "healed many that were sick of divers diseases." Recently a man told us with all seriousness that when he was a boy and heard this and similar passages read from the pulpit, he actually thought the reference was to diseases suffered by divers! The word "divers" is simply the obsolete spelling of "diverse." So the correct meaning is "various" (NIV).

Jesus also "cast out many devils." As we have noted a number of times, the Greek word means "demons," not devils.

The account of this incident concludes with the statement that Jesus was not permitting (imperfect tense) the demons to speak. This was His regular policy.

"What a glorious sunset scene that was! Many people that night in Capernaum had their first good, painless sleep in months. The touch of the Divine had brought healing and health" (Earle, *Mark*, p. 38).

IV. AN EARLY PRAYER TIME: Mark 1:35-39

A. The Master Praying: v. 35

Jesus had had a very busy day in Capernaum—probably a typical day! In the morning He had cast the demon out of a man in the synagogue. About noon He had healed Peter's mother-in-law. And in the evening He had ministered in both ways to a large crowd of people. He was doubtless weary when He finally retired.

But very early the next morning He got up and went out to a quiet spot for prayer. Typically, Mark piles up words to emphasize how early it really was. In fact, he uses three adverbs in succession. The first, *prioi*, means "in the morning, early." The second, *ennycha* (only here in New Testament) means "by night." The third, *lian* means "exceedingly." Mark alone notes that it was before daybreak. Of these three adverbs Vincent Taylor writes: "The strange temporal phrase appears to reflect the point of view of those within the house who discovered that Jesus was gone" (*The Gospel According to St. Mark*, p. 183). They probably wakened at dawn; but the Master had already left.

Jesus sought "a solitary place"

outside of the town, where He could pray without interruption. Often it is after our busiest and seemingly most successful occasions in Christian service that we most need to get alone with God. The point we dare not miss is that if Jesus needed to take time out for prayer, how much more do we! Bishop John C. Ryle comments: "A praying master, like Jesus, can have no prayerless servants" (*Expository Thoughts on the Gospels*, I, 18).

One of the greatest lessons we can learn from this incident is the importance of prayer. J. Newton Davies puts it this way: "To meet the tests and challenges of Jerusalem one must have a Bethany and a Mount of Olives. To live nobly in the living room of life depends on our having an inner chamber whose doors we can close and in whose silence we can hear the words of God by which alone man can live" ("Mark," *Abingdon Bible Commentary*, p. 1001).

It appears clear that Jesus was seeking guidance from His Father as to what His next move should be. Someone has well said, "Prayer is a holy conference with God." We need not only power, but direction. Jesus sent the Holy Spirit to give us both. But we must wait on Him to receive guidance.

B. The Disciples Seeking: vv. 36-37

"And Simon and they that were with him followed after him" (v. 36).

Typically, Mark uses here a strong verb—they "hunted him down." That this took some time is implied by the next clause: "And when they had found him" (v. 37). He was hidden away in a solitary place so that they had to search for Him.

They greeted Him with: "Everyone is looking for you!" (NIV). People were already gathering at Peter's house, eager for another big healing service.

C. The Need to Go Farther: vv. 38-39

But Jesus had received other directions from His Father. So He replied, "Let us go into the next towns that I may preach there also" (v. 38). He had come primarily to preach the gospel and save men's souls. The needs of the body must be kept secondary to those of the spirit. One of the most important factors in life is that of keeping our priorities straight. Healing has a place in the Christian ministry. But Jesus has given us a clear example: Healing must never take priority over preaching. Jesus turned His back on the crowd waiting to be healed—doubtless there were also curiosity-seekers—and went to other places to preach.

The word for "towns" is a compound, *komopoleis*, found only here in the New Testament. It literally means "village-cities." It probably refers to villages with large populations, but without city walls. Josephus claims that there were multitudes of towns in Galilee, the least of which contained fifteen-thousand inhabitants. That is probably an exaggeration. But it does indicate that Galilee was heavily populated in Jesus' day.

The last clause of verse 38, "for therefore came I forth"—"That is why I have come" (NIV)—has been debated as to its meaning. Many commentators refer it to His coming from heaven to earth. He came forth from the Father to proclaim God's message to men. His main mission was not healing but preaching. We favor this interpretation.

DISCUSSION QUESTIONS

1. Why was demon-possession common in Christ's day?
2. What may be the relationship today between demon-worship and demon-possession?
3. What influence has "The Exorcist" had on the situation?
4. How may demons be cast out?
5. What demonic forces operate in men's hearts?
6. How may these be cast out?

On the other hand, some good commentators say that Jesus was referring to His coming out of Capernaum that morning. Vincent Taylor even suggests a third interpretation: "It is best to conclude that Mark has in mind the mission of Jesus in Galilee" (*Mark*, p. 184).

That the first of these interpretations is preferable is supported by the parallel in Luke's Gospel (4:43): "for therefore am I sent." It hardly seems likely He would say that He was sent out of Capernaum to preach the gospel. But the New Testament reiterates the truth that Jesus was sent from God, sent from heaven to earth in order to bring the message of redemption to mankind.

Verse 39 is one of several summaries of Jesus' Galilean ministry: "So he traveled throughout Galilee, preaching in their synagogues and driving out demons" (NIV). Josephus says that in his day (the first century) there were "two hundred and forty towns and villages in Galilee" (*Life*, #45). While that may well be an overstatement, there were more of them than Jesus could give adequate attention to in the short span of His ministry (probably less than two years in Galilee). But the term "village-cities" would suggest that He concentrated on the large towns.

CONTEMPORARY APPLICATION

The question is often raised: Is there such a thing as demon-possession today? Some would claim that there is no such thing; it was just an ancient, superstitious explanation of insanity. Others go to the opposite extreme and assert that it is very common.

Probably, as is often the case, the truth lies midway between. It does seem likely that because of a great increase in Satan-worship in this country today, demon-possession has become increasingly widespread. But Christ still has power to cast out all demons.

February 6, 1977

POWER OVER SICKNESS AND DEATH

DEVOTIONAL READING	Luke 7:1-10

ADULTS

Topic: *Power over Sickness and Death*

Background Scripture: Mark 5:21-43; Luke 7:1-23

Scripture Lesson: Luke 7:11-23

Memory Verse: *"Go and tell John what you have seen and heard: the blind receive their sight, the lame walk, lepers are cleansed, and the deaf hear, the dead are raised up, the poor have good news preached to them."* Luke 7:22

YOUTH

Topic: *Facing Life's Crises*

Background Scripture: Mark 5:21-43; Luke 7:1-23

Scripture Lesson: Luke 7:11-23

Memory Verse: *When I am afraid, I put my trust in thee.* Psalm 56:3

CHILDREN

Topic: *Power over Death*

Background Scripture: Mark 5:21-43; Luke 7:1-23

Scripture Lesson: Luke 7:11-18

Memory Verse: *Even though I walk through the valley of the shadow of death, I fear no evil; for thou art with me.* Psalm 23:4

DAILY BIBLE READINGS

Mon., Jan. 31: A Leper Healed, Matthew 8:1-4.
Tues., Feb. 1: Healed and Forgiven, Matthew 9:1-8.
Wed., Feb. 2: Jairus's Daughter, Mark 5:21-23, 35-43.
Thurs., Feb. 3: Timid but Believing, Mark 5:25-34.
Fri., Feb. 4: A Great Faith, Luke 7:1-10.
Sat., Feb. 5: Sight to the Blind, Mark 8:22-26.
Sun., Feb. 7: A Friend Resurrected, John 11:33-45.

LESSON AIM

To help us understand and appreciate Jesus' power over sickness and death.

LESSON SETTING

Time: About A.D. 28

Place: Galilee

LESSON OUTLINE

Power over Sickness and Death

    I. An Anxious Father: Mark 5:21-24

172

II. Healing of the Woman with Hemorrhage: Mark 5:25-34

III. Raising of Jairus's Daughter: Mark 5:35-43

IV. Healing of the Centurion's Servant: Luke 7:1-10
    A. The Request for Healing: vv. 1-3
    B. The Plea of Friends: vv. 4-5
    C. The Faith of the Centurion: vv. 6-8
    D. The Reward of Faith: vv. 9-10

V. Raising of the Widow's Son: Luke 7:11-17
    A. Approaching Nain: v. 11
    B. The Sorrowing Mother: vv. 12-13
    C. The Miracle of Raising the Dead: vv. 14-15
    D. The Reaction of the People: vv. 16-17

VI. Jesus and John the Baptist: Luke 7:18-23
    A. John's Concern: vv. 18-20
    B. Jesus' Ministry: v. 21
    C. Jesus' Credentials: v. 22
    D. A Gentle Reproof: v. 23

SUGGESTED INTRODUCTION FOR ADULTS

All four Gospels present Jesus as the Conqueror of disease and death. They record at least twenty instances of His healing individuals—of all kinds of ailments, even blindness from birth. They also have numerous incidents of Jesus healing many people on certain occasions, such as the one we found in our last lesson (at the sunset healing service). Jesus was able to heal any kind of illness that confronted Him in His earthly ministry. And He is still able to heal every disease.

But He was also the mighty Conqueror over death. In the Gospels we have three incidents of Jesus raising the dead. Two of them are in today's lesson. The first was the daughter of Jairus, who had been dead only a few minutes. Unbelieving critics label this a case of natural resuscitation. The second was the son of the widow of Nain. He had been dead for a few hours. Yet Jesus was able to restore him to life. The third and climactic case is recorded in the eleventh chapter of John's Gospel. Lazarus had been dead four days—no one can doubt that *he* was really dead! But Jesus brought him back to life.

SUGGESTED INTRODUCTION FOR YOUTH

Our topic is: "Facing Life's Crises." In the passages of Scripture we study today these are the crises of sickness and death.

What do we do when someone gets sick? "Call the doctor," you say. Yes, that is the sensible thing. But why not also pray? Jesus Christ is "the same yesterday and today and forever," the Bible declares (Hebrews 13:8). If He could heal people while on earth, He can certainly heal people now. And He does. But we believe that often He chooses to heal through medicine and surgery.

We must remember that the medical situation in Jesus'

day was as different from ours as darkness is from light. We have in writing some of the ancient rabbis' prescriptions, and they are on the level of the witch doctors of today. So Jesus had to heal in order to meet the need.

But Christ is able to help us face all the different kinds of crises we meet. Whatever they are, we can face them successfully with Him.

CONCEPTS FOR CHILDREN

1. Death is seemingly the greatest tragedy of life.
2. But to die in Christ is victory, not tragedy.
3. However, death does bring sorrow to the loved ones left behind.
4. Jesus can minister effectively to that sorrow.

THE LESSON COMMENTARY

I. AN ANXIOUS FATHER:
Mark 5:21-24

All three Synoptic Gospels have a unique combination of miracles at this point. Jesus starts for the house of Jairus to heal his daughter. On the way a woman touches His robe and is healed. He continues to Jairus's house and restores to life his daughter, who had meanwhile died. The two miracles are sandwiched into one account.

Jesus had just delivered the Gadarene demoniac from demon-possession (5:1-20). That was on the east side of the Lake of Galilee. Now He returns to the busy west side of the lake. As usual, He found a big crowd waiting for Him as soon as He landed (v. 21).

A synagogue ruler named Jairus came hurrying to Him with an urgent plea. His daughter was at the point of death, and he, perhaps tearfully, begged Jesus to come and heal her. Most of the synagogue rulers seem to have been opposed to Jesus. But here was one who believed that Jesus could heal a desperate case of illness. Doubtless he had witnessed some of Jesus' miracles.

The Master did not hesitate, but compassionately set out with the distraught father. A great crowd followed Him (v. 24).

II. HEALING OF THE WOMAN WITH HEMORRHAGE:
Mark 5:25-34

There was a woman in the town who had been hemorrhaging for twelve years. The doctors had not been able to help her. In typical layman fashion, Mark tells it "just like it was." He says that she "had suffered many things of many physicians, and had spent all that she had, and was nothing bettered, but rather grew worse" (v. 26). Those were the facts! But Luke the physician has to protect his profession. He admits that she had spent all her money on doctors, but adds that "no one could heal her" (8:43, NIV). Hers was an incurable case.

That she could well have "suffered" many things from the physicians of that day is well documented. Here is a prescription given in the Jewish Talmud: "Take of the gum of Alexandria the weight of a zuzee; of alum the same; of crocus the same. Let them be bruised together, and given in wine to the woman that has an issue of blood. If this does not benefit, take of Persian onions three logs [pints]; boil them in wine, and give her to drink, and say, 'Arise from thy flux.' But if this do no good, take a handful of cummin, a handful of crocus, and a handful of fenugreek. Let these be boiled in wine and give them to her to drink, and say 'Arise from thy flux!' If these do no good, let them dig seven ditches, in which let them burn some cuttings of vines, not yet four years old. Let her take in her hand a cup of wine, and let them lead her away from this ditch, and make her sit down over that. And let them remove her from that, and make her sit down over another, saying to her at each remove, 'Arise from thy flux!' " (Quoted by Marvin R. Vincent, *Word Studies in the New Testament*, I, 189).

When this woman heard about Jesus, she came in "the press"—the Greek simply says "the crowd"—slipped up behind Him, and touched His cloak. Immediately she was healed. And she knew it; she felt it in her body (v. 29).

Just as suddenly, Jesus knew that "virtue" had gone out of Him (v. 30). The Greek word is *dynamis*, which means "power." Divine power, healing power, had gone out of Jesus. It cost Him something to heal people. And it still costs us to have a ministry of spiritual healing to others.

Jesus, turning around in the crowd, asked, "Who touched my clothes?" The disciples expostulated with their Master: "Why, everybody's touching you! What do you mean by asking, 'Who touched me?' " (paraphrased).

"But Jesus kept looking around"—imperfect tense—"to see who had done it" (v. 32, NIV). The woman began to tremble with fear. "According to the Levitical law (Lev. 15:19) she was unclean and her presence defiled all those she touched. Technically, she had rendered Jesus unclean! But how different was the actual case. Instead of her defiling Him, 'power' (*dynamis*, 'dynamite,' 'dynamic') had gone out of Him and healed her. Spirit-filled Christians ought to touch unclean people with victorious divine power, instead of being defiled by them" (Ralph Earle, *Mark*, Evangelical Commentary, p. 75).

The woman fell at His feet and "told him all the truth" (v. 33). With tender love Jesus said to her: "Daughter, thy faith hath made thee whole; go in peace, and be whole of thy plague" (v. 34). What matchless comfort these words must have brought to her heart!

III. RAISING OF JAIRUS'S DAUGHTER:
Mark 5:35-43

Meanwhile Jairus had been standing "on pins and needles," as it were, anxiously waiting for Jesus to get to his house and heal his daughter. It must have been very trying to him to watch Jesus talking to this woman!

To add to his frustration, just then some messengers from his home stepped up to him. " 'Your daughter is dead,' they said. 'Why bother the teacher any more?' " (v. 35, NIV). It seemed that the Master didn't care anyhow, the way He was stopping to talk!

But Jesus quickly calmed Jairus's fears. The best translation of verse 36 is: "Ignoring what they said, Jesus told the synagogue ruler, 'Don't be afraid; just believe' " (NIV). Jesus paid no attention to the death notice. Literally He said: "Stop being afraid; keep on believing."

Only Peter, James, and John were allowed to follow Jesus (v. 37). They were the three of the inner circle, who were also alone with Him on two other occasions: on the Mount of Transfiguration and in the Garden of Gethsemane.

When Jesus reached the synagogue ruler's house He found a great commotion, with people weeping and wailing loudly (v. 38).

The Master took command of the situation. First, He reproved the people: "Why all this commotion and wailing? The child is not dead but asleep" (v. 39, NIV). She was physically dead, but soon He would waken her from the sleep of death. Those who are in Christ will never be "dead"; they will "sleep in Jesus" (I Thessalonians 4:13-14).

The mourners "laughed him to scorn" (v. 40). Expelling the unbelievers from the room, Jesus took the parents and His three disciples and went in where the child was. Taking the young girl by the hand, He spoke just two words in Aramaic, *Talitha koum*, which means "Little girl, I say to you, get up" (v. 41, NIV). It has been beautifully suggested that these may have been the very words that the mother used each morning in calling her little daughter.

Immediately the girl got up and began to walk. "For she was of the age of twelve years" (v. 42) seems an odd statement. Perhaps it is put in to show that this "little girl" was old enough to walk. (There is a coincidence with the woman's twelve-year hemorrhage.)

Thoughtfully Jesus instructed the parents to give the child something to eat. He had performed the miracle of restoring her to life (cf. Luke 8:55); they must keep her alive. This is a lesson for us.

IV. HEALING OF THE CENTURION'S SERVANT: Luke 7:1-10

A. The Request for Healing: vv. 1-3

The seventh chapter of Luke follows his version of the so-called Sermon on the Mount. Now Jesus returns to Capernaum to continue His ministry of teaching and healing.

A centurion—Roman officer in charge of a "century" (a hundred soldiers)—had a servant whom he "valued highly" (NIV). This servant "was sick, and ready to die" (v. 2).

When the centurion heard about Jesus, he sent some of the Jewish elders to Him to ask Him to come and heal his servant.

B. The Plea of Friends: vv. 4-5

When the elders arrived where Jesus was "they pleaded earnestly with him, 'This man deserves to have you do this, because he loves our nation

and has built our synagogue'" (NIV). It is an interesting fact that all the centurions in the New Testament are spoken of in a favorable way. One thinks of Cornelius (Acts 10) and of the centurion who was kind to Paul (Acts 27:43). This is in contrast to both the governors above them and the common soldiers beneath. As with the case of Cornelius, this centurion was friendly to the Jews and probably worshiped with them. He had actually built a new synagogue for them.

C. The Faith of the Centurion: vv. 6-8

Jesus acceded to the request of the Jewish elders and started out with them for the centurion's house. But before He arrived there, the officer sent other friends to tell the Lord not to trouble Himself; the wealthy Roman centurion did not feel he deserved to have Jesus enter his home; in fact, he didn't consider himself worthy to come to Him in person.

Then this foreigner expressed a truly remarkable faith: "But say the word, and my servant will be healed" (v. 7, NIV). Frederic L. Godet comments: "How are we to explain the existence of such faith in this man? We must bear in mind the words of ver. 3: having *heard of Jesus*. The fame of the miracles of Jesus had reached even him. There was one cure especially, which Jesus had wrought at Capernaum itself . . . which presented a remarkable similarity to that which the centurion besought—the cure of the nobleman's son (John iv.). Perhaps his knowledge of this miracle is the most natural mode of explaining the faith implied in the message which he addresses to Jesus by the mouth of his friends" (*A Commentary on the Gospel of St. Luke*, I, 338).

The reasoning of the centurion (v. 8) was very logical. It shows keen insight and common sense. Plummer paraphrases it this way: "I know from personal experience what a word from one in authority can do. A word from my superiors secures my obedience, and a word from me secures the obedience of my subordinates. Thou, who art under no man, and hast authority over unseen powers, hast only to say a word and the sickness is healed" (*A Critical and Exegetical Commentary on the Gospel According to St. Luke*, International Critical Commentary, p. 196).

D. The Reward of Faith: vv. 9-10

Only twice are we told that Jesus "marveled"—once at the unbelief of his own fellow Jews at Nazareth, and here at the amazing faith of a foreigner. No wonder He exclaimed: "I have not found so great faith, no, not in Israel" (v. 9).

The Jews required signs before they would believe in Jesus. Not so the centurion: "His faith is greater than that of people who desire to see visible or tangible signs before they can believe" (J. Norval Geldenhuys, *Commentary on the Gospel of Luke*, New International Commentary on the New Testament, p. 221, n. 8).

When the messengers returned to the house, they found the servant "whole." The Greek means "in good health."

V. RAISING OF THE WIDOW'S SON: Luke 7:11-17

A. Approaching Nain: v. 11

Leaving Capernaum, Jesus came, with His disciples and many other followers, to Nain, where he raised the widow's son. The incident is recorded only by Luke, who emphasizes especially the compassion of Christ.

"*Nain* is now an Arab village called Nein. It is on the lower slope of a knoll called 'Little Hermon,' located between Mount Gilboa and Mount Tabor in the Plain of Esdraelon (which forms a natural boundary between Galilee and Samaria). It is five or six miles southeast of Nazareth and about twenty-five miles (a day's journey) from Capernaum. . . . While this place today is only a small village of about

two hundred inhabitants, the ruins of ancient Nain show that it was once a large town" (Ralph Earle, *Wesleyan Bible Commentary*, IV, 249). As one drives along the main highway today, he can see the village of Nein on the hillside.

B. The Sorrowing Mother: vv. 12-13

As Jesus approached "the gate of the city"—which shows that it was a walled town—He passed the cemetery, where tombs can still be seen in the hillside. Before He reached the gate, He met a funeral procession coming out of the city. We are told the dead man was "the only son of his mother, and she was a widow" (v. 12). That she was a widow could quickly be ascertained by the fact that no man walked with her. That the deceased was her only son was evident from the absence of young men mourning with her.

It is hard for us today to realize the full import of this. At that time a widow was often looked down on. Her oldest son took his father's place as the head of the household. He was his mother's only support, both socially and financially. But further, this only son had been the only one on whom she could shower her affection. "When he died, it seemed as if all the lights went out. Not only was she left to live alone, but she was bereft of all financial support. In those days a widow did not find a job in office, store, or factory. She faced not only loneliness but even the threat of starvation, except as her neighbors might come to her rescue. This was no ordinary funeral; it was a black, bleak one" (Earle, *Wesleyan Commentary*).

When "the Lord"—Luke's favorite designation for Jesus—saw the woman, He "had compassion on her." The Greek aorist is better translated, "was gripped with compassion" toward her. This was always Jesus' immediate reaction to human need. "He bore the sorrows of humanity not only on the cross in those last awful hours, but also on His heart during the days of His earthly ministry" (Earle, *Wesleyan Commentary*).

The first thing Jesus did was to speak to the mother's broken heart. "Don't cry," He said. This was no flippant remark, but a gentle admonition filled with divine love. He had a right to tell her not to weep, because He knew that in a few moments her sorrow would be turned into joy.

C. The Miracle of Raising the Dead: vv. 14-15

In accordance with Jewish custom, the mother was walking in front of the coffin. So Jesus addressed her first. Then He went on and touched "the bier." This was either an open wicker casket—the Jews did not use a closed one—or else a board on which the body was laid. Because of the lack of modern embalming techniques, and also the hot weather in Palestine, it was required that bodies must be buried on the day the person died. So this young man had been dead only a few hours.

When Jesus touched the coffin, the funeral procession came to a halt. Then the Lord again spoke words of power: "Young man, I say unto thee, Arise" (v. 14). This was a perfectly

absurd thing to say to a dead man— except that *Jesus* said it. Godet comments: "Among the Jews the bier was not covered; it was a simple plank, with a somewhat raised edge. The body, wrapped in its shroud, was therefore visible to all. Jesus lays His hand on the bier, as if to arrest this fugitive from life. The bearers, struck by the majesty of this gesture, which was at once natural and symbolical, stopped. There is a matchless grandeur in this *soi lego*: "*I say to thee, . . .* to thee who seemest no longer able to hear the voice of the living . . .'" (*Luke*, p. 341).

Then the miracle took place: "And he that was dead sat up, and began to speak. And he delivered him to his mother" (v. 15). Geldenhuys writes: "Because Jesus is the Lord of life and death and possesses all power over the invisible realm to which the spirit of the deceased youth had already departed, the young man's spirit is again joined to his body in obedience to the Lord's command. Out of His deep sympathy with the widowed mother Jesus does not ask the youth to follow Him but gives him back to his mother" (*Luke*, p. 223). She would need him!

D. The Reaction of the People: vv. 16-17

As would be expected, the witnesses to this miracle were struck with awe. They concluded that a great prophet had appeared among them and that God had visited His people to help them (v. 16).

The report of this spread "throughout all Judaea, and throughout all the region round about" (v. 17). Probably "Judaea" should here be taken in its wider connotation as "the land of the Jews"—that is, all Palestine. The surrounding region would then be Perea, the Decapolis, Syria, and Phoenicia (modern Lebanon).

Jesus is Lord of both life and death. When we are fully committed to Him we are safe for time and eternity.

DISCUSSION QUESTIONS

1. What lessons can we learn from the experience of Jairus?
2. What are some differences that might be noted between Jairus's daughter and the woman with the hemorrhage?
3. Name some spiritual applications that might be made.
4. What is true faith, as exemplified by the centurion?
5. What characteristics of Christ are obvious in the story of the widow's son at Nain?
6. What allowances should be made for John the Baptist?

VI. JESUS AND JOHN THE BAPTIST:
Luke 7:18-23

A. John's Concern: vv. 18-20

The disciples of John the Baptist told him what had taken place in Nain. At this time John was in prison and unable to travel. So he called two of his disciples and sent them to Jesus with the urgent query: "Are you the one who was to come, or should we expect someone else?" (v. 19, NIV). Dutifully the two men confronted Jesus with the question (v. 20).

How could John, who had seen the Spirit descend on Jesus at His baptism, and who had heard the Father's voice from heaven acclaiming Jesus as His Son, now question whether Jesus was the Messiah?

Three answers have been suggested. Chrysostom (fourth century) thought that the question was asked for the sake of John's disciples, not for his own sake. Luther and Calvin accepted this idea. Some have felt that John's own faith was failing. Plummer prefers a third view: that it was his patience, not his faith, that was failing. He was anxious for the Messiah to set up His kingdom and deliver the Jews from Roman bondage. Perhaps it was a combination of the second and third. We must remember that John was languishing in prison.

B. Jesus' Ministry: v. 21

Christ let the messengers from John stay with Him for awhile and observe His work. During that time "Jesus cured many who had diseases, sicknesses and evil spirits, and gave sight to many who were blind" (NIV). These disciples of John could be personal witnesses of what they had seen with their own eyes.

C. Jesus' Credentials: v. 22

The Master then instructed the messengers to return to John and tell him what they had seen and heard: "the blind see, the lame walk, the lepers are cleansed, the deaf hear, the dead are raised, to the poor the gospel is preached." The last clause is especially significant. "The gospel is preached" is all one word in Greek, *euangelizontai*. The poor were being evangelized. This was Jesus' greatest credential as Messiah—that He demonstrated divine love for the despised poor of earth.

D. A Gentle Reproof: v. 23

Jesus added: "And blessed is he, whosoever shall not be offended in me"—or "caused to stumble in me." Was Jesus' lack of political assertion a cause of stumbling to John? Perhaps so. But John must not allow it to be so. He must revise his concepts of the Messiah to fit the compassionate ministry of Christ.

CONTEMPORARY APPLICATION

Geldenhuys has a beautiful comment on the implications of Jesus' miracle at Nain. He writes: "In this story the Saviour's sympathy with the sorrowing and His absolute divine power over the invisible spirit-world are gloriously revealed. We see Him here as the loving Comforter, the Victor over death, and the Reuniter of separated dear ones. What He did here for the widowed mother and son He will one day do for all the faithful in a perfect and final form. He will bring full comfort, He will raise all His people in incorruptibility, and will reunite us, in the heavenly realm, with our loved ones who have died in Him" (*Luke*, p. 223).

POWER TO FORGIVE SIN

DEVOTIONAL READING	Mark 2:1-12

ADULTS

Topic: *Jesus Forgives Sin*

Background Scripture: Mark 2:1-12; Luke 7:36-50

Scripture Lesson: Luke 7:36-50

Memory Verse: *If we confess our sins, he is faithful and just, and will forgive our sins and cleanse us from all unrighteousness.* I John 1:9

YOUTH

Topic: *You Can Be Forgiven*

Background Scripture: Mark 2:1-12; Luke 7:36-50

Scripture Lesson: Luke 7:36-50

Memory Verse: *If we confess our sins, he is faithful and just, and will forgive our sins and cleanse us from all unrighteousness.* I John 1:9

CHILDREN

Topic: *The Need for Forgiveness*

Background Scripture: Mark 2:1-12; Luke 7:36-50

Scripture Lesson: Luke 7:36-39, 48-50

Memory Verse: *If we confess our sins, he is faithful and just, and will forgive our sins and cleanse us from all unrighteousness.* I John 1:9

DAILY BIBLE READINGS

Mon., Feb. 7: Sins White as Snow, Isaiah 1:11-18.
Tues., Feb. 8: Trangression Covered, Psalm 32:1-5.
Wed., Feb. 9: Faith Brings Forgiveness, Mark 2:1-5.
Thurs., Feb. 10: Power Proven, Mark 2:6-12.
Fri., Feb. 11: Forgiving and Forgiven, Matthew 18:23-35.
Sat., Feb. 12: Love and Forgiveness, Luke 7:41-48.
Sun., Feb. 13: Confession Brings Forgiveness, I John 1:1-10.

LESSON AIM   To help us appreciate Christ's free forgiveness of our sins.

LESSON SETTING

Time: About A.D. 28

Place: Capernaum and some other place in Galilee

LESSON OUTLINE

Power to Forgive Sin

I. Healing of the Paralytic: Mark 2:1-12
   A. The Place: v. 1
   B. The Crowd: v. 2

C. The Paralytic: vv. 3-4
D. The Pronouncement: v. 5
E. The Complaint: vv. 6-7
F. The Question: vv. 8-9
G. The Command: vv. 10-11
H. The Miracle: v. 12

II. Forgiveness of the Penitent: Luke 7:36-50
A. At Dinner in a Pharisee's House: v. 36
B. A Repentant Prostitute: vv. 37-38
C. A Critical Pharisee: v. 39
D. A Challenging Christ: v. 40
E. A Parable of Two Debtors: vv. 41-43
F. An Insulting Host: vv. 44-46
G. A Forgiven Penitent: vv. 47-48
H. A Critical Audience: v. 49
I. A Saved Woman: v. 50

SUGGESTED INTRODUCTION FOR ADULTS

The most basic need of every human being is for forgiveness. The Bible says, "All have sinned" (Romans 3:23). Therefore all have to be forgiven if they are going to enjoy peace here and heaven hereafter.

But forgiveness must be preceded by penitence. And it must bring a new life in Christ. Otherwise only the past is taken care of: the present and the future still threaten us.

Another prerequisite for forgiveness is faith. The paralytic had faith to be healed, or he would not have let his four friends carry him to Jesus. The woman had faith, or she would not have entered the Pharisee's house.

The story of the paralytic emphasizes the faith aspect particularly, that of the woman the aspect of repentance. But Jesus discerned that both of them had repentance and faith. And so He forgave their sins freely.

In seeking to help people find forgiveness we need to emphasize both of these preliminary requirements. If they are going to find a satisfactory experience with Christ they need sincere repentance and solid faith.

SUGGESTED INTRODUCTION FOR YOUTH

"You Can Be Forgiven." What a glorious, comforting truth! Many young people today are tired of their life of sin and want to find a sense of forgiveness for the past. But they don't know where to seek. If we have found forgiveness we should rejoice in it and try to help others find it. If we have not found it, the Savior waits to give it to us.

What a horrible life this would be if we could never find forgiveness! We ought to be eternally and daily thankful that Christ died for us on the cross so we could be forgiven. One of the central emphases of both the Old and New Testament is that "without the shedding of blood there is no remission (forgiveness) of sin." That is why Christ had to shed His blood for us, so that we could be saved. Thank God that you can be forgiven!

CONCEPTS FOR
CHILDREN

1. We all need forgiveness because we have all sinned.
2. The worst sinner can find forgiveness.
3. But even though we have not lived a wicked life, we still need forgiveness.
4. That is because sin is an inner attitude of wanting our own way rather than God's way.

THE LESSON COMMENTARY

I. HEALING OF THE PARALYTIC: Mark 2:1-12

A. The Place: v. 1

Jesus had been on a preaching tour of the towns of Galilee, but after some days returned to Capernaum. "It was noised that he was in the house" is simply, "It was heard, 'He is at home.'" The Greek could equally well be translated either way, since both direct and indirect discourse are expressed the same way in Greek.

B. The Crowd: v. 2

A big crowd gathered quickly. Probably most came out of curiosity, eager to see some more miracles. We may hope that many wanted to hear His teaching.

So many came that they filled the house—evidently Peter's house, which Jesus had now made His home. Finally "there was no room left, not even outside the door" (NIV). "He preached the word unto them" is literally "He was speaking to them the word." Although most of them may have been hoping to see a miracle, Jesus realized that what they needed far more was to hear the word of God preached. So He gave them what they needed, not necessarily what they wanted.

C. The Paralytic: vv. 3-4

"Some men came, bringing to him a paralytic, carried by four of them" (v. 3, NIV). "One sick of the palsy" (KJV) is all one word in Greek, *paralyticon*. Leave off the case ending, and you have our word "paralytic." Most of our medical terms come from the Greek, since the Greeks had the best physicians in the ancient world.

One of the outstanding characteristics of Mark's Gospel is the addition of vivid details that are not given by Matthew or Luke. While Mark's Gospel is the shortest of the four, usually his account of a dramatic incident in the life of Christ is longer than that found in the other two Synoptic Gospels. Such is the case here. Mark alone records the fact that the paralytic was carried by four men. He is also the only one who says (v. 2) that there was no longer any room because of the crowd.

In line with this, Mark now says, "And when they could not come nigh unto him for the press" (v. 4). That is, they could not push their way in through the door. Today "the press" means newsmen. All up-to-date translations simply say "the crowd," which is the meaning of the Greek word.

Luke (5:19) says that they "went upon the housetop." The homes in Palestine—until very recently, in Israel—were made of stone or sun-dried brick, because of the scarcity of lumber. Always there were stone steps on the outside leading up to the roof.

Mark tells what happened when they got to the housetop. He says that they "uncovered the roof where he [Jesus] was: and when they had broken it up, they let down the bed wherein the sick of the palsy lay." The Greek literally says, "They unroofed the roof"—that is, took off the top covering. "When they had broken it up" is one word in Greek. It means "having dug through." Luke says that they let him down through the tiles.

Mark uses a different word for bed than Matthew or Luke. They both use the common word for "couch"—something on which one reclines. But Mark has here four times (vv. 4, 9, 11,

12) the word *krabatton*, which comes from the Latin *grabatus*. It simply meant a rude "pallet" (NASB), or "mat" (NIV), not much more than a heavy blanket or quilt. Each of the four helpers took hold of a corner of this, using it as a stretcher.

"By a study of the structure of a typical Palestinian home a person can reconstruct the incident and clarify matters a great deal. The poorer people usually lived in one-story dwellings with a flat roof, reached by an outside stairway. The roof was made by laying beams, then covering them with brush or thatch. On this was spread dirt, which was rolled hard to shed the rain. Often grass grew in this soil, and goats sometimes were seen cropping the grass on these roofs. Sometimes slabs of tile or dried clay were laid across the beams to hold the dirt. This was evidently the case with the house in question (cf. Luke 5:19).

"The picture then becomes clear. The four men managed to get the helpless man up on the low, flat roof. There they uncovered a section of it, scraping away the dirt. Next they dug down through the brush and slabs which held the dirt, forming a hole big enough for lowering the paralytic on his pallet" (Ralph Earle, *Mark*, Evangelical Commentary, p. 42).

This incident emphasizes for us the need of persistence and perseverance in bringing people to Christ. We must not quit because of hindrances and obstacles.

Mark's vivid details doubtless reflect Peter's description of this incident. It was probably his house that had a hole dug in the roof, which he had to repair later! He remembered the episode very vividly—he was probably sitting near Jesus and, so, under the hole.

D. The Pronouncement: v. 5

"When Jesus saw their faith [the faith of the four, and probably also of the sick man] he said to the paralytic, 'Son, your sins are forgiven'" (NIV).

"Thy sins be forgiven thee" (KJV) sounds like a prayer or wish. But the Greek is clearly a declaration. In fact, many old Greek manuscripts have the perfect tense here, "Your sins have been forgiven." It was an accomplished fact when Jesus uttered the words of forgiveness. For, as our lesson topic suggests, He has "power to forgive sin."

The Jews of that day commonly held that all sickness was the direct result of sin (cf. John 9:2). That was the theory of Job's three "comforters." Probably this paralytic had a guilt complex. The first thing he needed was to be released from his burdened conscience. So Jesus took care of this matter at once. He assured the man that his sins were forgiven.

E. The Complaint: vv. 6-7

Some "scribes"—teachers of the Law—were sitting there—probably right up front, where they could see and hear everything. When they heard Jesus' pronouncement of forgiveness, they immediately bristled, saying to themselves: "Why does this fellow talk like that? He's blaspheming! Who can forgive sins but God alone?" (v. 7, NIV). (This is exactly what the Greek says.)

Was Jesus blaspheming? No, because He was God (John 1:1). It was the failure of the religious leaders to recognize this fact that caused the strong reaction.

Luke (5:17) tells us that "there were Pharisees and doctors of the law sitting by, which were come out of every town of Galilee, and Judaea, and Jerusalem." Some of them had walked a hundred miles to check on this new prophet from Nazareth, to find out what He was teaching. Now they had caught Him assuming the prerogatives of Deity. It was shocking!

F. The Question: vv. 8-9

They must have been further shocked when Jesus indicated that He was reading their thoughts. "Why reason ye these things in your hearts?"

He asked. Then He posed a twofold question: "Which is easier: to say to the paralytic, 'Your sins are forgiven,' or to say, 'Get up, take your mat and walk'?" (v. 9, NIV).

Which was easier? It was not a question of which was easier to perform, but which was easier "to say." Probably the scribes thought it would be easier to *say*, "Your sins are forgiven," since no one would know the results. But to say to a helpless paralytic, "Get up," would put Jesus "on the spot."

G. The Command: vv. 10-11

Jesus did not hesitate. He commanded the man to get up, pick up his mat and go home. And the man did so.

It is difficult for us to get the full force of Jesus' words in verse 10: "But that ye may know that the Son of man hath power on earth to forgive sins." The Jewish Talmud contains this rabbinical saying: "No one gets up from his sickbed until all his sins are forgiven." So when the paralytic obeyed Jesus' command and got up a well man, it was—according to the scribes' theology—a proof that his sins had been forgiven, as Jesus said they were!

H. The Miracle: v. 12

The man's obedience was immediate and so was his cure. As usual, the people marveled at what they had witnessed.

II. FORGIVENESS OF THE PENITENT:
Luke 7:36-50

A. At Dinner in a Pharisee's House: v. 36

Why this Pharisee invited Jesus to dinner we are not told. But Jesus accepted the invitation, went to the Pharisee's house, and "sat down to meat." The Greek simply says, "reclined"—that is, at the table. In the better homes of those days the custom was to recline on couches around the table while eating in a leisurely fashion.

John the Baptist was an ascetic, living out in the desert and eating food that was crude. But Jesus, who is our example, was not an ascetic. He lived a normal social life in the cities and evidently enjoyed, on occasion, dining in well-to-do homes. But it was always with a spiritual purpose!

B. A Repentant Prostitute: vv. 37-38

The better homes of that day were built around open courtyards. One can often view these from the street today, through an open door. It was easy for people to slip in from the outside.

And so that day there was an uninvited intruder, "a sinner." She was a "street-walker" in that city. But she was sick of her life of sin. So when she heard that Jesus was dining at this Pharisee's house, she came, bringing an "alabaster box of ointment"—better, an "alabaster jar of perfume" (NIV). It may very well have been the very perfume with which she had plied her trade. But now she was using it as a token of her sincere love and gratitude.

She "stood at his feet behind him weeping, and began to wash his feet with tears, and did wipe them with the hairs of her head" (v. 38). Obviously she could not have done this if Jesus was sitting at the table as we do today, with His feet under the table and with His shoes on. In those days they always removed their shoes or sandals when entering a house, as they still do in Japan. While eating they reclined on couches around the table, with their bare feet at the outside edge of the couch.

Not only did this woman wash Jesus' feet with her tears of repentance and wipe them with the hairs of her head, but she "kissed his feet." The form of the Greek compound verb in the imperfect tense suggests: "she kept on tenderly kissing his feet." Her love and gratitude were unbounded.

Not only all this, but she "anointed them with the ointment"—better, "poured perfume on them" (NIV).

This anointing of Jesus is not to be confused with that done later by Mary of Bethany, as recorded in Matthew 26:6-13, Mark 14:3-9, and John 12:2-8. That incident took place in Judea, this one in Galilee.

C. A Critical Pharisee: v. 39

It was a scene to make angels weep with joy (cf. 15:10)—"A sinner has come home." But the Pharisee met it with cold, cruel criticism. He reasoned to himself, "This man [the Greek, in the context, suggests a contemptuous "this fellow"] if he were a prophet, would have known who and what manner of woman this is that toucheth him: for she is a sinner."

"The self-righteous host was particularly disgusted that this woman 'toucheth him.' According to the rabbis no good man would ever in public talk to a woman—not even his own wife, mother, or sister—or let a woman get within six feet of him. Jesus was violating both rules. By letting this woman touch His feet, He rendered Himself ceremonially unclean. So thought the Pharisee. But instead Jesus made the sinful woman clean. The touch of divine power brings purity" (Ralph Earle, *Wesleyan Bible Commentary*, IV, 253).

Legalism always looks with critical eyes, picking flaws in other people's conduct. Love looks with compassionate eyes, appreciating every effort made to redeem the lost. Legalism misunderstands sin. Love knows the true horror of sin, and seeks to save.

D. A Challenging Christ: v. 40

The Pharisee sat as judge, condemning Jesus. But Christ is God's appointed Judge, and He proceeded to expose the Pharisee's true character. At the same time He acted as the woman's lawyer, defending her.

"Jesus answering said." He was answering the unspoken thoughts of the Pharisee, once more revealing His divine discernment. Augustine put it well: "He heard the Pharisee think-ing." And He challenged him out loud. Simon listened.

E. A Parable of Two Debtors: vv. 41-43

Sometimes the best way to answer people's unreasonable ideas is to tell a story. This is what Jesus did here, using a common experience out of life.

He told about a certain "creditor" (the Greek word means "moneylender") who had two debtors. One owed him five hundred "pence" (Greek, *denaria*), the other fifty. Since the Roman silver denarius was worth about twenty cents, these two sums represent respectively one hundred dollars and ten dollars. But since a denarius was a day's wage, these were large amounts of money for working people in those times. The first would be equivalent to four months' wages.

Neither man could pay, and the moneylender "frankly"—rather, "freely"—forgave them both. The Greek verb is based on the root *charis*, which means "grace." Plummer points out the implication: "In *echarisato*, 'he made them a present' of what they owed him, we trace the Pauline doctrine of free grace and salvation for all" (*A Critical and Exegetical Commentary on the Gospel According to St. Luke*, International Critical Commentary, p. 212). This is in line with the fact that the early church held that we find Paul's theology in Luke's writings.

Then Jesus asked the question, "Which of them will love him most?" With an air of supercilious indifference Simon replied, "I suppose that he, to whom he forgave most." Jesus agreed.

F. An Insulting Host: vv. 44-46

These three verses reveal the real attitude of the Pharisee toward Jesus. He invited Him to his home for dinner but did not extend to Him the common courtesy that any host of that day would show to a guest.

But first Jesus asked the Pharisee to look at the woman he had been treating with such contempt. He reminded His host that he had omitted the universal custom of washing the feet of a guest. In those days men wore open sandals and no socks. On the hot, dusty roads the traveler's feet would become grimy with dirt and perspiration. A thoughtful host would have a servant wash the feet of his guests. Simon had really insulted Jesus. In contrast, the repentant prostitute had washed His feet with her tears.

Simon had omitted the common courtesy of planting a kiss on the guest's cheek, apparently because he despised Jesus in his heart. But this woman had kept on kissing the Master's feet.

It was also the custom to pour a little olive oil on the head of a favored guest. Simon was bestowing no such honor on Jesus. But the woman had poured on Jesus' feet a far more costly perfume than olive oil.

Verse 45 seems to indicate that the woman entered the house the same time as Jesus did, or soon after, probably to escape detection. She may have been aware of Simon's lack of courtesy. At any rate, she more than made up for it.

G. A Forgiven Penitent: vv. 47-48

The first half of verse 47 is a bit difficult to explain. Are we for-given because we love God? Plummer writes: "We have to choose between two possible interpretations. 1. 'For which reason, I say to thee, her many sins have been forgiven, because she loves much.' . . . Her sins have been forgiven for the reason that her love was great; or her love won forgiveness. This is the interpretation of Roman Catholic commentators. . . . But it is quite at variance (a) with the parable which precedes; (b) with the second half of the verse, which ought in that case to run, 'but he who loveth little, wins little forgiveness'; (c) with verse 50, which states that it was *faith*, not love, which had been the means of salvation; a doctrine which runs through the whole of the New Testament. This cannot be correct. 2. 'For which reason I say to thee, her many sins have been forgiven (and I say this to thee) because she loved much'. . . . This statement, that her many sins have been forgiven, is rightly made to Simon, because he knew of her great sinfulness, he had witnessed her loving reverence, and he had admitted the principle that the forgiveness of much produces much love. This interpretation is quite in harmony with the parable, with the second half of the verse, and with verse 50" (*Luke*, p. 213).

Then Jesus said to the penitent woman, as He did to the paralytic, "Thy sins are forgiven" (v. 48). The Greek here is clearly the perfect tense. As Plummer points out, the force of this is "have been and remain forgiven." The perfect tense indicates completed action and, even more, a continuing state. The woman had accepted Jesus' teaching and found forgiveness. Now Jesus is speaking out for her rehabilitation in society. She is no longer a "sinner."

H. A Critical Audience: v. 49

Meanwhile the other guests, who were reclining at the table with Jesus, "began to say within themselves, Who is this that forgiveth sins also?" Again the "this" is contemptuous. Probably

---

DISCUSSION QUESTIONS

1. How is paralysis a symbol of sin?
2. What is the true relationship between sin and sickness?
3. Are there some who will never reach Jesus unless they are "carried" to Him?
4. What would happen if four people conspired together to bring a certain one to Christ?
5. Do we give up too easily?
6. What are evidences of true repentance?

most of these guests were self-righteous Pharisees, who shared the feelings of their host. Jesus was definitely not in the house of friends! His fellow guests evidently thought He was having delusions of grandeur, thinking He was God.

I. A Saved Woman: v. 50

Jesus said to the woman: "Thy faith hath saved thee; go in peace."

The last clause is literally, "Go into peace." Plummer comments: " 'Depart into peace,' i.e. into a lasting condition of peace: a Hebrew formula of blessing and of goodwill, with special fulness of meaning" (*Luke*, p. 214). What sweeter words could have come to a penitent prostitute?

CONTEMPORARY APPLICATION

The incident of the paralytic who was brought to Jesus is full of important lessons for us. Perhaps the significant point can be summed up in one short sentence: "The faith that works is the faith that *works!*"

We read that Jesus "saw their faith"—primarily the faith of the four friends. They showed their faith by what they did. It reminds us of James's dictum: "Faith without works is dead" (James 2:20).

These four men might be dubbed Brother Prayer, Brother Persistence, Brother Patience, and Brother Perseverance. Together they got the paralytic successfully to Jesus, and Jesus did the rest.

We need more patience and perseverance in winning souls to Christ. It is not easy, but it is rewarding. And perhaps we should "gang up" on individuals who are unsaved.

POWER TO TRANSFORM LIFE

DEVOTIONAL READING	Philippians 3:7-14

ADULTS

Topic: *Jesus Transforms Life*

Background Scripture: Mark 8:34-38; Luke 19:1-10

Scripture Lesson: Luke 19:1-10; Mark 8:34-36

Memory Verse: *"For the Son of man came to seek and to save the lost."* Luke 19:10

YOUTH

Topic: *A New You*

Background Scripture: Mark 8:34-38; Luke 10:1-10

Scripture Lesson: Luke 9:1-10; Mark 8:34-36

Memory Verse: *"For the Son of man came to seek and to save the lost."* Luke 19:10

CHILDREN

Topic: *A Changed Life*

Background Scripture: Luke 19:1-10

Scripture Lesson: Luke 19:1-10

Memory Verse: *"Whoever would save his life will lose it; whoever loses his life for my sake and the gospel's will save it."* Mark 8:35

DAILY BIBLE READINGS

Mon., Feb. 14: Bread from Heaven, John 6:41-51.
Tues., Feb. 15: "Like His Glorious Body," Philippians 3:17-21.
Wed., Feb. 16: Sight for the Blind, Mark 10:46-52.
Thurs., Feb. 17: Denying Self, Mark 8:34-38.
Fri., Feb. 18: Life-changing Decision, Luke 19:1-10.
Sat., Feb. 19: A Transformed Mind, Philippians 4:4-9.
Sun., Feb. 20: Pressing Forward, Philippians 3:7-14.

LESSON AIM

To help us understand and appropriate the life-transforming power of Christ.

LESSON SETTING

Time: Probably early in A.D. 30 (Luke 19:1-10); A.D. 29 (Mark 8:34-38)

Place: Luke: Jericho, in Judea; Mark: Galilee

LESSON OUTLINE

Power to Transform Life

    I. Zacchaeus the Tax Collector: Luke 19:1-4
       A. A Citizen of Jericho: v. 1

B. A Wealthy Tax Collector: v. 2
C. A Short Man: v. 3
D. An Eager Observer: v. 4

II. Zacchaeus the Host: Luke 19:5-7
    A. Jesus, a Self-Invited Guest: vv. 5-6
    B. Criticism of the Crowd: v. 7

III. Zacchaeus the Penitent: Luke 19:8

IV. Zacchaeus the Saved: Luke 19:9-10
    A. A True Son of Abraham: v. 9
    B. The Seeking Savior: v. 10

V. The Cost of Discipleship: Mark 8:34-38
   A. The Threefold Requirement: v. 34
   B. Losing to Save: v. 35
   C. The Value of the Human Soul: vv. 36-37
   D. A Warning Against Disowning Christ: v. 38

SUGGESTED INTRODUCTION FOR ADULTS

The lesson today consists of one outstanding incident in the life of Christ (from Luke), and one outstanding saying and its amplification. But these two are not in chronological order. The incident of Jesus and Zacchaeus took place in Jericho only about a week before Jesus' crucifixion. The saying on discipleship was given much earlier in northern Galilee. It comes between Peter's famous confession at Caesarea Philippi and the Transfiguration a week later. This was probably several months before Jesus reached Jericho on His way to Jerusalem. But both parts of the lesson have to do with Christ's power to transform men's lives.

We can *re*form ourselves, but only Christ can *trans*form us. There is a world of difference between these two changes. Reformation is mainly outward, but transformation is inward. We can change our lives, but only Christ can change our hearts. A Christian is a person with a changed heart and life.

SUGGESTED INTRODUCTION FOR YOUTH

"A New You." That's what you really want, and that's what Christ can make you!

But we have to cooperate. That is why Jesus laid down the principles of discipleship. We can't trust in "cheap grace." The cost of God's redeeming grace was the death of Christ on the cross. And the cost of discipleship is our identification with Him in that death (Galatians 2:20).

As Jesus put it, we have to lose our life in order to save it. He is not talking about physical death, but about death to our own desires and a willingness to accept His will for our lives. If we hang on to our lives, we ultimately lose them. If we turn them over to Christ, we save them for His highest and best for us.

1. Jesus confronts all of us, as He did Zacchaeus.
2. We must repent of our sins and make restitution for our wrongs if we are to be saved.
3. Only Jesus can really change our lives.
4. But we must ask Him to change us.

THE LESSON COMMENTARY

I. ZACCHAEUS THE TAX COLLECTOR:
Luke 19:1-4

A. A Citizen of Jericho: v. 1

"Jesus entered Jericho and was passing through" (NIV). This is what the Greek says. He had not "passed through" (KJV), but was "passing through" when this incident occurred.

Jesus had left Galilee and headed for Jerusalem for the last time (9:51). The intervening nine chapters are apparently devoted to His Perean ministry. The name *Perea* comes from the Greek preposition *peran*, "across," because this territory was across the Jordan from Judea. In modern times it has been called *Transjordan*. It is now the Hashemite Kingdom of Jordan, with Amman as its capital.

Crossing the Jordan River at some shallow spot, Jesus and His disciples came to the first Judean city, Jericho. Situated nearly a thousand feet below sea level, it was called "The City of Palm Trees"—which it still is to some extent. Cleopatra and Herod the Great had made it a famous city of that day. And here lived Zacchaeus.

B. A Wealthy Tax Collector: v. 2

This incident, found only in Luke's Gospel, fits in with the Lukan emphasis on the salvation of sinners. As Plummer puts it, "The case of Zacchaeus illustrates the special doctrine of this Gospel, that no one is excluded from the invitation to the Kingdom of God" (*A Critical and Exegetical Commentary on the Gospel According to St. Luke*, International Critical Commentary, p. 432).

The Hebrew name *Zacchaeus,* which shows that he was a Jew, means "pure" or "righteous." But apparently this man was not living up to his name very well.

"Chief among the publicans" is one word in Greek, *architelones*. Plummer writes: "This is evidently an official title, and means more than that Zacchaeus was a very rich tax-collector. . . . Perhaps we may render, 'Commissioner of Taxes.' The word occurs nowhere else, and the precise nature of the office cannot be ascertained. . . . Jericho, as a large frontier city, through which much of the carrying trade passed, and which had a large local trade in costly balsams, would be a likely place for a commissioner of taxes" (*Luke*, p. 433). We have already noted in lesson 6 of this quarter why "publican" (KJV) is an incorrect translation.

C. A Short Man: v. 3

As a man with a vigorous mind, Zacchaeus wanted to see who Jesus was. He may possibly have heard that in Galilee Christ had been kind to tax collectors and "sinners." At any rate, he was eager to see Him.

But he had one problem: he was short. And "the press" (the crowd) kept him from being able to see this notable visitor.

D. An Eager Observer: v. 4

Running on ahead to a point that he knew Jesus would pass, Zacchaeus climbed up into a "sycamore tree." Plummer says it was " 'A fig-mulberry,' quite a different tree from the fig and the mulberry and the common sycamore. Its fruit is like the fig, and its leaf like the mulberry, and hence its name"

(*Luke*). Tristram says that the fig-mulberry "recalls the English oak, and its shade is most pleasing. It is consequently a favourite wayside tree. . . . It is very easy to climb, with its short trunk, and its wide lateral branches forking out in all directions" (*Natural History of the Bible*, p. 398).

Zacchaeus did not let his status or his stature keep him from seeing Jesus. He is an example to us.

II. ZACCHAEUS THE HOST: Luke 19:5-7

A. Jesus a Self-Invited Guest: vv. 5-6

It is altogether likely that some of the crowd spotted Zacchaeus perched in the tree. They may have been looking up at him, even pointing to him. It is not impossible that someone may have called out his name. A rich man of high position—up a tree!

At any rate, when Jesus reached the place, He looked up, saw the man, and called to him. Frederic L. Godet comments: "There is something of pleasantness, and even of sprightliness, in the form: '*Make haste and come down; for to-day I must abide at thy house.*' The word *must* indicates that Jesus has recognised in him, on account of this eager desire which he has to see Him, the host whom His Father has chosen for Him at Jericho. Here there is a lost sheep to be found. It is the same unwearied conviction of His mission as in meeting with the Samaritan woman" (*A Commentary on the Gospel of St. Luke*, p. 216).

So Jesus invited Himself to be Zacchaeus's guest. In so doing He bestowed a high honor.

Zacchaeus "made haste, and came down, and received him joyfully" (v. 6). It must have been an interesting sight: the short, rich official almost tumbling out of the tree in his eagerness to welcome Jesus. Plummer comments: "He had made haste to see Christ: he must make haste to receive Him. . . . As in the case of Nathanael (Jn. i. 47), Jesus knew the goodness of the man's heart. Here supernatural

knowledge, necessary for Christ's work, is quite in place" (*Luke*, p. 434).

"Received" is a compound verb in the Greek, meaning "to receive under one's roof, receive as a guest, entertain hospitably" (Abbott-Smith, *Manual Greek Lexicon of the New Testament*, p. 460). Zacchaeus welcomed Jesus "with open arms," as it were. He quickly made it clear that he wanted Jesus to be his guest that night.

He received Him "joyfully." The Greek says "rejoicing." Zacchaeus was overjoyed that Jesus wanted to come to his house. Receiving Jesus is always a joyous experience.

B. Criticism of the Crowd: v. 7

It is a sad thing when "religious" people are unhappy about Jesus accepting sinners. But this is the picture we find frequently in the Gospels. Legalism is a denial of love, and it shows its true colors in incidents like this.

We read that "they all murmured." The verb is a strong compound, *die-gongyzon*. It sounded like the buzzing of the bees.

What was their complaint? "He has gone to be guest with a man that is a sinner." The Pharisees classified all tax collectors automatically as sinners. Bamberger writes: "The rabbinic sources repeatedly bracket tax collectors with robbers" (*Interpreter's Dictionary of the Bible*, IV, 522). So the people were not passing on Zacchaeus's character, but simply recognizing his position, which was opprobrious in their eyes.

"To be guest" is *katalysai*, which had the meaning of "loosing one's garments and resting from a journey." The idea was that Jesus was going to Zacchaeus's house to relax and rest for the night.

III. ZACCHAEUS THE PENITENT: Luke 19:8

When Zacchaeus heard the muttering of the crowd, he stood still. Then he made a bomb-shell announcement: "Behold, Lord, the half of my goods I give to the poor." That must have rocked his complaining critics back on their heels! Which one of them would do a thing like that?

What a man does with his money is often a test of his religion. Here was a notoriously rich man who was going to give half his possessions to the poor. He really had a new heart! Plummer comments: "The narrative represents this declaration as the immediate result of personal contact with the goodness of Christ. He is overwhelmed by Christ's condescension in coming to him, and is eager to make a worthy acknowledgment" (*Luke*, p. 434). So he goes "all out" in setting his financial record straight.

But generous giving does not compensate for wrongdoing. And so Zacchaeus promised to make restitution. The form of the Greek indicates that "if I have taken" means "if, as I know is the case, I have taken." Zacchaeus knew that he was guilty.

"I have taken . . . by false accusation" is one word in Greek. It is the verb *sychophanteo* (found only here and in 3:14), which literally means to "show figs." It has sometimes been explained as meaning to "inform" on those who were illegally exporting figs. But Plummer discounts this. He thinks the *sychophantes* was actually "one who *shows* figs by *shaking* the tree; i.e., who makes the rich yield money by intimidating them. Nowhere is *sycophantes* found in the sense of 'informer,' nor yet of 'sychophant.' It always denotes a 'false accuser,' especially with a view to obtaining money" (*Luke*, p. 93). Hunzinger, in the new *Theological Dictionary of the New Testament* (VII, 759), agrees that here it has the weaker meaning of "to extort something." Perhaps "if I have cheated anybody out of anything" (NIV) expresses it well.

What was Zacchaeus going to do about his cheating? "I will pay back four times the amount" (NIV). This was the penalty the Law prescribed for

one who had stolen a sheep (Exodus 22:1). But Plummer notes that this was "when a man was *compelled* to make reparation for a deliberate act of destructive robbery. . . . If the stolen property had not been consumed, double was to be paid (Exod. xxii. 4, 7). When the defrauder confessed and made *voluntary* restitution, the whole amount, with a fifth added, was sufficient (Lev. vi. 6; Num. v. 7)" (*Luke*, p. 435). So Zacchaeus was going more than the second mile.

Restitution is a proof of repentance. Both the inward repentance and the outward restitution are necessary to salvation.

IV. ZACCHAEUS THE SAVED: Luke 19:9-10

A. A True Son of Abraham: v. 9

In response to Zacchaeus's confession of guilt and promise of restitution Jesus declared, "Today salvation has come to this house" (NIV). This shows that the man had not previously been right with God, but now was.

Jesus added, "forsomuch as he also is a son of Abraham." Zacchaeus was a Jew, but he may well have been excommunicated from the synagogue as an unclean "sinner" because he was a tax collector, working for the Roman government. Jesus now reinstates him. Godet comments: "Zacchaeus is restored to this character which he had lost by his excommunication. He possesses it in a still higher sense than that in which he had lost it" (*Luke*, p. 218).

By his faith and obedience Zacchaeus had proved himself to be a *true* "son of Abraham." He was now not only a good Jew, but a saved individual.

B. The Seeking Savior: v. 10

This verse is usually called the key verse of Luke's Gospel. It sums up the whole thrust of what Renan called "the most beautiful book in the world."

The verse begins with *elthen*, "he came." Plummer notes: "First with emphasis: 'He *came* for this very purpose' " (*Luke*, p. 437). What was the purpose? "To seek and to save what was lost." Luke portrays Jesus as the seeking Shepherd.

Of the salvation portrayed in this story, J. Norval Geldenhuys writes: "Whosoever accepts Jesus wholeheartedly in his life and becomes personally acquainted with Him receives real salvation, a salvation which brings about an effective and practical revolution in his life, inwardly and outwardly. When Jesus comes into a person's life, and gains authority there, selfishness and dishonesty are irresistibly eradicated" (*Commentary on the Gospel of Luke*, New International Commentary on the New Testament, p. 471).

V. THE COST OF DISCIPLESHIP: Mark 8:34-38

A. The Threefold Requirement: v. 34

This Scripture must be understood in the light of its context. Peter had just made his great confession at Caesarea Philippi (v. 29): "Thou art the Christ"—that is, "the Messiah." On the basis of this, Jesus made His first prediction of His passion at Jerusalem: "And he began to teach them, that the Son of man must suffer many things, and be rejected of the elders, and of the chief priests, and scribes, and be killed, and after three days rise again" (v. 31).

As usual, Peter blurted out his immediate reaction: "Peter took him, and began to rebuke him" (v. 32). But Jesus turned and "rebuked Peter." The kindly disciple didn't want his Master to suffer. But Jesus told him that he was acting the part of Satan—"Satan" means "adversary"—expressing man's idea, not God's. As Messiah, Jesus had to suffer in order to save us.

Then Jesus called the crowd to Him, along with His disciples, and made this great pronouncement found in all three Synoptic Gospels: "If anyone would come after me, he must deny himself and take up his cross and follow me" (NIV).

What does it mean to deny oneself? Does it mean giving up candy during Lent, as a person once told us? Is it a matter of depriving oneself of some little thing he likes, in order to give to missions? Jesus did not say, "He must deny himself of this or that or the other." He said, "He must deny himself"—period! This is something far greater. It means that we give up the right to have our own way; we accept His way. It means that we say sincerely, "I do not live for myself." Rather, we live for God and others. We deny our own sovereignty and submit to His sovereignty as Lord of our lives. It is saying No to self and Yes to Him. That is true self-denial.

"In this saying, as in many others, Jesus cut squarely across the world's philosophy of life. Over the portals of the path leading to worldly success are the words: 'Assert yourself!' At the entrance of the pathway of eternal life one finds the words: 'Deny yourself!' The first, the philosophy of Friedrich Nietzsche, has plunged this generation into bloodshed and destruction. The second, the philosophy of Jesus Christ, the Healer of nations, leads to life eternal. The first marks the path of self-love; the second shows the way of

DISCUSSION QUESTIONS

1. Why was Zacchaeus treated as a "sinner"?
2. What are some of the advantages and disadvantages of being wealthy?
3. What should be our attitude toward the rich?
4. What good traits did Zacchaeus have?
5. What does self-denial involve?
6. What are some implications of taking up our cross?

divine love. Each person must choose which path he will take" (Ralph Earle, *Mark*, Evangelical Commentary, p. 107).

The second requirement of discipleship that Jesus laid down is that one must "take up his cross." Henry P. Swete says that this means "to put oneself into the position of a condemned man on his way to execution" (*The Gospel According to St. Mark*, p. 172). Ezra P. Gould agrees with this. He comments: "The criminal carried his own cross to the place of execution, and so, to take up the cross means to go to the place of death" (*A Critical and Exegetical Commentary on the Gospel According to St. Mark*, International Critical Commentary, p. 156).

Taking up our cross, then, means death to the self-willed self. It means going Jesus' way, the way of the cross.

"Deny" and "take up" are both in the aorist tense, suggesting crises in experience—a crucial conversion and a complete consecration to Christ. But "follow" is in the present tense of continuous action. Following Jesus is a lifelong assignment. But it must be preceded by denying self and even dying with Christ to our own will, that we may have His will. Then we must follow Him all the way.

B. Losing to Save: v. 35

Here we find one of the greatest principles of life: "For whosoever will save his life shall lose it; but whosoever shall lose his life for my sake and the gospel's, the same shall save it." The way to save oneself is to lose onself in God and in service to others. Every consecrated Christian knows the glorious reality of this. To lose oneself in living for others is to find the highest life inwardly and the largest life as our lives are multiplied in the lives of those we serve.

A. F. Hort gives a good paraphrase of the first part of this verse: "He that wishes to save what he calls his 'life' (i.e. life in the narrower sense) will lose his true 'life' (i.e. life in its highest sense)" (*Mark*, p. 122).

C. The Value of the Human Soul: vv. 36-37

These two verses consist of two unanswerable questions, unless the answer be a simple "Nothing." Suppose a man could gain the whole world but then had to leave it all and spend eternity in outer darkness, what profit would his former riches be to him? The human soul is worth more than any and all material possessions.

D. A Warning Against Disowning Christ: v. 38

If we are ashamed of Christ down here, He will disown us at His return. We either deny ourselves or we deny Him. Every person must make the choice between these two alternatives.

CONTEMPORARY APPLICATION

Today thousands of people are having their lives transformed by meeting Jesus. Some have been considered real "sinners" by Christian standards. Yet they have become model saints.

It is a thrill to hear the testimony of former actresses or entertainers when they tell of the complete change that has come to their inward lives. Where before there was frustration and futility, selfishness and emptiness, there is now fullness and fulfillment.

We should not neglect the up-and-outers any more than the down-and-outers. They both need Christ. And He who came to seek and save the lost can transform all of them.

POWER FOR CREATIVE LIVING

DEVOTIONAL READING	Colossians 2:16—3:4
ADULTS	Topic: *Religion Can Be Vital* Background Scripture: Mark 2:13—3:6; Luke 5:27—6:11 Scripture Lesson: Mark 2:23—3:6 Memory Verse: *Where the Spirit of the Lord is, there is freedom.* II Corinthians 3:17
YOUTH	Topic: *Religion Can Be Vital* Background Scripture: Mark 2:13—3:6; Luke 5:27—6:11 Scripture Lesson: Mark 2:23—3:6 Memory Verse: *Where the Spirit of the Lord is, there is freedom.* II Corinthians 3:17
CHILDREN	Topic: *What Is More Important?* Background Scripture: Mark 2:13—3:6; Luke 5:27—6:11 Scripture Lesson: Mark 2:23-28 Memory Verse: *"The sabbath was made for man, not man for the sabbath."* Mark 2:27
DAILY BIBLE READINGS	Mon., Feb. 21: Freedom from Infirmity, Matthew 12:9-14. Tues., Feb. 22: Freedom from Social Confines, Luke 5:27-32. Wed., Feb. 23: Freedom to a New Way, Luke 5:33-39. Thurs., Feb. 24: Freedom from Tradition, Luke 6:1-5. Fri., Feb. 25: Freedom to Minister, Luke 6:6-11. Sat., Feb. 26: Freedom Through the Son, John 8:31-38. Sun., Feb. 27: Freedom to Serve Christ, I Corinthians 7:17-24.
LESSON AIM	To help us learn the secret of creative living.
LESSON SETTING	Time: About A.D. 28 Place: In and around Capernaum

LESSON OUTLINE	Power for Creative Living
	
	I. The Call of Matthew: Mark 2:13-17
	   A. The Call: vv. 13-14
	   B. The Dinner: v. 15

C. The Critics: v. 16
D. The Answer: v. 17

II. **The Question About Fasting:** Mark 2:18-22
  A. The Complaint: v. 18
  B. The Defense: vv. 19-20
  C. The Comparison: vv. 21-22

III. **Plucking Grain on the Sabbath:** Mark 2:23-28
  A. Picking Heads of Wheat: v. 23
  B. Picking Flaws in Conduct: v. 24
  C. Pointing Out a Precedent: vv. 25-26
  D. Pointing Up Priorities: v. 27
  E. Proclaiming the Lord of the Sabbath: v. 28

IV. **Healing on the Sabbath:** Mark 3:1-6
  A. The Man with the Withered Hand: v. 1
  B. The Spying Critics: v. 2
  C. The Command of Christ: v. 3
  D. The Question of Christ: v. 4
  E. The Cure: v. 5
  F. The Conspiracy: v. 6

SUGGESTED INTRODUCTION FOR ADULTS

In Mark 2:1—3:6 five incidents are recorded in which Jesus faced severe criticism from the Pharisees. The first, the healing of the paralytic (2:1-12), we studied two weeks ago. The other four are found in today's lesson.

In the case of the paralytic, the Pharisees accused Jesus of blasphemy because He claimed to forgive the man's sins. At the feast in Levi's house they criticized Jesus for eating with "publicans and sinners" (2:16). In the next incident they complained because the disciples of Jesus were not observing a day of fasting (2:18). In the fourth incident they found fault with His disciples because they were plucking heads of wheat on the sabbath day (2:24). The last case involved healing on the sabbath, with Jesus Himself as the target again (3:2).

This opposition of the Pharisees to Jesus is one of the prominent features of the Synoptic Gospels. It became more severe as time went on, finally helping to bring about His death.

SUGGESTED INTRODUCTION FOR YOUTH

"Religion Can Be Vital." Tens of thousands of teenagers are finding that to be true. Religion is no longer a neglected nuisance; it is a vital factor in life for an increasing host of youth.

In the past, too many young people felt that religion was irrelevant; the church was a holdover from medieval times. But today's problems have driven many people back to God and the Bible for the only working solutions available. It is a great day to be alive!

What we need, and are finding increasingly prevalent, is not a narrow, legalistic traditionalism, but a new openness to the freedom of the Spirit. This is the religion of the New Testament, and it is the religion of tomorrow.

CONCEPTS FOR CHILDREN

1. Jesus is Lord of the sabbath.
2. So whatever pleases Him is all right for us to do on Sunday.
3. We worship on Sunday as "the Lord's Day."
4. This is because Jesus rose on the first day of the week.

THE LESSON COMMENTARY

I. THE CALL OF MATTHEW: Mark 2:13-17

A. The Call: vv. 13-14

"Once again Jesus went out beside the lake" (v. 13, NIV). Today "by the sea side" (KJV) would mean the Mediterranean coast. It was beside the Lake of Galilee that Jesus found His largest crowds and did much of His teaching.

"All the multitude resorted unto him, and he taught them." Both these verbs are in the imperfect tense of continuing action. Vincent Taylor comments: "The two imperfects indicate the coming and going of successive groups of hearers" (*Mark*, p. 202). It was a busy time.

As Jesus walked along, "he saw Levi the son of Alphaeus" (v. 14). Luke (5:27, 29) agrees with Mark in calling him Levi. Nowhere else in the New Testament is this name found. In its parallel passage, Matthew's Gospel (9:9) uses the name "Matthew," which occurs five times in the New Testament. That is the name by which he is generally known. Jesus may have given Levi the name Matthew when he became a disciple.

Levi was sitting at the "receipt of custom." This is one word in Greek, *telonion*, which could mean several things. It could have been a place where duty was paid on fish caught in the lake. In that case, Matthew would have been well acquainted with Peter and his associates in the fishing industry. Or it might have been a toll house on the busy caravan road from Damascus to the coast. Merchants coming into the territory of Herod Antipas, tetrarch of Galilee, would have to stop and pay customs duties. Again, the word could be translated "tax office." But that term today would conjure up a more elaborate situation than was probably the actual case. Perhaps "tax collector's booth" (NIV) would more nearly fit the picture. At any rate, Matthew had a position of responsibility. We note again that Jesus calls busy men.

To this tax collector Jesus said only two words: "Follow me." But this was enough. Levi "arose and followed him." Both these verbs are in the aorist tense, suggesting prompt, decisive action. There was no arguing or debating—just instant obedience. Luke (5:28) adds: "And he left all."

B. The Dinner: v. 15

The first thing that Matthew did was to have a farewell banquet at his house, with Jesus as the guest of honor. Luke says specifically: "And Levi made him a great feast in his own house" (5:29). The comment of Quesnel is appropriate: "Every sinner converted to Christ must endeavor to conduct his friends to Him. Fruitfulness is a certain proof of the reality of conversion" (quoted by Sadler, *Mark*, p. 34).

Jesus "sat at meat." The Greek literally says "was lying down"—that is, was reclining at the table. Vincent Taylor says that this custom was "universal in the time of Jesus" (*The Gospel According to Mark*, p. 204).

Many tax collectors and "sinners"—so dubbed by the Pharisees because they were not meticulously careful to keep all the detailed regulations for ceremonial cleanness—were reclining at the table with Jesus and His disciples. There were many of these who followed Christ. Evidently they felt their need of His help and flocked to Him—partly because He accepted them, whereas the Pharisees did not.

C. The Critics: v. 16

When the scribes and Pharisees—the best Greek text has "the scribes of the Pharisees," that is, "the teachers of the law who were Pharisees" (NIV)—saw Jesus eating with the "sinners" and tax collectors, they asked His disciples, "Why does he eat with tax collectors and 'sinners'?" (NIV). The added phrase "and drinketh" (KJV) is not in the best Greek text.

"Taxes in Palestine were oppressive in Jesus' day. Water, meat and salt were taxed. There were road taxes, city taxes, house taxes, besides the poll tax. It is not surprising that tax collectors were classed as robbers and ruffians, whose money was not acceptable for alms, and whose testimony was not valid in court" (Ralph Earle, *Mark*, Evangelical Commentary, p. 45).

They were hated throughout the Roman Empire. "But the tax collectors of Palestine were doubly hated. Not only were they considered extortioners, but they also represented the domination of a foreign power, and so were despised as traitors by the patriotic Jews. In addition, the pious ones held them in contempt because they were defiled by frequent contact with Gentiles and were careless about observing the ritual requirements of the law. So they were classed with the 'sinners' as unfit for association with righteous, God-fearing Jews" (Earle, *Mark*, pp. 45-46).

We find in this verse the first mention of the "Pharisees" in Mark's Gospel. They were a sect of separatists, as their name indicates. Begin-

ning in the Maccabean period (second century before Christ) they had the noble purpose of trying to oppose the increase of pagan Hellenism in Palestine. They insisted on close observance of the Law. But, as happens too often, they became more and more legalistic in their emphasis. By Jesus' day many of them had degenerated in spirit so far that He called them hypocrites.

D. The Answer: v. 17

When Jesus heard the complaint of the Pharisees, He answered their criticism. First He quoted an old proverb, whose meaning was obvious. The strong or healthy do not need a physician, but rather those who are ill. Then Jesus made the application: "I came not to call the righteous, but sinners." (The added phrase "to repentance" is not in the Greek.)

"It is the duty of a doctor to visit those afflicted with disease, even at the risk of contagion. How much more should He visit those diseased with sin, in order to save them. . . . Such was Jesus' reasoning with these critics" (Earle, *Mark*, p. 46).

Unfortunately, these religious leaders were not concerned for the salvation of "sinners." They tended to hold them in contempt and avoid contact with them.

But that has too often been the case with "pious" people in modern times as well. Our petty prejudices often form barriers that keep people out of the kingdom of God. We cannot afford to take an "offish" attitude toward sinners, lest we turn them away from Christ and His salvation. This is a terrible responsibility to face.

II. THE QUESTION ABOUT FASTING:
Mark 2:18-22

A. The Complaint: v. 18

Luke's Gospel says that the disciples of John (the Baptist) "fast often and make supplications" (5:33). Mark's Gospel (KJV) says that "the disciples of John and of the Pharisees"—the Greek says "the disciples of John and the Pharisees" (nominative case)—"used to fast." So they asked Jesus, "Why do the disciples of John . . . fast, but thy disciples fast not?" But the Greek represents Mark's usual characteristic of vividness. Literally it reads this way: "Now John's disciples and the Pharisees were fasting. Some people came and asked Jesus, 'How is it that John's disciples and the disciples of the Pharisees are fasting, but yours are not?' " (NIV).

Now the picture becomes clear. It was a fasting period for the Jews. Yet here were Jesus and His disciples *feasting*. Perhaps the disciples of John felt that it was particularly inappropriate for Jesus to be feasting while their own leader was languishing in prison, and also fasting.

The Mosaic Law prescribed only one fast day a year, the great Day of Atonement, Yom Kippur (Leviticus 23:27). But at the time of the captivity fasting received new emphasis among the Israelites. In Jesus' day the Pharisees prided themselves on fasting twice a week (Luke 18:12). *The Teaching of the Twelve Apostles* (second century), commonly called the *Didache*, says that the Jews fasted on Tuesday and Thursday, but Christians should fast on Wednesday and Friday. The result was that the church soon fell into the same rut of legalistic ceremonialism as had Judaism.

B. The Defense: vv. 19-20

In reply to their question, Jesus asked another: " 'Can the children of the bridechamber fast, while the bridegroom is with them?' " The word "children" here is misleading, for Jesus is talking about adults, not children. The Greek says "sons of the bridechamber"—a Hebraistic expression for associates of the bridegroom. Abbott-Smith says that this refers to "the bridegroom's friends who have charge of the nuptial arrangements" (*Manual Greek Lexicon of the New Testament*, p. 306). So the correct meaning is "the attendants of the bridegroom" (NASB), "the guests of the bridegroom" (NIV), or simply "wedding guests" (Goodspeed).

Jesus added, " 'As long as they have the bridegroom with them they cannot fast.' " William Lane comments: "The statement may be proverbial for any inappropriate action, since a wedding was a time of great joy and festivity, heralded by music and gala processions. To fast in the presence of the groom would be unthinkable" (*Gospel According to Mark*, The New International Commentary on the New Testament, pp. 109-10).

Jesus went on, however, to say: " 'But the days will come, when the bridegroom will be taken away from them, and then shall they fast in those days.' " Christ is the heavenly Bridegroom. One day He was taken away in His ascension. So fasting is appropriate for the church today, but will not be at the Marriage Supper of the Lamb!

C. The Comparison: vv. 21-22

These verses contain two brief parabolic statements (cf. Luke 5:36), in which Jesus drew two striking comparisons. They are very important for our understanding of the nature of true religion.

First He said: " 'No one sews a patch of unshrunk cloth on an old garment. If he does, the new piece will pull away from the old, making the tear worse' " (v. 21, NIV).

The point of this parable is obvious. If one tries to patch up an old "garment"—the Greek word is *himation*, outer cloak—with a piece of unshrunk cloth, the patch will shrink when the cloak is washed and pull away at the edges, making a more unsightly hole.

The second parable portrays the same truth with a different picture: " 'And no one pours new wine into old wineskins. If he does, the wine will burst the skins, and both the wine and the wineskins will be ruined. No, he pours new wine into new wineskins' " (v. 22, NIV). The translation "bottles"

(KJV) is misleading to the modern reader, who is used to glass bottles. But the people of Palestine in that day took the skin of a goat, sewed it together and used it as a container for wine. (One can still see these skins being used in the Holy Land.) When the grape juice fermented, it expanded and stretched the skin—as leather shoes stretch with wear. But if a person put fresh grape juice the next year into an old, stretched wineskin, he would be in trouble. As fermentation took place the wineskin could stretch no further and it would break open—with the loss of both wine and wineskin. Jesus' hearers were thoroughly familiar with the figure and caught the point quickly.

The new message of the Gospel could not be contained in the old, hardened, legalistic forms of Judaism. Christianity was to be a fresh, expanding movement. Jesus suggests that if Christianity had been forced to stay within the confines of Judaism, both religions would have perished.

III. PLUCKING GRAIN ON THE SABBATH: Mark 2:23-28

A. Picking Heads of Wheat: v. 23

"Corn fields" should be "grainfields" and "ears of corn" should be "heads of grain." In the United States "corn" means Indian corn, with "ears" six inches or more in length. But in the British Isles wheat is still called "corn." Consequently recent British versions of the New Testament and commentaries still say "corn fields" and "ears of corn." This presents a wrong picture to American readers.

Walking through the grainfields on the sabbath day (Saturday), the disciples were hungry (Matthew 12:1) and began to pluck some heads of grain. Luke (6:1) adds: "rubbing them in their hands."

B. Picking Flaws in Conduct: v. 24

The picayunish Pharisees began again to "pick" on Jesus' disciples.

They asked Him why His disciples were doing on the sabbath day what was unlawful. We must not assume that the Pharisees were accusing the disciples of stealing, for the Mosaic Law specifically said, "When you enter your neighbor's standing grain, then you may pluck the heads with your hand" (Deuteronomy 23:25, NASB). The criticism here was for doing manual labor on the sabbath. "In the eyes of the pedantic Pharisees plucking the grain was reaping, and rubbing off the husks or shells was threshing. Perhaps, also, blowing the loose chaff out of their hands was winnowing! Such was the narrow legalism of rabbinic interpretation" (Earle, *Mark*, p. 49). And this is the bane of legalism today. It makes mountains out of molehills.

C. Pointing Out a Precedent: vv. 25-26

In reply to the question of the Pharisees, Jesus asked them if they had never read what David did when he was hungry. He actually ate the "shewbread"—literally "bread of the Presence"—the consecrated bread that only the priests had a right to eat. This happened in the lifetime of Abiathar, who became high priest. His father Ahimelech was high priest at the time (I Samuel 21). Since Abiathar became the prominent high priest in the reign of David, his name is used here. To label this a blunder is unreasonable, for Mark certainly knew the Old Testament narrative.

D. Pointing Up Priorities: v. 27

The Pharisees could not quarrel with Jesus' statement in this verse. For one of their own rabbis said, "The Sabbath is delivered unto you, and ye are not delivered to the Sabbath." But Jesus made it more specific: "The sabbath was made for man, and not man for the sabbath." Human life is the most important thing on earth, and all other things must be subservient to it. This must always be the governing principle.

E. Proclaiming the Lord of the Sabbath: v. 28

Jesus regularly refers to Himself as "the Son of man"—probably a Messianic title. The statement of this verse is found in all three Synoptic Gospels. Someone has well said that Jesus is Lord of the sabbath "to own it, to interpret it, to preside over it and to ennoble it, by merging it in 'the Lord's day.' " So Jesus should be Lord of all we do on His day. We should keep it holy.

IV. HEALING ON THE SABBATH: Mark 3:1-6

This is the fifth of the controversies between Jesus and the Pharisees, and the second over the question of sabbath observance. In 2:23-28 it was a matter of working on the sabbath, here of healing (considered working).

A. The Man with the Withered Hand: v. 1

Again Jesus went into "the synagogue"—probably at Capernaum—and there was a man there who "had a withered hand"—Greek, "the hand having dried up." So he was not born that way.

B. The Spying Critics: v. 2

"They"—Luke (6:7) says "the scribes and the Pharisees"—"kept watching Jesus narrowly" (so the Greek) to see if He would heal the man on the sabbath, "that they might accuse him." Wycliffe (first English version of the Bible) caught the picture correctly when he translated the first clause: *Thei aspieden Hym*. The Pharisees were acting as spies to trap Jesus and have Him arrested.

The Jews allowed healing on the sabbath day only in cases of life or death. Obviously this affliction did not come under that category.

C. The Command of Christ: v. 3

Refusing to be intimidated by His enemies, Jesus said to the man, "Stand forth"—translated literally, "Rise into the midst," that is, "Stand up in front of everyone" (NIV). He deliberately made the affair fully public.

D. The Question of Christ: v. 4

The answer to Jesus' twofold question is utterly obvious; it could only be answered one way by any decent person. The Master thus put His critics on the spot. No wonder they "held their peace"—that is, "remained silent" (NIV).

E. The Cure: v. 5

"When he had looked round about on them with anger"—the aorist participle indicates a momentary flash of anger—"being grieved for the hardness of their hearts." The participle here is in the present tense of continuous grief. Swete well says: "The look was momentary, the sorrow habitual" (*Mark*, p. 50). We should always have anger against sin, but this should be mingled with grief for the sinner.

Jesus healed the man with a single word of command. Once more we see His power to heal.

F. The Conspiracy: v. 6

Instead of rejoicing that the afflicted man was cured, the Pharisees conspired with the Herodians—supporters of Roman rule in Palestine—to destroy Jesus. The Pharisees were ardent na-

---

DISCUSSION QUESTIONS

1. Why does Jesus call busy people into His service?
2. What did Matthew gain by leaving all to follow Jesus?
3. What is the place of fasting in the church today?
4. Why do new denominations (wineskins) come into being?
5. What principle should govern our use of the Lord's Day?
6. How may we "do good" on the sabbath?

tionalists and usually hated the Hero-dian "Quislings." But now the two united in their common opposition to Jesus.

CONTEMPORARY APPLICATION

What about the question of fasting? "Christ refused to endorse a legalistic institutional type of fasting. He clearly intended that fasting among Christians should not be a matter of duty or form. Rather, it should be spontaneous and from the heart. Fasting as a form has no spiritual value. As a means of divorcing oneself for a season from material things that one may give undivided attention to spiritual concerns, it has always been helpful. Performed as a duty it becomes legalistic and tends to spiritual pride. But as a spiritual exercise in connection with burdened, intercessory prayer it helps to develop one's spiritual muscles and tends to produce greater intensity and effectiveness in prayer" (Earle, *Mark*, p. 48).

THE LIFE AND MINISTRY OF JESUS: MARK AND LUKE (continued)

Unit IV: Jesus Teaches His Way

Unit V: Jesus Climaxes His Mission

Unit VI: Faith in Action: James

THE WAY OF UNSELFISH SERVICE

DEVOTIONAL READING	Luke 10:30-37

ADULTS

Topic: *The Way of Unselfish Service*

Background Scripture: Mark 10:35-45; Luke 10

Scripture Lesson: Mark 10:35-45

Memory Verse: *Whoever would be great among you must be your servant, and whoever, would be first among you must be slave of all.* Mark 10:43-44

YOUTH

Topic: *Committed to Serving Others*

Background Scripture: Mark 10:35-45; Luke 10

Scripture Lesson: Mark 10:35-45

Memory Verse: *Whoever would be great among you must be your servant, and whoever would be first among you must be slave of all.* Mark 10:43-44

CHILDREN

Topic: *Being Concerned*

Background Scripture: Mark 10:35-45; Luke 10

Scripture Lesson: Luke 10:29-37

Memory Verse: *. . . you shall love the Lord your God with all your heart, and with all your soul, and with all your mind, and with all your strength.* Mark 12:30

DAILY BIBLE READINGS

Mon., Feb. 28: The Apostle's Example, Acts 20:17-24.
Tues., Mar. 1: Declaring the Counsel of God, Acts 20:25-35.
Wed., Mar. 2: How to Be First, Mark 10:35-45.
Thurs., Mar. 3: Sent on a Mission, Luke 10:1-12.
Fri., Mar. 4: Mission Accomplished, Luke 10:17-22.
Sat., Mar. 5: The Love Commandment, Luke 10:23-29.
Sun., Mar. 6: The Good Samaritan, Luke 10:30-37.

LESSON AIM

To discover Jesus' way of unselfish service and learn to walk in this way.

LESSON SETTING

Time: About A.D. 29

Place: Near Jericho, on the way to Jerusalem

LESSON OUTLINE

The Way of Unselfish Service

  I. The Selfish Request: Mark 10:35-37
    A. The Blanket Proposal: v. 35

B. The Specific Question: v. 36
C. The Self-seeking Desire: v. 37

II. **The Challenging Answer:** Mark 10:38-40
A. The Penetrating Question: v. 38
B. The Superficial Answer: v. 39a
C. The Solemn Warning: v. 39b
D. The Divine Choice: v. 40

III. **The Indignant Colleagues:** Mark 10:41-45
A. The Self-righteous Ten: v. 41
B. The Pagan Way of Life: v. 42
C. The Christian Way of Life: vv. 43-44
D. The Example of Jesus: v. 45

IV. **The Good Samaritan:** Luke 10:25-37
A. The Occasion for the Parable: vv. 25-29
B. The Callousness of Religious Leaders: vv. 30-32
C. The Kindness of a Despised Samaritan: vv. 33-37

**SUGGESTED
INTRODUCTION
FOR ADULTS**

The first eight lessons of this quarter continue and complete the series on "The Life and Ministry of Jesus" as portrayed in Mark and Luke. Two units are studied, consisting of four lessons each: (1) "Jesus Teaches His Way"; (2) "Jesus Climaxes His Mission." The last five lessons of the quarter are from the Epistle of James.

What is the way that Jesus teaches? It is the way of unselfish service to others. This is the way He took when on earth, and it is the way we must take if we are going to follow Him. Ecclesiastical leaders who usurp and assert arbitrary authority prove thereby that they are not real followers of Christ.

Before one can be a leader, he must be a follower. Unless we are willing to be led, we cannot lead others. And as appointed leaders, in whatever capacity, we must always recognize that we have a Leader, the only one who has absolute authority. We must constantly let Him lead us, as we seek to lead others in a helpful way.

**SUGGESTED
INTRODUCTION
FOR YOUTH**

Ambition is a good thing. The person who lacks it never amounts to anything in life. There is a holy ambition to excel in the things of God, to function at our highest level in Christian service. Thank God for every evidence of this.

But there is also an unholy ambition. This is the self-seeking attitude that strives for position and honor. This is the ambition that demands acclaim and award.

What we need is to have our selfish, self-willed, self-centered ego crucified with Christ (Galatians 2:20). Then we are free to serve our Master with only one supreme desire—to please Him. Then we are happy to serve others in love, sincerely desiring their best good.

	1. We are to be good neighbors to those in need.
CONCEPTS FOR CHILDREN	2. We are to help them, even if they dislike us.
	3. Only Christ's love in us can enable us to do this.
	4. We show our love for God by loving others.

THE LESSON COMMENTARY

I. THE SELFISH REQUEST: Mark 10:35-37

A. The Blanket Proposal: v. 35

James and John, the sons of Zebedee, were among the first four whom Jesus called to leave their vocations and follow Him. They were fishermen, as were their partners Andrew and Peter, who were also brothers.

They came to Jesus, addressing Him as "Master" (KJV). But the Greek word clearly means "teacher." *Master* does not connote that meaning today. The Greek word *didaskalos* occurs fifty-eight times in the New Testament. In the King James Version it is translated "master" forty-seven times, "teacher" ten times, and "doctor" once. It should always be "teacher"—its regular meaning in the Greek of that day.

"Teacher," they said, "we want you to do for us whatever we ask" (NIV). This was a childish request. We have all heard children say, "Promise me you'll do what I tell you." The obvious answer is, "You'll have to tell me first." These grown men were giving a sad demonstration of their immaturity. We have no right to put God "on the spot" in this way.

B. The Specific Question: v. 36

Jesus did what any wise parent would do in such a situation: He required a specific request. "What do you want me to do for you?" he asked (NIV). To give a blanket promise to a *carte blanche* proposal is absurd. People can get themselves into serious trouble by doing such a silly thing.

C. The Self-seeking Desire: v. 37

Suppose Jesus had said Yes to the first proposal of these two ambitious disciples—what a quandary He would have been in! For now they proceeded to ask for the two coveted seats beside Him in His "glory." Matthew (20:21) says "kingdom." As they headed for Jerusalem (v. 32) they expected Jesus to set up His Messianic kingdom there. They wanted to be the first to get in their bid for the highest political positions in the new regime. The seat to the right of the king was the place of highest honor, and the one on his left was second place. The two sons of Zebedee were eager to get these prize positions.

This showed how carnally selfish they were. Instead of saying, "Lord, can we be of any service to you?" they asked for honor and preferment. What about the other disciples? Might not some of them possibly be better qualified? Specifically, what about Peter? It is very likely that the sons of Zebedee were jealous of Peter's growing prominence—as recently exhibited at Caesarea Philippi (Matthew 16:13-19)—and they were anxious now to "steal a march" on him. What these two men sadly needed was the Holy Spirit to cleanse their hearts from their carnal spirit of self-seeking. This finally happened to them on the day of Pentecost (Acts 15:8-9).

We need constantly to put our motives under the scrutiny of Christ. Do we want a certain position for our own honor, or so that we may have a greater opportunity to serve others in love?

II. THE CHALLENGING ANSWER: Mark 10:38-40

A. The Penetrating Question: v. 38

The first reply of Jesus to their request was, " 'You don't know what you are asking' " (NIV). In the light of verse 39 one is tempted to translate this: "You don't know what you are asking for!" And the Greek would support this. The verb *aiteo* carries the idea of asking for something specific: "Itemize your requests."

There is a striking truth here. Many a man has asked or sought for a position of high honor, little dreaming what that position would cost him— sometimes his life. It is far safer and wiser to let God choose for us. When we accept His will for our lives, we know that He will give what is best. When we choose our own way we have to take the consequences, and we have no one to blame but ourselves.

Then Jesus asked a twofold question: "Can ye drink of the cup that I drink of? and be baptized with the baptism that I am baptized with?" It was a solemn, probing question, that should have stopped the disciples short in their tracks!

B. The Superficial Answer: v. 39a

Unfortunately, these two imma- ture men failed to realize the implica- tions of Jesus' query. Blithely they answered, "We can."

In the parallel account in Matthew 20:22 the question is translated ". . . Are ye able?" and the reply, "We are able." (The Greek is exactly the same in both Gospels.) From this has come the song "We Are Able," which is sung thoughtlessly by many people who know nothing of real consecration.

The facts are that when the dis- ciples said, "We can," they were not facing reality. When Jesus was arrested in the garden, they all forsook Him and fled.

Incidentally, it is obvious that the first part of verse 39 belongs with verse 38. The verse division is correct in Matthew but incorrect in Mark. The verse divisions in the New Testament, made centuries ago, are not well done.

C. The Solemn Warning: v. 39b

The prediction that Jesus made here did come true. James became the first apostolic martyr (Acts 12:2). John was exiled to Patmos, and there is even a legend that he died by means of boiling oil. Both these brothers suffered for their Lord.

The figure of drinking the cup (that is, its contents) was a familiar one to Jewish people (Psalm 75:8). Baptism would also be understood as referring to overwhelming floods of sorrows (cf. Isaiah 43:2). Today we speak of deep suffering as a "baptism of fire." Alford suggests that "cup" may refer more to the inner, spiritual agony of Christ, while "baptism" may have to do with His outer persecution and afflictions.

D. The Divine Choice: v. 40

Those who are prepared to fill positions will be assigned them. James Morison writes: "The degree of exalta- tion in ultimate glory is not to be a matter of capricious or arbitrary deter- mination. It must be regulated by the degree of the spirit of self-sacrifice during probation" (*A Critical Com- mentary on the Gospel According to St. Matthew*, p. 294). God alone knows whom to choose. A. B. Bruce comments: "Favouritism has no place here; It depends on fitness" (*Exposi- tor's Greek Testament*, I, 257).

III. THE INDIGNANT COL- LEAGUES: Mark 10:41-45

A. The Self-righteous Ten: v. 41

The expression "the ten" is found only here in the New Testament. When they heard about the request of the two brothers, they were "indignant" ("much displeased," KJV). Bruce writes: "The ten were 'mad' at the two; pitiful exhibition in the circumstances, fitted to make Jesus doubt His choice of such men" (*Expositor's Greek Testament*, I, 257).

The sad truth is that this was probably not righteous indignation. One is tempted to wonder if some of the other disciples may have been angry because they hadn't been smart enough to think of asking Jesus for those positions before James and John made their request. There seems no doubt that envy and jealousy were behind much of the indignation they felt.

B. The Pagan Way of Life: v. 42

These disciples were in great need of some pointed teaching. So Jesus called them together. He warned them that their attitude was pagan, not Christian. They needed a new slant on life. They belonged to a new order and must act accordingly.

To the ten Jesus said: "You know that those who are regarded as rulers of the Gentiles lord it over them, and their high officials exercise authority over them" (NIV). The last two verbs are interesting. "Lord it over" (*katakyrieuo*) is found in the parallel passage (Matthew 20:25) and also in Acts 19:16 and I Peter 5:3. But the other verb (*katexousiazo*) occurs only in this saying of Jesus in Matthew and Mark. They are compounded of *kyrios*, "lord," and *exousia*, "authority." The pagan way is for rulers to show their authority and lord it over their subjects.

C. The Christian Way of Life: vv. 43-44

Emphatically Jesus asserted: "Not so with you. Instead, whoever wants to become great among you must be your servant, and whoever wants to be first must be slave of all" (NIV). The King James Version has "minister" and "servant." But today *minister* means "pastor" to most people. The

Greek word is *diaconos*. Later it did come to have in ecclesiastical circles the technical sense of "deacon." But in Jesus' day it meant a servant. Its early use was for one who waited on tables. Clearly Christ was talking here about a servant, not a minister in the modern sense.

And then Jesus added: "If you really want to be first, then become the slave of all" (paraphrased). The Greek word translated "servant" in the King James Version is *doulos*, which means "bondservant," or "slave." What Jesus was emphasizing was this: The way up is down. "In the kingdom of God greatness is measured by service, not by self-assertiveness. Eternity will furnish a startling revelation of God's appraisal of who are the greatest. It is striking to realize that many shining stars in public life may be low in the heavenly scale, while some obscure, unheard of saints who have lived sacrificial lives will become the 'five star generals' " (Ralph Earle, *The Gospel According to Mark*, p. 131).

Are we willing to serve others, regardless of earthly reward? That is the true test of our devotion.

D. The Example of Jesus: v. 45

"Ministered unto" and "to minister" are the verb *diaconeo*. The better translation is: "For even the Son of Man did not come to be served, but to serve, and to give his life a ransom for many" (NIV). He Himself is the great example of what He taught.

This is the greatest single theological passage in Mark's Gospel. It clearly teaches the doctrine of vicarious atonement.

The Greek word translated "ransom" is particularly significant. It is *lytron*, coming from the verb *lyo*, "loose." So its basic idea is that of a release. Then it came to mean what *ransom* does now, the means by which the release is gained.

In his epochal work, *Light from the Ancient East*, Deissmann shows that in the first century the word *lytron* was the regular term for the redemption money paid for freeing a slave (pp. 327-28). The word occurs in the New Testament only here and in the parallel passage in Matthew (20:28). The cognate verb *lytroo* is used three times and means "redeem." The noun *lytrosis* (which also appears three times) means "redemption."

The word *for* in this verse is also very significant. The Greek preposition is *anti*, which we have taken over in the sense of "against." But James Moulton and George Milligan in their *Vocabulary of the Greek Testament*—the standard work in the field—write: "By far the commonest meaning of *anti* is the simple 'instead of' " (p. 46). Scholarly commentators agree.

Recently we worked carefully through the Septuagint of Isaiah, while our Committee on Bible Translation was finalizing the translation of that prophecy in the New International Version. We were amazed to see how frequently *anti* can mean nothing else than "instead of" or "in the place of."

This clearly indicates that Mark 10:45 teaches the doctrine of substitutionary atonement. On the cross Christ died in our place. He gave His life's blood as a ransom for our sins, redeeming us from the slavery of sin.

DISCUSSION QUESTIONS

1. What were the motives of James and John?
2. What are the profits and perils of ambition?
3. What principles should guide our asking from God?
4. What are some risks involved in following Christ?
5. How should Christians exercise authority?
6. What does it mean to be a slave to all?

IV. THE GOOD SAMARITAN: Luke 10:25-37

A. The Occasion for the Parable: vv. 25-29

Jesus, as we just saw, pointed to His own life of sacrificial service as the supreme example of the truth He was teaching His disciples—that unselfish service is the sign of true greatness. But He also gave the Parable of the Good Samaritan as an example on the purely human level.

It all started when a "lawyer"—an expert in the Law of Moses—stood up to test Jesus. He asked a very pertinent question: "Master [rather, "Teacher"] what shall I do to inherit eternal life?" (v. 25).

Appropriately Jesus referred him to the Law, asking him, "How do you read it?" (v. 26, NIV)—that is, "What does it say to you?" The teacher of the Law rose to the occasion and gave the correct reply, citing the two greatest commandments of the Mosaic Law (cf. Mark 12:28-31). Jesus complimented him and asserted, "This do, and thou shalt live" (v. 28).

But this typical lawyer wanted to argue. More than that, he wanted "to justify himself" (v. 29). Was his conscience troubling him a bit as to whether he loved his neighbor as himself? If not, it should have been! So he asked the question, "And who is my neighbour?" The most this word could mean was certainly a fellow Jew!

B. The Callousness of Religious Leaders: vv. 30-32

The Parable of the Good Samaritan is one of the best known of Jesus' parables, though it is found only in Luke's Gospel. Christ told about a man who "was going down from Jerusalem to Jericho" (NIV)—not "went down" (KJV), for he was waylaid on the road. On the famous Jericho road he "fell into the hands of robbers" (NIV)—not "thieves" (KJV). They stripped off his clothes, beat him, and left him half dead.

"A priest happened to be going down the same road" (v. 31, NIV). When he saw the victim lying there, he passed by on the other side. After all, he had just finished his stint of ministering in the temple at Jerusalem, and he had no further responsibility! (Thousands of priests lived in Jericho at this time.)

Then a Levite happened by. When he saw the body, he too passed by on the other side. He may have reasoned that the man was past help anyhow.

These two men illustrate what is too often the attitude of the church and its leaders. If people come to our services we will gladly help them, but we have no responsibility outside the walls of our building. Thank God, this attitude is changing today, and visitation evangelism is being promoted widely.

The attitude of the Levite is also too common. We are quick to dismiss some sinners as "hopeless." They may be helpless—many are—but they are not hopeless, and we should not treat them as such.

C. The Kindness of a Despised Samaritan: vv. 33-37

Then along came a Samaritan, perhaps a businessman. When he saw the victim, he could have said: "Well, he's a Jew. These Jews hate and despise me for being a Samaritan. Why should I do anything for this fellow?"

Instead, he "had compassion on him" and "went to him" and "bound up his wounds" (vv. 33-34). He poured in wine for an antiseptic and olive oil for a healing balm. Then he set the man on his own donkey, carried him to an inn, "and took care of him." He believed in a "follow-up program"— the supreme importance of which is being increasingly recognized today.

After the Samaritan had nursed the poor Jew through the night, he had to leave the next morning on business. But before he left he took out two denarii—worth two days' wages—and gave them to the host with the admonition to "take care of him," promising to pay any further expenses on his return.

It has well been pointed out that we find in this parable three philosophies of life. That of the robbers was: "What's yours is mine, and I'll take it." That of the priest and Levite was: "What's mine is mine, and I'll keep it." That of the Samaritan was: "What's mine is yours, and we'll share it." These can be summarized more briefly as: (1) "Beat him up"; (2) "Pass him up"; (3) "Pick him up." Too often the church has been guilty of the second. We are challenged to adopt the third.

The lawyer had asked, "Who is my neighbor?" Jesus turned this around and asked, "Which of the three was a neighbor to the man in need?"

The proud religionist couldn't say, "The Samaritan"; but he had to admit: "He that shewed mercy on him" (v. 37). Then Jesus firmly commanded, "Go, and do likewise." In other words, "Be a neighbor to the man in need."

When Jesus told the Parable of the Good Samaritan, He was describing His own ministry. Judaism, in the person of the priest and Levite, was failing to minister in love to the poor people in their sin and desperate need. But Jesus had "compassion" on the crowds, as often mentioned in the Gospels. Also He came where we were, in His incarnation, and met our need fully.

But we must not forget the challenge, "Go, and do thou likewise." That is our daily duty.

CONTEMPORARY APPLICATION

Victor Hugo is credited with having said: "Power corrupts. Absolute power corrupts absolutely." The illustrations of this truth are innumerable.

Many men have started their careers with a genuine desire to serve the public. But as they were elected to positions of authority, the feel of power gradually possessed them. Instead of being free to act in love, they became prisoners of their own selfish ambitions. They began to assert their authority in more and more arbitrary fashion. Finally they became dictators, if not despots. And in the process their personalities were ruined.

Jesus indicated that the two essential characteristics of true greatness are humility and service. This is His way.

THE WAY OF AUTHENTIC PRAYER

DEVOTIONAL READING	Luke 13:31-35

ADULTS

Topic: *The Way of Genuine Prayer*

Background Scripture: Luke 11:1-13; 18:1-14

Scripture Lesson: Luke 18:1-14

Memory Verse: *Ask, and it will be given you; seek, and you will find; knock, and it will be opened to you.* Luke 11:9

YOUTH

Topic: *Prayer That Is Genuine*

Background Scripture: Luke 11:1-13; 18:1-14

Scripture Lesson: Luke 18:1-14

Memory Verse: *Ask, and it will be given you; seek, and you will find; knock, and it will be opened to you.* Luke 11:9

CHILDREN

Topic: *When We Pray*

Background Scripture: Luke 11:1-14; 18:1-4

Scripture Lesson: Luke 11:5-13

Memory Verse: *Rejoice always, pray constantly.* I Thessalonians 5:16-17

DAILY BIBLE READINGS

Mon., Mar. 7: Teach Us to Pray, Luke 11:1-4.
Tues., Mar. 8: The Importunate Friend, Luke 11:5-13.
Wed., Mar. 9: The Model Prayer, Matthew 6:5-15.
Thurs., Mar. 10: Prayer for Forgiveness, II Chronicles 6:36-42.
Fri., Mar. 11: The Unrighteous Judge, Luke 18:1-8.
Sat., Mar. 12: The Pharisee and the Publican, Luke 18:9-14.
Sun., Mar. 13: Jesus' Prayerful Lament, Luke 13:31-35.

LESSON AIM

To help us follow our Teacher in the way of genuine prayer.

LESSON SETTING

Time: About A.D. 29

Place: Perhaps Perea, east of the Jordan

LESSON OUTLINE

The Way of Authentic Prayer

    I. An Exemplary Prayer: Luke 11:1-4
      A. The Example of Jesus: v. 1

B. Prayer for God's Kingdom: v. 2
C. Prayer for Our Needs: vv. 3-4

II. **Importunate Prayer:** Luke 11:5-8
A. The Request: vv. 5-6
B. The Reply: v. 7
C. The Reward: v. 8

III. **Persevering Prayer:** Luke 11:9-13
A. Assurance of Answer: vv. 9-10
B. A Human Father: vv. 11-12
C. The Divine Father: v. 13

IV. **Persistent Prayer:** Luke 18:1-8
A. The Purpose of the Parable: v. 1
B. The Widow's Request: vv. 2-3
C. The Judge's Reaction: vv. 4-5
D. The Divine Assurance: vv. 6-8

V. **Sincere Prayer:** Luke 18:9-14
A. The Purpose of the Parable: v. 9
B. The Self-righteous Prayer: vv. 10-12
C. The Penitent Prayer: v. 13
D. The Results of the Two Prayers: v. 14

SUGGESTED INTRODUCTION FOR ADULTS

Luke's Gospel is outstandingly the Gospel of Prayer. This is shown in two ways, both in the example and in the teaching of Jesus—that is, in what He did and said.

First, the example. Six times Luke mentions Jesus as praying where the other Gospels do not. The first is at His baptism (3:21). The second is after healing a man full of leprosy (5:16). The third is before the choosing of His twelve apostles (6:12). The fourth is before Peter's confession at Caesarea Philippi (9:18). The fifth is at the Transfiguration (9:29). The sixth is at the beginning of our lesson for today, as the occasion for the giving of the so-called Lord's Prayer.

In the second place, we have Jesus' teaching on prayer presented more fully in Luke's Gospel. Luke alone gives the three great parables of prayer that constitute the bulk of our lesson today. Jesus was a man of prayer. He wants to teach us to pray.

SUGGESTED INTRODUCTION FOR YOUTH

It has sometimes been said that prayer is the breath of the spiritual life. Paul said, "Pray without ceasing" (I Thessalonians 5:17). This does not mean, of course, that one is praying consciously all the time. That would be impossible. But just as we mustn't stop eating if we are going to remain alive, so we mustn't stop praying if we are going to stay alive spiritually. We must pray every day.

If there is any time above all others when we should be utterly sincere, it is when we are talking to God. For He knows our thoughts as fully as people understand our words—even more so. Sincerity and humility should characterize our every approach to God.

<table>
<tr><td>CONCEPTS FOR
CHILDREN</td><td>1. Jesus is our great Example of prayer.
2. He talked frequently to His Father in heaven.
3. Prayer is our acknowledgment that we need God's help.
4. It is also an act of adoration and worship.</td></tr>
</table>

THE LESSON COMMENTARY

I. AN EXEMPLARY PRAYER: Luke 11:1-4

A. The Example of Jesus: v. 1

"One day Jesus was praying in a certain place" (NIV). We are not told where this was. The previous incident, in the home of Martha and Mary, was probably in Bethany, near Jerusalem. Jesus was coming toward the close of His earthly ministry.

When He finished praying, one of His disciples said to Him, "Lord, teach us to pray, as John also taught his disciples." There is no mention elsewhere of John the Baptist teaching his followers to pray, but it is perfectly logical that he should have done so.

The disciple literally said, "Lord, teach us to be praying." He did not say, "Lord, teach us *how* to pray," though this is probably implied. But one can only learn to pray by praying. It is helpful to read good books on prayer. But no amount of reading on the subject can take the place of actually engaging in this exercise. As in many other areas of life, it is only practice that makes perfect. "Lord, teach us *to pray*."

B. Prayer for God's Kingdom: v. 2

In verses 2-4 we find Luke's form of what is commonly called "The Lord's Prayer." It is considerably briefer than the form found in Matthew (6:9-13). This is true even in the King James Version. But the best Greek text of Luke, based on the

earliest manuscripts, is even shorter. Here is what the Greek text actually says, as translated in the Revised Standard Version: "Father, hallowed be thy name. Thy kingdom come. Give us each day our daily bread; and forgive us our sins, for we ourselves forgive every one who is indebted to us; and lead us not into temptation."

God is addressed here simply as "Father." This highlights the fact that we can come to our heavenly Father as we do to our human father, with confidence and the assurance that He is listening to us and wants to help us.

There are two petitions in this verse. The first is "Hallowed be thy name." The Greek literally says, "Let your name be sanctified." In the Mishnah one finds the rabbinical expression "the sanctification of the name." In the Hebrew Old Testament the word *name* signifies more than it does today. F. W. Farrar writes: "The '*name*' of God is used for all the attributes of His Being" (*Mark*, Cambridge Greek Testament, p. 260).

We who are called Christians bear the name of Christ. Do we sanctify that name by Christlike living, or do we desecrate that sacred name by unchristlike living? That is one of the greatest challenges that confronts us every day. Anyone who faces it realistically will pray repeatedly, "Lord, help me!" Only the indwelling Holy Spirit can enable us to sanctify our Lord's holy name by our deeds, words, and thoughts.

The second petition is "Your kingdom come." Matthew's Gospel adds:

"Your will be done on earth as it is in heaven." It is thought that some later scribe added it in Luke as a harmonization with the more familiar form in Matthew.

Actually, these two petitions mean much the same thing. Plummer says that "Thy kingdom come" means "Thy sway be extended from heaven to this world (now ruled by the adversary), so as to extirpate wickedness" (*A Critical and Exegetical Commentary on the Gospel According to St. Luke*, International Critical Commentary, p. 295). It is almost universally agreed that *kingdom* does not mean a "realm" but rather the "reign" of God.

C. Prayer for Our Needs: vv. 3-4

We should always pray first for God's glory and kingdom, not selfishly for our own desires. But our heavenly Father wants us, having worshiped Him, to present our personal needs to Him. He is interested in each of His children, even in their material needs.

So we are told to pray, "Give us day by day our daily bread" (v. 3). The Greek word for "daily" is *epiousion*. Plummer comments: "We are still in ignorance as to the origin and exact meaning of this remarkable word. It appears here first in Greek literature ..." (*Luke*). It has been variously translated as "for the coming day," "continual," "for the day," or "daily." Probably the last is best.

Luke's wording here says that we are to pray for the forgiveness of our "sins." The Greek word is *harmartias*, the most common term for sin in the New Testament (172 times, all but 2 times translated "sin" in the King James Version). Matthew (6:12) has, "Forgive us our debts." But Jesus probably spoke in Aramaic, and in that language the same word is used for *debt* and *sin*. Every sin is a debt for which God holds us responsible.

The last petition is "And lead us not into temptation." The added item, "but deliver us from evil" (KJV) was probably imported from Matthew. It is not found in our two oldest Greek manuscripts of the New Testament (fourth century), and Origen (third century) says that it and the last part of verse 2 (KJV) were not in the Greek manuscripts of his day.

"Lead us not into" probably means "keep us from." Instead of being over-confident, we should humbly pray to be kept from temptation.

II. IMPORTUNATE PRAYER: Luke 11:5-8

A. The Request: vv. 5-6

After giving the so-called Lord's Prayer, Jesus followed with what is known as the Parable of the Importunate Friend at Midnight. Farrar makes the helpful observation: "Although idle repetitions in prayer are forbidden, persistency and importunity in prayer—wrestling with God, and not letting Him go until He has blessed us—are here distinctly taught" (*Mark*, p. 261).

Jesus told about a man going to a friend's house at midnight and saying, "Friend, lend me three loaves." The Greek word for "lend" is not the common one, meaning "to lend on interest," as a business transaction, but one found only here in the New Testament. Joseph H. Thayer says it means, "grant the use of, as a friendly act" (*Greek-English Lexicon of the New Testament*, p. 125).

Why three loaves? The man would need one for his guest, one for himself as he courteously ate with him, and a third to offer as a second helping. The "loaves" of that day were the size of a small pancake.

The man continued his plea by explaining his predicament. A friend of his on a journey had suddenly appeared at his door at midnight, "and I have nothing to set before him." This does not imply a home of poverty. In those days of no refrigeration it was the custom to grind the wheat or barley each morning and bake fresh bread, using it all that day.

B. The Reply: v. 7

From inside the house the neighbor answered, "Don't bother me" (NIV). The door had been shut and barred for the night. "My children are with me in bed" would be literally true, for in a Palestinean home the whole family lay on a padded quilt on the hard dirt floor and were all covered by one big blanket. If the father got up he would disturb the entire family. So he concluded, "I can't get up and give you anything" (NIV). The request was unreasonable and the reply was an emphatic, "Nothing doing!"

C. The Reward: v. 8

Jesus declared: "Though he will not rise and give him, because he is his friend, yet because of his importunity he will rise and give him as many as he needeth." The Greek word for "importunity" is *anaideian*, found only here in the New Testament. It literally means "shamelessness." A. B. Bruce says that it suggests here "the total disregard of domestic privacy and comfort shown by persistent knocking; very indecent from the point of view of the man in bed" (*Expositor's Greek Testament*, I, 548).

III. PERSEVERING PRAYER: Luke 11:9-13

A. Assurance of Answer: vv. 9-10

In the English the three key words of verse 9 form an acrostic:

Ask
Seek
Knock

However, this is not true in the Greek. We have here three stages in prayer. First, Jesus says, "Ask, and it shall be given you." We find this same truth stated in Mark 11:24 and John 16:24. Verses 9 and 10 here are closely paralleled in Matthew 7:7-8.

If the answer to one's asking is not forthcoming, then one should "seek" until he finds. This suggests more earnest, continued prayer. If there is still no satisfaction, then one should begin to "knock." Now we are in the realm of desperate, agonizing prayer.

Plummer comments: "The three commands are obviously taken from the parable, and they form a climax of increasing earnestness. They are all present imperatives: '*Continue* asking, seeking, knocking'" (*Luke*, p. 299).

Verse 10 gives the assurance that if we do keep on asking, seeking and knocking, we will, without fail, be rewarded. Sometimes we have to seek the Lord's will over a period of time before it becomes clear. But even closed doors will be opened if we continue to knock in earnest prayer.

B. A Human Father: vv. 11-12

Luke gives three examples of how a human father would *not* treat his son—giving him a stone when he asked for bread, a serpent when he asked for a fish, or a scorpion when he asked for an egg. Matthew has just the first two. Plummer observes: "The meaning here is, that in answer to prayer God gives neither what is useless (a stone) nor what is harmful (a serpent or scorpion)" (*Luke*, p. 300).

C. The Divine Father: v. 13

"Being evil" simply underscores the fact that the best of parents are "evil" compared with God in His perfect holiness. Jesus said that if earthly parents would give good gifts to their children, "how much more will your heavenly Father give the Holy Spirit to them that ask him?" Matthew says that He will give "good things." But Luke here shows his special interest in the Holy Spirit, who is "the summum bonum," the highest good, "and the supreme object of desire for all true disciples"

(Bruce, *Expositor's Greek Testament*, I, 548).

IV. PERSISTENT PRAYER: Luke 18:1-8

A. The Purpose of the Parable: v. 1

An unusual feature is found as a preface here—the purpose of the parable is stated. "Then Jesus told his disciples a parable to show them that they should always pray and not give up" (v. 1, NIV). "Not to faint" (KJV) may well be translated "not to lose heart." We are not to be discouraged if our prayers are not answered immediately.

B. The Widow's Request: vv. 2-3

This parable is known by two names because there are two main characters in it: The Unjust Judge or The Importunate Widow. The latter name emphasizes the main point of the parable: persistence in praying.

The parables of Jesus are illustrations of truth put in story form, which makes them easier to remember. So here we are told that in a certain city there was a judge who "feared not God, neither regarded man" (v. 2). He had no reverence for God or respect for men. Wonderful qualifications for a judge!

In the same city was a widow. She "kept coming to him with the plea, 'Grant me justice against my adversary' " (v. 3, NIV)—that is, "protect me from his attacks."

In those days widows had very few legal rights. They were at the mercy of unscrupulous money-grabbers. Plummer comments: "Typical of defencelessness: she had neither a protector to coerce, nor money to bribe the unrighteous magistrate. The O.T. abounds in denunciations of those who oppress widows" (*Luke*, p. 412). Farrar writes: "The necessity for *special* justice and kindness to widows rose from the fact that in the East they were of all classes the most defenceless and oppressed" (*Mark*, p. 328).

C. The Judge's Reaction: vv. 4-5

"She came" (v. 3) and "he would not" (v. 4) are both in the imperfect tense in the Greek: "he continued refusing, just as she continued coming" (Plummer).

This judge was utterly shameless in his sin. He said to himself, "Even though I don't fear God or care about men, yet because this widow keeps bothering me, I will see that she gets justice, so that she won't eventually wear me out with her coming" (NIV). He was not concerned at all about her but only about himself.

The King James Version has at the end of verse 5: "lest by her continual coming she weary me." But this is a very weak translation. The Greek verb literally means "give me a black eye." This could be taken literally—which is unlikely!—or figuratively: "ruin my reputation in town." But since he didn't care what people thought, we probably have to rule this out also. Plummer says, "There is no doubt that 'annoy greatly' is the meaning here" (*Luke*, p. 413). But "wear me out" (RSV, NASB, NIV) perhaps captures the idea best. He was afraid the woman would give him ulcers!

D. The Divine Assurance: vv. 6-8

Luke likes to refer to Jesus as "the Lord." Now Christ makes the application of the parable. If the unjust judge would finally give justice, how much more will a holy God "bring about justice for his chosen ones, who cry out to him day and night? Will he keep putting them off? I tell you, he will see that they get justice, and quickly" (NIV). God sometimes seems to delay, but He always acts on time.

This section ends with a note of warning: "Nevertheless when the Son of man cometh, shall he find faith on the earth?" This note is sounded at several other places in the New Testament (Matthew 24:12, 22; II Thessalonians 2:3; II Peter 3:3-4). We need to keep our hearts constantly ready for our Lord's return.

V. SINCERE PRAYER:
Luke 18:9-14

A. The Purpose of the Parable: v. 9

Both of these parables on prayer in chapter 18 have the purpose stated. In this case Jesus was speaking "to some who were confident of their own righteousness and looked down on everybody else" (NIV).

B. The Self-righteous Prayer: vv. 10-12

This parable is known as that of The Pharisee and the Publican. The term *publican* (KJV) is not quite accurate. In the Roman Empire the *publicani* were wealthy men who were assigned the taxation of large areas. But the so-called publicans of the Gospels were the local tax collectors in the towns and cities of Palestine and should be designated as such.

The Pharisee "stood"—aorist tense, "took his stand"—in a prominent place, where he could be seen and heard. Then he "prayed thus with himself." He was not praying to God in his heart, though his lips addressed the Deity.

Instead of praising God, he praised himself: "God, I thank you that I am not like all other men—robbers, evil-doers, adulterers—or even like this tax collector" (NIV). One can hardly imagine the conceited egotism of this proud, self-righteous Pharisee. But there are some people who are so blind to their own faults that they think they are perfect—in a class all by themselves. And these are the very ones who constantly see faults in others.

The last part of verse 11 shows the diabolical depravity of this man's heart. Perhaps with a sneer in his voice he cast his contempt on the tax collector. We must always remember that contempt is unchristian.

Self-righteousness is one of the worst sins that the human heart can be guilty of. It is putting ourselves on a pedestal with God.

On the positive side, the Pharisee reminded God: "I fast twice in the week, I give tithes of all I possess" (v. 12). But legalism is not righteousness in God's sight. Righteousness is love in the heart.

The central word in the Pharisee's prayer is "I." It occurs twice in verse 11 and three times in verse 12. The Pharisee was self-centered not God-centered and others-centered.

C. The Penitent Prayer: v. 13

The tax collector felt unworthy to come into God's presence or to be near this pious Pharisee. So he stood "afar off." Ashamed even to look up toward heaven, he beat his breast and cried out, "God be merciful to me a sinner." He was the picture of penitence and abject humility. Farrar writes: "The Jews usually stood with arms outspread, the palms turned upwards, as though to receive the gifts of heaven, and the eyes raised" (*Mark*, p. 332). But the tax collector was so overwhelmed with his own spiritual need that he simply cried for mercy, feeling he didn't deserve it.

D. The Results of the Two Prayers: v. 14

Jesus said that the tax collector went home justified rather than the Pharisee. And then He stated the general principle: "For everyone who exalts himself will be humbled, and he who humbles himself will be exalted"

DISCUSSION QUESTIONS

1. What should be our attitude as we approach God in prayer?
2. How should we address Him?
3. What "vain repetitions" should we avoid?
4. Why does God sometimes delay the answer?
5. What are the benefits of persistent prayer to us?
6. What is the logic of humility?

(NIV). "Abased" and "humbleth" (KJV) are the same verb in the Greek. This is a universal principle in life.

The way up is down. If we humble ourselves in God's sight He will lift us up.

CONTEMPORARY APPLICATION

Years ago an editorial in a Monday newspaper in Boston described a service in Trinity Church the day before. Included was this comment: "It was the most beautiful prayer ever prayed to a Boston audience."

The editor spoke better than he knew. The prayer was prayed to the cultured audience, not to God.

So it was with the Pharisee. Plummer comments: "There is no prayer, even in form; he asks God for nothing, being thoroughly satisfied with his present condition. And only in form is this utterance a thanksgiving; it is self-congratulation. He glances at God, but contemplates himself. Indeed he almost pities God, who but for himself would be destitute of faithful servants" (*Luke*, p. 417). It is a perfect example of what a prayer ought not to be!

THE WAY OF FORGIVING LOVE

DEVOTIONAL READING	Psalm 103:11-14
ADULTS	Topic: *The Way of Forgiving Love* Background Scripture: Luke 15 Scripture Lesson: Luke 15:17-32 Memory Verse: *He arose and came to his father. But while he was yet at a distance, his father saw him and had compassion, and ran and embraced him and kissed him.* Luke 15:20
YOUTH	Topic: *Love That Forgives* Background Scripture: Luke 15 Scripture Lesson: Luke 15:17-32 Memory Verse: *He arose and came to his father. But while he was yet at a distance, his father saw him and had compassion, and ran and embraced him and kissed him.* Luke 15:20
CHILDREN	Topic: When We Forgive Background Scripture: Luke 15 Scripture Lesson: Luke 15:11-20 Memory Verse: *Be kind to one another, tenderhearted, forgiving one another, as God in Christ forgave you.* Ephesians 4:32
DAILY BIBLE READINGS	Mon., Mar. 14: Brothers Seek Forgiveness, Genesis 50:15-21. Tues., Mar. 15: Forgive an Erring Brother, II Corinthians 2:5-11. Wed., Mar. 16: Rejoice When the Lost Is Found, Luke 15:1-10. Thurs., Mar. 17: Forgiving the Prodigal, Luke 15:11-24. Fri., Mar. 18: The Unforgiving Spirit, Luke 15:25-32. Sat., Mar. 19: God's Mercy and Forgiveness, Psalm 103:1-10. Sun., Mar. 20: God's Everlasting Love, Psalm 103:11-18.
LESSON AIM	To help us see the true nature of forgiving love and how to practice it.
LESSON SETTING	Time: About A.D. 29 Place: Perhaps Perea, east of the Jordan

The Way of Forgiving Love

LESSON OUTLINE

I. **The Prodigal Son:** Luke 15:11-24
   A. The Possessor: vv. 11-12
   B. The Prodigal: v. 13
   C. The Pauper: vv. 14-16
   D. The Penitent: vv. 17-19
   E. The Pardoned: vv. 20-24

II. **The Parsimonious Son:** Luke 15:25-32
   A. Inquisitive: vv. 25-27
   B. Angry: v. 28
   C. Self-righteous: v. 29
   D. Jealous: v. 30
   E. Reproved: vv. 31-32

SUGGESTED INTRODUCTION FOR ADULTS

One of the main emphases of Luke's Gospel is on lostness and salvation. In the fifteenth chapter we have three parables illustrating this: The Lost Sheep (vv. 3-7), The Lost Coin (vv. 8-10), and The Lost Son (vv. 11-32). The first is found also in Matthew 18:12-14, in briefer form. The other two are recorded only in Luke's Gospel.

It has been pointed out that we find here a hint of the part that each of the three Persons of the Trinity play in our salvation. In the Parable of the Lost Sheep we see Christ on the mountainsides of His earthly ministry— Temptation, Transfiguration, Travail (Gethsemane), and Tragedy (Calvary)—seeking the lost sheep of the human race, and finding it. In the Parable of the Lost Coin the woman (v. 8) typifies the Holy Spirit seeking diligently for every lost soul. In the Parable of the Lost Son we see the Father waiting longingly and lovingly for the prodigal's return.

There is another element here that is typical of Luke's Gospel—the emphasis on joy, as reflected in the first two chapters and elsewhere (e.g., 10:21). The shepherd who found his lost sheep called together his friends and neighbors for a time of rejoicing (v. 6). The woman who found her lost coin did the same (v. 9, where "friends" is feminine in the Greek). And the happy father put on a big feast (vv. 23, 32).

SUGGESTED INTRODUCTION FOR YOUTH

Our lesson for today really contains two lessons: (1) God is ready to forgive us, no matter what we have done, if we sincerely repent and ask His forgiveness; (2) we should forgive others gladly and fully, as God has forgiven us.

No matter what others do to us, we must forgive them freely, for God has forgiven us of far greater sins. We show our gratitude to Him by forgiving others.

CONCEPTS FOR CHILDREN

1. God loves us and is ready to forgive all our sins.
2. We should be sorry for our sins and ask His forgiveness for doing wrong.

3. Because He forgives us, we should forgive others.
4. True love always expresses itself in forgiveness.

THE LESSON COMMENTARY

I. THE PRODIGAL SON:
Luke 15:11-24

A. The Possessor: vv. 11-12

We usually speak of Luke 15:11-32 as the Parable of the Prodigal Son. But actually two sons are pictured here, as verse 11 suggests. Instead of The Lost Son we have Two Lost Sons.

This takes us back to the opening verses of the chapter, which give us the occasion and setting for the three parables that make up the chapter's contents. The tax collectors and "sinners"—called this by the religious leaders because they did not scrupulously observe the Law—were gathering around Jesus to listen to Him (v. 1). The Pharisees and the teachers of the Law muttered, "This man receiveth sinners and eateth with them" (v. 2).

It was against this haughty, self-righteous attitude of the Pharisees that Jesus gave the three parables. He especially painted their picture in His description of the older brother—the last part of our lesson.

The younger of the two sons said to his father, "Father give me my share of the estate" (v. 12, NIV). So the father divided his property between the two sons. The older one got two-thirds of the family estate (Deuteronomy 21:17). But the younger one was happy with his third. Plummer gives evidence to show that in that day it was sometimes the custom to give the sons their inheritance long before the death of the father (A Critical and Exegetical Commentary on the Gospel According to St. Luke, International Critical Commentary, p. 372).

B. The Prodigal: v. 13

The proud possessor became a profligate prodigal. The younger son turned his newly acquired property into money and "set off for a distant country and there squandered his wealth in wild living" (NIV). He wanted to get as far away from home as he could. Probably the young rebel said to himself, "I'm not going to have my father telling me what to do any longer; I'm going to be my own boss." But he found what many youth have discovered since: that the meanest master anyone can have is his own willful self.

"With riotous living" is in the Greek: "living asotos." This Greek adverb, found only here in the New Testament, is defined by G. Abbott-Smith as "wastefully," but "not necessarily dissolute" (Manual Greek Lexicon of the New Testament, p. 66). But William F. Arndt and F. Wilbur Gingrich say "dissolutely, loosely" (Greek-English Lexicon of the New Testament, p. 119). T. W. Manson writes: "The Greek adverb translated 'with riotous living' may mean that he spent his money 'extravagantly,' or that he spent it on dissolute pleasures, or both" ("The Sayings of Jesus," The Mission and Message of Jesus, p. 579). We would say, "Certainly both!" It would be hard to believe that he did not go into deep sin.

The prodigal not only "wasted his substance" materially, but he also wasted the inner substance of his soul spiritually. The great tragedy of America is not only the multiplied billions of dollars spent on liquor every year, but what the drinking of that liquor does to millions of lives and homes. When we sin we destroy ourselves and sometimes others.

C. The Pauper: vv. 14-16

"A fool and his money are soon parted." It wasn't long until the prodigal found himself a pauper, without a penny in his pocket. He had "spent all" and he "began to be in want."

The real tragedy was that he had not only an empty pocketbook but also an empty heart. There was no one to love him, no one to care for him. All that was left inside was a haunting loneliness, a sense of frustration and futility. This young man had had every opportunity that one could ask for, but he "blew it" all. Now he had nothing left but the realization of failure.

Added to the problem of his lack of any money was the fact of a severe famine in the land. When we run away from God we find that troubles multiply. "The way of transgressors is hard" (Proverbs 13:15).

Desperate for something to eat, "he went and hired himself out to a citizen of that country, who sent him to his fields to feed pigs" (v. 15, NIV). This was not only very humiliating for one who had been brought up in a well-to-do home, but it was doubly distressing for a Jew. In the Mosaic Law pork is definitely forbidden as "unclean" meat. This young man had never been around pigs before, and now he had to stoop to the disgraceful job of feeding them. He had really hit bottom!

But still there was no food. "He longed to fill his stomach with the pods that the pigs were eating, but no one gave him anything" (v. 16, NIV). These were the dry pods of the carob tree, not well fitted for human consumption. There is an appropriate rabbinical saying: "When the Israelites are reduced to eating carob-pods, then they repent." Another fits the situation perfectly: "When a son (abroad) goes barefoot (through poverty), then he remembers the comforts of his father's house" (Manson, "Sayings of Jesus," p. 580). This young man had to face a black, blank wall before he was willing to turn around.

D. The Penitent: vv. 17-19

"When he came to himself" is the literal Greek. The same expression is found in Latin, and it is good idiomatic English today. The young man had been acting as if he were out of his mind. But, then, in a very real sense, sin *is* insanity. The Bible tells us that "the wages of sin is death" (Romans 6:23). When a person deliberately goes on sinning he is committing spiritual suicide. This is insane.

"When he came to his senses," he remembered how good things were back home. His father's hired servants had an over-abundance of food—"and here I am starving to death!" (NIV). At last he was thinking intelligently and wisely.

So he made a resolution, "I will arise and go to my father" (v. 18). He had to get up from his sin and selfishness, his poverty and hunger, and head home.

He knew that he had no reason to expect that he would be received back into the family. After all, he had taken his share of the estate and "blown it." He had no basis for asking for forgiveness and mercy. He had no legal rights to any property. What was there to go back to? But he couldn't stay any longer where he was—and now he didn't want to; he had had enough.

So he planned carefully what he would say to his father. First, "I have sinned." This is the one essential confession that every sinner must make. "Against heaven" means "against God." In the last analysis, every sin we commit is against God, against His eternal love. But he had also sinned "before thee"—against his father.

Then he would say, "And am no more worthy to be called thy son: make me as one of thy hired servants" (v. 19). This is the only place he felt that he was fit to have—and he was right! He had hurt his father deeply and had disgraced the family. He now deserved nothing better than a servant's lowly status. After all, that would be a big improvement on what he was experiencing where he was.

E. The Pardoned: vv. 20-24

"And he arose, and came to his father." Both verbs are in the aorist tense, suggesting instantaneous action. He lost no time in putting feet to his thoughts.

It is not enough to make good resolutions; we must carry them out, or they are of no value whatever. Many people resolve to change their lives, to make a new beginning. But they go no further, and so are still lost. There is a time for words; but there is also a time for action, or the words will be lost in limbo.

Concerning the young man of the parable, Plummer writes: "The repentance is as real as the fall. He prepares full confession, but no excuse; and, having made a good resolution, he acts upon it without delay" (*Luke*, p. 375).

While the son was still a long way off, his father saw him coming down the road. In spite of the rags and haggard appearance, there was something familiar about his walk.

We might have expected the father to be angry and disgusted. Instead he "had compassion"—the aorist tense suggests that he was "gripped with compassion"—this was his immediate reaction. He "ran, and fell on his neck, and kissed him." The last verb is a compound, meaning that he "kissed him tenderly." The father's heart was overflowing with love toward his lost son, who was now safe. "As yet the son has said nothing, and the father does not know in what spirit he has returned; but it is enough that he *has* returned. The father has long been watching for this" (Plummer, *Luke*, p. 375).

The son would have been less than human if he had not been overcome with emotion. This warm, affectionate welcome was far beyond what he had any right to expect. But as soon as he could get his voice he made his honest, humble confession (v. 21). How unworthy he was to be the son of such a generous father!

According to the generally accepted Greek text of verse 21, the son never finished his speech (cf. v. 19). Plummer comments: "He had not counted on his father's love and forgiveness when he decided to make this request; and now emotion prevents him from meeting his father's generosity with such a proposal" (*Luke*, p. 375). Perhaps so. But we somewhat prefer the suggestion of R. V. G. Tasker: "The prodigal is interrupted by his father, and so prevented from completing his carefully prepared speech!" (*Greek New Testament*, p. 422).

By now, apparently, they' were nearing the house. The father said to his servants: "Quick! Bring the best robe and put it on him. Put a ring on his finger and sandals on his feet" (v. 22, NIV). "Quick" is in the best Greek text. The word for "robe" (*stole*) means a long and stately robe. The son was to have the very best to replace his rags and cover his emaciated body.

The "ring" (*daktylion*, only here in the New Testament) has special significance. This was probably the signet-ring, with the family emblem on it. It meant that the returned son was fully reinstated and was authorized to transact business in his father's name. And that is the way God treats every repentant sinner. He does not half-forgive us or put us on probation. Rather, He forgives us fully, and immediately gives us all the privileges of sonship in His family. And that is the way we should forgive others.

With regard to the "sandals," Plummer writes: "The *hypodemata* were marks of a freeman, for slaves went barefoot." He continues: "None of the three things ordered are necessaries. The father is not merely supplying the wants of his son, who has returned in miserable and scanty clothing. He is doing him honour" (*Luke*, p. 376).

The father also ordered the servants to bring the fattened calf and kill it. "Let's have a feast and celebrate" (v. 23, NIV). "Calf" is in the singular. Plummer comments: "There is only one, reserved for some special occasion. But there is no occasion better than this" (*Luke*, p. 376).

This reminds us of verse 7: "I tell you that in the same way there is more rejoicing in heaven over one sinner who repents than over ninety-nine righteous persons who do not need to repent" (NIV).

Why the great celebration? "For this my son was dead, and is alive again; he was lost, and is found" (v. 24). As far as the father was concerned, the son had been dead and lost; now he was alive and found.

II. THE PARSIMONIOUS SON: Luke 15:25-32

A. Inquisitive: vv. 25-27

While all this was going on, the older brother had been out in the field. Probably now it was getting toward evening, and he was returning. As he neared the house he heard music and dancing. So he summoned one of the servants and asked what was going on. The servant told him that his brother had returned home and his joyful father had put on a big celebration in gratitude for having him back safe and sound.

B. Angry: v. 28

The older brother's reaction to the prodigal's return is in startling contrast

to that of his father. He was angry and refused to go into the house and join the celebration.

Evidently the servant reported this to the father, who went out and "entreated him." The Greek is literally "was pleading with him." This suggests that the older brother interrupted his father. He had built up so much pressure inside that he exploded.

C. Self-righteous: v. 29

"Angry and sullen, the older son gave vent to his feelings in a very unlovely and unloving tirade. He showed that he was far from being a true son of his generous-hearted father" (Ralph Earle, *Wesleyan Bible Commentary*, IV, 296). Here is what he said: "Look! All these years I've been slaving for you and never disobeyed your orders. Yet you never gave me even a young goat so I could celebrate with my friends" (NIV). That is the way he felt about "life with father"; it was slavery! Poor fellow, he didn't understand the meaning of love.

On his statement that he had never disobeyed his father, Plummer makes this comment: "The blind self-complacency of the Pharisee, trusting in his scrupulous observance of the letter of the Law, is here clearly expressed. This sentence alone is strong evidence that the elder brother represents the Pharisees rather than the Jewish nation as a whole, which could hardly be supposed to make so demonstrably false a claim" (*Luke*, p. 378).

Here is legalism at its worst—proud, self-righteous, obsessed with slavelike duty, unhappy, condemning others, self-centered.

D. Jealous: v. 30

"But when this son of yours who has squandered your property with prostitutes comes home, you kill the fattened calf for him!" (NIV). He refused to say, "My brother." Contemptuously he says, "This son of

---

DISCUSSION QUESTIONS

1. How do teenagers show the attitude of the younger son: "Give me all of life now"?
2. What is the price one pays for wanting to experience everything in youth?
3. What is true repentance?
4. How are we to treat repentant sinners?
5. How are church members sometimes like the Pharisees?
6. How may we avoid this wrong attitude?

yours." Jealousy generates hate. The older brother shows no respect for his father's feelings, but castigates him severely. Legalism is lack of love.

E. Reproved: vv. 31-32

The patience of this father is amazing. Tenderly he says, "My son" (NIV). The Greek word for "son" here is *teknon*, which literally means "child." (The usual word for "son" in this parable, and elsewhere in the New Testament, is *whios*.) Though the older brother was so angry that he would not even courteously say, "Father," yet his father now answers his insolent tirade with tender affection. He showed genuine love to both sons!

The message was also gentle: "You are always with me, and everything I have is yours" (NIV). Not just a young goat—he could have had the whole flock!

These words of the father are full of meaning for us as Christians. We should remember them if we are ever tempted to think that our heavenly Father is treating others of His children better than He is treating us—that they are getting more from Him. If so, it is entirely our fault! He tells us that all He has belongs to us. We are "heirs of God and joint-heirs with Christ" (Romans 8:17). We can have as much heavenly blessing as we want. It is carelessness and selfishness that rob us of the abundant blessings that are ours for the asking.

The father concluded: "But we had to celebrate and be glad, because this brother of yours was dead and is alive again; he was lost and is found" (v. 32, NIV). The older brother had said contemptuously, "This son of yours . . ." With gentle reproof the father answers, "This brother of yours. . . ." It was a rebuke to the Pharisees. The tax collectors and "sinners," whom they despised, were really their brother Jews. Jesus scores the Pharisees for their legalistic lack of love.

CONTEMPORARY APPLICATION

There are two lost sons in this parable, and both are significant for us today. The younger son was lost way out in the world, far from home. But the older son was lost right in the home. His hateful attitude showed that his heart was bad; he was not a true son.

Today we have two types of sinners for whom we should be concerned. There are those who have run away from God, and we follow them with our prayers. If they repent and return, we should receive them warmly, with forgiving love.

But too often we forget those who are lost at home—in our Christian homes and in our churches. They are there in body, but not in spirit. They need our prayers, too.

THE WAY OF RESPONSIBLE STEWARDSHIP

DEVOTIONAL READING	Luke 12:42-48

ADULTS

Topic: *The Way of Responsible Stewardship*

Background Scripture: Mark 12:41-44; Luke 16:10–17:10

Scripture Lesson: Luke 16:10-15; Mark 12:41-44

Memory Verse: *He who is faithful in a very little is faithful also in much; and he who is dishonest in a very little is dishonest also in much.* Luke 16:10

YOUTH

Topic: *My Christian Stewardship*

Background Scripture: Mark 12:41-44; Luke 16:10–17:10

Scripture Lesson: Luke 16:10-15; Mark 12:41-44

Memory Verse: *He who is faithful in a very little is faithful also in much; and he who is dishonest in a very little is dishonest also in much.* Luke 16:10

CHILDREN

Topic: *Giving Your Best*

Background Scripture: Mark 12:41-44

Scripture Lesson: Mark 12:41-44

Memory Verse: *God loves a cheerful giver.* II Corinthians 9:7

DAILY BIBLE READINGS

Mon., Mar. 21: The Wicked Tenants, Mark 12:1-12.
Tues., Mar. 22: Caesar's or God's, Mark 12:13-17.
Wed., Mar. 23: The Unjust Steward, Luke 16:1-9.
Thurs., Mar. 24: God or Mammon, Luke 16:10-17.
Fri., Mar. 25: Doing One's Duty, Luke 17:7-10.
Sat., Mar. 26: The Widow's Mite, Mark 12:41-44.
Sun., Mar. 27: Much Given, Much Required, Luke 12:42-48.

LESSON AIM

To show us as Christians how we may be good stewards of what God has given us.

LESSON SETTING

Time: About A.D. 29

Place: Perhaps Perea, east of the Jordan

The Way of Responsible Stewardship

LESSON OUTLINE

I. A Man and His Money: Luke 16:10-15
   A. Honest Stewardship: vv. 10-12
   B. Serving God or Money: v. 13
   C. Divine Versus Human Values: vv. 14-15

II. The Rich Man and Lazarus: Luke 16:19-31
   A. Differences in This Life: vv. 19-21
   B. Differences in the Next Life: vv. 22-26
   C. Concern for Lost Relatives: vv. 27-31

III. The Poor Widow's Mite: Mark 12:41-44
   A. The Large Gifts of the Wealthy: v. 41
   B. The Small Gift of the Poor Widow: v. 42
   C. The True Measure of Giving: vv. 43-44

SUGGESTED INTRODUCTION FOR ADULTS

Stewardship constitutes a very important phase of the Christian's life. Giving and spirituality are closely connected.

We have seen this demonstrated in churches. More than once a pastor who was concerned about the low spiritual ebb of his church has launched a campaign of vigorous giving to missions. As the people loosened their purse strings their hearts were opened and enlarged. They found the truth of Jesus' words, "It is more blessed to give than to receive" (Acts 20:35). When the people gave, they rejoiced. Almost overnight there was a new, vibrant atmosphere of blessing in the church.

The same thing happens to individuals. Selfishness is a stifling, choking, strangling thing. Misers are never happy people. Generosity in giving is a great means of spiritual grace. Everyone who has tried it knows this.

SUGGESTED INTRODUCTION FOR YOUTH

It is never too soon for a young person to begin practicing Christian stewardship. As soon as we receive an allowance or earn a little money in any way, we should begin to tithe. A tenth of what we get belongs to the Lord and should be given to Him. It is well to start this habit of tithing while young. As soon as we give our hearts to the Lord we should give Him our pocketbooks, too.

Christian stewardship means that all we are and all we have belongs to the Lord. Our talents, time, and money are all His, to be used as He directs. So stewardship involves offerings as well as tithes. If we give generously to the Lord, He will give generously to us. Try it!

CONCEPTS FOR CHILDREN

1. The poor widow gave all she had to the Lord.
2. Sometime the Lord may ask us to give Him all we have, to test our love.
3. We should learn to give while we are small.
4. God wants us to give gladly, not grudgingly.

THE LESSON COMMENTARY

I. A MAN AND HIS MONEY:
Luke 16:10-15

This chapter begins (vv. 1-8) with what may be called "The Parable of the Shrewd Manager." It is a familiar story. The manager of a certain rich man was accused of wasting his possessions. So the boss called his employee on the carpet and demanded an explanation. The manager made a quick deal with his master's debtors, discounting their bills heavily so that they would be obligated to him and take care of him when his present job was terminated. His "master" (NIV) ("the lord" [v. 8, KJV] does *not* mean Jesus) "commended the unjust steward because he had done wisely"—better, "because he had acted shrewdly" (NIV).

Then Jesus commented: "For the people of this world are more shrewd in dealing with their own kind than are the people of the light" (NIV). God expects us to use the intelligence He has given us. We are to be prudent and far-sighted in dealing with others.

The application of the parable is given in verse 9: "I tell you, use worldly wealth to gain friends for yourselves, so that when it is gone, you will be welcomed into eternal dwellings" (NIV). Matthew 25:40 may help us to interpret this. When we give to the needy we are laying up treasures in heaven.

The first section of our lesson today (vv. 10-15) gives a further explication and application. Alfred Plummer comments: "To prevent possible misunderstanding owing to the commendation of a dishonest servant, Christ here insists upon the necessity of fidelity in dealing with worldly possessions. He shows clearly that it is not the dishonesty of the steward which is commended as an example, but his prudence in using present opportunities as a means of providing for the future" (*A Critical and Exegetical Commentary on the Gospel*

According to St. Luke, International Critical Commentary, pp. 384-85).

A. Honest Stewardship: vv. 10-12

"That which is least" means "very little." Ray Summers writes: "The *very little* of verse 10 refers to material things and the *much* refers to spiritual things. Faithfulness in the use of material possessions is followed correspondingly by faithfulness in the higher stewardship of spiritual things. By the same principle, dishonesty in the use of material possessions is followed correspondingly by dishonesty in the higher stewardship of spiritual things" (*Commentary on Luke*, p. 191).

Though verse 10 states a common principle that operates in this life, the above interpretation seems justified by the parallel in verse 11. "*Very little* and *much* (v. 10) seem to be explained as meaning *unrighteous mammon* and *true riches* (v. 11). The *very little* relates to this life, the *much* to the next" (Ralph Earle, *Wesleyan Bible Commentary*, IV, 299).

In a similar vein Frederic L. Godet writes: "Our Lord's thought is therefore this: God commits to man, during his earthly sojourn in the state of probation, goods belonging to Him, which are of less value (earthly things); and the use, faithful or unfaithful, just or unjust, which we make of these settles the question whether our true patrimony (the goods of the Spirit, of which the believer himself receives only the earnest here below) shall or shall not be granted to him above" (*A Commentary on the Gospel of St. Luke*, II, 169).

In verse 11 "unrighteous mammon" is contrasted with "the true riches"—literally, "the genuine thing." Richard C. H. Lenski comments: "Mammon is, indeed, not the genuine thing, transient, fleeting, deceptive as it is, bound presently to give out altogether (v. 9). They are fools who place that estimate upon it. 'The genuine thing' is that which never gives out, never disappoints. It is left unnamed, but by analogy it is all our spiritual and heavenly wealth" (*Interpretation of St. Luke's Gospel*, p. 834).

Mammon is here described as "unrighteous." This may be for two reasons: (1) wealth is often accumulated by unjust means; (2) its use is too often an abuse.

Jesus goes on to say in verse 12: "And if ye have not been faithful in that which is another man's, who shall give you that which is your own?" But "another man's" in the Greek is simply "another's." The contrasts in verses 10 and 11 are continued. "*Another's* means God's, for everything we have here on earth belongs to Him, not to us. In a sense we shall enjoy in eternity what is our *own*" (Earle, *Wesleyan Commentary*, IV, p. 299)— our heavenly inheritance.

Plummer summarizes this paragraph thus: "The case sketched in these three verses (10-12) is that of a wealthy owner who educates his son for managing the estate to which he is heir, and proves his fitness for it by allowing him to have control of something that is of little value except as an instrument for forming and discerning character. If the son proves faithless in this insignificant charge, he is disinherited" (*Luke*, p. 387).

B. Serving God or Money: v. 13

"Servant" is literally "houseservant" (*oiketes*, from *oikos*, "house"). "Serve" is literally "be a slave to" (*douleuein*). Plummer points out the force of this: "To be a *servant* to two masters is possible, and is often done. But to be at the absolute disposal of two masters is not possible" (*Luke*, p. 387). A household slave cannot belong to two different owners. We cannot really live with divided loyalties, or they will tear us apart.

Then Jesus makes the application: "You cannot be a slave to God and money." Ultimately one or the other will get our full loyalty.

As has often been pointed out, we are to be the masters of our money; we are not to let our money master us. One has only to watch those who work incessantly day and night to make all the money they can, to see what a horrible slavery this is. They allow themselves to be deprived of family life, of leisure to enjoy God's beauties in nature, of all that is highest and best in life.

C. Divine Versus Human Values: vv. 14-15

"The Pharisees, who loved money, heard all this and were sneering at Jesus" (v. 14, NIV). "Who loved money" is literally "being money-lovers"—*philargyroi*, compounded of *philos*, "lover," and *argyros*, "money" (literally, "silver"). The politically minded Sadducees were more given to living in ostentatious wealth. But the Pharisees, at least some of them, were money-grabbers.

". . . were sneering at" ("derided," KJV) is literally "were turning up their noses at" Jesus. It was a contemptuous, and contemptible, attitude. Plummer writes: "The covetousness of the Pharisees is independently attested, and they regarded their wealth as a special blessing for their carefulness in observing the Law. Hence their contempt for a teaching which declared that there is danger in wealth, and that as a rule it promotes unrighteousness. They considered themselves an abiding proof of the connexion between riches and righteousness: moreover, they had their own explanation of the reason why a Rabbi who was poor declaimed against riches" (*Luke*, pp. 387-88).

Jesus accused the Pharisees of justifying themselves "before men" (v. 15). But not before God, for "God knoweth your hearts." He could read there the covetousness which caused them to amass wealth for their own selfish purposes.

Then Jesus declared: "For that which is highly esteemed among men is abomination in the sight of God." The phrase "in the sight of" translates the same single Greek word (*enopion*) that is rendered "before" with "men."

"Abomination" ("detestable," NIV) is a strong Greek word, *bdelygma*. It is used frequently in the Septuagint (especially Isaiah) for the abominations of idolatry. This is the only place in the New Testament where it is used in the general sense of something detestable. "It meant originally that which greatly offends the nostrils" (Plummer, *Luke*, p. 388). One cannot help wondering if this was Jesus' answer to the fact that the Pharisees turned up their noses at Him. This attitude was a stench in God's nostrils.

II. THE RICH MAN AND LAZARUS:
Luke 16:19-31

A. Differences in This Life: vv. 19-21

"There was a rich man who was dressed in purple and fine linen and lived in luxury every day" (v. 19, NIV). In those days purple dye was derived from a shellfish in the Mediterranean. Naturally it was very scarce and expensive. That is why "purple" came to be used as a symbol for royalty. Only the rich could afford it.

At the gate of this rich man, who had all he wanted every day, a poor beggar named Lazarus was laid. So desperate was he for food that he would gladly have eaten whatever fell from the rich man's table. There is no evidence that either the rich man or his servants showed any pity for the helpless beggar.

Added to hunger was a further misery: His body was covered with sores—the Greek says literally, "being ulcerated." Dogs "licked his sores" (v. 21). Many commentators feel that this was the ultimate in his misery. But we would agree with Lenski's suggestion: "These dogs licked the beggar's sores

as they would have licked their own, to clean and ease them with their soft tongues. Dogs did that, no one else would" (*Luke*, p. 848).

B. Differences in the Next Life: vv. 22-26

Finally "the beggar died, and was carried by the angels into Abraham's bosom." He probably had no funeral; nothing is said about his burial, or any earthly pallbearers (he had heavenly ones). In contrast, "the rich man also died, and was buried." We may be sure that his funeral was marked by great pomp and ceremony, with many eulogies pronounced over his dead body. What good did they do him?

But on the other side of death the situation was in the sharpest possible contrast to the earthly scene. Now the roles of the two men were reversed: "In hell, where he was in torment, he looked up and saw Abraham far away, with Lazarus by his side" (v. 23, NIV).

Lazarus's suffering on earth had been severe. But it was nothing at all compared with the torment the rich man was now enduring. Being a Jew he cried out, "Father Abraham," begging him to send Lazarus with a drop of water to cool his tongue—"for I am tormented in this flame" (v. 24). He who had done nothing (recorded) for the poor beggar during his lifetime, was now asking Lazarus to help him!

"Son, remember" (v. 25) are words filled with significance. As a "son of the Law" (Hebrew *Ben-Torah*, Aramaic *Bar-Mitzvah*) the rich man had known the right way. But he had made money his god. The ultimate torment in hell will be the memory of wasted opportunities. The saddest words ever spoken are "It might have been," or "If only I had."

But now it was too late. Abraham declared that between Paradise and Inferno, to use Dante's designations, there was a great chasm fixed, so that no one could cross over (v. 26). The language here underscores the fact that in the next life there is no second chance—though in this life there may be a thousand chances to repent and change our destiny. At death our eternal abode is permanently decided, with no opportunity for reconsideration. What we do in this life determines where we spend eternity. It is a solemn lesson that should be learned before it is too late to change.

C. Concern for Lost Relatives: vv. 27-31

When the rich man realized that there was absolutely no help or hope for him, he recalled his five brothers, who were still alive on earth. He knew that they were following the same path he had taken. So he begged Abraham to send Lazarus back to earth to warn them (vv. 27-28).

Abraham's reply was: "They have Moses and the Prophets [the Jewish Scriptures, our Old Testament] let them listen to them" (v. 29, NIV). The Sacred Scriptures are all we need, if we will obey them.

When the rich man protested that if someone from the dead went to his brothers they would repent (v. 30), Abraham answered: "If they hear not Moses and the prophets, neither will they be persuaded, though one rose from the dead" (v. 31). This statement receives striking confirmation from an incident in Christ's life. When He raised Lazarus from the dead—the sameness of name is probably only an interesting coincidence—the Jewish leaders instead of believing Him wanted to kill Lazarus because he was influencing people toward Jesus (John 12:10-11).

III. THE POOR WIDOW'S MITE: Mark 12:41-44

A. The Large Gifts of the Wealthy: v. 41

Jesus had just condemned the teachers of the law ("the scribes") for their pride and hypocrisy (vv. 38-39) and especially because they "devour widow's houses, and for a pretext make long prayers" (v. 40). They would take mortgages on the homes of poor, helpless widows, and then foreclose those mortgages, cruelly leaving the widows entirely destitute.

In striking contrast to all of this, we are told about a widow who gave her all. The setting was very dramatic.

Jesus sat down opposite "the treasury" (v. 41). This was located in the Court of the Women.

The temple area of Jesus' day covered about twenty-five or thirty acres and consisted of a series of courts. One would first enter the largest area, called the Court of the Gentiles. Here Jesus could teach vast crowds.

Between this and the Court of the Women was a marble wall with nine gateways. Each had a sign over it, written in Greek. One of these was discovered in 1871. It reads: "No foreigner may enter within the balustrade and enclosure around the Sanctuary. Whoever is caught will render himself liable to the death penalty which will inevitably follow." So it was only Jews who were permitted in the Court of the Women. Jewish men were allowed to go beyond this into the Court of Israel. It is said that the Court of Women could hold fifteen thousand people.

The "treasury" consisted of thirteen large brass receptacles for money. They are called in the Hebrew "trumpets," because of their trumpet-shaped mouths. Nine of them were for the

---

DISCUSSION QUESTIONS

1. What is the real nature and purpose of money?
2. Of what value is earthly wealth?
3. Why is the tithe still a fair minimum standard?
4. What principles should govern our giving of offerings?
5. How did the rich man show poor stewardship?
6. What is our "fair share" in giving?

regular temple tax. The other four were labeled for offerings for the purchase of wood, incense, temple decorations, and burnt offerings. Probably priests stood by to supervise the people's giving.

Jesus sat down and was watching the crowd putting money into these receptacles. It must have been an interesting study of human nature, observing the faces of the different people who came. He especially noted how the wealthy threw in large amounts, probably hoping to be honored for it.

B. The Small Gift of the Poor Widow: v. 42

A widow came and threw in "two mites, which make a farthing"—"two very small copper coins, worth only a fraction of a penny" (NIV). She had only two *lepta*, but she gave both. The *lepton* was the smallest copper coin, worth only about a fourth of a cent. (It is still the smallest unit of monetary value in Greece today, where a fifty-lepta coin equals about a cent and a half of United States money.) For the sake of his Roman readers—it is usually thought that this Gospel was written to the Romans—Mark says that the two lepta equaled one *quadrans*, a Roman coin worth about half an American penny. This would be a rather small amount on any treasurer's book!

C. The True Measure of Giving: vv. 43-44

But this was not a small amount on God's records. Jesus must have startled His disciples when He called them to Him and proclaimed: "I tell you the truth, this poor widow has put more into the treasury than all the others" (v. 43, NIV).

How could He say this? Verse 44 gives some clues: "They all gave out of their wealth; but she, out of her poverty, put in everything—all she had to live on" (NIV).

She gave more than all the others in two ways: (1) in proportion to what she had; (2) in the spirit she showed. A. M. Hunter says, "The greatest gift is that which costs the giver most" (*Gospel According to Saint Mark*, p. 121).

"Giving is not measured so much by what is given as by what is left. God is not impressed with large amounts but by a sacrificial spirit of devotion. The rich cast in 'out of that which was abounding to them.' The poor widow gave out of her lack, her want, her real poverty. Her gift weighed more in God's scales than the costly gifts of the wealthy. . . . A good rule for giving is: 'Give till you feel it' " (Ralph Earle, *Gospel According to Mark*, p. 152).

Lenski puts it well: "The widow's gift, though copper, was entirely gold in the eyes of the Lord" (*Luke*, p. 559). This is the divine assessment.

CONTEMPORARY APPLICATION

In this world it is the big gifts that receive prominent notice. A billionaire gives five million to some cause, and it is trumpeted loudly in the press. Few stop to think of how poor the man must be with only 995 million left!

On the heavenly books the story is far different. A person who gave to missions the last five dollars he or she had, not knowing when or how it would be replaced, is a far more generous giver in God's sight. And He is the one who keeps the final records and will give the final rewards.

Our responsibility is to be faithful in our stewardship—not only of money, but of time and talents as well. Above all, we must give in a spirit of love.

JESUS OFFERS HIMSELF

DEVOTIONAL READING	John 3:14-21

ADULTS

Topic: *Jesus Offers Himself*

Background Scripture: Mark 11:1-11; 14:1—15:41

Scripture Lesson: Mark 11:7-10; 14:32-36; 15:33-39

Memory Verse: *Father, all things are possible to thee; remove this cup from me; yet not what I will, but what thou wilt.* Mark 14:36

YOUTH

Topic: *Jesus Gives His Life*

Background Scripture: Mark 11:1-11; 14:1—15:41

Scripture Lesson: Mark 11:7-10; 14:32-36; 15:33-39

Memory Verse: *Father, all things are possible to thee; remove this cup from me; yet not what I will, but what thou wilt.* Mark 14:36

CHILDREN

Topic: *Jesus Is Crucified*

Background Scripture: Mark 11:1-11; 14:1—15:41

Scripture Lesson: Mark 14:32-38; 15:24-25

Memory Verse: *I am the good shepherd. The good shepherd lays down his life for the sheep.* John 10:11

DAILY BIBLE READINGS

Mon., Mar. 28: "Hosanna in the Highest," Mark 11:1-11.
Tues., Mar. 29: God's Will Be Done, Mark 14:32-42.
Wed., Mar. 30: Jesus Is Betrayed, Mark 14:43-50.
Thurs., Mar. 31: Condemned to Death, Mark 14:53-65.
Fri., Apr. 1: Delivered to Be Crucified, Mark 15:6-15.
Sat., Apr. 2: Death on the Cross, Mark 15:33-39.
Sun., Apr. 3: Exaltation Through the Cross, Philippians 2:5-11.

LESSON AIM

To help us see that following in Jesus' way means full commitment to the will of God, regardless of the cost.

LESSON SETTING

Time: April of A.D. 30 (or 33, as some hold)

Place: Jerusalem and its surroundings

LESSON OUTLINE

Jesus Offers Himself

I. The Triumphal Entry: Mark 11:7-10
   A. Riding a Colt: v. 7

B. A Royal Carpet: v. 8
C. A Royal Welcome: vv. 9-10

II. The Agony in Gethsemane: Mark 14:32-42
    A. The Eight Outside: v. 32
    B. The Three Inside: v. 33
    C. The Overwhelming Sorrow: v. 34
    D. The Prayer of Submission: vv. 35-36
    E. The Admonition to Watch and Pray: vv. 37-38
    F. The Second Prayer: vv. 39-40
    G. The Imminent Arrest: vv. 41-42

III. The Crucifixion: Mark 15:22-39
    A. The First Three Hours: vv. 22-32
    B. The Last Three Hours: v. 33
    C. The Cry of Dereliction: v. 34
    D. The Reaction of the Bystanders: vv. 35-36
    E. The Death of Christ: vv. 37-38
    F. The Testimony of the Centurion: v. 39

SUGGESTED INTRODUCTION FOR ADULTS

After four lessons on "Jesus Teaches His Way," we now complete our twenty-one-week study of the life and ministry of Jesus with the fifth and final unit, "Jesus Climaxes His Mission." This brings us to the end of the story in the Gospels of Mark and Luke.

Since this is Palm Sunday, it is appropriate that we should study today the so-called Triumphal Entry of Jesus into Jerusalem. But since next Sunday is Easter, we have to include the agony in Gethsemane and the Crucifixion, in order to come to the Resurrection next week. The last two sessions of the unit will be devoted to Jesus' assurance to His disciples that He was the Risen Lord, and to His commissioning them to carry on His ministry.

In the lesson today we have the greatest contrast imaginable—between the Triumphal Entry on the one hand, and Gethsemane and Calvary on the other. But both were in the Father's will for His Son.

SUGGESTED INTRODUCTION FOR YOUTH

What does Palm Sunday mean? It means celebration. It is the cry, "Hosanna! The King has come!"

We should rejoice today that the Savior of the world has come indeed. But we have to face the somber fact that just as many people rejected Him then, so the masses reject Him now.

And so the Triumphal Entry was followed by Gethsemane and Calvary. And we will find that some of our highest moments of rejoicing will be followed by hours of agonizing prayer. It is always costly to say, "Thy will be done." For Jesus it meant death on the cross. And for all of us it will mean being crucified with Him (Galatians 2:20).

CONCEPTS FOR CHILDREN

1. We should join in praising Jesus, as children did on that first Palm Sunday (Matthew 21:15-16).

2. We should not deny that we belong to Jesus, as Peter did.
3. Jesus loved us and gave His life for us.
4. We should respond to that love by giving ourselves to Him.

THE LESSON COMMENTARY

I. THE TRIUMPHAL ENTRY: Mark 11:7-10

A. Riding a Colt: v. 7

It was the Sunday (first day of the week) before the crucifixion. Jesus had come from Galilee, by way of Perea, and was now approaching Jerusalem. As He came near Bethphage and Bethany, neighboring villages on the slopes of the Mount of Olives (v. 1), He sent two of his disciples on ahead to get a colt for Him to ride (v. 2). Since Matthew (21:1) only mentions Bethphage, it would seem that it was there they found the colt tied at a doorway. They untied it and brought it to Jesus.

In lieu of a saddle, the disciples threw their outer cloaks over the colt (v. 7). Then Jesus sat on it. We are told in both Mark (v. 2) and Luke (19:30) that it was a colt that no one had ever ridden. To ride an unbroken colt would ordinarily be a difficult feat, but the Creator was in full command. God had told Adam to have dominion over all animal life (Genesis 1:28). By his sin of disobedience, he forfeited this authority, at least in a measure. But the Perfect Man had perfect authority over creation.

In choosing a donkey on which to ride into Jerusalem, Jesus was purposefully fulfilling the Messianic prophecy of Zechariah 9:9, as we are told in Matthew 21:4 (NIV):

"Say to the daughter of Zion,
'See, your king comes to you,
gentle and riding on a donkey,
  on a colt, the foal of a donkey.' "

A. M. Hunter puts the matter well: "This prophecy Jesus now deliberately acted out. By his action he proclaimed that he was the Messiah, but a Messiah contrary to all their dreaming, a Messiah without arms or an army, who was riding in lowly pomp that road of the spirit marked out for the Servant of the Lord, a road upon which ever darker fell the shadow of a cross" (St. Mark, Cambridge Greek Testament, p. 109).

This was a Messianic act of the highest possible significance. Jesus was publicly presenting Himself to the Jewish nation as its Messiah.

B. A Royal Carpet: v. 8

Many of the people spread their cloaks on the road, to form a carpet on which the King could ride. Others, more restrained, laid on the path a litter of leaves that they had cut in the fields nearby. All were paying their highest respect to Jesus as He rode down the western slope of the Mount of Olives on His way into Jerusalem.

C. A Royal Welcome: vv. 9-10

Some were eagerly running on ahead of Him, while others were following behind the donkey. But all were crying out enthusiastically: "Hosanna; Blessed is he that cometh in the name of the Lord."

"Hosanna" is a Hebrew word literally meaning "Save now" or "Save, we pray." But here it seems to be an exclamation of praise, like "God save the King!" (Or, Queen!) In place of "Hosanna in the highest" (v. 10; Matthew 21:9), Luke (19:38) has "glory in the highest." That is the way Luke explained "Hosanna" for his Greek readers. The whole account in Luke's Gospel (see 19:37) shows that here it was an expression of rejoicing, rather than a prayer.

All four Gospels have "Blessed is he that cometh in the name of the Lord." The Messiah was often referred to as "the Coming One," which is the literal Greek here. So the crowd was definitely welcoming Jesus as the long-expected Messiah who would come to deliver God's people from their enemies. Very probably the hope that day was that Jesus would ride into Jerusalem in triumph and overthrow the Roman rulers. This is shown in the people's cry (only found in Mark): "Blessed is the coming kingdom of our father David!" (v. 10, NIV; cf. II Samuel 7:11-16). But He had come to set up a spiritual kingdom, not a political one.

Someone may ask, "Where do we get the name 'Palm Sunday'?" This comes from John's account of the Triumphal Entry. He says (12:13) that the people took "branches of palm trees"—symbols of victory.

It has sometimes been said that the same people cried "Hosanna!" on Sunday and "Crucify him!" on Friday (15:13-14). But on Sunday it was primarily the Galilean pilgrims to the Passover, who has seen his miracles (cf. Luke 19:37). On Friday it was the people of Jerusalem.

II. THE AGONY IN GETHSEMANE: Mark 14:32-42

A. The Eight Outside: v. 32

After the Last Supper (vv. 17-21) and the inauguration of the Lord's Supper (vv. 22-25), Jesus went out with His disciples to the Mount of Olives, just east of Jerusalem (v. 26). On the way He predicted that Peter would thrice deny his Master (vv. 27-31).

Finally (v. 32) they came to "a place" ("a piece of ground") named "Gethsemane." This is a Hebrew term

meaning "oil-press." The name is given only here and in Matthew 26:36. In John 18:1, 26 it is called a "garden." But probably a better translation is "olive grove" (NIV). The name Gethsemane indicates that it was a place where olive oil was pressed out of the olives—for which the Mount of Olives was named. We do not know the exact location of Gethsemane, but we do know that it was an olive grove on the slopes of the Mount of Olives. The "Garden of Gethsemane" kept today by the Franciscan friars is a beautiful spot for meditation and prayer. One can kneel under a gnarled olive tree thought to be over a thousand years old. It would not, however, be the same tree as in Jesus' day, for Josephus says that Titus cut down all the trees on the east side of the city of Jerusalem.

Before entering the olive grove, which may have been enclosed by a rustic stone wall, Jesus said to eight of His disciples, "Sit ye here, while I shall pray." They were to be on guard at the gate of the grove.

B. The Three Inside: v. 33

Taking with Him Peter, James, and John, Jesus went inside the enclosure. These three were the only disciples with Him when He raised Jairus's daughter from the dead (5:37). They also were alone with Him on the Mount of Transfiguration (9:2), where they witnessed His glory. Now they alone were to view His agony.

By our attitude we determine how close we will be to Christ. There were more than five hundred at one time who saw Jesus after His resurrection (I Corinthians 15:6). Of these only 120 tarried in the upper room (Acts 1:15). There were 12 apostles. With Judas Iscariot gone, 8 of them had to wait outside Gethsemane. Only the 3 who constituted the inner circle were privileged to be with Jesus on the three occasions. Are we willing to pay the price of belonging to the inner circle near the Master?

As Jesus entered the olive grove, He began "to be sore amazed, and to be very heavy"—better, "to be deeply distressed and troubled" (NIV). Both of these infinitives are strong verbs in the Greek. The first can be translated "terrified." Jesus was entering into terrific emotional suffering. Henry B. Swete says: "Long as He had foreseen the Passion, when it came clearly into view its terrors exceeded his anticipations" (*The Gospel According to St. Mark*, p. 322).

C. The Overwhelming Sorrow: v. 34

To the three disciples that were closest to Him Jesus opened His heart and said, "My soul is overwhelmed with sorrow to the point of death" (NIV). In other words, He was saying to them: "My sorrow is killing me; it's crushing the life out of me." He begged them to stay there and watch. In this hour of deepest soul agony He craved their companionship. But they failed Him! The shadow of the cross was falling across His soul, but the disciples were oblivious to it. They had not yet caught the significance of His three predictions of the coming passion.

D. The Prayer of Submission: vv. 35-36

Jesus "went forward a little" (Luke says "a stone's throw"). The statement that He "went a little farther" has great spiritual significance. Throughout His earthly ministry He was always going "a little farther" to help people. Now, at the close, He went a little farther in suffering in order to save us.

Finally, He "fell on the ground." Mark uses here the imperfect tense of continuous action: "He was falling." This may suggest that He was staggering, stumbling under the crushing load of the world's sin, until He finally fell prostrate on the ground. No wonder this is called the Holy of Holies of the Gospels, and we must draw the inner curtain of reverence across this sacred scene.

What was Jesus' prayer? "That, if it were possible, the hour might pass from him." He was beginning to sense what Calvary would mean, and the picture was so horrible that He instinctively cried out for release. We must remember that Jesus was human as well as divine. His humanity shrank from the deep darkness ahead.

His actual prayer is recorded for us in verse 36. "Abba" is the Aramaic word for "Father." It is followed by *pater*, the Greek word for "Father." As is almost always true when one is under deep emotional stress, Jesus cried out in the familiar language of His childhood home. We have no way of knowing whether He used both languages here, or whether Mark adds *pater* as an explanation of *abba* for his Gentile readers.

What was the "cup" from which He asked to be delivered? "Some scoffers have called Jesus a coward. They have remarked that while martyrs have gone singing to the stake, He cringed at the thought of the cross and shrank from impending death. But such have not entered at all into the mysteries of Calvary. His was no martyr's death. It was not physical suffering that He dreaded, but separation from His Father's face when He took man's place as a condemned sinner. It was the premonition of that moment when He would cry out, 'My God, my God, why hast thou forsaken me?' that caused Him now to pray, 'Take away this cup from me'" (Ralph Earle, *The Gospel According to Mark*, Evangelical Commentary, p. 170).

But His prayer did not end there. Its conclusion was: "Nevertheless not what I will, but what thou wilt." The highest prayer that any Christian can pray is, "Not my will, but thine, be done." In praying this we are following Christ.

E. The Admonition to Watch and Pray: vv. 37-38

Coming back from His first period of agonizing prayer, Jesus found the three disciples sleeping. Reprovingly He said to boastful Peter: "Simon [calling him by his human name] are you asleep? Could you not keep watch for one hour?" (v. 37, NIV). Then He said to all three: "Watch and pray so that you will not fall into temptation. The spirit is willing, but the body is weak" (v. 38, NIV).

F. The Second Prayer: vv. 39-40

This was the same (v. 39) as the first. Once more, when He returned, He found the disciples asleep.

G. The Imminent Arrest: vv. 41-42

In the Greek exactly the same words in the same order can be a declaration or a question. Common sense shows that the middle of verse 41 should be taken as a question. The King James Version is very awkward here: "Sleep on now. . . . Rise up, let us go." The correct translation is: "Are you still sleeping and resting? Enough! The hour has come. Look, the Son of Man is betrayed into the hands of sinners. Rise! Let us go! Here comes my betrayer!" (NIV). That makes sense.

III. THE CRUCIFIXION: Mark 15:22-39

A. The First Three Hours: vv. 22-32

"Golgotha" is the Aramaic word for "skull." It may well refer to a

---

DISCUSSION QUESTIONS

1. Why did Jesus present Himself as He did in the Triumphal Entry?
2. What two reactions were there to this?
3. Why did Jesus pray so long in Gethsemane?
4. Why did the Father let Him suffer so?
5. Why was Christ forsaken on the cross?
6. What is the full meaning of His death?

---

skull-shaped rock outside the north wall of Jerusalem.

Jesus was crucified at "the third hour"—that is, nine o'clock in the morning (v. 25). "The written notice of the charge against him read: THE KING OF THE JEWS" (v. 26, NIV). Two "robbers"—not "thieves" (KJV)—were crucified with Him, one on each side (v. 27). Thus Jesus was "numbered with the transgressors" (v. 28), as Isaiah had prophesied (53:12).

"Those who passed by hurled insults at him, shaking their heads" (v. 29, NIV). With callous cruelty they mocked Him and challenged Him to come down from the cross. Saddest of all, the chief priests and the teachers of the Law (interpreters of Scripture) mocked His claim to be the Messiah (vv. 31-32). To top it all off, the robbers crucified with Him "heaped insults on him" (v. 32, NIV). It was the world's worst hour. But it became, redemptively, the best hour the world had ever seen.

B. The Last Three Hours: v. 33

From noon until three o'clock "there was darkness over the whole land." This is recorded in all three Synoptic Gospels. This could not have been an ordinary eclipse of the sun, for the Passover always comes at the time of full moon. (Every Jewish month began with a new moon, and the Passover was on the fourteenth.) It may be that very heavy storm clouds, suggesting God's judgment, covered the sky.

C. The Cry of Dereliction: v. 34

The darkness over the land was only a symbol of the midnight blackness that enshrouded Christ's soul. This is evidenced by His cry (in Aramaic): "My God, my God, why hast thou forsaken me?" That is the wail of a lost soul! It would seem that Jesus, in His human consciousness, felt as though He had been forever forsaken by the Father. Richard C. H. Lenski writes: "All that we can say is that only thus, by Jesus' being actually forsaken, could the full price of our redemption be paid" (*Interpretation of St. Mark's Gospel*, p. 718). It was the ultimate price, and "Jesus paid it all."

D. The Reaction of the Bystanders: vv. 35-36

Listening to Jesus' cry in Aramaic, some who stood near the cross said, "Listen, he's calling Elijah" (v. 35, NIV). "Probably this remark was just a cruel joke, a piece of heartless mockery. It is not likely that they actually misunderstood Jesus, whether he spoke in Aramaic or Hebrew. What they meant perhaps was: 'This poor deluded "Messiah" thinks Elijah will come to his rescue' " (Earle, *Mark*, p. 185).

Someone, probably a soldier, filled a sponge with sour wine—which was the common drink of day laborers (Ruth 2:14) and private soldiers—attached it to a stick and raised it to Jesus' mouth (v. 36). "Let alone" on the lips of this man might mean, "Let me alone." Ezra P. Gould suggests this explanatory paraphrase for the last part of verse 36: "Let me give him this and so prolong his life, and then we shall get an opportunity to see whether Elijah comes to help him or not" (*A Critical and Exegetical Commentary on the Gospel According to St. Mark*, International Critical Commentary, p. 295). Matthew 27:49 may be reporting the earlier admonition to the soldier to leave Jesus alone.

E. The Death of Christ: vv. 37-38

Jesus cried out with a loud voice and then "gave up the ghost" (v. 37). The Greek has only one word, *exepneusen*—literally, "He breathed out." Today we would say it this way: "With a loud cry, Jesus breathed his last" (NIV). Plummer comments: "No Evangelist says that Christ 'died'; He gave up His life by an act of will, *He yielded up His spirit*" (*Mark*, Cambridge Greek Testament, p. 359). The single Greek word could be translated, "He expired."

Apparently at the moment of Jesus' death, "the curtain of the temple was torn in two from top to bottom" (v. 38, NIV). This was the inner veil in front of the Holy of Holies, not the outer veil in front of the Holy Place. "The significance of this startling event is given clearly in Hebrews 9:1-14; 10:19-22. It symbolized the fact that the way was now opened for every follower of Christ to enter the very presence of God. . . . The rending of the veil would be observed by the priest ministering in the temple at the time of the offering of the evening sacrifice. . . . This may be one explanation for the fact related in Acts 6:7 that many of the priests were converted to Christianity" (Earle, *Mark*, p. 186).

F. The Testimony of the Centurion: v. 39

It is interesting to note that every centurion mentioned in the New Testament is shown in a favorable light. This centurion—a Roman officer in charge of one hundred soldiers—was on duty at the cross. When he witnessed Christ's death, he said, "Truly this man was the Son of God." There is no article before the Greek word for "son"; so the phrase could be translated "a son of God." This seems to be the force of Luke's report of what the centurion said: "Certainly this was a righteous man" (23:47). "A son of God" would mean "a godly man." We have no way of knowing which this pagan Roman officer intended his words to mean.

CONTEMPORARY APPLICATION

Christianity, like Christ, is not always on parade. There are moments of triumph, of enthusiastic crowds. But often the greatest work of the kingdom is done, not by the man who shines in public, but by the agonizing intercessor behind the scenes.

So for all of us individually as Christians there will be the times of public rejoicing. But there will also be the hours of agony. Each of us must have our personal Gethsemane, when we pray with all our hearts, "Not my will, but thine, be done." And all of us must have our Calvary, where we are crucified with Christ (Galatians 4:4).

JESUS LIVES!

(EASTER)

DEVOTIONAL READING	I Corinthians 15:12-19

ADULTS

Topic: *Jesus Lives!*

Background Scripture: Mark 15:42—16:8; Luke 23:50—24:12

Scripture Lesson: Mark 15:42—16:8

Memory Verse: *He has risen, he is not here; see the place where they laid him.* Mark 16:6

YOUTH

Topic: *Jesus Lives!*

Background Scripture: Mark 15:42—16:8; Luke 23:50—24:12

Scripture Lesson: Mark 15:42—16:8

Memory Verse: *He has risen, he is not here; see the place where they laid him.* Mark 16:6

CHILDREN

Topic: *Our Risen King*

Background Scripture: Mark 15:42—16:8; Luke 23:50—24:12

Scripture Lesson: Mark 16:1-8

Memory Verse: *He is not here; for he has risen, as he said. Come, see the place where he lay.* Matthew 28:6

DAILY BIBLE READINGS

Mon., Apr. 4: Buried in a Borrowed Tomb, Luke 23:50—24:12.
Tues., Apr. 5: Sealed and Guarded, Matthew 27:62-66.
Wed., Apr. 6: News of the Resurrection, Luke 24:1-12.
Thurs., Apr. 7: Appearance to Mary Magdalene, John 20:11-18.
Fri., Apr. 8: Paid to Tell a Lie, Matthew 28:11-15.
Sat., Apr. 9: "The Resurrection and the Life," John 11:17-27.
Sun., Apr. 10: What If No Resurrection? I Corinthians 15:12-19.

LESSON AIM

To help us see the importance of Christ's resurrection and its significance for us.

LESSON SETTING

Time: Probably April 9, A.D. 30

Place: Jerusalem

Jesus Lives!

LESSON OUTLINE

I. **The Burial of Jesus:** Mark 15:42-47
   A. Joseph's Request: vv. 42-43
   B. Pilate's Surprise: vv. 44-45
   C. Careful Burial: v. 46
   D. The Watching Women: v. 47

II. **The Resurrection of Jesus:** Mark 16:1-8
   A. The Devoted Women: vv. 1-2
   B. A Problem Solved: vv. 3-4
   C. The Angel at the Tomb: v. 5
   D. The Startling Announcement: v. 6
   E. The Message to the Disciples: v. 7
   F. The Amazed Women: v. 8

SUGGESTED INTRODUCTION FOR ADULTS

In the Lesson Setting we suggested that the resurrection of Jesus may well have taken place on April 9, A.D. 30. Some may wonder how we can arrive at such a precise date.

The answer is, by astronomical calculations. Jesus was crucified at the time of the Jewish Feast of the Passover. The Passover lamb was killed on the afternoon of the fourteenth of the month Nisan and eaten that evening, which would be the fifteenth. (The Jewish day ran from sunset to sunset, not midnight to midnight as ours does.) Every Jewish month began with the new moon. So astronomers can calculate the year on which the fifteenth of the month would fall on a Friday, and then give it an exact date in terms of our solar calendar. (The Jews had a lunar calendar.) The early church held that Jesus was crucified on Friday. The Gospels definitely place the resurrection on Sunday morning.

SUGGESTED INTRODUCTION FOR YOUTH

Jesus lives! That is the foundation of our Christian faith. Had Jesus not risen, our faith would be "useless," as Paul says (I Corinthians 15:14, NIV). It is the risen, living Lord who is our Savior.

Mohammed is dead. Confucius is dead. Gautama, the Buddha, is dead. But Christ is alive! That is the unique glory of the Christian religion—something that no other religion can boast. It alone has a Founder who was divine, the Son of God. But also, only its founder died to atone for the sins of the world and then rose from the dead to be the living Savior of mankind. Let us rejoice today in the utterly incomparable message of Easter: "Jesus lives!"

CONCEPTS FOR CHILDREN

1. It would have been nice to have been in Jerusalem on that first Easter Sunday.
2. But most of the people in Jerusalem did not see Jesus that day—only a handful of disciples did.
3. We can have a real Easter now with the risen Lord.
4. The risen Jesus wants to live in our hearts.

THE LESSON COMMENTARY

I. THE BURIAL OF JESUS:
Mark 15:42-47

A. Joseph's Request: vv. 42-43

"It was Preparation Day" (v. 42, NIV). The reason this is capitalized and without the article (contra. KJV) is twofold. First, there is no article in the Greek. Second, this was the official name of Friday. In fact the Greek word here, *paraskue*, is used today in the Greek Orthodox Church for Friday. Incidentally, this is a strong argument supporting the traditional date of the crucifixion as being on Friday, not Wednesday (the day that some people contend for).

Paraskue ("preparation") is defined as indicating "the day before the sabbath." This is all one word in Greek, *pro-sabbaton* (from *pro*, "before," and *sabbaton*, "sabbath"). The Jewish sabbath was Saturday; so this clearly means Friday.

Now we are ready to interpret the word "even" (v. 42)—today we would say "evening." This term means different things in different parts of the United States. The writer, who was brought up in Massachusetts, well remembers his first experience of this in Indiana. A friend said, "I'll be over to see you this evening"—and then showed up at two o'clock in the afternoon! We soon learned that in the Midwest "evening" meant any time after the noon meal, whereas in New England it began not sooner than 6:00 P.M.

It is obvious that "the even" in this passage means late afternoon. (The Greek word is the adjective "late.") For the Jewish sabbath began at sunset Friday night and ended at sunset Saturday. In the twenty-four hours between these no law-abiding Jew could carry any kind of burden, such as the body of Jesus would have been. That is why Joseph hurried to Pilate to take care of the burial before sunset. Luke (23:54) indicates this

more precisely: "It was Preparation Day, and the Sabbath was about to begin" (NIV). What Joseph did he must do quickly.

Joseph of Arimathea (v. 43) is so called because he was "from" (so the Greek) the village of Arimathea. "The exact site is uncertain, but it is thought to be identical with the modern Rentis, twenty miles NW of Jerusalem. . . . It may be the same as the OT Ramathaim, where the prophet Samuel lived (I Sam. 1:1)" (*Zondervan Pictorial Encyclopedia of the Bible*, I, 301).

Joseph is further described as "an honourable counsellor." This means "a prominent member of the Council" (NIV)—that is, of the Sanhedrin, the supreme court of Israel. Matthew (27:57) says that he was "a rich man," and Luke that he was "a good and upright man" (23:50, NIV). Both of these expressions fit well with Mark's description. Alfred Plummer comments: "Only a person of good position and bearing would have had much hope of at once being admitted to an audience with Pilate" (*St. Mark*, Cambridge Greek Testament, p. 362).

We read further that Joseph "also waited for the kingdom of God." This reminds us of Simeon, who was "waiting for the consolation [the deliverance] of Israel" (Luke 2:25) and Anna, who spoke about the baby Jesus "to all them that looked for redemption in Jerusalem" (Luke 2:38). It is obvious that there were many devout souls in Israel at that time who were waiting eagerly for the coming of the promised Messiah.

Joseph went in "boldly" to Pilate. Plummer puts it well: "It required courage to go to the Procurator on such an errand. He was no relation of the Crucified, and therefore had no claim to this favour, and his being a member of the Sanhedrin might be fatal. The Sanhedrin had that day driven Pilate to condemn an innocent person to death—a humiliating and exasperating thought for a Roman judge. . . . Above all, there was danger as to what the Sanhedrin would do, when they heard of Joseph's visit to the Procurator. But reverence and affection for the Master gave him the necessary courage" (*Mark*, pp. 362-63).

Luke tells us that Joseph "had not consented to their decision and action" (23:51, NIV). But Pilate would have had no way of knowing this. John describes Joseph as a "disciple of Jesus, but secretly for fear of the Jews" (19:38). But this time he overcame his fears and risked his life to bury Jesus. If he had not done so, Jesus' body would have been thrown with those of the two robbers into a common grave for criminals. The pious Jews felt very strongly about burying their bodies sacredly.

"Craved" (KJV) is an over-translation of the simple verb *aiteo*, which is rendered "ask" in forty-eight out of the seventy-one times it occurs in the New Testament. Only here is it translated "crave."

B. Pilate's Surprise: vv. 44-45

"Pilate was surprised to hear that he was already dead. Summoning the centurion, he asked him if Jesus had already died" (v. 44, NIV). Jesus was crucified at nine o'clock in the morning; so He had been on the cross less than nine hours. It was common for criminals to hang on a cross for two or three days before they expired from hunger and weakness.

When Pilate learned from the centurion that Jesus was already dead (cf. v. 39), "he gave the body to Joseph" (v. 45). William Lane writes: "The release of the body of one condemned of high treason, and especially to one who was not an immediate relative, was wholly unusual and confirms the tenor of the Gospel account of the Roman trial (Ch. 15:1-15). Only if Pilate had no reservations concerning Jesus' innocence of the charge . . . but had pronounced sentence begrudgingly

to placate the irate mob, would he have granted the request of the councillor" (*The Gospel According to Mark*, The New International Commentary on the New Testament, p. 579).

The verb here translated "gave" (*doreo*) occurs elsewhere in the New Testament only in II Peter 1:3-4, where it is used of divine favors given to man. It literally means to "present" or "bestow." Because Pilate realized he had done wrong, he gave the body to Joseph as a free gift, without charging the usual fee.

Instead of the normal Greek word for "body" (*soma*), Mark alone uses *ptoma*, a fallen body, a "corpse." This is what Pilate considered it to be—a mere corpse to dispose of.

C. Careful Burial: v. 46

John adds an interesting item here. He says of Joseph of Arimathea: "He was accompanied by Nicodemus, the man who earlier had visited Jesus at night. Nicodemus brought a mixture of myrrh and aloes, about seventy-five pounds. Taking Jesus' body, the two of them wrapped it, with the spices, in strips of linen. This was in accordance with Jewish burial customs" (19:39-40, NIV). The last sentence indicates—though none of the Gospels mentions it—that Jesus' body was first carefully washed. So important was this ceremonial rite that it was even permitted on the sabbath.

We are told that Joseph "bought fine linen." Plummer suggests: "Joseph may have done this and made arrangement with Nicodemus before going to the Procurator. Both were members of the Sanhedrin and had agreed to act together" (*Mark*, p. 363).

After they had wrapped the body in the linen, with the spices (not mentioned by Mark), they laid it in a tomb cut out of rock. It was a new tomb, never used before (John 19:41). Plummer notes: "Rock-hewn tombs are common round about Jerusalem, and would commonly be used for well-to-do persons. . . . One wall would be cut with a stone shelf, on which the Body was laid, and a large stone, circular like a millstone, would be lying flat against the outside rock, ready for closing the opening. Two men might roll it into its place, but to roll it back would be a difficult task for women" (*Mark*, pp. 363-64).

D. The Watching Women: v. 47

Two women were carefully observing all this. Their devotion to Jesus was so deep that they could not leave the spot until the body of Jesus had been placed out of sight. (Where were the men?)

One of the two was Mary Magdalene. She was the last to leave the tomb on Friday evening and the first there on Sunday morning (John 20:1). The other was "Mary the mother of Joses," already mentioned in verse 40. They had endured the traumatic experience of seeing the heart-rending death of Jesus.

II. THE RESURRECTION OF JESUS: Mark 16:1-8

A. The Devoted Women: vv. 1-2

Luke tells us that after the women had seen where Jesus was buried "they went home and prepared spices and perfumes. But they rested on the Sabbath in obedience to the commandment" (23:56, NIV). Here we are told that "when the Sabbath was over" these two women "bought spices so that they might go to anoint Jesus' body" (v. 1, NIV). These two statements supplement, rather than contradict, each other. On Friday afternoon after the late burial there would be very little time left for preparing the spices before the sabbath day of rest began at sunset. In obedience to the Fourth Commandment (Exodus 20:8-11), they ceased all labor until the sabbath ended at sunset on Saturday. Then they hurried to the market to buy some "spices." The Greek word is *aroma*, which has come directly over into English. It is found

in the New Testament only in connection with Jesus' burial (Mark 16:1; Luke 23:56; 24:1; John 19:40). These acts showed the aroma of love for Jesus that these people had.

The purpose of all this is well described by Lane: "Spices were not used for mummification, which was not a Jewish custom, but to offset the odors from decomposition. It is not uncommon to find in Palestinian tombs dating to the first century such funerary objects as perfume bottles, ointment jars and other vessels of clay and glass designed to contain aromatic oils. The desire of the women to 'anoint' the body indicates that the oils were to be poured over the head. ... Since in the climate of Jerusalem deterioration would occur rapidly, the visit of the women with the intention of ministering to the corpse after two nights and day must be viewed as an expression of deep devotion" (*Mark*, p. 585). It should be noted, however, that Joseph and Nicodemus had poured in a heavy dose of spices as they wrapped His body in linen. But the women wanted to add their love-offering to this.

With only about a half hour of daylight after sunset on Friday night, the women barely got their buying done before dark. So they had to return home and wait until morning.

But "very early in the morning the first day of the week, they came unto the sepulchre at the rising of the sun" (v. 2). All four Gospels agree that the tomb was found empty on Sunday morning.

B. A Problem Solved: vv. 3-4

As the women were walking toward the garden tomb (cf. John 19:41), they "were saying" (imperfect tense) to each other, "Who shall roll us away the stone from the door of the sepulchre?" Anyone who has handled millstones (as this writer did in early life on the farm) knows that they are not meant for women to move. And this one was probably in a deep groove.

When they came in sight of the sepulcher, they saw to their surprise and joy that the big stone had already been rolled away. What a relief! Now they could carry out their mission.

C. The Angel at the Tomb: v. 5

Since the large stone that had covered the entrance was rolled back, the women entered the tomb. As they did so they were frightened to see "a young man sitting on the right side, clothed in a long white garment." Such appearances of angels are common in the Old Testament. Regarding the mention of them in the Gospels, Geoffrey Bromiley has this to say: "The function of angels is best seen from their part in the saving mission of Jesus Christ. It is natural that they should be present both when he came to earth and at his resurrection and ascension. They are also to accompany him at his return in glory (Matt. 24:31). They do not do the real work of reconciliation. But they declare and accompany, and they summon man to participate in their work of praise (cf. Luke 1:46)" ("Angel," *Baker's Dictionary of Theology*, Everett F. Harrison, ed., pp. 41-42).

Matthew has more to say about why this angel came. He relates it this way: "There was a violent earthquake, for an angel of the Lord came down from heaven and, going to the tomb, rolled back the stone and sat on it. His appearance was like lightning, and his clothes were white as snow. The guards were so afraid of him that they shook and became like dead men" (28:2-4, NIV).

This explains two things. The first is why the stone was rolled back from the doorway of the tomb. The second is why the women did not encounter the Roman guard: The frightened men had already fled. Matthew alone tells about them.

The basic historic fact of Easter is the empty tomb. This important discovery is reported in all four Gospels. But, as John's Gospel indicates, it was not a grave robbery; it was a resurrection. John saw the evidence and believed (John 20:8).

D. The Startling Announcement: v. 6

The last word in verse 5 is "they were affrighted" (one word in Greek). Now the angel says to the women, "Be not affrighted" (the same verb). It is a strong compound, *ekthambeo*, used in the New Testament only by Mark (9:15; 14:33; 16:5, 6), always in the passive. It means "be terrified."

The angel's next words may well have been in the form of a question: "Jesus you are seeking, the Nazarene, the Crucified? He has risen! He is not here. See the place where they laid Him." In the Greek the words are almost staccato in utterance. For instance, "He has risen" is one word in Greek. It is in the aorist tense of instant reaction: "You are too late; He is already risen." Matthew (28:6) and Luke (24:6) both have the reverse order: "He is not here; He has risen." But Mark puts the important fact first and then gives the evidence. "He is risen. Do you doubt that? The tomb is empty; look at the place where the Body was laid" (Plummer, *Mark*, p. 368).

DISCUSSION QUESTIONS

1. Do we have any people today like Joseph of Arimathea? In what way?
2. Who was last at the tomb on Friday night and first on Sunday morning? Why?
3. Where were the men on Sunday morning?
4. Why did God speak through angels then, but not now?
5. What is the importance of the resurrection for us?
6. How should we demonstrate the resurrection in our lives?

E. The Message to the Disciples: v. 7

"But go, tell his disciples and Peter, 'He is going ahead of you into Galilee. There you will see him, just as he told you' " (NIV). All three Synoptic Gospels give the command to the women to convey this message to the sorrowing disciples. But Mark alone adds the words "and Peter." It will be remembered that the early church is unanimous in saying that Mark's Gospel gives us the preaching of Peter. He was the one who had denied his Lord three times and then wept bitterly. To him the death of Jesus was a crushing blow. He could never forgive himself, and he felt sure that Jesus could not forgive him. Those words "and Peter" came to him like life out of death. He exulted in the fact that the risen Christ had by these words indicated that He still loved His failing disciple. What joy must have sprung up in Peter's heart. As the song goes, "It's just like Jesus to roll the clouds away."

The message from Christ to His disciples was: "I will meet you in Galilee." That was where they had spent most of the time with Him in His earthly ministry. Now they were to have a grand reunion there!

F. The Amazed Women: v. 8

"Trembling and bewildered, the women went out and fled from the tomb. They said nothing to anyone, because they were afraid" (NIV). The latter sentence must be taken as describing their first reaction: They were too afraid to tell anyone what had happened. But we know that they later carried out the command given to them. Matthew (28:8) says that with fear and great joy they "ran to bring his disciples word." Luke (24:9) says that they "told all these things to the eleven, and to all the rest." Probably Mark's statement means that they said nothing to any outsider.

CONTEMPORARY APPLICATION

On Good Friday of 1968 we were in Jerusalem. We stood on a balcony overlooking the place where Pilate is supposed to have tried Jesus. Below us many different religious groups were clustering around heavy wooden crosses that would be carried in the long procession from Pilate's Praetorium to the traditional Calvary in the Church of the Holy Sepulcher. We went down and walked in the procession.

Exactly a week later we arrived in Athens, only to discover that we were just in time to see the Greek Orthodox celebration of Good Friday. From the balcony of our room in the King George Hotel we looked out over Constitution Square. There we saw the air filled with colorful balloons. On each one was the word *EGEIRE*, "He rose!"—printed in large Greek letters.

What a thrill! Good Friday was only the prelude to Easter Sunday. As the Good Friday procession—patriarch, archbishops, bishops and all—passed in front of our balcony, we thanked God for the glorious truth: "Christ is risen!"

JESUS ASSURES HIS DISCIPLES

DEVOTIONAL READING	I Corinthians 15:1-11

ADULTS

Topic: *Surprised by Joy!*

Background Scripture: Luke 24:13-35

Scripture Lesson: Luke 24:13-16, 25-35

Memory Verse: *They said to each other, "Did not our hearts burn within us while he talked to us on the road, while he opened to us the scriptures?"* Luke 24:32

YOUTH

Topic: *Surprised by Joy!*

Background Scripture: Luke 24:13-35

Scripture Lesson: Luke 24:13-16, 25-35

Memory Verse: *They said to each other, "Did not our hearts burn within us while he talked to us on the road, while he opened to us the scriptures?"* Luke 24:32

CHILDREN

Topic: *Jesus Cheers His Disciples*

Background Scripture: Luke 24:13-35

Scripture Lesson: Luke 24:13-15, 28-32

Memory Verse: *Weeping may tarry for the night, but joy comes with the morning.* Psalm 30:5

DAILY BIBLE READINGS

Mon., Apr. 11: An Unrecognized Traveler, Luke 24: 13-24.
Tues., Apr. 12: The Recognized Lord, Luke 24:25-35.
Wed., Apr. 13: Witness for the Risen Lord, Acts 3:11-16.
Thurs., Apr. 14: Telling Good News to Gentiles, Acts 10:34-43.
Fri., Apr. 15: The Essence of the Gospel, I Corinthians 15:1-11.
Sat., Apr. 16: Made Alive in Christ, I Corinthians 15:20-28.
Sun., Apr. 17: A New Kind of Body, I Corinthians 15:35-41.

LESSON AIM

To help us see what the living presence of the risen Lord meant to the first disciples and what it can mean to us today.

LESSON SETTING

Time: April of A.D. 30

Place: Jerusalem and the nearby village of Emmaus

Jesus Assures His Disciples

LESSON OUTLINE

SUGGESTED INTRODUCTION FOR ADULTS

In last Sunday's lesson we saw that it was women, not men, who were last at the cross on Friday afternoon and first at the empty tomb on Sunday morning. Matthew (28:9) and John (20:14-18) both indicate clearly that it was these same faithful women who were the first to see Jesus on that glorious Easter morn. Their superior devotion had paid off.

There is no question that women, perhaps because of a mother instinct, seem capable of a higher love and deeper devotion than most men. The history of the church of Jesus Christ is replete with examples of sacrificial consecration. Many mission fields have been largely staffed with single women. Where were the men? Many small, struggling churches in America would not have survived if it had not been for praying women. They will get their due reward in heaven.

Today we study about Jesus' appearances to men, which came later in the day. He gave to His disciples the assurance of His living presence.

SUGGESTED INTRODUCTION FOR YOUTH

Surprised by Joy! That is the title of C. S. Lewis's spiritual autobiography. He tells how he was an unbeliever, proud of his intellectual superiority. For him Christ was only a myth, a superstitious belief of naive minds.

But then something happened! One day he met the risen, living Lord. He surrendered his life to Him. The result was that he became to the intellectuals of our day the mightiest witness of the reality of the Christian faith. For instance, his book *Miracles* is one of the most powerful defenses of the authenticity of the miracles in the Gospels.

We, too, can meet the Miracle Man, Jesus, and have ample, satisfying assurance that He is the living Lord. Then our lives will also be transformed.

CONCEPTS FOR CHILDREN

1. After the crucifixion the disciples were very sad.
2. Their Leader, on whom they had leaned, had fallen.
3. Jesus was quick to change their sorrow to joy.
4. His living presence was all the assurance they needed.

THE LESSON COMMENTARY

I. SAD HEARTS:
Luke 24:13-24

A. Two Disciples on the Road to Emmaus: vv. 13-14

The women who discovered the empty tomb on Sunday morning heard the angels' announcement that Jesus had risen (vv. 1-6). The angels also reminded them that Jesus Himself had told them in Galilee that He would be crucified, but would rise again on the third day (v. 7). Remembering His words now, the women hurried to tell the remaining eleven apostles and their associates about what they had seen and heard (vv. 8-10).

The reaction of the men was typical: "But they did not believe the women, because their words seemed to them like nonsense" (v. 11, NIV). Oh, you know, these women! But Peter did have enough grace to go and check the matter (v. 12). Sure enough, he found the grave clothes there, but no body. "He went away, wondering to himself what had happened" (NIV). The whole thing was very bewildering.

Against this background we have the story of the two disciples on their way to Emmaus. They were among "all the rest" (v. 9) to whom the women reported.

It was "that same day" (v. 13), the first Easter Sunday, that two of Jesus' disciples (not apostles) "were going" (NIV, imperfect tense) "to a village called Emmaus." The distance from Jerusalem was "about threescore furlongs" (KJV)—"about seven miles"

(NIV). The Greek word for "furlong" is *stadion*, which first meant a course on which foot races were held, with tiers of seats for spectators. The Latin form was *stadium*, adopted in English for a place where athletic events are held. Since the Greek race course measured about 607 feet in length, the word *stadion* came to signify this length of measurement, as here in this passage. Sixty of these would be about 36,420 feet, or approximately seven miles. The village of El Kubeibeh, seven miles northwest of Jerusalem on the road to Lydda, is the most likely site.

As the two disciples walked along they were talking about what had happened in the last few days. It had been an exciting, but exhausting, weekend.

B. An Unexpected Companion: vv. 15-16

"As they talked and discussed these things with each other, Jesus himself came up and walked along with them; but they were kept from recognizing him" (NIV).

In the King James Version "talked" (v. 14) and "communed" (v. 15) both translate the same Greek verb. The variation in translation comes from the Latin Vulgate, which had an unfortunate influence on the King James Version. It should be "talked" in both places (cf. NIV).

While the two disciples were discussing the startling events of that morning, Jesus joined them on the road, appearing unexpectedly from behind them. They assumed that He was coming from Jerusalem (v. 18).

Why did they not recognize Him? Alfred Plummer gives a reasonable answer: "There is no *need* to assume a special act of will on the part of Christ, 'who would not be seen by them till the time when he saw fit.' They were preoccupied and had no expectation of meeting Him, and there is good reason for believing that the risen Saviour had a glorified body which was not at once recognized. . . . But it is quite possible that the Evangelist understands the non-recognition of Jesus here and the recognition of Him afterwards (ver. 31) to be the results of Divine volition" (*A Critical and Exegetical Commentary on the Gospel According to St. Luke*, International Critical Commentary, p. 552). In any case, their vision was restrained—literally, "their eyes were being held"—so that they did not know who He was. It would seem reasonable to conclude that if He had looked exactly as He did before His crucifixion, they would have recognized Him during the fairly long period they were with Him—probably an hour or more.

C. A Surprising Conversation: vv. 17-18

"He asked them, 'What are you discussing together as you walk along?' "They stood still, their faces downcast."

This translation of verse 17 (NIV) represents the best Greek text, found in the oldest manuscripts. Stunned by Jesus' question, the two disciples stopped. For a few moments they stood there, sad and perplexed.

Then one of them, named Cleopas, spoke up. We do not know anything further about this man. Some have tried to identify him with Clopas (John 19:25). But Plummer points out that "Clopas" is Aramaic, whereas "Cleopas" is Greek. The other person's name is not given.

Cleopas countered Jesus' question with one in reply: "Are you the only one living in Jerusalem who doesn't know what things have happened there in these days?" (v. 18, NIV). Richard C. H. Lenski says that this was "really not an answer to Jesus' question but an incredulous, exclamatory question because of what appeared like impossible ignorance on Jesus' part" (*Interpretation of St. Luke's Gospel*, p. 1182).

The King James Version has "Art thou only a stranger in Jerusalem?" But Lenski writes: "The verb *paroikeis* means to dwell as a *paroikos*, as one who is not a native but has come in from the outside . . . the verb here refers to a Jew who had been born and reared elsewhere but was now residing in the Holy City" (*Luke*, p. 1182). Such a person should surely know about the exciting events in Jerusalem.

D. A Disappointed Hope: vv. 19-21

Still probing, Jesus asked a further question: "What things?" Almost in unison, perhaps interrupting each other, "they" answered. It was a long reply.

First, they identified the subject of their discussion. It was "Jesus of Nazareth"—literally, in the oldest Greek text, "Jesus the Nazarene." Among the Jews of that day "Jesus" (Greek equivalent of the Hebrew "Joshua," or, Yehoshuah) was a common name. So this Jesus had to be identified by His hometown.

The disciples described Him as "a prophet mighty in deed and word before God and all the people" (v. 19). One of the titles of the Messiah was "prophet" (Deuteronomy 18:15). The whole description here reflects the faith of these two men that Jesus was the Messiah. But that faith had now been badly shaken. For the one they had expected to set up His kingdom in Jerusalem had instead been "condemned to death" and "crucified" (v. 20). This was a traumatic shock, and they hadn't recovered from it yet.

Verse 21 expresses their disappointed hope in plaintive tones: "But we had hoped that he was the one who was going to redeem Israel. And what is more, it is the third day since all this took place" (NIV). They did not seem to remember His threefold prediction that after His crucifixion He would rise again on the third day. This truth simply had not registered.

Regarding this reply of the men, Lenski writes: "It was just what Jesus wanted, namely that these two should express themselves fully and thus enable Jesus to clear up the very things that were so dark and perplexing to them and all the rest of the men. Jesus chose these two because they were two and could serve as two witnesses, not only to testify that they had seen him, but to testify to all that he was telling them about the Scripture prophecies regarding his death and his resurrection" (*Luke*, p. 1183). Cleopas and his companion probably filled an important place in giving this witness. Luke alone records this incident, which he may very well have learned directly from Cleopas.

E. An Empty Tomb: vv. 22-24

The men went on to say that some women in their group of Jesus' followers had gone to the tomb early that morning and found the body gone. They amazed the men by reporting that they saw angels, who declared that Jesus was alive (v. 23). Two of the men had gone to the tomb to check the women's report (cf. John 20:3). Sure enough, the tomb was opened and empty—"but him they saw not" (v. 24).

Lenski comments: "This is the sad ending. The fact that the women had seen him (Matt. 28:9, 10), also Mary Magdalene (John 20:18), apparently failed to satisfy the men. The very excitement with which the women reported what they had seen made the men think that they were nervously upset, had imagined things, and ought not to be believed beyond the verifiable fact that the body was indeed gone" (*Luke*, pp. 1186-87).

How long Cleopas and his companion had known Jesus, we cannot tell. But they had seen enough of Him and His miracles, and had been sufficiently impressed by His teaching, to believe deeply in Him. But now He was gone!

II. SLOW HEARTS: Luke 24:25-27

A. The Suffering Messiah: vv. 25-26

"Fools" is too strong a translation here. Four very different words are translated "fool" in the King James Version. This is the weakest one. Elsewhere (in the KJV) it is rendered "foolish" (Galatians 3:1, 3; I Timothy 6:9; Titus 3:3), and that is the way it should be translated here: "How foolish you are, and how slow of heart that you do not believe all that the prophets have spoken!" (NIV). The Greek adjective refers not to moral folly, but to mental dullness. It literally means "mindless."

These men, as devout Israelites, believed the prophets in general. But they had failed to believe "all" that the prophets had spoken. Plummer says: "There is special point in the *pasin*. Like most Jews, they remembered only the promises of the glories of the Messiah, and ignored the predictions of His sufferings" (*Luke*, p. 555). Charles R. Erdman writes: "It is noticeable that Jesus did not chide them for refusing to accept his own words, or those of their friends, or those of angels; they were rebuked for not believing the Old Testament. They had accepted it in part; as men often accept just so much as suits their prejudices and tastes and notions; but they failed to believe in all that the prophets had spoken, and particularly the predictions of Jesus' atoning death, and of his return to the heavenly glory which he would share when he ascended" (*Gospel of Luke*, Commentaries on the New Testament, p. 225).

And so He asked the question: "Ought not Christ [literally, "the

Christ" that is, "the Messiah"] to have suffered these things, and to enter into his glory?" (v. 26). The problem with the Jews was that they expected the Messiah to come in glorious power, deliver them from foreign oppression, and set up his kingdom of righteousness and peace. They were expecting a political kingdom. Jesus had failed to meet their expectations. What they needed to realize was that their sacred Scriptures taught that the Messiah was to suffer and die. This is what Jesus now proceeded to show them.

B. Christ in All the Scriptures: v. 27

"And beginning with Moses and all the Prophets, he explained to them what was said in all the Scriptures concerning himself" (NIV). The term "Scriptures," of course, means the Hebrew Scriptures, our Old Testament. The word "Prophets" is capitalized (NIV) because it refers to a fixed section of the Jewish Bible. But often the whole of the Hebrew Scriptures was referred to as "Moses and the Prophets," as here.

What a treat it would have been to have heard this discourse of Jesus! But by a diligent study of the Old Testament, with the help and illumination of the Holy Spirit who inspired it, we can have the same knowledge that Jesus imparted to these two disciples.

He would have called their attention especially to Psalm 22, which graphically describes His crucifixion, and Isaiah 53, which declares that the Suffering Servant of the Lord would die an atoning death for sinners. Other passages point in the same direction. Today we can find Christ in all the Scriptures.

III. SEEING HEARTS: Luke 24:28-32

A. Urgent Hospitality: vv. 28-29

"As they approached the village to which they were going, Jesus acted as

if he were going farther. But they urged him strongly, 'Stay with us, for it is nearly evening; the day is almost over.' So he went in to stay with them" (NIV). "Abide" and "tarry" (v. 29, KJV) are the same verb in the Greek.

Frederic L. Godet comments on these verses: "When Jesus *made* as if He would continue His journey, it was not a mere feint. He would have really gone, but for that sort of constraint which they exercised over Him. Every gift of God is an invitation to claim a greater. . . . But most men stop very quickly on this way; and thus they never reach the full blessing" (*A Commentary on the Gospel of St. Luke*, III, 355).

What a blessing these two men would have missed if they had not insisted on this Stranger coming into their home! And how much we miss when we casually let spiritual opportunities go by, not caring enough to take time and make the effort to include Christ in our schedule. It is claimed that verse 29 furnished the inspiration for Lyte's dying hymn: "Abide with me, fast falls the eventide."

B. Recognition of the Guest: vv. 30-31

"As he sat at meat with them" (KJV) is literally "as he reclined with them," which means "when he was at the table with them" (NIV). It was the custom then in better homes to recline on couches around the table as they ate.

Acting as host, Jesus "took bread, and blessed it, and brake, and gave to them." Lenski comments: "It was all perfectly natural, the result of the relation that had been established on the journey when Jesus acted as the teacher and the two disciples as his pupils. Neither of them thought it odd that Jesus should proceed as he did" (*Luke*, p. 1192). Perhaps they had decided from His teaching of the Scriptures that He must be a rabbi, and so it was natural that He should pronounce the blessing at the beginning of the meal.

And then the miracle happened! "Their eyes were opened"—the opposite of their being "held" (v. 16). Now for the first time they really saw Him. They "knew" (KJV) or "recognized" (NIV) Him. It was a most dramatic moment.

But then He suddenly disappeared, was no longer seen by them. It is probably useless to speculate as to the nature of Jesus' postresurrection body. The Gospel accounts indicate that He appeared and disappeared without warning.

Probably these disciples had seen Jesus bless and break bread many times. When He performed this familiar function before them, they suddenly recognized who He was. Godet comments: "No doubt the influence exercised on their heart by the preceding conversation and by the thanksgiving of Jesus, as well as the manner in which He broke and distributed the bread, had prepared them for this awaking of the inner sense. The sudden disappearance of Jesus had a supernatural character. His body was already in course of glorification, and obeyed more freely than before the will of the spirit" (*Luke*, p. 355).

DISCUSSION QUESTIONS

1. Are we ever guilty of failing to recognize Christ's presence with us?
2. How can we become more conscious of it?
3. How does Christ reveal Himself to us today?
4. How would you evaluate the historical evidence for the resurrection of Jesus?
5. What are some ways that Christ is revealed in the Old Testament?
6. How do we *know* the reality of the resurrection?

C. Experience in Retrospect: v. 32

Now the experience along the road came into focus with new meaning. The two men recollected how their hearts had burned within them as they listened to His exposition of the Scriptures.

IV. SHARING HEARTS: Luke 24:33-35

A. The Report in Jerusalem: vv. 33-34

This experience was too wonderful to enjoy alone; the disciples must share it. So, although it was late in the day, the two men got up from the table and hurried back to Jerusalem. The seven miles would take them about two hours. So it is not unreasonable to hold that they may have arrived soon after dark.

When they got back to Jerusalem they found "the Eleven" (NIV). This was evidently a name used for the apostles after the defection of Judas. We know from John 20:24 that Thomas was absent this first Sunday night. But still the ten present would be referred to as "the Eleven."

Before the two from Emmaus had a chance to tell what had happened to them, they were greeted by exciting news from the Jerusalem disciples: "It is true! The Lord has risen and has appeared to Simon" (v. 34, NIV). Paul lists this appearance to Peter as the first postresurrection appearance that he mentions (I Corinthians 15:5). For obvious reasons he considered it to be of primary importance. As we have already noted, Peter doubtless lived in the depths of despair from early Friday morning, when he denied his Lord, until Jesus met him on that Easter Sunday. It is evident that this happened after the Emmaus disciples left Jerusalem that day (perhaps about noon), because they had not heard about it. But Jesus would be eager to show His love by getting Peter "off the hook" as soon as possible. We can be certain that He assured Peter of full forgiveness and restoration to divine favor.

B. The Report from Emmaus: v. 35

Then it was the turn of the two men from Emmaus to tell about the conversation on the road and how Jesus "was recognized by them when he broke the bread" (NIV). So the certainty of Christ's resurrection was confirmed from both sides. What a time of rejoicing they must have had in the upper room that evening!

CONTEMPORARY APPLICATION

Charles R. Erdman has a good comment for us here. He writes: "No story tells us more impressively the truth that a divine Saviour walks beside us all the way of our earthly journey. It is pathetic that our eyes are so often dimmed by unbelief that we fail to realize his presence. We walk and are sad while we might be rejoicing in his companionship. It may be as the Scriptures are opened to us, or as we meet to break bread in his name, that our blindness will be removed; and surely when the journey ends and we enter the home toward which we are moving, we shall see him face to face, and the vision will not fade in deepening twilight, but grow more glorious through the eternal day" (*Luke*, p. 225).

JESUS COMMISSIONS HIS FOLLOWERS

DEVOTIONAL READING	John 20:19-31

ADULTS

Topic: *Jesus Commissions His Followers*

Background Scripture: Mark 16:9-20; Luke 24:36-52

Scripture Lesson: Luke 24:44-53

Memory Verse: *Repentance and forgiveness of sins should be preached in his name to all nations.* Luke 24:47

YOUTH

Topic: *Action Plan for Christians*

Background Scripture: Mark 16:9-20; Luke 24:36-53

Scripture Lesson: Luke 24:44-53

Memory Verse: *Repentance and forgiveness of sins should be preached in his name to all nations.* Luke 24:47

CHILDREN

Topic: *Winning Friends for Jesus*

Background Scripture: Mark 16:9-20; Luke 24:36-53

Scripture Lesson: Luke 24:44-53

Memory Verse: *Go therefore and make disciples of all nations, baptizing them in the name of the Father and of the Son and of the Holy Spirit.* Matthew 28:19

DAILY BIBLE READINGS

Mon., Apr. 18: Appearance by the Lake, John 21:1-14.
Tues., Apr. 19: Get Back to the Work, John 21:15-23.
Wed., Apr. 20: The Great Commission, Matthew 28:16-20.
Thurs., Apr. 21: Preach Repentance and Remission, Luke 24:36-49.
Fri., Apr. 22: Witnesses to the World, Acts 1:1-11.
Sat., Apr. 23: Sent to the Gentiles, Acts 26:12-18.
Sun., Apr. 24: Write to the Churches, Revelation 1:9-20.

LESSON AIM

To look at the commission that Jesus gave His disciples and see its application to us.

LESSON SETTING

Time: April and May of A.D. 30

Place: Jerusalem and the Mount of Olives

LESSON OUTLINE

Jesus Commissions His Followers

I. The Appearance of Jesus: Luke 24:36-37
  A. The Greeting of Peace: v. 36
  B. The Terror of the Disciples: v. 37

258

II. **The Proof of His Bodily Presence:** Luke 24:38-43
   A. Flesh and Bones: vv. 38-40
   B. Eating Food: vv. 41-43

III. **The Presentation of Scripture:** Luke 24:44-47
   A. Christ in the Old Testament: v. 44
   B. Opening the Disciples' Minds: v. 45
   C. A Suffering, Resurrected Messiah: v. 46
   D. The Gospel Message to All Nations: v. 47

IV. **The Needed Preparation:** Luke 24:48-49
   A. Witnessing These Things: v. 48
   B. Power from on High: v. 49

V. **The Ascension:** Luke 24:50-53
   A. The Benediction: v. 50
   B. The Ascending Christ: v. 51
   C. The Worshiping Disciples: vv. 52-53

SUGGESTED INTRODUCTION FOR ADULTS

The so-called Great Commission is given most clearly and fully in Matthew 28:18-20. This is picked up very briefly in Mark 16:15. But the two oldest Greek manuscripts of the New Testament (Vaticanus and Sinaiticus, from the fourth century) do not have the last twelve verses of Mark's Gospel (16:9-20). Leading church fathers of the second and third centuries show no knowledge of these verses, and Jerome (late fourth century) wrote: "Almost all the Greek copies do not have this concluding portion." Verses 9-20 are put in brackets in the New American Standard Bible, which was translated entirely by evangelical scholars. The New International Version, also done only by evangelicals, separates them with a note indicating that the earliest manuscripts omit them.

So the commission of Jesus to His disciples comes to us primarily through Matthew and secondarily through Luke. As we shall see, the account of Luke's Gospel is shorter and less specific.

SUGGESTED INTRODUCTION FOR YOUTH

What is the "Action Plan for Christians"? The answer of this lesson is: We are to be empowered by the Holy Spirit and are to be witnesses of the risen, living Lord, whose forgiveness is to be preached to all nations. This means that we must know the spiritual reality of the resurrection, must be filled with the Spirit and must take our God-appointed place in world evangelism. This begins at Jerusalem (Luke 24:47)—our hometown—and extends around the world. Some will be called by the Head of the church to witness in the homeland. Others will be called to go to the ends of the earth. Our responsibility is to hear the call and fulfill our commission.

CONCEPTS FOR CHILDREN

1. The Great Commission is for all of us.
2. Even children can help to win others to Christ by inviting them to Sunday school.

3. For our witness to be effective we must be Christlike.
4. We can tell what Jesus has done for us.

THE LESSON COMMENTARY

I. THE APPEARANCE OF JESUS: Luke 24:36-37

F. W. Farrar writes: "This is one of the most remarkable appearances of the Risen Christ. His intercourse with them on this occasion consisted of a greeting (36); a reproach and consolation (38); a demonstration of the reality of His person (39-43); an opening of their understandings (44-46); an appointment of the Apostles to the ministries of remission and witness (47-48); a promise of the Spirit, for the fulfilment of which they were to wait in Jerusalem (49)" (*St. Luke*, Cambridge Greek Testament, p. 405).

A. The Greeting of Peace: v. 36

While the disciples were still talking about Jesus' appearances to Peter and the two men of Emmaus, suddenly He was standing right in front of them. His immediate greeting was "Peace be with you" (NIV). The regular greeting of the Jews was "Shalom" (Peace). In John's account of this same appearance on that first Sunday night this greeting is repeated (20:19, 21). This is God's typical greeting to those who love Him.

Richard C. H. Lenski comments: "Jesus says at once: 'Peace to you!' But this common Oriental form of greeting, which implies only a kindly human wish when it is spoken by ordinary lips, means infinitely more when it is spoken by him who died and rose for us. As is the person, so is the word. When Jesus says 'peace' he actually gives what the word says. It is not a lovely looking package that is empty inside but one that is filled with heavenly reality that is far more beautiful than the covering in which it is wrapped" (*Interpretation of St. Luke's Gospel*, p. 1197).

B. The Terror of the Disciples: v. 37

In spite of Jesus' comforting greeting, the disciples "were startled and frightened, thinking they saw a ghost" (NIV). The first verb (found only here and in 21:9) literally means "being terrified." The second one is also a strong expression in the Greek—"having become filled with fear." They were really scared at the sight of what they thought was a ghost.

John tells us (20:19) that where the disciples were assembled that evening the doors were locked for fear of the Jews. The disciples believed that Jesus had indeed risen (vv. 34-35). But they did not expect Him to come through closed doors. Lenski writes: "We do not know by how much the glorified form of Jesus differed from his appearance in his earthly life, and not even whether he always appeared in the same form during the forty days. May we say that a majesty and an exaltation were now evident in the old familiar form and face, such as the disciples had not seen before? Simon and the two Emmaus disciples had seen him, but we have no details about the former case and know that in the other Jesus became invisible just as he was recognized" (*Luke*, p. 1198).

The truth is that we do not know too much about the exact nature of Jesus' postresurrection body. But the next verses tell us of one aspect, the physical.

II. THE PROOF OF HIS BODILY PRESENCE: Luke 24:38-43

A. Flesh and Bones: vv. 33-40

Jesus said to His disciples, "Why are you troubled, and why do doubts rise in your minds?" (v. 38, NIV). There is a solemn truth implied here: Jesus reads our thoughts like an open book. As He had often done before, the Master had to reprove His disciples for their unbelief.

Then He told them to do two things (v. 39): (1) "Behold my hands and my feet, that it is I myself"; (2) "Handle me, and see." Concerning the first, Alfred Plummer writes: "This seems to imply that His feet, as well as His hands had been nailed" (A Critical and Exegetical Commentary on the Gospel According to St. Luke, International Critical Commentary, p. 559). His feet had not simply been tied to the cross, as some have averred. And about both of the commands A. B. Bruce has this to say: "Jesus shows His hands and feet with the wounds to satisfy them of His identity. . . . Then He bids them touch Him . . . to satisfy themselves of His substantiality" (Expositor's Greek Testament, I, 649).

The purpose of their touching Him is clearly indicated in the latter part of verse 39: "A ghost does not have flesh and bones, as you see I have" (NIV). Some have suggested that since blood is not mentioned here, Jesus' resurrection body had flesh and bones but not blood: His blood had all been shed on the cross. But verse 43 specifically says that He ate food. This would be impossible without circulation of blood. Nor can we conceive of a live physical body without blood coursing through its veins. This sort of argument from silence is contrary to common sense.

The disciples could actually touch Jesus' body and see that it was solid material substance. They were not looking at a phantom.

Having said this, Jesus showed them His hands and feet (v. 40). It was a dramatic moment, a never-to-be-forgotten experience.

B. Eating Food: vv. 41-43

"And while they still did not believe it because of joy and amazement, he asked them, 'Do you have anything here to eat?' " (v. 41, NIV). It was just too good to be true that He was alive!

The use of "meat" (KJV) for "food" does not communicate accurately today. The Greek word brosimon (only here in New Testament) is an adjective meaning "eatable." So the whole expression means "anything to eat."

The disciples responded to Jesus' implied request. "They gave him a piece of broiled fish" (v. 42, NIV). The added words "and of an honeycomb" (KJV) are found only in very late medieval Greek manuscripts; all the early manuscripts omit them. It is clear that they are not a part of the original text of Luke's Gospel, but were added by a later scribe.

Jesus took the piece of fish and ate it in their presence (v. 43). Thus He proved conclusively to His disciples that He was not a phantom, not a ghost, but that He had a real body. His was not just a spiritual resurrection; it was a bodily resurrection. Farrar comments: "This was one of the 'infallible proofs' appealed to in Acts i. 3; compare John xxi. 12, 13; 'who did eat and drink with Him after He rose from the dead,' Acts x. 41" (Luke, p. 406).

Some people have raised their eyebrows at Jesus' action here. But Plummer handles the problem well. He writes: "The objection that, if Jesus took food in order to convince them that He was no mere spirit, when food was not necessary for the resurrection-body, He was acting deceitfully, does not hold. The alternative—'either a ghost, or an ordinary body needing food'—is false. There is a third possibility: a glorified body, capable of receiving food. Is there any deceit in taking food, which one does not want, in order to place others, who are needing it, at their ease?" (Luke, p. 56).

As noted before, we really know very little about the nature of the glorified body. And there is the possibility that Jesus' postresurrection body was an intermediate one, that He was glorified at His ascension.

III. THE PRESENTATION OF SCRIP-TURE:
Luke 24:44-47

A. Christ in the Old Testament: v. 44

Jesus reminded His disciples that He had previously taught them "these words"—that is, about His death and resurrection. At that time they had not understood what He was talking about (Luke 9:44-45).

Concerning the clause "while I was yet with you," Farrar makes this comment: "Important as showing that the forty days between the Resurrection and the Ascension were not *intended* to be a continuous sojourn with the disciples, or an integral portion of the Lord's human life" (*Luke*, p. 406). After His resurrection Christ was not "with" His disciples as He had been during the previous three years; rather, He came and went, from time to time.

Now He asserts that all that was written about Him "must" be fulfilled. God's Word cannot fail. Divine sovereignty is wrapped up in the word "must." God's purposes *will* be carried out.

The word translated "written" is in the perfect passive participle in the Greek. The full force of this grammatically is that these things "have been written and still stand written"—"The scripture cannot be broken" (John 10:35).

Jesus referred to the things written "in the law of Moses, and in the prophets, and in the psalms"—the entire Old Testament. Sometimes the Jews referred to their sacred Scriptures (our Old Testament) as simply "the Law and the Prophets" (cf. v. 27). In later times they divided them into three parts. The first was "the Law"—the first five books (Pentateuch), Genesis through Deuteronomy. The second division was "the Prophets."

This included the "former prophets"—Joshua, Judges, Samuel, Kings—and the "latter prophets"—Isaiah, Jeremiah, Ezekiel, and the Twelve (that is, the twelve Minor Prophets, thought of as one book). The third division was sometimes referred to as simply "the rest of the books"—that is, the remaining books of our Old Testament—but later became known as "the Writings." Of these, the largest and most important was "the Psalms," which are especially rich in Messianic prophecies.

B. Opening the Disciples' Minds: v. 45

Jesus had talked to His disciples about these things on several previous occasions, while He was still with them. But at that time their minds were closed: "And they understood none of these things: and this saying was hid from them, neither knew they the things which were spoken" (18:34). Now Jesus "opened their minds so that they could understand the Scriptures" (NIV).

About the Greek verb for "opened" A. T. Robertson writes: "The same verb as that in verses 31 and 32 about the eyes and the Scriptures. Jesus had all these years been trying to open their minds that they might understand the Scriptures about the Messiah and now at last he makes one more effort in the light of the Cross and the Resurrection. They can now see better the will and way of God, but they will still need the power of the Holy Spirit before they will fully know the mind of Christ" (*Word Pictures in the New Testament*, I, 296-97). This was clearly demonstrated by Peter's sermon on the day of Pentecost.

C. A Suffering, Resurrected Messiah: v. 46

Jesus showed His disciples how the Scriptures (Old Testament) taught that the Messiah would suffer and would rise from the dead the third day. He had told them this before (9:22; 18:31-33), but they had not understood it. Now they were beginning to comprehend.

D. The Gospel Message to All Nations: v. 47

In a sense this verse could be called a summary of the Book of Acts. We find the first clear preaching of the gospel in the sermon of Peter in Jerusalem on the day of Pentecost. There the apostle told his Jewish audience: "Repent, and be baptized every one of you in the name of Jesus Christ for the remission of sins" (Acts 2:38). The rest of Acts records this preaching going out from Jerusalem to all nations. And that is still going on today.

"Repentance" is our part; "remission" is God's part. He cannot do His part until we do ours. The Greek word for "remission" is *aphesis*, which means "dismissal, release," and then "pardon, remission of penalty" (G. Abbott-Smith, *Manual Greek Lexicon of the New Testament*, p. 70). Our more common word for this today is "forgiveness" (NIV), which is the way *aphesis* is translated six times in the King James Version.

It is only in Jesus' name that we can have the forgiveness of sins. This is because of His atoning death for us and His resurrection as our living Savior.

IV. THE NEEDED PREPARATION: Luke 24:48-49

These two verses (in reverse order) remind us of Acts 1:8: "But you will receive power when the Holy Spirit comes on you; and you will be my witnesses in Jerusalem, and in all Judea and Samaria, and to the ends of the earth" (NIV).

A. Witnessing These Things: v. 48

The idea that the disciples were "witnesses" of what they had heard and seen is prominent in the early part of Acts (1:8; 2:32; 3:15; 4:33; 5:30-32, etc.). We need to remember that a witness can only tell what he *knows*.

B. Power from on High: v. 49

"The promise of my Father" is the Holy Spirit (Joel 2:28; John 14:26). The disciples were not to start right out preaching; they were not yet ready to do this. Instead, they were to "tarry" (literally, "sit") in Jerusalem until they were "endued" (literally, "clothed") "with power from on high." This is what came to them on the day of Pentecost (Acts 1:8; 2:1-4). No one is fully equipped to witness until He has been filled with the Holy Spirit.

V. THE ASCENSION: Luke 24:50-53

A. The Benediction: v. 50

A careful comparison with John 20:19-23 would seem to indicate that all of our lesson thus far (vv. 36-49) is related to Jesus' appearance on that first Sunday night (the day of His resurrection). But now we shift to a different time and place.

The statement that He led them out "as far as to Bethany" (KJV) is better translated "out to the vicinity of Bethany" (NIV). Frederic L. Godet says that the Greek expression *heos pros* "signifies not *as far as*, but *to*

DISCUSSION QUESTIONS

1. What part did the ascension play in the plan of redemption?
2. Why did Jesus demonstrate the fact of His resurrection?
3. How can we discover Christ in the Old Testament?
4. What passages are particularly pertinent?
5. How may we be Christ's witnesses?
6. What part does the Holy Spirit have in this?

about, in the direction and even to the neighbourhood of" (*A Commentary on the Gospel of St. Luke*, p. 366). Acts 1:12 seems to indicate that the ascension took place on the Mount of Olives. Of course, Bethany was on the eastern slope of the Mount of Olives, but it seems likely that Jesus ascended from the top of the mount, the traditional place.

Incidentally, Luke is the only one who describes the ascension for us (Luke 24:50-53; Acts 1:9-11). We owe much to this careful, Spirit-inspired historian.

At the climax of Jesus' last meeting with His disciples on earth, He "lifted up his hands, and blessed them." This was the crowning benediction of His three years' ministry among them.

B. The Ascending Christ: v. 51

As Jesus was blessing them, He separated from them and was being taken up into heaven. Acts 1:9 adds: "And a cloud received him out of their sight." He was gone—but only in His physical body. Farrar puts it well: "The withdrawal of His Bodily Presence preceded His Spiritual Omnipresence" (*St. Luke*, p. 408).

We are reminded of the words of Jesus to His disciples in the upper room: "It is for your good that I am going away. Unless I go away, the Counselor will not come to you; but if I go, I will send him to you" (John 16:7, NIV). While in the flesh Jesus could only be in one place at one time. In the Spirit He is with all His people everywhere all the time.

C. The Worshiping Disciples: vv. 52-53

The first reaction of the disciples was a spontaneous worship of their risen, ascended Lord. Then they returned to Jerusalem (half a mile away) "with great joy." Instead of sorrowing at the departure of their Master, they now rejoiced because they believed what He had told them. Acts 1:11 adds the promise of His return, which doubtless thrilled them greatly.

Did these disciples immediately separate themselves from Judaism? Verse 53 shows that the answer is No. They were "continually in the temple, praising God" (NIV). (There is only one verb here in the earliest Greek manuscripts.)

This does not contradict the statement in Acts 1:13-14 about their continuing in prayer in an upper room in Jerusalem. What it means is that they participated in the morning (9:00 A.M.) and evening (3:00 P.M.) prayers in the temple every day (Acts 3:1).

CONTEMPORARY APPLICATION

The Great Commission was not only to the twelve apostles, who formed the nucleus of the church of Jesus Christ. It is to His church today. We are to carry the Good News to every nation.

The early church found that a proper division of labor was necessary if the Body of Christ was to function efficiently and effectively (Acts 6:1-4). The same is true today. If everyone went as a missionary or into full-time pastoral or evangelistic work, who would pay the bills? Consecrated laymen who support the program of the church for winning the lost are just as truly carrying out Christ's commission as are those who go.

TESTS OF FAITH

DEVOTIONAL READING	Psalm 73:2-17

ADULTS

Topic: *Tests of Faith*

Background Scripture: James 1:1-18

Scripture Lesson: James 1:1-15

Memory Verse: *Blessed is the man who endures trial, for when he has stood the test he will receive the crown of life which God has promised to those who love him.* James 1:12

YOUTH

Topic: *Tests of Faith*

Background Scripture: James 1:1-18

Scripture Lesson: James 1:1-15

Memory Verse: *Blessed is the man who endures trial, for when he has stood the test he will receive the crown of life which God has promised to those who love him.* James 1:12

CHILDREN

Topic: *We Can Trust God*

Background Scripture: James 1:1-18

Scripture Lesson: James 1:4-8

Memory Verse: *For the Lord is good;*
his steadfast love endures forever,
and his faithfulness to all generations. Psalm 100:5

DAILY BIBLE READINGS

Mon., Apr. 25: Steadfastness Amidst Hard Trials, James 1:2-8.
Tues., Apr. 26: Holding Your Ground Against Odds, James 1:12-18.
Wed., Apr. 27: Tested with Divine Permission, Job 1:6-12.
Thurs., Apr. 28: "Man Is Born to Trouble," Job 5:1-7.
Fri., Apr. 29: Relying on God in Trouble, Job 5:8-16.
Sat., Apr. 30: Faith Shining Through, Job 19:23-29.
Sun., May 1: Reward for Passing the Test, I Peter 5:6-10.

LESSON AIM

To help us see the value of trials in developing perseverance.

LESSON SETTING

Time: The Epistle of James was probably written about A.D. 60—some say about A.D. 45.

Place: Probably Jerusalem

Tests of Faith

LESSON OUTLINE

After twenty-one sessions on the life and ministry of Jesus as recorded in Mark's and Luke's Gospels, we now devote the five remaining lessons of the quarter to the Epistle of James—which happens conveniently to have five chapters. The lessons will cover the entire book.

As we shall see, this Epistle echoes many of the teachings of Jesus, especially those on practical living. It has many affinities with the Book of Proverbs, which is part of the Wisdom Literature of the Old Testament. In its emphasis on social justice it reminds us of some of the Minor Prophets, especially the three from the eighth century B.C.—Hosea, Amos, and Micah. As far as the New Testament is concerned, it most closely resembles the Sermon on the Mount (Matthew 5—7).

**SUGGESTED
INTRODUCTION
FOR ADULTS**

The unit of five lessons is entitled "Faith in Action." James was incurably practical. He ridicules a theoretical faith as worthless. The only faith that works is the faith that *works*. An intellectual belief that does not produce good action is not real faith.

James is the first of the seven General Epistles in the New Testament. These follow Hebrews, which in turn is preceded by the thirteen Pauline Epistles. Before those are the Four Gospels and Acts. These with Revelation make up our New Testament.

SUGGESTED
INTRODUCTION
FOR YOUTH

Looking at the total span of life, youth is probably the time of greatest testing. Adolescence is the period of preparation for adulthood. Young people cannot be blamed for feeling that life is hard—it is! That they are having a hard time—they are!

And the fact that adults have messed things up so badly doesn't make it any easier for young people. Crime among the youth, and corruption in high places. What can a young person do?

James gives the only answer: We must stand the tests of life victoriously, regardless of what others do. Then we shall receive the crown of life.

CONCEPTS FOR
CHILDREN

1. We *can* trust God; He will not let us down.
2. Trusting Him means leaning our whole weight on Him.
3. Trusting also involves obeying; only those who obey can trust.
4. We must believe Him and not doubt Him.

THE LESSON COMMENTARY

I. SALUTATION AND GREETINGS:
James 1:1

There is a striking difference between ancient letters and those of our time. We begin a letter by saying "Dear So-and-So," and place our own name at the close. The result is that sometimes we begin reading a letter and it doesn't make any sense to us. Suddenly we stop and ask ourselves the question, "Who wrote this?" So we turn over to the end to find out!

The ancients were much more sensible than we at this point: They always put their own name first, where it is needed. All of Paul's Epistles—as well as those of James, Peter, John, and Jude—begin with the name of the author. This was the universal custom of that day, as we know from the myriads of papyrus letters from that period that have been dug up.

But who was this "James"? The early church held that it was James the brother of our Lord. He is mentioned twice in the Gospels (Matthew 13:15; Mark 6:3) as a brother of Jesus. Paul refers to him in Galatians 1:19, when he says: "I saw none of the other apostles, only James, the Lord's brother" (NIV).

Soon after His resurrection Jesus appeared to James (I Corinthians 15:7), who thereupon believed in Him—up to that time His brothers had not accepted Him as the Messiah (John 7:5). The result was that he and his brothers waited in the upper room for the coming of the Holy Spirit (Acts 1:14). He later became the leader of the Jewish Christian church in Jerusalem (Acts 12:17). Also he presided at the Council of Jerusalem, as is clearly indicated in Acts 15:13-20. When Paul went up to Jerusalem the last time, Luke writes: "And the day following Paul went in with us unto James; and all the elders were present" (Acts 21:18).

Since Josephus indicates that James the Lord's brother was put to death in A.D. 62 or 63, the Epistle must have been written not later than this time. Some scholars prefer about A.D. 45.

The author describes himself as a "servant [literally, "slave"] of God and of the Lord Jesus Christ." Jude, in his Epistle, likewise calls himself "a servant of Jesus Christ," adding: "and a brother of James" (v. 1). Paul (Romans 1:1; Titus 1:1) and Peter (II Peter 1:1) refer to themselves as both "servant" and "apostle." Only James and Jude use "servant" alone. J. B. Mayor comments: "So far as it goes, this peculiarity of the epistles of the two brothers, James and Jude, is (1) in favour of the view that neither of them was included in the number of the Twelve; (2) it shows that the writer of this epistle was so well known that it was unnecessary alike for him and for his brother to add any special title to distinguish him from others who bore the same name" (*Epistle of St. James*, p. 29).

The Epistle is addressed to "the twelve tribes"—"the Christian church conceived as the true Israel, inheriting the rights of the ancient people of God" (J. H. Ropes, *A Critical and Exegetical Commentary on the Epistle of St. James*, International Critical Commentary, p. 118). These are spoken of as "scattered abroad"— Greek, "in the Diaspora" (dispersion). Probably James, the head of the Jerusalem church, was primarily writing to Jewish Christians. He was their acknowledged leader.

The greeting in this Epistle consists of only one word, "Greetings." In the Greek this is *chairein*. It is a striking fact that we find this word for greeting only twice elsewhere in the New Testament—in the letter to the governor written by Claudius Lysias (Acts 23: 26) and in the Jerusalem council letter written by James (Acts 15:23). The latter is certainly some evidence in favor of this Epistle being written by the same James.

Chairein is the regular greeting found in the many papyrus letters of that period. Paul changed it to the great Christian word *charis*, "grace," at the beginning of his Epistles, and added "peace." Peter does the same (I Peter 1:2; II Peter 1:2). We do not know why James stuck to the common Greek greeting, but it supports his authorship.

II. PERSEVERANCE UNDER TRIAL:

James 1:2-4

A. Rejoicing in Trials: vv. 2-3

It is evident that those to whom James was writing were undergoing severe trials—probably persecution for their Christian faith. For right away he writes: "Consider it pure joy, my brothers, whenever you face trials of many kinds" (v. 2, NIV). How can they do that? "Because you know that the testing of your faith develops perseverance" (v. 3, NIV).

The word for "temptation" (KJV) is *peirasmois*, which was used to describe the testing of metals. Ropes says of its use here: "In the passage before us *peirasmois* evidently means 'trials,' i.e., adversities, which befall us from without and against our will. According to James (vv. 13ff.) 'temptations' spring mainly from within and could not be a subject for rejoicing. . . . What James has in mind is the strain put upon faith in Providence and in a good God by the fact that God permits his people to fall into distress of various kinds" (*James*, p. 133).

In line with the literal meaning of *peirasmois*, C. H. Lenski writes: "We should regard trials as tests of our Christian faith. If we have true faith we ought to be glad to have it tested out and proved to be genuine. If I have genuine gold coins I shall welcome any test to which they may be subjected" (*Interpretation of Hebrews and James*, p. 525).

It is agreed by all Bible scholars that "patience" (v. 3, KJV) is not an adequate translation for the Greek word *hypomone*. For instance, Leslie C. Mitton writes: "*Hypomone* . . . usually indicates not so much patience toward awkward people, but steadfastness and endurance in trying circumstances. . . . It occurs again, at 5:11, of the 'steadfastness' of Job. Job's 'patience' was outstanding, not in the sense of his forbearance towards friends and acquaintances, but in his continuing steadfastness of faith in spite of the most distressing sequence of disasters" (*James*, p. 23).

B. Perseverance and Perfection: v. 4

"But let patience [perseverance] have her perfect work, that ye may be perfect and entire, wanting nothing." Perseverance produces Christian maturity. The Greek word for "perfect" is *teleios*. It comes from *telos*, "end." So it properly means "having reached its end, finished, mature, complete, perfect" (G. Abbott-Smith, *Manual Greek Lexicon of the New Testament*, p. 442). Of the two adjectives here Mitton writes: " 'Perfect' means 'having reached full development.' 'Complete' means 'with no unfinished part' " (*James*, p. 24).

III. WARNING AGAINST DOUBT: James 1:5-8

A. Asking God for Help: v. 5

What is meant by "wisdom"? Ropes says that it is "the supreme and divine quality of the soul whereby man knows and practises righteousness" (*James*, p. 139). It comes from God alone (Proverbs 2:6). So if we sense our lack of it, we should ask Him to supply it.

God gives to all men "liberally." Ropes comments on the Greek adverb *haplos* (only here in New Testament): "Properly means 'simply,' but here clearly shown by what follows to have a moral sense, 'graciously,' 'bounteously,' 'generously' " (*James*, pp. 139-40). It may mean "without bargaining."

Also God "upbraideth not"; He gives "without finding fault" (NIV). Mayor writes: "It is not meant that God never upbraids . . . but that where there is sincere repentance He freely gives and forgives whatever may have been the past sin" (*James*, p. 40). Ropes says that the Greek expression

here "describes God's giving as full and free, in contrast to the meanness which after a benefaction calls it unpleasantly to the mind of the one benefited. That this disagreeable trait of human nature was prominent in ancient times is attested . . ." (*James*, p. 140).

B. Asking in Faith: v. 6

"But when he asks, he must believe and not doubt, because he who doubts is like a wave of the sea, blown and tossed by the wind" (NIV). Of the Greek participle translated "wavering" (KJV) Ropes says that it means "doubting," or "divided." He further remarks that "he that wavereth" or "he who doubts" is "a man whose allegiance wavers, not one tormented by speculative intellectual questionings, which do not fall within James's horizon. This is indicated by v. 7, which shows . . . that the kind of waverer whom James has in mind fully *expects* to receive some benefit from God" (*James*, pp. 140-41). God does not punish us for intellectual doubts, that go with a questioning mind, but He does for moral doubts that show a fault in our character.

C. Danger of Doubt: vv. 7-8

Such a man, doubting God's Word, has no right to expect that he will receive anything from the Lord. He is trifling, insincere in his praying. We are to be frank and honest with God, as He is with us.

James says that this kind of a person is "double-minded" (v. 8)— literally, "double-souled" (*dipsychos*). Lenski says that the adjective "is a new Greek formation so that some think that it was coined by James; it is used often after the time of James as if it caught men's fancy. This word is certainly expressive of just what James means by the figure he used in v. 6: a *psyche* that seems like two by flying in opposite directions. This is enhanced by the verbal 'unstable' (not placed

down to stand solidly) in all his ways.'
A weak wobbler does not wobble
merely in one respect" (James, p.
532).

God does not want us to be a "Mr.
Two-face." He wants simplicity and
honesty of character, a one-souled man.

IV. FRAILTY OF HUMAN LIFE:
James 1:9-11

A. The Lowly Brother: v. 9

"The brother in humble circumstances ought to take pride in his high
position" (NIV). Ropes comments:
"The writer returns to the peirasmoi
(trials) of v. 2. That these fall heavily on
the poor man is not an evil for him but
an elevation, of which he should boast
as a privilege" (James, p. 144).

B. The Rich Man: v. 10

"But the one who is rich should
take pride in his low position, because
he will pass away like a wild flower"
(NIV). Both the poor and the rich
should boast, or be happy, in their
place in life.

W. E. Oesterley notes that there
are two possible interpretations of
verses 9-10. The first is this: "Let the
brother who is 'humble,' i.e., belonging to the lower classes and therefore
of necessity (in those days) poor, glory
in the exaltation which as a Christian
he partakes of; but let him who was
rich glory in the fact that, owing to his
having embraced Christianity, he is
humiliated" (Expositor's Greek Testament, IV, 424).

Oesterley himself prefers a more
general application: "These verses
simply contain a wholesome piece of
advice to men to do their duty in that
state of life unto which it shall please
God to call them; if the poor man
becomes wealthy, there is nothing to be
ashamed of, he is to be congratu-
lated; if the rich man loses his wealth,
he needs comfort—after all, there is
something to be thankful for in escaping the temptations and dangers to
which the rich are subject" (Expositor's Greek Testament, IV, p. 425).

C. The Fading Away: v. 11

In the last part of verse 10 the rich
man is compared to "the flower of the
grass"—that is, "a wild flower" (NIV)
of the field. This thought is elaborated
in verse 11. When the sun rises and the
scorching winds from the desert blow
in on the flowers, they wither and die.
So it will be with the rich man; he will
wither or fade away while he is going
about his business. How often this
happens in life today!

V. REWARD   FOR   PERSEVER-
ANCE:
James 1:12

"Blessed is the man who perseveres
under trial, because when he has stood
the test, he will receive the victor's
crown, the life God has promised to
those who love him" (NIV).

"Crown of life" (KJV) is a good
example of the genitive of apposition—
"the crown that is life." That is,
eternal life is the highest reward that
God could give to those who persevere
to the end.

Why "the victor's crown" (NIV)?
Because the Greek word here is not
diadema, a royal crown ("diadem"),
but stephanos, the laurel wreath given
to the one who was victorious in the
ancient Greek games and races. So we
who run the race of life successfully,
in spite of all the tests and trials that
beset us, will receive the victor's
crown. We shall have the supreme
reward—living forever in the presence
of our Lord who has made it all
possible.

VI. NATURE OF TEMPTATION:
James 1:13-15

A. Not from God: v. 13

When we are being tempted to do
wrong we should never say, "God is
tempting me." For God cannot be
tempted by evil things and He tempts
no one. He does test us with hard trials
at times, as He tested Job. But as in
the case of that ancient man of God,

He does it for our own good (cf. vv. 2-3). We should always carefully make this distinction: God tests, but Satan tempts. In the first instance the purpose is good; in the second it is evil.

"God cannot be tempted" is literally, "God is untemptable." This "has perhaps a twofold application: God cannot be tempted to do evil Himself, nor can He be tempted with the wish to tempt men" (Oesterley, *Expositor's Greek Testament*, IV, 428). This verse supports the doctrine, asserted strongly in both the Old and New Testaments, that God is holy. The holiness of God is the bedrock foundation on which our faith rests.

B. Enticement of Evil Desire: v. 14

The source of temptation is not God but our own "evil desire" ("lust," KJV). It is primarily not from without but from within.

Two interesting verbs are used here. The first is "drawn away," the second "enticed." Originally the first was used of fishing, the second of hunting. Later the second was used for the seductions of a prostitute. Oesterley writes: "Both the participles might be transferred, from their literal use in application to hunting or fishing, to a metaphorical use of alluring to sensual sin, and thus desire entices the man from his self-restraint as with the wiles of a harlot, a metaphor maintained by the words which follow, 'conceived,' 'beareth,' 'bringeth forth'" (*Expositor's Greek Testament*, IV, 428).

In a similar vein Ropes says: "These words were applied to the hunter or, especially, the fisherman, who 'lures' his prey from its retreat ...and 'entices' it ... by bait ... to his trap, hook, or net" (*James*, p. 156).

C. Consequences of Evil Desire: v. 15

"Then, after desire has conceived, it gives birth to sin; and sin, when it is full-grown, gives birth to death" (NIV). This is the tragic sequence of

temptation: desire, sin, death. The only way to avoid the final, eternal consequence is to stop temptation at its very beginning. We must do as Joseph did when seduced by Potiphar's wife: flee from it.

We must be very clear in our distinction between temptation and sin. Temptation does not become sin until we give our consent to it. No matter how strong and forceful the temptation may be, it is not sin until we say Yes. Mayor writes: "Sin is the result of the surrender of the will to the soliciting of *epithymia* (desire) instead of the guidance of reason." He goes on to say: "Sin when full-grown, when it has become a fixed habit of determining the character of the man, brings forth death" (*James*, p. 55).

VII. SOURCE OF ALL GOOD:
James 1:16-18

A. The Unchanging Father: vv. 16-17

James warns us: "Don't be deceived, my dear brothers" (v. 16, NIV). Evidently there was a false teaching abroad in that day to the effect that God tempts people. James says that this is not true.

"Every good gift and every perfect gift" (v. 17) is literally "All good giving and every perfect gift" (Mayor, *James*). James declares that these are from above, from the Father of lights, "with whom is no variableness, neither

---

DISCUSSION QUESTIONS

1. What is the value of trials?
2. What is the difference between testing and temptation?
3. What are some consequences of doubt?
4. What does it mean to be "double-minded"?
5. How is man like the flower of the field?
6. How can we persevere under trial?

shadow of turning"—"who does not change like shifting shadows" (NIV). The idea seems to be that of a "shadow cast by turning," as the shadow on a sundial. The sun and the moon are constantly changing, as we view them. But the Father of these heavenly lights, the One who is the eternal Source of all light, is unchanging. He is always the same, unswerving.

B. The Gift of Life: v. 18

The greatest gift that God has given us is life—His life. He is the Source of both life and light.

CONTEMPORARY APPLICATION

As we noted in the Lesson Commentary, the only way to escape the seductiveness of temptation is to flee from it, as Joseph did from Potiphar's wife. But how do we do this?

If there is some circumstance or person that is luring us to evil, we can flee quickly, and must! But what if the temptation is entirely inward?

The answer is that we can flee from it by turning our attention immediately to something else. Recall some pleasant experience, some happy, exciting event—the more exciting the better! Soon our mind is absorbed with this pleasant memory. We can only think of one thing at a time. Let's fill our minds with good thoughts.

A FAITH THAT WORKS

DEVOTIONAL READING	Psalm 40:1-8

ADULTS

Topic: *A Faith That Works*

Background Scripture: James 1:19—2:26

Scripture Lesson: James 2:14-26

Memory Verse: *Religion that is pure and undefiled before God and the Father is this: to visit orphans and widows in their affliction, and to keep oneself unstained from the world.* James 1:27

YOUTH

Topic: *A Faith That Works*

Background Scripture: James 1:19—2:26

Scripture Lesson: James 2:14-26

Memory Verse: *Religion that is pure and undefiled before God and the Father is this: to visit orphans and widows in their affliction, and to keep oneself unstained from the world.* James 1:27

CHILDREN

Topic: *Belief in Action*

Background Scripture: James 1:19—2:26

Scripture Lesson: James 2:14-17

Memory Verse: *Be doers of the word, and not hearers only, deceiving yourselves.* James 1:22

DAILY BIBLE READINGS

Mon., May 2: Listening, the First Step to Faith, James 1:19-20; Proverbs 1:8-9; 4:10-13.

Tues., May 3: Receive the Word with Meekness, James 1:21; 4:10; Proverbs 16:19-20.

Wed., May 4: The Word: A Guide for the Faithful, James 1:22-25; Psalm 17:4-5; 119:28-29, 105.

Thurs., May 5: Faith Leads to Works of Love, James 1:26-27; I Thessalonians 1:5-12.

Fri., May 6: Impartiality, an Attribute of Faith, James 2:1-13.

Sat., May 7: Restrained Words Essential to Faith, Proverbs 17:4-10, 27-28.

Sun., May 8: Faith and Works Inseparable, James 2:14-24.

LESSON AIM

To help us understand what the true faith is and how we can have a faith that really works.

273

LESSON SETTING

Time: About A.D. 60 (or 45)

Place: Probably Jerusalem

A Faith That Works

LESSON OUTLINE

I. Listening and Doing: James 1:19-27
A. Quick to Listen, Slow to Speak: vv. 19-21
B. Listening and Doing: vv. 22-25
C. True Religion: vv. 26-27

II. Favoritism Forbidden: James 2:1-13
A. Discrimination Against the Poor: vv. 1-4
B. Unreasonableness of Favoring the Rich: vv. 5-7
C. Favoritism Is Sin: vv. 8-11
D. Mercy and Judgment: vv. 12-13

III. Faith and Works: James 2:14-26
A. Faith Without Works: vv. 14-17
B. Faith Shown by Works: vv. 18-19
C. Example of Abraham: vv. 20-23
D. Justified by a Faith That Works: v. 24
E. Example of Rahab: v. 25
F. Faith Without Works Is Dead: v. 26

SUGGESTED INTRODUCTION FOR ADULTS

As we noted last week, we are in a unit of five lessons covering the Epistle of James. The printed portions cannot include all the text, for obvious reasons. But in order that the study of James may be complete, we are covering all the intervening material in our Lesson Commentary. There is a great value in studying the Bible by books, not isolated verses or sections of Scripture. So we are including every verse of James in our study.

Our lesson today deals with one of the most crucial questions in practical theology: How can a person be justified before God? The Roman Catholic Church has, to all intents and purposes, said: "By faith *and* works." Protestantism has countered with the assertion: "By faith *alone*." Which is right?

According to our Scripture lesson today both are right and both are wrong! We hope that this statement will make sense after we finish our study of this important passage.

SUGGESTED INTRODUCTION FOR YOUTH

The title of our lesson today is "A Faith That Works." It can be put in a nutshell: The faith that works is the faith that *works*. It is not a dead, lifeless faith, without any deeds; it is a faith that does something. It is not a mere theoretical faith; it is a practical faith. It not only says, but does. It is not only in the head, but in the heart—and it shows itself in the life. This is true faith, saving faith.

There are two kinds of religion today. One emphasizes

believing alone; the other puts all the accent on action—usually social (and sometimes political) activism. Proponents of each side stand there throwing rocks—or at least mud—at each other. James shows us in our lesson today what true faith is.

CONCEPTS FOR CHILDREN

1. Faith and love go together.
2. We must not only believe in God, but also show love to others.
3. We should look for opportunities to do this.
4. Real belief is belief in action.

THE LESSON COMMENTARY

I. LISTENING AND DOING: James 1:19-27

A. Quick to Listen, Slow to Speak: vv. 19-21

Who of us has not erred at this point? Instead of listening, we keep on talking, and so we don't learn much! For listening is one of the main avenues of learning.

Too much talking and too little listening used to be one of the main faults of counselors, and it is often the besetting sin of Christians. People sense that we are happy and seem to be making it in life; so they come to us, hoping for help. Immediately we tell them that they ought to do this and that and the other. But first they needed to unload their minds and hearts—and we didn't give them a chance! Today it is recognized that one of the main roles of counseling is listening.

But the last part of verse 19, "slow to anger," indicates that the main application of this verse is that we should think more and talk less. Especially when someone offends us and we feel like making a sharp reply, we should be "quick to listen, slow to speak, and slow to become angry" (NIV).

James goes on to say, "For man's anger does not bring about the righteous life that God desires" (v. 20, NIV). The true Christian life is one of "longsuffering, gentleness, goodness"

(Galatians 5:22), not angry words to each other. Anger produces strife and quarreling, not God's righteousness in our lives.

"Superfluity of naughtiness" (v. 21, KJV) is surely a quaint expression, but it is hardly contemporary speech. The Greek simply says "abundance of evil." A more meaningful rendering of this verse would be: "Therefore, get rid of all moral filth and the evil that is so prevalent, and humbly accept the word planted in you, which can save you" (NIV).

B. Listening and Doing: vv. 22-25

"Do not merely listen to the word, and so deceive yourselves. Do what it says" (v. 22, NIV). That puts it right on the line! In verses 19-21 James emphasizes the importance of listening. Now he says that after we have listened we must do something as a result. Hear what God says to us in His Word, and then do it!

If we merely listen to the Word and don't do what it says, we are like a man "who looks at his face in a mirror ["glass" (KJV) is wrong, since they did not have glass mirrors then, but metal mirrors]—[but] "goes away and immediately forgets what he looks like" (v. 24, NIV). The man who will be blessed is the one who looks into "the perfect law of liberty"—the law that gives freedom—and continues to order his life in accordance with the law (v. 25).

"Law of liberty" is a striking phrase. What our generation desperately needs to learn is that there is no true liberty without law. As we obey the law we find true freedom; we are free to live a happy, useful life.

C. True Religion: vv. 26-27

"If anyone considers himself religious and yet does not keep a tight rein on his tongue, he deceives himself and his religion is worthless" (v. 26, NIV). The truth of this statement is so clear that it hardly calls for comment. One of the quickest ways to lose our religion is out through our lips!

Verse 27 is unique in the New Testament. It tells us that true religion is twofold. It is love in action, ministering to the needs of orphans and widows—the helpless victims in ancient society. But it also means keeping oneself "unspotted from the world." Liberals have usually emphasized the former and Conservatives the latter. James says that we must do both if we are to have the religion that meets God's approval.

II. FAVORITISM FORBIDDEN: James 2:1-13

A. Discrimination Against the Poor: vv. 1-4

"My brothers, as believers in our glorious Lord Jesus Christ, don't show favoritism" (v. 1, NIV). "Respect of persons" (KJV) is one word in the Greek—*prosopolempsia*. Literally it means "face-receiving." This is an Old Testament way of expressing the idea of showing partiality or favoritism. James condemns this as wrong.

Then he gives a concrete example: "Suppose a man comes into your meeting wearing a gold ring and fine clothes, and a poor man in shabby clothes also comes in" (v. 2, NIV). The Greek word for "meeting" (KJV, "assembly") is *synagoge*. This is the common word in the Gospels and Acts for the Jewish place of meeting for worship. In Revelation we find mention of

the "synagogue of Satan" (Revelation 2:9; 3:9), referring to the Jewish persecution of Christians. Only here in the New Testament is it used for a Christian congregation, though this usage is found in several second-century writers. The regular word for church (in the New Testament) is *ecclesia*.

James goes on: "If you show special attention to the man wearing fine clothes and say, 'Here's a good seat for you,' but say to the poor man, 'You stand there,' or, 'Sit on the floor by my feet,' have you not discriminated among yourselves and become judges with evil thoughts?" (vv. 3-4, NIV). "Judges of evil thoughts" (KJV) sounds like judging other people's thoughts, but obviously the meaning here is that of the believer himself thinking wrongly. J. H. Ropes suggests that the sense is: "You have passed judgments (i.e., on rich or poor) prompted by unworthy motives" (*A Critical and Exegetical Commentary on the Epistle of St. James*, International Critical Commentary, p. 193). It is very easy to show partiality toward those who are wealthy, but it is unchristian.

B. Unreasonableness of Favoring the Rich: vv. 5-7

James now shows how illogical this attitude is. He first reminds his readers that God has chosen those who are materially poor but spiritually rich as heirs of the Kingdom He has promised to those who love Him. This does not mean that poverty guarantees piety. But in both the Old Testament and the Gospels we find the idea that too often the rich are ungodly, whereas many poor people lean on God. There are always exceptions, of course, like Joseph of Arimathea and Joseph.

The unreasonableness of favoring the wealthy is indicated pointedly by three questions in verses 6-7: "Is it not the rich who are exploiting you? Are they not the ones who are dragging you into court? Are they not the ones who are slandering the noble name of him to whom you belong?" (NIV). Why honor those who oppress you and persecute you? It doesn't make sense!

C. Favoritism Is Sin: vv. 8-11

Not only is favoritism unreasonable; it is wrong. James declares that it is sin. He says that if we really keep "the royal law" found in Scripture, "Love your neighbor as yourself," we are doing well. "But if you show favoritism, you sin and are convicted by the law as lawbreakers" (v. 9, NIV). How many of us are guilty of this sin of favoritism? If we are, we should repent, ask God's forgiveness, and change our ways.

The Jewish Christians whom James was addressing might well answer, "But we keep most of the Law (of Moses)." James declares, "If you stumble at one point, you are guilty of all"—that is, "the law as a whole" (v. 10). You only have to break one law to become a lawbreaker.

For instance, says James, the God who commanded, "Do not commit adultery," also said, "Do not murder." If you break either *one* of these, you are a guilty lawbreaker.

D. Mercy and Judgment: vv. 12-13

"Speak and act as those who are going to be judged by the law that gives freedom" (v. 12, NIV). Why? Because "judgment without mercy" will be shown to the one who has not shown mercy to others.

James concludes this paragraph by saying, "Mercy triumphs over judgment!" (v. 13b, NIV). Ropes comments: "This gives the converse of the previous sentence (v. 13a). As the unmerciful will meet with no mercy, so a record of mercy will prevent condemnation" (*James*, p. 202). The "judgment" here is God's judgment.

Anyone familiar at all with English literature cannot help recalling Portia's speech in Shakespeare's *Merchant of Venice*, beginning, "The quality of mercy is not strained." It is one of the most powerful passages in all literature on the importance of mercy in "seasoning" justice. But Jesus said it most graphically: "Blessed are the merciful, for they shall obtain mercy" (Matthew 5:7).

III. FAITH AND WORKS: James 2:14-26

A. Faith Without Works: vv. 14-17

Now we come to the very heart of the Epistle of James. He asks: "What doth it profit, my brethren, though a man say he hath faith, and have not works? can faith save him?" (v. 14).

On the surface this looks like a flat contradiction of one of the main doctrines of the New Testament—salvation by faith. When the Philippian jailor asked Paul and Silas, "What must I do to be saved?" they replied, "Believe on the Lord Jesus Christ, and thou shalt be saved" (Acts 16:30-31). And we are all familiar with John 3:16. How can we reconcile all this with James?

The first "faith" in verse 14 has no article with it, but the second one does. Often in Greek the definite article has the force of a demonstrative pronoun—"that" or "this." The application is brought out in the New International Version: "What good is it, my brothers, if a man claims to have faith but has no deeds? Can such faith save him?" The point is that "that kind of faith"—a faith that is not evidenced in deeds—cannot save a person.

James proceeds to illustrate what he means: "Suppose a brother or sister is without clothes and daily food. If one of you says to him, 'Go, I wish you well; keep warm and well fed,' but does nothing about his physical needs, what good is it?" (vv. 15-16, NIV).

We have noted before that James is incisively and insistently practical. He declares that for a Christian to say to a person who is cold and hungry, "Keep warm and well fed" is the height of hypocrisy. And yet have we not come perilously near to being guilty of this as a church and as individuals? We have

been interested in people's souls, but not their bodies. We are eager to minister to their spiritual needs, but too often we have been oblivious to their physical needs.

Fortunately there is an increasing awareness among evangelical Christians that our evangelism would sometimes be more effective if backed up by an interest in the total man. Starving people may need to be fed with physical food before we try to feed them with the gospel. An empty stomach that is howling for help may drown out the words of spiritual life. The National Association of Evangelicals and other such groups are grappling realistically with this problem and seeking to meet this challenge. But we need a personal as well as organizational sense of responsibility at this point.

James concludes his illustration by saying: "Even so faith, if it hath not works, is dead, being alone" (v. 17). True faith produces action. If there is no action there is no real faith. That is the main point that James is making here.

B. Faith Shown by Works: vv. 18-19

"Yea, a man may say, Thou hast faith, and I have works: shew me thy faith without thy works, and I will shew thee my faith by my works" (v. 18). The last part might possibly be misunderstood as meaning a faith that comes by works, as some have erroneously held. But in the Greek "by my works" comes first: "And I by my works will show you my faith." Clearly what James is doing is asserting that good deeds are an essential and inevitable evidence of genuine faith. If a man claims to have faith and does not demonstrate it in his outward life, his profession of faith is false.

That intellectual belief will not save anyone is shown in a surprising, almost shocking way, in verse 19: "You believe that there is one God. Good! Even the demons believe that—

and shudder" (NIV). It should be noted that the translation "devils" (KJV, NEB) is incorrect. The New Testament very clearly indicates that there is only one "devil" (*diabolos*) but that there are many "demons" (*daimonia*). The distinction should always be made, as it always is in the original Greek.

In 1741 John Wesley preached before the elite of Oxford University on the subject, "The Almost Christian." When he told that cultured, "Christian" audience that mere intellectual belief was no more than the faith of demons, his audience was enraged. It is not surprising that he was told he could not preach there again, even though it was his assignment as a Fellow of Lincoln College.

C. Example of Abraham: vv. 20-23

James is aware that some of his readers may still be unconvinced. So he writes on: "You foolish man, do you want evidence that faith without deeds is useless?" (v. 20, NIV). And then he proceeds to give two Old Testament examples as proof.

The first is that of Abraham. He is cited in the New Testament as the great man of faith, the father of the "faithing" ones. But how did he show his faith? By obedience! And so James asks: "Was not Abraham our father justified by works, when he had offered Isaac his son upon the altar?" (v. 21). Obedience is the greatest demonstration and proof of faith. The mountain peak of Abraham's faith came when he went ahead with God's command to offer his son Isaac on an altar of sacrifice. Only at the last moment, when he had fully proved his obedience, did God stay his hand from actual execution.

Then James makes the application: "Seest thou how faith wrought with his works, and by works was faith made perfect?" (v. 22). Thus was fulfilled the Scripture that says: "Abraham believed God, and it was credited to him as righteousness" (v. 23, NIV). He demonstrated his faith by his deed. The result was that he was called "the Friend of God." What an honor for an Old Testament saint! We are reminded of Jesus' words to His disciples: "Henceforth I call you not servants ... but I have called you friends" (John 15:15). A friend is one in whom we confide, one we can trust. That is the way God treats us.

At first glance it seems that the statement of James in verse 21 that Abraham was justified by works is in direct contradiction with Paul's assertion that Abraham was justified by faith (Romans 4:1-5). As is well known, Martin Luther was severely plagued by this problem.

D. A. Hayes, in his book *New Testament Epistles*, gives great help at this point. He says that Paul and James are using three key terms—faith, works, justified—in quite different ways and that a recognition of this fact resolves the problem of seeming contradiction.

He suggests that James is using the term "faith" in the sense of mental acceptance. Such a faith cannot save us, for demons have that kind of faith in Jesus. But when Paul talks about faith he means moral commitment, and that kind of faith brings salvation.

How about "works"? Paul is thinking of the dead works of the Law, a formal and ceremonial observance of the Law of Moses. He asserts strongly that by the works of the Law no man will be justified (Romans 3:20). But James is thinking of works of love, the good deeds that genuine faith produces. If there are no good deeds, there is no real faith.

And now to "justification." Paul is concerned with initial justification, when a sinner becomes accepted with God. But James is thinking about final justification before God at the final judgment. Only those who have demonstrated their faith in good deeds will pass the test then (Revelation 20:12).

When we recognize these differences in emphasis, the seeming contradiction fades away. Words mean different things to different people and in differing circumstances.

D. Justified by a Faith That Works: v. 24

James states his conclusion clearly: "Ye see then how that by works a man is justified, and not by faith only." Now we can understand what he means. If we expect to live forever in God's presence, or even to have His approbation here, we must back up our profession of faith by a life of good deeds. If Christ really dwells within, He will live out His life of good works in us.

Mental assent to the truths of the gospel is not enough. There must be a *moral consent* to do the will of God in our daily lives.

For ten years John Wesley worked hard to live as he thought a Christian should live. He even came as a missionary to the Indians in America. But when he returned disillusioned to England, the Moravian Peter Boehler asked him if he knew that his sins were forgiven. Wesley replied that he knew Christ died for the sins of the world. "But do you know that he died for *your* sins?" Wesley was not satisfied until he found the answer in his own inner experience of conversion.

E. Example of Rahab: v. 25

We said that James gives two examples of justification in the Old

---

DISCUSSION QUESTIONS

1. What are some advantages of listening, not talking?
2. What illustration of hearing and doing is found at the close of the Sermon on the Mount?
3. How is true religion described?
4. What are some of the consequences of favoritism?
5. How may we carry out our social responsibilities?
6. How would you define faith?

Testament. The first was that of Abraham; the second is Rahab. Though she had been a "prostitute" (NIV), she was justified when she gave lodging to the Israelite messengers and sent them safely off to the hills. She demonstrated her faith by what she did. That is the whole point that James is making.

F. Faith Without Works Is Dead: v. 26

James compares faith to the human body, and works to the spirit.

We might expect the opposite analogy to be more logical. But Ropes explains it this way: "To the mind of James faith and works co-operate to secure justification, and by works faith is kept alive. So the body and the spirit co-operate to secure continued life, and by the spirit the body is kept alive" (*James*, p. 225).

It is obvious that James had been plagued by the antinomianism of his day—rejecting all law. Faith and obedience can never be separated in Christian experience.

CONTEMPORARY APPLICATION

In Matthew 25 we find three parables on preparedness for the return of Christ. The first, the Ten Virgins, emphasizes the absolutely essential preparation of an up-to-date, warm spiritual experience if we are not going to miss out on the Marriage Supper of the Lamb. The second, the Talents, shows the need for active, faithful service if we are going to be ready for the Second Coming. The third, the Sheep and the Goats, stresses the importance of social action (in a Christian sense) as a part of the preparation. Have we fed the hungry, clothed the destitute, visited the sick and imprisoned?

Evangelical Christians have always stressed the first preparation—inner experience of personal salvation. Many have been not only devout in spirit but devoted in service. But too often we have neglected our social responsibility.

SPEAKING WITH WISDOM

DEVOTIONAL READING	Proverbs 2:1-15

ADULTS	Topic: *Speaking with Wisdom* Background Scripture: James 3 Scripture Lesson: James 3:6-18 Memory Verse: *The wisdom from above is first pure, then peaceable, gentle, open to reason, full of mercy and good fruits, without uncertainty or insincerity.* James 3:17

YOUTH	Topic: *Speaking with Wisdom* Background Scripture: James 3 Scripture Lesson: James 3:16-18 Memory Verse: *The wisdom from above is first pure, then peaceable, gentle, open to reason, full of mercy and good fruits, without uncertainty or insincerity.* James 3:17

CHILDREN	Topic: *The Way to Be Wise* Background Scripture: James 3 Scripture Lesson: James 3:13-18 Memory Verse: *If any of you lacks wisdom, let him ask God, who gives to all men generously.* James 1:5

DAILY BIBLE READINGS	Mon., May 9: The Power of the Tongue, James 3:1-6. Tues., May 10: The Changeableness of the Tongue, James 3:7-12. Wed., May 11: False and True Wisdom, James 3:13-18. Thurs., May 12: "The Lord Gives Wisdom," Proverbs 2:1-15. Fri., May 13: Wisdom's Call, Proverbs 8:1-9. Sat., May 14: Wisdom's Teachings, Proverbs 8:10-21. Sun., May 15: Christ, the Wisdom of God, Proverbs 8:22-31.

LESSON AIM	To help us guide our lives by true wisdom.

LESSON SETTING	Time: About A.D. 60 (or 45) Place: Probably Jerusalem

SUGGESTED INTRODUCTION FOR ADULTS

It is generally agreed, even by secular writers, that the third chapter of James contains the greatest passage on the tongue to be found in all literature. It is graphic and vivid.

There is no more striking way in which we reveal our wisdom or lack of it than in the way we use our tongues. As soon as we open our mouths we advertise ourselves—for better or for worse!

It is sometimes said that silence is golden; speech, at best, can only be silver. But the great preacher in Constantinople in the fourth century was a man named John, who was called Chrysostom—Greek for "Golden-mouthed."

In the Book of Proverbs we find this beautiful statement: "A word fitly spoken is like apples of gold in pictures of silver" (Proverbs 25:11). That is what we should desire our speech to be, whether in public or in private. The wise man is one who knows what to say, and how and when to say it. We should all of us pray for true wisdom at this point.

SUGGESTED INTRODUCTION FOR YOUTH

To a great extent our words betray our thoughts. So we need to be careful what we think. But we especially need to be careful what we say. For people judge us in large measure by what they hear us saying. On this point we cannot be too careful.

More than any other book in the New Testament, the

Epistle of James resembles the Wisdom Literature of the Old Testament. The author is concerned that his readers will possess and demonstrate the true wisdom that comes from God, not the false wisdom of the carnal mind.

We need to reread James 1:5. All of us lack wisdom in some ways. We need to ask God for His wisdom.

CONCEPTS FOR CHILDREN

1. All of us lack sufficient wisdom in ourselves.
2. So we need to ask God to give us wisdom.
3. He has promised to give it to us generously.
4. True wisdom is marked by humility.

THE LESSON COMMENTARY

I. THE PENALTY OF BEING A TEACHER: James 3:1-2

A. Not Many Should Be Teachers: v. 1

"My brethren, be not many masters" (KJV). What does this mean? The truth is that 90 percent of those who read this verse today don't know what it means!

The Greek word translated "master" here is *didaskalos*, which simply means "teacher." Yet in the King James Version it is translated "master" forty-seven times and "teacher" only ten times—plus "doctor" once (Luke 2:46). In 1611 "master" was used for a teacher, but that translation does not communicate the correct meaning to the modern reader.

What the Greek literally says is: "Do not many of you become teachers." Why? "Because you know that we who teach will be judged more strictly" (NIV). The Greek word for "condemnation" (KJV) is *crima*, which simply means "judgment." (The word that means "condemnation" is *katacrima*.) James says that if we try to teach others what to do, we are under greater responsibility to do exactly the right thing ourselves. This idea is carried over into the second verse, where he warns us that we all fail sometimes.

B. We All Stumble: v. 2

The King James Version says, "For in many things we offend all"—that is, offend all people. Obviously this is not true. But "all" in the Greek is not in the accusative (objective) case; it is in the nominative case. What the Greek clearly says is, "For in many things we all offend"—"We all stumble in many ways" (NIV)—which *is* true. Not one of us can say that we never give offense by anything that we do or say. The Greek word meaning "stumble" occurs twice in this verse. We have already had it in 2:10.

With regard to the first statement of this verse J. H. Ropes says: "All men stumble, and of all faults those of the tongue are the hardest to avoid. Hence the profession of teacher is the most difficult mode of life conceivable" (*A Critical and Exegetical Commentary on the Epistle of St. James*, International Critical Commentary, p. 228).

James goes on to say that if anyone does not "stumble in word" (literal Greek)—"If anyone is never at fault in what he says" (NIV)—he is "a perfect man, able also to bridle the whole body." The Greek verb for "bridle" is *chalinagogeo* (only here and in 1:26). It is compounded of the noun *chalinos*, "bridle" (cf. v. 3) and the verb *ago*, "lead." Hence it literally means "lead with a bridle," and so "keep in check" (NIV). This is a high standard.

II. THREE ILLUSTRATIONS OF THE TONGUE:
James 3:3-6

A. A Bit in a Horse's Mouth: v. 3

Following up the metaphor of bridling the whole body, James writes: "Behold, we put bits in the horses' mouths, that they may obey us; and we turn about their whole body." Today very few people *drive* horses, but many still *ride* them. And so the figure of a bit in a horse's mouth is still a fairly familiar one. The rider pulls on the bridle rein and gets results. Not only does the horse's head turn in the desired direction, but his entire body turns also, big though it be. And this is all accomplished by pulling on one end of the small metal bit in his mouth.

What is the application? J. B. Mayor puts it this way: "By the bridle in the mouth we turn the horse as we will, so by controlling our words we can regulate our whole activity" (*Epistle of St. James*, p. 108). Ropes says simply: "It is with men as with horses: control their mouth and you are master of all their action" (*James*, p. 229).

B. A Rudder on a Ship: vv. 4-5a

"Or take ships as an example. Although they are so large and are driven by strong winds, they are steered by a very small rudder wherever the pilot wants to go" (NIV). The Queen Elizabeth, which made its last regular runs in 1968, was nearly a thousand feet long and had a displacement of eighty-three thousand tons. It was a floating palatial hotel. Yet one who has stood at the stern could not help being amazed at how small a rudder turned this mammoth craft.

James says, "Likewise the tongue is a small part of the body, but it makes great boasts" (v. 5a, NIV). The point that the writer is making here is

that though the tongue is very small in comparison with the entire body, yet what the tongue says can affect the body as a whole. For instance, a man can say the wrong thing in a few words, or even one word, and thereby bring death to his body. The importance of the tongue is all out of proportion to its size.

C. A Spark in a Forest: vv. 5b-6

The Greek word for "matter" (v. 5b, KJV) is *hyle*. It is true that in later Greek writings it sometimes had the philosophical connotation of "matter" in the sense of material substance Latin, *materia*). But the average reader of the King James Version today would take the statement of verse 5b as meaning that a little fire kindles a big "affair." This is not what the Greek says.

Actually the first meaning of *hyle* is "wood, forest, woodland." It sometimes meant "wood, timber, fuel" (G. Abbott-Smith, *Manual Greek Lexicon of the New Testament*, p. 455). Ropes comments: "The abundant references in ancient literature to forest fires, sometimes with direct references to the smallness of the spark which leads to vast destruction, and the repeated use of this comparison in ethical discussions make it likely that *hylen* here means 'forest' rather than 'fuel' " (*James*, p. 232).

Every year the papers tell about, and television portrays, forest fires that destroy thousands of acres of valuable timberland. And it is well known that many of these devastating fires were started by a smoker throwing away a lighted cigarette or dropping a hot match. We ourselves have traced a brush fire to its source, picked up the warm ashes at the starting point, and discovered a strong tobacco smell.

The language of verse 6 is shockingly strong, but not too strong. A few words from the tongue can start a destructive conflagration that will wipe out thousands of people and even destroy a nation.

James asserts that the tongue "corrupts the whole person, sets the whole course of his life on fire, and is itself set on fire by hell" (NIV). Only Satan could be responsible for the Satanic effects of some hellish things that people say these days. The whole course of life seems set on fire by "hell" (Gehenna, the place of continual burning). These are solemn words of warning.

III. TAMING THE TONGUE: James 3:7-8

A. Tamable Animals: v. 7

James declares that "all kinds of animals, birds, reptiles and creatures of the sea are being tamed and have been tamed by man" (NIV). This, of course, is a striking fact that most of us have witnessed at some time or other. It is astonishing to see trained animals from the forests and sea perform unbelievable feats—to say nothing of domesticated animals.

B. Untamable Tongue: v. 8

This is a startling statement: "But the tongue can no man tame; it is an unruly evil, full of deadly poison." One thinks of gossipers, with their restless evil talk. One also thinks of men who have acid tongues that can blister and burn opponents. Poisonous lies from the human tongue have destroyed many a man's reputation and wiped out whole careers. The language here is literally, horribly true.

IV. WRONG USE OF THE TONGUE: James 3:9-12

A. For Both Praise and Cursing: vv. 9-10

"With the tongue we praise our Lord and Father, and with it we curse men, who have been made in God's likeness" (v. 9, NIV). The word "praise" or "bless" (KJV) may be used here as a reflection of the fact that whenever the Jews mentioned the name "God" they customarily added, "Blessed be He." And yet those who did this would perhaps soon after that get angry and curse a fellowman. This meant that out of the same mouth came blessing and cursing. No wonder that James said, "My brethren, these things ought not so to be" (v. 10).

B. Contrary to Nature: vv. 11-12

James illustrates the unreasonableness and unnaturalness of this by three different figures. First he asks, "Can both fresh water and salt water flow from the same spring?" (v. 11, NIV). The form of the Greek indicates that the answer is "No. It cannot, can it?" And of course we know that this is the way of nature: One spring is salty, another sweet.

In verse 12 James introduces two other illustrations from nature and then closes the verse by stating positively what he had strongly implied in question form in verse 11. He writes: "Can the fig tree, my brethren, bear olive berries? either a vine, figs? so can no fountain both yield salt water and fresh."

Olives, figs, and grapes are the three most common fruits of the Mediterranean world. One can drive past miles of continuous olive groves, as we did last summer in Greece. The Mount of Olives was so called because it was largely covered with olive trees. And fig orchards are very common. As for vineyards, they cover the whole hillsides throughout the Middle East.

But no one ever saw olives growing on fig trees or figs appearing on grape vines. Nature is not so confused as men's actions!

James concludes this section by returning to the question of verse 11. He now asserts categorically: "Neither can a salt spring produce fresh water" (NIV). If the spring of our heart is evil, then evil will come out.

V. WRONG KIND OF WISDOM: James 3:13-16

A. The Truly Wise Man: v. 13

"Wise man" is one word in Greek, *sophos*. Of this word Ropes says: "The technical term for the Teacher (cf. v. 1): in Jewish usage one who has a knowledge of practical moral wisdom, resting on a knowledge of God. The words of James relate to the ideal to be maintained by a professional Wise Man and Teacher, not merely to the private wisdom of the layman" (*James*, p. 244).

This seems confirmed by the next Greek noun *epistemon*, translated "understanding" (NIV) or "endued with knowledge." Mayor says that this is "used in classical Greek for a skilled or scientific person as opposed to one who has no special knowledge or training" (*James*, p. 126).

"Conversation" (KJV) means "manner of living," not talk. Three different Greek words in the New Testament are translated by "conversation" in the King James Version, and not one of them means "conversation" as we use that term today.

Mayor notes that there are two emphases here: "deeds *versus* words, gentleness and modesty *versus* arrogance and passion. What this passage means is: 'let him show his deeds in meekness of wisdom,' that is, 'let him give practical proof (of his being wise) from his life and conduct in the meekness which proceeds from and is the true mark of wisdom'" (*James*, p. 126).

People who think they are wise— that is, "wise-acres" who make "wise-cracks"—are proud and often arrogant. But true wisdom is always marked by humility.

In the Bible, both Old Testament and New, wisdom is not primarily an intellectual matter; it is basically moral. The wise man is not the one who knows the most in science and literature, for instance, but the person who knows how to order his life in obedience to God's will.

Again, while knowledge may be mainly intellectual, wisdom is practical. It is knowing how to use the knowledge that one has.

B. False Wisdom: vv. 14-16

"But if you harbor bitter envy and selfish ambition in your hearts, do not boast about it or deny the truth" (v. 14, NIV). There is nothing on earth much more bitter than envy or jealousy. It will cause people to take hateful attitudes that they had never dreamed of having.

The Greek word translated "selfish ambition" (KJV, "strife") is *eritheia*, which basically means "party spirit." It is a mixture of ambition, rivalry, and strife. Thousands of times it has caused disunity and division in the church. James especially warns church leaders against being guilty of this.

If you have this wrong attitude, James says, don't boast, "and lie not against the truth." Mayor puts it well: "If you have bitterness you cannot be truly wise, for wisdom is shown by gentleness; your profession therefore is a lie" (*James*, p. 127).

It would seem that even in the first century rivalry and strife were threatening the church. And the guilty ones claimed to be wise!

James does not hesitate to place strong labels on this false wisdom. He asserts that it does not come "from above"—that is, "from heaven" (NIV) —"but is earthly, sensual, devilish" (v. 15).

The first adjective is clear enough. It is *epigeios*, "of the earth," and so, "earthly." Ropes says: "*epigeios* seems to mean here 'derived from the frail and finite world of human life and affairs'" (*James*, p. 247).

The second adjective, *psychice* (from which we get *psychic*), is a little more difficult. *Psyche* is the Greek word for "soul." So this adjective literally means "soulish." But what is that?

Throughout the New Testament this adjective is used to describe what is opposed to the spiritual, or at least contrasted with it. For this reason the New International Version has "unspiritual" here. Some would translate it "natural."

The third adjective is *daimoniodes*, from *daimonion*, "demon." So it essentially means "demonic," which is basically the same as "devilish." This false wisdom comes from hell, not heaven.

Ropes makes a good summary of the three adjectives. He writes: "These three words, 'earthly, sensual, devilish,' describe the so-called wisdom, which is not of divine origin, in an advancing series—as pertaining to the earth, not to the world above; to mere nature, not to the Spirit; and to the hostile spirits of evil, instead of God" (*James*, p. 248).

What is the effect of all this? James says, "For where envying and strife is, there is confusion and every evil work" (v. 16), Jealousy and selfish ambition always produce confusion—in the home, the church, the community, and the nation, as well as in international affairs.

The Greek word translated "confusion'" is *akatastasia*. It basically means "instability," then "confusion" or "tumult." It also means "disturbance" or "disorder" (NIV). Ropes says, "The word seems to have something of the bad associations of our word 'anarchy,' and has to bear much weight in this sentence" (*James* p. 248).

The Greek word for "evil" here is a very strong one, *phaulon*. Literally it means "vile."

VI. RIGHT KIND OF WISDOM: James 3:17-18

A. Pure and Peaceable: v. 17

This is a beautiful verse, probably the best description of heavenly ("from above") wisdom to be found in all literature. It comes to us by inspiration of the Holy Spirit.

It is "first pure." This statement is of utmost importance. It graphically underscores the fact that true wisdom is basically moral, not mental.

What a contrast to much of the boasted wisdom of our day! In high academic circles in our country it has become fashionable to ridicule whatever is pure and clean. The Free Speech Movement, which soon became "the filthy speech movement," started on the campus of one of our largest universities. Wisdom has become a synonym for cleverness—and there is no one more clever than the devil.

But the second characteristic follows right behind it in importance; it is "peaceable." Unfortunately, there are religious people who glory in the fact that they are "pure," but their censorious, contentious words are hardly "peaceable."

The same could be said concerning the third adjective, "gentle." The Greek word *epieikes* has a spread of meaning. Ropes defines it as: "reasonable," "considerate," "moderate," "gentle." He adds: "We have no words in English which are full equivalents of the Greek" (*James*, p. 249).

"Easy to be entreated" is also a rare virtue in some religious circles. The Greek is all one word, *eupeithes*, "easily persuaded." It can be translated "willing to yield." It means "submissive" (NIV), the opposite of "obstinate."

This heavenly wisdom is further defined as "full of mercy and good fruits, without partiality and without hypocrisy"—"impartial and sincere" (NIV). This is the wisdom that God gives us and requires that we show in our daily lives.

B. Result of True Wisdom: v. 18

"The fruit of righteousness" is "the reward which righteous conduct

---

DISCUSSION QUESTIONS

1. Why should we not be too eager to be teachers?
2. What responsibility must we accept as teachers?
3. Why cannot the tongue be tamed?
4. What should be the relation of our language in church to our language on the street?
5. How can we display true wisdom?
6. What is the connection between purity and peace?

brings" (Ropes). Such is shown only in peace. That is, righteousness must be peaceable to bring a reward. But only those who practice peace are sowing real righteousness. In the Bible righteousness and peace always go together.

CONTEMPORARY APPLICATION

How are we going to control our tongues? That is one of the greatest challenges facing all of us.

The psalmist prayed that the Lord would set a watch before his lips. That might well be our prayer every day, and especially in times of crisis and provocation.

Reading God's Word will help us to think right thoughts, and our words are the expression of our thoughts. A mind that is filled with the Word of God is much less apt to say wrong things.

There is a close connection between the tongue and the peace that is emphasized in the last part of the lesson. The best way to hold our peace in our hearts is to "hold our peace" with our tongues!

May 22, 1977

GUIDELINES TO FAITH

DEVOTIONAL READING	Psalm 124

ADULTS

Topic: *Guidelines to Faith*

Background Scripture: James 4:1—5:6

Scripture Lesson: James 4:1-10, 13-17

Memory Verse: *Whoever knows what is right to do and fails to do it, for him it is sin.* James 4:17

YOUTH

Topic: *Guidelines to Faith*

Background Scripture: James 4:1—5:6

Scripture Lesson: James 4:1-10, 13-17

Memory Verse: *Whoever knows what is right to do and fails to do it, for him it is sin.* James 4:17

CHILDREN

Topic: *Ways for Following Jesus*

Background Scripture: James 4:1—5:6

Scripture Lesson: James 4:3-8, 10

Memory Verse: *Trust in the Lord with all your heart, and do not rely on your own insight. In all your ways acknowledge him, and he will make straight your paths.* Proverbs 3:5-6

DAILY BIBLE READINGS

Mon., May 16: Christ or the World, James 4:1-10.
Tues., May 17: Render No Rash Judgments, James 4:11-12.
Wed., May 18: "If the Lord Wills," James 4:13-17.
Thurs., May 19: Beware of Ill-gotten Gain, James 5:1-6.
Fri., May 20: Examples of Faith, Hebrews 11:32-40.
Sat., May 21: "The Outcome of Your Faith," I Peter 1:3-9.
Sun., May 22: "Our Help Is . . . the Lord," Psalm 124.

LESSON AIM

To help us see and follow some of the guidelines for Christian living.

LESSON SETTING

Time: About A.D. 60 (or 45)

Place: Probably Jerusalem

LESSON OUTLINE

Guidelines to Faith

I. The Sin of Quarreling: James 4:1-3
   A. The Source of Quarreling: v. 1

289

B. Quarreling and Fighting: v. 2a
C. Asking with Wrong Motives: vv. 2b-3

II. The Sin of Worldliness: James 4:4-6
A. Enmity Against God: v. 4
B. Opposed by the Spirit: v. 5
C. More Grace Available: v. 6

III. The Need of Submission: James 4:7-10
A. Submission to God: v. 7
B. Drawing Near to God: v. 8
C. Humility and Exaltation: vv. 9-10

IV. The Sin of Slander: James 4:11-12

V. The Sin of Boasting: James 4:13-17
A. The Uncertainty of Life: vv. 13-14
B. Bowing to God's Will: vv. 15-16
C. Sins of Omission: v. 17

VI. The Sin of Selfish Wealth: James 5:1-6
A. Hoarding Wealth: vv. 1-3
B. Failing to Pay Wages: v. 4
C. Living in Luxury: vv. 5-6

SUGGESTED INTRODUCTION FOR ADULTS

In the first chapter of his Epistle James exhorts his readers to persevere in spite of trials. In the second chapter he warns against favoritism and shows the importance of good deeds as an evidence of faith. In the third chapter he talks about taming the tongue and discusses the nature of true wisdom.

When we come to our study of chapter 4 in today's lesson we find a startling, actually shocking, contrast. James pictures a quarreling, worldly, slandering, boasting people. Can these be Christians?

A reasonable view would seem to be that these sins were creeping into the congregations of Christian Jews in the Dispersion. James was deeply concerned about what he saw or heard about. So he warns these erring Christians of the seriousness of their wrong attitudes. In doing so he speaks most nearly like the thundering prophets of the Old Testament—Amos, Micah, Hosea, and Isaiah.

SUGGESTED INTRODUCTION FOR YOUTH

"Anyone, then, who knows the good he ought to do and doesn't do it, sins" (4:17, NIV). Our memory verse today constitutes a real challenge.

When we talk about "sins" we are apt to think about lying, stealing, adultery, murder, and the like. But Christians need to realize that there are sins of omission as well as sins of commission. When we fail to do the good we ought to do, we are guilty of sinning.

This raises the level of our thinking. It places upon us a higher responsibility. We not only need to watch our thoughts, words, and deeds, but we must be careful to see that we are daily doing what God wants us to.

CONCEPTS FOR
CHILDREN

1. Being a Christian means following Jesus.
2. We need to find ways we can follow Him.
3. When we follow Him we find peace and joy.
4. We should avoid things that displease Him.

THE LESSON COMMENTARY

I. THE SIN OF QUARRELING: James 4:1-3

A. The Source of Quarreling: v. 1

"What causes fights and quarrels among you? Don't they come from your desires that battle within you?" (NIV).

The first noun here is *polemos*, which literally means "war" (cf. KJV). G. Abbott-Smith says that in the New Testament it is often equivalent to *mache* (the second noun here), which means "a fight, battle," but that here in James it is used "hyperbolically, of private quarrels" (*A Manual Greek Lexicon of the New Testament*, p. 370). The second noun, *mache*, meant "a fight." But in the New Testament it has always the sense of "a strife, contention, quarrel" (Abbott-Smith, p. 280). J. B. Mayor says of the two Greek terms: "These need not be limited to their narrow sense: the former denotes any lasting resentment, the latter any outburst of passion" (*The Epistle of St. James*, p. 133).

The Greek word for "desires" is *hedonon*, from which we get "hedonism" ("love of pleasure"). It is correctly translated "pleasures" at the end of verse 3 (NIV). The translation "lusts" in both places (KJV) is perhaps too strong. J. H. Thayer says that the term here means "desires for pleasure" (*Greek-English Lexicon of the New Testament*, p. 276). So it is wrong desire that causes fights and quarrels among people. And these desires "war in your members." This may mean that they operate in the sphere of our body, or simply that they "battle within you."

B. Quarreling and Fighting: v. 2a

"You want something, but don't get it. You kill and covet, but you cannot have what you want. You quarrel and fight" (NIV). In this last sentence we have verbs corresponding to the first two nouns in verse 1, but in reverse order.

"Covet" sounds like an anticlimax after "kill." It seems best to put a period between them. (The early Greek manuscripts have no punctuation marks.) The New American Standard Bible probably has the best translation: "You lust and do not have; so you commit murder. And you are envious and cannot obtain; so you fight and quarrel." That gives the sense correctly.

With regard to the verb meaning "kill" or "murder," J. H. Ropes says: "No weaker sense is possible, and none is here necessary, for James is not describing the condition of any special community, but is analyzing the result of choosing pleasure instead of God. The final issue of the false choice is flagrant crime" (*A Critical and Exegetical Commentary on the Epistle of St. James*, International Critical Commentary, pp. 254-55).

C. Asking with Wrong Motives: vv. 2b-3

"Ye have not, because ye ask not." What a challenging statement! How many of God's blessings do we miss simply because we do not come to Him in humble petition for our needs. Our heavenly Father wants us to ask!

But what about the petitions that haven't been answered? James says, "When you ask, you do not receive, because you ask with wrong motives, that you may spend what you get on your pleasures" (v. 3, NIV).

Commenting on verses 2 and 3, Ropes says: "So long as men allow their lives to be governed by ... [the desire for pleasures], their desire is sure to be unsatisfied. The only sure source from which men can always receive is God. By choosing pleasure as their aim, men cut themselves off from this source. . . . James' principle is: Make the service of God your supreme end, and then your desires will be such as God can fulfil in answer to your prayer (cf. Mt. 6:31-33). Then there will be none of the present strife. . . . Desire for pleasure, when made the controlling end, leads to violence, for longings then arise which can only be satisfied by the use of violence, since God, from whom alone come good things (1:17), will not satisfy them" (*James*, p. 258).

II. THE SIN OF WORLDLINESS: James 4:4-6

A. Enmity Against God: v. 4

The King James Version has "ye adulterers" (masculine) "and adulteresses" (feminine). But the oldest and best Greek manuscripts all have just the feminine form, which is undoubtedly the original reading.

The reason the feminine form alone is used goes back to the Old Testament figure of Israel as the wife of Yahweh (Jehovah). In the New Testament we find, especially in Ephesians and Revelation, the beautiful concept of the church as the bride of Christ. James is here speaking in the metaphorical sense, as the context clearly indicates, and for that only the feminine form could be used. "Adulteresses" are those who have broken their vows to Christ, who have flirted with the world and therefore have been untrue to their Husband.

This is shown by the rest of the verse: "Know ye not that the friendship of the world is enmity with God? whosoever therefore will be a friend of the world is the enemy of God." In the Old Testament it was idolatry that constituted spiritual adultery. Israel was often guilty of leaving her true husband and following false gods (cf. Hosea 2:2). But in the New Testament it is friendship with the world.

What is meant by worldliness? Too often it has been defined primarily in terms of the way one dresses. Others, more reasonably, have said that it is conformity to the pagan customs of secular society. But the matter goes deeper than either of these. Worldliness is an inner spirit of love for the world and its pleasures (cf. v. 3). It is a set of mind, an attitude of the heart. A person may be straight-laced in dress and conduct, and yet be very worldly because he is thinking as the man of the world thinks, not as Christ thinks. John puts it clearly in his First Epistle (2:15): "Love not the world, neither the things that are in the world. If any man love the world, the love of the Father is not in him." James is here using "the world" in the same sense that John does, and John derived it from Jesus, who said of His disciples: "They are not of the world, even as I am not of the world" (John 17:16). Being "of the world" means sharing the spirit of the world.

B. Opposed by the Spirit: v. 5

It must be stated first of all that the apparent quotation in this verse is not found in this exact form anywhere in the Old Testament. But the thought that God is a jealous lover of His own is clearly indicated (cf. Exodus 20:5-6). Mayor well says: "We have other instances of quotations in the New Testament which remind us rather of the general sense of several passages than of the actual words of any one particular passage in the Old Testament" (*James*, p. 140).

A more difficult problem is the meaning of the words cited here. The New International Version offers three possible interpretations. The text reads: "that the spirit he caused to live in us tends toward envy." The margin gives two alternatives: "that God jealously longs for the spirit that he made to live in us; *or* that the Spirit he caused to live in us longs jealously." Our own preference would be in exactly the reverse order!

Mayor discusses the problem at

great length. We would agree with him when he says that the view "which makes the human spirit the subject, seems to me entirely to destroy the meaning of the passage" (*James*, p. 114)—even though this is found in the King James Version and in the New International Version.

Rather than being the human spirit as sinfully jealous, we believe that it is the Holy Spirit as jealous for our good. Mayor would translate it: "The Spirit which he made to dwell in us jealously yearns for the entire devotion of the heart" (*James*, p. 141). He also suggests that this was the interpretation "most favoured by the early church" (p. 142). John Wesley explained it this way: "*The spirit of love that dwelleth in all* believers *lusteth against envy*—Gal v. 17; is directly opposite to all those unloving tempers which necessarily flow from the friendship of the world" (*Explanatory Notes upon the New Testament*, p. 866).

C. More Grace Available: v. 6

But—"he giveth more grace." This is the basis of the beautiful song by that title. No matter what happens to us, God's abundant grace is available to us at all times.

How is this related to the context? Ropes comments: "God makes rigorous requirements of devotion, but gives gracious help in order that men may be able to render the undivided allegiance which he exacts" (*James*, p. 265). He further observes: "The quotation from Prov. 3:34 illustrates and confirms the main position of the preceding passage, vv. 1-5, namely, that God will not yield to Pleasure a part of the allegiance of men's hearts, but that by his grace he enables men to render to him undivided allegiance" (*James*, p. 266).

The quotation from Proverbs is in the last part of this verse. This important Old Testament truth is cited also in I Peter 5:5. God's grace is given abundantly to those who are humble.

III. THE NEED OF SUBMISSION: James 4:7-10

A. Submission to God: v. 7

True humility is not striking a pious pose, or putting on an air of self-depreciation. Those can both be manifestations of a proud heart that is seeking compliments. Real humility is total submission to the will of God. We are willing to be nothing, that He may be everything.

But we are not to submit to the devil. Rather, we are to "resist" him—Greek, "stand up" against him. Ropes paraphrases this, in the light of the context, "Take a bold stand in resisting temptations to worldliness sent by 'the prince of this world' (Jn. 14:30), and you will be successful" (*James*, p. 268).

B. Drawing Near to God: v. 8

God took the iniative in drawing near to us at Bethlehem and preeminently at Calvary. Now it is our responsibility to reciprocate by drawing near to Him in responding love and in complete devotion. When we do, He comes close to us.

"Cleanse your hands, ye sinners; and purify your hearts, ye double-minded." The first and most obvious application of this twofold command is that the first part (the hands) refers to the outward life. New Testament Christianity demands clean living; it makes no place for a life that is immoral in any sense of the word.

But we must also have pure hearts. Jesus declared that it is the pure in heart who will see God (Matthew 5:8). This shows that the inner life as well as the outer life must be pure.

We have already had the term "double-minded" in this Epistle (1:8). We noted that it literally means "double-souled." It may well be taken to describe those who have a mind to serve Christ, but also a mind to serve self (cf. Romans 8:5-7).

So we have a twofold emphasis here. The "sinner" needs to have his sins washed away and live a clean life.

The "double-minded" Christians need to have their hearts purified from all love of the world.

C. Humility and Exaltation: vv. 9-10

"Grieve, mourn and wail. Change your laughter to mourning and your joy to gloom" (v. 9, NIV). This is addressed primarily to the sinner, but also the Christian who is not fully dedicated to Christ. The one needs to mourn over his *sins*; the other needs to mourn over the *sin* in his heart that seeks to lead him astray. We know that sin grieves the heart of a holy, loving God, and it should grieve our hearts as His children.

"Humble yourselves in the sight of the Lord, and he shall lift you up" (v. 10). The way up is down. If we exalt ourselves, God will humble us. But if we humble ourselves, He will lift us up.

When we humble ourselves, we are following Christ, our Leader. The best commentary on this verse is Philippians 2:5-8: "Let this mind be in you, which was also in Christ Jesus. . . ." We are then told how He humbled Himself to be the Servant of mankind and finally to die on the cross.

IV. THE SIN OF SLANDER: James 4:11-12

"Brothers, do not slander one another" (NIV)—literally, "Do not talk against each other, brothers." The one who talks against his brother or judges him is talking against the Law and judging it. It is not our business to judge the Law, but to obey it.

Then James declares: "There is only one Lawgiver and Judge, the one who is able to save and destroy. But you—who are you to judge your neighbor?" (v. 12, NIV). We can almost hear James exclaiming: "Who do you think you are—God?"

The facts of the case are that when we sit in judgment on others we are usurping God's place. He alone is Judge. All of us must stand before His judgment seat. We have no right to assume divine authority. To make oneself God is the worst sin that the human heart can commit. Yet some earnest Christians come perilously close to becoming guilty at this point.

V. THE SIN OF BOASTING: James 4:13-17

A. The Uncertainty of Life: vv. 13-14

The sin that is condemned in verse 13 is altogether too common a one, even among Christians. How easy it is to declare what we are going to do during the next year! "Today or tomorrow we will go to this or that city, spend a year there, carry on business and make money" (NIV).

James has a sharp answer: "Why, you do not even know what will happen tomorrow" (v. 14, NIV). We don't even know that we will be alive! What right, then, have we to assert categorically what we are going to do in the future?

Then James asks a very probing, penetrating question: "What is your life?" And he gives an incisive answer: It is "a mist" that "appears" for a short time and then "disappears"—this reflects the play on words of the verbs in the Greek. Life is as fleeting and fragile as a bit of mist that comes and then goes. In our day of so many sudden deaths we ought to be very conscious of this fact.

DISCUSSION QUESTIONS

1. How can we avoid quarreling?
2. What is worldliness?
3. How may we guard against it?
4. What does submission to God involve?
5. Why is boasting a senseless sin?
6. What are some of the perils of being rich?

B. Bowing to God's Will: vv. 15-16

Instead of talking like the man in verse 13, we should say, "If the Lord will, we shall live, and do this or that" (v. 15). This is the basis of our use of "D.V."—Latin, *Deus Vole*, "God willing." Like all other religious practices, this can become a meaningless formality. But the spirit of it should always dominate our thinking. All our planning should be in the frame of reference of "D.V."

The next verse is sad to contemplate: "As it is, you boast and brag. All such boasting is evil" (NIV). It is evident that not all the early Christians were walking humbly with their God!

C. Sins of Omission: v. 17

This verse is one that should disturb our consciences. It is almost frightening! If we fail to do the good we know we should do, we sin. It makes us feel like crying out, "Lord, have mercy on me!" But it should make us seek ways to serve others.

VI. THE SIN OF SELFISH WEALTH: James 5:1-6

A. Hoarding Wealth: vv. 1-3

This is a vivid description of the rich man who is resting in a false sense of self-congratulation and security. James declares that all his possessions are soon to perish. There is nothing more pathetically stupid than for a man to spend a whole lifetime hoarding a fortune for his last days, and then be so sick he can't enjoy it—and finally to die and leave it all. Yet this is what happens over and over again.

B. Failing to Pay Wages: v. 4

This was evidently altogether too common a sin in the Old Testament times (cf. Leviticus 19:13), and it carried over into the Jewish-Christian church. James declares that these unpaid wages "cry out" against those who are guilty, and the Lord hears these cries.

C. Living in Luxury: vv. 5-6

The greatest of all sins is selfishness. This is the thing for which James condemns the wealthy. They too often live in luxury with no concern for the poor. There are exceptions!

CONTEMPORARY APPLICATION

The sins for which James scored the professing Christians of the first century are all too common today. Quarreling among church members is a tragic disgrace to the name of Christ, who is the Prince of Peace. Worldliness, too, is still prevalent in the church. Church members talking against each other—how often does that happen? And how about boasting?

What we need to do is to examine our own hearts individually to make sure that we are not guilty of these sins. The Epistle of James is still pertinent today.

May 29, 1977

AN ENDURING FAITH

DEVOTIONAL READING	Psalm 57

ADULTS

Topic: *An Enduring Faith*

Background Scripture: James 5:7-20

Scripture Lesson: James 5:7-11, 13-20

Memory Verse: *We call those happy who were steadfast.* James 5:11

YOUTH

Topic: *Faith That Lasts*

Background Scripture: James 5:7-20

Scripture Lesson: James 5:7-11, 13-20

Memory Verse: *We call those happy who were steadfast.* James 5:11

CHILDREN

Topic: *Being Patient*

Background Scripture: James 5:7-20

Scripture Lesson: James 5:7-11

Memory Verse: *You also be patient.* James 5:8

DAILY BIBLE READINGS

Mon., May 23: Faith and Patience, James 5:7-11.
Tues., May 24: Fathers of Faith, Hebrews 11:13-22.
Wed., May 25: Wonder-working Faith, James 5:13-15; Hebrews 11:11-12.
Thurs., May 26: The Community of Faith, James 5:16-20.
Fri., May 27: Sheltered by His Shadow, Psalm 91:1-11.
Sat., May 28: Help from Heaven, Psalm 57:1-6.
Sun., May 29: When Faith Is Rewarded, Psalm 57:7-11.

LESSON AIM

To help us have a faith that will endure to the end, so that we may be saved.

LESSON SETTING

Time: About A.D. 60 (or 45)

Place: Probably Jerusalem

LESSON OUTLINE

An Enduring Faith

I. Patience in Suffering: James 5:7-11
   A. The Example of the Farmer: v. 7
   B. Patient Waiting for the Parousia: v. 8
   C. No Grumbling: v. 9

296

D. The Example of the Prophets: v. 10
E. The Example of Job: v. 11

II. **Telling the Simple Truth:** James 5:12

III. **Prayer for the Sick:** James 5:13-16
A. Prayer and Praise: v. 13
B. Prayer and Anointing with Oil: v. 14
C. The Prayer of Faith: v. 15
D. The Effectual Prayer: v. 16

IV. **The Example of Elijah:** James 5:17-18

V. **Converting the Sinner:** James 5:19-20

SUGGESTED INTRODUCTION FOR ADULTS

We have noted that James is everlastingly practical. That shows up markedly in this closing part of his Epistle. He deals with several practical problems in the Christian life.

Suffering is a universal experience of mankind. Every person suffers some time in some way. And this suffering can be destructive and devastating, or it can be constructive and healing. It all depends on our attitude toward it.

Suffering requires patience. But when it is faced properly it *produces* patience. The person who suffers is richer and stronger for having suffered, provided he uses his suffering as a stepping stone to higher heights of faith and perseverance. Prayer is the secret. Here James shows us how to pray in faith. That kind of prayer is effectual.

SUGGESTED INTRODUCTION FOR YOUTH

The things that man makes don't last very long. Cars, clothes, furnishings, appliances—they all wear out.

But we can have one thing that does last, and that is our faith. Instead of weakening and wearing out, it can grow stronger and firmer as the years and decades roll by.

Faith brings patience in suffering. We all have to suffer in one way or another—physically, socially, psychologically. But our faith will grow if we keep close to Christ and lean our whole weight on Him. For that is what faith means. He will never let us down. Faith in Him can hold us firm throughout life.

CONCEPTS FOR CHILDREN

1. Farmers have to be patient in waiting for their crops to grow.
2. So we should be patient in letting the fruit of good character grow in our lives.
3. We also need to be patient with each other.
4. Prayer will help us to be patient.

THE LESSON COMMENTARY

I. PATIENCE IN SUFFERING: James 5:7-11

A. The Example of the Farmer: v. 7

We have all heard of children who have planted seeds in a garden and then want to dig them up to see if they are growing. The farmer knows better. Every year he plants crops and then waits for weeks to see much evidence of it. Added to that will be months of waiting until harvest. "See how the farmer waits for the land to yield its valuable crop and how patient he is for the fall and spring rains" (NIV).

We need to have similar patience. This can be applied to two spheres. One is in our sowing the seed of God's Word. We may have to wait patiently for a long time before it produces the crop of conversion in the hearts of those to whom we witness. So we must keep on praying and not push things too fast—give time for the Spirit to work.

The other sphere is the growing of the fruit of the Spirit (Galatians 5:22-23) in our lives. It takes time for fruit to grow. We don't plant an apple or peach tree and then go out the next day to look for fruit on it. We know that it will take at least a year or two before any fruit appears. So we should wait patiently for the fruit of the Spirit to grow in our lives and in the lives of those for whom we are concerned.

Regarding the "early and the latter rain" (KJV), J. H. Ropes says: "The 'early rain' normally begins in Palestine in late October or early November, and is anxiously awaited because, being necessary for the germination of the seed, it is the signal for sowing. In the spring the maturing of the grain depends on the 'late rain,' light showers falling in April and May. Without these, even heavy winter rains will not prevent failure of the crops" (*A Critical and Exegetical Commen-*

tary on the Epistle of St. James, International Critical Commentary, p. 295).

B. Patient Waiting for the Parousia: v. 8

In the first part of verse 7 we read: "Be patient therefore, brethren, unto the coming of the Lord." Verse 8 reads: "Be ye also patient; stablish your hearts: for the coming of the Lord draweth nigh."

The word for "coming" is *parousia*, which occurs twenty-four times in the New Testament. Twenty-two times it is translated "coming." Twice (II Corinthians 10:10; Philippians 2:12) it is rendered "presence," which is the primary meaning of the word—literally "being beside." It is used once for the coming of human beings, in I Corinthians 16:17. Elsewhere in the New Testament (twenty-one times) it refers to the return of Christ. It is the most usual term in the New Testament for the Second Coming.

The secular use of *parousia* is interesting. Adolf Deissmann writes: "From the Ptolemaic period down into the 2nd. century A.D. we are able to trace the word in the East as a technical expression for the arrival or the visit of the king or the emperor" (*Light from the Ancient East*, p. 368). It is understandable, then, why the Second Coming is commonly called in English "The Parousia."

How are we to wait for the return of our Lord? James says that we are to be patient and "stand firm" (NIV). We need to wait patiently because He has tarried so long and we do not know when He will actually come. But James assures us that His coming is near.

This thought is elaborated in II Peter 3:4, 8-10. Because so many centuries have gone by since the angels at His ascension said that He would come back (Acts 1:11), people say that He never will. But Peter reminds us that "one day is with the Lord as a thousand years, and a thousand years as one day" (II Peter 3:8). On God's calendar only two days have gone by. So we can be patient.

C. No Grumbling: v. 9

Once more James makes a very practical application: "Don't grumble against each other, brothers, or you will be judged. The Judge is standing at the door!" (NIV). Christ is coming soon. The word translated here "grumble" literally means "groan." J. B. Mayor comments: "The word denotes feeling which is internal and unexpressed" (*The Epistle of St. James*, p. 162).

Ropes points out the fact that "grudge" (KJV) at that time meant "complain." The sentence then means, "Do not blame one another for the distress of the present soon-to-be-ended age." He continues: "We ought to cultivate patience in general, and we ought not to blame one another for our unmerited distress, for we should recognize that it is part of the inevitable and temporary evil of the present age" (*James*, p. 297). If we blame others, the Judge will blame us!

D. The Example of the Prophets: v. 10

For the third time (cf. vv. 7, 9) James addresses his readers as "brothers." He does it again in verse 12. It is clear that he is writing to professing Christians.

He points to the prophets as examples of patience in the face of suffering. To what prophets was he referring? Mayor says, "Noah, Abraham, Jacob, Moses, Isaiah, Jeremiah are preeminent patterns of endurance" (*James*, p. 163).

The Epistle to the Hebrews says that some of "the prophets" (11:32) "had trial of cruel mockings and scourgings, yea, moreover of bonds and imprisonment; they were stoned, they were sawn asunder, were tempted, were slain with the sword: they

wandered about in sheepskins and goatskins, being destitute, afflicted, tormented" (11:36-37). Tradition says that Isaiah was sawed in two, while still alive. It was not easy to be a true prophet of God.

E. The Example of Job: v. 11

"As you know, we consider blessed those who have persevered. You have heard of Job's perseverance and have seen what the Lord finally brought about. The Lord is full of compassion and mercy" (NIV).

This translation brings out the fact that the verb "persevered" and the noun "perseverance" are from the same root in Greek. We have become accustomed to thinking of "the patience of Job" (KJV). The Greek word, however, does not denote the passive virtue of patience but the positive virtue of perseverance.

Actually, Job was not patient. He speaks impatiently again and again in the Book of Job. He became so tried with his three friends—false "comforters"—that he said to them, "No doubt but ye are the people, and wisdom shall die with you" (12:2). Again he cried out, "Miserable comforters are ye all" (16:2). But the important thing is that he persevered to the end in his trust in God.

"...have seen the end of the Lord" (KJV) is a literal translation of the Greek, but seems rather meaningless in English. Some have referred it to the death, resurrection, and ascension of Jesus—the end of His life on earth. But that does not seem to fit into the context. "Seen" probably implies "in the story of Job." Ropes suggests that "the end of the Lord" means "the conclusion wrought by the Lord to his troubles" (*James*, p. 299). This would refer to the double reward that God gave Job when his excruciating trials were ended in triumphant faith.

"Pitiful" (KJV) hardly connotes today the sense of the Greek word here. It is a strong compound, meaning at least "very kind" and at most "full of compassion" (NIV). We now use "pitiful" in a derogatory sense, as when we say, "This is a pitiful mess."

"Of tender mercy" (KJV) brings out well the force of the last (single) word in this verse. God is full of mercy, or we all would be lost.

II. TELLING THE SIMPLE TRUTH: James 5:12

This verse seems like a strange intrusion between the discussion of patience (vv. 7-11) and of prayer (vv. 13-18). So it is omitted in the printed lesson. But James must have felt the need for inserting this warning at this point.

The verse is a very clear reflection of Jesus' teaching in the Sermon on the Mount, where it is developed more fully (Matthew 5:34-37). In both places we are told that we should not have to swear that we are telling the truth; we should simply state the truth without oath. "Let your 'Yes' be yes, and your 'No,' no" (NIV) is almost exactly the same as "Simply let your 'Yes' be 'Yes,' and your 'No,' 'No' " (Matthew 5:37, NIV). "Anything beyond this comes from the evil one" becomes in James "or you will be condemned" (NIV).

Swearing in court actually implies a double standard of morals—when you are not under oath you don't have to tell the truth! Jesus and James are both opposed to this falsity.

III. PRAYER FOR THE SICK: James 5:13-16

A. Prayer and Praise: v. 13

"Is any of you in trouble? He should pray. Is anyone happy? Let him sing songs of praise" (NIV). Our lives should be a mixture of prayer and praise.

What do we do when we find ourselves "suffering evil" (literal Greek)? Do we find fault, complain, get discouraged? Or do we pray? The other things will do nothing to help either our spirits or the unpleasant

circumstances. Prayer can help in both ways. It has the subjective value of making us feel better and also the objective value of changing things around us, when that is in God's will.

Actually, praise helps prayer. Sometimes the clouds are so dark that it seems we can't pray our way through. There is nothing that will dispel the dark clouds of doubt or depression any faster than praising the Lord for what He has already done.

B. Prayer and Anointing with Oil: v. 14

Verses 14-16 constitute the greatest and most specific passage in the New Testament on praying for the physical healing of believers.

The instructions given in this verse are plain and simple. The sick person is to call for "the elders of the church." This expression might have different applications in different denominations. It probably does not mean just the older men of the church in general, but rather appointed officials. Some churches have both teaching elders and ruling elders in each congregation. In other denominations the term *elder* means an ordained minister. Whatever the connotation, these elders should be called to pray over the sick person.

They are to "anoint him with oil in the name of the Lord" (NIV). Oil is a type of the Holy Spirit. The anointing is to indicate to the sick one that his healing will be the work of the Spirit on his body (cf. Romans 8:11).

C. The Prayer of Faith: v. 15

"And the prayer of faith shall save the sick." The Greek verb translated "save" here is *sozo*. In the Gospels and the first part of Acts it is used mostly for physical healing. In the latter part of Acts and in the Epistles it usually denotes spiritual salvation. But here we find a reflection of the earlier usage.

It is the Lord who raises the sick person. He can also forgive the sins of the sick one—which in some cases may have led to the illness.

An important question poses itself in this verse: Is it the Lord's will to heal all His children who are sick? This is a rather touchy issue, but we feel that it needs to be faced realistically.

Many people today give a positive answer to this question. We remember many years ago hearing this startling statement made in the pulpit: "If you are where you ought to be spiritually, you will be well physically." This is surely a cruel blow to godly people in the congregation who may be suffering in body.

In more recent times we have heard it said: "You have no right to pray for healing 'if it is God's will'; it is His will to heal everyone!" We should simply like to register our conviction that it is never wrong to pray, "if it is Your will."

Those who talk this way seem to have forgotten such sainted blind hymn-writers as Fanny Crosby and George Matheson. And how about the semi-invalid condition of Frances Ridley Havergal, who out of her physical sufferings and weakness wrote hymns that have blessed millions of Christians?

But perhaps the most striking answer is found right in the New Testament. The great apostle Paul suffered from "a thorn in the flesh"—clearly a physical affliction (II Corinthians 12:7). Three times he begged the Lord to remove it. But the answer was: "My grace is sufficient for thee: for my strength is made perfect in weakness." What was Paul's reaction? "Most gladly therefore will I rather glory in my infirmities, that the power of Christ may rest upon me" (v. 9).

What, then, did James mean when he said, "And the prayer of faith shall save the sick"? It is our conviction that we can pray in faith only when the Holy Spirit enables us to believe a certain thing. When it is His will to heal, He will give us "the prayer of faith," and healing will result. This is what we can affirm from our own experience.

D. The Effectual Prayer: v. 16

This verse states an important condition that is usually bypassed in times of prayer for healing. James writes: "Confess your faults [the Greek says "sins" (*hamartias*)] one to another, and pray one for another, that ye may be healed." May it be that some people are not healed simply because this divine directive is not carried out? We have had the experience of pleading with people to meet this requirement before we prayed for someone's healing, only to be met with silence.

"The prayer of a righteous man is powerful and effective" (NIV). (There is no "fervent" in the Greek.) Let us pray in faith.

IV. THE EXAMPLE OF ELIJAH: James 5:17-18

"Elijah was a man just like us. He prayed earnestly that it would not rain, and it did not rain on the land for three and a half years. Again he prayed, and the heavens gave rain, and the earth produced its crops" (NIV).

"Elias" (KJV) is the Greek form of "Elijah." When we find Old Testament names in the New Testament, we should always give them the familiar Hebrew form, as is done in most modern versions. This is especially important in the public reading of the Scriptures, so that the listeners will get the connection.

Elijah was just like us. That ought to encourage us. If he had enough

---

DISCUSSION QUESTIONS

1. Why do we need patience?
2. What are some of the benefits of patience?
3. What is the relation of patience and perseverance?
4. Why does God heal the sick?
5. What is our part in this?
6. How does confession of sin help?

302   AN ENDURING FAITH

faith to stop the rain for three and a half years as a judgment for Ahab's wickedness (I Kings 17:1), should we not be able to exercise faith for the miracle of healing, when it is in God's will? The Old Testament narrative indicates that Elijah was following divine instructions; so he was able to pray the prayer of faith.

V. CONVERTING THE SINNER:
James 5:19-20

This is the fifth time that we have found "brothers" in this lesson. James is addressing his fellow Christians.

If a believer wanders from the truth, the one who brings him back from his wandering will save a soul from death. It is just as important to restore the backslider as to get a sinner saved. Too often while we are bringing new converts in through the front door we are at the same time losing others out the back door. That back door needs to be locked!

What does it mean when it says that the one who brings back the wanderer will "hide a multitude of sins"? A. F. Harper calls attention to the parallel in I Peter 4:8 and notes that both passages are derived from Proverbs 10:12. He writes: "The applications in these two other places give the clue to the meaning here. In Proverbs the sins covered are social consequences.... Peter urges charity (love) because love covers, or prevents, sins of anger and retaliation in the other person. So here we understand that it is the sins of the erring man and the social evils resulting from his sins that are covered" (*Beacon Bible Commentary*, X, 249).

CONTEMPORARY APPLICATION

Prayer and praise are the normal breath of the spiritual person. If we did more praying we would do less criticizing. If we did more praising we would do less complaining.

With most of us it is true that we do too much talking to others and too little talking to God. We air our problems to others—sometimes to our own embarrassment and to the embarrassment of the church. If we would go to God with our troubles and find our solutions from Him, it would save much trouble.

FROM SLAVERY TO NATIONHOOD

AN ENSLAVED PEOPLE

DEVOTIONAL READING	Psalm 102:12-22

ADULTS

Topic: *An Enslaved People*

Background Scripture: Exodus 1—2

Scripture Lesson: Exodus 1:7-14; 2:11-15a

Memory Verse: *Out of the depths I cry to thee, O Lord! Lord, hear my voice! Let thy ears be attentive to the voice of my supplications!* Psalm 130:1

YOUTH

Topic: *Oppression Endured*

Background Scripture: Exodus 1—2

Scripture Lesson: Exodus 1:7-14; 2:11-15

Memory Verse: *Out of the depths I cry to thee, O Lord! Lord, hear my voice! Let thy ears be attentive to the voice of my supplications!* Psalm 130:1

CHILDREN

Topic: *In Slavery*

Background Scripture: Exodus 1—2

Scripture Lesson: Exodus 1:7-14; 2:11-15

Memory Verse: *And the people of Israel groaned under their bondage and cried out for help, and their cry under bondage came up to God.* Exodus 2:23b

DAILY BIBLE READINGS

Mon., May 30: A Deliverer Is Born, Exodus 2:1-10.
Tues., May 31: Dependence on God for Deliverance, Psalm 44:1-8.
Wed., June 1: Set Free from Our Enemies, Psalm 69:13-18.
Thurs., June 2: Prisoners Set Free, Psalm 102:18-22.
Fri., June 3: Freedom from Distress, Psalm 118:1-6.
Sat., June 4: God Hears and Remembers, Exodus 2:16-25.
Sun., June 5: Made Free Through Christ, John 8:31-36.

LESSON AIM

To help us see the need of people who are oppressed in various ways.

LESSON SETTING

Time: Around 1500 B.C. (Some scholars prefer a later time.)

Place: Egypt and Midian

An Enslaved People

I.   The Israelites in Egypt: Exodus 1:1-7
     A. The First Two Generations: vv. 1-6
     B. The Rapid Growth: v. 7

II. The Oppressing Pharaoh: Exodus 1:8-10
     A. A New Dynasty: v. 8
     B. Israelite Threat: vv. 9-10

III. The Oppressed People: Exodus 1:11-14
     A. Harsh Slavery: v. 11
     B. Continued Growth: v. 12
     C. Hard Labor: vv. 13-14

LESSON OUTLINE

IV. Pharaoh's Plot Against Israel: Exodus 1:15-22

V.   A Coming Deliverer: Exodus 2:1-10
     A. The Birth of Moses: vv. 1-4
     B. The Childhood of Moses: vv. 5-9
     C. In Pharaoh's Palace: v. 10

VI. The Attempted Deliverance: Exodus 2:11-15a
     A. Killing an Egyptian Oppressor: vv. 11-12
     B. Acting as Arbitrator: v. 13
     C. Repulsed and Threatened: v. 14
     D. The Threat of Pharaoh: v. 15a

VII. Moses in the Land of Midian: Exodus 2:15b-22

VIII. God's Compassion on Oppressed Israel: Exodus
      2:23-25

We have just finished a five-session study of the Epistle of James, which was probably all written at one time. Now we come to something quite different. The lessons of this quarter span a period of many centuries, roughly from about 1600-1000 B.C. They trace the history of the Israelites from slavery to nationhood. Mostly they deal with the time from the call of Moses, the deliverer and first leader of Israel, to Saul, the nation's first king.

SUGGESTED INTRODUCTION FOR ADULTS

The quarter's lessons are divided into three units. The first unit is called "A People in Need of Deliverance." Four sessions are devoted to the slavery in Egypt, the call of Moses, the Exodus, and the celebration of freedom. The second unit (five sessions), entitled "God Creates a Covenant People," deals first with what happened at Sinai—the giving of the Law and the building of the tabernacle—and the conquest of Canaan and the failure of the Israelites to keep God's covenant. The third unit, consisting of four sessions, views the logical consequence: "The Struggle to Survive." It takes us from the time of Joshua's closing message to Israel, through the period of the judges, to the anointing of Saul as the first king of Israel. This study of the beginnings of Israelite history is full of lessons for us today.

SUGGESTED INTRODUCTION FOR YOUTH

"Oppression Endured"—that has been the experience of large numbers of people for at least the last four thousand years. In today's lesson we study about an enslaved people in Egypt. Oppressed by harsh bondage, they cried out for deliverance.

This was about fifteen hundred years before Christ. The tragic truth is that far more than fifteen hundred years after Christ slavery was still practiced.

Let's face it: Slavery is inhuman! All human beings are made in the image of God, with the right—within certain divinely ordained limits—to freedom of choice. Slavery is dehumanizing; it destroys human personality. We must treat all human beings as real persons.

CONCEPTS FOR CHILDREN

1. Submission to parents is not slavery!
2. Children dislike restrictions, yet feel the need for dependency on their parents.
3. We need a proper balance of submission and freedom.
4. We should not try to dominate others.

THE LESSON COMMENTARY

I. THE ISRAELITES IN EGYPT: Exodus 1:1-7

A. The First Two Generations: vv. 1-6

The Book of Exodus begins by recapitulating the move of Jacob and his sons from Canaan to Egypt. We are told that his sons and their families totaled seventy in number (v. 5). The same figure is given in Genesis 46:27 and Deuteronomy 10:22. But Stephen, speaking before the Jewish Sanhedrin, said that there were seventy-five (Acts 7:14). How can we harmonize these?

The answer is simple. The seventy people were the eleven sons of Jacob and their families. Jacob himself made seventy-one. When we add Joseph, his wife, and his two children, we get seventy-five. This was the total number of the first group of Israelites in Egypt.

Finally "Joseph died, and all his brethren, and all that generation" (v. 6). This statement probably includes the children of Joseph and his brothers.

B. The Rapid Growth: v. 7

The Israelites had large families and so multiplied rapidly. They became a strong people, until it seemed that "the land was filled with them." This created a problem for the Egyptians.

II. THE OPPRESSING PHARAOH: Exodus 1:8-10

A. A New Dynasty: v. 8

"Now there arose up a new king over Egypt, which knew not Joseph." From the records of the history of that time we know that this was not only a new king, but a new dynasty.

Thoughtful people have sometimes wondered how Joseph, a foreigner released from prison, could have become the prime minister of Egypt, second only to the reigning Pharoah in power (Genesis 41:39-44). He belonged to a far different race than the Egyptians. He was from Asia, and they were in Africa. (The term *Pharoah* is not a proper name for a single individual. Rather, it was a title for the ancient Egyptian rulers, similar to *Caesar* or *Czar* in later times.)

Now we know the answer. When Joseph was taken to Egypt that country was ruled by a foreign dynasty, the Asiatic Hyksos kings. They were in control of that country from about 1730 to 1570 B.C. These kings were of Semitic origin, as Joseph was. So they treated Jacob and his family with great respect, giving them the best land in Egypt, in the fertile Nile Delta (Genesis 47:6). The Hyksos are sometimes called "the shepherd kings." So they welcomed the sons of Jacob with their flocks and herds.

But about 1570 the Egyptians expelled the foreign Hyksos rulers and installed a native Egyptian dynasty again. This was probably the "new king which knew not Joseph." The new dynasty would naturally turn against the favorites of the previous dynasty, just as today a new party in power throws out of office the members of the previous party—the spoils of victory. This has happened from time immemorial!

B. Israelite Threat: vv. 9-10

The new Pharaoh was concerned about the rapid growth of the Israelites in numbers and influence. It probably was an exaggeration, but he declared: "Behold, the people of the children of Israel are more and mightier than we" (v. 9). George Rawlinson says: "Ancient Egypt must have had a population of seven or eight millions, which would imply nearly two millions of adult males, whereas the adult male Israelites, near a century later, were no more than six hundred thousand (chap. xii. 37). Wicked men do not scruple at misrepresentation when

they have an end to gain" ("Exodus," *Ellicott's Commentary on the Whole Bible*, I, 193).

In any case, something had to be done about the situation. So Pharaoh proposed: "Come on, let us deal wisely with them" (v. 10). Craftily the king suggested a plan of action.

The Pharaohs were always afraid of invasion from the north (the continent we now call Asia). The Israelites were living in the land of Goshen, in the eastern section of the Delta. Pharaoh was fearful that they might join an attacking army and make a strike for freedom, leaving Egypt. Rawlinson comments: "The Pharaohs of the nineteenth dynasty were excessively jealous of the withdrawal from Egypt of any of their subjects, and endeavoured both to hinder and to recover them. Immigration was encouraged, emigration sternly checked. The loss of the entire nation of the Hebrews could not be contemplated without extreme alarm" ("Exodus," *Ellicott's*, p. 193). (In all honesty we should state that Rawlinson prefers a later date for the oppression and Exodus. But his comment is relevant for the earlier time.)

III. THE OPPRESSED PEOPLE: Exodus 1:11-14

A. Harsh Slavery: v. 11

How did the Egyptians cope with the situation? They set over the Israelites "taskmasters" to afflict them with their burdens (v. 11). The Hebrew means "chiefs of tributes." Rawlinson says that the Egyptian term for this occurs "on the monument representing brick-making, which has been supposed by some to be a picture of the Hebrews at work. . . . Among the tasks set the labourers in the representation above alluded to are the carrying of huge lumps of clay and of water-jars on one shoulder, and also the conveyance of bricks from place to place by means of a yoke" ("Exodus," *The Pulpit Commentary*, I, 10-11).

On the expression "to afflict them" Rawlinson writes: "This was the object of the whole proceeding. It was hoped that severe labour under the lash would produce so much suffering that the number of the Israelites would be thinned, and their multiplication stopped. Humanly speaking, the scheme was a 'wise' one—i.e., one likely to be successful" ("Exodus," *Ellicott's*, p. 193).

B. Continued Growth: v. 12

"But the more they afflicted them, the more they multiplied and grew." This not only was true in the case of the ancient Israelites; it has also been true many times in the history of the church. Christians thrive on persecution; it just deepens their devotion. It is actually a fact that the church grows more both numerically and spiritually in times of persecution than it does in times of plenty. The greatest threat to the church is not affliction but affluence. As in the case of Job, the devil often defeats his own purposes when he makes it hard for God's people.

The Egyptians were "grieved" because of the Israelites. Rawlinson comments: "The word *grieved* very insufficiently renders the Hebrew verb, which 'expresses a mixture of loathing and alarm' " ("Exodus," *Pulpit*, p. 11). They were afraid of the Israelites and so they hated and despised them. They were angry because these slaves continued to prosper.

C. Hard Labor: vv. 13-14

"And the Egyptians made the children of Israel to serve with rigour." Rawlinson says: "The word translated *rigour* is a very rare one. It is derived from a root which means 'to break in pieces, to crush.' The 'rigour' would be shown especially in the free use of the stick by the taskmaster, and in the prolongation of the hours of work" ("Exodus," *Pulpit*, p. 11).

Elaborating elsewhere on this a bit, he writes: "Forced labour in Egypt was of a very severe character. Those condemned to it worked from morning to night under the rod of a taskmaster, which was freely applied to their legs or backs, if they rested their weary limbs for a moment. . . . The heat of the sun was great; the burthens which the labourers had to carry were heavy, and the toil was incessant. Death often resulted from the excessive work. According to Herodotus a single monarch, Neco, destroyed in this way 120,000 of his subjects" ("Exodus," *Ellicott's*, p. 193). Facing the very impressive ruins of the four great temples at Baalbec (between Beirut and Damascus) the traveler today is told that two hundred thousand workmen were employed to build them in Roman times and that one hundred thousand perished in the process.

"And they made their lives bitter with hard bondage, in morter, and in brick" (v. 14). Rawlinson comments: "While stone was the material chiefly employed by the Egyptians for their grand edifices, temples, palaces, treasuries, and the like, brick was also made use of to a large extent for inferior buildings, for tombs, dwelling-houses, walls of towns, forts, enclosures of temples, etc." As regards "all manner of service in the field," he writes: "There is no country where care and labour are so constantly needed during the whole of the year. . . . Success depends upon a system of irrigation that requires constant labour and unremitting attention." He adds: "If the 'labour in the field' included, as Josephus supposed . . . , the cutting of canals, their lives would indeed have been 'made bitter.' There is no such exhausting toil as that of working under the hot Egyptian sun, with the feet in water, in an open cutting, where there can be no shade, and scarcely a breath of air, from sunrise to sunset, as forced labourers are generally required to do" ("Exodus," *Pulpit*, p. 11). No wonder there have been violent revolutions under such conditions!

IV. PHARAOH'S PLOT AGAINST ISRAEL:
Exodus 1:15-22

When he saw that harsh slavery didn't decimate the Israelites, Pharaoh hit on another scheme. He told the two Hebrew midwives to kill all the baby boys born to the Israelitish women. This would be a very simple matter, such as suffocating the new-born child.

"But the midwives feared God" (v. 17). So they saved the male babies, defying the king's command. They feared God more than they feared Pharaoh. God's people have always survived and prospered on that principle.

When the king reprimanded them—evidently he had his secret police observing—the midwives answered that the Hebrew women were more "lively" than the Egyptian mothers and gave birth before the arrival of the midwife. Scholars agree that this may very likely have been true to a great extent.

Because they feared Him, God blessed the midwives and "made them houses"—that is, gave them children of their own, who grew up to comfort and sustain them. This was a fitting reward for those who refused to bring suffering to mothers of other children.

Finally Pharaoh got desperate. He ordered all male Hebrew babies thrown into the river. Obviously this order was not carried out either.

V. A COMING DELIVERER:
Exodus 2:1-10

A. The Birth of Moses: vv. 1-4

Moses' father and mother were both of the tribe of Levi (v. 1), from which the priests were later drawn. A child was born to them, and the mother observed that he was a "goodly child." So she hid him for three months (v. 2).

When she saw that it was no longer possible to escape detection, she tried a desperate expedient. She put the baby in "an ark of bulrushes"—literally, "a chest of papyrus"—which she daubed with "slime" (bitumen) and "pitch" (a vegetable substance), and laid in the "flags" along the river's bank, to keep it from floating away. Moses' older sister stood guard (v. 4).

B. The Childhood of Moses: vv. 5-9

When Pharaoh's daughter came down to wash herself in the sacred Nile, she spotted the object in the river and sent her maid to bring it. Providentially, as soon as the chest was opened the baby cried. This touched the heart of Pharaoh's daughter, who also observed, "This is one of the Hebrews' children" (v. 6).

Quickly Moses' sister asked if she might get a Hebrew woman to nurse the baby (v. 7). When Pharaoh's daughter said, "Go," the girl lost no time in bringing Moses' mother! So the child was given a godly training by his own mother, though how long he lived with his parents we do not know.

C. In Pharaoh's Palace: v. 10

Moses was adopted by Pharaoh's daughter and brought up in the palace as "her son." He may well have been an heir to the throne of Egypt, so that he was given a careful education and perhaps a thorough training in how to rule. All this would stand him in good stead when he was called by God to be the first leader of His people.

The best commentary on this verse is found in Stephen's speech in Acts: "And Moses was learned in all the wisdom of the Egyptians, and was mighty in words and in deeds" (Acts 7:22). Egypt was the great center of wisdom literature, especially at a somewhat later date, and "all the wisdom of the Egyptians" would be comprehensive. There was perhaps no other place on earth where Moses could have received better "book knowledge" than in Pharaoh's palace. This was a wonderful preparation for his writing the first five books of the Bible!

But he was also mighty in "deeds." This would have included military training and whatever was known then about logistics. This fitted him as leader of the Israelites for forty years in the wilderness.

VI. THE ATTEMPTED DELIVER-ANCE:
Exodus 2:11-15a

A. Killing an Egyptian Oppressor: vv. 11-12

We learn from Acts 7:23 that Moses was not only "grown" (v. 11) but forty years old when this incident took place. Deciding to visit his brother Israelites, he was shocked to see "an Egyptian smiting an Hebrew, one of his brethren." He looked around and saw no one in sight. So "he slew the Egyptian, and hid him in the sand" (v. 12).

Once more Stephen interprets the passage for us. He puts it this way: "And seeing one of them suffer wrong, he defended him, and avenged him that was oppressed, and smote the Egyptian; for he supposed his brethren would have understood how that God by his hand would deliver them: but they understood not" (Acts 7:24-25).

To get a full understanding of what was involved, we need to turn to the Epistle to the Hebrews. There we read: "By faith Moses, when he was come to years, refused to be called the son of Pharaoh's daughter; choosing rather to suffer affliction with the people of God, than to enjoy the pleasures of sin for a season" (11:24-25). At forty years of age Moses made the decision to identify himself with his own oppressed people.

B. Acting as Arbitrator: v. 13

The next day Moses went out to visit his fellow Israelites again. This time he found two of them quarreling. To the one "that did the wrong" (so the Septuagint; the Hebrew has "the

wicked one") Moses said, "Wherefore smitest thou thy fellow?" (literally, "thy neighbor"). Stephen says that he tried to unify them again, saying, "Sirs, ye are brethren; why do ye wrong one another?" (Acts 7:26). Moses was simply trying to intervene helpfully in an argument that had come to blows.

C. Repulsed and Threatened: v. 14

Typically, the man who was in the wrong snarled at Moses, "Who made thee a prince and a judge over us? intendest thou to kill me, as thou killedst the Egyptian?" Horrified, Moses realized that his impetuous act of the day before had been seen after all.

D. The Threat of Pharaoh: vv. 15a

How Pharaoh learned of this we do not know. But "murder will out!" Understandably the king was determined to kill Moses. This becomes more logical if we assume the fact, implied in Hebrews 11:24-25 that Moses had already made his decision and had left Pharaoh's palace. Now he had taken his people's side and killed an Egyptian. Clearly he was an outlaw!

VII. MOSES IN THE LAND OF MIDIAN:
Exodus 2:15b-22

"But Moses fled from the face of Pharaoh, and dwelt in the land of Midian" (v. 15b). Again we need to get the inspired comment of the writer of Hebrews: "By faith he forsook Egypt, not fearing the wrath of the king" (11:27). This is the other side of the picture. He was motivated most by the desire to escape death so that he could yet deliver his people. So he went into hiding. We have already noted Stephen's comment: "For he supposed his brethren would have understood how that God by his hand would deliver them: but they understood not" (Acts 7:25).

The mistake that Moses made was

in attempting the deliverance in his own way. What he needed to do was to wait on the Lord until he had discovered God's way. His long years in exile gave him this opportunity better than life in the palace.

We do not know exactly where "the land of Midian" was. The Midianites were a nomadic people, roaming widely over the area between Egypt and Palestine. But it seems clear that the expression here refers to a part of the peninsula of Sinai.

This was a desert region, where wells were scarce; so Moses "sat down by a well" (v. 15). He was hot and thirsty from his walk across the searing sands. But he had no way of drawing water from the well.

Just then the seven daughters of the priest of Midian came and drew water for their father's flock (v. 16). But shepherds drove them away, seeking to take the water for their own flocks. It was a man's world, and a rough one for women! But chivalrous Moses interfered, helping the girls to water their flock (v. 17).

When they returned home their father asked them, "How is it that ye are come so soon to day?" (v. 18). This shows that the shepherds were in the daily habit of hindering the girls. Moses was probably dressed in fine Egyptian clothes (of royalty?), and so they were afraid of him.

When his daughters replied that an Egyptian man had helped them (v. 19), the priest immediately sent them back to bring Moses home for supper (v. 20). He was evidently pleased with the newcomer. The result was that Moses remained in the priest's home and married one of his daughters (v. 21). To this union a son was born. Moses gave him the name Gershom—"a stranger here"—saying, "I have been a stranger in a strange land" (v. 22). At last he had found a safe haven of rest.

It should be pointed out that Moses did not marry a pagan wife. The Midianites were descended from Midian, the son of Abraham by his second wife Keturah (Genesis 25:1-2). The later accounts in Exodus (chap. 18) show that this priest of Midian was a worshiper of the true God.

VIII. GOD'S COMPASSION ON OPPRESSED ISRAEL: Exodus 2:23-25

Finally the oppressing Pharaoh died, although apparently a ruler at least as bad succeeded him. "The children of Israel sighed by reason of their bondage, and they cried, and their cry came unto God by reason of the bondage" (v. 23). The word "sighed" is better translated "groaned." The oppressive yoke of slavery was too heavy to bear.

But "God heard their groaning" (v. 24), as He always hears the cries of His people. He "remembered his covenant with Abraham, with Isaac, and with Jacob." He had promised these venerable patriarchs that their descendants would be in number like the stars of the sky and the sands of the seashore. And God cannot break His covenant. He had also promised them that their seed would possess the land of Canaan. The time had now come to see that this promise was carried out.

"God looked upon the children of

DISCUSSION QUESTIONS

1. Why did God permit Jacob and his family to go down into Egypt?
2. Was there some danger of their being absorbed into the culture of Canaan and losing their identity?
3. What are some of the benefits of tribulation?
4. How did God prepare Moses for his task?
5. How may we find God's will for our tasks?
6. What is our responsibility to the oppressed?

Israel" in compassion (v. 25), and "had respect unto"—literally "knew"—them. He knew all about their trials and tears, their hardships and heartbreak, their suffering and sorrow. Now He was ready to act in their behalf.

CONTEMPORARY APPLICATION

It is never God's will that human beings, made in His image, should be enslaved or even oppressed. God is love, and His love reaches out to all mankind.

While actual slavery is a rare thing today, oppression is still altogether too common. Often this oppression is not physical, but psychological and social—which may be worse.

What are we to do about it? Some "social action" programs today are too much like Moses' first attempt to free his people—meeting violence with violence. Christ's way is to meet hatred with love. What we need to do is to wait on God, as Moses finally did, and find His plan and method for freeing the oppressed. If we take His way we will have His help.

A LEADER CALLED

DEVOTIONAL READING	Psalm 105:1-3, 26-39

ADULTS

Topic: *A Leader Called*

Background Scripture: Exodus 3—4

Scripture Lesson: Exodus 3:1-12

Memory Verse: *Then the Lord said, "I have seen the affliction of my people who are in Egypt, and have heard their cry because of their taskmasters."* Exodus 3:7

YOUTH

Topic: *A Leader Called*

Background Scripture: Exodus 3—4

Scripture Lesson: Exodus 3:1-12, 19

Memory Verse: *Then the Lord said, "I have seen the affliction of my people who are in Egypt, and have heard their cry because of their taskmasters."* Exodus 3:7

CHILDREN

Topic: *A Leader Called*

Background Scripture: Exodus 3—4

Scripture Lesson: Exodus 3:1-12, 19

Memory Verse: *Then the Lord said, "I have seen the affliction of my people who are in Egypt . . . and have come down to deliver them out of the hand of the Egyptians."* Exodus 3:7-8

DAILY BIBLE READINGS

Mon., June 6: "The Lord . . . Has Sent Me," Exodus 3:13-17.
Tues., June 7: A Leader Needs Tools, Exodus 4:1-5.
Wed., June 8: A Mouth and a Rod, Exodus 4:10-17.
Thurs., June 9: We Are Called to Freedom, Galatians 5:1, 13-15.
Fri., June 10: The Lord Remembers, Psalm 105:7-15.
Sat., June 11: The Lord Sends Deliverers, Psalm 105:16-25.
Sun., June 12: He Led Forth His People, Psalm 105:26-37.

LESSON AIM | To help us see how God calls and commissions His leaders.

LESSON SETTING

Time: About 1450 B.C. (or, as some prefer, 1300 B.C.)

Place: Mount Sinai and Egypt

A Leader Called

SUGGESTED INTRODUCTION FOR ADULTS

Someone has well said: "The world is looking for better machines; God is looking for better men." When people have a project that needs to be done, they seek to build a bigger computer or perfect some device that will do the job. But God always seeks out and calls a man or woman.

It is men and women that have changed history. We realize that it took machines to bring us, for better or worse—perhaps we should say for better *and* worse—into our modern industrial age. But who made the machines that have changed civilization? The answer is, "Men."

In Moses' day there was a whole nation that needed to be led out of Egyptian bondage. In a very unlikely place—on the backside of the desert—he found a man to do the job. But for eighty years He had been preparing that man for exactly that place.

God still has challenging, "impossible" jobs to be done. Many of us can look back and see how God prepared us for the work we are now doing. Let us be quick to hear God's call and eager to do the work He assigns to us.

SUGGESTED INTRODUCTION FOR YOUTH

It is a great honor to be called by God as a leader in any part of His enterprise. To be called to preach, to teach, to be a missionary—there is no greater honor on earth. But it is also an honor to be called by God to a place of responsible leadership as a layman (man or woman) in a local church. Because we cannot shine in the pulpit or in public is no excuse for sitting down listlessly in the pew and doing nothing.

Remember the man with one talent (Matthew 25:14-30). Those who had received the five talents and the two talents doubled what had been given them. But the one-talent man hid his master's money in the ground.

God calls all of us to useful service. Let us hear and heed His call. And let us be willing to spend the necessary years in preparation, as Moses did, so that we can do our assigned work with God's help.

CONCEPTS FOR CHILDREN

1. God calls even young children to definite service (see Contemporary Application).
2. A genuine call will become more clear and certain as the years pass.
3. We should obey God's call, not make excuses.
4. Where God guides, He provides.

THE LESSON COMMENTARY

I. THE PLACE OF THE CALL: Exodus 3:1-3

A. The Backside of the Desert: v. 1

In 2:18 the priest of Midian is called *Reuel*. But here and in the later chapters of Exodus he is referred to as *Jethro*. But this poses no problem. Many Bible characters are known by two names (e.g., Jacob-Israel, John-Mark, Saul-Paul, Levi-Matthew).

Moses, the man who had been brought up in Pharaoh's palace and trained for the royal throne of Egypt, is tending a flock of sheep way out on the backside of the desert. Incredible! But it is true.

How long did Moses take care of his father-in-law's sheep? Stephen gives us the answer: He tell us that it was forty years (Acts 7:30). What a waste of time! No, not in God's planning.

Moses' life was divided into three equal segments of forty years each (Acts 7:23, 30, 36). Most of the first forty years was spent in Pharaoh's palace. As we noted in our last lesson, Moses received here a thorough education and also a specific training in

kingship. He was being prepared for the throne of one of the great empires of that day. This was of inestimable value to him when he was called to found a new nation and lead it for the first forty years of its history. Most important of all, it was God's Chosen People that he must mold into a nation.

But this secular training in Egypt was not enough. If Moses was going to be the leader of God's people, he must have a spiritual preparation. And this he found in the lonely solitude of the desert. Sitting for endless hours during thousands of days—for forty years!—he had plenty of time to think and pray. At Pharaoh's court he had not only learned to read and write, but he had become acquainted with the best literature of his day. But he needed to know more than *how* to write; he needed to know *what* to write. The all-important story of the beginnings of both the human race and the chosen race, as recorded in Genesis, may well have come to his mind by the Spirit of God during these years of meditation.

But there was another important

lesson that Moses needed to learn. He
was facing forty years of leading a
fickle and stubborn people across the
wilderness. In that same desert of Sinai
he led sheep for forty years. From this
he gained a much-needed acquaintance
with the area. But he also learned lessons of patience in leadership that he
desperately needed (compare his killing
of the Egyptian in last week's lesson).

Moses had had the best university
education available. And then God
sent him to seminary—on the backside
of the desert. There he completed his
training.

One day he led his flock "to the
mountain of God, even to Horeb."
This is more familiarly known to us as
Mount Sinai. It was here that the Israelites, shortly after escaping from
Egyptian bondage, would spend some
time. There they would receive the
Law and build the tabernacle. So it
was especially appropriate that Moses
should receive his call at this very spot.

The exact location of Mount Sinai
is still debated. Traditionally it is
placed near the southern tip of the
Sinai Peninsula. But it may have been
farther north.

B. The Burning Bush: v. 2

Later God Himself was to appear
to Moses on top of Mount Sinai. But
at this time "the angel of the Lord
[Hebrew, "an angel of the Lord"] appeared unto him in a flame of fire out
of the midst of a bush"—literally, "out
of the midst of the acacia" (a very
common tree in that area, used later
for building the tabernacle).

Very naturally, the fire caught Moses' attention. He looked, and to his
astonishment discovered that though
the bush was on fire it was not being
consumed. Ordinarily a thorn bush
such as this would burn up quickly.

C. The Curiosity of Moses: v. 3

Moses could hardly believe his
eyes. So he decided to go over and
have a closer look at this very strange
phenomenon.

On the expression "I will now turn

aside" George Rawlinson makes this
comment: "A minute touch, indicating that Moses is the writer. He
remembers that the bush did not grow
on the track which he was pursuing,
but lay off it, and that he had to 'turn
aside,' in order to make inspection"
(*Ellicott's Commentary on the Whole
Bible*, I, 198).

II. THE VOICE OF GOD:
Exodus 3:4-6

A. Calling a Man: v. 4

"When the Lord saw that he
turned aside to see." How often we
miss God's appointments because we
do not take time to look and listen!
One shudders to think of missed opportunities for blessing to ourselves
and others, just because we are too
busy to stop. "Be still, and know that
I am God" (Psalm 46:10). That is a
verse that I need! Do you?

Because Moses stopped by, "God
called unto him out of the midst of
the bush, and said, Moses, Moses."
Rawlinson writes: "The double call
implies urgency. Compare the call of
Samuel (I Sam. iii. 10)" ("Exodus,"
The Pulpit Commentary, I, 55).

God knows each of our names and
He knows exactly where we are. Our
responsibility is to listen when He calls
and answer, as Moses did, "Here am I"
(cf. Isaiah 6:8).

B. Holy Ground: v. 5

As Moses hurried to look more
closely at the unusual sight, God spoke
a word of warning: "Draw not nigh
hither." Rawlinson comments: "The
awful greatness of the Creator is such
that his creatures, until invited to draw
near, are bound to stand aloof. Moses,
not yet aware that God himself spoke
to him, was approaching the bush too
close, to examine and see what the
'great thing' was" ("Exodus," *Pulpit*,
p. 55).

The Lord added, "Put off thy
shoes from off thy feet." The word
"shoes" should be "sandals." Rawlinson says: "Shoes were not worn com-

monly, even by the Egyptians, until a late period, and would certainly not be known in the land of Midian at this time. The practice of putting them off before entering a temple, a palace, or even the private apartments of a house, was, and is, universal in the East" ("Exodus," *Pulpit*, p. 55).

Anyone who has traveled much in the East can attest to the truth of this last statement. In Japan shoes are always taken off and left outside the door of a home. In Korea we took off our shoes even before entering the house of a missionary. In India one must remove his shoes before going to the platform or standing in the pulpit (at least this was true in the 1960s). And every traveler to the Middle East knows that he takes off his shoes before entering a Moslem mosque.

This sign of reverence was especially important in Moses' case. For God said to him, "The place whereon thou standest is holy ground." It is only God's presence that makes any place holy.

What lessons does this have for us? It reminds us that when we come into God's presence—in our private devotions, in family worship, or in the church sanctuary—we should take off our shoes of contact with the world and set our minds on heavenly things. We must be reverent in His presence.

C. The God of the Fathers: v. 6

When God identified Himself as "the God of Abraham, the God of Isaac, and the God of Jacob" it flooded Moses' mind with the stories of those men that he has recorded for us in the Book of Genesis. God had marvelously led each of these three partriarchs, and had given them amazing promises about their descendants. Now these promises were about to be fulfilled in a new and larger way than ever before.

It was one of the great historical moments in the history of divine revelation. No wonder that "Moses hid his face; for he was afraid to look upon God."

III. GOD'S CONCERN FOR HIS PEOPLE: Exodus 3:7-9

A. Observing Their Affliction: v. 7

"I have surely seen" is literally, "Seeing I have seen"—a typical Hebraism expressing both certainty and continuance. The Israelites probably felt that no one cared about their condition. But God was keeping His eye on the situation every moment. And now had come the time to act. His leader was ready.

God not only had "seen" the affliction of His people, but he had "heard" their cry. Much of their torment came from cruel "taskmasters." The Hebrew has a different word from that translated the same way in 1:11. There the "taskmasters" were high officials who acted as superintendents of large groups of workers. But here the word for "taskmasters" suggests cruelty and might be rendered "oppressors" (as in Zechariah 9:8). It refers to the foremen in charge of small gangs of workers, who beat them unmercifully. The suffering Israelites were crying out in their anguish, though it seemed that no one heard. But God did!

B. Coming to Deliver Them: v. 8

God declared, "I am come down to deliver them out of the hand of the Egyptians." This is somewhat of an anthropomorphism, God accommodating Himself to the language and understanding of men. But the very expression has a fitting application to what God did at Bethlehem and Calvary. In the person of His Son, Jesus Christ, He came down to earth and died on the cross to deliver mankind from the slavery of sin.

God was now visiting His people "to bring them up out of that land unto a good land." Palestine is literally "up" from Egypt in two senses. It is north on the map, and most of it is at a higher elevation. The land of Egypt lies along the Nile River, which inundates the surrounding countryside each year. Most of Egypt is close to sea level. In contrast to that, Jerusalem is at an elevation of about three thousand feet. The bulk of Palestine proper is a rather high plateau, more healthful than the climate of Egypt.

Palestine is also described as a "large" land. What may be called Palestine proper—north to south some two hundred miles from Dan to Beersheba, and west to east about fifty miles from the Mediterranean Sea to the Jordan River—is relatively small. But God had promised a much larger territory to Abraham (Genesis 15:18-21), and David and Solomon's kingdoms were extensive (I Kings 4:21).

The phrase "flowing with milk and honey" occurs here for the first of many times in the Old Testament. It was probably a proverbial expression for "a land of plenty." The twelve spies sent to investigate the land of Canaan came back with the report: "Surely it floweth with milk and honey" (Numbers 13:27). It had a greater variety of fruits and other foods than did the land of Egypt, where wheat was the main crop.

Palestine was originally a land of ten nations (Genesis 10:15-20; 15:19-21). It is more often referred to as the land of "seven nations" (e.g., Deuteronomy 7:1). Here and in Judges 3:5 only six are mentioned. The Girgashites are omitted as being apparently the least important of the seven. All of these nations the Israelites had to displace.

C. Hearing Their Cry: v. 9

This verse repeats what was said in verse 7. It serves as a connecting link to verse 10.

IV. MOSES' CALL AND COMMISSION:
Exodus 3:10

The call was clear: "Come now." The commission was explicit: "I will send thee unto Pharaoh, that thou mayest bring forth my people the children of Israel out of Egypt."

At forty years of age Moses was ready—so *he* thought—to strike a blow for the freedom of his people. But that attempt proved abortive. Now, at eighty years of age, he was older and wiser, and much less eager to tackle the job.

It wasn't a matter of his being too old and senile. For Moses lived his most vigorous life of service during the next forty years of bringing the Israelites out of Egypt and leading them through the wilderness. It was simply that he appreciated now the human impossibility of the task.

But where God guides, God provides. When the Lord tells us to do something, our responsibility is to obey. It is His responsibility to furnish the power necessary to carry out the assignment. God never commands us to do anything that He will not enable us to do.

V. MOSES' FOUR OBJECTIONS:
Exodus 3:11—4:17

A. "Who Am I?": 3:11-12

When confronted with this gigantic assignment, this impossible task, Moses replied in consternation, "Who am I, that I should go unto Pharaoh, and that I should bring forth the children of Israel out of Egypt?" Forty years before it would have been a simple thing to enter the presence of the great sovereign of Egypt, for Moses had been brought up in the royal palace. But now? That was something else! For forty years he had been out in the distant hinterland, caring for a few sheep—just a common shepherd.

But Moses was given all the answer he needed: "Certainly I will be with thee" (v. 12). It is not who *we* are, but who *God* is! When we face that fact realistically, we realize that no assignment God gives us is impossible.

The Lord gave Moses a special "token," or sign. When Moses had led the Israelites out of Egypt, they would worship God at "this mountain"—

Mount Sinai. The fulfillment of this sign would be an assurance to Moses that God would be with him all the way. All Moses had to do was obey.

B. "What Shall I Say?": 3:13-22

Still Moses hesitated. His mind was filling up with obstacles. He was much more problem-conscious than promise-conscious. And that is too often our trouble.

So Moses envisioned the time when he would tell the Israelites that the God of their fathers had sent him to deliver them. They would ask, "What is his name?" What should he reply to that?

Thereupon came one of the greatest revelations of God in the entire Old Testament. At the burning bush God revealed Himself to Moses as "I AM THAT I AM." The basic meaning is, "I am that which I am." Rawlinson comments: "My nature, i.e., cannot be declared in words, cannot be conceived of by human thought. I exist in such sort that my whole inscrutable nature is implied in my existence. I exist, as nothing else does—necessarily, eternally, really. If I am to give myself a name expressive of my nature, so far as language can be, let me be called 'I AM' " ("Exodus," *Ellicott's*, p. 200).

Then God told Moses to call together "the elders of Israel" (v. 16) and take them with him to Pharaoh (v.

18). He warned Moses that Pharaoh would refuse; but God would win.

C. "They Will Not Believe Me": 4:1-9

We have to be careful about what our unbelief may do to us. The Lord told Moses, "And they shall hearken to thy voice" (3:18). Now Moses declares, "They will not believe me, nor hearken unto my voice" (4:1). He was making God out to be a liar! And that is really what we do when we doubt His promises.

The Lord replied by asking Moses a question: "What is that in thy hand?" (v. 2). And He is saying the same thing to us. We say that we have nothing; we can't do anything. He says, "What's that in your hand?" We all have something God can use.

Moses replied briefly, "A rod." Probably his tone of voice implied: "Just a walking stick; that's nothing!" But God used it to work a miracle that would impress the doubting Israelites. He also gave Moses a second "sign." When he put his hand inside his robe and pulled it out again, it was white with leprosy. When he repeated the act, it was healed. If the people of Israel still doubted Moses, he was to perform a third sign: pour some river water on the ground and it would become blood (v. 9). This would surely convince them that he was God's messenger.

D. "I Am Not Eloquent": 4:10-17

Moses was still hedging. This time he objected: "I am not eloquent"—literally, "No man of words am I." He added: "Neither heretofore, nor since thou has spoken unto thy servant" (v. 10). This almost sounds like a complaint: "If you want me to be your spokesman, why don't you help me to speak easily?"

God answered with a reproving question: "Who hath made man's mouth?" (v. 11). He then repeated the command, with an assuring promise: "Now therefore go, and I will be with

---

DISCUSSION QUESTIONS

1. What are some ways in which God makes known His call to us?
2. What should our response always be?
3. What is God's concern today for oppressed people?
4. How can we help?
5. What did Moses lose by his objections?
6. What is true humility, in contrast to false humility?

thy mouth, and teach thee what thou shalt say" (v. 12).

There is really no excuse for Moses' answer to this. His reply was actually insulting: "O my Lord, send, I pray thee, by the hand of him whom thou wilt send" (v. 13)—but not me! Literally it was, "Pray send by whom thou wilt"—"A curt, impatient, and scarcely reverent speech" (Rawlinson, "Exodus," *Ellicott's*, p. 203).

No wonder that "the anger of the Lord was kindled against Moses" (v. 14)! God informed him that because of his unwillingness to accept the full assignment, his brother Aaron would become the public spokesman. Thus Moses lost some of the blessing and service that God had for him.

VI. MOSES' RETURN TO EGYPT:
Exodus 4:18-31

When Moses announced to his father-in-law that he must return to his people in Egypt, the old priest graciously said, "Go in peace" (v. 18). So Moses took his wife and two sons on a donkey and headed back home (v. 20).

The Lord warned Moses that Pharaoh's heart would be hardened (v. 21), so that he would not let the people go (cf. 7:13, 22; 8:15, 32; 9:7, 34, 35). But Moses was to warn him that if he refused to release Israel, God's firstborn, then Pharaoh's own firstborn son would die (vv. 22-23). And that, of course, is exactly what happened.

Evidently Moses had neglected to circumcise his second son. As punishment he became fatally ill (v. 24). His wife quickly performed the necessary task, though with loathing and protest (v. 25). Then Moses got well (v. 26).

Working at the other end of the line, the Lord told Aaron to go out into the wilderness to meet Moses. He did so and met him at Mount Sinai (v. 27), where Moses reported all that had happened (v. 28).

When all the elders of Israel had been brought together (v. 29), Aaron acted as Moses' spokesman (v. 30). "And the people believed" (v. 31), as God had told Moses they would. Humbly they "bowed their heads and worshipped."

CONTEMPORARY APPLICATION

God still calls men today. And He makes His call clear to those who will listen.

Perhaps the writer may be allowed a word of personal testimony. As a young child I felt a call to preach. I cannot remember my first consciousness of it, but it became a growing conviction throughout the years. At twenty-one years of age I spent the summer holding revival meetings in the mountains of Kentucky. (My home was in Massachusetts.)

As a senior in college I was praying alone in the chapel one evening during the dinner hour, deeply burdened for the spiritual life of the students. As clear as an audible voice came the call: "I want you to teach Bible here at E.N.C." And so in 1933 I began as instructor in Greek New Testament and have been teaching the New Testament, Greek and English, ever since.

In 1939 the Lord spoke again: "I want you to write a book." I had never dreamed of being an author. But I obeyed, never suspecting it would mean thirty books in the next thirty-five years. It pays to answer God's call! He knows far better than we what is best for each of our individual lives and what is best for the Kingdom. And there is never any conflict between these two.

June 19, 1977

LET MY PEOPLE GO

DEVOTIONAL READING	Exodus 6:2-8

ADULTS

Topic: *Let My People Go*

Background Scripture: Exodus 5—13

Scripture Lesson: Exodus 11:1-6; 13:17-22

Memory Verse: *And Moses said to the people, "Fear not, stand firm, and see the salvation of the Lord, which he will work for you today."* Exodus 14:13

YOUTH

Topic: *Bondage Broken*

Background Scripture: Exodus 5—13

Scripture Lesson: Exodus 11:1-6; 13:17-22

Memory Verse: *And Moses said to the people, "Fear not, stand firm, and see the salvation of the Lord, which he will work for you today."* Exodus 14:13

CHILDREN

Topic: *Let My People Go*

Background Scripture: Exodus 5—13

Scripture Lesson: Exodus 11:1-6; 13:17-22

Memory Verse: *Let my people go, that they may serve me.* Exodus 9:13

DAILY BIBLE READINGS

Mon., June 13: "I Will Bring You Out," Exodus 6:2-8.
Tues., June 14: The Lord's Passover, Exodus 12:1-11.
Wed., June 15: The First Passover, Exodus 12:14-20.
Thurs., June 16: After Four Hundred Thirty Years, Exodus 12:40-47.
Fri., June 17: A Sign of Deliverance, Isaiah 19:19-22.
Sat., June 18: A Prayer for Deliverance, Psalm 44:20-26.
Sun., June 19: Led Forth with Joy, Psalm 105:38-45.

LESSON AIM

To help us see how God works out His purposes in spite of man's opposition.

LESSON SETTING

Time: Around 1450 B.C. (or 1300 B.C.)

Place: Egypt

LESSON OUTLINE

Let My People Go

  I. **One More Plague:** Exodus 11:1-3
     A. Announcement of the Last Plague: v. 1

B. Collecting Unpaid Wages: v. 2
C. Greatness of Moses: v. 3

II. **Death of the Firstborn:** Exodus 11:4-6
A. A Fatal Midnight: v. 4
B. All the Firstborn: v. 5
C. A National Mourning: v. 6

III. **Institution of the Passover:** Exodus 12:1-28

IV. **Escape from Egypt:** Exodus 12:29-51

V. **Dedication of the Firstborn:** Exodus 13:1-16

VI. **Following the Appointed Route:** Exodus 13:17-19
A. Avoiding Philistia: v. 17
B. Through the Wilderness: v. 18
C. Taking Joseph's Bones: v. 19

VII. **The Symbol of God's Presence:** Exodus 13:20-22
A. On the Edge of the Wilderness: v. 20
B. A Pillar of Cloud and of Fire: v. 21
C. An Unfailing Presence: v. 22

SUGGESTED INTRODUCTION FOR ADULTS

Our last lesson ended with the Israelites believing Moses and worshiping God (4:31). But then things took a bad turn.

Moses and Aaron went in and told Pharaoh: "Thus saith the Lord God of Israel, Let my people go, that they may hold a feast unto me in the wilderness" (5:1). With typical arrogance Pharaoh answered: "Who is the Lord, that I should obey his voice to let Israel go? I know not the Lord, neither will I let Israel go" (5:2). That began a battle between the Lord and Pharaoh that fills the next eight chapters of Exodus. It was a long duel, but God won.

Reacting to the request of Moses and Aaron, Pharaoh imposed harder work on the Israelites. They were now required to find their own straw for making bricks (5:7). When production fell because of this, they were beaten (5:14). The Israelite foremen complained to Pharaoh, but his harsh reply was, "Ye are idle, ye are idle" (5:17). The result was that the people of Israel turned against Moses and Aaron and blamed them (5:20-21). It was Moses' darkest hour, and he complained to God (5:22-23).

But the Lord assured Moses that He would still carry out His promise to deliver His people (6:1). He would now reveal himself as Jehovah (6:3), or *Yahweh*. This is the Hebrew word that is translated *Lord* in the Old Testament. It is the personal name of God as the God who keeps the covenant.

Once more the people refused to listen to Moses because of their "anguish of spirit" and "cruel bondage" (6:9). Only God's promises sustained this severely tested leader.

(We would suggest that teachers of adult classes read this time the "Suggested Introduction for Youth," as well.)

One of Satan's favorite devices to defeat young people spiritually is to suggest compromises. This is what Pharaoh did. He first said, "Stay in the land" (8:25). So he says to the young people, "Stay in the world; you don't have to change your life-style." Then Pharaoh suggested, "Don't go very far away" (8:28). So Satan says today: "Don't go too far in your religion; take it easy!" His third compromise was, "Leave your families behind" (10:11). The fourth was, "Leave your flocks and herds behind" (10:24). But God wants our *all.*

1. People without Christ are in bondage to sin.
2. God wants to deliver everyone from this bondage.
3. Satan tries to hold on to us.
4. But Christ can set us free.

THE LESSON COMMENTARY

I. ONE MORE PLAGUE:
Exodus 11:1-3

A. Announcement of the Last Plague: v. 1

The Lord announced to Moses: "Yet will I bring one plague more upon Pharaoh, and upon Egypt; afterwards he will let you go hence." The time had come for the final showdown.

This would be the tenth plague, for nine had already taken place. The first plague was that of turning the waters of the Nile River into blood (7:19-25). This lasted for a week, with the people searching for water to drink. Since the Egyptians worshiped the Nile as a god, this was a blow to their religion. The Lord had already said to Moses, "And the Egyptians shall know that I am the Lord" (7:5). One purpose of the ten plagues was to expose their pagan gods as weak and worthless, unable to stand before the power of the true God.

The second plague was that of frogs (8:1-7) throughout the country. A few frogs is all right, but these "cov-ered the land of Egypt" (8:6). Pharaoh relented momentarily (8:8). But when the plague ended, he once more became stubborn (8:15).

This brought on the third plague, lice on man and beast (8:16-19). The fourth plague was that of flies (8:20-24). Now a new thing took place. The Israelites had suffered with the Egyptians in the first three plagues, but a separation was then made. They were to be immune from the other seven plagues (8:22-23).

The fifth plague was that of murrain (9:1-7), an epidemic pestilence that killed the cattle in Egypt. Even though Pharaoh ascertained that the Israelites were protected from this calamity, he still refused to let the people go (9:7).

The sixth plague was that of boils on both people and animals (9:8-12). The seventh was hail (9:13-26). Heeding the advice of Moses, some of the Egyptians saved their servants and animals by keeping them indoors, but the disbelieving ones paid no attention (9:19-21). The land of Goshen was immune (9:26). Again Pharaoh relented and promised to let the Israelites go (9:27-28). But when the destructive storm ceased, once more the wicked king hardened his heart (9:34-35).

The eighth plague consisted of swarms of locusts that destroyed all vegetation in Egypt (10:12-15). The ninth was darkness that covered the whole land, except where the Israelites lived (10:21-23).

B. Collecting Unpaid Wages: v. 2

The Lord instructed Moses to have the Israelitish men and women "borrow" from their neighbors jewels of silver and gold. Some people claim to find an ethical problem in the word "borrow" here. Clearly the Israelites had no intention of returning these valuables.

The solution is simple: The Hebrew word translated "borrow" only means "ask." The Israelites were just collecting a bit of the wages that were due them for their many years of hard labor. It was fully justifiable.

But what was the purpose of this? We find the answer later, in 35:21-24. When the tabernacle was being built, there was need for considerable amounts of gold and silver. Moses asked for an offering to supply this material. We read: "And they came, both men and women, as many as were willing hearted, and brought bracelets, and earrings, and rings, and tablets, all jewels of gold" (35:22). The jewelry donated by the Egyptians was now given to the Lord.

C. Greatness of Moses: v. 3

"The Lord gave the people favour in the sight of the Egyptians." By now any thinking Egyptian could see that the true God was on Israel's side; the plagues had proved that. Even Pharaoh's servants had remonstrated with the king: "How long shall this man be a snare unto us? let the men go, that they may serve the Lord their God; knowest thou not yet that Egypt is destroyed?" (10:7). Though Pharaoh refused to pay attention, his people had a healthy respect for the Israelites.

"Moreover the man Moses was very great in the land of Egypt." Greatness is always costly. Moses had paid a high price in winning this place of honor. He was hated and opposed by Pharaoh. He was blamed by his own people for their increased hardships. The only one he had to lean on was God Himself. True greatness always emerges out of trial.

It must have seemed to the Egyptians that Moses was as great as Pharaoh himself. For this champion of the Israelites confronted the king boldly and was winning the field.

II. DEATH OF THE FIRSTBORN: Exodus 11:4-6

A. A Fatal Midnight: v. 4

The darkest hour in the life of an individual or nation is often referred to as midnight. Now a midnight for Egypt had come. God was going to visit the nation in judgment. It would be a fatal hour for an important segment of the population.

B. All the Firstborn: v. 5

"And all the firstborn in the land of Egypt shall die." This terrible stroke of divine judgment would reach all the way from the palace of Pharaoh down to the humblest home in Egypt. It would include the firstborn of "the maidservant that is behind the mill"— the small handmill in every home used for grinding grain each morning to make the bread for the day.

Concerning the term "firstborn" George Rawlinson writes: "The Hebrew word translated *firstborn* is applied only to males; and thus the announcement was that in every family the eldest *son* should be cut off. In Egypt, as in most other countries, the law of primogeniture prevailed—the eldest son was the hope, stay, and support of the household, his father's companion, his mother's joy, the object of his brothers' and sisters' reverence. The firstborn of the Pharaoh bore the title of . . . 'hereditary crown prince,' and succeeded his father, unless he died or was formally set aside during his father's lifetime. Among the nobles, estates were inherited, and sometimes titles descended to the firstborn. No greater affliction can be conceived, short of the general destruction of the people, than the sudden death in every family of him round whom the highest interests and fondest hopes clustered" ("Exodus," *Ellicott's Commentary on the Whole Bible*, I, 226).

Also "all the firstborn of beasts" would die. This was particularly significant because the Egyptians worshiped certain animals as gods.

C. A National Mourning: v. 6

The result of the death of the firstborn son in every home would be a great national mourning such as had never taken place or ever would take place. In every home "throughout all the land" there would literally be "a great cry," a loud, unsuppressed wailing and weeping.

Moses went on to say: "But against any of the children of Israel shall not a dog move his tongue, against man or beast: that ye may know how that the Lord doth put a difference between the Egyptians and Israel" (v. 7). This would be proof that God was supreme.

Verse 8 seems to indicate that the message of verses 4-8 was addressed to Pharaoh, a continuation of 10:29. For Moses says, "All these thy servants shall come down unto me." The verse ends with the statement: "And he went out from Pharaoh in a great anger."

Rawlinson comments: "Moses makes his last appeal—utters his last threats. The Pharaoh had bidden him 'see his face no more' (chap. x. 28), and he has accepted the warning, and declared, 'I will see thy face again no more' (chap. x. 29). It is the last interview—the last interchange of speech. Moses had to deliver himself of a mes-

sage. Hardened as his heart is, Pharaoh is yet to be allowed 'a place for repentance.' . . . If Pharaoh had even now relented, it was not too late. . . . But he had 'hardened himself,' and then 'been hardened,' until, practically, the time for relenting was gone by. He remained obdurate, and 'would not let the children of Israel go out of his land' (verse 10)" ("Exodus," *Ellicott's*, p. 226).

III. INSTITUTION OF THE PASSOVER:
Exodus 12:1-28

Now that the interviews with Pharaoh were over, the Lord gave to Moses and Aaron careful instructions about the Passover. "This month [the month of the exodus from Egypt] shall be unto you the beginning of months: it shall be the first month of the year to you" (v. 2). Because the Israelites had a lunar, not solar, calendar, this month spans parts of our March and April. This is the beginning of the Jewish religious year. The civil year begins with a New Year's day in the fall.

The Israelites were to kill a lamb and sprinkle its blood on the side posts and upper frame of their doorways (v. 7). Then they were to eat the Passover lamb that evening (v. 8).

The name "Passover" was due to the fact that as God passed through the land of Egypt that night killing all the firstborn males (v. 12), "when I see the blood, I will pass over you" (v. 13). Every year thereafter the Israelites were to observe the Passover as "a memorial" (v. 14) of that eventful night. For seven days they were to eat unleavened bread (v. 15). The children were to be instructed in the meaning of this rite (vv. 27-28).

IV. ESCAPE FROM EGYPT:
Exodus 12:29-51

Finally, after much warning, the tenth plague struck. "At midnight the Lord smote all the firstborn in the land of Egypt, from the firstborn of Pharoah that sat on the throne unto the firstborn of the captive that was in the dungeon; and all the firstborn of cattle" (12:29). As was predicted, "there was a great cry in Egypt; for there was not a house where there was not one dead" (12:30). It was truly a nation in mourning.

At long last Pharaoh gave in completely. He sent word to Moses and Aaron to take the Israelites and leave, "bag and baggage"—"also take your flocks and your herds, as ye have said; and be gone" (v. 32). This is what he had previously refused to permit (10:24). Then he added plaintively, "And bless me also." He had had enough of divine curse on him for his sin.

God had told Moses that after the tenth plague Pharaoh "shall surely thrust you out hence altogether" (11:1). Now this was literally fulfilled: "And the Egyptians were urgent upon the people, that they might send them out of the land in haste; for they said, We be all dead men" (12:33). There was no further talk of compromise or delay.

In spite of the rush of getting off, the Israelites took time to "borrow" (ask) from the Egyptians the jewelry and clothes they would need later (v. 35). The Lord gave them favor with the Egyptians, who freely gave their former slaves whatever they requested; "and they spoiled the Egyptians" (v. 36), as the Lord had said they would (3:22).

The Israelites journeyed from Rameses (v. 37)—a city they had helped to build (1:11)—and came to Succoth (the location of this city is uncertain). We are told that there were "about six hundred thousand on foot that were men, beside children." From this it had usually been assumed that at least two million Israelites left Egypt (cf. Numbers 1:3-46).

"And a mixed multitude went up also with them" (v. 38). These may have been other enslaved people in Egypt, or even possibly some native Egyptians. In any case the "mixed multitude" proved later to be a hindrance (Numbers 11:4).

Verse 40 states that the Israelites were in Egypt for 430 years (cf. Genesis 15:13; Acts 7:6). Now at last that long sojourn was ended.

"This is that night of the Lord to be observed of all the children of Israel in their generations" (v. 42). Therefore specific instructions are given for the observance of the annual Passover (vv. 43-50).

V. DEDICATION OF THE FIRST-BORN:
Exodus 13:1-16

Because the Israelites' firstborn males, both human and animal, had been delivered from death in Egypt, the Lord said to Moses, "Sanctify unto me all the firstborn" (v. 2). The word *sanctify* means to "set apart as sacred." Since the Lord had saved the firstborn, they were His. Later the Levites were selected to take their place (Numbers 3:40-51).

Evidently the firstborn male animals were to be sacrificed to the Lord. But since unclean animals could not be offered on the altar, "every firstling of an ass thou shalt redeem with a lamb," or else break the donkey's neck (v. 13). Every firstborn child was to be redeemed with money (cf. Numbers 3:47).

If a son asked why this was being done, his father was to tell him: "It came to pass, when Pharaoh would hardly let us go, that the Lord slew all the firstborn in the land of Egypt, both the firstborn of man, and the firstborn of beast: therefore I sacrifice to the Lord all that openeth the matrix, being males; but all the firstborn of my children I redeem" (v. 15). Thus the oldest son would feel a special sense of belonging to God.

VI. FOLLOWING THE APPOINTED ROUTE:
Exodus 13:17-19

A. Avoiding Philistia: v. 17

When Pharaoh finally released the Israelites, "God led them not through the way of the land of the Philistines, although that was near." He was fearful that they would be so frightened at the sight of enemy armies that they would turn back to Egypt.

The rejected route is thus identified by Rawlinson: "The starting point of the journey being Tanis or Rameses, in the Eastern Delta, not far from the sea, he sees that the shortest, and apparently the easiest, route for the Israelites to have pursued would have been that which led along the coast, from Tanis to Pelusium, thence to . . . Gaza, Ascalon, and Ashdod, the chief towns of the Philistines. The distance along this line was not more than about 200 miles, and might have been accomplished in a fortnight" ("Exodus," *Ellicott's*, p. 236).

The Philistines were a foreign people who had settled on the Mediterranean coast in the southern part of Palestine. Rawlinson says of them: "The Philistines were a powerful and warlike race half a century after this, in the time of Joshua, and were masters of the five important cities of Gaza, Ascalon, Ashdod, Gath, and Ekron, which seem to have formed a confederacy (Josh. xiii. 3). It would appear that their strength was already considerable, and that the Israelites, though perhaps more numerous, were incapable of coping with them, being wholly unaccustomed to war" ("Exodus," *The Pulpit Commentary*, I, 305).

DISCUSSION QUESTIONS

1. What are some ways in which God guides us?
2. What part does the Word of God play in this?
3. How can we be aware of God's presence today?
4. Why does God sometimes lead us by what seems a hard way?
5. What does the Passover typify to us?
6. What part did patience play in the life of Moses?

B. Through the Wilderness: v. 18

Instead of the seashore route, "God led the people about, through the way of the wilderness of the Red sea." As anyone can readily see by looking at a map, this was rather a circuitous route to take to Palestine. But sometimes the longest way around is the safest way home!

"The wilderness of the Red sea"— or "Reed Sea"—is perhaps the same as "the wilderness of Sinai," what is now called the Sinai Peninsula. This extends a long way from north to south. We cannot now be certain as to exactly how far south the Israelites went.

There were evidently some definite advantages in taking this southern route. Rawlinson writes: "Kalisch shows the wisdom of this course—how it gave time for the nation to be 'gradually accustomed to fatigues and hardships by a long and tiresome march in the desert'—to learn obedience to their chief—and finally to be 'trained to military discipline and martial virtue by occasional expeditions against the weaker tribes of the desert' " ("Exodus," *Pulpit*, pp. 305-06).

"The children of Israel went up harnessed out of the land of Egypt." The word "harnessed" suggests suits of metal armor, which is very unlikely. Rawlinson writes: "The best explanation is, that the word here means 'organized,' 'in military order.' . . . It was clearly necessary, to prevent confusion, that a military order should have been adopted, and there are not wanting indications that during the year of contention with Pharaoh such an organization was introduced and proceeded with. (See chaps. iv. 29, 31, vi. 26, xii. 3, 21, 51). It must have been brought to a high pitch of perfection for the Exodus to have taken place, as it seems to have done, without serious confusion or entanglement" ("Exodus," *Ellicott's*, p. 236).

C. Taking Joseph's Bones: v. 19

"Moses took the bones of Joseph with him." In the next to last verse of

Genesis (50:25) we find that Joseph had bound the Israelites by oath to carry his bones back to Canaan. This showed tremendous faith on his part: "God will surely visit you." We read in Genesis 50:26 that Joseph's body was embalmed and placed in a casket in Egypt. This was befitting his position as prime minister.

VII. THE SYMBOL OF GOD'S PRESENCE:
Exodus 13:20-22

A. On the Edge of the Wilderness: v. 20

The people left "Succoth," which means "booths," and "encamped in Etham, in the edge of the wilderness." Both of these places are of uncertain location. They were somewhere near the eastern edge of the fertile Delta. From now on it would be wilderness most of the way.

B. A Pillar of Cloud and of Fire: v. 21

In verse 18 it is stated that God "led" the people. Now we are told how He did it. He went before them by day in a pillar of cloud, or smoke, to guide them. At night He preceded them in a pillar of fire, which provided both guidance and light. It was an ideal arrangement.

The relation to the times is indicated by Rawlinson, who writes: "There is little doubt that fire and smoke signals were already used by commanders of armies for much the same purpose as that which God now accomplished in this way. The Egyptian documents of the period contain indications of the usage; and it is found among the Arabians, the Greeks, and the Persians. . . . The miracle was thus, in a certain sense, founded upon an existing custom, with the difference that God here gave the signals miraculously, which were wont to be given in a natural way by the human leaders of armies. He thus constituted himself the general of the host" ("Exodus," *Pulpit*, pp. 310-11).

"To go by day and night" means "so that they might march by day and by night." Because of the great heat of the desert region it was necessary that much of the marching be done at night (cf. Numbers 9:21).

C. An Unfailing Presence: v. 22

The pillar of cloud by day and the pillar of fire by night not only provided guidance and light, but they were also symbols of God's presence, like the Shekinah in the tabernacle. And this sign of God's presence stayed with them all the way across the wilderness (Nehemiah 9:19), though it is not mentioned distinctly after Numbers 16:42. The cloud hovered over the tabernacle by day and the fire by night (Numbers 9:15-16). When the cloud moved, the Israelites moved; when it stayed over the tabernacle, they remained where they were (Numbers 9:17-23).

CONTEMPORARY APPLICATION

"Let my people go" has numerous applications today—some of them explosive. This is because there are still oppressed peoples in the world today, that cannot live a life of normal freedom.

One of the worst offenders is Russia. It is not only a matter of "Save Soviety Jewry"—though that is still a crucial issue. But the Jews are not the only ones who cannot get permission to leave that country. There are many citizens who have sought to leave in recent years, but were held as though they were prisoners. The startling case of Simas Kudirka, a Lithuanian, received much publicity a few years ago. It was representative of thousands who are unjustly denied their rightful freedoms. Such people deserve our prayers for deliverance.

CELEBRATION OF FREEDOM

DEVOTIONAL READING	Psalm 136:1, 13-26
ADULTS	Topic: *Celebration of Freedom* Background Scripture: Exodus 14—15 Scripture Lesson: Exodus 14:21-25, 30-31; 15:1-3, 20-21 Memory Verse: *Who is like thee, O Lord, among the gods? Who is like thee, majestic in holiness, terrible in glorious deeds, doing wonders?* Exodus 15:11
YOUTH	Topic: *Freedom Celebrated* Background Scripture: Exodus 14—15 Scripture Lesson: Exodus 14:21-25, 30-31; 15:1-3, 20-21 Memory Verse: *Who is like thee, O Lord, among the gods? Who is like thee, majestic in holiness, terrible in glorious deeds, doing wonders?* Exodus 15:11
CHILDREN	Topic: *A Song of Victory* Background Scripture: Exodus 14—15 Scripture Lesson: Exodus 14:21-25, 30; 15:2 Memory Verse: *The Lord is my strength and my song, and he has become my salvation.* Exodus 15:2
DAILY BIBLE READINGS	Mon., June 20: God's Instruction to Moses, Exodus 14:1-9. Tues., June 21: The Flight of the Israelites, Exodus 14:10-20. Wed., June 22: The Deliverance of Israel, Exodus 14:21-29. Thurs., June 23: Moses' Song of Deliverance, Exodus 15:1-10. Fri., June 24: Praise to the Deliverer, Psalm 136:1-3, 10-15. Sat., June 25: A Song of Trust, Psalm 27:1-5. Sun., June 26: Praise to the Lord of Lords, Psalm 136:16-26.
LESSON AIM	To remind us that we should celebrate the victories that God gives us.
LESSON SETTING	Time: The traditional date of the Exodus in 1447 B.C. W. F. Albright and many other archaeologists prefer a later date, about 1295 B.C.

Celebration of Freedom

I. The Egyptian Pursuit of Israel: Exodus 14:1-12
    A. The Hardening of Pharaoh's Heart: vv. 1-4.
    B. The Massive Pursuit: vv. 5-9
    C. The Terrified Israelites: vv. 10-12

II. The Divine Intervention: Exodus 14:13-20
    A. Moses' Words of Assurance: vv. 13-14
    B. God's Directions to Moses: vv. 15-18
    C. The Divine Barrier: vv. 19-20

LESSON OUTLINE

III. The Crossing of the Red Sea: Exodus 14:21-25
    A. The Parting of the Waters: v. 21
    B. The Passage of the Israelites: v. 22
    C. The Punishment of the Egyptians: vv. 23-25

IV. The Destruction of the Egyptians: Exodus 14:26-29

V. The Deliverance of the Israelites: Exodus 14:30-31

VI. The Song of Celebration: Exodus 15:1-21
    A. Moses' Song: vv. 1-3
    B. God's Mercy: vv. 4-19
    C. Miriam's Music: vv. 20-21

SUGGESTED INTRODUCTION FOR ADULTS

Throughout the Old Testament we see abundant evidence that the Exodus was considered to be the greatest event in Israel's history. It was here that the nation began. A multitude of helpless, oppressed slaves in Egypt became a mighty nation under God.

One is reminded of John Wesley's *Journal.* Frequently one finds such expressions as "ten years ago" or "forty years ago," and they all point back to his evangelical conversion experience in the upper room on Aldersgate Street in London. That was in the evening of May 24, 1738. It marked the great turning point in Wesley's life.

So the Israelites looked back to the Exodus as the day of their redemption. All that followed was possible only because they had been delivered from Egyptian bondage.

We, too, should celebrate our deliverance from the bondage of sin. We should never cease to praise God for it.

SUGGESTED INTRODUCTION FOR YOUTH

Everybody—well, almost everybody—likes a happy celebration. And what should we celebrate more than the fact that Jesus is our Savior, that He has redeemed us from our sins?

Too often in the past, religion has been a rather solemn, somber affair. That has turned many people off. Christians should be the happiest people in the world. When we sincerely, joyously play that part, people are turned on.

It has always been hard for us to understand why a stadium should be turned into a mass victory rally of shouting, waving people, and yet there must be no emotional reaction to the freedom that Christ has brought us. Let's celebrate to His glory as a free people.

CONCEPTS FOR CHILDREN

1. God wants to give us freedom from sin, as He gave the Israelites freedom from slavery.
2. Their deliverance was a miracle, and so is ours.
3. They celebrated their deliverance with singing.
4. We should also celebrate in song.

THE LESSON COMMENTARY

I. THE EGYPTIAN PURSUIT OF ISRAEL:
Exodus 14:1-12

A. The Hardening of Pharaoh's Heart: vv. 1-4

In the Book of Exodus we find three recurring expressions. Sometimes we read that Pharaoh's heart was hardened. At other times it says that the Lord hardened Pharaoh's heart. Then again we find the statement that Pharaoh hardened his heart. Perhaps these are different ways of expressing the same phenomenon. One of the difficult theological questions is the relationship of divine sovereignty and human freedom. Though divine sovereignty is certainly the dominant Biblical emphasis, man's freedom of choice is also emphasized strongly. We cannot blame God for our wrong choices. Made in the image of God, man has a free will that can function within certain divinely ordained limits.

God told Moses that He would harden Pharaoh's heart, so that he would pursue the escaping Israelites. But the result would be "that the Egyptians may know that I am the Lord" (v. 4).

B. The Massive Pursuit: vv. 5-9

When Pharaoh heard that the Israelites had fled the country, he and his servants said, "Why have we done this, that we have let Israel go from serving us?" (v. 5). In view of the events described in the previous chapters, this question seems utterly absurd. But though illogical, it is not impossible. Even today people have a convenient way of forgetting the past and acting foolishly.

So Pharaoh called for his chariot. He proceeded to muster an impressive army of "six hundred select chariots, and all the other chariots of Egypt with officers over all of them" (v. 7, NASB). The Egyptians had now lost six hundred thousand slaves (12:37), and all the public building projects had suddenly come to a standstill. This was too much to take! Pharaoh must have known that the Israelites would put up a big struggle, rather than be recaptured. So he was not taking any chances. He used his strongest military force, his chariots.

"The children of Israel went out with an high hand" (v. 8)—"i.e., confidently, boldly, perhaps somewhat proudly, as having brought the Egyptians to entreat them to take their departure (chap. xii. 33)" ("Exodus," *Ellicott's Commentary on the Whole Bible*, I, 238).

This boldness soon suffered a setback: "But the Egyptians pursued after them, all the horses and chariots of Pharaoh, and his horsemen, and his army" (v. 9). This seems to indicate three arms of the Egyptian military force—chariots, cavalry, and infantry. It is true that the contemporary monuments do not picture a cavalry in Egypt at that time, though there was such a thing later (II Chronicles 12:3). So it has been suggested that the Hebrew word translated "horsemen" refers to the riders in the chariots. In his two commentaries on Exodus, Rawlinson oscillates between these two ideas. We cannot be sure which is correct.

In any case, Pharaoh's military force overtook the Israelites as they were camped "by the sea," beside two towns of eastern Egypt unknown today.

C. The Terrified Israelites: vv. 10-12

When the Israelites saw the approaching Egyptian army, "they were sore afraid"—"they became very frightened" (NASB)—and cried out to the Lord (v. 10). That was a proper thing to do under such crucial circumstances.

But the next thing was *not* proper. The Israelites launched a complaint against Moses, the first of an endless series that continued throughout the wilderness journeys. They asked Moses if there were no graves in Egypt, that he should bring them out to lie unburied in the wilderness. And then, with typical ingratitude, they reminded him that they had told him in Egypt, "Let us alone, that we may serve the Egyptians" (v. 12). They preferred slavery in Egypt to death in the wilderness.

It was this kind of people that Moses had to put up with for forty years. It is a great tribute to his noble character that he stayed with them through it all.

II. THE DIVINE INTERVENTION: Exodus 14:13-20

A. Moses' Words of Assurance: vv. 13-14

What marvelous faith this man displayed! To the terrified Israelites he said: "Fear ye not, stand still, and see the salvation of the Lord, which he will shew to you to day" (v. 13). He then assured them that they would never see these Egyptian enemies again. And they never did!

Moses concluded: "The Lord shall fight for you, and ye shall hold your peace" (v. 14). These words have been a great consolation to God's people in all ages. When we face an impossible situation, as the Israelites did, we can place the whole thing in His hands and let Him take care of it.

B. God's Directions to Moses: vv. 15-18

"Why are you crying out to me?" (v. 15, NASB). Nothing has been said about this. Lange offers this suggestion: "Moses outwardly was silent; but Jehovah heard how he inwardly cried to Him. The confidence, therefore, which he displayed to the people was founded on a fervent inward struggle of spirit. While therefore Jehovah's word is no reproof, there is something of a contrast in what follows: Speak unto the children, etc. That is: No further continuance of the spiritual struggle; forward into the Red Sea!" (John Peter Lange, "Exodus," *Commentary on the Holy Scriptures*, p. 49).

Now Moses was given specific directions. He was to lift up his rod, stretch it out over the sea, and the waters would part, with the result that the Israelites could cross on dry land (v. 16). The Lord told him that the Egyptians would try to follow, but "I will be honored through Pharaoh and all his army, through his chariots and his horsemen" (v. 17, NASB). Just how this would happen is not stated here.

God went on to say, "And the Egyptians shall know that I am the Lord" (v. 18). George Rawlinson comments: "All Egypt would learn of the destruction of the host, and the circumstances under which it occurred, whose miraculous nature could not be concealed. And the consequence would be a wide recognition of the superior might of Jehovah, the God of Israel, over that of any of the Egyptian deities" ("Exodus," *The Pulpit Commentary*, I, 335).

C. The Divine Barrier: vv. 19-20

The angel of God, symbolized by the pillar of cloud, moved to a position behind the Israelites, in the direction of the Egyptians, and stopped between the two camps.

The situation is thus described by Rawlinson: "This movement alone was calculated to alarm the latter, and prevent them from stirring till near daybreak; but the better to secure their inaction, the pillar was made to overshadow them with a deep and preternatural darkness, so that it became almost impossible for them to advance. Meanwhile, on the side which was turned toward the Israelites the pillar presented the appearance of a bright flame, lighting up the whole encampment, and rendering it as easy to make ready for the march as it would have been by day" ("Exodus," *Pulpit*, p. 339).

III. THE CROSSING OF THE RED SEA:
Exodus 14:21-25

A. The Parting of the Waters: v. 21

When Moses obediently (cf. v. 16) stretched out his hand over the sea, "the Lord caused the sea to go back by a strong east wind all that night, and made the sea dry land, and the waters were divided." It is clearly indicated here that God used natural means (a strong east wind blowing all night) to produce a supernatural miracle (a path through the sea). In view of what is said here it seems reasonable to hold that where the Israelites crossed there was a shallow part of "the sea" (perhaps near the Bitter Lakes) and that this powerful east wind was employed by the Lord to blow the water back from this spot.

B. The Passage of the Israelites: v. 22

As the Israelites crossed on dry ground, "the waters were a wall unto them on their right hand, and on their left." Probably most of us have seen literalistic pictures of high walls of water on both sides of the marching Israelites. The truer picture is probably that of *deep* water on both sides of the dry land, effectually protecting the Israelites from being attacked on either flank. This exactly fits what is described here. The deep water would be like barriers, acting as walls of protection.

C. The Punishment of the Egyptians: vv. 23-25

The Egyptians evidently discovered that the Israelites were escaping across the waters. So they pursued them "to the midst of the sea" (v. 23). It was Pharoah's cavalry and chariots that did this; the infantry probably stayed in camp.

"In the morning watch [between 2:00 and 6:00 A.M.] the Lord looked unto the host of the Egyptians through the pillar of fire and of the cloud, and troubled the host of the Egyptians"— "brought the army of the Egyptians into confusion" (NASB)—(v. 24). Rawlinson suggests: "By some terrible manifestation of His presence and of his anger, proceeding from the pillar of the cloud in their front, God threw the Egyptians into consternation and confusion. A panic terror seized them." Going on to verse 25, he writes: "Then followed a second difficulty. The progress of the chariots was obstructed. According to the present reading of the Hebrew text, the wheels parted from the axles, which would naturally bring the vehicles to a stand. According to the LXX and a reading found in the Samaritan Pentateuch, the wheels 'became entangled,' as they would if they sank up to the axles in the soft ooze" ("Exodus," *Ellicott's*, p. 240).

In either case, the ground over which the Israelites had passed was soon covered with a confused mass of horses and chariots. What terror must have struck the hearts of the Egyptians! They cried out, "Let us flee from the face of Israel; for the Lord fighteth for them against the Egyptians" (v. 25). But it was too late.

God had said that they would know that He was the Lord. Now this was being demonstrated. Israel's Lord was the supreme God of all power.

IV. THE DESTRUCTION OF THE EGYPTIANS:
Exodus 14:26-29

Once more God commanded Moses to stretch out his hand over the sea—this time "that the waters may come again upon the Egyptians, upon their chariots, and upon their horsemen" (v. 26). When Moses obeyed, "the sea returned to his strength when the morning appeared" (v. 27). To their horror, the Egyptians saw the waters coming in upon them from both sides. They tried to flee. But it was to no avail: "The Lord overthrew the Egyptians in the midst of the sea."

The returning waters "covered the chariots, and the horsemen, and all the host of Pharaoh" (v. 28). It will be noticed that the last *and* is in italics in the King James Version, which means that it is not in the original Hebrew. It should be *even* (NASB), rather than *and*. That is, the charioteers and cavalrymen were drowned, but not the infantrymen. They were probably still in camp. But Pharaoh's military force was knocked out, so that there was no danger of his pursuing the Israelites farther.

V. THE DELIVERANCE OF THE ISRAELITES:
Exodus 14:30-31

"Thus [by this supernatural means] the Lord saved Israel that day out of the hand of the Egyptians; and Israel saw the Egyptians dead upon the seashore" (v. 30). It was a sight they would never forget. Their powerful enemy, whose pursuit had struck terror to their hearts, was now literally "washed up" on the shore. The peril was over. It was a salvation that marked a new beginning for the nation.

"And Israel saw that great work"— better, "power"—that the Lord had shown in wiping out the Egyptians. The result was that "the people feared the Lord, and believed the Lord, and his servant Moses" (v. 31).

The Israelites needed to witness this miracle. Up to this time they had been a doubting, vacillating people. If they were going to cross the wilderness and conquer Canaan, they needed to be strengthened in their faith—both in God and in their human leader, Moses.

VI. THE SONG OF CELEBRATION:
Exodus 15:1-21

A. Moses' Song: vv. 1-3

Victory calls for celebration. The Israelites had just won a miraculous victory over the Egyptians. The latter's military force had been wiped out. And yet the Israelites had not raised a hand in self-defense. It was all of the Lord. If ever a victory deserved a spontaneous celebration, this was it.

And so Moses and the Israelites sang a song of praise to the Lord. They began with the words: "I will sing unto the Lord, for he hath triumphed gloriously: the horse and his rider hath he thrown into the sea" (v. 1).

It was a remarkable triumph—no fighting, no effort on the part of Israel, just trust in the Lord. But faith had brought the victory—primarily Moses' faith, shown in obedience. Had he not spread out his hand over the waters they would not have parted,

DISCUSSION QUESTIONS

1. Why did God harden Pharaoh's heart?
2. How does Satan try to keep us enslaved in sin?
3. How can we be delivered?
4. To what limits will God go in saving His people?
5. What part should singing play in our lives?
6. What is the value and importance of praise?

and the Israelites would not have escaped. How much depended on this one man!

Moses led the people in a further expression of praise and gratitude: "The Lord is my strength and song, and he is become my salvation" (v. 2). Christians of all ages have joined in singing this. If the Lord is all three of these things to us we will be a strong, happy, victorious people.

"I will prepare him an habitation" is better translated, "I will praise Him" (NASB). This preserves the parallelism of the Hebrew poetry here, as reflected in the New American Standard Bible:

> This is my God,
> and I will praise Him;
> My father's God,
> and I will extol Him.

The song continued: "The Lord is a man of war: the Lord is his name." The Hebrew for *Lord* is *Yahweh* (or, "Jehovah"). Rawlinson writes: "In the very name, Jehovah, is implied all might, all power, and so necessarily the strength to prevail in battle. The name, meaning 'the Existent,' implies that nothing else has any real existence independently of Him; and if no existence, then necessarily no strength" ("Exodus," *Ellicott's*, p. 242).

We have called this "Moses' Song." Rawlinson makes this observation: "With his usual modesty, Moses does not say that he composed the magnificent ode . . . ; but it is scarcely conceivable that it can have had any other author. It bears a close resemblance to the Egyptian religious poetry, with which Moses—and probably no other Israelite of the time—would have been familiar from his early training; and it breathes the elevated tone of religious sentiment that was scarcely shared

with Moses by any contemporary" ("Exodus," *Ellicott's*, p. 241).

B. God's Mercy: vv. 4-19

This is the theme of the song. It is highlighted in verse 13: "Thou in thy mercy hast led forth the people which thou hast redeemed: thou hast guided them in thy strength unto thy holy habitation." This is prophetic of what God was going to do, in leading them all the way to the Promised Land. On the way they would meet the rulers of Edom and Moab, but God would put His fear on them—as well as on the inhabitants of Canaan (v. 15). This last part was literally fulfilled (Joshua 2:9; 5:1). Moses was assured that God would, without fail, plant His people safely in their own land (v. 17).

The last part of the song (v. 19) echoes the first part (vv. 4-12). It celebrates the overthrow of Pharaoh's host in the Red Sea.

C. Miriam's Music: vv. 20-21

Miriam "the sister of Aaron" (and so of Moses as well) was a "prophetess." Even in the Old Testament women held this status, as also in the New Testament (Acts 21:9).

She took a "timbrel," or tambourine, and led the women in dances of joy. Even today in the Middle East, one sees women dancing together (as at wedding feasts) and men dancing together, but in separate groups.

Verse 21 is very similar to verse 1. Probably this was a refrain that was repeated throughout the song of praise. "Answered" may suggest that the singing was at least partly antiphonal, perhaps between the men and the women.

CONTEMPORARY APPLICATION

Singing songs of praises to God for His salvation should always be a vital part of our worship. One of the great assets of Protestant worship has always

been congregational singing. May the time never come when we pay choirs to do our singing for us!

And this singing should be joyous.

It is universally recognized that one of the powerful factors in the success of the Evangelical Revival of the eighteenth century was the joyful, spontaneous singing of the Methodist congregations. There is something very contagious about the joy of the Lord as expressed in song.

CALLED INTO COVENANT

DEVOTIONAL READING	Deuteronomy 6:4-15

ADULTS

Topic: *Called into Covenant*

Background Scripture: Exodus 19—20; Deuteronomy 10—12

Scripture Lesson: Exodus 19:2-9; Deuteronomy 11:8-9, 18-19

Memory Verse: *Now therefore, if you will obey my voice and keep my covenant, you shall be my own possession among all peoples; for all the earth is mine, and you shall be to me a kingdom of priests and a holy nation.* Exodus 19:5-6

YOUTH

Topic: *The Basis of a New Community*

Background Scripture: Exodus 19—20; Deuteronomy 10—12

Scripture Lesson: Exodus 19:2-9; Deuteronomy 11:8-9, 18-19

Memory Verse: *Now therefore, if you will obey my voice and keep my covenant, you shall be my own possession among all peoples; for all the earth is mine, and you shall be to me a kingdom of priests and a holy nation.* Exodus 19:5-6

CHILDREN

Topic: *Learning God's Ways*

Background Scripture: Exodus 19; Deuteronomy 10—12

Scripture Lesson: Exodus 19:2-9; Deuteronomy 11:18-21

Memory Verse: *. . . what does the Lord your God require of you, but to fear the Lord your God, to walk in all his ways, to love him, to serve the Lord your God with all your heart and with all your soul.* Deuteronomy 10:12

DAILY BIBLE READINGS

Mon., June 27: The Tablets and the Ark, Deuteronomy 10:1-5
Tues., June 28: What the Lord Requires, Deuteronomy 10:12-22.
Wed., June 29: Reasons for Love and Obedience, Deuteronomy 11:1-8.
Thurs., June 30: Remove all Hindrances, Deuteronomy 12:1-7.
Fri., July 1: Meeting with God, Deuteronomy 12:1-7.
Sat., July 2: A Word of Warning, Deuteronomy 12:29-32.

Sun., July 3: The Covenant Relationship, Deuteronomy
6:4-15.

LESSON AIM

To help us understand what it means to be God's covenant people.

LESSON SETTING

Time: About 1447 B.C. (or 1295 B.C.)

Place: Mount Sinai

LESSON OUTLINE

Called into Covenant

I. Israel's Arrival at Sinai: Exodus 19:1-2

II. Moses on the Mount: Exodus 19:3-6
   A. Reminder of Deliverance: vv. 3-4
   B. A Covenant People: v. 5
   C. A Holy Nation: v. 6

III. Moses and the People: Exodus 19:7-9
   A. Reporting God's Words: v. 7
   B. Response of the People: v. 8
   C. Reporting the People's Words: v. 9

IV. Preparation for Receiving the Law: Exodus 19:10-25

V. The Ten Commandments: Exodus 20:1-17

VI. Keeping the Law: Deuteronomy 11:8-9
   A. Condition for Possessing the Land: v. 8
   B. Condition for Continuing in the Land: v. 9

VII. The Land of Canaan: Deuteronomy 11:10-17

VIII. Importance of the Law: Deuteronomy 11:18-19
   A. Storing It in One's Heart: v. 18
   B. Teaching It to the Children: v. 19

**SUGGESTED
INTRODUCTION
FOR ADULTS**

Today we begin our study of a new unit, "God
Creates a Covenant People." This happened at Mount
Sinai, where the Law was given to Moses. The Law indicated the conditions of the covenant. If the people
obeyed the Law, they would receive the benefits of the
covenant. If they refused to obey, they would suffer the
consequences.

It was a high moment in the life of the Israelites. They
had been redeemed from Egyptian bondage. They had
been delivered from the enemy miraculously at the Red
Sea. Now as a redeemed people they entered into a
covenant with God, to obey His law and do His will.

It is not enough for us to have our sins forgiven, to
know that we are adopted into the family of God. We

must enter into full covenant relationship with Him, solemnly agreeing to do His will with our whole heart.

Being a Christian is more than having our sins forgiven. It is more than experiencing a joyous relief because the past is all put under the blood, the guilt is gone, the slavery of sin is ended. Being a Christian involves entering into a covenant with God that we will keep His commandments. It means giving our will in full surrender to His will. It means that we no longer belong to ourselves; we are God's own possession, for Him to do with as He desires.

Being a Christian involves a full commitment to Christ. When we have made that, we are God's free people, His covenant people today.

1. God instructed the Israelites to teach their children.
2. Boys and girls need to know the Bible so that they will know what pleases the Lord.
3. But we must also obey Him.
4. That is how we follow God's ways.

THE LESSON COMMENTARY

I. ISRAEL'S ARRIVAL AT SINAI: Exodus 19:1-2

It was in the third month after the Exodus from Egypt that the Israelites reached Mount Sinai. There they "camped before the mount" (v. 2).

Since our last lesson they had tasted the bitter waters of Marah, which were made sweet for them (15:22-26). They also had camped for a while at an oasis called Elim, where there were twelve wells and seventy palm trees (15:27).

In the Wilderness of Sin the people had complained to Moses because of a shortage of food (16:1-3). In response to this, God sent quails for meat in the evening and manna for bread in the morning (16:4-36).

In Rephidim there was no water for the people to drink (17:1). Again the Israelites "grumbled against Moses" (NASB) for bringing them out of Egypt (16:3). God directed their leader to strike a rock, and water

gushed out to satisfy their thirst (16:4-7).

The first enemies encountered by the Israelites in the wilderness were the Amalekites. They attacked Israel (17:8). Moses appointed Joshua as general of Israel's army. As the spiritual leaders, Moses, his brother Aaron, and an associate named Hur went to the top of a hill overlooking the field of battle. When Moses held up his hands, Israel prospered, but when he let them down, Amalek prevailed. So Aaron and Hur held up his hands until sunset. Thus Amalek was defeated and came under divine curse (17:9-16).

Chapter 18 records the visit of Moses' father-in-law, Jethro. He gave his son-in-law wise advice about organizing his administration of justice.

Now the Israelites were at Sinai. Here they spent about a year (cf. Numbers 10:11-12). During that time they received God's Law through Moses. They also built the tabernacle, a task which probably consumed a considerable amount of time.

II. MOSES ON THE MOUNT:
Exodus 19:3-6

A. Reminder of Deliverance: vv. 3-4

Moses climbed the mountain to be in God's special presence. In response, the Lord spoke from the top of the mount and gave him a message for the Israelites. They were to remember how God had miraculously destroyed the Egyptians, but had borne His own people "on eagles' wings" and brought them to Himself. This is a beautiful expression to describe God's loving care. George Rawlinson writes: "Compare Deut. xxxii. 11, 'As an eagle stirreth up her nest, fluttereth over her young, spreadeth abroad her wings, taketh them, *beareth them upon her wings.*' When its young are first fledged, the eagle is said to assist them in their flight by flying beneath them, so that they may settle upon its wings or back, if necessary. God means that He has bestowed upon His people the same tender and powerful care, has borne them up mightily when they might have fallen, supported their first flight as fledglings, and so saved them from disaster" ("Exodus," *Ellicott's Commentary on the Whole Bible*, I, 256).

B. A Covenant People: v. 5

Here we have the heart of God's message through Moses. If the Israelites would obey God's voice and keep His covenant, they would be His "peculiar treasure" above all other peoples of the earth. In the King James Version the word *peculiar* is used five times in the Old Testament (Exodus 19:5; Deuteronomy 14:2; 26:18; Psalm 135:4; Ecclesiastes 2:8) and twice in the New Testament (Titus 2:14; I Peter 2:9). In none of these cases does it carry the meaning which

it has for us today—"unusual or eccentric; strange, queer, odd." The Hebrew and Greek words translated "peculiar" mean "for one's own possession." If we substituted *precious* for *peculiar* we would have a meaningful translation. There are over two hundred words like this in the King James Version that are used in a very different way from their present meaning. God does not want a "peculiar" people, but a *precious* people.

C. A Holy Nation: v. 6

God said also that the Israelites would "be unto me a kingdom of priests and an holy nation." This combination is picked up in I Peter 2:9 and applied to the New Israel, the church. We are to be a "royal priesthood." The Protestant Reformation rightly emphasized the priesthood of all believers, on the basis of this passage. We can all come directly to God through Christ.

The basic meaning of *holy* is "set apart to God, sacred." But when applied to people it also has the moral connotation of "pure, sanctified."

III. MOSES AND THE PEOPLE:
Exodus 19:7-9

A. Reporting God's Words: v. 7

When Moses came down from Mount Sinai he summoned "the elders of the people." These are the "rulers" or judges whom Moses had appointed at the urging of his father-in-law (18:24-26). He wanted their assistance in communicating God's words effectively to the people. So he first told them what the Lord's message was.

B. Response of the People: v. 8

The people were always quick to say that they would obey all of God's commands; but often they were slow in carrying out their promises. Unfortunately, they have many successors in the church today!

C. Reporting the People's Words: v. 9

Having told the people what God had said, Moses now told the Lord what the people had promised. God's presence was symbolized by "a thick cloud," hiding Him, as it were, from the people's gaze. By this the people knew that it was the Lord who was speaking.

IV. PREPARATION FOR RECEIVING THE LAW: Exodus 19:10-25

What we have described here is the spectacular pageantry of an inaugural ceremony. God was making a covenant with His people and inaugurating the age of the Law. It was a most significant moment in Israel's history and one that called for an impressive demonstration of God's presence.

God told Moses to "sanctify" the people for two days (v. 10), and on the third day He would "come down in the sight of all the people upon mount Sinai" (v. 11). The term *sanctify* here evidently means "purify." Rawlinson comments: "Sanctification is twofold—outward and inward. The real essential preparation for approach to God is inward sanctification; but no external command can secure this. Moses was therefore instructed to issue directions for outward purification; and it was left to the spiritual insight of the people to perceive and recognize that such purity symbolized and required internal purification as its counterpart" ("Exodus," *Ellicott's*, p. 257).

Moses was also instructed to set bounds around the holy mount. Any person or animal that touched the precipitous mountain would be put to death (vv. 12-13).

The third day was an exciting time. Perhaps the people were wakened by the roar of thunder. When they pulled aside their tent flaps, they saw a thick cloud (cf. v. 9) enveloping the top of the mountain and heard the sound of a trumpet "exceeding loud" (v. 16). Billows of smoke rose from the mount, because the Lord descended on it in power. Added to all this was a severe earthquake, which shook the mountain violently (v. 18).

Why all this divine pyrotechnic display? God wanted His people to have a vivid sense of His holiness and majesty so that they would reverence Him properly. He also wanted them to realize the incomparable importance of this occasion of giving the Law.

As the sound of the trumpet became longer and louder, Moses spoke and God answered him. He called Moses to the top of the mount to receive the Law (v. 20). To make doubly sure that the people did not carelessly touch the sacred mountain, God told Moses once more to go down and warn them (v. 21).

This was an epoch in the history of religion. The true God was making a covenant with His redeemed people and giving them the Law that would bind that covenant. This was an occasion they would never forget.

V. THE TEN COMMANDMENTS: Exodus 20:1-17

Because the main religious danger that confronted the Israelites was from the surrounding pagan polytheism, the first two commandments speak to this situation. The first and basic commandment is: "Thou shalt have no other gods before me" (v. 3). The true God must have our supreme devotion. Idolatry was specifically forbidden in the second commandment: "Thou shalt not make unto thee any graven image" (v. 4). Because of its importance in the face of the culture of that day, this prohibition is elaborated (vv. 5-6).

The third commandment is: "Thou shalt not take the name of the Lord thy God in vain" (v. 7). The fourth, "Remember the sabbath day, to keep it holy," is also elaborated. Sabbath observance was one of the strongest emphases of Judaism, as we see reflected in the Gospels.

The first four commandments have to do with man's duties to God. They actually occupy more space than the remaining six, which deal with man's duties to his fellowman. "Honour thy father and thy mother" (v. 12) is the first commandment with a promise, as Paul noted (Ephesians 6:2).

The sixth, seventh, and eighth commands forbid three crimes that are being committed with increasing frequency today—murder, adultery, and theft. The ninth warns against bearing false witness, and the tenth against covetousness.

When the people saw and heard the striking manifestations of God's power and presence, they "stood afar off" in reverential fear (v. 18). They were afraid that if they came near to God they would die (v. 19).

Moses sought to comfort them and at the same time to warn them: "Fear not; for God is come to prove you, and that his fear may be before your faces, that ye sin not" (v. 20).

VI. KEEPING THE LAW:
Deuteronomy 11:8-9

A. Condition for Possessing the Land: v. 8

Obedience is the price of strength. God said that if the Israelites would keep all His commandments, they would be strong and take possession of the land of Canaan. Disobedience always brings weakness and defeat.

B. Condition for Continuing in the Land: v. 9

It was not only God's will that the Israelites should conquer Canaan, the land He had promised to Abraham, Isaac, and Jacob, but that also they should dwell there for the rest of time. It was only because of their sin and disobedience that they were taken into captivity out of their land by the Assyrians (722 B.C.) and the Babylonians (586 B.C.). The history of Israel is a vivid commentary on this verse. Obey

and stay, or disobey and depart. This is what happened dramatically in the history of God's people.

VII. THE LAND OF CANAAN
Deuteronomy 11:10-17

Though Moses had never seen the Promised Land, yet with prophetic faith he assured the people that it "is not like the land of Egypt from which you came, where you used to sow your seed and water it with your foot like a vegetable garden" (v. 10, NASB). W. L. Alexander makes this comment: "Canaan was not like Egypt, a country that depended for its fertility on being irrigated by man's labour or by artificial processes, but was a land where the supply and distribution of water was provided for in natural reservoirs and channels, by means of which the rain which God, who cared for the land, sent plentifully on it, was made available for useful purposes. In Egypt there is little or no rain, and the people are dependent on the annual overflowing of the Nile for the proper irrigation of fields; and as this lasts only for a short period, the water has to be stored and redistributed by articifical means, often of a very laborious kind" ("Deuteronomy," *The Pulpit Commentary*, pp. 194-95). (It does rain once in a great while in northern Egypt, as we discovered one day when caught in a sudden shower at the Pyramids near Cairo!)

The reference to watering the land "with your foot" is intriguing. The New American Standard Bible explains in a marginal note: "I.e., probably a treadmill." As one travels along the Nile River today one can see water being pumped up from the river for irrigating the land. Sometimes the power is furnished by donkeys or camels.

But W. M. Thomson in his fascinating work, *The Land and the Book*, gives a description which perhaps fits better the situation in the time of Moses. He writes: "The reference, perhaps, is to the manner of conducting the water about from plant to plant and from furrow to furrow. I have often watched the gardener at this fatiguing and unhealthy work. When one place is sufficiently saturated, he pushes aside the sandy soil between it and the next furrow with his foot, and thus continues to do until all are watered" (II, 279).

In contrast to Egypt, the land of Canaan "is a land of hills and valleys, and drinketh water of the rain of heaven" (v. 11). It is "a land which the Lord thy God careth for" (v. 12), from the beginning of the year to the end of it. God had chosen a good land for His people.

But their enjoyment of it was dependent on their obedience (v. 13). If they loved God and obeyed His commandments, then He would give them rain in due season, "the first rain and the latter rain" (v. 14). The first rain is that "which falls from the middle of October to the end of December, which prepares the soil for the seed, and keeps it moist after the seed is sown." The latter rain "falls in March and April, about the time when the grain is ripening for harvest" ("Deuteronomy," *Pulpit*, p. 195). This would give them good crops of wheat—not "corn" (KJV)—and grapes and olive oil. But if they disobeyed, God would banish them from the land (vv. 16-17).

DISCUSSION QUESTIONS

1. Why do we need to recall our conversion experience?
2. What is God's covenant with us in Christ?
3. What does it mean to be "holy"?
4. How should be prepare ourselves for coming into God's presence each Sunday morning?
5. What is the importance of the Ten Commandments today?
6. What are the conditions for our retaining our covenant relationship to God?

VIII. IMPORTANCE OF THE LAW: Deuteronomy 11:18-19

A. Storing It in One's Heart: v. 18

The Israelites were told to lay up in their hearts these commandments that God was giving them. They were not to forget them, but live by them daily.

They were also instructed to "bind them for a sign upon your hand, that they may be as frontlets between your eyes." The Israelites later took this very literally. They made phylacteries (see Matthew 23:5), which they wore strapped on their forehead and left wrist. These were small boxes containing strips of parchment, on which were inscribed Exodus 13:2-10, 11-17 and Deuteronomy 6:4-10, 13-22. These were worn during times of prayer. Even today at the famous West Wall in Jerusalem—until 1967 called the Wailing Wall—one can see tables holding phylacteries. As men come to pray, they fasten these on their foreheads and wrists.

B. Teaching It to the Children: v. 19

The Israelites were to teach God's commandments to their children, "speaking of them when thou sittest in thine house, and when thou walkest by the way, when thou liest down, and when thou risest up." This reminds us of the supreme importance of having religious devotions in our homes. It is essential that every Christian home should have family worship each evening, when all can be present. In most homes today, it is difficult to get this in satisfactorily in the morning, with people leaving at different times for work or school. Right after the evening meal or just before bedtime for the children is usually best.

But what about "when thou risest up"? A good practice is to have a few verses of the Bible read at the breakfast table, followed by a prayer that includes the usual "blessing" or "grace" or "thanks." We need to impress on our children a love for God's Word.

CONTEMPORARY APPLICATION

One of the finest things that a Christian can do is to memorize Scripture. It is amazing how much one can store up in his mind or heart if he gives reasonable attention to this.

We read of a very busy preacher who suddenly found himself one day flat on his back in a hospital bed. His first reaction was one of frustration that he was unable to be doing his accustomed work.

Lying there, too weak to hold a Bible in his hand, he began to repeat the twenty-third Psalm. He came to the second verse: "He maketh me to lie down." That was as far as he got. The Holy Spirit seemed to put a period there, and said, "I wanted you to lie down and listen to me; you have been too busy with your work."

Lying awake at night, sick, traveling, working—there are many times when memorized Scripture can be a great blessing to us. When we can't *read* our Bibles, we can recall from memory those passages we have stored in our hearts and minds.

A WORSHIPING PEOPLE

DEVOTIONAL READING	Psalm 150

ADULTS

Topic: *A Worshiping People*

Background Scripture: *Exodus 33:1—36:1; 40*

Scripture Lesson: *Exodus 33:9-16; 35:29*

Memory Verse: *My presence will go with you, and I will give you rest.* Exodus 33:14

YOUTH

Topic: *New Patterns of Worship*

Background Scripture: *Exodus 33:1—35:22; 40:1-38*

Scripture Lesson: *Exodus 33:9-16; 35:29*

Memory Verse: *My presence will go with you, and I will give you rest.* Exodus 33:14

CHILDREN

Topic: *Worshiping God*

Background Scripture: *Exodus 33—40*

Scripture Lesson: *Exodus 33:7-17; 35:20-22*

Memory Verse: *O magnify the Lord with me, and let us exalt his name together!* Psalm 34:3

DAILY BIBLE READINGS

Mon., July 4: An Encounter with God, Exodus 33:18-23.
Tues., July 5: Preparation for Worship, Exodus 34:12-17.
Wed., July 6: Thanksgiving for Deliverance, Psalm 114.
Thurs., July 7: Testimony of the Redeemed, Psalm 107:1-9.
Fri., July 8: A Hymn of Faith, Psalm 108.
Sat., July 9: Sing a New Song, Psalm 98:1-6.
Sun., July 10: An Anthem of Praise, Psalm 150.

LESSON AIM

To help us see some things that are involved in true worship.

LESSON SETTING

Time: About 1440 B.C.

Place: Mount Sinai

LESSON OUTLINE

A Worshiping People

    I. A Rebellious People: Exodus 33:1-3

II. **A Repentant People:** Exodus 33:4-8
   A. Stripping Off Their Ornaments: vv. 4-6
   B. Seeking God's Favor: vv. 7-8

III. **A Worshiping People:** Exodus 33:9-11
   A. The Symbol of God's Presence: v. 9
   B. The Response of the People: v. 10
   C. The Man of God: v. 11

IV. **An Accompanying Presence:** Exodus 33:12-16
   A. Moses' Concern: v. 12
   B. Moses' Petition: v. 13
   C. The Promised Presence: v. 14
   D. The Necessity for the Divine Presence: vv. 15-16

V. **A Place of Worship:** Exodus 35:4-35
   A. A Willing Offering: vv. 4-19
   B. A Generous Offering: vv. 20-29
   C. The Willing Workmen: vv. 30-35

SUGGESTED INTRODUCTION FOR ADULTS

In last week's lesson we studied about the giving of the Ten Commandments at Sinai (Exodus 20). This was followed by setting out in minute detail the moral demands of daily living (chaps. 21—23). Then God called for Moses, his close associates, and the seventy elders of the people to come to Him at the mount (24:1). Finally Moses went up on the mountain and spent forty days in God's presence (24:18).

This time the Lord gave him instructions about building the tabernacle as a place of worship (chaps. 25—27). Precise specifications were given for the ark (25:10-16), the mercy seat (25:17-19), the cherubim (25:20-22), the table of showbread (25:23-30), and the golden lampstand (25:31-39). Moses was warned, "And see that you make them after the pattern for them, which was shown to you on the mountain" (25:40, NASB). Chapter 26 gives the specifications for the tabernacle building, and chapter 27 for the altar of sacrifice and the outer court. Chapters 28-30 describe the clothing and work of the priests.

SUGGESTED INTRODUCTION FOR YOUTH

The last sixteen chapters of Exodus (25—40) are taken up largely with the detailed instructions for building the tabernacle and then with the actual construction. This suggests that God places a high premium on the matter of worship.

Today we have new patterns of worship. But the necessity and importance of worship still remain.

Every once in a while we hear it suggested that the church, as such, is passé, that we don't need the church any more—we should forget about beautiful sanctuaries and lovely organ music, and meet on hillsides or in private homes.

But a proper place and time for worship are helpful, as

most people find. Instead of abandoning our buildings, we should seek to make God's presence more real there.

CONCEPTS FOR CHILDREN

1. We are saved through believing in Jesus.
2. But our spiritual life is nurtured by worship.
3. True worship is responding in love to God's love for us.
4. Children can bring offerings of love to God.

THE LESSON COMMENTARY

I. A REBELLIOUS PEOPLE: Exodus 33:1-3

The Lord told Moses to go up to the Promised Land—"thou and the people which thou hast brought up out of the land of Egypt" (v. 1). It was really God who had delivered them from Egyptian slavery and from Pharaoh's host. But they had rebelled against Him. So He now refers to them as the people Moses had brought up from Egypt.

He does promise to "send an angel before thee," who would drive out the inhabitants of Canaan (v. 2). Again he reminds the Israelites that the country He is giving them is "a land flowing with milk and honey" (v. 3). But He gives a solemn warning: "I will not go up in the midst of thee; for thou art a stiffnecked people: lest I consume thee in the way." The Israelites were "obstinate" (NASB), or "stubborn." They had rebelled against God.

How had they shown this obstinacy? The previous chapter (32) tells the story in detail. Moses had stayed on Mount Sinai for forty days (24:18). The people became restless; where was their leader?

Finally they said to Aaron—the next in command—"Up, make us gods, which shall go before us; for as for this Moses, the man that brought us up out of the land of Egypt, we wot not what is become of him" (v. 1). ("Wot" is old English for "know.")

It is impossible to explain Aaron's defection at this point. He took the people's gold earrings, melted them, and made a golden calf. Aaron built an altar in front of it, and the people joined in a drunken, sensual orgy (v. 6).

On the mountain, meanwhile, God informed Moses of what had happened. Calling them "a stiffnecked people" (v. 9), the Lord proposed to destroy them all and make of Moses a great nation (v. 10). Only the unselfish plea of this man of God (vv. 11-13) saved the people (v. 14). There is no greater intercessory prayer in the Bible than that contained in verses 31-32.

II. A REPENTANT PEOPLE: Exodus 33:4-8

A. Stripping Off Their Ornaments: vv. 4-6

"When the people heard these evil tidings, they mourned" (v. 4). In obedience to Moses' command (v. 5), they "stripped themselves of their ornaments by the mount Horeb" (v. 6)—that is, Mount Sinai. In verse 4 it says, "No man did put on his ornaments." There is no real conflict between this and the next two verses. "Put off" (v. 5) means "leave off"—that is, put them aside altogether. This is what the people proceeded to do. They were so filled with fear at the threat of destruction (v. 5) that they were willing to give up wearing any ornaments, as a sign of their true repentance.

This was a real sacrifice for them. Oriental people in general have been fond of wearing jewelry, and the

Egyptians were especially noted for this. George Rawlinson writes: "To strip himself of his ornaments was a great act of self-denial on the part of an Oriental; but it was done commonly in the case of mourning on account of a family bereavement, and sometimes in the case of national misfortunes" ("Exodus," *Ellicott's Commentary on the Whole Bible*, I, 314).

B. Seeking God's Favor: vv. 7-8

"Moses took the tabernacle and pitched it without the camp ... and called it the Tabernacle of the congregation" (v. 7). But the tabernacle was not yet built (40:2)! The correct translation here is: "Moses used to take the tent and pitch it outside the camp ... and he called it the tent of meeting" (NASB). Until the tabernacle was completed he pitched a tent—perhaps his own—for a temporary place of meeting with God. Everyone who "sought the Lord" would go out to this tent to pray.

When Moses went out to the tent of meeting, all the people were in the habit of standing at attention at the entrances of their tents. They watched their leader and prophet until he entered the tent. It was a mark of respect for him and reverence for God. In worship today we tend to be too casual in the presence of the King of kings.

III. A WORSHIPING PEOPLE: Exodus 33:9-11

A. The Symbol of God's Presence: v. 9

"And it came about, whenever Moses entered the tent, the pillar of cloud would descend and stand at the entrance of the tent; and the Lord would speak with Moses" (NASB). While the Israelites camped at the foot of Mount Sinai, the pillar of cloud usually enveloped the top of the mountain (19:16, 20; 20:21; 24:15-18; 34:5). But this symbol of God's presence came down each time Moses approached the tent of meeting.

It will be noticed that *the Lord* is in italics in the King James Version, indicating that it is not in the original. The voice came out of the cloud, where God's special presence dwelt.

This is the same pillar of cloud that had led the fleeing Israelites to the Red Sea and protected them there. After the miraculous crossing, it had continued to lead them each day as they journeyed toward the mount of God.

B. The Response of the People: v. 10

"When all the people saw the pillar of cloud standing at the entrance of the tent, all the people would arise and worship, each at the entrance of his tent" (NASB). It is probable that Moses went out to the tent at a given time each day, and the people were watching for him at this time.

"Worshipped" is literally "bowed themselves down." The people sensed God's presence and bowed their heads reverently before Him.

Reverence seems to be almost a lost art today. Some people even attend the Sunday morning worship service dressed in casual fashion. As is usually the case, the way they are dressed affects the way they act. The practice of wearing one's "Sunday best" to church is still a wholesome one. And bowing our heads in silent prayer when we sit down in the pew is a recognition of the fact that we expect to find God's presence in the sanctuary.

C. The Man of God: v. 11

"And the Lord spake unto Moses face to face, as a man speaketh unto his friend." We find this idea again in Numbers 12:8 and Deuteronomy 34:10. Rawlinson comments: "This is clearly spoken of as a privilege peculiar to Moses; but in what exactly the pecularity consisted is not apparent. Some special closeness of approach is no doubt meant—some nearness such as had been enjoyed by no mortal previously" ("Exodus," *Ellicott's*, p. 315).

When Moses returned to camp each time, his servant Joshua stayed at the tent. The leader's presence was needed in the camp. Rawlinson writes: "He left, however, his personal attendant ('minister'), Joshua, to watch and guard the sacred structure during his absence. It is remarkable that the trust was committed to Joshua, rather than to Aaron, or any of the Levites. Probably the reason for this was, that Joshua alone had no part in the idolatry of the calf" ("Exodus," *The Pulpit Commentary*, II, 350).

IV. AN ACCOMPANYING PRESENCE:
Exodus 33:12-16

A. Moses' Concern: v. 12

The Lord had said to Moses, "I will send an angel before thee ... for I will not go up in the midst of thee" (vv. 2-3). This brought a deepening concern to Moses. Who was this angel that was going to take the place of God's presence?

Since the Lord was conversing with Moses as with a friend (v. 11), this mere man felt bold enough to say, "See, you tell me to bring these people up to Canaan, but you haven't told me whom you are sending with me. Yet you say that you know me by name and that I have found favor in your sight" (my own translation).

B. Moses' Petition: v. 13

In the light of all this, Moses makes his plea: "Shew me now thy way, that I may know thee." He wants to understand God better. In order that he may continue to find favor with the Lord, he wants to know the Lord's ways, to follow them.

In speaking to Moses, God had called the Israelites "thy people, which thou broughtest out of the land of Egypt" (32:7; cf. 33:1). Moses now becomes bold enough to say, "Consider that this nation is thy people." It

was not Moses' choice to lead the Israelites out of Egypt; God had specifically called him to this task and given him this assignment. So he was perfectly justified in saying, "No, Lord, they are your people." The pastor who is called to the ministry can say the same thing when the going is hard.

C. The Promised Presence: v. 14

Moses' prayer was answered. The Lord assured him: "My presence shall go with thee, and I will give thee rest." Basically this perhaps meant that God would give the people rest in Canaan.

But this is one of the most beautiful promises in the Old Testament for Christians. What words could be more comforting for us when the future looks fearsome and forbidding? And Moses needed these words personally.

D. The Necessity for the Divine Presence: vv. 15-16

It may be that the "thee" in God's promise left Moses not yet quite satisfied. He wanted to be sure that God's presence was going with the people as well as with him.

So he said to the Lord: "If Thy presence does not go with us, do not lead us up from here. For how then can it be known that I have found favor in Thy sight, I and Thy people? Is it not by Thy going with us, so that we, I and Thy people, may be distinguished from all other people who are upon the face of the earth?" (NASB).

On the word "distinguished" Rawlinson makes this comment: "God's presence with them would distinguish them from all the other nations of the earth—place them in a category alone and apart from all others" ("Exodus," *Pulpit*, p. 352).

This is an important truth for us today. It is only God's presence in our hearts and lives that distinguishes us from other people. It is nothing in *us*, but all of *Him*.

God evidently granted Moses his request in full. For we read in verse

17: "I will also do this thing of which you have spoken; for you have found favor in My sight, and I have known you by name" (NASB). The last expression emphasizes Moses' close personal relationship to God.

V. A PLACE OF WORSHIP:
Exodus 35:4-35

A. A Willing Offering: vv. 4-19

The tabernacle built at Mount Sinai was an expensive structure. It was to be a building worthy of the King of kings and Lord of lords. So no cheap materials were used in building it.

All this required sacrificial offerings from the people. They were to offer with "a willing heart" (v. 5). That is still the Number One requirement for all giving to the Lord. In the New Testament we read: "Each man should give what he has decided in his heart to give, not reluctantly or under compulsion, for God loves a cheerful giver" (II Corinthians 9:7, NIV). The Greek word for "cheerful" is *hilaros*, from which we get "*hilarious*."

God is not so much concerned about the amount we give as the spirit in which we give. We owe the tithe to the Lord, and we must pay it. But above that it is "free will offerings" that please the Lord.

The first offering for the tabernacle was to consist of metals—gold, silver, and brass (or bronze, or copper). The gold was a symbol of Deity, the silver of redemption, and the brass of judgment. A study of the typology of the tabernacle will show how well these fit.

After this came offerings of materials to be used in the construction of the tabernacle: "blue, purple and scarlet material, fine linen, goats' hair, and rams' skins dyed red, and porpoise skins, and acacia wood" (vv. 6-7, NASB). Added to this was: "Oil for the light, and spices for anointing oil, and for the sweet incense, and onyx stones, and stones to be set for the ephod, and for the breastplate" (vv. 8-9).

Besides giving these items, there was much work to be done. So the Lord said through Moses: "And let every skillful man among you come, and make all that the Lord has commanded" (v. 10, NASB). There follows a long list of the things to be made (vv. 11-19).

B. A Generous Offering: vv. 20-29

The people responded beautifully, as God's own people always do to the challenge of definite need. We read: "And they came, every one whose heart stirred him up, and every one whom his spirit made willing, and they brought the Lord's offering to the work of the tabernacle of the congregation, and for all his service, and for the holy garments. And they came, both men and women, as many as were willing hearted, and brought. . . ." (vv. 21-22). It must have been a wonderful sight!

The women not only brought what they had on hand; they worked hard to get things ready. The account says: "And all the women that were wise hearted did spin with their hands, and brought that which they had spun, both of blue, and of purple, and of scarlet, and of fine linen. And all the women whose heart stirred them up in wisdom spun goats' hair" (vv. 25-26).

DISCUSSION QUESTIONS

1. Why did the Israelites go into idolatry right at Mount Sinai?
2. What are some modern idolatries?
3. How do we show true repentance?
4. Why could Moses approach God's presence?
5. How does God's presence bring rest?
6. What spiritual benefit is there in giving?

This is all summed up in verse 29: "The children of Israel brought a willing offering unto the Lord, every man and woman, whose heart made them willing to bring for all manner of work, which the Lord had commanded to be made by the hand of Moses." This went on and on. For we read further: "And they brought yet unto him free offerings every morning" (36:3).

As often happens today when the spirit of giving comes on a congregation, the people were so generous that the needs were more than met. Moses was informed: "The people bring much more than enough for the service of the work, which the Lord commanded to make" (36:5). The workmen had more materials than they could use.

The upshot was that a new order had to be given: "Let neither man nor woman make any more work for the offering of the sanctuary. So the people were restrained from bringing" (v. 6). The people had really given hilariously!

C. The Willing Workmen: vv. 30-35

The generous offering of the people notwithstanding, the tabernacle could not have been constructed without the skilled work of men who were fitted for such a task. Fortunately there were such available. The Lord had called a man of the tribe of Judah, "And he hath filled him with the spirit of God, in wisdom, in understanding,

and in knowledge, and in all manner of workmanship" (v. 31). Rawlinson comments: "By 'wisdom' is probably meant the power to invent and originate artistic forms; by 'understanding,' the ability to appreciate artistic suggestions received from others; by 'knowledge,' acquaintance with the methods and processes of art" ("Exodus," Ellicott's, p. 306). With regard to the expression "in all manner of workmanship," Rawlinson goes on: "He was also to possess that wonderful dexterity of hand on which the power of artistic execution mainly depends."

Bezaleel was to "devise curious works" (v. 32) and "make any manner of cunning work" (v. 33). Obviously "curious" and "cunning" are not used in the same way that we use those terms today. The latter probably means "inventive" (NASB). The former has to do with intricate designs.

With regards to Bezaleel's skill, Rawlinson makes this comment: " 'Every good gift and every perfect gift [intellectual power no less than others] is from above, and cometh down from the Father of lights' (James i. 17). Artistic ability is a Divine gift, a very precious gift, best employed in God's direct service, and always to be employed in subordination to His will, as an improving, elevating, and refining—not as a corrupting—influence" ("Exodus," Ellicott's, p. 306). The great tragedy of our day is that art students and professionals too often prostitute their gifts in sensual productions.

CONTEMPORARY APPLICATION

The Israelites had "a pillar of cloud" as their guide. While they camped for months at the foot of Mount Sinai, the cloudy pillar acted as a symbol of God's presence with them.

In this Christian age we do not need any such visible sign. The Holy

Spirit in our hearts is our Guide. He makes the presence of God real to us.

We should treasure this Divine Presence and do nothing to grieve the Holy Spirit. We need Him every day as our Paraclete, our Helper in every way. That is our only safety.

July 17, 1977

THE FULFILLMENT OF THE PROMISE DELAYED

DEVOTIONAL
READING

Psalm 77:1-15

ADULTS

Topic: *Unbelief Delays Covenant Fulfillment*

Background Scripture: *Numbers 13—14*

Scripture Lesson: *Numbers 13:30—14:10a*

Memory Verse: *And the Lord said to Moses, "How long will this people despise me? And how long will they not believe in me, in spite of all the signs which I have wrought among them?"* Numbers 14:11

YOUTH

Topic: *Promises Delayed*

Background Scripture: *Numbers 13—14*

Scripture Lesson: *Numbers 13:30—14:10a*

Memory Verse: *And the Lord said to Moses, "How long will this people despise me? And how long will they not believe in me, in spite of all the signs which I have wrought among them?"* Numbers 14:11

CHILDREN

Topic: *When Courage Fails*

Background Scripture: *Numbers 13—14*

Scripture Lesson: *Numbers 13:30—14:10a*

Memory Verse: *Create in me a clean heart, O God, and put a new and right spirit within me.* Psalm 51:10

DAILY BIBLE
READINGS

Mon., July 11: The Choosing of the Spies, Numbers 13:1-3, 17-20.
Tues., July 12: The Searching of the Land, Numbers 13:21-29.
Wed., July 13: God's Displeasure with a Faithless People, Numbers 14:26-31.
Thurs., July 14: The Penalty for Lack of Faith, Numbers 14:32-37.
Fri., July 15: The Reward for Faith, Joshua 14:6-11.
Sat., July 16: Forty Years of Delay, Psalm 95:6-11.
Sun., July 17: Israel Provokes God, Numbers 14:10b-19.

LESSON AIM

To help us see the destructive effects of unbelief.

LESSON SETTING

Time: Probably about 1400 B.C.

Place: Kadesh-Barnea is identified with an oasis made by four springs, located approximately fifty miles southwest

353

of Beersheba and about fifty miles from the Mediterranean (*Zondervan Pictorial Encyclopedia of the Bible*, III, 775).

The Fulfillment of the Promise Delayed

SUGGESTED INTRODUCTION FOR ADULTS

It was "the twentieth day of the second month, in the second year" (10:11) that the Israelites broke camp and left Mount Sinai, after nearly a year there (cf. Exodus 19:1). Almost immediately they fell to complaining (11:1), and God had to punish them at Taberah. More surprising still, we find Miriam and Aaron rebelling against the authority of Moses (12:1-2). As a result Miriam was punished with an advanced case of leprosy (12:10).

In connection with this incident we are told: "Now the man Moses was very meek, above all the men that were upon the face of the earth" (12:3). This does not mean that he was a pusillanimous coward. Over and over again he showed great courage in leading the people. True meekness is not striking a pious pose or acting humble. Rightly understood, meekness is submissiveness to the will of God. Moses was the meekest man because he always wanted God's will carried out. Meekness is not weakness but mighty strength in doing the divine will.

SUGGESTED INTRODUCTION FOR YOUTH

Why did the Israelites spend nearly forty years wandering in the desert of Sinai? Because they disbelieved and disobeyed the Lord.

We need to realize that unbelief leads to disobedience, and disobedience always results in punishment. We cannot afford to doubt God's promises; it costs too much! The story of the Israelites is marked by instance after instance of unbelief and disobedience, with sad consequences.

It takes courage to believe and obey. But there is no other way to live life successfully and happily. Sometimes obedience may seem costly, but disobedience always costs more in the end. Let's believe God!

CONCEPTS FOR CHILDREN

1. The majority is not always right.
2. In our story today, two men were right and the other ten were wrong.
3. It takes courage to stand against the majority.
4. Faith will give us the courage we need.

THE LESSON COMMENTARY

I. THE SENDING OF THE TWELVE SPIES:
Numbers 13:1-25

In Deuteronomy 1:22 we are told that the people requested the sending of twelve men to investigate the land of Canaan. Here we are told that the Lord ordered it. But there is no contradiction. Moses would naturally ask the Lord about it, and he was told to go ahead. So he selected one man from each tribe.

Since Canaan was north of Kadesh-Barnea, it seems strange to find Moses commanding the spies to go "southward" (v. 17). But the Hebrew word for "southward" is *Negev*, which is still the name for the southern part of Palestine (Israel). The correct translation is: "Go up there into the Negev; then go up into the hill country" (NASB). The central part of Palestine is a high plateau.

The twelve men were to inspect the country, to see whether the inhabitants were "strong or weak, few or many" (v. 18). They were to check the land, to see whether it was "good or bad" (v. 19), "fat or lean" (v. 20). They were urged to be "of good courage, and bring of the fruit of the land."

In obedience to this command, the spies moved up into the Negev and came to Hebron. This was an ancient city (v. 22) and is still an important town about twenty miles south of Jerusalem. Abraham had lived there (Genesis 13:18).

When they came to the valley (or "wadi") of Eschol, they found one cluster of grapes so large that it took two men to carry it (v. 23). This was vivid proof of the fruitfulness of Canaan. We are told that the place was called "Eshcol" (Hebrew for "cluster") because of this (v. 24). The men also took back some pomegranates and figs. These were probably things that were not available to the Israelites in Egypt.

The twelve men spent "forty days" searching the land (v. 25). The number forty is a significant one in the Bible. Elijah fasted forty days (I Kings 19:8), as did Jesus (Matthew 4:2). Moses spent forty days on Mount Sinai receiving the Law (Exodus 24:18). It was forty years that the Israelites spent in the wilderness (Numbers 32:13).

II. THE REPORT OF THE SPIES:
Numbers 13:26-33

A. The Majority Report: vv. 26-29

The twelve men returned "to Moses, and to Aaron, and to all the congregation of the children of Israel" (v. 26) at Kadesh. They presented their report and showed the fruit they had brought back with them. They all agreed that it was surely a land flowing with milk and honey (v. 27), as they had been told it would be (Exodus 3:8).

Unfortunately, they did not stop there. They went on to say, "Nevertheless the people be strong that dwell in the land, and the cities are walled, and very great; and moreover we saw the children of Anak there" (v. 28). These are described in verse 33 as "giants."

The land was in the possesssion of powerful nations (v. 29). In the Negev the Amalekites were in control. They had already attacked the Israelites before the latter reached Mount Sinai (Exodus 17:8). The Hittites, Jebusites, and Amorites lived in the hill country, and the Canaanites along the coast.

B. The Faith of Caleb: v. 30

Distressed about the negative reaction of his colleagues, and the effects it had on their audience, Caleb quieted the people. His attitude was that of faith: "Let us go up at once, and possess it; for we are well able to overcome it." He did not deny the difficulties—we don't solve our problems that way. But he took God into the picture; and so he said, "We can do it." This is always the attitude of faith.

Basically, there are two ways that we can face difficult or dangerous situations: with fear or with faith. If we assess everything from merely the human side, we throw up our hands and cry in despair, "Impossible!" If we take God into consideration, we say, "With God all things are possible" (Matthew 19:26) and "All things are possible to him that believeth" (Mark 9:23). That is the attitude of faith, which is always based on the promises of God. With Him we *can* and *will* win.

C. The Unbelief of the Majority: vv. 31-33

The other spies protested, "We are not able to go up against this people; for they are stronger than we are" (v. 31). From 14:6 we know that Joshua was on Caleb's side; so it was a majority of ten against a minority of two.

"We can't" is the dismal cry of the doubters. The believer says, "We can." Paul was a great man of faith. He wrote: "I can do all things through Christ which strengtheneth me" (Philippians 4:13).

It is not wrong to say, "They are stronger than we." Militarily that was true in the case of the Israelites versus the Canaanites. The inhabitants of Canaan were great fighters and had fortified cities with high walls (v. 28). And it is true in many of our situations today. We gain nothing by ignoring or underrating our opposition. That is unrealistic.

But the whole point is this: If we are on God's side, God is on our side. And "If God be for us, who can be against us?" (Romans 8:31). With Him, we are stronger than all our opponents put together.

The unbelieving men, ten of the spies, "brought up an evil report of the land which they had searched" (v. 32). They said that it was "a land that eateth up the inhabitants thereof." What is meant by this? Thomas Whitelaw writes: "This cannot mean that the people died of starvation, pestilence, or other natural causes, which would have been contrary to facts and to their own report. It must mean that the population was continually changing through internecine wars, and the incursions of fresh tribes from the surrounding wastes. The history of Palestine from first to last testifies to the constant presence of this danger. The remarkable variation in the lists of the tribes inhabiting Canaan may be thus accounted for" ("Numbers," *The Pulpit Commentary*, p. 145).

The Israelites spies were also impressed with the fact that "all the people whom we saw in it are men of great size" (NASB). They were frightened by the prospect of facing them in battle.

This idea is further developed and elaborated in verse 33: "There also we saw the Nephilim (the sons of Anak are part of the Nephilim); and we became like grasshoppers in our own sight, and so we were in their sight" (NASB). The Septuagint (Greek translation of Old Testament) has for the first part *tous gigantas*, "the gigantic ones." Whitelaw comments: "The Nephilim are, without doubt, the primeval tyrants mentioned under that name in Gen. vi. 4. The renown of these sons of violence had come down from those dim ages, and the exaggerated fears of the spies saw them revived in the gigantic forms of the Beni-Anak" ("Numbers," *Pulpit*, p. 145). (*Ben* is the Hebrew word for "son.")

The ten spies said that they felt like grasshoppers in contrast with the descendants of Anak. We don't know how tall the Anakim were. But Goliath is described as over nine feet tall (I Samuel 17:4). There were giants in those days, as there are some today.

III. THE REACTION OF THE PEOPLE:
Numbers 14:1-4

A. Weeping at Night: v. 1

Many people have wept all night, or nearly so, without sinning. But the Israelites were shedding tears of unbelief and rebellion. Instead of believing God's promises, they were influenced by the ten spies, who were cowardly unbelievers.

B. Grumbling Against Moses: vv. 2-3

Again the Israelites were murmuring or complaining "against Moses and against Aaron" (v. 2). They started this ungodly, ungrateful business soon after they left Egypt. Repelled by the bitter waters of Marah, "the people murmured against Moses, saying, What shall we drink?" (Exodus 15:24). A little later they "murmured against Moses and Aaron in the wilderness" (Exodus 16:2) because food was scarce. They were a complaining, grumbling crowd. In Rephidim "the people murmured against Moses" (Exodus 17:3) when they found no water to drink.

The King James Version sometimes uses the name "God" when it is not in the original. This occurs fifteen times in the New Testament in the phrase, "God forbid." The Greek simply says, "May it not be." So here the correct translation is: "Would that

we had died in the land of Egypt! Or would that we had died in this wilderness!" (NASB).

It is difficult for us to understand how the Israelites could be so ungrateful as to forget God's wonderful, miraculous deliverance of them from Egyptian bondage. This had become so unbearable that they had cried to the Lord for help, and He had come to their rescue. Now they forget it all and complain about the hardships they encounter. They were too easily affected by their feelings at the moment.

But how often that is true of Christians today! They rejoice in their newfound faith in Christ. Then when the way gets hard and difficulties appear, they tend to complain and find fault.

"Wherefore hath the Lord brought us unto this land" (v. 3) is more accurately translated, "Why is the Lord brining us into this land" (NASB). They were not yet in the land of Canaan. In fact, because of their unbelief, this generation never entered the Promised Land.

Pessimistically the men expected "to fall by the sword," while their wives and children would be taken as plunder by the enemy. When we insist on looking on the dark side of life, everything looks black. But we are to blame for taking this wrong attitude.

On the language of verses 2-4 Robert Jamieson makes this comment: "Such insolence to their generous leaders, and such base ingratitude to God, show the deep degradation of the Israelites, and the absolute necessity of the decree that debarred that generation from entering the promised land. They were punished by their wishes being granted to die in that wilderness. . . . The sinfulness and insanity of their conduct are almost incredible. Their conduct, however, is paralleled by too many amongst ourselves, who shrink back from the smallest difficulties, and rather remain slaves to sin than resolutely try to surmount the obstacles that lie in their way to the Canaan above" (*A Commentary Criti-*

cal, *Experimental and Practical on the Old and New Testaments*, by Robert Jamieson, A. R. Fausset, and David Brown, I, 548).

C. Rebelling Against Moses: v. 4

The complaining spirit of the people exploded into open rebellion. They proposed to appoint another "captain" and return to Egypt. Nehemiah 9:17 says they actually chose him. Whitelaw writes: "It was a height of rebellion to which they had never risen before. They had lamented that they had not died in Egypt, and they had wished themselves back in Egypt, but they had never proposed to take any overt steps toward returning thither. Nothing less than an entire and deliberate revolt was involved in the wish to elect a captain for themselves. . ." ("Numbers," *Pulpit*, p. 146).

IV. THE RESPONSE OF THE LEADERS:
Numbers 14:5-9

A. Moses and Aaron: v. 5

"Then Moses and Aaron fell on their faces before all the assembly of the congregation of the children of Israel." Nothing is said here about praying. So Whitelaw may be correct when he says: "It was not, however, in this case an attitude of intercession, but the instinctive action of those who await in silent horror a catastrophe which they see to be inevitable; it testified to all who saw it that they were overwhelmed with shame and sorrow in view of the awful sin of the people, and of the terrible punishment which must follow" ("Numbers," *Pulpit*, p. 146).

Perhaps we should not rule out altogether the other interpretation. Jamieson thinks that Moses and Aaron fell on their faces "as humble and earnest suppliants, either to the people, entreating them to desist from so perverse a design, or rather to God, as the usual and only refuge from the violence of that tumultuous and stiff-necked rabble, and a hopeful means of softening and impressing their hearts" (JFB, *Commentary*, p. 548).

B. Caleb and Joshua: vv. 6-9

The two men who wanted to obey God's call to go into Canaan "rent their clothes" (v. 6). We find this frequently in the Old and New Testaments as an expression of deep grief or consternation (e.g., Genesis 37:29, 34; Job 1:20; Matthew 26:35).

Caleb and Joshua then pleaded with the people to reconsider. They reminded them that the land the spies had investigated was "an exceeding good land" (v. 7). They urged faith and obedience: "If the Lord is pleased with us, then He will bring us into this land and give it to us—a land which flows with milk and honey" (v. 8, NASB). The opening expression of this verse was also used by Moses (Deuteronomy 10:15). It gives the only condition. If God is pleased with our attitude toward Him—if it is one of faith and obedience—then He will unfailingly give us victory and success. If there is failure, it is only because we have earned His disfavor by our wrong attitude.

Coming right to the point, Caleb and Joshua pleaded with the people: "Only do not rebel against the Lord" (v. 9, NASB). Rebellion brings God's wrath down on the guilty rebels. It is hard to see why the Israelites were not willing to respond to this plea for

---

DISCUSSION QUESTIONS

1. What was the purpose of spying out the land?
2. When is it safe to follow the majority?
3. What price does the minority have to pay?
4. How do we demonstrate our faith?
5. What is the cost of disobedience?
6. Why is complaining dangerous?

obedience, and thus receive God's blessing.

The two men continued: "'. . . and do not fear the people of the land, for they shall be our prey" (NASB)— literally, "food." That is, "We shall devour them" (cf. 24:8).

"Their defence is departed from them" is literally "Their shadow is turned, or departed." Jamieson comments: "The departing of the shadow was regarded as an indication of some evil. . . . So that the meaning of the phrase, 'their defence is departed' from them, is, that the favour of God was now lost to those whose iniquities were full (Gen. xv. 16), and transferred to the Israelites" (JFB, *Commentary*, p. 549). The shadow which had protected the inhabitants of Canaan from God's wrath was now removed, "and the Lord is with us."

V. THE DIVINE DISPLEASURE: Numbers 14:10-37

The reaction of the Israelites to the earnest, sincere plea of Caleb and Joshua is almost unbelievable. To our amazement we read: "But all the congregation bade stone them with stones" (v. 10). How could the people be so rebellious?

Neither Moses and Aaron, nor Caleb and Joshua, had to respond to this. God Himself intervened: "And the glory of the Lord appeared in the tabernacle of the congregation before all the children of Israel." The dazzling sight must have struck terror to the hearts of these stubborn rebels.

Moses was now faced with one of the great crises of his life, but he came through with flying colors. The Lord revealed His deep displeasure at the Israelites (v. 11) and then said to him, "I will smite them with the pestilence, and disinherit them, and will make of thee a greater nation and mightier than they" (v. 12).

If Moses felt any momentary temptation of ambition or pride, it is not indicated. Instead he reasoned with the Lord that if He did this, the Egyptians would hear about it and would say that God was unable to bring the Israelites into Canaan and therefore He destroyed them (vv. 13-16). Then Moses pleaded for God to show mercy to the sinful people (vv. 17-18). The climax of his prayer was: "Pardon, I beseech thee, the iniquity of this people according unto the greatness of thy mercy, and as thou hast forgiven this people, from Egypt even until now" (v. 19).

Moses' prayer was answered. The Lord said, "I have pardoned according to thy word" (v. 20). But because the people had ten times rebelled against His will (v. 22), they would not be allowed to enter Canaan (v. 23). The people were to be informed that their request to die in the wilderness would be granted (vv. 28-29). Only Caleb and Joshua, of that generation, would enter the Promised Land (v. 30).

CONTEMPORARY APPLICATION

Disbelief and disobedience are always costly. The tragedy is that too often the results affect far more than the guilty ones. Sometimes church congregations have refused to follow their leaders in going forward to new conquests for Christ. The doubting cowards themselves have suffered. But one trembles to think of the souls that may be lost because of their failure to carry out God's plans.

Faith and obedience go together. We all, as Christians, are challenged every day to believe God's promises and obey His commands.

CLAIMING THE PROMISED LAND

DEVOTIONAL READING	Joshua 3:9-17

ADULTS

Topic: *Claiming the Promised Land*

Background Scripture: *Joshua 3—6; 14:1-5*

Scripture Lesson: *Joshua 4:4-7; 5:10-12; 6:1-3; 11:23*

Memory Verse: *Be strong and of good courage; be not frightened, neither be dismayed; for the Lord your God is with you wherever you go.* Joshua 1:9

YOUTH

Topic: *Claiming the Promise*

Background Scripture: *Joshua 3—6; 14:1-5*

Scripture Lesson: *Joshua 4:4-7; 5:10-12; 6:1-3; 11:23*

Memory Verse: *Be strong and of good courage; be not frightened, neither be dismayed; for the Lord your God is with you wherever you go.* Joshua 1:9

CHILDREN

Topic: *Into the Promised Land*

Background Scripture: *Joshua 3—6; 14:1-5*

Scripture Lesson: *Joshua 4:1-7; 5:10-12*

Memory Verse: *I will give thanks to the Lord
with my whole heart;
I will tell of all thy wonderful deeds.*
Psalm 9:1

DAILY BIBLE READINGS

Mon., July 18: A Jordan to Cross, Joshua 3:1-9.
Tues., July 19: The Crossing of the Jordan, Joshua 4:10b-18.
Wed., July 20: A New and Holy Land, Joshua 5:10-15.
Thurs., July 21: The Siege of Jericho, Joshua 6:12-16.
Fri., July 22: The Fall of Jericho, Joshua 6:17-25.
Sat., July 23: The Roll Call of the Faithful, Hebrews 11:1, 24-31.
Sun., July 24: The Parting of the Waters, Joshua 3:9-17.

LESSON AIM

To help us see how we may claim what God has promised to us.

LESSON SETTING

Time: About 1400 B.C. (or 1250 B.C.)

Place: The Jordan River and nearby Jericho

360

Claiming the Promised Land

LESSON OUTLINE

SUGGESTED INTRODUCTION FOR ADULTS

The Greek word for "beginning" is *Genesis*. So that is the name of the first book of our Bible, which describes the beginnings of human life and of the Chosen People.

The second book is called *Exodus*, after the Greek word *Exodos*, which means "a going out." The third is *Leviticus*, which describes the duties of the Levitical priests. The fourth is called *Numbers* because it records two numberings of the Israelites. The first census was taken at Sinai (chap. 1), the second before they entered Canaan (chap. 26).

Last week's lesson was taken from the Book of Numbers; today's lesson is from the Book of Joshua. In between is Deuteronomy. This comes from two Greek words—*deuteros*, "second," and *nomos*, "law." The Book of Deuteronomy records the second giving of the Law, this time to the new generation that was to enter Canaan. The Book of Joshua describes the conquest of Canaan (chaps. 1—12) and the division of the land (chaps. 13—24). In today's lesson we study the beginning of the conquest of Canaan.

SUGGESTED INTRODUCTION FOR YOUTH

The Memory Selection for today (Joshua 1:9) is a combined command and promise. It is one of the greatest verses in the Bible for young people. God's personal promise to Joshua can be His personal promise to us.

Joshua was facing the greatest challenge of his life.

Moses was dead (1:2), and the new leader had to take over. How could he do it?

It is well for us to be conscious of our own inadequacy to face the demands of life. But then we need to listen to God's promise that He will be with us. And He gives all the adequacy we need to live victoriously. "I am with you" is all we need to hear.

CONCEPTS FOR CHILDREN

1. Memorials help us to remember the past.
2. We should each remember the time when Jesus came into our heart.
3. Like the Jewish Passover, the Lord's Supper is a memorial.
4. It reminds us of Christ's death for us on the cross.

THE LESSON COMMENTARY

I. CROSSING THE JORDAN:
Joshua 3

After forty years in the wilderness, the Israelites at last reached the Jordan River (v. 1), the eastern border of the Promised Land. The people were told that they were to follow the ark, "for ye have not passed this way heretofore" (v. 4). There is a sense in which every day faces us with a new path to be walked, and we need divine guidance. But there are also special crises in our lives when we face the challenge of a new career and especially need God's help.

The seven nations that dominated the Promised Land at that time are all named in verse 10. God promised to stop the course of the Jordan River long enough for the Israelites to cross over into Canaan (v. 13), just as He had parted the waters of the Red Sea for them to escape Egypt. The new miracle would be a sign to them that they would, without fail, conquer the land God had promised to them (v. 10). This would give them the necessary courage to meet their enemies.

As soon as the priests carrying the ark stepped into the swiftly flowing river (v. 15) the waters stopped flowing (v. 16). It took faith to take this first step. Often God asks us to move forward into the impossible before He acts in response to our faith.

We are told that the Jordan was overflowing its banks. It was March or April ("first month" of the Jewish year, 4:19), and the springtime rains—plus the melting snows of Mount Hermon, where the Jordan River begins—were causing the flood conditions. This made the miracle even greater.

Verse 16 says that the waters coming down from the north "rose up upon an heap very far from the city Adam, that is beside Zaretan." In 1927 an earthquake caused a landslide in the narrow gorge near this point, which blocked the river so that it did not flow down past Jericho for twenty-one hours. It is obvious that this is what happened here. God caused an earthquake which dammed up the river so that the Israelites were able to cross it "right against Jericho." It was a miracle.

II. THE MEMORIAL BY THE JORDAN:
Joshua 4:1-7

A. The Divine Instructions: vv. 1-3

When all the people had finished crossing the Jordan River (v. 1)—something that would take several hours with such a large crowd—the Lord gave Joshua some new instructions. He was to take twelve stones from the bed of the Jordan, right where the priests had stood still with the ark while the people crossed over (3:17), and erect a memorial at their first lodging place in the Promised Land (v. 3).

B. The Twelve Men: v. 4

Obediently Joshua chose twelve men, one from each of the twelve tribes of Israel, to carry out this assignment. In the Old Testament there is a great deal of emphasis on the twelve tribes of Israel—one for each of the twelve sons of Jacob, who was renamed Israel (Genesis 32:28). This was to underscore the solidarity of the people of God. Reflecting this fact, Jesus chose twelve apostles. In Revelation 4:4 the twenty-four elders represent God's people of all time: Israel of the Old Testament (twelve tribes), plus the church of the New Testament (symbolized by the twelve apostles).

C. The Twelve Stones: v. 5

"Pass over before the ark of the Lord your God into the midst of Jordan" poses a problem, since the people had all reached the west bank of the river, except for the priests who still held the ark near the eastern shore. Probably the correct sense is: "Cross again to the ark" (NASB). That is, the twelve men were to go back to the place where the ark was being held by the priests.

Each man was to take a stone on his shoulder. This suggests that the stones were large and heavy. Together they would make a cairn, a pile of huge stones.

D. The Meaning of the Memorial: vv. 6-7

"Let this be a sign among you, so that when your children ask later, saying, 'What do these stones mean to you?' " (v. 7, NASB). When the future generations inquired about the reason for the pile of stones, they were to be told what it symbolized. The use of

stones as a memorial is an ancient custom, still perpetuated in the use of gravestones.

The pile of stones by the Jordan has long since been lost to sight. But the Passover still continues. J. J. Lias writes: "The passover, the law itself, as well as certain outward and visible memorials, were to be the guarantee to future ages of the truth of the history related in the Books of Moses and Joshua. The monument has disappeared, but the observance of the passover and the whole law by the Jews now, more than 3,000 years after the events related in these books, is a perpetual standing witness of the truth of the record. In like manner the Christian passover, the sacrament of the Lord's Supper, is appealed to by Christians of every denomination as a proof of the substantial truth of the narrative of the Gospels" ("Joshua," *The Pulpit Commentary*, p. 62).

In answer to the question of verse 6, the Israelites were to say that the stones were a "memorial" of the miraculous crossing of the Jordan (v. 7). The waters of the river had been "cut off before the ark of the covenant of the Lord." The stones would testify to this fact.

There was evidently a second memorial heap of stones, described in verse 9. C. H. Waller comments: "It would seem that we are to understand two cairns to have been set up, one on either side of the river, to mark the place where the Israelites crossed. The western cairn was in Gilgal, the other on the opposite side, at the edge of the overflow, where the priests had stopped. The only difficulty lies in the words . . . *in the midst of Jordan.* The phrase, like many other Hebrew phrases, is used in a different way from that in which we use it. The words 'in the middle of the Jordan' to an English reader appear to mean half-way between the banks. But if the river were divided, and half of it had recoiled many miles toward the north, and the rest flowed away to the south, any one standing between these two parts of the river might be said to stand *in the midst of Jordan.* . . . It is perfectly clear from chap. iii. 8 that the priests stood at the brim of the overflow. That spot and no other would be the particular spot which it would be most interesting to mark. . ." ("Joshua," *Ellicott's Commentary on the Whole Bible,* II, 113).

III. THE NEW LIFE IN CANAAN: Joshua 5:10-12

A. The First Passover in the Promised Land: v. 10

Verses 2-9 tell of the circumcising of the male Israelites who had been born in the wilderness. All the males that came out of Egypt had been circumcised, but those who were old enough to fight in the army had all died in the wilderness (vv. 4-6), as God had predicted they would (Numbers 14:29). Now the new generation had to be circumcised, in conformity with God's command to Abraham (Genesis 17:9-11).

Making their first permanent camp at Gilgal, the Israelites "kept the passover on the fourteenth day of the month at even in the plains of Jericho." These two significant religious rites have their parallels in Christianity. For Christians, baptism takes the place of circumcision, and the Lord's Supper takes the place of the Passover. We are baptized as a public testimony to the fact that we belong to Christ. We partake of the Lord's Supper in remembrance of Christ's redeeming death for us on the cross.

B. New Food in Canaan: v. 11

"And on the day after the Passover, on that very day, they ate some of the produce of the land, unleavened cakes and parched grain" (NASB). After forty years of eating manna in the wilderness, it must have been a welcome change to eat the fresh produce of Canaan. God has better spiritual food for us, as we move forward in His will to enter new levels of the Christian life.

C. Cessation of the Manna: v. 12

It was soon after they left Egypt that God began to provide the Israelites with manna fresh every morning, except on the sabbath day (Exodus 16:4-5). It is described as "like coriander seed, white; and the taste of it was like wafers made with honey" (Exodus 16:31). God had graciously provided a delicious daily diet for His people. But the best of food can become tiresome after a while.

One lesson from this verse is that God will provide for us what we cannot provide for ourselves. But when the time comes that we can, He expects us to work and earn our food.

IV. THE CAPTAIN OF THE LORD'S HOST: Joshua 5:13-15

As Joshua was near Jericho he looked up and saw a strange sight: Opposite him stood a man with a drawn sword in his hand. Courageously Joshua went over to him and asked, "Art thou for us, or for our adversaries?" (v. 13). Perhaps Joshua was standing on a rise of ground scanning the country to see which way he should move next.

The stranger answered, "Nay; but as captain of the host of the Lord am I now come" (v. 14). Waller comments: "Jehovah will take part in this conflict, *not as an ally or an adversary, but as commander-in-chief.* It is not Israel's quarrel, in which they are to ask the Divine assistance. It is the Lord's own quarrel, and Israel and Joshua are but a division in His host. The wars of Israel in Canaan are always represented by the Old Testament as 'the wars of the Lord.' It would be well to remember this aspect of the story. The conquest of Canaan is too often treated as an enterprise of the Israelites, carried out with great cruelties, for which they claimed the Divine sanction. The Old Testament presents the matter in an entirely different light. The war is a Divine enterprise, in which human instruments are employed, but so as to be entirely subordinate to the Divine will" ("Joshua," *Ellicott's*, p. 116).

Meekly Joshua said to this captain, "What saith my lord unto his servant?" Instead of a challenge to a stranger, it was now submission to a leader. The real captain of the Lord's host was not Joshua but Jesus Christ, appearing in one of the Christophanies of the Old Testament.

The answer to Joshua's question was, "Remove your sandals from your feet, for the place where you are standing is holy" (v. 15, NASB). This reminds us, of course, of Moses' experience at the burning bush, where God said to him the same words (Exodus 3:5). This shows that it was the Lord Himself, not an angel, who was speaking to Joshua. And He stood there with a drawn sword, as the symbol of victory.

V. THE CONQUEST OF JERICHO: Joshua 6

A. The Closed City: v. 1

"Now Jericho was tightly shut because of the sons of Israel; no one went out and no one came in" (NASB). The Hebrew suggests that the gates had not only been closed, but securely locked with bars and bolts. We are told that when the kings of the land heard that the Jordan had miraculously dried up so that the Israelites could cross over "their heart melted, neither was there spirit in them any more, because of the children of Israel" (5:1). This would be particularly true of Jericho, whose rulers knew that the city had been visited by two Israelite spies (2:1-2). At that time Rahab had reported to the spies: "I know that the Lord hath given you the land, and that your terror is fallen upon us, and that all the inhabitants of the land faint because of you" (2:9). The people of Jericho had heard about the miraculous crossing of the Red Sea and the destruction of the Amorite kings (2:10). Now there was no courage left in Jericho (2:11), just watchful waiting.

B. The Promise of Victory: v. 2

The assurance could hardly have been more specific and encouraging: "See, I have given Jericho into your hand, with its king and the valiant warriors" (NASB). Joshua no longer had to wonder what would happen next. The first city that confronted the Israelites in the land of Canaan would be given them as a free gift from God. What an encouragement!

C. The Plan of Conquest: vv. 3-5

The command was very clear: "You shall march around the city, all the men of war circling the city once. You shall do so for six days" (v. 3, NASB). Seven priests were to march ahead of the ark, carrying seven trumpets of rams' horns (v. 4). On the seventh day the Israelites were to march around the city seven times. Then the priests were to blow a loud signal on their trumpets, the people were to shout with all their might, and the walls would fall (v. 5). The city would then be in their hands.

Waller suggests a reason for the silent marching. He writes: "The meaning of this proceeding becomes clearer when we remember that the centre of the procession is the written law of God. The ark is the vessel that contains it. The armed men that precede it are its executioners. The priests who blow the trumpets are its heralds. It was this law that had brought Israel over Jordan; this law was henceforth to be established in Canaan; this law that was about to take vengeance on the transgressors. The whole law of Moses is but the expansion of the Decalogue; and the Pentateuch contains an ample statement of the transgressions which had brought the inhabitants of Canaan under the ban of the Divine law. The seven days' march round Jericho, in absolute silence, was well calculated to impress on the inhabitants the lesson of 'the forbearance of God.' . . . For several generations the long-suffering of God had waited, while 'the iniquity of the Amorites was not yet full.' . . . But now the longsuffering of God had waited long enough. The shout that burst from the lips of Israel was a signal that He would wait no longer" ("Joshua," *Ellicott's*, p. 117).

D. Carrying Out Instructions: vv. 6-16

Joshua communicated God's orders to the priests (v. 6) and the people (v. 7). And so the procession started. In front were the armed men, followed by the priests blowing their trumpets for the march (v. 9). Behind the priests with the trumpets was the ark (v. 8). Behind the ark came the rearguard (v. 9). The whole thing must have made an impressive sight as the long procession marched all the way around the walls of Jericho and returned to camp (v. 11). The second day they did the same thing, and so on through six days (vv. 12-14).

The seventh day they started early, marching around the city seven times (v. 15). On the seventh circuit of the walls, the priests blew their trumpets as the signal for the people to shout (v. 16).

E. The Spoils Devoted to the Lord: vv. 17-19

"And the city shall be under the ban, it and all that is in it belongs to the Lord" (v. 17, NASB). The people were warned not to touch any of the spoils of the city, lest they bring a curse on the camp of Israel (v. 18). All the silver and gold, and the articles of bronze and iron, were consecrated to the Lord and must go into His treasury (v. 19).

F. The Destruction of Jericho: vv. 20-21

When the people shouted, "the wall fell down flat" (v. 20). The armed men quickly penetrated the city and took possession of it. "And they utterly destroyed everything in the city, both man and woman, young and old, and ox and sheep and donkey, with the edge of the sword" (v. 21, NASB). They also burned the city with fire (v. 24).

In accordance with instructions (v. 17), Rahab and all her family were saved (v. 25). She had fastened the scarlet line in her window on the wall, as the spies had told her to do (2:15-21)—a symbol of redemption.

VI. MISSION ACCOMPLISHED: Joshua 11:23

From Jericho in the valley the Israelites marched into the hills and took Ai (chap. 8). Later, in the famous "long day" (10:12-14), Joshua and his forces defeated the armies of five Amorite kings, including the kings of Hebron and Jerusalem (chap. 10). In 10:40 we read: "Thus Joshua struck all the land, the hill country and the Negev and the lowland and the slopes and all their kings. He left no survivor, but he utterly destroyed all who breathed, just as the Lord, the God of Israel, had commanded" (NASB).

The king of Hazor—far to the north—enlisted the help of many neighboring kings to defeat the Israelites. We read: "And they came out, they and all their armies with them, as many people as the sand that is on the seashore, with very many horses and chariots" (11:4, NASB). But the Lord gave Joshua a great victory over them (11:6-17). He also destroyed the Anakim (11:21-22), the dreaded giants.

DISCUSSION QUESTIONS

1. What is the value of founding memorials?
2. Why do we need to look back to the past?
3. Does God want us to live on manna all our lives?
4. What is typified by the new food in Canaan?
5. How do we win our spiritual victories?
6. Why did God destroy the inhabitants of Canaan?

Then comes the summary in 11:23. The whole land was conquered by Joshua. His next assignment was to divide the land among the tribes.

CONTEMPORARY APPLICATION

"There remaineth therefore a rest to the people of God" (Hebrews 4:9). The context shows that this rest is something we may enjoy here in this life. It is our heritage in Christ. It is the Promised Land that we are to claim by faith.

The idea of Canaan as a type of heaven is deeply imbedded in our hymnology. But the Israelites fought by far their greatest and most numerous battles in Canaan, not in the wilderness. Will we be fighting battles in heaven? The idea is preposterous.

The Biblical concept of Canaan is that it typifies the place of victory and rest that we can reach by a complete surrender of our will to God's will. Then we can live in Canaan right here on earth.

July 31, 1977

DIFFICULTY IN KEEPING THE COVENANT

DEVOTIONAL READING	Psalm 51:1-12

ADULTS

Topic: *Difficulty in Keeping the Covenant*

Background Scripture: Judges 1—3

Scripture Lesson: Judges 2:13-23

Memory Verse: *The people of Israel did what was evil in the sight of the Lord, forgetting the Lord their God.* Judges 3:7

YOUTH

Topic: *Difficulty in Keeping the Covenant*

Background Scripture: Judges 1—3

Scripture Lesson: Judges 2:13-23

Memory Verse: *The people of Israel did what was evil in the sight of the Lord, forgetting the Lord their God.* Judges 3:7

CHILDREN

Topic: *Disobeying God's Ways*

Background Scripture: Judges 1—3

Scripture Lesson: Judges 2:11-12, 16-22

Memory Verse: *Create in me a clean heart, O God, and put a new and right spirit within me.* Psalm 51:10

DAILY BIBLE READINGS

Mon., July 25: The Problems of Judah and Benjamin, Judges 1:16-21.
Tues., July 26: The Compromise of Joseph, Judges 1:22-26.
Wed., July 27: A New Generation, Judges 2:6-12.
Thurs., July 28: The Internal Struggle, Romans 7:15-25.
Fri., July 29: Walk in the Spirit, Galatians 5:16-25.
Sat., July 30: The Perils of the Righteous, Psalm 11.
Sun., July 31: A Sinner's Plea, Psalm 51:1-12.

LESSON AIM

To help us see the danger of our failing to keep God's covenant.

LESSON SETTING

Time: Around 1300 or 1200 B.C.

Place: The land of Canaan (Palestine)

LESSON OUTLINE

Difficulty in Keeping the Covenant

I. Weeping Over Failure: Judges 2:1-5

368

II. A Faithful Generation: Judges 2:6-10
     A. Joshua's Generation: vv. 6-7
     B. Joshua's Death and Burial: vv. 8-9
     C. A New Generation: v. 10

III. Forsaking God: Judges 2:11-13

IV. Punishment for Sin: Judges 2:14-15

V.   Divine Mercy for Sinners: Judges 2:16-19
     A. Raising Up Deliverers: v. 16
     B. Refusal to Listen: v. 17
     C. Respite for a Time: v. 18
     D. Return to Idolatry: v. 19

VI. Divine Judgment: Judges 2:20-23
     A. No More Help: vv. 20-21
     B. Obedience Tested: vv. 22-23

VII. Oppression and Deliverance: Judges 3

SUGGESTED INTRODUCTION FOR ADULTS

Joshua is the book of conquest; Judges is the book of failure. It would be difficult to find a greater contrast. And one follows immediately after the other.

In the first part of chapter 1 we find a brighter picture than in most of the rest of the book. The Israelites asked the Lord who should fight against the Canaanites (v. 1). The Lord said, "Judah" (v. 2). The tribe of Judah, with help from Simeon (v. 3), did a magnificent job of conquering Jerusalem, Hebron, and the south country (vv. 4-11), including the coastal cities (v. 18).

But then comes a sad tale of failure. "The children of Benjamin did not drive out the Jebusites that inhabited Jerusalem" (v. 21). This is followed by the monotonous refrain: "Neither did . . . drive out . . ."—Manasseh (v. 27), Ephraim (v. 29), Zebulun (v. 30), Asher (v. 31), Naphtali (v. 33)—everyone of them failed to drive out the pagan inhabitants of the territories that had been assigned to them. From now on the Book of Judges is a story of repeated failures.

SUGGESTED INTRODUCTION FOR YOUTH

The Book of Joshua describes the kind of Christian life that God wants all of us to live. It is a story of conquest and victory, of inheriting the possession that God provides for His people. All this came through obedient faith.

The Book of Judges is a sad contrast. Here we find defeat and failure on almost every page. Even though God delivered His people over and over again, they quickly lapsed once more into idolatry and sin.

Too many professing Christians live in the Book of Judges instead of the Book of Joshua. Their spiritual experience is an unending series of ups and downs. This need not be, if we will believe and obey God.

| CONCEPTS FOR CHILDREN | 1. God wants us to live victorious lives.
2. If we trust and obey Him, He will give us victory.
3. Doubting leads to disobedience, which is sin.
4. God still loves us and wants to forgive. |

THE LESSON COMMENTARY

I. WEEPING OVER FAILURE: Judges 2:1-5

"An angel of the Lord came up from Gilgal to Bochim" (v. 1). There has been a great deal of discussion as to the identity of this "angel." The Hebrew word—as also the Greek word in the New Testament—means "messenger." So some have thought that a human messenger is meant, especially since it says "came up." But F. W. Farrar says: "This notice is by no means *decisive* against the conclusion that an angel is intended. The writer may mean to intimate that the Angel Prince of the host (Ex. xxiii. 20-23), the Angel of the Covenant, left his station in the camp of Gilgal and came up to the new camp or assembly of the people in Central Palestine" ("Judges," *Ellicott's Commentary on the Whole Bible*, II, 179). Farrar's conclusion is: "It seems probable, therefore, that by 'the angel of the Lord' the writer meant 'the captain of the Lord's host,' who appeared to Joshua at Jericho (Josh. v. 13-15)" (p. 179).

The message from the Lord began with a reminder: "I made you go up out of Egypt, and have brought you unto the land which I sware unto your fathers; and I said, I will never break my covenant with you" (v. 1). God had been good to His people.

The Israelites had been commanded by the Lord not to make any covenant with the inhabitants of the Promised Land, and to break down the pagan altars. "But ye have not obeyed my voice" (v. 2). They had violated the conditions of the divine covenant. As a result, God now said: "I will not drive them out from before you; but they shall be as thorns in your sides, and their gods shall be a snare unto you" (v. 3).

When the people heard this pronouncement of judgment, they "lifted up their voice, and wept" (v. 4). Because of that the place was called "Bochim" (v. 5), which means "Weepers." The location of this place is unknown, but the statement that they "sacrificed there unto the Lord" may suggest that it was near Shiloh, where the tabernacle was.

II. A FAITHFUL GENERATION: Judges 2:6-10

A. Joshua's Generation: vv. 6-7

Verses 6-9 are almost identical with Joshua 24:28-31 (in somewhat different order), as a close comparison will show. In both places we find this summary of the close of Joshua's life.

The last chapter of the Book of Joshua contains that great leader's final charge to Israel, after the land had been divided among the tribes. Then he dismissed the people to go to their various allotted places (see verse 6 here).

Verse 7 tells us that the people served the Lord during the days of Joshua and of the elders who outlived him. A. C. Hervey writes: "This verse is the epitome of the religious history of Israel from the time of the expostulation of the angel till the dying off of all those who had been elders in the time of Joshua. It probably includes some forty or fifty years from the entrance into Canaan, namely, about thirty years of Joshua's lifetime, and ten, fifteen, or twenty years after Joshua's death" ("Judges," *Pulpit Commentary*, p. 21).

It has often been pointed out that verse 7 describes the typical situation in new religious movements. After the founder is gone, the work seems to lag and some deviations take place. Yet it need not be so, and there are exceptions.

"All the great works of the Lord" would include the plagues in Egypt, the parting of the Red Sea, the provision of food and water at various times, the dividing of the waters of the Jordan, the fall of Jericho, and the defeat of enemy armies. God's miraculous power had been demonstrated over and over again on behalf of His people.

The consciousness of the supernatural is still needed by Christians. When we have seen God work, we cannot doubt His Word.

B. Joshua's Death and Burial: vv. 8-9

Moses lived 120 years (Deuteronomy 34:7). The second leader fell ten years short of this (he lived to be 110 years old). Hervey comments: "Caleb was eighty-five years old, he tells us (Josh. xiv. 10), when he went to take possession of Hebron, forty-five years after the spies had searched Canaan from Kadesh-Barnea, and consequently some time in the seventh year of the entrance into Canaan. Joshua was probably within a year or two of his contemporary" ("Judges," *Pulpit*, p. 21). This would suggest that Joshua's death came about thirty years after the Israelites entered the Promised Land.

The great leader was buried in his own allotted inheritance, in Timnath-heres, or Timnath-serah (as it is called in Joshua 19:50). The form given here means "portion of the sun." It may be the modern Tibneh, about six miles from Shiloh. The location of "the hill Gaash" is uncertain.

C. A New Generation: v. 10

When all the people of Joshua's generation had died, "there arose another generation after them, which knew not the Lord, nor yet the works which he had done for Israel." Hervey says: "The memory of God's great works gradually faded away, and with this memory their influence upon the

hearts of the people. The seductions of idolatry and the influence of heathen example were ever fresh and powerful. Had the people obeyed the voice of the Lord, the idolatry and the idolaters would have been out of the way" ("Judges," *Pulpit*, p. 21).

Disobedience always gets us into trouble. God had commanded the Israelites to destroy every vestige of idol-worship in the territories they conquered. If they had done so, their children would not have gone astray. Obedience is the prime requirement of the Christian life.

III. FORSAKING GOD: Judges 2:11-13

"The children of Israel did evil in the sight of the Lord" (v. 11). The context shows that this evil was particularly apostasy—forsaking God and going into idolatry.

This is indicated by the last part of this verse: "served Baalim." The masculine plural ending of Hebrew nouns is *im*. So "Baalim" means "the Baals" (NASB). Robert Jamieson writes: "The plural is used, to include all the gods of the country, the Phoenician idolatry being the prevalent superstition of Syria" (Robert Jamieson, A. R. Fausset, and David Brown, *A Commentary Critical, Experimental and Practical on the Old and New Testaments*, II, 74-75).

The word *Baal* means "lord" or "possessor." Farrar comments: "The splendour of the worship, as well as its sensual and orgiastic character, made it very attractive to the *backsliding* Israelites" ("Judges," *Ellicott's*, p. 181).

"And they forsook the Lord God of their fathers . . . and followed other gods, of the gods of the people that were round about them" (v. 12). This seems to confirm the fact that "Baalim" included many gods.

Baal was popularly thought of as the god of fertility. Since the Israelites were dependent on crop production for their food supply, they tended to worship the gods that went under this name.

Along with Baal they worshiped "Ashtaroth" (v. 13). It should be noted that *oth* is the feminine plural ending of Hebrew nouns. So "Baalim" and "Ashtaroth" may represent the male and female deities. Jamieson says of "Ashtaroth": "... also a plural word, denoting all the female divinities, especially Ashtarte, the Syrian Venus, whose rites were celebrated by the most gross and revolting impurities" (JFB, *Commentary*, p. 75). This is why the later prophets speak out so strongly against this pagan worship.

IV. PUNISHMENT FOR SIN:
Judges 2:14-15

Regarding these two verses Farrar says: "The language of the sad summary which follows should be compared with that of very similar passages which we find in various parts of the Bible" ("Judges," *Ellicott's*, p. 181). Some of these are Deuteronomy 32; II Kings 17; Psalm 106:34-35; Jeremiah 11:2-10.

Concerning "spoilers" (v. 14), Adam Clarke says: "Probably marauding parties of the Canaanites, making frequent incursions in their lands, carrying away cattle, spoiling their crops" (*Commentary on the Holy Bible*, abridged edition, p. 267).

One of the most shocking statements is that God "sold them into the hands of their enemies round about." He had redeemed them from Egyptian bondage. When they revolted against Him, He sold them to new enemies.

Previously God had been for them. But now "the hand of the Lord was against them" (v. 15). This is what the Lord "had sworn unto them" (see Leviticus 26:14-39). It is a sad picture indeed.

V. DIVINE MERCY FOR SINNERS:
Judges 2:16-19

A. Raising Up Deliverers: v. 16

This verse sounds the keynote of the book called Judges. The Lord raised up judges to deliver His people from their oppressors.

The word *judges* may not be the happiest translation. These were not magistrates in court but usually generals in battle. However, the term *judges* is probably so deeply imbedded in the English versions of this book that it would be hard to dislodge it.

Jamieson says of these leaders: "The judges who governed Israel were strictly God's vicegerents in the government of the people, He being the supreme ruler. Those who were thus elevated retained the dignity, at first apparently during the public crisis only, but afterwards so long as they lived; but there was no regular unbroken succession of judges till the days of Samuel, who had transmitted the judicial office as hereditary to his sons. Individuals, prompted by the inward irresistible impulse of God's Spirit, when they witnessed the depressed state of their country, were roused to achieve its deliverance. It was usually accompanied by a special call; and the people, seeing them endowed with extraordinary courage or strength, accepted them as delegates of heaven, and submitted to their sway. Frequently they were appointed only for a particular district, and their authority extended no farther than over the people whose interests they were commissioned to protect. They were without pomp, equipage, or emoluments attached to the office. They had no power to make laws, for these were given by God; nor to explain them, for that was the province of the priests; but they were officially upholders of the law, defenders of religion, avengers of all crimes, particularly of idolatry and its attendant vices" (JFB, *Commentary*, p. 75).

B. Refusal to Listen: v. 17

Even though God showed His compassionate love in raising up deliverers for the people, still they would not listen to these "judges." Instead "they went a whoring ["played the harlot" (NASB)] after other gods ... ; they turned quickly out of the way which their fathers had walked in." The Israelites were perennial backsliders.

On the word *whoring* Adam Clarke comments: "Idolatry, or the worship of strange gods, is frequently termed adultery, fornication, and whoredom in the sacred writings. As many of their idolatrous practices were accompanied with impure rites, the term was not only metaphorically but literally proper" (*Commentary*, p. 267).

The aptness of the figure is evident. Israel was the wife of Jehovah (Yahweh). When the Israelites turned to other gods, they committed spiritual adultery. In the same way, the church is the bride of Christ. When we as Christians turn away from Him to follow other loves—pleasure, money, etc.—we too are guilty of spiritual adultery.

C. Respite for a Time: v. 18

Again the "judges" are clearly represented as being deliverers. Throughout the lifetime of the judge God delivered the people from their enemies.

How can it be said that the Lord "repented"? Adam Clarke's explanation is excellent: "He changed His purpose towards them; He purposed to destroy them because of their sin; they repented and turned to Him, and He changed this purpose" (*Commentary*, p. 267).

D. Return to Idolatry: v. 19

The statement of this verse seems hard to believe. How could the Israelites forget all that God had done for them and turn again to idolatry as soon as the divinely given deliverer died? But that is what they did every time!

They were "stubborn." This is one of the worst sins of the human heart. Stubborn refusal to obey God is the very heart of sin.

VI. DIVINE JUDGMENT: Judges 2:20-23

A. No More Help: vv. 20-21

Again we read that "the anger of the Lord was hot against Israel" (v. 20;

cf. v. 14). He now declared that because they had transgressed His covenant and refused to listen to Him, "I also will not henceforth drive out any from before them of the nations which Joshua left when he died" (v. 21). Joshua had obeyed, and God had given him constant victory over the enemies of Israel. Disobedience would now bring defeat.

B. Obedience Tested: vv. 22-23

The purpose of leaving these nations in the land would be "in order to test Israel by them, whether they will keep the way of the Lord to walk in it as their fathers did, or not" (v. 22, NASB).

Exodus 23:29-30 and Deuteronomy 7:22 suggest an auxiliary reason why God did not drive out all of the nations at once—the wild beasts would have multiplied too rapidly before the Israelites were able to occupy all the land. But there was also an element of judgment, as indicated here.

VII. OPPRESSION AND DELIVERANCE: Judges 3

Among the "nations" left to test the Israelites (v. 1) were "five lords of the Philistines" (v. 3)—over the cities of Gaza, Ashdod, Askelon, Gath, and Ekron on the southern coast of Palestine. Later, in the days of King Saul, these became the worst enemies of Is-

DISCUSSION QUESTIONS

1. Why did the Israelites fail to occupy all the Promised Land?
2. What are main secrets of victory? of failure?
3. What are some warnings for us in this lesson?
4. How is God's mercy shown?
5. What is the greatest threat to Christians today?
6. Does the Book of Judges describe normal Christian experience?

rael. The "Canaanites" were also along the coastal plain. The "Sidonians" were on the northern coast. The "Hivites" are here located as being in the far north. So the Israelites had possession of the central plateau, the backbone of Palestine.

One big mistake that the people made was to intermarry with the pagan inhabitants of the land (vv. 5-7). This led to idolatry and immorality.

Beginning with verse 8 we find the main feature of the Book of Judges—a recurring series, almost a constant sequence, of disobedience, depression, and deliverance. Sin leads to captivity, and then repentance leads to restoration. That is the story of this book.

In this chapter we read about the first three judges—Othniel, Ehud, and Shamgar. The last one is mentioned only briefly (v. 31).

In connection with the other two we have oppression and then deliverance. The first oppression lasted eight years (v. 8). When the people cried out to God for help, He raised up a deliverer—Othniel, a nephew of Caleb (v. 9). "The Spirit of the Lord came upon him" (v. 10) and he delivered the Israelites from the king of Mesopotamia. As a result, "the land had rest forty years" (v. 11).

Again we find the people doing evil (v. 12). This resulted in their being oppressed by the king of Moab for eighteen years (v. 14).

Once more they cried out for mercy, and God raised up another deliverer, Ehud (v. 15). He assassinated the king of Moab and set Israel free, winning a great battle (v. 29). This time the land had rest for eighty years (v. 30). God's mercy was always greater than the punishment.

CONTEMPORARY APPLICATION

Christians are still tempted to worship the gods of the pagan people around them: fame, fortune, pleasure, power—ad infinitum. But when they do so, they soon find themselves in serious trouble. It is still true that the way of the transgressor is hard.

One important truth in this lesson is that sin always brings divine punishment, sooner or later. At the same time, we find emphasized the fact that God is quick to forgive and restore those who call on Him.

RENEWING THE COVENANT

DEVOTIONAL READING	Deuteronomy 26:1-10

ADULTS

Topic: *Renewing the Covenant*

Background Scripture: Deuteronomy 26; Joshua 24

Scripture Lesson: Joshua 24:19-28

Memory Verse: *If you be unwilling to serve the Lord, choose this day whom you will serve, whether the gods your fathers served in the region beyond the river, or the gods of the Amorites in whose land you dwell; but as for me and my house, we will serve the Lord.* Joshua 24:15

YOUTH

Topic: *Model of Commitment*

Background Scripture: Deuteronomy 26; Joshua 24

Scripture Lesson: Joshua 24:19-28

Memory Verse: *The Lord our God we will serve, and his voice we will obey.* Joshua 24:24

CHILDREN

Topic: *Renewing the Covenant*

Background Scripture: Deuteronomy 26; Joshua 24

Scripture Lesson: Joshua 24:19-28

Memory Verse: *This day the Lord your God commands you to do these statutes and ordinances; you shall therefore be careful to do them with all your heart and with all your soul.* Deuteronomy 26:16

DAILY BIBLE READINGS

Mon., Aug. 1: "The Sacrifice Acceptable," Psalm 51:12-19.
Tues., Aug. 2: A Pledge of Loyalty, Joshua 24:14-25.
Wed., Aug. 3: Choices Make a Difference, Deuteronomy 30:15-20.
Thurs., Aug. 4: Confidence in God, Job 13:1-15.
Fri., Aug. 5: A Reminder of Commitment, Joshua 24:26-31.
Sat., Aug. 6: The Sacrifice of Commitment, Matthew 12:46-50.
Sun., Aug. 7: Gesture of Thanksgiving, Deuteronomy 26:1-10.

LESSON AIM	To help us see the value of renewing our covenant with God.
LESSON SETTING	Time: Perhaps around 1350 or 1200 B.C.

Renewing the Covenant

   I. A Meeting for Renewal: Joshua 24:1

  II. A Resumé of History: Joshua 24:2-13
       A. A Reference to the Forefathers: vv. 2-4
       B. A Reminder of the Exodus: vv. 5-7
       C. A Recollection of the Wilderness Battles: vv. 8-10
       D. A Rehearsal of the Conquest of Canaan: vv. 11-13

LESSON OUTLINE

 III. A Challenge to Serve the Lord: Joshua 24:14-18
       A. The Great Choice: vv. 14-15
       B. The Pledge of the People: vv. 16-18

  IV. A Dialogue with the People: Joshua 24:19-25
       A. Joshua's Warning: vv. 19-20
       B. The People's Promise: v. 21
       C. The Ban on Idolatry: vv. 22-23
       D. The Covenant with the People: vv. 24-25

   V. The Monument to the Covenant: Joshua 24:26-28

SUGGESTED INTRODUCTION FOR ADULTS

Deuteronomy 26, the background Scripture for to-day's lesson, gives some of the requirements of God's covenant with Israel. Since the Lord was giving His people the Land of Promise, they were to give back to Him the first portion of all their produce (v. 2). They were to present it to the priest with a ceremony in which they confessed: "My father was a wandering Aramean, and he went down to Egypt and sojourned there, few in number; but there he became a great, mighty and populous nation" (v. 5, NASB).

On the third year in the land, when the crops had finally come in, the people were to pay the tithe of all their increase (v. 12). As a result they could expect God's blessing on them in the Promised Land (v. 15).

The Israelites were to be God's special covenant people, His treasured possession (vv. 18-19). This required their obedience (v. 16).

SUGGESTED INTRODUCTION FOR YOUTH

In order to face the future successfully, we need to look back at God's dealings with us in the past. When we see how miraculously He delivered us from a life of slavery to sin, we know that He can keep us from sin now. The victories of the past give faith for the future.

One of Satan's most powerful weapons against the young Christian is discouragement. Recalling God's faith-fulness in bygone days fills our hearts with courage for the unknown tests that are ahead.

Our only safety lies in complete commitment to Christ. We need to accept and obey God's covenant with us.

	1. If we feel that we have failed, we should ask God's forgiveness.
CONCEPTS FOR CHILDREN	2. Then we should renew our commitment.
	3. Obedience builds faith.
	4. Children can have a meaningful relationship to God.

THE LESSON COMMENTARY

I. A MEETING FOR RENEWAL: Joshua 24:1

Now that the land of Canaan had been conquered and had been allotted to the people, "Joshua gathered all the tribes of Israel to Shechem." This was an ancient Canaanite town located about thirty miles north of Jerusalem, in the hill country of Ephraim. It was Abraham's first stopping place in the Promised Land, and he built an altar there (Genesis 12:6-7). Later Jacob purchased land and erected an altar there (Genesis 33:18-20). So it was natural that the Israelites should make this place a rallying point for religious purposes.

At Shechem Joshua "called for all the elders of Israel, and for their heads, and for their judges, and for their officers; and they presented themselves before God." It was a solemn assembly, involving all the representatives of the various tribes. It would have been impossible for all the people to come.

II. A RESUMÉ OF HISTORY: Joshua 24:2-13

A. A Reference to the Forefathers: vv. 2-4

The citizens of our country have been deeply involved in celebrating its Bicentennial Year. The people of the United States felt that it was important for us to recall and review the days of our beginnings as a nation.

If this is true for Americans, how much more true it was for the Israelites. They were the Chosen People of God, heirs to the promises made to the patriarchs. These promises were now being fulfilled.

Abraham is mentioned first, as the father of the nation. He had lived in Ur of the Chaldees, "the other side of the flood" (vv. 2-3). This phrase should be translated "beyond the River" (NASB)—that is, the Euphrates, thought of as the most significant river in that day. Abraham had come from Mesopotamia, where he and his relatives "served other gods" (v. 2).

Isaac, his son, had succeeded Abraham (v. 3). He, in turn, had two sons, Jacob and Esau (v. 4). God assigned Mount Seir, southeast of the Dead Sea, to Esau and his descendants (the Edomites). Jacob and his children went down to Egypt.

B. A Reminder of the Exodus: vv. 5-7

We have already noted that the Exodus from Egypt was considered by the Israelites to be the most important event in their history. So here, in this brief historical resumé, it is given three verses.

The story of the Exodus begins with Moses and Aaron, and the ten plagues on the Egyptians. But it was God who brought the Israelites out of Egypt (v. 5). The vividness of the Red Sea experience is underscored (vv. 6-7). God held back the Egyptian forces by darkness until the Israelites had crossed safely over. Then He caused the Egyptians to be drowned in the returning waters.

C. A Recollection of the Wilderness Battles: vv. 8-10

East of the Jordan lived the Amorites, who fought against the Israelites (v. 8). But God defeated these enemies and gave their land to Israel.

Then the king of the Moabites waged a war against the Israelites (v. 9). Though he tried to win by having Balaam curse Israel, God intervened and delivered His people (v. 10).

D. A Rehearsal of the Conquest of Canaan: vv. 11-13

The first city captured west of the Jordan River was Jericho (v. 11). But after this great victory, the Israelites were attacked by the seven nations of Canaan, all named here. God, however, delivered them over to the Israelites. The Lord even sent the "hornet" to defeat the Amorite kings. C. H. Waller comments: "There appears no reason for taking this word in any other than a literal sense" ("Joshua," *Ellicott's Commentary on the Whole Bible*, II, 158).

III. A CHALLENGE TO SERVE THE LORD: Joshua 24:14-18

A. The Great Choice: vv. 14-15

In verses 2-13 God is speaking to Israel through His servant. But now Joshua makes his own plea to the people. He exhorts them to "fear the Lord, and serve him in sincerity and in truth: and put away the gods which your fathers served on the other side of the flood ["beyond the River" (NASB)] and in Egypt" (v. 14). It would appear that some of the Israelites were still worshiping the pagan gods of their ancestors, or had taken up with the false deities of Egypt. Perhaps they did this along with participating publicly in the worship of the true God of Israel. They were not serving Him "in sincerity and in truth."

This exhortation is still relevant today. People go to church on Sunday. But too many during the week serve the false gods of money, pleasure, or selfish ambition.

Then Joshua throws out a strange challenge to these vacillating Israelites: "And if it seem evil unto you to serve the Lord, choose you this day whom ye will serve" (v. 15). They had two

alternatives: "the gods which your fathers served which were beyond the River, or the gods of the Amorites in whose land you are living" (NASB). Both the ancient and contemporary gods were worthless—no gods at all.

What about Joshua himself? He had already made a firm and irrevocable decision: "But as for me and my house, we will serve the Lord." J. J. Lias observes: "Here speaks the sturdy old warrior, who had led them to victory in many a battle. He invites them, as Elijah did on another even more memorable occasion, to make their choice between the false worship and the true, between the present and the future, between the indulgence of their lusts and the approval of their conscience. But as for himself, his choice is already made" ("Joshua," *The Pulpit Commentary*, p. 350).

B. The Pledge of the People: vv. 16-18

As usual, the people responded with firm words of promise: "Far be it from us that we should forsake the Lord to serve other gods" (v. 16, NASB). But the Book of Judges, as we have already seen, gives a sad spectacle of backsliding.

The people acknowledged that the Lord had brought the nation out of Egypt and had provided for them in the wilderness (v. 17). He had driven out before them the inhabitants of Canaan, here referred to as "the Amorites" (v. 18). It appears clear that this was a general designation for people on both sides of the Jordan River.

The Israelites concluded with the assertion: "We also will serve the Lord, for He is our God" (v. 18). It will be noted that *therefore* (KJV) is in italics, indicating that it is not in the original.

IV. A DIALOGUE WITH THE PEOPLE: Joshua 24:19-25

A. Joshua's Warning: vv. 19-20

At first sight the reply of Joshua seems strange: "Ye cannot serve the

Lord: for he is an holy God; he is a jealous God" (v. 19). But Waller gives this excellent explanation: "Jehovah will not consent to be served as one God among many: the very thing which Israel was doing at the moment, which they meant to do, and did do, with rare intervals, down to the Babylonish captivity, when the evil spirit of (literal) idolatry was expelled for evermore. Israel always maintained the worship of Jehovah (except in *very evil* times) as the national Deity, but did not abstain from the recognition and partial worship of other national deities of whom they were afraid, and whom they thought it necessary to propitiate. Therefore Joshua's argument is perfectly intelligible, and was entirely necessary for those times" ("Joshua," *Ellicott's*, p. 159).

Joshua added for good measure: "He will not forgive your transgressions and your sins." The Hebrew word for "transgressions" here signifies a "breach of covenant." If they persisted in this, divine forgiveness would be impossible.

How can a "holy" God be "jealous"? This has been a problem to some readers of the Bible. That is because we usually think of jealousy in a bad sense. But Lias offers the true explanation: "The meaning is that God will not permit others to share the affections or rights which are His due alone" ("Joshua," *Pulpit*, p. 352). The fact is that there is no genuine, holy love in marriage without a jealous concern for the affection of the companion of our special love.

Joshua went on to say: "If you forsake the Lord and serve foreign gods, then He will turn and do you harm and consume you after He has done good to you" (v. 20, NASB). In the King James Version the word *strange* usually means "foreign," as here and in the case of Solomon's "strange wives" (I Kings 11:8). This is one of over two hundred words in the 1611 version that convey a wrong meaning to the modern reader.

On the last clause of verse 20 Lias comments: "This implies what has been before stated, that it is not God who is inconsistent, but man; not God who has changed His mind, but man who has changed his" ("Joshua," *Pulpit*, p. 352).

B. The People's Promise: v. 21

The people's answer was: "Nay; but we will serve the Lord." Waller makes this astute observation: "Being brought to the point, no other answer was possible. If they must give up Jehovah or the idols, the idols must go first" ("Joshua," *Ellicott's*, p. 159). If only they had fulfilled this affirmation, how different their future history would have been!

C. The Ban on Idolatry: vv. 22-23

Apparently Joshua put the best construction possible on the people's promise of obedience. He simply reminded them that what they said would stand as a witness against them (v. 22). Lias observes: "Joshua has not disguised from them the difficulty of the task they have undertaken. Like a true guide and father, he has placed the case fully and fairly before them, and they have made their choice. He reminds them that their own words so deliberately uttered will be for ever witnesses against them, should they afterwards refuse to keep an engagement into which they entered with their eyes open. They do not in any way shrink from the responsibility, and by accepting the situation as it is placed before them, render it impossible henceforth to plead ignorance or surprise as an excuse for their disobedience" ("Joshua," *Pulpit*, p. 352).

On the basis of their promise to obey, Joshua issued the clear command to put away the foreign gods that they still retained (v. 23). We would feel better if we could read here that they carried out this order, as we find in the days of Jacob (Genesis 35:4) and David (II Samuel 5:21). Of course, silence does not prove that they failed. But an oral promise is never enough; it must be implemented by obedient action. The Book of

Judges suggests that these foreign gods were not fully put away.

D. The Covenant with the People: vv. 24-25

In response to Joshua's command, the people reiterated their pledge of verse 21, but with added emphasis: "The Lord our God will we serve, and his voice will we obey" (v. 24). But they did not specifically say that they would get rid of their pagan gods, and it appears that they failed to do so.

This was Joshua's last chance to address the nation as a whole, through its representative leaders. So he took advantage of the situation to make "a covenant with the people that day" (v. 25). The Hebrew literally says that he "cut a covenant" with them. This refers to the custom of dividing animal sacrifices into two parts, as Abraham did when God made a covenant with him that his descendants would inherit the Promised Land (Genesis 15:9-21). Now that they were in the land, it was fitting that the people should "cut"— that is, solemnly make and ratify—a covenant with the Lord.

V. THE MONUMENT TO THE COVENANT: Joshua 24:26-28

The word for "statute" in verse 25 comes from a root meaning "to cut,"

DISCUSSION QUESTIONS

1. What is the value of recalling our past?
2. What happens to our future when we forget our past?
3. How does recollection strengthen faith?
4. What are the pagan gods that seduce us now?
5. In what ways may we renew our covenant?
6. What does it mean to "serve the Lord"?

---

and was used for engraving inscriptions in stone. So we read here that Joshua not only "wrote these words in the book of the law of God," but that he "took a great stone, and set it up there under an oak, that was by the sanctuary of the Lord" (v. 26). This may have been the very same oak tree under which Jacob buried the "foreign gods" that his household had acquired (Genesis 35:2-4)—a very appropriate place for the Israelites to make a covenant that they would put away their pagan idols and worship the true God alone.

It is not said whether there was an inscription on this "stone." But we know that stones were commonly used for inscriptions. There is the case of the Ten Commandments written on tablets of stone. Archaeology has discovered many stone inscriptions from this period.

Joshua told the people, "Behold, this stone shall be a witness unto us, [or, "against us" (NASB)]" (v. 27). Whenever they saw the stone they would be reminded of the covenant they had made to serve the Lord, and Him alone. If they ever returned to idolatry, as they did, the stone would stand there as a witness against them. Shechem was conveniently located near the center of the land, where the people would often see the stone.

Concerning the statement that the stone had "heard all the words of the Lord which he spake unto us," Lias writes: "Joshua speaks by a poetical figure of the stone, as though it had intelligence. The stone was taken from the very place where they stood, and within earshot of the words which had been spoken. Thus it became a more forcible memorial of what had occurred than if it had been brought from far" ("Joshua," *Pulpit*, p. 354).

Having delivered his last charge to the people, Joshua now let them return home. They had every reason to remember his words.

Lias gives a beautiful description of this event. He writes: "The whole scene must have been a striking one. The aged warrior, full of years and honours, venerable from his piety and courage and implicit obedience, addresses in the measured, perhaps tremulous, accents of age the representatives of the whole people he has led so long and so well. Around him are the ancient memories of his race. Here Abraham pitched his tent in his wanderings through Canaan. Here was the first altar built to the worship of the one true God of the land. Here Jacob had buried the teraphim [household gods], and solemnly engaged his household in the worship of the true God. Here was the second foothold the children of Abraham obtained in the promised land (see ver. 32), a foretaste of their future inheritance. . . . No other place could combine so many solemn memories; none could more adequately remind them of the fulness of blessing God had in store for those who would obey His word; none could be fitter to impress upon them the duty of worshipping God, and Him alone" ("Joshua," *Pulpit*, p. 354).

CONTEMPORARY APPLICATION

It is very easy for us, in the midst of the hectic living of modern times, to become careless about our devotion to God. "The world is too much with us." It invades the privacy or our bedrooms through radio, and the communion of our family rooms through television.

So from time to time we need to renew our covenant with God. This can be done privately in our home or publicly at church. These renewals deepen our devotion and strengthen our faith.

GIDEON: GOD'S COURAGEOUS MAN

DEVOTIONAL READING	Judges 6:11-16

ADULTS

Topic: *Gideon: God's Courageous Man*

Background Scripture: Judges 6—8

Scripture Lesson: Judges 7:2-8, 20-21

Memory Verse: *Gideon said to them, "I will not rule over you, and my son will not rule over you; the Lord will rule over you."* Judges 8:23

YOUTH

Topic: *Profile of Courage*

Background Scripture: Judges 6—8

Scripture Lesson: Judges 7:1-8, 20-21

Memory Verse: *Gideon said to them, "I will not rule over you, and my son will not rule over you; the Lord will rule over you."* Judges 8:23

CHILDREN

Topic: *Gideon: God's Courageous Man*

Background Scripture: Judges 6—8

Scripture Lesson: Judges 7:1-8, 19-21

Memory Verse: *Wait for the Lord;
let your heart take courage;
yea, wait for the Lord.* Psalm 27:14

DAILY BIBLE READINGS

Mon., Aug. 8: Gideon and God's Army, Judges 7:1-8.
Tues., Aug. 9: Gideon, a Man of Conquests, Judges 7:9-21.
Wed., Aug. 10: Bold Witnesses, Acts 4:5-13.
Thurs., Aug. 11: The Danger of Popularity, Luke 6:20-26.
Fri., Aug. 12: Trusting God, Psalm 46.
Sat., Aug. 13: The Man of God, Proverbs 16:1-7.
Sun., Aug. 14: Called to Serve, Judges 6:11-16.

LESSON AIM

To challenge us to see what God can do with one man who is totally committed.

LESSON SETTING

Time: Probably around 1150 B.C.

Place: In the territory of Manasseh, in the central part of Palestine

LESSON OUTLINE

Gideon: God's Courageous Man

    I. Gideon's Call: Judges 6:11-24
       A. The Message of the Angel: vv. 11-16

B. The Concern of Gideon: vv. 17-19
C. The Miracle of Assurance: vv. 20-24

II. Gideon's First Assignment: Judges 6:25-32
A. The Command: vv. 25-26
B. Carrying It Out: v. 27
C. The Consequences: vv. 28-32

III. Gideon's Fleece: Judges 6:33-40

IV. Gideon's Army: Judges 7:1-8
A. The First Reduction: vv. 1-3
B. The Second Reduction: vv. 4-6
C. The Assurance of Victory: vv. 7-8

V. Gideon's Fears Allayed: Judges 7:9-14

VI. Gideon's Victory: Judges 7:15-25
A. The Plan of Battle: vv. 15-18
B. Execution of the Plan: vv. 19-20
C. The Success of the Plan: vv. 21-25

SUGGESTED INTRODUCTION FOR ADULTS

Gideon was the sixth judge described in the Book of Judges. He was preceded by Othniel (3:8-11), Ehud 3:12-30), Shamgar (3:31), and Deborah and Barak (4:1—5:31). In connection with these judges, or deliverers, God gave the land rest for forty years (3:11), eighty years (3:30), and forty years (5:31). These periods were preceded by times of oppression by the enemy. The first oppression lasted eight years (3:8), the second eighteen years (3:12-14), and the third twenty years (4:1-3).

Chapter 6 begins with the account of the fourth oppression, which lasted for seven years (v. 1). The Midianites, with the help of others, ravaged the land of Israel and destroyed all the crops, leaving the countryside desolate (vv. 2-6). When the people cried to God for help, He reminded them of His faithfulness and their unfaithfulness (vv. 7-10).

The story of Gideon covers three chapters (6—8). Due to limitations of time, we shall be able to treat only the first two in our exposition.

SUGGESTED INTRODUCTION FOR YOUTH

Gideon is one of the most colorful characters of history. With three hundred men he met and defeated an immense army. Who ever heard of such a thing as that?

The explanation, of course, is that God worked a mighty miracle. It was He who dispersed the enemy.

But God had to have a man to lead in this achievement. And Gideon was "God's Courageous Man." He is a "Profile of Courage." What about us? God still seeks men to do His work. But such men are scarce!

CONCEPTS FOR CHILDREN

1. God works through men who will let Him.
2. Gideon was willing to attempt the impossible.

3. This was because he was ready to believe and obey.
4. Only with God can we meet the difficulties of life.

THE LESSON COMMENTARY

I. GIDEON'S CALL:
   Judges 6:11-24

A. The Message of the Angel: vv. 11-16

One day "Gideon was beating out wheat in the wine press in order to save it from the Midianites" (v. 11, NASB). This was in "Ophrah." The exact location of this town is uncertain, but it was in central Palestine, in the territory of Manesseh.

An angel of the Lord appeared to him, greeting him with the assuring and yet challenging words: "The Lord is with thee, thou mighty man of valour" (v. 12). Gideon's response was almost a protest: "Oh my lord, if the Lord is with us, why then has all this happened to us?" (v. 13, NASB). When Gideon saw the angel sitting under the oak tree, he probably thought he was a stranger. And so he addressed him as "my lord," which in Biblical language would be equivalent to "sir."

Gideon went on: "And where are all His miracles which our fathers told us about . . . ? But now the Lord has abandoned us and given us into the hand of Midian" (NASB). It seems likely that Gideon had been thinking gloomy thoughts as he beat out the wheat in secret.

The angel's answer was startling: "Go in this thy might, and thou shalt save Israel from the hand of the Midianites: have not I sent thee?" (v. 14). The problem which was depressing him was to be solved, and he was the one through whom the action was to take place. Thrilling? Yes, but also frightening.

Incredulous, Gideon replied, "Oh my Lord, wherewith shall I save Israel?" (v. 15). His family was poor, "and I am the least in my father's house." He had no army with which to defeat the enemy and deliver Israel.

It was "the Lord"—Jehovah or Yahweh—who answered, "Surely I will be with thee, and thou shalt smite the Midianites as one man" (v. 16). The Scriptures emphasize over and again the glorious fact that all we need is God with us, to do what He commands.

B. The Concern of Gideon: vv. 17-19

In spite of the Lord's assurance, Gideon wanted to be sure. So he asked for a "sign" (v. 17)—some miracle of power—to certify the fact that it was really God's message that he was hearing. He requested the angel to wait while he went and got a "present" (v. 18). The Hebrew word means "offering" and is used throughout the Book of Leviticus for the meal offering presented to God in the tabernacle. Verse 19 indicates that it was a rather elaborate sacrificial offering that Gideon prepared and presented.

C. The Miracle of Assurance: vv. 20-24

The angel told Gideon to place everything on a rock. When he did so, the angel touched the sacrifice with the tip of his staff. Immediately fire came out of the rock and consumed the sacrifice and offering (v. 21).

This frightened Gideon (v. 22). But the Lord assured him that all was well (v. 23). Comforted, Gideon built there an altar to the Lord, and called it

"Jehovah-shalom"—"The Lord is Peace" (v. 24, NASB).

II. GIDEON'S FIRST ASSIGNMENT:
Judges 6:25-32

A. The Command: vv. 25-26

In the Old Testament we find God speaking to His people in a variety of ways. So here we have Him sending Gideon a message in the daytime through an angel and then "the same night" (v. 25) speaking to him—perhaps in a dream, though that is not stated.

God usually prepares His servants for gigantic tasks by "breaking them in" with less formidable assignments. So it was with Gideon. To defeat the powerful Midianites and deliver the oppressed Israelites was a frightening prospect. To encourage his faith, as well as test his obedience, the Lord gave him first an easier, but still a dangerous, job to do.

And so he was told: "Take your father's bull and [probably better than "even" (KJV)] a second bull seven years old, and pull down the altar of Baal which belongs to your father, and cut down the Asherah that is beside it" (v. 25, NASB). Then he was to erect an altar to the Lord, in place of the altar to Baal, and sacrifice the second bullock on the new altar (v. 26). This would be a very daring and dangerous thing to do.

B. Carrying It Out: v. 27

In those days men of means had many servants. So Gideon "took ten men of his servants and did as the Lord had said unto him." In spite of the extreme danger, this man obeyed.

But "he feared his father's household" so he carried out his assignment by night. In the culture of that day it was a very serious crime for one to defy his father's authority. But here was Gideon destroying not only his father's property but also his father's

god. It is no wonder that he did it under cover of darkness.

C. The Consequences: vv. 28-32

The next morning the men of the city discovered that the altar and the nearby Asherah (wooden symbol of a female deity) had been destroyed during the night. When they learned that Gideon had done it, they said to Joash, "Bring out thy son, that he may die" (v. 30).

In spite of the fact that Joash had apparently been worshiping Baal, he now took the part of Gideon. Scornfully he asked, "Will ye plead for Baal? will ye save him?" (v. 31). If Baal was really a god, he ought to be able to defend himself. The logic was unanswerable! The idea of defending deity was preposterous.

On verse 31 F. W. Farrar has this good comment: "These words of Joash were extraordinarily bold and cunning. Possibly the brave act of his son may have roused his conscience, and Gideon may have told him that he had acted under Divine guidance. But he saves his son's life, not by excusing his act, but by feigning such a zeal for Baal as to denounce it as a blasphemous impiety to suppose that Baal will not avenge his own insult—an impiety *so* monstrous, that the man who was guilty of it should be at once put to death" ("Judges," *Ellicott's Commentary on the Whole Bible*, II, 208).

III. GIDEON'S FLEECE:
Judges 6:33-40

About this time the Midianites, Amalekites, and their allies gathered together in the valley of Jezreel—between Samaria and Galilee—to attack the Israelites (v. 33). "But the Spirit of the Lord came upon Gideon" (v. 34)—as He later came upon Samson (14:6, 19; 15:14). He "blew a trumpet" (a ram's horn) as a signal for war. The men of his own tribe, Manasseh, as well as the surrounding tribes of Asher, Zebulun, and Naphtali, gathered to him.

But Gideon, though obeying God's call (v. 14), was still afraid to meet the massive forces of the enemy. He wanted added assurance that God would be with him. So he put out a "fleece" (v. 37). If the fleece was wet with dew and the ground around it dry, then he would know that God was going to save Israel by his hand. The next morning he found that the test had been amply met (v. 38). Still needing added assurance, he reversed the test, with equally positive results (vv. 39-40). Now he was sure of God's will.

IV. GIDEON'S ARMY:
Judges 7:1-8

A. The First Reduction: vv. 1-3

Gideon is now called Jerubbaal (v. 1; cf. 6:32). He and his army got up early—as we always should to do God's work—"and pitched beside the well of Harod." Unfortunately, the exact location of this well is unknown. But we are told that it was south of the Midianite army in the valley of Jezreel.

The next word from the Lord was startling, almost shattering. God told Gideon that his hastily assembled army was too large for Him to use. If the Israelites defeated the Midianites they would take the credit to themselves, boasting, "Mine own hand hath saved me" (v. 2).

So the Lord told Gideon to make this announcement: "Whoever is afraid and trembling, let him return and depart from Mount Gilead" (v. 3, NASB). We can imagine Gideon's feelings as he saw twenty-two thousand men walk away, leaving him an army of only five thousand for meeting the vast forces of several enemy nations.

The logic of this move, however, is clear. In the heat of the battle these fearful, trembling ones would have turned and fled, disrupting the whole affair and bringing defeat to the Israelites (cf. Deuteronomy 20:8). God cannot use weak doubters in His army today; He needs men and women of strong faith. Better ten thousand courageous warriors than thirty-two thousand, with two-thirds of them already

afraid of the enemy. Nevertheless, Gideon's heart must have sunk within him as he watched the twenty-two thousand men leave him.

There is an interesting parallel here from Tacitus, the Roman historian. He wrote: "The ancients had observed that even when there are many legions it is always the few that win the battle" (*Annals*. xiv. 36). The same thing has always been true in the work of the church.

B. The Second Reduction: vv. 4-6

The worst—and best—was yet to come. To Gideon's astonishment and chagrin, the Lord said to him, "The people are yet too many" (v. 4). He was told to bring his men down to "the water"—the spring of Harod—and God would "try" (better, "test") them there. The battles of the Lord have always been won by people who have been tested and proved true. That is why we should not object to the tests when they come.

Obediently Gideon brought his ten thousand men to the spring of Harod, from which doubtless a brook was flowing. Then the Lord indicated the nature of the test. Those who scooped up the water in their hand and lapped it like a dog were to be put in one group, and those who got down on their knees to drink were separated into another group. Three hundred men passed the test; the other ninety-seven hundred failed (v. 6).

What was the difference? A. C. Hervey puts it this way: "It showed a much more soldierly and self-controlled spirit just to quench the thirst by lapping the water out of the palm of the hand, than to kneel down and drink without stint out of the spring itself. The Lord saw the difference of character indicated by the two actions, and chose his instruments accordingly" ("Judges," *The Pulpit Commentary*, p. 73).

The ones who scooped up the water with their hand were keeping themselves on the alert, watching constantly for any surprise attack by the enemy. The ones who knelt down to put their faces in the water and drink copiously were not watching, and so were not good soldiers. There is a warning here to all of us.

C. The Assurance of Victory: vv. 7-8

At the close of the test, with the two groups separated, the Lord told Gideon that by the three hundred men who lapped He would save Israel and give the Midianites into his hand. The rest of the people were to go home (v. 7).

Hervey comments: "The same principles which run through the choice of God's instruments on the other occasions appear here. The instruments are to be such in quality or in quantity as to make it quite manifest that the excellency of the power is God's, not man's; and yet the instruments themselves are to be conspicuous for their rare excellence." He further says: "And so here the overthrow of the hosts of Midian by three hundred Israelites was manifestly the effect of the power of God fighting on their behalf. But yet what a marvelous heroism was there in those three hundred! what strength of purpose, what iron-firmness of nerve, to see about thirty thousand of their comrades leave them in the face of the myriads of their foes; to remain quietly at their post, and, when the time came, to leave their camp and pour down into the plain" ("Judges," *Pulpit*, pp. 73-74).

The first part of verse 8 seems a bit ambiguous: "So the people took victuals (food) in their hand, and their trumpets." Who were "the people"?

The New American Standard Bible makes it specific: "So the 300 men took the people's provisions and their trumpets into their hands"—that is, from the 9,700. This translation seems to be well supported. F. W. Farrar writes: "The E. V. [English Version] here differs from most of the ancient versions (e.g., the LXX, the Chaldee, the Vulgate, etc.), which render it, 'And they (the 300) took the provisions and trumpets of the people (the 9,700) in their hands.' This is also the

explanation of Rabbi Kimchi, Levi Ben Gerson, etc. Provisions would be scarce in the neighbourhood of so vast a host, and it would be the desire of all that the brave 300 should be well supplied. The reason for taking 300 rams' horns would soon appear; and, indeed, but for this verse we might well wonder how each of the 300 came to have a horn of his own. Their 'pitchers' were probably those in which the provisions had been carried" ("Judges," *Ellicott's*, p. 211).

The last clause of verse 8 is significant. Gideon had only three hundred men left, "and the host of Midian was beneath him in the valley." What a frightening sight!

V. GIDEON'S FEARS ALLAYED: Judges 7:9-14

Gideon had every right to be afraid. Yet that night the Lord said to him: "Arise, get thee down unto the host; for I have delivered it into thine hand" (v. 9).

But God is gracious and compassionate. So He said to His general, "If you are afraid, take your servant and visit the camp of the enemy" (v. 10).

The enemies' forces covered the Plain of Jezreel "like grasshoppers for multitude" (v. 12). Gideon's task was ridiculous, utterly impossible!

But he and his servant arrived at the edge of the camp just in time to hear a man telling his dream to a fellow soldier. In this dream he had seen

---

DISCUSSION QUESTIONS

1. Why did the Lord choose Gideon?
2. What were some of his assets and liabilities?
3. Are we justified in putting out a "fleece"?
4. Why did God test Gideon's obedience with a lesser task?
5. What is the relation of divine power and human instrument?
6. What is the relation of faith and obedience?

a small biscuit of barley bread come tumbling into the Midianite camp, and it knocked over a whole tent! More amazing still, the enemy soldier gave a divinely inspired interpretation: "This is nothing else save the sword of Gideon the son of Joash, a man of Israel; for into his hand hath God delivered Midian, and all the host" (v. 14).

VI. GIDEON'S VICTORY:
Judges 7:15-25

A. The Plan of Battle: vv. 15-18

When Gideon heard the dream and its interpretation, he appropriately "bowed in worship" (v. 15, NASB). Then he ordered the attack.

What could three hundred men do against an innumerable host of the enemy? Gideon adopted a wise strategy: "He divided the three hundred men into three companies" (v. 16). This was a common stratagem of that day (I Samuel 11:11; II Samuel 18:2; Job 1:17).

But Gideon did something more. "He put trumpets and empty pitchers into the hands of all of them, with torches inside the pitchers" (v. 16, NASB). Farrar comments: "These torches are simply of wood dipped in turpentine or pitch, which are not easily extinguished" ("Judges," Ellicott's, p. 212).

Gideon told all his men to follow his lead. When he and his hundred men blew their trumpets, the rest were to join in. Farrar observes: "Hearing the sound of three hundred ram's horns, the Midianites would naturally suppose that they were being attacked by three hundred companies" ("Judges," Ellicott's, p. 212). Usually there was only one trumpeter for each company, to signal the attack.

B. Execution of the Plan: vv. 19-20

Gideon and his company of one hundred men reach the outside of the enemy camp "in the beginning of the middle watch" (v. 19). This would be about ten o'clock, for the ancient Israelites divided the night into three watches of four hours each.

When Gideon and his group blew their ram's horns, the rest did the same. They also broke their pitchers, so that the torches shone brightly (v. 20). Holding the torches in their left hands and the trumpets in their right hands, they shouted, "The sword of thy Lord, and of Gideon."

C. The Success of the Plan: vv. 21-25

It was a shattering sound and a blazing sight in the quiet and darkness of the night. No wonder that "all the host ran, and cried, and fled" (v. 21). It seemed that the end of the world had come. In the confusion and terror some enemy soldiers even killed each other (v. 22).

Soon the Israelites of several tribes were pursuing the fleeing Midianites (v. 23). The two leaders of Midian, Oreb and Zeeb, were captured and slain (v. 25). God had given His faithful servant an overwhelming victory.

CONTEMPORARY APPLICATION

Even when the Lord does a miraculous work for His people, there are always some who will find fault. Here we find the men of Ephraim blaming Gideon for not enlisting them in his army at first. But he showed a beautiful spirit in pacifying their anger (8:1-3). It is a good example to us in treating our critics.

The Israelites asked Gideon to rule over them (8:22). With magnificent humility he replied: "I will not rule over you, neither shall my son rule over you: the Lord shall rule over you" (v. 23). That should be our attitude. God alone must be Lord.

SAMSON: STRUGGLE AGAINST OPPOSITION

DEVOTIONAL READING | Psalm 27

ADULTS

Topic: *Samson: Struggle Against Opposition*

Background Scripture: Judges 13—16

Scripture Lesson: Judges 13:1; 16:23-30

Memory Verse: *The Lord is my light and my salvation; whom shall I fear? The Lord is the stronghold of my life; of whom shall I be afraid?* Psalm 27:1

YOUTH

Topic: *Samson: Struggle Against Opposition*

Background Scripture: Judges 13—16

Scripture Lesson: Judges 13:1; 16:23-30

Memory Verse: *The Lord is my light and my salvation; whom shall I fear? The Lord is the stronghold of my life of whom shall I be afraid?* Psalm 27:1

CHILDREN

Topic: *Against the Wrong*

Background Scripture: Judges 13—16

Scripture Lesson: Judges 13:1; 16:23-30

Memory Verse: *O Lord God, remember me, I pray thee, and strengthen me.* Judges 16:28

DAILY BIBLE READINGS

Mon., Aug. 15: The Need for Salvation, Psalm 54.
Tues., Aug. 16: Refuge from Danger, Psalm 43.
Wed., Aug. 17: Suffering in Service, II Corinthians 11:21-33.
Thurs., Aug. 18: Security in Christ, Romans 8:35-39.
Fri., Aug. 19: Rely on God, Psalm 125.
Sat., Aug. 20: A Promise of Hope, Zechariah 3.
Sun., Aug. 21: A Divine Revelation, Judges 13:6-14.

LESSON AIM | To help us see how God can use ordinary men to do a great work, if they are obedient to His will.

LESSON SETTING

Time: About 1100 B.C.

Place: The western part of Palestine

Samson: Struggle Against Opposition

SUGGESTED INTRODUCTION FOR ADULTS

In our lessons for this quarter the two outstanding judges, Gideon and Samson, have been selected for study. We found that three chapters of the Book of Judges (6—8) are devoted to the story of Gideon. Today we note that four chapters (13—16) tell the story of Samson.

There is considerable contrast between these two men. Gideon is introduced as a grown man; Samson's birth and childhood are announced beforehand. Gideon defeated the enemy miraculously with a tiny army; Samson single-handedly destroyed the enemy by miraculous feats of physical strength. Gideon lived a consistently godly life; Samson's life was marred by immorality and a spirit of personal vengeance.

This is one of the most astonishing aspects of today's lesson. Samson was anything but an example of godly living. Yet God used him to deliver His people from the Philistines. And God still seems to use strange instruments at times.

Actually, Samson's life is for us more an occasion of warning than of example. But we see God's grace in opposition to man's sin.

SUGGESTED INTRODUCTION FOR YOUTH

What lessons can young people learn from the life of Samson? At the outset we can say that Samson's life shows us largely what we ought *not* to be and do.

In his youth Samson was demanding, prankish, undisciplined, and vengeful. He quickly resorted to violence and destruction, motivated by anger and revenge. And yet God used him to defeat the oppressing Philistines. His great physical prowess was the cause of his greatest glory, but it also became the occasion of his downfall.

The main lesson for us is that disobedience always leads to destruction. Samson broke his vows and thereby ultimately destroyed himself. The path of self-indulgence is suicidal.

CONCEPTS FOR CHILDREN

1. Samson's father and mother obeyed God and carefully guarded the life of their child.
2. But Samson became selfish and willful.
3. He won many great victories in his life.
4. But his heroism was marred by sin.

THE LESSON COMMENTARY

I. FORTY YEARS OF OPPRESSION:
Judges 13:1

The statement in the first half of this verse is a sadly recurring refrain in the Book of Judges (cf. 2:11; 3:7; 4:1; 6:1; 10:6). The Israelites were certainly "bent to backsliding" (Hosea 11:7). It is interesting to note that the word *backsliding* occurs no less than fourteen times in Jeremiah—and elsewhere in the Old Testament only in Hosea (three times). But the experience of backsliding is found throughout the Book of Judges.

This time the Lord delivered the disobedient Israelites "into the hand of the Philistines forty years." This was the sixth and longest oppression (cf. 3:8, 14; 4:3; 6:1; 10:8). The Israelites paid a heavy penalty for their unfaithfulness to God.

The "Philistines" are thought to have come from the Island of Crete and to have settled on the southeast coast of Palestine (Canaan) at about 1200 B.C. For the next two centuries they were the main enemies of the Israelites, especially during the days of Saul and the early reign of David.

II. SAMSON'S BIRTH:
Judges 13:2-25

A. The Angel's Announcement:
vv. 2-23

Zorah, in the tribal territory of Dan, was a town about halfway between Jerusalem and the Mediterranean coast. Here lived a man named Manoah and his barren wife (v. 2).

The angel of the Lord appeared to the wife and assured her that she was to have a child (v. 3). In preparation for this she was to abstain from drinking alcoholic beverages and avoid all unclean food (v. 4). The boy was to be from birth a "Nazirite" (*not* "Nazarite," KJV), never cutting his hair (v. 5). He would begin to deliver Israel from the Philistines.

The Nazirite vow was threefold. It demanded not only letting the hair grow long, but also avoiding drinking wine or touching anything unclean (Numbers 6:2-21). Samson broke all three of these vows.

The woman told her husband that "a man of God" had come to her, "and his appearance was like the appearance of the angel of God, very awesome" (v. 6, NASB). She also reported the promise of the angel and his instructions about the strict life she was to live (v. 7). This was because the boy was to be a Nazirite all his life.

Manoah wanted this confirmed for him personally. So he prayed to the Lord that the angel would return and "teach us what to do for the boy who is to be born" (v. 8, NASB). He showed a proper concern for carrying out the divine will.

God answered this prayer and sent the angel again—once more to the wife (v. 9). She quickly ran and called her husband (v. 10). Meanwhile the angel waited.

When Manoah inquired about further directions (v. 12), the angel repeated what he had already told the wife (vv. 13-14). She was to fulfill the first two requirements of the Nazirite vow (as given in Numbers), avoiding alcoholic drinks and unclean foods. As a woman, the long hair was automatic.

Still uncertain about the identity of the visitor, Manoah asked permission to prepare a "kid" (young goat) to feed him (v. 15). The angel declined, telling Manoah to offer his burnt offering to the Lord (v. 16). The husband and wife did not yet know that they were talking with an angel.

Curious about the whole thing, Manoah asked the visitor for his name (v. 17). The answer was: "Why do you ask my name, seeing it is wonderful?" (v. 18, NASB). The King James Version has: "seeing it is secret." A. C. Hervey comments: "The Hebrew word does not mean secret, but wonderful, as it is rendered in Isa. ix. 6, and elsewhere" ("Judges," The Pulpit Commentary, p. 139).

This introduces an interesting possibility. In Isaiah 9:6 the coming Messiah is called "Wonderful Counselor" (NASB). Could this appearance of "the angel of the Lord" have been a Christophany—an appearance of the Son of God in human form in Old Testament times?

When Manoah offered the kid, with a meal offering—not, as the King James Version has it: "meat offering," for it was ground grain—the angel "did wonderously" (v. 19). This is the same root as "wonderful" in verse 18; the connection is lost in the King James Version. The angel was living up to his name!

Verse 20 describes what happened. When the flame on the altar went up toward heaven, "the angel of the Lord ascended in the flame of the altar." This shows that it was not an ordinary human body that had been seen. The sight was so overwhelming that Manoah and his wife "fell on their faces to the ground." Then they knew that it was an angel (v. 21).

Struck with fear, Manoah said to his wife, "We shall surely die, because we have seen God" (v. 22). As often happens, the wife gave her husband a sensible answer. She said, "If the Lord had desired to kill us, He would not have accepted a burnt offering and a grain offering from our hands, nor would He have showed us all these things, nor would He have let us hear things like this at this time" (v. 23, NASB). This was logical.

B. The Birth of Samson: v. 24

In due time the child was born and named Samson. The meaning of this word is uncertain. We are further told that "the child grew, and the Lord blessed him."

C. The Stirring of the Spirit: v. 25

"And the Spirit of the Lord began to move him at times in the camp of Dan" (Hebrew, Mahaneh-dan). Concerning the verb here, F. W. Farrar notes: "Literally, to agitate or thrust him. . . . The word implies vehement and overwhelming impulses to noble deeds . . . which, however, only came over him 'at times' (chaps xiv. 6, xv. 14, xvi. 20)" ("Judges," Ellicott's Commentary on the Whole Bible, II, 241). The New American Standard Bible has "began to stir him."

The experience of Samson is not to be identified, of course, with the filling with the Spirit described in the New Testament. In the case of Samson, the Spirit of the Lord came on him intermittently, stirring and empowering him to do great deeds.

III. SAMSON AND THE PHILISTINES: Judges 14:1—15:20

A. Getting a Wife: 14:1-4

Samson "went down" from his home in the foothills "to Timnath"—a Philistine town on the maritime plain (v. 1). There he saw a Philistine woman who fascinated him. He went back home and told his parents about her, adding, "Get her for me as a wife" (v. 2, NASB). This, of course, reflects the custom of that time that parents arranged all marriages and paid a dowry (Genesis 24:4-12).

Quite naturally, Samson's father and mother protested: "Is there no woman among the daughters of your relatives, or among all our people, that you go to take a wife from the uncircumcised Philistines?" (v. 3, NASB). Marriage with the Canaanites was specifically prohibited (Exodus 34:16; Deuteronomy 7:3-4), and this would apply to the pagan Philistines.

But Samson insisted: "Get her for me, for she looks good to me" (NASB). The parents did not realize that the Lord was allowing this to happen so that "he" (v. 4), Samson, would have "an occasion against the Philistines." Farrar observes: "All that can be meant is that in this marriage God was overruling the course of events to the furtherance of His own designs" ("Judges," Ellicott's, p. 242).

B. Killing a Lion: 14:5-9

Although Samson's parents did not approve the proposed marriage, on his insistence they went down with him to Timnath (v. 5). Had they spoiled him by giving in to his desires since childhood? The picture of Samson that we see in these chapters suggests that the answer is Yes.

Suddenly a young lion roared against him. The Spirit of the Lord "came mightily upon him, and he rent him as he would have rent a kid" (v. 6), though he had no weapon in his hand. Surprisingly, he did not tell his parents about it.

This raises a little problem. If the three were walking together, how would the parents not know of it? Hervey makes this suggestion: "Samson had left the road along which his father and mother were walking, at a pace, perhaps, too slow for his youthful energy, and had plunged into the vineyards" (Pulpit, p. 149). There a lion unexpectedly confronted him.

"And he went down, and talked with the woman; and she pleased Samson well" (v. 7). Farrar comments: "His father and mother seem to have preceded him, and made the betrothal arrangements; otherwise he would not have been allowed by Eastern custom to talk with her" ("Judges," Ellicott's, p. 243).

"After a time he returned to take her" (v. 8). On the way he stopped to see the carcass of the lion he had killed, and he found a swarm of bees and some honey in the dead body. This shows that considerable time had passed in the interval. Samson took some of the honey in his hands and shared it with his parents (v. 9).

C. Propounding a Riddle: 14:10-20

"So his father went down unto the woman" (v. 10), to make the final arrangements for the wedding. Samson put on a great feast for his bride, as was the custom. These usually lasted at least a week.

Thirty companions had been selected for the bridegroom (v. 11). To them Samson propounded a riddle and made a proposal. If they could guess the riddle within the seven days of the feast, he would give them thirty "sheets"—rather, linen shirts—and thirty changes of clothes (v. 12). If they could not explain the riddle they would have to give him the same amount (v. 13).

For six days they were nonplussed. Finally on "the seventh day"—or "the fourth day" (NASB)—they went to the bride and threatened to burn her and her father's house if she did not extract the answer from Samson (v. 15). So she wept before him, begging him (v. 16) for "seven days, while their feast lasted" (v. 17). This suggests that the companions' request was made earlier than the last day.

On the seventh day she exerted extra pressure, and Samson finally told her. She quickly informed the men and they gave Samson the correct answer. Angrily he replied, "If ye had not plowed with my heifer, ye had not found out my riddle" (v. 18). Again the Spirit of the Lord came on him (v. 19). He killed thirty men of Ashkelon and in this way obtained the clothing to pay for his wager. But Samson's wife was given to his best man (v. 20).

D. Avenging a Wrong: 15:1-8

Some time later Samson went down to get his wife, whom he had left in anger (14:19). But her father turned him away (vv. 1-2).

Thoroughly enraged by this, Samson caught three hundred foxes, tied a lighted torch to each pair of tails, and let the frantic animals loose in the standing grain of the Philistines. Not only was the wheat burned, but the vineyards and olive orchards as well (vv. 33-5).

After ascertaining who the culprit was and his motive for the crime, the Philistines came and burned the bride and her father (v. 6)—the very thing she had tried to avoid (14:15). This provoked Samson again, and he sought revenge on those who had killed his wife (v. 7). He "smote them hip and thigh with a great slaughter" (v. 8).

E. Killing a Thousand Men: 15:9-17

A large army of Philistines then came up against Judah, demanding that Samson be surrendered to them (vv. 9-10). Three thousand men of Judah waited on Samson (v. 11). After a promise that they themselves would not kill him (vv. 12-13), he submitted to be bound with two new cords and handed over to the Philistines.

But when his enemies shouted triumphantly at the sight of their arch foe in bonds, "the Spirit of the Lord came mightily upon him" (v. 14), and he easily broke the cords that held him. Finding the fresh jawbone of a donkey, he proceeded to kill a thousand men with it (v. 15). Typically,

when he was done with it, he threw it away (v. 17). It seems he was utterly undisciplined.

F. Ruling for Twenty Years: 15:18-20

This great "hero" too often acted like a baby. Feeling thirsty after the big massacre, he thought he was going to die of thirst (v. 18)! "But God split the hollow place that is in Lehi so that water came out of it" (v. 19, NASB). This translation is preferable to "an hollow place in the jaw" (KJV). We already have "Lehi," the Hebrew word for "jaw," used as a place name (v. 9) and it should be taken that way here.

Samson "judged Israel"—the southwestern part of it—for twenty years. But he was mainly a warrior.

IV. SAMSON'S FEAT OF STRENGTH: Judges 16:1-3

The pathetic moral weakness of this physically strong man is revealed in the first verse here. Going down to Gaza, the southernmost Philistine city, he committed sin with a prostitute.

When the men of that city heard that he was in town, they surrounded the place and lay in wait for him at the city gate. They "kept silent all night, saying, 'Let us wait until the morning light, then we will kill him' " (v. 2, NASB).

Samson lay still until midnight. At that time he rose "and took hold of the doors of the city gate and the two posts and pulled them up along with the bars; then he put them on his shoulders and carried them up to the top of the mountain which is opposite Hebron" (v. 3, NASB). Once more he had escaped the efforts of the Philistines to kill him.

This was a tremendous feat of strength. But it was more. Farrar comments: "The carrying away the *gate* of his enemies would be understood in the East as a very peculiar insult" (*Ellicott's*, p. 249).

V. SAMSON AND DELILAH:
Judges 16:4-22

This is the saddest chapter in the life of Samson. We have already seen that he had a weakness for wicked women. Now he became infatuated with a worthless character named Delilah (v. 4).

This woman was willing to be used by the Philistine lords to bring about the destruction of her lover. Such a person deserves no respect whatever.

It was all for a handsome bribe—"eleven hundred pieces of silver" (v. 5). So she went to work on him, begging him to tell her the secret of his great strength (v. 6). Three times he deliberately lied to her (v. 7-14). But the last time (v. 13) he came perilously close to revealing the secret. Too bad a red light didn't flash in his consciousness!

Finally, when she had "pressed him daily with her words, and urged him, so that his soul was vexed unto death" (v. 16), he told her all the truth (v. 17). She put him to sleep and had his long hair cut off (v. 19). This time he was captured by the Philistines. They put out his eyes and took him to Gaza, where they made him operate a grindstone in the prison (v. 21).

VI. SAMSON'S LAST FEAT AND DEATH:
Judges 16:23-30

A. Disgraced by the Philistines: vv. 23-25

The Philistine lords held a great celebration in the temple of their god, Dagon, to rejoice over the fact that their feared enemy was at last at their mercy (v. 23). The people praised their god for delivering Samson over to them (v. 24).

"When their hearts were merry"— perhaps with much drinking—they said, "Call for Samson, that he may make us sport" (v. 25). Hervey writes: "It is not certain whether the idea conveyed is that of the A.V., that Samson

was brought there to be as it were baited by the populace, jeered and jested at, reviled and reproached, perhaps struck or pelted; or whether the words do not simply mean *to dance with music*" ("Judges," *Pulpit*, p. 174). Probably we are justified in putting the worst construction on the situation here.

B. Praying for Help: vv. 26-28

Samson had been brought inside and set between two pillars. Because he was blind, a boy led him by the hand. Now Samson asked the boy to let him feel the pillars, so that he could lean against them (v. 26).

The temple was filled with people, with about three thousand on the roof (v. 27). Both men and women were there, watching.

Then Samson prayed for God to give him miraculous strength just this one more time, so that he could be avenged on the Philistines for gouging out his two eyes.

C. Dying with Great Destruction: vv. 29-30

Samson's prayer was answered. Putting his right hand on one pillar and his left on the other, he bent with all his might against them. The pillars gave way, and the entire temple collapsed. Both the people on the roof

---

DISCUSSION QUESTIONS

1. Why did God choose Samson?
2. Where may his parents have failed?
3. What is the importance of proper discipline for children in producing self-discipline?
4. What were Samson's weaknesses?
5. How can we guard against them?
6. How did God use Samson for His purposes?

and those inside were killed. This would probably be about five thousand. "So the dead which he slew at his death were more than they which he slew in his life" (v. 30).

But what a way for a great hero to die—in disgrace and shame! If only he had walked straight and obeyed God, the end would have been different.

CONTEMPORARY APPLICATION

The life of Samson is full of warning for all of us. It teaches us that we cannot be complacent over the fact that God may have used us in a great way in His work. Great feats of power are no substitute for purity. If we transgress God's laws, we pay a heavy penalty for it.

Samson is a sad example of selfishness and willfulness. The only safe way to live is in complete obedience to God's will every day. Disobedience is too costly for us to afford. Deeds of service are no substitute for living a godly life.

PROLOGUE TO NATIONHOOD

DEVOTIONAL READING	Psalm 110

ADULTS

Topic: *Give Us a King*

Background Scripture: Judges 21:25; I Samuel 7—10

Scripture Lesson: I Samuel 8:1-9; 10:1

Memory Verse: *The people of Israel said to Samuel, "Do not cease to cry to the Lord our God for us, that he may save us from the hand of the Philistines."* I Samuel 7:8

YOUTH

Topic: *The Appeal of Conformity*

Background Scripture: Judges 21:25; I Samuel 7—10

Scripture Lesson: I Samuel 8:1-9; 10:1

Memory Verse: *The people of Israel said to Samuel, "Do not cease to cry to the Lord our God for us, that he may save us from the hand of the Philistines."* I Samuel 7:8

CHILDREN

Topic: *Give Us a King*

Background Scripture: Judges 21:25; I Samuel 7—10

Scripture Lesson: I Samuel 8:1, 3-7, 10-20; 10:1

Memory Verse: *O Israel, trust in the Lord! He is their help and their shield.* Psalm 115:9

DAILY BIBLE READINGS

Mon., Aug. 22: The Call of Abraham, Genesis 12:1-9.
Tues., Aug. 23: Covenant Through Moses, Exodus 19:1-9.
Wed., Aug. 24: "This Nation Is My People," Exodus 33:12-23.
Thurs., Aug. 25: A Circuit Judge, I Samuel 7:12-17.
Fri., Aug. 26: Prologue to Nationhood, I Samuel 8:1-9.
Sat., Aug. 27: "Long Live the King," I Samuel 10:17-24.
Sun., Aug. 28: The Lord Rules, Psalm 110.

LESSON AIM

To illustrate the importance of seeking God's will, individually and nationally.

LESSON SETTING

Time: About 1050 B.C.

Place: Various cities in Palestine

LESSON OUTLINE

Prologue to Nationhood

   I. No King in Israel: Judges 21:25

397

II. **Give Us a King:** I Samuel 8:1-5
   A. Samuel's Sons as Judges: vv. 1-2
   B. Their Wicked Conduct: v. 3
   C. The Request of the People: vv. 4-5

III. **Rejecting the Lord as King:** I Samuel 8:6-9
   A. Samuel's Displeasure: v. 6
   B. The Lord's Answer: vv. 7-8
   C. The Lord's Instructions: v. 9

IV. **The Price of Having a King:** I Samuel 8:10-18

V. **The Pride of Having a King:** I Samuel 8:19-22

VI. **The Choice of Saul as King:** I Samuel 9:1-27

VII. **The Anointing of Saul as King:** I Samuel 10:1

VIII. **The Preparation of Saul as King:** I Samuel 10:2-16

IX. **The Inauguration of Saul as King:** I Samuel 10:17-25
   A. Samuel's Reminder: vv. 17-19
   B. Selection of Saul: vv. 20-22
   C. God Save the King: vv. 23-25

SUGGESTED INTRODUCTION FOR ADULTS

Samuel was the fifteenth and last of the judges of Israel. He is also sometimes called the first of a long succession of prophets.

The Lord used Samuel to bring a real revival in Israel. The people had been without the ark—the symbol of God's presence—for twenty years (I Samuel 7:2). Samuel urged the people to put away "the Baalim and the Ashtaroth" (vv. 3-4)—the pagan male and female deities—and serve the Lord only. They obeyed, at least temporarily.

Then Samuel called on all Israel to meet him at Mizpeh, so that he might pray to the Lord for them (v. 5). There the people fasted and confessed, "We have sinned against the Lord" (v. 6). It is also stated that "Samuel judged the children of Israel in Mizpeh." This town, now spelled "Mizpah," seems to have been between Bethel and Jerusalem.

In answer to Samuel's prayer (v. 9), the Lord gave Israel a great victory over the Philistines, so that they ceased to threaten the safety of the Israelites (vv. 10-13). This continued throughout the life of Samuel.

"Samuel judged Israel all the days of his life" (v. 15). He was an itinerant judge, making an annual circuit of Bethel, Gilgal, and Mizpah (v. 16). His home, as main headquarters, was in Ramah (v. 17), where he was born (1:19-20). It was also between Bethel and Jerusalem.

SUGGESTED INTRODUCTION FOR YOUTH

Our lesson today illustrates "the appeal of conformity." The Israelites wanted to be like other nations. So they asked for a king—and paid a high price for royalty.

The price of conformity is always high. If we want to be conformed to the world, instead of being transformed by Christ (Romans 12:1-2), we sacrifice the spiritual to the material. And that is a dead-end street, ending in failure, frustration, and futility.

CONCEPTS FOR CHILDREN

1. The Israelites wanted a king, to satisfy their pride.
2. The only safe way in life is to want God's will.
3. The things of the world look appealing, but they do not really satisfy.
4. The Israelites suffered for wanting their own way.

THE LESSON COMMENTARY

I. NO KING IN ISRAEL:
Judges 21:25

"In those days there was no king in Israel: every man did that which was right in his own eyes." This is the key verse of the Book of Judges. It occurs at the very end of the book and near the middle (17:6). With no monarchy, there was anarchy.

The spiritual lesson is clear. When there is no recognized authority, things go to pieces. No society can endure and prosper without some kind of leadership. It is true in the home, at school, in business, in the church, and in the nation. Without authority, there is no freedom.

The Book of Judges describes a period of transition between the time of Moses and Joshua—a theocratic government under God's appointed leaders, who ruled for Him—and the period of the monarchy. In the latter the law of hereditary succession prevailed. The result was that many of the kings were weak or wicked—or both. Their willful selfishness brought on Israel's captivity.

II. GIVE US A KING:
I Samuel 8:1-5

A. Samuel's Sons as Judges: vv. 1-2

When Samuel became "old," probably about seventy, he appointed his sons judges over Israel. This was a very

unwise thing for him to do. He should have let God choose the next judge. Nepotism—favoring of close relatives (literally, nephews)—has been practiced not only in secular politics but unfortunately in church circles as well. It should be avoided like the plague!

Samuel had two sons. The older was named Joel, which means "Jehovah is God." The younger was Abiah, which means "Jehovah a Father." These names express the faith of the godly prophet.

The two sons "were judges in Beersheba." This city is in the southern desert, far from Samuel's home and near the Philistine territory.

B. Their Wicked Conduct: v. 3

Unfortunately, the sons did not follow in the footsteps of their father. From all we know of him, his character was beyond reproach. But his sons were greedy for money. They took bribes and perverted justice—a sin that is expressly forbidden in the Law (Exodus 23:6-8; Deuteronomy 16:19). H. D. M. Spence comments: "It is strange that the same ills that ruined Eli's house, owing to the evil conduct of his children, now threatened Samuel. The prophet-judge, however, acted differently to the high priestly judge. The sons of Samuel were evidently, through their father's action in procuring the election of Saul, quickly deposed from their authority. The punishment seems to have been successful in correcting the corrupt tendencies of these men, for we hear in after days of the high position occupied at the court of David by the distinguished descendants of the noble and disinterested prophet" ("Judges," *Ellicott's Commentary on the Whole Bible*, II, 321).

C. The Request of the People: vv. 4-5

Concerned about the situation, the elders of Israel came in a group to Samuel at Ramah. Since he was old and his sons unworthy to succeed him, the elders reminded him: "Thy sons walk not in thy ways" (v. 5). R. Payne Smith notes: "These words show that the elders had the most perfect confidence in Samuel. They felt that he would not connive at the wickedness of his sons, but would do what was right by the nation. Thus they had everything to hope from the father's justice, while if they waited till his death the sons might resist what was virtually their deposition" ("I Samuel," *The Pulpit Commentary*, p. 143).

Then they made their plea: "Now make us a king to judge us like all the nations." These words are almost an exact quotation of Deuteronomy 17:14, following which are given instructions as to how a king should be selected: He must be one whom God would choose. So the elders may have felt that they were justified in asking for a king. But the motive was wrong—to be "like all the nations." They were supposed to be God's holy people.

III. REJECTING THE LORD AS KING:
I Samuel 8:6-9

A. Samuel's Displeasure: v. 6

"But the thing displeased Samuel." Smith comments: "And justly so. For, in the first place, they had determined to have a king without consulting the will of God. . . . Samuel did make it a matter of prayer; the elders were actuated solely by political motives. And, secondly, they undervalued their own religious privileges. They wanted

a king such as the heathen had, whereas something far better and higher was possible for them, namely, a king who would be the representative of Jehovah" ("Judges," *Pulpit*, p. 143).

We cannot deny that personal disappointment may have colored Samuel's first reaction. After all, he was human. But he did the right thing—he prayed to the Lord about it.

B. The Lord's Answer: vv. 7-8

The Lord told Samuel to accede to the people's demands and appoint a king. He went on to say: "They have not rejected thee, but they have rejected me, that I should not reign over them" (v. 7). They were not looking for a theocratic king, who would enforce the divine law. Rather, they were asking for a soldier-king, such as the surrounding nations had. They had rejected God as their king by not seeking His guidance in all this. They wanted their own style of king, rather than that God should rule over them.

This is the way they had acted with Moses, from the time they left Egypt (v. 8). They had forsaken the true God and served pagan deities. They were now treating Samuel as they had treated Moses.

C. The Lord's Instructions: v. 9

Samuel was told to do what the people requested. But he was to solemnly warn them what the consequences would be. They demanded a king. They must be told what this involved—what it would mean to have a human ruler who considered himself to be the final authority, whose word was law. They needed to know what they were getting.

IV. THE PRICE OF HAVING A KING:
I Samuel 8:10-18

Samuel warned the people that their king would draft their sons into his service as charioteers and horsemen (v. 11), and as farmers and artisans (v. 12). He would take their daughters to be "perfumers and cooks and bakers" (v. 13, NASB). He would take the best of their fields, vineyards, and olive groves, and give them to his servants (v. 14). He would take a tenth of their seed and vineyards to give to his officers and servants (v. 15). He would confiscate their menservants, maidservants, choice young men and donkeys, and use them for his work (v. 16). He would take a tenth of their flocks, and the people would be his slaves (v. 17).

When all this happened, the people would cry out in agony, but God would not listen to them—because they had refused to listen to Him. This is the sad price of self-will and disobedience.

V. THE PRIDE OF HAVING A KING:
I Samuel 8:19-22

In spite of all this warning, given in good faith, we read: "Nevertheless the people refused to obey the voice of Samuel; and they said, Nay; but we will have a king over us" (v. 19). They were stubborn and willful. Having made up their minds, they were not going to change.

Again their wrong motive comes through clearly: "That we also may be like all the nations; and that our king may judge us, and go out before us, and fight our battles" (v. 20). They were not looking for a wise, godly man to lead them as a nation in following God's ways. What they wanted was military protection, forgetting that God had miraculously given this to them under His servant Samuel (7:7-12). They quickly forgot the Lord's goodness to them.

When Samuel reported the people's words to the Lord (v. 21), he was once more told to do what they requested. So Samuel dismissed the assembly (v. 22).

VI. THE CHOICE OF SAUL AS KING:
I Samuel 9:1-27

It was now Samuel's assignment to appoint a king over Israel. But where would he find the right man? Chapter 9 gives the answer in interesting detail.

We are first introduced to a Benjamite, whose name was Kish. He had a son named Saul, who stood head and shoulders above the people (v. 2).

Some of Kish's donkeys had strayed away. So he sent Saul and a servant to find the lost animals (v. 3).

After a fruitless search, Saul was ready to go home (vv. 4-5). But the servant suggested that they first consult "a man of God" (vv. 6-8). The writer explains that in that day a prophet was called "a Seer" (v. 9).

As we often find in both the Old Testament and the New, God had been working at the other end. The previous day He had told Samuel, the "man of God," that He was sending to him a Benjamite whom he was to anoint as "prince" (NASB) of His people, to save them from the Philistines (vv. 15-16). When Saul approached Samuel, the Lord said to the prophet, "Behold, the man of whom I spoke to you! This one shall rule over My people" (v. 17, NASB).

Samuel identified himself to Saul and informed him that he was to eat with him, adding that the lost donkeys had already been found. Then he startled his guest by saying, "And on whom is all the desire of Israel? Is it not on thee, and on all thy father's house?" (v. 20). Though Saul protested his humble status (v. 21), he was given the head place at the table and the favorite food.

He was also Samuel's guest that night. We are told that the two men talked on the roof (v. 25), probably of Samuel's house. The Septuagint adds: "And they spread a bed for Saul upon the roof, and he lay down."

What were they talking about that evening? Probably the prophet had two purposes in mind. First, he wanted to sound Saul out, to see what his thinking was like. But he would very likely also be eager to share with this young man the importance of letting God have His way, of recognizing His sovereign authority over Israel. He did not, of course, disclose the divine secret.

VII. THE ANOINTING OF SAUL AS KING:
I Samuel 10:1

The next morning "at daybreak ... Samuel called to Saul on the roof, saying, 'Get up, that I may send you away.' So Saul arose, and both he and Samuel went out into the street" (9:26, NASB). The prophet asked Saul to send his servant on ahead, while he shared "the word of God" with his young guest (9:27).

Then the eventful moment came. "Samuel took the flask of oil, poured it on his head, kissed him and said, 'Has not the Lord anointed you a ruler over His inheritance?' " (10:1, NASB). Smith comments: "A strong affirmation often takes the form of a question, especially when, as probably was the case here, surprise is manifested. Saul, on whom the occurrences of the previous day must have come as strange and unintelligible marvels, was no doubt still more embarrassed when one so old and venerable, both in person and office, as Samuel solemnly consecrated him to be Israel's prince ... and gave him the kiss of fealty and allegiance" ("Judges," *Pulpit*, p. 175).

DISCUSSION QUESTIONS

1. What happens when everyone does as he pleases?
2. What are some of the perils of democracy?
3. What is the greater evil of autocracy?
4. Why do great men's sons often fail?
5. What are some dangers of conformity?
6. What are some lessons we can learn from Samuel's life?

VIII. THE PREPARATION OF SAUL AS KING:
I Samuel 10:2-16

To quiet Saul's doubts and convince him that his appointment was from God, Samuel gave him three signs. The first was that near Rachel's tomb he would find two men who would inform him that the lost donkeys had been found and that his father was concerned about him (v. 2). The second was that on the road he would meet three men going to Bethel, who would give him food (vv. 3-4). The third was that when he came to "the hill of God" he would meet a group of prophets. The Spirit of the Lord would come upon Saul, and he would prophesy with them and "be turned into another man" (vv. 5-6). "And it shall be when these signs come to you, do for yourself what the occasion requires; for God is with you" (v. 7, NASB).

Samuel gave Saul one further instruction: He was to go down to Gilgal and wait seven days, until Samuel arrived to offer sacrifices (v. 8). This became the occasion of Saul's first disobedience and the beginning of his downfall (13:8-14).

In verses 9 and 10 two things are said to have happened to Saul. First, as he left Samuel, "God gave him another heart." Second, "the Spirit of God came upon him." We are also informed that "all those signs came to pass that day." Saul had every reason to be assured that God had selected him to be the ruler of Israel.

On the statement "God gave him another heart" (v. 9), Smith writes: "The Hebrew is remarkable: 'When he turned his shoulder to go from Samuel, God also turned for him another heart,' i.e. God turned him round by giving him a changed heart. He grew internally up to the level of his changed circumstances. No longer had he the feelings of a husbandman, concerned only about corn and cattle; he had become a statesman, a general, and a prince" ("Judges," *Pulpit*, p. 176). God never calls people to extraordinary positions of service without equipping them for their tasks.

IX. THE INAUGURATION OF SAUL AS KING:
I Samuel 10:17-25

A. Samuel's Reminder: vv. 17-19

"And Samuel called the people together unto the Lord to Mizpeh" (v. 17)—rather, "Mizpah." We have already seen that it was here that God had given the Israelites a great, miraculous victory over the Philistines (7:5-12). So this was a fitting place to come before the Lord and inaugurate the new king. Spence makes this further comment: "The words, 'unto the Lord,' probably signify that the mysterious Urim and Thummim, by which inquiry was used to be made of the Eternal, had been brought there by the high priest . . ." ("Judges," *Ellicott's*, p. 333).

Samuel reminded the people that it was the Lord, the God of Israel, who had brought His people up out of Egypt, delivering them from the Egyptians and all their other enemies (v. 18). But they had rejected their God and asked for a king (v. 19). So the next step was to select the king. Samuel ordered: "Therefore present yourselves before the Lord by your tribes, and by your thousands" ("your clans" [NASB]).

B. Selection of Saul: vv. 20-22

As the representatives of all the tribes came near, "the tribe of Benjamin was taken" (v. 20)—better, "was taken by lot" (NASB). The custom was to pray and ask God to guide the drawing of lots. The Hebrew word here may indicate that they drew the

"lots" from a vessel, and the drawing indicated that the tribe of Benjamin was the one from which the king would come.

Then the various families of the tribe came forward, and the "Matrite family" (NASB) was taken. Further drawing of lots narrowed it down to Saul the son of Kish (v. 21). But he could not be found.

Only Samuel and Saul knew beforehand who would be selected. Evidently Saul felt so unworthy of the honor that he hid himself among the baggage—as the Lord revealed to the people (v. 22). One could wish that in his later life Saul had continued to show the becoming humility he exhibited here. But, "power corrupts."

C. God Save the King: vv. 23-25

Some ran, found Saul, and brought him before Samuel. As he stood there, it was noticeable that he stood a head higher than the rest of the people (v. 23). His appearance was impressive.

Then Samuel presented to the people their new king: "Do you see him whom the Lord has chosen? Surely there is no one like him among all the people" (NASB). In response the people shouted, "Long live the king!" (v. 24, NASB). This is closer to the Hebrew than "God save the king" (KJV), which is the modern salute to the British monarch. The original here is well represented in the French cry, "*Vive le roi!*"

Before letting the people go, Samuel took advantage of the opportunity to tell the people "the ordinances of the kingdom" (v. 25, NASB). He wrote these in a book and placed it before the Lord, where it would be a constant reminder to the people.

CONTEMPORARY APPLICATION

Favoritism is the bane of politics. It is the one black mark we have against that great man of God, Samuel. Few men have been able to resist the temptation to put their own children forward, to the disadvantage of others. Blood still runs thicker than water.

Samuel should have recognized the fact that his own sons were unworthy to succeed him. In fact, he should not have sought to have a family succession in power. This is always the problem with hereditary monarchy.

But it also shows up in church. A great and godly leader will promote his son as successor, and then the whole cause suffers. We should always want the most worthy person for every position.

FURTHER STUDY HELPS

Galatians

Barnes, Albert. *Barnes' Notes on the New Testament: II Corinthians and Galatians*. Grand Rapids: Baker Book House, 1949.

Burton, Ernest DeWitt. *A Critical and Exegetical Commentary on the Epistle to the Galatians*. International Critical Commentary. Edinburgh: T. & T. Clark, 1921.

Hamilton, Floyd E. *The Epistle to the Galatians*. Shield Bible Study Series. Grand Rapids: Baker Book House, 1959.

Hendriksen, William. *New Testament Commentary: Galatians*. Grand Rapids: Baker Book House, 1968.

Hogg, C. F., and Vine, W. E. *The Epistle to the Galatians*. Grand Rapids: Kregel Publications, 1921.

Howard, R. E., and others. "Galatians through Philemon." *Beacon Bible Commentary*. Kansas City: Beacon Hill Press, 1965.

Lenski, R. C. H. *The Interpretation of St. Paul's Epistles to the Galatians, to the Ephesians, and to the Philippians*. Columbus, OH: Wartburg Press, 1946.

Luther, Martin. *A Commentary on St. Paul's Epistle to the Galatians*. Translated by Theodore Graebner. Grand Rapids: Zondervan Publishing House, n.d.

Tenney, Merrill C. *Galatians: The Charter of Christian Liberty*. Grand Rapids: Wm. B. Eerdmans Publishing Co., 1957.

Wuest, Kenneth S. *Galatians in the Greek New Testament*. Grand Rapids: Wm. B. Eerdmans Publishing Co., 1944.

Romans

Archer, Gleason L., Jr. *The Epistle to the Romans*. Shield Bible Study Series. Grand Rapids: Baker Book House, 1959.

Barnes, Albert. *Barnes' Notes on the New Testament: Romans*. Grand Rapids: Baker Book House, 1949.

Beet, Joseph Agar. *A Commentary on St. Paul's Epistle to the Romans*. London: Hodder & Stoughton, 1900.

Bruce, F. F. *The Epistle of Paul to the Romans*. The Tyndale New Testament Commentaries. Grand Rapids: Wm. B. Eerdmans Publishing Co., 1963.

Dayton, Wilber T. "The Epistle of Paul to the Romans," *Wesleyan Bible Commentary*. Vol. 5. Grand Rapids: Wm. B. Eerdmans Publishing Co., n.d.

Denney, James. "St. Paul's Epistle to the Romans," *The Expositor's Greek Testament*, vol. 2. Grand Rapids: Wm. B. Eerdmans Publishing Co., n.d.

Erdman, Charles R. *The Epistle of Paul to the Romans*. Philadelphia: Westminster Press, 1925.

Godet, F. *Commentary on the Epistle to the Romans*. Grand Rapids: Zondervan Publishing House, 1956 (reprint).

Greathouse, William. "Romans," *Beacon Hill Commentary*, vol. 8. Kansas City: Beacon Hill Press, 1968.

Griffith Thomas, W. H. *St. Paul's Epistle to the Romans*. Grand Rapids: Wm. B. Eerdmans Publishing Co., 1946.

Lenski, R. C. H. *The Interpretation of St. Paul's Epistle to the Romans*. Columbus: Wartburg Press, 1945.

Moule, H. C. G. *The Epistle of St. Paul to the Romans*. The Expositor's Bible. New York: A. C. Armstrong, 1906.

Murray, John. *The Epistle to the Romans*, 2 vols. The New International Commentary on the New Testament. Grand Rapids: Wm. B. Eerdmans Publishing Co., 1959.

Sanday, William, and Headlam, A. C. *A Critical and Exegetical Commentary on the Epistle to the Romans.* International Critical Commentary. Edinburgh: T. & T. Clark, 1895.

Mark

Alexander, J. A. *Commentary on the Gospel of Mark.* Grand Rapids: Zondervan Publishing House, n.d.

Barnes, Albert. *Barnes' Notes on the New Testament: Matthew–Mark.* Grand Rapids: Baker Book House, 1949.

Bruce, A. B. "The Synoptic Gospels," *The Expositor's Greek Testament,* vol. 1. Grand Rapids: Wm. B. Eerdmans Publishing Co., n.d.

Earle, Ralph. "Matthew, Mark, Luke," *The Wesleyan Bible Commentary,* vol. 4. Grand Rapids: Wm. B. Eerdmans Publishing Co., 1964.

Earle, Ralph, and others. "Matthew through Luke," *Beacon Bible Commentary.* Kansas City: Beacon Hill Press, 1964.

Gutzke, Manford G. *The Go Gospel: A Discussion Guide to the Book of Mark.* Grand Rapids: Baker Book House, 1975.

Hendriksen, William. *New Testament Commentary: Exposition of the Gospel According to Mark.* Grand Rapids: Baker Book House, 1975.

Lane, William. *The Gospel According to Mark.* The New International Commentary on the New Testament. Grand Rapids: Wm. B. Eerdmans Publishing Co., 1974.

Morgan, G. Campbell. *The Gospel According to Mark.* New York: Fleming H. Revell, 1927.

Morison, James. *A Practical Commentary on the Gospel According to St. Mark.* 6th ed. London: Hodder & Stoughton, 1889.

Rawlinson, A. E. J. *St. Mark.* Westminster Commentaries. London: Methuen & Co., 1925.

Swete, Henry Barclay. *The Gospel According to St. Mark.* Greek text. London: Macmillan & Co., 1898.

Taylor, Vincent. *The Gospel According to St. Mark.* Greek text. London: Macmillan & Co., 1952.

Luke

Arndt, William F. *The Gospel According to St. Luke.* St. Louis: Concordia Publishing House, 1956.

Barnes, Albert. *Barnes' Notes on the New Testament: Luke and John.* Grand Rapids: Baker Book House, 1949.

Brownson, William C. *Distinctive Lessons from Luke.* Grand Rapids: Baker Book House, 1974.

Earle, Ralph, and others. "Matthew through Luke," *Beacon Bible Commentary.* Kansas City: Beacon Hill Press, 1964.

Geldenhuys, Norval. *Commentary on the Gospel of Luke.* The New International Commentary on the New Testament. Grand Rapids: Wm. B. Eerdmans Publishing Co., 1951.

Godet, F. L. *Commentary on the Gospel of Luke.* Grand Rapids: Zondervan Publishing House, n.d.

Lenski, R. C. H. *The Interpretation of St. Luke's Gospel.* Columbus, OH: Wartburg Press, 1946.

Plummer, Alfred. *A Critical and Exegetical Commentary on the Gospel According to St. Luke.* The International Critical Commentary. Edinburgh: T. & T. Clark, 1896.

Summers, Ray. *Commentary on Luke.* Waco, TX: Word Books, 1972.

James

Barnes, Albert. *Barnes' Notes on the New Testament: James—Jude*. Grand Rapids: Baker Book House, 1949.

Krutza, W. J., and DiCicco, P. P. *Living That Counts: A Study Guide to the Book of James*. Grand Rapids: Baker Book House, 1972.

Mayor, Joseph B. *The Epistle of St. James*. Greek text. Grand Rapids: Zondervan Publishing House, n.d.

Ropes, James Hardy. *A Critical and Exegetical Commentary on the Epistle of St. James*. The International Critical Commentary. Edinburgh: T. & T. Clark, 1916.

Ross, Alexander. *The Epistles of James and John*. The New International Commentary on the New Testament. Grand Rapids: Wm. B. Eerdmans Publishing Co., 1954.

Taylor, Richard, and others. "Hebrews through Revelation." *Beacon Bible Commentary*. Kansas City: Beacon Hill Press, 1967.

Zodhiates, Spiros. *The Labor of Love*. 3 vols. Grand Rapids: Wm. B. Eerdmans Publishing Co., 1960.

Exodus—I Samuel

Barnes, Albert. *Barnes' Notes on the Old Testament: Exodus—Ruth*. Grand Rapids: Baker Book House, 1949.

Barnes, Albert. *Barnes' Notes on the Old Testament: Samuel—Esther*. Grand Rapids: Baker Book House, 1949.

Davis, John J. *The Birth of a Kingdom: Studies in Samuel and Kings*. Grand Rapids: Baker Book House, 1970.

Davis, John J. *Moses and the Gods of Egypt: Studies in Exodus*. Grand Rapids: Baker Book House, 1971.

Ellicott, Charles John, ed. *Commentary on the Whole Bible*. 8 vols. Grand Rapids: Zondervan Publishing House, 1954.

Jamieson, Robert; Fausset, A. R.; and Brown, David. *A Commentary Critical, Experimental and Practical on the Old and New Testaments*. 6 vols. Grand Rapids: Wm. B. Eerdmans Publishing Co., 1945 (reprint).

Livingston, George, and others. "Genesis through Deuteronomy," *Beacon Bible Commentary*. Kansas City: Beacon Hill Press, 1969.

Mulder, Chester O., and others. "Joshua through Esther," *Beacon Hill Commentary*, Kansas City: Beacon Hill Press, 1965.

Spence, H. D. M., and Exell, Joseph S., eds. *The Pulpit Commentary*. 23 double vols. Grand Rapids: Wm. B. Eerdmans Publishing Co., 1950 (reprint).